A HISTORY OF THE JEWS

OTHER BOOKS BY PAUL JOHNSON

Modern Times
A History of the English People

A HISTORY OF THE JEWS

PAUL JOHNSON

1817

HARPER & ROW, PUBLISHERS New York
Cambridge, Philadelphia, San Francisco, Washington
London, Mexico City, São Paulo, Singapore, Sydney

LIBRARY OF CONGRESS CATALOG CARD NUMBER: 85-42575
ISBN: 0-06-015698-8

87 88 89 90 91 10 9 8 7 6 5 4 3 2

*This book is dedicated
to the memory of
Hugh Fraser,
a true Christian gentleman
and lifelong friend of the Jews*

Contents

Part Three: Cathedocracy

Part Four: Ghetto

Part Five: Emancipation

Part Six: Holocaust

Part Seven: Zion

Acknowledgments

This is a personal interpretation of Jewish history. The opinions expressed (and any errors) are my own. But my debt to many scholars will be clear to anyone who looks at the source notes. I am particularly grateful to the editors of the *Encyclopaedia Judaica*, which has proved an indispensable guide, and to the valuable compilation edited by H. H. Ben Sasson, *A History of the Jewish People*. My understanding has been illuminated by the monumental studies of S. W. Baron, S. D. Goitein and G. G. Scholem, and I have also been greatly helped by the works of such historians as Cecil Roth, Alexander Marx, Alexander Altmann, Hyam Maccoby, Jonathan I. Israel, Michael Marrus, Ronald Sanders, Raul Hilberg, Lucy Davidowicz, Robert Wistrich and Martin Gilbert. On Jewish beliefs and opinions I have found particularly useful books by Samuel Belkin, Arthur A. Cohen and Meyer Waxman. Chaim Raphael and Hyam Maccoby both generously read the entire text and made many helpful suggestions and corrections. I am also much indebted to the copy editor, Peter James, and to my son, Daniel Johnson, who worked on the text, and especially to my editor at Weidenfeld & Nicolson, Linda Osband, who on this as on earlier occasions has rendered my book incomparable services. Finally I must thank Lord Weidenfeld for his courage in making it possible for me to tackle this vast and daunting subject.

Prologue

Why have I written a history of the Jews? There are four reasons. The first is sheer curiosity. When I was working on my *History of Christianity*, I became aware for the first time in my life of the magnitude of the debt Christianity owes to Judaism. It was not, as I had been taught to suppose, that the New Testament replaced the Old; rather, that Christianity gave a fresh interpretation to an ancient form of monotheism, gradually evolving into a different religion but carrying with it much of the moral and dogmatic theology, the liturgy, the institutions and the fundamental concepts of its forebear. I thereupon determined, should opportunity occur, to write about the people who had given birth to my faith, to explore their history back to its origins and forward to the present day, and to make up my own mind about their role and significance. The world tended to see the Jews as a race which had ruled itself in antiquity and set down its records in the Bible; had then gone underground for many centuries; had emerged at last only to be slaughtered by the Nazis; and, finally, had created a state of its own, controversial and beleaguered. But these were merely salient episodes. I wanted to link them together, to find and study the missing portions, assemble them into a whole, and make sense of it.

My second reason was the excitement I found in the sheer span of Jewish history. From the time of Abraham up to the present covers the best part of four millennia. That is more than three-quarters of the entire history of civilized humanity. I am a historian who believes in long continuities and delights in tracing them. The Jews created a separate and specific identity earlier than almost any other people which still survives. They have maintained it, amid appalling adversities, right up to the present. Whence came this extraordinary endurance? What was the particular strength of the all-consuming idea which made the Jews different and kept them homogeneous? Did its continuing power lie in its essential immutability, or its capacity to adapt, or both? These are sinewy themes with which to grapple.

My third reason was that Jewish history covers not only vast tracts of time but huge areas. The Jews have penetrated many societies and left their mark on all of them. Writing a history of the Jews is almost like writing a history of the world, but from a highly peculiar angle of vision. It is world history seen from the viewpoint of a learned and intelligent victim. So the effort to grasp history as it appeared to the Jews produces illuminating insights. Dietrich Bonhoeffer noticed this same effect when he was in a Nazi prison. 'We have learned', he wrote in 1942, 'to see the great events of world history from below, from the perspective of those who are excluded, under suspicion, ill-treated, powerless, oppressed and scorned, in short those who suffer.' He found it, he said, 'an experience of incomparable value'. The historian finds a similar merit in telling the story of the Jews: it adds to history the new and revealing dimension of the underdog.

Finally the book gave me the chance to reconsider objectively, in the light of a study covering nearly 4,000 years, the most intractable of all human questions: what are we on earth for? Is history merely a series of events whose sum is meaningless? Is there no fundamental moral difference between the history of the human race and the history, say, of ants? Or is there a providential plan of which we are, however humbly, the agents? No people has ever insisted more firmly than the Jews that history has a purpose and humanity a destiny. At a very early stage in their collective existence they believed they had detected a divine scheme for the human race, of which their own society was to be a pilot. They worked out their role in immense detail. They clung to it with heroic persistence in the face of savage suffering. Many of them believe it still. Others transmuted it into Promethean endeavours to raise our condition by purely human means. The Jewish vision became the prototype for many similar grand designs for humanity, both divine and man-made. The Jews, therefore, stand right at the centre of the perennial attempt to give human life the dignity of a purpose. Does their own history suggest that such attempts are worth making? Or does it reveal their essential futility? The account that follows, the result of my own inquiry, will I hope help its readers to answer these questions for themselves.

PART ONE

Israelites

The Jews are the most tenacious people in history. Hebron is there to prove it. It lies 20 miles south of Jerusalem, 3,000 feet up in the Judaean hills. There, in the Cave of Machpelah, are the Tombs of the Patriarchs. According to ancient tradition, one sepulchre, itself of great antiquity, contains the mortal remains of Abraham, founder of the Jewish religion and ancestor of the Jewish race. Paired with his tomb is that of his wife Sarah. Within the building are the twin tombs of his son Isaac and his wife Rebecca. Across the inner courtyard is another pair of tombs, of Abraham's grandson Jacob and his wife Leah. Just outside the building is the tomb of their son Joseph.[1] This is where the 4,000-year history of the Jews, in so far as it can be anchored in time and place, began.

Hebron has great and venerable beauty. It provides the peace and stillness often to be found in ancient sanctuaries. But its stones are mute witnesses to constant strife and four millennia of religious and political disputes. It has been in turn a Hebrew shrine, a synagogue, a Byzantine basilica, a mosque, a crusader church, and then a mosque again. Herod the Great enclosed it with a majestic wall, which still stands, soaring nearly 40 feet high, composed of massive hewn stones, some of them 23 feet long. Saladin adorned the shrine with a pulpit. Hebron reflects the long, tragic history of the Jews and their unrivalled capacity to survive their misfortunes. David was anointed king there, first of Judah (II Samuel 2:1–4), then of all Israel (II Samuel 5:1–3). When Jerusalem fell, the Jews were expelled and it was settled by Edom. It was conquered by Greece, then by Rome, converted, plundered by the Zealots, burned by the Romans, occupied in turn by Arabs, Franks and Mamluks. From 1266 the Jews were forbidden to enter the Cave to pray. They were permitted only to ascend seven steps by the side of the eastern wall. On the fourth step they inserted their petitions to God in a hole bored 6 feet 6 inches through the stone.

Sticks were used to push the bits of paper through until they fell into the Cave.[2] Even so, the petitioners were in danger. In 1518 there was a fearful Ottoman massacre of the Hebron Jews. But a community of pious scholars was re-established. It maintained a tenuous existence, composed, at various times, of orthodox Talmudists, of students of the mystic kabbalah, and even of Jewish ascetics, who flogged themselves cruelly until their blood spattered the hallowed stones. Jews were there to welcome, in turn, the false Messiah, Shabbetai Zevi, in the 1660s, the first modern Christian pilgrims in the eighteenth century, secular Jewish settlers a hundred years later, and the British conquerors in 1918. The Jewish community, never very numerous, was ferociously attacked by the Arabs in 1929. They attacked it again in 1936 and virtually wiped it out. When Israeli soldiers entered Hebron during the Six Day War in 1967, for a generation not one Jew had lived there. But a modest settlement was re-established in 1970. Despite much fear and uncertainty, it has flourished.

So when the historian visits Hebron today, he asks himself: where are all those peoples which once held the place? Where are the Canaanites? Where are the Edomites? Where are the ancient Hellenes and the Romans, the Byzantines, the Franks, the Mamluks and the Ottomans? They have vanished into time, irrevocably. But the Jews are still in Hebron.

Hebron is thus an example of Jewish obstinacy over 4,000 years. It also illustrates the curious ambivalence of the Jews towards the possession and occupation of land. No race has maintained over so long a period so emotional an attachment to a particular corner of the earth's surface. But none has shown so strong and persistent an instinct to migrate, such courage and skill in pulling up and replanting its roots. It is a curious fact that, for more than three-quarters of their existence as a race, a majority of Jews have always lived outside the land they call their own. They do so today.

Hebron is the site of their first recorded acquisition of land. Chapter 23 of the Book of Genesis describes how Abraham, after the death of his wife Sarah, decided to purchase the Cave of Machpelah and the lands which surrounded it, as a burying-place for her and ultimately for himself. The passage is among the most important in the entire Bible, embodying one of the most ancient and tenaciously held Jewish traditions, evidently very dear and critical to them. It is perhaps the first passage in the Bible which records an actual event, witnessed and described through a long chain of oral recitation and so preserving authentic details. The negotiation and ceremony of purchase are elaborately described. Abraham was what might now be termed an alien, though a resident of long standing in Hebron. To own freehold land in the place he required not merely the power of purchase but the public consent of the community. The land was owned by a dignitary called Ephron the Hittite, a West Semite and Habiru of Hittite origin.[3] Abraham had first to secure the formal agreement of the community, 'the children of Heth', 'the people of the land', to make the transaction; then to bargain with Ephron about the price, 400 shekels (i.e. pieces) of silver; then to have the coins, 'current money with the merchant', weighed out and handed over before the communal elders.

This was a memorable event in a small community, involving not merely transfer of ownership but change of status: the ritualistic bowings, the dissimulations and false courtesies, the hardness and haggling, are all brilliantly conveyed by the Bible narrative. But what strikes the reader most, what lingers in the mind, are the poignant words with which Abraham begins the transaction: 'I am a stranger and a sojourner with you'; then, when it was concluded, the repeated stress that the land 'was made sure unto Abraham for a possession' by the local people (Genesis 23:20). In this first true episode in Jewish history, the ambiguities and the anxieties of the race are strikingly presented.

Who was this Abraham, and where did he come from? The Book of Genesis and related Biblical passages are the only evidence that he existed and these were compiled in written form perhaps a thousand years after his supposed lifetime. The value of the Bible as a historical record has been a matter of intense argument for over 200 years. Until about the year 1800, the predominant view, among scholars and layfolk alike, was fundamentalist: that is, the Bible narratives were divinely inspired and true in whole and in detail, though many scholars, both Jewish and Christian, had maintained for centuries that the early books of the Bible in particular contained many passages which should be understood as symbols or metaphor rather than as literal fact. From the early decades of the nineteenth century, a new and increasingly professional 'critical' approach, the work mainly of German scholars, dismissed the Old Testament as a historical record and classified large parts of it as religious myth. The first five books of the Bible, or Pentateuch, were now presented as orally transmitted legend from various Hebrew tribes which reached written form only after the Exile, in the second half of the first millennium BC. These legends, the argument ran, were carefully edited, conflated and adapted to provide historical justification and divine sanction for the religious beliefs, practices and rituals of the post-Exilic Israelite establishment. The individuals described in the early books were not real people but mythical heroes or composite figures denoting entire tribes.[4]

Thus not only Abraham and the other patriarchs, but Moses and Aaron, Joshua and Sampson, dissolved into myth and became no more substantial than Hercules and Perseus, Priam and Agamemnon, Ulysses and Aeneas. Under the influence of Hegel and his scholarly followers, Jewish and Christian revelation, as presented in the Bible, was reinterpreted as a determinist sociological development from primitive tribal superstition to sophisticated urban ecclesiology. The unique and divinely ordained role of the Jews was pushed into the background, the achievement of Mosaic monotheism was progressively eroded, and the rewriting of Old Testament history was pervaded by a subtle quality of anti-Judaism, tinged even with anti-Semitism. The collective work of German Biblical scholars became the academic orthodoxy, reaching a high level of persuasiveness and complexity in the teachings of Julius Wellhausen (1844–1918), whose remarkable book, *Prolegomena to the History of Ancient Israel*, was first published in 1878.[5] For half a century Wellhausen and his school dominated the approach to Biblical study, and many of his ideas influence the historian's reading of the Bible even today. Some outstanding twentieth-century scholars, such as M. Noth and A. Alt, retained this essentially sceptical approach, dismissing the pre-conquest traditions as mythical and arguing that the Israelites became a people only on the soil of Canaan and not before the twelfth century BC; the conquest itself was largely myth too, being mainly a process of peaceful infiltration.[6] Others suggested that the origins of Israel lay in the withdrawal of a community of religious zealots from a Canaanite society they regarded as corrupt.[7] These and other theories necessarily discarded all Biblical history before the Book of Judges as wholly or chiefly fiction, and Judges itself as a medley of fiction and fact. Israelite history, it was argued, does not acquire a substantial basis of truth until the age of Saul and David, when the Biblical text begins to reflect the reality of court histories and records.

Unfortunately, historians are rarely as objective as they wish to appear. Biblical history, which for Christians, Jews and atheists alike involves beliefs or prejudices which go to the very root of our being, is an area where objectivity is peculiarly difficult, if not quite impossible, to achieve. Moreover, scholarly specialities involve their own *déformations professionnelles*. During the nineteenth and for much of the twentieth centuries, Biblical history was controlled by the text scholars, whose instinct and training was and is to atomize the Biblical narratives, identify the sources and motives of those who assembled them, select the few authentic fragments on this basis, and then reconstruct events in the light of comparative history. With the development of modern scientific archaeology, however, a counter-vailing force has been exerted, for the bias of the archaeologists is to use the ancient texts as guides and seek confirmation in the physical remains. In Greece and Asia Minor, the discovery and excavation of Troy, of Knossos and other Minoan sites in Crete, and of the Mycenaean cities of the Peloponnese, together with the unearthing and deciphering of ancient court records found in some of them, have rehabilitated the Homeric tales as historical records and enabled scholars to perceive growing elements of reality beneath the legendary veneer. So, in Palestine and Syria, the investigation of ancient sites, and the recovery and translation of a vast number of legal and adminis-trative records, have tended strongly to restore the value of the early Biblical books as historical narratives. The work of W. F. Albright and Kathleen Kenyon in particular has given us renewed confidence in the actual existence of places and events described in the early Old Testament books.[8] Equally important, the discovery of contemporary archives from the third and second millennia BC has thrown new light on hitherto obscure Biblical passages. Whereas, fifty years ago, any early passage from the Bible was assumed to be mythical or symbolic, the onus of proof has now shifted: increasingly scholars tend to assume that the text contains at least a germ of truth and see it as their business to cultivate it. This has not made the historical interpretation of the Bible any easier. Both the fundamentalist and the 'critical' approach had comforting simplicities. Now we see our Bible texts as very complex and ambiguous guides to the truth; but guides none the less.

The Jews are thus the only people in the world today who possess a historical record, however obscure in places, which allows them to trace their origins back into very remote times. The Jews who worked the Bible into something approaching its present shape evidently thought that their race, though founded by Abraham, could trace forebears even further and called the ultimate human progenitor Adam. In our present state of knowledge, we must assume that the very earliest chapters of the book of Genesis are schematic and symbolic rather than factual descriptions. Chapters 1–5, with their identification of such concepts as knowledge, evil, shame, jealousy and crime, are explanations rather than actual episodes, though embedded in them are residual memories. It is hard, for instance, to believe that the story of Cain and Abel is complete fiction; Cain's reply, 'Am I my brother's keeper?', has the ring of truth, and the notion of the shamed and hunted man, with the mark of guilt upon him, is so powerful as to suggest historic fact. What strikes one about the Jewish description of creation and early man, compared with pagan cosmogonies, is the lack of interest in the mechanics of how the world and its creatures came into existence, which led the Egyptian and Mesopotamian narrators into such weird contortions. The Jews simply assume the pre-existence of an omnipotent God, who acts but is never described or characterized, and so has the force and invisibility of nature itself: it is significant that the first chapter of Genesis, unlike any other cosmogony of antiquity, fits perfectly well, in essence, with modern scientific explanations of the origin of the universe, not least the 'Big Bang' theory.

Not that the Jewish God is in any sense identified with nature: quite the contrary. Though always unvisualized, God is presented in the most emphatic terms as a person. The Book of Deuteronomy, for instance, is at pains to draw a distinction between the despised pagan peoples, who worship nature and nature-gods, and the Jews who worship God the person, warning them 'lest thou lift up thine eyes unto heaven, and when thou seest the sun, and the moon, and the stars, even all the host of heaven, shouldest be driven to worship them'.[9] Moreover, this personal God, from the start, makes absolutely clear moral distinctions, which his creatures must observe, so that in the Jewish version of early man moral categories are present and imperative from the very beginning. This again differentiates it sharply from all pagan accounts. The prehistoric sections of the Bible thus constitute a kind of moral fundament, upon which the whole of the factual structure rests. The Jews are presented, even in their most primitive antecedents, as creatures capable of perceiving absolute differences between right and wrong.

The notion of a moral universe superimposed on the physical one determines the treatment of the first truly historical episode in the Bible, the description of the Flood in Genesis 6. There can now be no doubt that some kind of huge inundation did occur in Mesopotamia. The first corroboration of the Biblical account took place in 1872 when George Smith of the British Museum discovered a version of the Deluge in cuneiform tablets found by A. H. Layard in 1845–51 at Kuyunjik in the library of the Palace of Sennacherib, confirmed by further tablets found in the Palace of Ashurbanipal.[10] This was in fact a late-Assyrian version, interpolated at the end of a much earlier epic known as *Gilgamesh*, which deals with an ancient Sumerian ruler of Uruk, in the fourth millennium BC. Before the Assyrians, both the

Babylonians and the distant Sumerians treasured memories of a great flood. In the 1920s, Sir Leonard Woolley found and excavated Ur, an important Sumerian city of the fourth and third millennia BC, which is mentioned in the Bible at the very end of its prehistoric section.[11] While investigating the earlier archaeological levels at Ur, Woolley made prolonged efforts to unearth physical evidence of a dramatic flood. He found an alluvial deposit of 8 feet which he dated 4000 to 3500 BC. At Shuruppak he came across another impressive alluvial deposit, and an 18-inch one at a similar stratum at Kish. But these datings, and Ur's, did not match.[12] Surveying the various sites which had been explored by the early 1960s, Sir Max Mallowan concluded that there had, indeed, been a giant flood.[13] Then in 1965 the British Museum made a further discovery in its deposits: two tablets, referring to the Flood, written in the Babylonian city of Sippar in the reign of King Ammisaduqa, 1646–1626 BC.

The importance of this last discovery was that it enables us to focus on the figure of Noah himself. For it relates how the god, having created mankind, regretted it and decided to drown it by flood; but Enki, the water-god, revealed the catastrophic plan to a certain priest–king called Ziusudra, who built a boat and so survived.[14] Ziusudra was undoubtedly a real person, king of the south Babylonian city of Shuruppak about 2900 BC, in which capacity he figures in the earliest column of the Sumerian king-list. At the site of Shuruppak itself there is evidence of a phenomenal flood, though the dating does not correspond with Woolley's flood at Ur.[15] The saviour-figure of Ziusudra, presented in the Bible as Noah, thus provides the first independent confirmation of the actual existence of a Biblical personage.

There is, however, a fundamental difference between the Biblical presentation of the Flood and the Babylonian–Sumerian epics. Noah, unlike Ziusudra, is a moral figure, anchored firmly in the scheme of values which the Book of Genesis identifies from the very beginning. Moreover, whereas the *Gilgamesh* story recounts isolated episodes lacking a unifying moral and historical context, the Jewish version sees each event as involving moral issues and, collectively, bearing witness to a providential design. It is the difference between secular and religious literature and between the writing of mere folklore and conscious, determinist history.

Moreover, not only is Noah the first real man in Jewish history: his story foreshadows important elements in Jewish religion. There is the Jewish god's obsession with detail, in the construction and loading of the ark. There is the notion of the one righteous man. Even more important, there is the Jewish stress on the supreme importance of human life, because of the imaginative relationship of man to God, which occurs in the key verse 6 of Genesis 9: 'Whoso sheddeth man's blood, by man shall his blood be shed: for in the image of God made he man.' This might be termed the central tenet of Jewish belief, and it is significant that it occurs in conjunction with the Flood, the first historic event for which there is non-Biblical confirmation.

The passages dealing with the Flood also contain the first mention of a covenant and the earliest reference to the land of Canaan.[16] But these themes recur far more emphatically when we progress through the post-diluvian king-lists and reach the patriarchs. We can now return to our question about Abraham's identity and provenance. What the Bible says, in Chapters 11–25 of Genesis, is that Abraham, originally Abram, ultimately descended from Noah, migrated from 'Ur of the Chaldees', first to Haran, then to various places in Canaan, travelling to Egypt in time of famine but returning to Canaan and ending his days at Hebron where he made his first landed purchase.

The substance of this Biblical account is history. The reference to the Chaldees is anachronistic since the Chaldeans did not penetrate southern Mesopotamia until towards the end of the second millennium BC, and Abraham is dated much earlier, closer to its beginning. The Chaldeans were inserted to identify Ur to readers of the Bible in the first millennium BC.[17] But there is no reason at all to doubt that Abraham came from Ur, as the Bible states, and this already tells us a lot about him, thanks to the work of Woolley and his successors. To begin with, it associates him with an important city, not the desert. Hegelians like Wellhausen and his school, with their notion of determinist progression from primitive to sophisticated, from desert to city, saw the Hebrews originally as pastoralists of the simplest kind. But the Ur Woolley excavated had a comparatively high level of culture. He found there, in the grave of 'Meskalamdug, Hero of the Good Land', a superb helmet made in the form of a wig from solid gold, the locks of hair in relief, and a religious standard for religious processions, decorated with shells and lapis lazuli. He found too a giant ziggurat, the temple raised on multiple platforms which, it is fair to conjecture, inspired the story of the Tower of Babel. This was the work of Ur Nammu of the Third Dynasty (2060–1950 BC), a great lawgiver and builder, who had himself portrayed on a stele, a fragment of which we possess, as a workman carrying a pick, trowel and measuring-dividers.

It is likely that Abraham left Ur after the time of this king, and so carried within him to Canaan tales of the ziggurat to heaven as well as the much earlier Flood story. When did he make this voyage? Dating the patriarchs is not such a hopeless task as was once supposed. In Genesis, antediluvian datings are, of course, schematic rather than actual but genealogies are not to be despised, any more than the other early king-lists of antiquity. The pharaoh-lists provided by such sources as Manetho, an Egyptian priest who lived in Hellenistic times, c. 250 BC, enable us to date Egyptian history with reasonable confidence as far back as the First Dynasty, 3000 BC. Berossus, a Babylonian priest who corresponds roughly to Manetho, gives us a similar king-list for Mesopotamia, and archaeology has unearthed others. If we examine the lists of ante- and post-diluvian names in Genesis, we find two groups with ten names on each, though the datings vary as between the near-original Hebrew Massoretic text, the Greek Septuagint and the Samaritan Pentateuch. These groupings are similar to non-Biblical literary records and the Biblical 'long' datings are akin to lives of the Sumerian kings before the flood at Shuruppak. The earliest king-list gives only eight ante-diluvian kings, but Berossus has ten, fitting the Genesis pattern. The link between the two is perhaps Abraham, who brought the tradition with him.

It is difficult to anchor the Mesopotamian king-lists, like the Egyptian, in absolute time, but the consensus is now to date Sargon and the Old Akkadian period to 2360–2180 BC, the lawgiver Ur-Nammu and the Third Dynasty of Ur to the end of the second millennium or the beginning of the first, and Hammurabi, who is unquestionably an authentic statesman and law-codifier, to the precise regnal period of 1728–1686 BC. The evidence suggests that the Genesis patriarch narratives belong to the period between Ur-Nammu and Hammurabi, the outside limits being 2100–1550 BC, that is the Middle Bronze Age. They certainly cannot be later, in the Late Bronze Age, because that would date them to the Egyptian empire of the New Kingdom, and the patriarchal sections make no mention of an Egyptian imperial presence in Canaan. Albright struggled with the problem of Abraham's dating for most of his professional life, pushing him backwards and forwards between the twentieth century BC and the seventeenth, finally concluding that he could not have lived before the twentieth or after the nineteenth. This dating seems reasonable.[18]

The ability to give a rough dating to the patriarchs enables us to relate them both to archaeological records and to the various literary archives which have now emerged from Bronze Age Syria and Mesopotamia. These last are important because they enable us not only to confirm but to explain episodes in the patriarchal stories. The archaeological finds include the investigation by Kathleen Kenyon of roadside tombs outside Jericho, which resemble the cave-tomb burials described in Genesis 23 and 35:19–20, and Nelson Glueck's archaeological survey of the Negev, which uncovered many Middle Bronze Age settlements of the patriarchal type.[19] Glueck noted that many of these settlements were destroyed some time after 1900 BC, which confirms the hints of ravaging we get in Genesis 14.

The literary finds are very considerable and suggestive. In 1933 A. Parrot excavated the ancient town of Mari (modern Tell Harari) on the Euphrates 17 miles north of the Syria–Iraq border, and found an archive of 20,000 items.[20] This was followed by the transcription of a similar archive of clay tablets at ancient Nuzi, near Kirkuk, the city of the Hurrians – the Horites of the Bible – who formed part of the Kingdom of Mitanni.[21] A third archive of 14,000 tablets was discovered at Ebla (modern Tell Mardikh) in north Syria.[22] These archives cover a large span of time, those at Ebla being somewhat before the time of the patriarchs, those at Nuzi, sixteenth, fifteenth century BC, being somewhat after, while the Mari tablets, end-nineteenth century BC to mid-eighteenth century, coincide closely with the most probable dating. Together they help us to create a picture of the patriarchal society which illuminates the Bible text. One of the strongest objections to the contention of Wellhausen and others that the early Bible books were compiled and edited to suit the religious beliefs of a much later age has always been that many episodes in them do no such thing. They embody customs which were evidently strange and inexplicable to the later editors of the first millennium BC who, in their reverence for the text and traditions handed down to them, simply copied them out, without any attempt at rationalization. Some passages remain mysterious to us, but many others are now explicable in the light of the tablets.

Thus both the Ebla and the Mari tablets contain administrative and legal documents referring to people with patriarchal-type names such as Abram, Jacob, Leah, Laban and Ishmael; there are also many suggestive expressions and loan-words related to Hebrew.[23] Moreover, these unknown litigants of the early second millennium BC faced exactly the same kind of difficulties, arising from childlessness, divorce, inheritance and birthrights, as their Biblical namesakes. Abraham's despairing plan to make one of his retainers his heir, for lack of his own, and his proposal for the adoption of Eleazer as heir-presumptive, reflect closely Nuzi practices. Nuzi also produces exact parallels with Abraham's dealings with his wife Sarah and his resort to her maid Hagar as a licensed concubine as a result of Sarah's failure to have a child – and, indeed, of the unhappy domestic consequences which followed. Nuzi marriage contracts, indeed, specifically provide for these contingencies. One Nuzi tablet attests the sale of birthright by an elder to a younger brother in return for three sheep, just as Esau transferred his to Jacob for a mess of pottage.[24] A Nuzi tablet also provides an instance of the binding power of the oral disposition of property, in the form of a death-bed blessing – thus illuminating the remarkable scene in Genesis 27, when Jacob and his mother Rebecca conspire to deceive his father, Isaac, and get his dying nomination as heir. Most strikingly of all, perhaps, the Nuzi archives explain the baffling Biblical account of Jacob's relations with Laban, which we now know to have been a common adoption problem. The heirless Laban adopted Jacob as his son, as well as his son-in-law; then he had sons of his own. A tablet from Nuzi reads:

The adoption tablet of Nashwi, son of Arshenni. He adopted Wullu, son of Pohishenni. . . . When Nashwi dies, Wullu shall be heir. Should Nashwi beget a son, he shall divide equally with Wullu, but Nashwi's son shall take Nashwi's gods. But if there be no son of Nashwi then Wullu shall take Nashwi's gods. And Nashwi has given his daughter Nuhuya as wife to Wullu. And if Wullu takes another wife he forfeits Nashwi's land and buildings.[25]

The Nuzi tablets show that family gods were like title-deeds, with symbolic legal value: we now understand that Rachel stole Laban's teraphim-gods to redress what she felt to be an unfair legal provision. The Mari tablets, again, give examples of the legal ritual of confirming a covenant by slaughtering an animal, just as Abraham confirmed his covenant with God in Genesis 15:9–10.[26]

We can thus begin to place Abraham and his descendants in their true historical context. At the end of the third millennium BC, civilized international society was disrupted by incursions from the East. These invaders caused great trouble in Egypt; and in settled Asia, archaeology reveals an absolute break in continuity in towns such as Ugarit, Byblos, Megiddo, Jericho and old Gaza, indicating pillage and abandonment.[27] These peoples, moving from Mesopotamia towards the Mediterranean, spoke West Semitic languages, of which Hebrew is one. A particular group is referred to, in Mesopotamian tablets and inscriptions, by the ideogram SA.GAZ, or as Hapiru, Habiru. Late Bronze Age Egyptian sources also speak of Abiru or Habiru. By this term they were not referring to Bedouin or desert-dwellers, who existed then as now, for they had a different term for this category. Habiru seems to have been a term of abuse used of difficult and destructive non-city-dwellers who moved from place to place. They were not regular tribes, migrating regularly with the flocks according to the cycles of the seasons, as they still do today in parts of Asia Minor and Persia. Their culture was superior to most desert tribes. Precisely because they were not easy to classify, they puzzled and annoyed the conservative Egyptian authorities, who knew exactly how to deal with genuine nomads. Sometimes they served as mercenaries. Some held jobs as government employees. They worked as servants, or as tinkers and pedlars. They were donkey-folk who moved in caravan, or merchants. Sometimes they acquired considerable wealth in the form of flocks and followers: then they might endeavour to settle, acquire land and form petty kingships.

Each group of Habiru had a sheikh or war-chief, who on occasion could launch an attack with as many as 2,000 followers. When they got the chance to settle and build, their leader called himself a king, and they attached themselves to the great king of the region. Apart from Egypt, a centralized autocracy of immemorial antiquity even in the nineteenth century BC, no king was powerful on his own. Hammurabi of Babylon had always ten or fifteen kings in attendance. It was a matter of fine judgment for a regional monarch whether to allow Habiru kings to settle and become (in effect) feudatories, or to beat them off.[28]

The same dilemma confronted petty local kings, already settled, who had formed part of an earlier wave of immigrants. Abraham was the leader of one of these immigrant Habiru groups, a substantial chief, with '318 trained servants born in his house'. In Genesis 12 we see him dealing with a major authority, Egypt; in Genesis 14 he and his men serve as mercenaries with the petty King of Sodom. His relations with settled authorities, large and small, always contain an element of unease and are marked by deceptions, such as his repeated pretence that his wife Sarah is his sister: we now know from the tablets that a wife with the legal status of a sister commanded more protection than an ordinary wife.[29] Pasture was limited; water was often scarce. If a Habiru group flourished in settlement, its very wealth became a source of conflict – an almost uncanny adumbration of later Jewish problems in the diaspora. Genesis 13:6–11 shows Abraham and his nephew Lot obliged to separate: 'And the land was not able to bear them, that they might dwell together; for their substance was great, so that they could not dwell together.' Genesis 21:22–31 shows Abraham, at Beersheba, involved in a dispute over water-rights with the men of Abimelech, the local king, a dispute resolved by a covenant sealed by animal sacrifice. Abraham's relations with Abimelech, though sometimes tense and always legalistic, were peaceful. It was sometimes in the interests of the settled kings to tolerate the Habiru, as a source of mercenaries. But if the 'strangers and sojourners' grew too numerous and powerful, the local king had to tell them to move on, or risk being overwhelmed himself. Thus we find Abimelech telling Abraham's son, Isaac: 'Go from us; for thou art much mightier than we.'[30]

All this Genesis material dealing with the problems of immigration, of water-wells and contracts and birthrights, is fascinating because it places the patriarchs so firmly in their historical setting, and testifies to the Bible's great antiquity and authenticity. But it is mingled with two other types of material which constitute the real purpose of the Bible narratives: the depiction of individuals, the ancestors of the people, in a moral context and, still more important, the origin and development of their collective relationship with God. The vividness and realism with which the patriarchs and their families are depicted in these ancient tales is perhaps the most remarkable aspect of the work and is without parallel in the literature of deep antiquity. There are archetypes of humanity, like Ishmael – 'And he will be a wild man; his hand will be against every man, and every man's hand against him'[31] – but no stereotypes: each character leaps vibrantly from the text.

Still more remarkable is the attention devoted to women, the leading role they often play, their vivacity and emotional power. Abraham's wife, Sarah, is the first person in history recorded as laughing. When, as an old woman, she is told she will bear the much wanted son, she did not believe it but 'laughed within herself, saying, After I am waxed old shall I have pleasure, my lord being old also?' (Genesis 18:12): her laughter is bitter-sweet, sad, ironic, even cynical, a foretaste of so much Jewish laughter through the ages. When the son, Isaac, was born, however, 'Sarah said, God hath made me to laugh, so that all who hear will laugh with me' – and her laughter is joyful and triumphant, communicating her delight to us over the distance of four millennia. Then there is the story of how Isaac, a gentle and meditative man, who loved his mother Sarah deeply, secured a wife to take her place – the shy but kind-hearted and loving Rebecca; and this is the first tale in the Bible to move us. Still more stirring, though not strictly from the time of the patriarchs, is the Book of Ruth, describing the affection and devotion between two sorrowing and solitary women, Naomi and her daughter-in-law Ruth. Their emotions are so tenderly and faithfully conveyed that one instinctively believes that a woman set them down. Certainly, the Song of Deborah, which constitutes Chapter 5 of the Book of Judges, with its multitude of feminine images and its triumphant vindication of female strength and courage, must be the lyrical work of a woman. Yet it is clear from internal evidence that this was one of the earliest sections of the Bible to be written down and it seems to have attained more or less its present form not later than 1200 BC.[32] These early Bible records testify to the creative role played by women in the shaping of Hebrew society, to their intellectual and emotional strength, and to their high seriousness.

Yet the early Bible is above all a statement of theology: an account of the direct, often intimate, relationship between the leaders of the people and God. Here the role played by Abraham is determinant. The Bible presents him as the immediate ancestor of the Hebrew people and founder of the nation. He is also the supreme example of the good and just man. He is peace-loving (Genesis 13:8–9), though also willing to fight for his principles and magnanimous in victory (14:22), devoted to his family and hospitable to strangers (18:1), concerned for the welfare of his fellow men (18:23), and above all God-fearing and obedient to divine command (22:12; 26:5). But he is not a paragon. He is a deeply human and realistic personality, sometimes afraid, doubtful, even sceptical, though ultimately always faithful and carrying out God's instructions.

If Abraham was the founder of the Hebrew nation, was he also the founder of the Hebrew religion? In Genesis he appears to inaugurate the special Hebrew relationship with a God who is sole and omnipotent. It is not clear whether he can accurately be called the first monotheist. We can dismiss Wellhausen's Hegelian notions of the Jews, symbolized by Abraham, moving out of their primitive desert background. Abraham was a man familiar with cities, complex legal concepts, and religious ideas which, for their day, were sophisticated. The great Jewish historian Salo Baron sees him as a proto-monotheist, coming from a centre whose flourishing moon-cult was becoming a crude form of monotheism. The names of many of his family, Sarah, Micah, Terah, Laban, for instance, were associated with the moon-cult.[33] There is in the Book of Joshua a cryptic reference to Abraham's idolatrous ancestry: 'even Terah, the father of Abraham . . . served other gods'.[34] The Book of Isaiah, reproducing an ancient tradition otherwise unrecorded in the Bible, says that God 'redeemed Abraham'.[35] The movements of the Semitic peoples westwards, along the arc of the fertile crescent, is usually presented as a drift under the pressure of economic forces. But it is important to grasp that Abraham's compulsion was religious: he responded to an urge he believed came from a great and all-powerful, ubiquitous God. It is possible to argue that, though the monotheistic concept was not fully developed in his mind, he was a man striving towards it, who left Mesopotamian society precisely because it had reached a spiritual impasse.[36]

Abraham may perhaps be most accurately described as a heno-theist: a believer in a sole God, attached to a particular people, who none the less recognized the attachment of other races to their own gods. With this qualification, he is the founder of the Hebrew religious culture, since he inaugurates its two salient characteristics: the covenant with God and the donation of The Land. The notion of the covenant is an extraordinary idea, with no parallel in the ancient Near East. It is true that Abraham's covenant with God, being personal, has not reached the sophistication of Moses' covenant on behalf of an entire people. But the essentials are already there: a contract of obedience in return for special favour, implying for the first time in history the existence of an ethical God who acts as a kind of benign constitutional monarch bound by his own righteous agreements.[37]

The Genesis account, with its intermittent dialogue between Abraham and God, suggests that Abraham's grasp and acceptance of the momentous implications of his bargain were gradual, an example of the way in which the will of God is sometimes revealed in progressive stages. The truth was finally brought home to Abraham, as described in Genesis 22, when God tests him by commanding him to sacrifice his only son, Isaac.[38] This passage is an important milestone in the Bible, as well as being one of the most dramatic and puzzling in the entire history of religion, because it first raises the problem of theodicy, God's sense of justice. Many Jews and Christians have found the passage unconscionable, in that Abraham is commanded to do something not only cruel in itself but contrary to the repudiation of human sacrifice which is part of the bedrock of Hebrew ethics and all subsequent forms of Judaeo-Christian worship. Great Jewish philosophers have struggled to make the story conform to Jewish ethics. Philo argued that it testified to Abraham's detachment from custom or any other ruling passion except the love of God, his recognition that we must give God what we value most, confident that, God being just, we will not lose it. Maimonides agreed that this was a test case of the extreme limits of the love and fear God rightfully demands. Nahmanides saw it as the first instance of the compatibility of divine foreknowledge and human free will.[39] In 1843 Sören Kierkegaard published his philosophical study of this episode, *Fear and Trembling*, in which he portrays Abraham as a 'knight of faith', who has to renounce for God's sake not only his son but his ethical ideals.[40] Most Jewish and Christian moral theologians reject this view, implying an unacceptable conflict between God's will and ethical ideals, though others would agree that the episode is a warning that religion does not necessarily reflect naturalistic ethics.[41]

From the viewpoint of a historian, the tale makes perfect sense because Abraham, as we know from contemporary archives, came from a legal background where it was mandatory to seal a contract or covenant with an animal sacrifice. The covenant with God was of such transcendent enormity that it demanded something more: a sacrifice of the best-loved in the fullest sense, though as the subject of the sacrifice was a human being, it was made abortive, thereby remaining valid but formal and ritualistic rather than actual. Isaac was chosen as the offering not only because he was Abraham's most precious possession but because he was a special gift of God's, under the covenant, and remained God's like all the rest of his gifts to man. This underlines the whole purpose of sacrifice, a symbolic reminder that everything man possesses comes from God and is returnable to him. That is why Abraham called the place of his act of supreme obedience and abortive sacrifice, the Mount of the Lord, an adumbration of Sinai and a greater contract.[42] It is significant of the importance of the event that, for the first time, the Bible narratives introduce the note of universalism into God's promises. He not only undertakes to multiply Abraham's offspring but now also adds: 'And in thy seed shall all the nations of the earth be blessed.'[43]

We are now close to the notion of an elect nation. The Old Testament, it is important to grasp, is not primarily about justice as an abstract concept. It is about God's justice, which manifests itself by God's acts of choice. In Genesis we have various examples of the 'just man', even the only just man: in the story of Noah and the Flood, in the story of the destruction of Sodom, for example. Abraham is a just man too, but there is no suggestion that God chose him because he was the only one, or in any sense because of his merits. The Bible is not a work of reason, it is a work of history, dealing with what are to us mysterious and even inexplicable events. It is concerned with the momentous choices which it pleased God to make.[44] It is essential to the understanding of Jewish history to grasp the importance the Jews have always attached to God's unrestricted ownership of creation. Many Jewish beliefs are designed to dramatize this central fact. The notion of an elect people was part of God's purpose to stress his possession of all created things. Abraham was a crucial figure in this demonstration. The Jewish sages taught: 'Five possessions has the Holy One, blessed be He, made especially his own. These are: the Torah, Heaven and earth, Abraham, Israel and the Holy Sanctuary.'[45] The sages believed that God gave generously of his creation, but retained (as it were) the freehold of everything and a special, possessive relationship with selected elements. Thus we find:

The Holy One, blessed be He, created days, and took to Himself the Sabbath; He created the months, and took to Himself the festivals; He created the years, and chose for Himself the Sabbatical Year; He created the Sabbatical years, and chose for Himself the Jubilee Year; He created the nations, and chose for Himself Israel. . . . He created the lands, and took to Himself the Land of Israel as a heave-offering from all the other lands, as it is written: 'The earth is the Lord's, and the fullness thereof.'[46]

The election of Abraham and his descendants for a special role in God's providence, and the donation of the land, are inseparable in the Biblical presentation of history. Moreover, both gifts are leasehold, not freehold: the Jews are chosen, the land is theirs, by grace and favour, always revocable. Abraham is both a real example and a perpetual symbol of a certain fragility and anxiety in Jewish possession. He is a 'stranger and sojourner' and remains one even after God's election, even after he has elaborately purchased the Cave of Machpelah. This uncertainty of ownership is transferred to all his descendants: as the Bible repeatedly reminds us. Thus God tells the Israelites: 'And the land is not to be sold in perpetuity, for all land is Mine, because you are strangers and sojourners before me'; or again, the people confess: 'For we are strangers before you, and sojourners like all our forefathers'; and the Psalms have David the King say: 'I am a stranger with thee, and a sojourner, as all my fathers were.'[47]

All the same, the promise of the land to Abraham is very specific and it comes in the oldest stratum of the Bible: 'To your descendants I give this land from the river of Egypt to the great river, the river Euphrates, the land of the Kenites, the Kenizzites, the Kadmonites, the Hittites, the Perizzites, the Rephaim, the Amorites, the Canaanites, the Girgashites and the Jebusites.'[48] There is some confusion about the frontiers, since in a later passage God promises only a portion of the larger gift: 'And I will give unto thee, and to thy seed after thee, the land wherein thou art a stranger, all the land of Canaan.'[49] On the other hand, this latter gift is to be 'a perpetual possession'. The implication, here and in later passages, is that the election of Israel can never be revoked, though it can be suspended by human disobedience. As the Lord's promise is irrevocable, the land will ultimately revert to Israel even if she loses it for a time.[50] The notion of the Promised Land is peculiar to Israelite religion and, for the Israelites and the Jews later, it was the most important single element in it. It is significant that the Jews made the five early books of the Bible, the Pentateuch, into the core of their Torah or belief, because they dealt with the Law, the promise of the land, and its fulfilment. The later books, despite all their brilliance and comprehensibility, never acquired the same central significance. They are not so much revelation as a commentary upon it, dominated by the theme of the promise fulfilled.[51] It is the land that matters most.

If Abraham established these fundamentals, it was left to his grandson, Jacob, to bring into existence a distinct people, Israel, his name, and the race, being inextricably linked.[52] There has always been a problem of what to term the ancestors of the Jews. 'Hebrews' is unsatisfactory, though it is often necessary to use it, for the term Habiru, from which it presumably derives, described more a way of life than a specific racial group. Moreover, it was pejorative. 'Hebrew' does indeed occur in the Pentateuch, meaning 'the children of Israel', but only when used by the Egyptians or by the Israelites themselves in the presence of Egyptians. From about the second century BC, when it was so used by Ben Sira, 'Hebrew' was applied to the language of the Bible, and to all subsequent works written in this language. As such it gradually lost its pejorative overtone, so that both to Jews themselves and to sympathetic gentiles, it sometimes seemed preferable to 'Jew' as a racial term. In the nineteenth century, for example, it was much used by the Reform movement in the United States, so that we get such institutions as the Hebrew Union College and the Union of American Hebrew Congregations. But the ancestors of the Jews never by choice called themselves Hebrews. When they became conscious of a national identity, the term they used, normative in the Bible, is Israelites or children of Israel, and it is this which gives Jacob his main significance.

Yet it is curious, and characteristic of the difficulties which have always surrounded Jewish identity and nomenclature, that the first mention of the term, when Jacob was divinely renamed Israel – the moment when the nation was born, as it were – occurs in what is perhaps the most mysterious and obscure passage in the entire Bible, Jacob's night-long struggle with the angel. The term 'Israel' may mean he who fights Gods, he who fights for God, he whom God fights, or whom God rules, the upright one of God, or God is upright. There is no agreement. Nor has anyone yet provided a satisfactory account of what the incident means. It is evident that the earliest editors and transcribers of the Bible did not understand it either. But they recognized it as an important moment in their history and, far from adapting it to suit their religious understanding, reproduced it verbatim because it was Torah, and sacred. The career of Jacob is described at great length in Genesis, and was indeed remarkable. He was quite unlike his grandfather Abraham: a dissimulator, a machiavellian, a strategist rather than a fighter, a politician, an operator, as well as a dreamer and visionary. Jacob prospered mightily and became a much more substantial man than Abraham or his father Isaac. He eventually had himself laid to rest beside the tombs of his forebears, but in the meantime he set up columns or built altars over a wide range of territory. He is described as still a 'stranger' in Canaan like his father.[53] Indeed, all his sons, except the last, Benjamin, seem to have been born in Mesopotamia or Syria. But it is during his lifetime that these links with the east and north were finally severed, and his followers began to think of themselves as linked in some permanent way to Canaan, so that even if they go to Egypt in time of famine, the divine dispensation is that they will return, inexorably.

As the eponymous national leader, Jacob–Israel was also the father of the twelve tribes which in theory composed it. These tribes, Reuben, Simeon (Levi), Judah, Issachar, Zebulun, Benjamin, Dan, Naphtali, Gad, Asher, Ephraim and Manasseh, were all descended from Jacob and his sons, according to Biblical tradition.[54] But in the Song of Deborah, which as we have noted is very ancient, only ten tribes are listed – Ephraim, Benjamin, Machir, Zebulun, Issachar, Reuben, Gilead, Dan, Asher and Naphtali. The context is bellicose, and it may be that Simeon, Levi, Judah and Gad were not listed by Deborah because they were not due to take part in the fight. The number twelve may be a convention: the same number is used for the sons of Ishmael, Nahor, Joktan and Esau.[55] Groupings of twelve tribes (sometimes six) were common in the eastern Mediterranean and Asia Minor in the later Bronze Age. The Greeks called them amphictyons, from a term meaning 'to dwell about'. The unifying factor might not be common ancestry but common devotion to a particular shrine. Many text scholars in the nineteenth and twentieth centuries dismissed the notion of common descent from Jacob and preferred to see the tribal groups of distant and disparate origins organizing themselves as an amphictyony around the Israelite shrines which were being established about this time.[56] But all these West Semitic groups moving into Canaan had common origins and were interrelated; they shared memories, traditions and revered ancestors. Working out the specific tribal histories of all the groups mentioned in the Bible would be impossibly complicated, even if the materials existed.[57] The salient point is that Jacob–Israel is associated with the time at which the Israelites first became conscious of their common identity but within the structure of a tribal system which was already ancient and dear to them. Religious and family links were equally strong, and inextricable in practice, as they were to be throughout Jewish history. In Jacob's day, men still carried their household gods about with them, but it was already becoming possible to think in terms of a national God too.

Abraham had his own religious beliefs, but he courteously paid tribute, being 'a stranger and sojourner', to local deities, known generically as 'El'. Thus he paid tithe to El Elyon at Jerusalem, and he acknowledged El Shaddai at Hebron and El Olan at Beersheba.[58] Jacob's adoption of the name Israel (or Isra-el) marks the point at which Abraham's God becomes located in the soil of Canaan, is identified with Jacob's progeny, the Israelites, and is soon to become the almighty Yahweh, the god of monotheism.

The dominance of Yahweh as the overwhelming focus of Israelite religion – the prototype of the sole 'God' which all Jews, Christians and Moslems worship today – was slowly confirmed during the next phase of the people's history, the movement into Egypt and the dramatic escape from Egyptian bondage. The Bible narrative, ending Genesis with the death of Joseph, then taking up the story again with its disastrous consequences at the beginning of the Book of Exodus, seems to suggest that the nation as a whole went down into Egypt. But this is misleading. It is quite clear that even in Jacob's time many of the Habiru or Hebrews, whom we must now call Israelites, were beginning to settle permanently in Canaan, and even to acquire territory by force. In Genesis 34 we read that Jacob's sons, Simeon and Levi, made a violent and successful assault on the king and city of Shechem, and this suggests the first Israelite possession of a sizeable town, which may well have become the earliest seat of the national God.[59] Shechem was already a city in the nineteenth century BC since it is mentioned in an Egyptian document from the reign of Sesostris III (1878–1843 BC) and later acquired Cyclopaean walls. It is in fact the first city of Canaan referred to in the Bible (Genesis 12:6–7) and Abraham got the divine promise there. Shechem is near the modern Nablus, a name derived from the new city, or Neapolis, which Vespasian built in 72 AD after the reconquest of Palestine. We can identify the site from references in Josephus, writing about 90 AD, and Eusebius, writing before 340 AD, who says ancient Shechem is in the suburbs of Neapolis near Jacob's Well. Clearly Shechem was not merely taken but remained in the hands of Jacob's family, since on his death-bed he bequeathed it to his son Joseph: 'I have given to thee one portion above thy brethren, which I took out of the hand of the Amorite with my sword and with my bow.'[60]

That a large number of the Israelites remained in Canaan is certain, and there is external confirmation that they were active and warlike. The Egyptian documents known as the Amarna Letters, which can be accurately dated 1389–1358 BC, from a time when the pharoahs of the Egyptian New Kingdom were nominally sovereign in Palestine, though their power was slipping, deal with local vassals and their enemies in the region. Some refer to a Hebrew called Labaya or Lion Man; others are actually by him. He caused great difficulties for the Egyptian authorities and their allies; as with all other Habiru, in Egyptian experience, he was hard to control, a nuisance. He eventually met a violent death in the reign of Pharaoh Akhenaten. But in his lifetime he was in control of a small kingdom around Shechem, and his sons inherited his possessions.

So far as we know, in fact, the Israelite–Hebrews were in control of Shechem throughout the time their brethren were in Egyptian bondage. There is no reference to it being taken during Joshua's conquest, yet as soon as the Israelite invaders got into the hills north of Jerusalem they enacted or re-enacted the ceremony of the covenant at Shechem, the place where Abraham first made it.[61] The implication is that it was already, and had long been, in the hands of people they recognized as their co-religionists and racial kin. Shechem was thus, in a sense, the original central shrine and capital of Israelite Canaan. The point is important, since the continuous existence of a sizeable Israelite population in Palestine throughout the period between the original Abrahamite arrival and the return from Egypt makes the Biblical Book of Exodus, which clearly describes only a part of the race, and the conquest narrated in the Book of Joshua, far more credible.[62] The Israelites in Egypt always knew they had a homeland to return to, where part of the population was their natural ally; and this fifth column within the land, in turn, made the attempt to seize Canaan by a wandering band less of a forlorn venture.

So the sojourn in and Exodus from Egypt, and the desert wanderings that followed, involved only part of the Israelite nation. Nevertheless this phase was of crucial importance in the evolution of their religious and ethical culture. Indeed, it was the central episode in their history, and has always been recognized by Jews as such, because it saw emerge for the first time, in transcendent splendour, the character of the unique God they worshipped, his power to deliver them from the greatest empire on earth and to give them a bounteous land of their own; and it also revealed the multitude of his exacting demands which, in return, he expected them to meet. Before they went to Egypt, the Israelites were a small folk almost like any other, though they had a cherished promise of greatness. After they returned, they were a people with a purpose, a programme and a message to the world.

The period opens and closes with two of the most mesmeric characters in the history of the Jews, Joseph and Moses, archetypes of men whose strengths and achievements were to illuminate Jewish history again and again. Both were younger sons, part of that group – Abel, Isaac, Jacob, David and Solomon were other examples – which it seems the peculiar purpose of the Bible to exalt. The Bible shows most leaders born without place or power but raised to it by their own efforts, themselves the product of acts of divine grace.[63] The Bible sees a peculiar virtue in powerlessness, appropriate to a people which has seldom possessed power, and suffered much from its exercise; but it also sees virtue in achievement, and achievement as the sign of virtue, especially of those once weak and lowly. Both Joseph and Moses had no rights of birth, and narrowly survived vulnerable childhoods or youth; but both had the God-endowed qualities to bring them to greatness by their own efforts.

But there the resemblance ends. Joseph was the great minister–statesman of an alien ruler, the pattern of many Jews over the next 3,000 years. He was clever, quick, perceptive, imaginative; a dreamer, but more than a dreamer, a man with the creative ability to interpret complex phenomena, to forecast and foresee, to plan and administer. Quiet, industrious, able in all economic and financial affairs, the master also of many forms of arcane knowledge, he knew well how to serve power and exploit it on behalf of his people. As pharaoh said to him, 'there is none so discreet and wise as thou art'.[64] Joseph occupies a great deal of space in Genesis, and he clearly fascinated the early scribes who first sorted out these many tales and then blended them together with considerable art and symmetry. But there is no doubt about his historicity. Indeed, some of the more romantic episodes in his life have echoes in Egyptian literature. His attempted seduction by Potiphar's wife, who in her fury at her rejection by him resorts to slander and has him thrown into prison, occurs in an ancient Egyptian narrative called *The Tale of the Two Brothers*, which first reached written form in a papyrus manuscript dated 1225 BC. Foreigners frequently rose high at the Egyptian court. In the fourteenth century BC, Joseph's career was paralleled by a Semite with the name of Yanhamu, Egyptian high commissioner in the empire under the Pharaoh Akhenaten. Later, in the thirteenth century, the marshal of Pharaoh Meneptah's court was a Semite called Ben Ozen.[65] Most of the Egyptian detail in the Joseph narrative appears to be authentic.

That West Semites came into Egypt in large numbers is certain. They began to penetrate the Nile Delta as early as the end of the third millennium BC. These immigrants usually came peacefully; sometimes willingly in search of commerce and work; sometimes driven by hunger – for the Nile was much the most regular provider of grain surpluses – and sometimes as slaves. There is a famous passage in an Egyptian papyrus, Anastasi VI, in which Egyptian frontier guards notify the palace of a tribe passing through in search of pasture and water. Papyrus No. 1116a in Leningrad shows a gracious pharaoh donating rations of wheat and beer to headmen identified as coming from Ashkelon, Hazor and Megiddo. For a time, indeed, from the eighteenth to the sixteenth centuries BC, Egypt had a dynasty of foreign rulers called the Hyksos. Some of their names seem Semitic – Khyan, Yakubher, for example. In the first century AD the Jewish historian Josephus, trying to buttress the Exodus story, quoted Manetho to link it with the eventual expulsion of the Hyksos in the mid-sixteenth century. But the Egyptian detail in the Bible would fit more neatly with a later period.

Indeed there is pretty convincing evidence that the period of Egyptian oppression, which finally drove the Israelites to revolt and escape, occurred towards the last quarter of the second millennium BC, and almost certainly in the reign of the famous Rameses II (1304–1237 BC). At the opening of the Book of Exodus, it said of the Egyptians: 'Therefore they did set over them taskmasters to afflict them with their burdens. And they built for Pharaoh store-cities, Pithom and Rameses.'[66] Rameses II, the greatest builder of the nineteenth-dynasty New Kingdom rulers – indeed the most prolific builder since the pyramid-creators of the Old Kingdom – engaged in tremendous building-works at Pithom, the modern Tell er-Rataba in the Wadi Tummilat, and in the place he called after himself, Rameses or Pi Ramesu, the modern San el-Hagar on the Tanatic arm of the Nile.[67] These nineteenth-dynasty pharaohs came from this part of the Delta, to which they transferred the central government, near the Biblical land of Goshen. Vast numbers of forced or slave labourers were employed. A papyrus from Rameses II's reign, Leiden 348, states: 'Distribute grain rations to the soldiers and to the Habiru who transport stones to the great pylon of Rameses.'[68] But it is not probable that the exodus itself took place in Rameses' reign. It seems more likely that the Israelites broke out under his successor, Merneptah. A victory stele of this pharaoh has survived and been dated 1220 BC. It relates that he won a battle beyond Sinai, in Canaan, and refers to the defeated as 'Israel'. He may not have won, as pharaohs often presented their defeats or stalemates as triumphs, but it is clear that he fought some kind of engagement with the Israelites outside his territory, so they had already left. This is the first non-Biblical reference to Israel. Taken in conjunction with other evidence, such as calculations based on I Kings 6:1 and Judges 11:26,[69] we can be reasonably sure that the Exodus occurred in the thirteenth century BC and had been completed by about 1225 BC.

The stories of the plagues of Egypt, and the other wonders and miracles which preceded the Israelite break-out, have so dominated our reading of Exodus that we sometimes lose sight of the sheer physical fact of the successful revolt and escape of a slave-people, the only one recorded in antiquity. It became an overwhelming memory for the Israelites who participated in it. For those who heard, and later read, about it, the Exodus gradually replaced the creation itself as the central, determining event in Jewish history. Something happened, at the frontiers of Egypt, that persuaded the eye-witnesses that God had intervened directly and decisively in their fate. The way it was related and set down convinced subsequent generations that this unique demonstration of God's mightiness on their behalf was the most remarkable event in the whole history of nations.

Despite intensive investigations over many years, we really have no idea where the hand of the Lord saved Israel from pharaoh's army.[70] The critical phrase is 'at the sea of reeds' or 'at the sea'. This could mean one of the salt lakes, or the northern end of the Suez Gulf, or even the top of the Gulf of Aqaba; another alternative is the Serbonian Sea (Lake Sirbonis) in northern Sinai, which in effect is a lagoon of the Mediterranean.[71] What we do know is that the frontier was heavily defended in places and policed throughout. The episode which saved the Israelites from pharaoh's fury, and which they saw as divine redemption, was so stupendous as to become for them and their progeny the dynamic of their whole spiritual existence. Ask yourselves, Moses said to them, since the day God created man, 'whether there hath been any such thing as this great thing, or hath been heard like it?' Has God ever before 'assayed to go and take him a nation from the midst of another nation, by temptations, by signs and by wonders, and by war, and by a mighty hand and a stretched-out arm, and by great terrors, according to all that the Lord your God did for you in Egypt before your eyes?' In Exodus, Moses has God himself point to the stupendous wonder of his acts, and show how they relate to his plans for them as a people: 'Ye have seen what I did to the Egyptians, and how I bare you on eagles' wings and brought you unto myself. Now therefore, if ye will obey my voice in deed, and keep my covenant, then ye shall be a peculiar treasure unto me above all people: for all the earth is mine. And ye shall be unto me a kingdom of priests, and an holy nation.'[72]

This overwhelming event was matched by the extraordinary man who made himself the leader of the Israelite revolt. Moses is the fulcrum-figure in Jewish history, the hinge around which it all turns. If Abraham was the ancestor of the race, Moses was the essentially creative force, the moulder of the people; under him and through him, they became a distinctive people, with a future as a nation. He was a Jewish archetype, like Joseph, but quite different and far more formidable. He was a prophet and a leader; a man of decisive actions and electric presence, capable of huge wrath and ruthless resolve; but also a man of intense spirituality, loving solitary communion with himself and God in the remote countryside, seeing visions and epiphanies and apocalypses; and yet not a hermit or anchorite but an active spiritual force in the world, hating injustice, fervently seeking to create a Utopia, a man who not only acted as intermediary between God and man but sought to translate the most intense idealism into practical statesmanship, and noble concepts into details of everyday life. Above all, he was a lawmaker and judge, the engineer of a mighty framework to enclose in a structure of rectitude every aspect of public and private conduct – a totalitarian of the spirit.

The books of the Bible which recount his work, especially Exodus, Deuteronomy and Numbers, present Moses as a giant conduit through which the divine radiance and ideology poured into the hearts and minds of the people. But we must also see Moses as an intensely original person, becoming progressively, through experiences which were both horrific and ennobling, a fierce creative force, turning the world upside down, taking everyday concepts accepted unthinkingly by countless generations and transforming them into something totally new, so that the world becomes a quite different place in consequence, and there can be no turning back to the old ways of seeing things. He illustrates the fact, which great historians have always recognized, that mankind does not invariably progress by imperceptible steps but sometimes takes a giant leap, often under the dynamic propulsion of a solitary, outsize personality. That is why the contention of Wellhausen and his school that Moses was a later fiction and the Mosaic code a fabrication of the post-Exilic priests in the second half of the first millennium BC – a view still held by some historians today – is scepticism carried to the point of fanaticism, a vandalizing of the human record. Moses was beyond the power of the human mind to invent, and his power leaps out from the page of the Bible narrative, as it once imposed itself on a difficult and divided people, often little better than a frightened mob.

Yet it is important to note that Moses, though an outsize figure, was in no sense a superhuman one. Jewish writers and sages, fighting against the strong tendency in antiquity to deify founder-figures, often went out of their way to stress the human weaknesses and failings of Moses. But there was no need; it is all in the record. Perhaps the most convincing aspect of the Biblical presentation is the way in which it shows Moses as hesitant and uncertain almost to the point of cowardice, mistaken, wrong-headed, foolish, irritable and, what is still more remarkable, bitterly conscious of his shortcomings. It is very rare indeed for a great man to confess: 'I am slow of speech, and of a slow tongue.'[73] Lack of articulation is about the last disqualification a lawgiver and statesman will admit. Still more striking are the images of Moses as an isolated, rather desperate and inefficient figure, struggling with the burdens of a huge role he has reluctantly accepted but grimly seeks to discharge. Exodus 18 shows him conscientiously sitting in judgment, from dawn till dusk, hearing cases brought to him by the people. His father-in-law Jethro, on a visit, asks indignantly: 'Why sittest thou thyself alone, and all the people stand by thee from morning until even?' Moses replies wearily: 'Because the people come unto me to inquire of God! When they have a matter, they come unto me; and I judge between one and another, and I do make them know the statutes of God, and his laws.' To this Jethro replies: 'The thing that thou doest is not good. Thou will surely wear away, both thou, and this people that is with thee.' So he proposes the creation of a regular, trained judiciary, and Moses, being in many ways a modest man, with the magnanimity to solicit and follow good advice, does as the old man proposes.[74]

Moses, as he comes to us from the Bible, is a deeply appealing mixture of the heroic and the human, who dealt in tremendous certitudes which concealed all kinds of doubts and sometimes sheer bewilderment. Because of his position, he had to keep up a brave front of omniscience; because he had to keep his fissiparous horde together, he was obliged to thunder confidently, even when unsure, and to display publicly a relentlessness he did not feel in his heart. So his image was stern, his watchword 'Let the Law bend the mountain.' There is no doubt truth in the early aggadic tradition that Aaron was more popular than his far greater brother: when Aaron died, everyone wept, but when Moses died only the menfolk mourned.[75] With the Bible record, readers today have perhaps a clearer picture of Moses' whole character than the men and women who actually followed him.

Moses was not only the most influential of all the Jews of antiquity before Christ; he was also the only one to make a considerable impact on the ancient world. The Greeks conflated him with their own gods and heroes, especially Hermes and Musaeos; he was credited with inventing Hebrew writing, seen as the prelude to Phoenician script and so of Greek. Eupolemus said he was the first wise man in the history of mankind. Artapanos credited him with organizing the Egyptian system of government and inventing all kinds of warlike and industrial machinery. Aristobulus thought that both Homer and Hesiod drew inspiration from his works, and there was a general view among many ancient writers that mankind as a whole, and Greek civilization in particular, owed much to his ideas.[76] Not surprisingly, Jewish writers of antiquity endorsed this tradition of Moses as a leading architect of ancient culture. Josephus says he invented the very word 'law', then unknown in Greek, and was the first legislator in world history.[77] Philo accused both philosophers and lawgivers of plundering or copying his ideas, Heraclitus and Plato being the chief culprits.[78] Still more striking is the assertion of the pagan writer Numenius of Apamea (second century AD) that Plato was just a Moses who spoke Greek.[79] The ancient writers were not merely convinced of Moses' existence: they saw him as one of the formative figures of world history.

But there was also a tendency among pagan writers, from the second half of the first millennium BC, to see Moses as a baleful figure, the creator of a form of religion which was strange, narrow, exclusive and anti-social. Moses is strongly associated with the very earliest stirrings of systematic anti-Semitism. Hecataeus of Abdera (fourth century BC), who wrote a history of Egypt (now lost), accused him of secluding his followers from other men, and encouraging xenophobia. Manetho (c. 250 BC) first put about the extraordinarily persistent legend that Moses was not a Jew at all but an Egyptian, a renegade priest of Heliopolis, who commanded the Jews to kill all the Egyptian sacred animals and set up alien rule.[80] The notion of the rebellious Egyptian priest, leading a revolt of outcasts including lepers and negroes, became the fundamental matrix of anti-Semitism, the Ur-libel, embroidered and repeated through the centuries with extraordinary persistence. It is reproduced, for instance, twice in anti-Semitic passages in Karl Marx's letters to Engels.[81] It is curious, too, that Sigmund Freud, certainly no anti-Semite, based his last work, *Moses and Monotheism*, on Manetho's story that Moses was an Egyptian and a priest, adding the common speculation that his religious ideas were derived from the monotheistic sun-cult of Akhenaten, and much pseudo-factual nonsense of his own.[82]

Wherever else Moses got his ideas, whether religious or legal (and the two, of course, were inseparable in his mind), it was certainly not Egypt. Indeed the work of Moses can be seen as a total repudiation of everything that ancient Egypt stood for. As with Abraham's migration from Ur and Haran to Canaan, we must not assume that the Israelite exodus from Egypt was dictated purely by economic motives. This was not just an escape from hardship. There are indeed hints in the Bible that the hardships were endurable; Moses' horde often hankered for 'the flesh-pots of Egypt'. Life in Egypt, throughout the second millennium BC, was more gracious (as a general rule) than in any other part of the ancient Near East. The motive for the Exodus was political, certainly. The Israelites in Egypt were a large and awkward minority, and a growing one. The opening of Exodus has pharaoh say 'to his people' that the Israelites are becoming 'more and mightier than we: come, let us deal wisely with them, lest they multiply'.[83] Egyptian fear of Israelite numbers was the principal motive for their oppression, which was specifically designed to reduce their ranks. Pharaonic slavery was, in a sinister way, a distant adumbration of Hitler's slave-labour programme and even of his Holocaust: there are disturbing parallels.

So the Exodus was an act of political separation and resistance; but it was also, and above all, a religious act. For the Israelites were distinct, and were seen and feared by the Egyptians as distinct, precisely because they rejected the whole weird and teeming pantheon of Egyptian gods, and the entire spirit of Egyptian spirituality, which in its own way was as intense and all-pervasive as the dawning religion of Israel. Just as Abraham felt that religion in Ur had come to an impasse, so the Israelites and their leader Moses, who saw more clearly than the rest, found the world of Egyptian religious belief and practice suffocating, insufferable, odious and evil. To leave was to break out not just of physical slavery but of an airless spiritual prison: the lungs of Israel in Egypt craved for a fiercer oxygen of truth, and a way of life which was purer, freer and more responsible. Egyptian civilization was very ancient and very childish, and the Israelite escape from it was a bid for maturity.

In this maturing process, the Israelites were of course acting, in the long run, not just for themselves, but for the whole of humanity to come. The discovery of monotheism, and not just of monotheism but of a sole, omnipotent God actuated by ethical principles and seeking methodically to impose them on human beings, is one of the great turning-points in history, perhaps the greatest of all. How great can be seen by considering the Egyptian world-view which the Israelites rejected. The Egyptians were extraordinarily skilful in using their hands and they had impeccable visual taste, but their intellectual notions were archaic in the extreme. They found it difficult or impossible to grasp general concepts. They had little sense of cumulative, as opposed to repetitive, time, and so no true grasp of history. The notion of linear progress was incomprehensible to them. Their conceptual distinctions between life and death, between the human, animal and vegetable worlds, were fragile and insecure. Their beliefs had more in common with the cyclical and animistic religions of the orient and Africa than anything we are accustomed to call religion in the West. Heaven and earth were different in degree, not kind, and heaven was ruled through a king in whom the creator was incarnate and of whom pharaoh was the earthly manifestation. Society in both heaven and earth was stable and static and necessarily so, and any form of change was aberrant and evil. It was very characteristic of this static society that it had no sense of impersonal law, and therefore no codified let alone written law at all. The pharaoh was the source and master of the law, his judges – there were courts, of course – sitting vicariously to enact his arbitrary judgments.

The world-view in the Mesopotamian cultures of the third and second millennia BC was very different. It was much more dynamic, but also more confused. They rejected the notion of a single god as the ultimate source of power. Unlike the Egyptians, who were constantly adding new gods to their pantheon if theological difficulties arose, they believed all the leading gods had been created. The community of these gods exercised final authority, chose the head of the pantheon (such as Marduk) and made humans immortal when desirable. Heaven was thus in a continuous state of restlessness, like human society. Indeed, each was a replica of the other, with the ziggurat a connecting link. But the human monarch was not divine – it was rare for Mesopotamian societies at this stage to believe in god-kings – nor was he absolute; he was accountable to the gods.[84] The monarch could not enact or dispense law arbitrarily. In fact the individual was protected by cosmic law, which was unalterable.[85] Being dynamic, and therefore offering the idea of progress, ideas current in ancient Mesopotamian society were much preferable to the dead hand of Egypt. They offered hope, as opposed to the resignation or fatalism of Afro-Asian norms, which Egypt so strikingly exemplified. Whereas the pyramid was the tomb of a dead god–king, the ziggurat–temple was a living bond between earth and heaven. On the other hand, these ideas provided no ethical basis for life, and they led to a great deal of uncertainty as to what the gods stood for or wanted. Their delight and anger was arbitrary and inexplicable. Man was endlessly and blindly seeking to propitiate them by sacrifices.

In one important respect, these Mesopotamian societies, spreading out into the West, were becoming more sophisticated. They were developing forms of scripts far more efficient than the Egyptian hieroglyph and its derivatives, and they rightly saw this invention as a source of power. They believed, therefore, that writing down a law strengthened its force and made it numinous. From the end of the third millennium onwards legal systems grew in density and complexity, and were reflected not only in masses of individual legal documents but in written legal codes, the spread of the Akkadian script and language encouraging rulers to compile their laws in societies as widely separated as Elam and Anatolia, among the Hurrians and the Hittites, at Ugarit and on the Mediterranean littoral.

The earliest version of the Mosaic code, which we presume to have been promulgated about 1250 BC, was thus part of a tradition which was already ancient. The first code, discovered among texts in the Museum of the Ancient Orient in Istanbul, dates from about 2050 BC, the work of Ur Nammu, 'king of Sumer and Akkad', the Third Dynasty of Ur. This states, among other things, that the god Nanna chose Ur Nammu to rule, and he got rid of dishonest officials and established correct weights and measures. Abraham must have been familiar with its provisions. Another code, which Abraham may have known too, dates from about 1920 BC: two tablets now in the Iraq Museum, from the ancient kingdom of Eshnuna, written in Akkadian, list about sixty property regulations laid down by the god, Tiskpak, and transmitted through the local king. Far more comprehensive are the early nineteenth-century BC tablets, mainly in the University of Pennsylvania, which give the code of King Lipt-Ishrar of Idi, written (like Ur Nammu) in Sumerian; and, most impressive of all, the code of Hammurabi, found in 1901 at Susa, east of Babylon, written in Akkadian on a 6-foot-high diorite slab, now in the Louvre, and dated 1728–1686 BC.[86] Other, later law-codes include a Mid-Assyrian set of clay tablets unearthed by German archaeologists in the years before the First World War at Qalat Shergat (ancient Ashur), which probably go back to the fifteenth century BC, and are perhaps the closest in date to the original Mosaic code.[87]

In collecting and codifying Israeli law, therefore, Moses had ample precedent. He had been brought up at court; he was literate. To set down the law in writing, to have it carved in stone, was part of the liberating act of fleeing from Egypt, where there was no statutory law, to Asia, where it was by now the custom. None the less, though the Mosaic code was in this sense part of a Near Eastern tradition, its divergences from all other ancient codes are so many and so fundamental as to make it something entirely new. Firstly, the other law-codes, though said to be inspired by God, are given and worded by individual kings, such as Hammurabi or Ishtar; they are thus revocable, changeable and essentially secular. By contrast, in the Bible, God alone writes the law – legislation throughout the Pentateuch is all his – and no Israelite king was ever permitted, or even attempted, to formulate a law-code. Moses (and, much later, Ezekiel, transmitter of the law reforms) was a prophet, not a king, and a divine medium, not a sovereign legislator. Hence, in his code there is no distinction between the religious and the secular – all are one – or between civil, criminal and moral law.[88]

This indivisibility had important practical consequences. In Mosaic legal theory, all breaches of the law offend God. All crimes are sins, just as all sins are crimes. Offences are absolute wrongs, beyond the power of man unaided to pardon or expunge. Making restitution to the offended mortal is not enough; God requires expiation too, and this may involve drastic punishment. Most law-codes of the ancient Near East are property-orientated, people themselves being forms of property whose value can be assessed. The Mosaic code is God-oriented. For instance, in other codes, a husband may pardon an adulterous wife and her lover. The Mosaic code, by contrast, insists both must be put to death.[89] Again, whereas the other codes include the royal right to pardon even in capital cases, the Bible provides no such remedy. Indeed, in capital cases it repudiates the notion of 'rich man's law': a murderer, however rich, cannot escape execution by paying money, even if his victim is a mere servant or slave, and there are many other crimes where God's anger is so great that financial compensation is not enough to appease the divine wrath. Where, however, the intention is not to wound or kill or sin grievously, and the injury is the unintended consequence of mischievous behaviour, God is less offended, and the laws of compensation apply. The offender then 'shall pay as the judges determine'. This applied, the Mosaic code laid down, in the case where a man strikes a woman and she has a miscarriage, or when death follows a culpable accident, and in all lesser cases, 'eye for eye, tooth for tooth, hand for hand, foot for foot',[90] a much misunderstood passage, which simply means that strict compensation for the injury is due. On the other hand, where the degree of culpability for an injury, though accidental, is criminal, the capital law must take its course. Thus an ox which gores a man to death is simply forfeit, and the owner unpunished; but if he knows his beast is dangerous, and he has failed to take proper measures, and a man is killed in consequence, the owner must suffer capitally.[91]

This last provision, known as 'The Law of the Goring Ox', testifies to the huge importance the Mosaic code attaches to human life. There is a paradox here, as there is in all ethical use of capital punishment. In Mosaic theology, man is made in God's image, and so his life is not just valuable, it is sacred. To kill a man is an offence against God so grievous that the ultimate punishment, the forfeiture of life, must follow; money is not enough. The horrific fact of execution thus underscores the sanctity of human life. Under Mosaic law, then, many men and women met their deaths whom the secular codes of surrounding societies would have simply permitted to compensate their victims or their victims' families.

But the converse is also true, as a result of the same axiom. Whereas other codes provided the death penalty for offences against property, such as looting during a fire, breaking into a house, serious trespass by night, or theft of a wife, in the Mosaic law no property offence is capital. Human life is too sacred where the rights of property alone are violated. It also repudiates vicarious punishment: the offences of parents must not be punished by the execution of sons or daughters, or the husband's crime by the surrender of the wife to prostitution.[92] Moreover, not only is human life sacred, the human person (being in God's image) is precious. Whereas, for instance, the Mid-Assyrian code lists a fierce series of physical punishments, including facial mutilation, castration, impalement and flogging to death, the Mosaic code treats the body with respect. Physical cruelty is reduced to the minimum. Even flogging was limited to forty strokes, and must be carried out 'before the face' of the judge, 'lest, if he should exceed, and beat him above these with many stripes, then thy brother should seem vile unto thee'.[93] The fact is, the Mosaic code was far more humane than any other, because, being God-centred, it was automatically man-centred also.

The core of the Mosaic code was the Decalogue, the statements of God related by Moses (Deuteronomy 5:6–18) and entitled 'the ten words or utterances' (Deuteronomy 4:13). The supposed original versions of these commands is given in Exodus 20:2–14. There are many unresolved problems and obscurities in the texts. It seems likely that in their original form the commands were simple, even terse, and only later elaborated. The earliest form, as given directly by Moses, has been reconstructed as follows, falling naturally into three groups, one to four covering the relations between God and man, six to ten dealing with relations between men, and the fifth, acting as a bridge between the two, dealing with parents and children. Thus we get: 'I am YHWH your God; You shall have no other gods besides me; You shall not make yourselves a graven image; You shall not take the name of YHWH in vain; Remember the Sabbath day; Honour your father and your mother; You shall not kill; You shall not commit adultery; You shall not steal; You shall not bear false witness; You shall not covet.'[94] Some of these ethical rules are common to other ancient Near Eastern civilizations: there is, for instance, an Egyptian document known as the 'Protestations of Guiltlessness', in which a dead soul, at the final judgment, recites a list of offences not committed.[95] But for a comprehensive summary of right conduct to God and man, offered to, accepted by and graven upon the hearts of an entire people, there is nothing in antiquity remotely comparable to the Ten Commandments.

The Decalogue was the basis of the covenant with God, first made by Abraham, renewed by Jacob and now renewed again, in a solemn and public manner, by Moses and the entire people. Modern research shows that the Mosaic covenant, set out briefly in Exodus 19–24 and again more elaborately in the Book of Deuteronomy, follows the form of an ancient Near Eastern treaty, such as those drawn up by the Hittites. It has a historical prolegomenon, setting out the purpose, followed by the nature of the undertaking, the divine witnesses, benefits and curses, the text and the deposit of the tablets on which it is written.[96] But the Mosaic covenant is unique in being, not a treaty between states, but a God–people alliance. In it, in effect, the ancient Israelite society merged its interests with God's and accepted Him, in return for protection and prosperity, as a totalitarian ruler whose wishes governed every aspect of their lives. Thus the Decalogue is merely the heart of an elaborate system of divine laws set out in the books of Exodus, Deuteronomy and Numbers. In late antiquity, Judaic scholars organized the laws into 613 commandments, consisting of 248 mandatory commandments and 365 prohibitions.[97]

This Mosaic legal material covers an immense variety of subjects. By no means all of it dates from Moses' time, let alone in the form it has come down to us. Some of it deals with settled agriculture, for instance, and must date from the period after the conquest of Canaan. It is conjectured that this was simply taken over from Canaanite law, ultimately of Sumerian, Babylonian, Assyrian and Hittite origin.[98] But the Israelites were already becoming a very legal-minded people, quite capable of innovation, or of transforming the notions they found around them so thoroughly as to constitute novelty. The old theory that the mass of the Mosaic material derives from post-Exilic times can now be dismissed. The technical book of Leviticus, highly ritualistic and providing the legal basis for organized religious and civic life among the Israelites, fits in very well with what we know of the political history of the Israelites in the thirteenth and twelfth centuries

BC. The same can be said for Deuteronomy, which is a popular presentation for a general audience of the priestly writings in Leviticus. The material concerns such matters as diet, medicine, rudimentary science and professional practice, as well as law. Much of it is highly original but all of it is consistent with non-Biblical material, covering similar topics, which was composed in the Near East in the Late Bronze Age, or had already been circulating for centuries.

But though in some ways the Israelites of Moses' time were typical of their age, certain marked characteristics were emerging. The Mosaic laws were very strict in sexual matters. For instance, the Ugaritic laws, revealed in the Ras Shamra tablets, permitted fornication, adultery, bestiality and incest in certain circumstances.[99] The Hittites would allow some forms of bestiality (though not incest). The Egyptians regarded consanguinity as relatively unimportant. The Israelites, by contrast, banned all irregular forms of sex, and they had a list of forbidden degrees of marriage, including affinity as well as consanguinity.[100]

The Israelites seem to have derived some of their dietary laws from the Egyptians, but there were many differences. Israelites, like Egyptians, were forbidden creatures from the sea which had no fins or scales. Pious Egyptians, however, were not supposed to eat fish at all. On the other hand they could, and did, eat many kinds of water-fowl, which the Israelites were forbidden. But they, like the Egyptians, could eat doves, pigeons, geese and other domestic fowl, partridges and quail. There seems to have been some kind of crude scientific basis, rather than pure superstition, for most of the Mosaic rules. Predatory and carnivorous animals were regarded as risky, and forbidden; 'clean' animals were, on the whole, exclusively vegetarian, cloven-footed and ruminant – moufflon, antelope, roebuck, ibex, fallow-deer and gazelle. Swine were forbidden because they were dangerous when eaten undercooked, harbouring parasitic organisms. The Israelites would not touch raptors or vultures either. They classified the camel as unclean because it was valuable. What is more difficult to understand is why they banned hares and coneys.

Israelite laws on hygiene usually followed Egyptian practice. There is a great deal of medical lore in the Mosaic material, and much of this also comes from Egypt, which had a medical tradition going back at least to Imhotep, around 2650 BC. Four of the most important Egyptian medical papyri, even in the copies we possess, were earlier than or contemporary with the Mosaic era. Medical empiricism was often enacted in ancient legal codes of the second millennium BC – in the law of Hammurabi, for instance, written about 500 years before

Moses' day. But the famous section in the Bible dealing with leprosy, which sets down the diagnostic and therapeutic duties of a special category of priests, is unique.

What is also unique, and already in Mosaic times possessing a long history, is the Israelite stress on circumcision. This practice was not used among the Canaanites or Philistines, or the Assyrians and Babylonians. The Edomites, Moabites and Ammonites used it, and so did the Egyptians. But none of these societies attached transcendent importance to the custom, and one has the impression it was generally dying out in the second millennium BC. This in itself attests the antiquity of the Israelite custom, which is first mentioned as being performed by Abraham as part of his original covenant. The great French scholar, Père de Vaux, believed that the Israelites first used it as an initiation rite before marriage.[101] For those ancient societies which practised it, this was its function, and it was performed around the age of thirteen. But Moses' son was circumcised at birth by his mother Zipporah (Exodus 4:24–6), and the ceremonial removal of the foreskin on the eighth day after birth was then enshrined in the Mosaic legislation (Leviticus 12:3). Thus the Israelites divorced the rite from its link to male puberty and, in accordance with their already marked tendency to historicize custom, made it an indelible symbol of an historic covenant and membership of a chosen people.[102] They kept up the tradition, going back to Abraham, that ancient flint knives must be used.[103] The law of circumcision was retained, long after all other early societies had abandoned it, as an indelible sign of the unity between the people and their beliefs. It was not just, as Tacitus was to sneer, to make Jews different. But of course it did this too, and was another element added to the growing pattern of anti-Semitism.[104]

The Sabbath was the other great and ancient institution which differentiated the Israelites from other peoples, and was also the seed of future unpopularity. The idea seems to have been derived from Babylonian astronomy, but its rationale in the Books of Exodus and Deuteronomy is variously stated as commemorating God's rest after creation, the liberation of Israel from Egyptian slavery and the humanitarian need to give labourers, especially slaves and beasts of burden, some respite. The day of rest is one of the great Jewish contributions to the comfort and joy of mankind. But it was a holy day as well as a rest-day, being increasingly associated in the minds of the people with the belief in the elect nation of God, so that eventually Ezekiel has God present it as designed to differentiate Jews from others: 'Moreover also I gave them my sabbaths, to be a sign between me and them, that they might know that I am the Lord that sanctify them.'[105] So this, too, became an element in the belief of other peoples that the Jews held aloof from the rest of humanity.

The Israelites were already in the process of becoming very distinctive, and in certain critical respects they were spiritually in advance of their age. But they were still a primitive people by the standards of advanced societies in 1250 BC. Even in their spirituality they retained many backward elements, and continued to do so for centuries. Indeed, being both historically minded and legalistic, they were inclined to formalize and cling to old superstitions. There were many taboos, for instance, concerning sex, blood and battle.[106] Belief in magic was ubiquitous and institutionalized. Moses not only talked to God face to face and presided over stupendous miracles, he also performed magic tricks. Staffs and rods which turned into snakes, the vulgar commonplace of ancient Near Eastern magic, were part of Israelite religion too, and sanctified from the age of Moses and Aaron onward. The earlier prophets, at least, were expected to perform, and often wore the magician's apparatus. We read of charismatic cloaks or mantles, as worn by Elijah and inherited by Elisha. Zedekiah made himself a pair of magic iron horns.[107] Samson illustrated the belief that hair was a locus of power, and this was reflected in ritual tonsure.[108] Prophets practised ecstasy states and may have used incense and narcotics to produce impressive effects.[109] In one book of the Bible alone the performances recorded include a magnet trick, a water trick, imposing disease, curing it, an antidote to poison, a bringing-back to life, causing lightning to strike, expanding an oil jar and feeding a multitude.[110]

All the same the Israelites were the first people to bring their reason systematically to bear on religious questions. From Moses' day onwards, and throughout their history, rationalism was a central element in Jewish belief. In a sense, it is *the* central element, for monotheism is itself a rationalization. If supernatural, unearthly power exists, how can it be, as it were, radiated from woods and springs, rivers and rocks? If the motions of the sun and moon and stars can be predicted and measured, and thus obey regular laws, how can they be the source of unnatural authority, since they too are plainly part of nature? Whence, then, comes the power? Just as man learns to lord it over nature, animal and inanimate, must not divine power, *a fortiori*, be living and personal? And if God lives, how can his power be arbitrarily and unequally divided into a pantheon of deities? The idea of a limited god is a contradiction. Once the process of reason is applied to divinity, the idea of a sole, omnipotent and personal God, who being infinitely superior to man in power, and therefore virtue, is consistently guided in his actions by systematic ethical principles, follows as a matter of course. Looking back from the perspective of the twentieth century, we see Judaism as the most conservative of religions. But in its origins it was the most revolutionary. Ethical monotheism began the process whereby the world-picture of antiquity was destroyed.

Granted the concept of a sole, omnipotent God, the Israelites rightly deduced that he could not be, as the pagan gods were, part of the world, or even the whole; he was not one of the forces which sustained the universe, or even all of them. His dimensions were infinitely greater: the entire universe was his mere creation. The Israelites thus attributed a far greater power and distance to God than any other religion of antiquity. God is the cause of all things, from earthquakes to political and military disasters. There is no other source of power, demons being God-activated; divinity is indivisible, unique, single. And, since God is not merely bigger than the world, but infinitely bigger, the idea of representing him is absurd.[111] It stands to reason, then, that to try to make an image of him is insulting. The Israelite ban on images, though not the oldest part of their religion, is very ancient and emerged soon after the cult of monotheism became established. It became the fiery symbol of the religion's puritan fundamentalists, the aspect they found most difficult to impose on the nation as a whole, the most obvious, visible difference between the Israelite religion and all others, and the dogma the rest of the world most resented, since it meant that strict Israelites, and later Jews, could not honour their gods. It was closely linked not just to Israelite exclusiveness but to aggression, since they were told not merely to forswear images but destroy them:

> You shall tear down their altars, and break their pillars, and cut down their Asherim (for you shall worship no other God , for the Lord, whose name is Jealous, is a Jealous God), lest you make a covenant with the inhabitants of the land, and when you play the harlot after their gods and sacrifice to their gods and one invites you, you eat of his sacrifice, and you take of their daughters for your sons, and their daughters play the harlot after their gods and make your sons play the harlot after their gods.

This passage from Exodus reflects a terrible fear and fanaticism.[112]

Moreover, the Israelites were wrong to suppose – if they did suppose – that the use of images was a form of religious infantilism. Most Near Eastern religions of antiquity did not regard idols of wood or stone or bronze as gods in themselves. They saw the image as a practical means whereby the ordinary, simple worshipper can visualize the divinity and achieve spiritual communion with him. This has always been the Roman Catholic justification for the use of images, not just of God but of saints. In moving from paganism, the Israelites were clearly right to insist on a greater intellectualization of the deity, a move towards the abstract. It was part of their religious revolution. But intellectualization is difficult, and the Israelites themselves did not despise visual aids, albeit verbal images. The Bible abounds with anthropomorphism of the deity.

There is a further contradiction. How can man be made in God's image, if the image of God is unimaginable, and therefore forbidden? Yet the idea of man as conceived in the divine image is as central to the religion as the ban on idols. In a way, it is the foundation of its morality, being an enormously comprehensive principle.[113] As man is in God's image, he belongs to God; the concept helps man to grasp that he does not possess real and permanent ownership even over himself, let alone over anything else he receives from God's bounty. His body is a leasehold; he is answerable to God for what he does to and with it. But the principle also means that the body – man – must be treated with respect and even dignity. Man has inalienable rights. Indeed, the Mosaic code is a code not only of obligations and prohibitions but also, in embryonic form, of rights.

It is more: it is a primitive declaration of equality. Not only is man, as a category, created in God's image; all individual men are also created in God's image. In this sense they are all equal. Nor is this equality notional; it is real in one all-important sense. All Israelites are equal before God, and therefore equal before his law. Justice is for all, irrespective of other inequalities which may exist. All kinds of privileges are implicit and explicit in the Mosaic code, but on essentials it does not distinguish between varieties of the faithful. All, moreover, shared in accepting the covenant; it was a popular, even a democratic, decision.

Thus the Israelites were creating a new kind of society. Josephus later used the term 'theocracy'. This he defined as 'placing all sovereignty in the hands of God'.[114] The sages were to call it 'taking on the yoke of the Kingdom of Heaven'.[115] The Israelites might have magistrates of one kind or another but their rule was vicarious since God made the law and constantly intervened to ensure it was obeyed. The fact that God ruled meant that in practice his law ruled. And since all were equally subject to the law, the system was the first to embody the double merits of the rule of law and equality before the law. Philo called it 'democracy', which he described as 'the most law-abiding and best of constitutions'. But by democracy he did not mean rule by all the people; he defined it as a form of government which 'honours equality and has law and justice for its rulers'.[116] He might have called the Jewish system, more accurately, 'democratic theocracy', because in essence that is what it was.[117]

In the age of Moses, then, the Israelites were strengthening and confirming a tendency we have already noted to be subversive of the existing order. They were a servile people, who rose up against their Egyptian master, the most ancient and autocratic monarchy in the world. They fled into the desert, and received their laws in mass popular assembly, not in some long-established city but on the bare mountainside from a wild leader who did not even call himself a king. We do not know where Moses' Mount Sinai was. It may have been a still-active volcano. The present monastery of Sinai has always been a Christian site; it goes back certainly to the fourth century AD, and perhaps to about 200 years before. But even that was 1,450 years after Moses came down from the mountain. It is likely that, after the Israelites settled in Canaan, the Mosaic Sinai remained a pilgrimage site for generations. But the tradition eventually lapsed and the site fell out of memory, and it is most improbable that the early Christians went to the right place. All the same, this dramatic place, with its fierce and terrible beauty, has poetic aptness. It is the right setting for the formative act of a revolutionary people who did not recognize the cities, power and wealth of the day, and who were able to perceive that there is a moral order superior to the order of the world. Later, in a dramatic passage, Deutero-Isaiah was to express the Jewish exaltation of powerlessness in the person of the Suffering Servant of the Lord, who in the end is victorious; and later still, a Jewish sectarian, St Paul, was to ask: 'Hath not God made foolish the wisdom of the world?' and to quote the Scriptures: 'For it is written, I will destroy the wisdom of the wise, and will bring to nothing the understanding of the prudent.'[118] But the spring of this tradition opened at Sinai.[119]

With their long experience of being strangers and sojourners, for the Israelites their exodus from Egypt and their wanderings in the desert and mountain country of Sinai were nothing new. But this episode, of perhaps half a century, tended to confirm their singularity, their antinomianism, their apartness. It is curious, as the Jewish historian Salo Baron has pointed out, that the God they worshipped, despite his epiphany on Mount Sinai, remained portable, as in Abraham's days: he dwelt in the Ark, a kind of large, elaborate dog-kennel, or was present in the tabernacle in the tent, or operated through the casting-lots, Urim and Tummin.[120] This movable core was present even during the period of the Temple, and the idea that God has no fixed abode was easily <u>resumed</u> after the Temple fell and has been paramount ever since in Judaism. It fits more naturally into the Jewish notion of the universal and ubiquitous but invisible God. It reflects too an extraordinary adaptability in the people, a great skill in putting down roots quickly, pulling them up and re-establishing them elsewhere, an admirable tenacity of purpose irrespective of the setting. As Baron has put it, 'The religious and ethnic power of perseverance, rather than the political power of expansion and conquest, became the corner-stone of Jewish belief and practice.'[121]

Nevertheless, it must be stressed again that the Israelites, though inclined to restlessness, were not desert nomads, by origin or inclination. Even their Sinai wanderings were not truly nomadic. The bulk of the Exodus narratives, covering some thirty-seven years, centre on the conquest of Kadesh or Qadesh, which was rich and well-watered and was taken from the settled Amalekites. Some other sites mentioned in Exodus have been tentatively identified. But plotting the wanderings on the map, though often attempted and undoubtedly entertaining, can produce nothing more than conjecture.[122] One interesting theory is that the Levite tribe, to which Moses himself belonged and which soon claimed the exclusive right to the priesthood, was the first to settle in Kadesh and there elaborated the new religion. The other tribes were already in Canaan. The last to force its way into the Promised Land were the tribe of Joseph, from Egypt, and the Levites of Kadesh, who had been reformed by Moses as an instrument for the fervent worship of Yahweh. Under its dynamic impulse, the new Israelite society came into being, religion being the catalyst.[123] It is plausible but undemonstrable.

With the entry into and conquest of Canaan, however, the pattern of historical events begins to clarify as more and more archaeological evidence confirms or illuminates the Biblical record. The Book of Joshua, called after the Israelites' first great military commander, can now be regarded as essentially an historical account, though with important qualifications. Joshua, son of Nun of the tribe of Ephraim, was Moses' security chief, acting as his bodyguard at Sinai and commanding the guard of the tent. He established his military reputation during the wanderings in a desperate encounter at Rephidim with a band commanded by the sheikh Amalek. Moses commanded Joshua to 'go out, fight with Amalek', while he himself stood 'on top of the hill with the rod of God in mine hand'. Aaron and Hur held up the old prophet's hands to encourage the warriors, 'and his hands were steady until the going down of the sun. And Joshua discomfited Amalek and his people with the edge of the sword.'[124] Just before his death, Moses transferred the leadership to Joshua and 'set him over the congregation' at a solemn public ceremony. This made him a prophet as well as a general: 'And Joshua the son of Nun was full of the spirit of wisdom; for Moses had laid his hands upon him.'[125]

Thus Joshua began and to a great extent completed the conquest of Canaan. He may not have commanded all the Israelites, at any rate at the beginning. Nor did he conduct a full-scale invasion. Much of the settlement was a process of infiltration, or reinforcement of affiliated tribes who, as we have seen, already held such towns as Shechem. But there were numerous skirmishes and several spectacular sieges. The Canaanites were a higher material civilization than the Israelites and must have had much better weapons as well as strongly built stone cities. There is an air of desperation about the Israelites' conquest and this helps to explain why they were so ruthless when they took a town.

The first place to fall, after the crossing of the Jordan, was Jericho, one of the most ancient cities in the world. The excavations of Kathleen Kenyon and carbon-dating show that it goes back to the seventh millennium BC. It had enormous walls in the Early and Middle Bronze Ages, and the strength of its defences produced one of the most vivid passages in the Bible. Joshua the prophet–general ordered the priests to carry the Ark round the city, with their ram's-horn trumpeters, on six consecutive days; and on the seventh, 'when the priests blew with the trumpets', he commanded to all the people: 'Shout; for the Lord hath given you the city.' Then 'the people shouted with a great shout, that the walls fell down flat, so that the people went up into the city.'[126] Owing to erosion, the Kenyon researches threw no light on how the walls were destroyed; she thinks it may have been an earthquake which the Israelites attributed to divine intervention. The Bible narrative says: 'And they utterly destroyed all that was in the city, both man and woman, young and old, and ox and sheep and ass, with the edge of the sword.' Miss Kenyon established that the city was certainly burnt at this time and that, in addition, it was not reoccupied for a very long time afterwards, which accords with Joshua's determination that no one should rebuild it, and his threat: 'Cursed be the man before the Lord, that riseth up and buildeth this city Jericho.'[127]

Joshua did not storm a city if he could avoid it. He preferred to negotiate a surrender or better still an alliance and peaceful settlement. This was what happened, for instance, at Gibeon. But its inhabitants, he discovered, had deceived him over the terms of their covenant, and though he saved them from Israelite vengeance, he 'made them that day hewers of wood and drawers of water for the congregation'.[128]

Gibeon, says the Bible, was a 'great city', 'one of the royal cities'. Its precise location was finally established after the Second World War by the American archaeologist James Pritchard. There are no fewer than forty-five references to Gibeon in the Bible and Pritchard was able to confirm many of them. It was the centre of a fine wine-producing area, and the city had underground cellars for storing wine in nine-gallon vats. On the handles of no fewer than twenty-five of these Pritchard found the letters gb'n – Gibeon.[129] The loss of the city was regarded as so important that five Amorite city-kings tried to retake it. Joshua came to its rescue from Gilgal, 'and all the men of war with him, and all the mighty men of valour' – he now had a small regular army – and defeated the Amorites in a hectic battle fought during a hailstorm: 'they were more which died from hailstones than they whom the children of Israel slew with the sword'. Then followed a dramatic scene, according to the Bible record. Joshua needed daylight to complete the destruction of the Amorite army, so he prayed to the Lord for the weather to clear: 'Sun, stand thou still upon Gibeon; and thou, Moon, in the valley of Ajalon. And the sun stood still, and the moon stayed, until the people had avenged themselves upon their enemies.'[130]

Joshua then went on to achieve a still more important victory over Jabin, King of Hazor, who had tried to create a coalition in the northern part of Canaan to keep out the Israelite intruders. He collected an enormous army, 'even as the sand that is upon the sea-shore in multitude', but the Lord 'burnt their chariots with fire'. Then Joshua 'turned back, and took Hazor, and smote the king thereof with the sword. . . . And they smote all the souls that were therein with the edge of the sword, utterly destroying them: there was not any left to breathe: and he burnt Hazor with fire.'[131] Hazor was thoroughly excavated by the Israeli archaeologist–general, Yigael Yadin, in 1955–9. He found a vast and splendid town, with a lower section of 200 acres and a citadel of 24 acres, housing perhaps over 50,000 people. There were strong gates and massive walls. Here, again, the evidence of burning and destruction during the thirteenth century BC, the time of the Israelite conquest, is entirely consistent with the Biblical record. Among the debris Yadin found a deliberately mutilated temple stele of the moon-god Baal Hamman with the uplifted hands symbolizing his wife Tanit; so evidently Joshua's men had carried out the injunction to 'tear down their altars'.[132]

Despite Joshua's spectacular victories, however, the conquest of Canaan was by no means complete at the time of his death. The consolidation of the Israelite settlement, the reduction of the remaining towns, and the final occupation of the coast took more than two centuries, 1200–1000 BC, and was not accomplished until the unified kingdom of Israel came into being at the end of the millennium. The different Israelite tribes acted independently of each other, and sometimes fought. They had a variety of enemies: Canaanite enclaves, incursive Bedouin tribes, the new menace of the Philistines pushing in from the coast. They also had to take over from the Canaanites they had beaten, restore the cities, work the land. In the Book of Joshua, God says to them: 'I have given you a land for which ye did not labour, and cities which ye built not, and ye dwell in them; of the vineyards and oliveyards which ye planted not do ye eat.'[133] This is abundantly confirmed by excavations which show the Israelites strikingly inferior to their Canaanite predecessors in civil technology, notably building and pottery.[134] The children of Israel had a lot to learn.

Moreover, Palestine, though small, is a country of great variety, broken up into forty different geographical and climatic units.[135] That is what helps to give the land its extraordinary fascination and beauty. But it also tended to perpetuate tribal divisions and impede unity. The Israelite tradition, already strongly entrenched, of equality, communal discussion, acrimonious debate and argument, made them hostile to the idea of a centralized state, with heavy taxes to pay for a standing army of professionals. They preferred tribal levies serving without pay. The Book of Judges, covering the first two centuries of the settlement, gives the impression that the Israelites had more leadership than in fact they were prepared to tolerate. The 'judges' were not national rulers, holding power in succession. Normally they ran only one tribe each, and some may have been contemporaries. So every military coalition had to be negotiated on an *ad hoc* basis, summed up in the words of Barak, the chief of the Kedesh–Naphtali, to Deborah the warrior–prophetess: 'If thou wilt go with me, then I will go; but if thou wilt not go with me, then I will not go.'[136] The Book of Judges, though undoubted history and full of fascinating information about Canaan in the Late Bronze Age, is flavoured with mythical material and fantasy and presented in a confused fashion, so that it is difficult to work out a consecutive history of the period.

This may not matter very much, for what the Book of Judges does convey is much more important. First it illuminates the essentially democratic and meritocratic nature of Israelite society. It is a book of charismatic heroes, most of whom are low-born, obtaining advancement through their own energy and abilities, which are brought out by divine favour and nomination. Thus, when Eblon the King of Moab, the oasis-sheikh who 'possessed the city of palm trees', oppressed part of the Benjaminites, 'the Lord raised them up a deliverer' in the shape of Ehud, 'a man left-handed', always a grave disadvantage in those times, especially for a poor man. Ehud was too lowly to have a weapon. So he 'made him a dagger which had two edges, of a cubit length', hid it 'under his raiment' and got the local Israelites to contribute to a gift, by which he obtained admission to the sheikh. Eblon was 'a very fat man', who was 'sitting in a summer parlour, which he had for himself alone'. Ehud took out his home-made weapon, thrust it into the sheikh's belly 'and the fat closed upon the blade, so that he could not draw the dagger out of his belly; and the dirt came out'. This successful political assassination, carried out with great daring and skill, made Ehud a local commander, who then went on to subdue Moab: 'And the land had rest fourscore years.'[137]

Not only poor, left-handed men, but even women rose to heroism and so to command. Deborah, another figure from the oasis-country, was a fiery religious mystic, who prophesied and sang. She 'dwelt under the palm tree' and local folk 'came up to her for judgment'. This extraordinary woman, married to one Lapidoth (though we hear nothing of him), organized a coalition army against Jabin, one of the senior kings of Canaan, and destroyed his army. As if this were not enough, the defeated Canaanite general, Sisera, took refuge in the tent of the still more ferocious Israelite woman Jael, 'wife of Heber the Kenite' (Cain-ite). Jael gave him a bed, allowed him to fall asleep, then pulled out a tent-peg, 'took an hammer in her hand, and went softly unto him, and smote the nail into his temples, and fastened it into the ground'.[138] Whereupon Deborah, in the special sing-song tone which was the mark of the prophet, burst into a victory hymn, a savage and beautiful poem which descants on this appalling and treacherous act of violence.

Then there was Jephthah, lowliest of all, the son of a prostitute, who was thrust out of his father's house, while still young, by his elder brothers because of his mother's trade. Jephthah had no choice but to dwell in the badlands and form a band: 'And there were gathered vain men to Jephthah, and went out with him.'[139] When the Ammonites attacked, this bandit leader, in a reversal of the natural order which was becoming typical of Israelite history, was sought out by the prominent members of the local Israelite establishment, who asked him to become their war-captain. He agreed, on condition he remained their leader in peace too. After a surprising attempt to negotiate a peaceful agreement – the stories in Judges are never without unusual twists, and this passage contains a fascinating glimpse into contemporary diplomatic–religious procedure –

Jephthah swore a great oath to the Lord to solicit his help. Having received it, he defeated the enemy in battle and took twenty cities 'with a very great slaughter. Thus the children of Ammon were subdued.' But the terms of his oath were to sacrifice to the Lord whoever met him from his house when he returned home, and in the event this was his only child and daughter, who 'came out to meet him with timbrels and dances'. So in this strange and horrible story, Jephthah feels obliged to fulfil his vow and sacrifice his child, and the daughter meekly accepts her fate, stipulating only a respite of two months so that she and her maidens 'may go up and down upon the mountain, and bewail my virginity, I and my fellows'.[140] We do not even know the name of this innocent and tragic creature.

Strangest of all are the three chapters of the Book of Judges which describe the rise and fall, and the martyr's death, of Samson. He was another low-born member of society, a Nazarite, with wild, long hair, dedicated, in some way now obscure to us, to divine service. There is no question that Samson, despite the mythical elements in the narrative, which turn him into an Israelite Hercules, is a real person, a curious mixture of juvenile delinquent and hero, a strongman and a half-wit, with a paranoid streak of violence, a love of vandalism and arson, and a taste for low debauchery and wicked women. He is the outstanding example of the point which the Book of Judges makes again and again, that the Lord and society are often served by semi-criminal types, outlaws and misfits, who become by their exploits folk-heroes and then in time religious heroes. Israel was by its religious nature a puritanical society, but it is remarkable how often the Lord turns to sinners or responds generously when they turn to him. Thus Samson, disgraced, blinded and with fetters of brass, shouts to the Lord: 'O Lord God, remember me, I pray thee, and strengthen me, I pray thee, only this once, O God, that I may be avenged of the Philistines for my two eyes.'[141] God apparently responded, though the Bible does not actually say so. Some of Samson's exploits are the least plausible recorded in Judges, but the background to his story is authentic. The pressure of the Philistines from the coast was then just beginning to be felt, but there was no warfare between them and the Israelites, and Samson does not lead an army. On the contrary: there is constant contact and trade, even intermarriage, and this is attested by the archaeological evidence, such as the Philistine artifacts found in the Israelite town of Beth-Shemesh.[142] The marvels of Judges are always built upon a substratum of truth.

This raises the second point about the period. The Israelites were enlarging the imaginative gifts we have already noticed, and seen from this point of view Judges is one of the greatest collections of short stories in the whole of world literature. There is an underlying unity of theme but an astonishing variety of incident. The economy of means is admirable. Vivid characters are sketched in a sentence or two and leap from the page; an ingeniously selected detail brings the background to life; the narrative is swift and deft.

There is also a feature of the Bible which we notice here for the first time: the superfluous but unforgettable detail. Thus in Chapter 12 we are told that the escaping Ephraimites who were taken at the Jordan passage were forced to say the word 'Shibboleth' because the Gileadites knew they could not pronounce the sibilant 'sh'; hence when they said 'Sibboleth' they were identified and slaughtered.[143] The detail is not in any way important to the story, but it struck the narrator so forcibly – as it strikes us – that he could not bear to leave it out. We find this instinct again in the story of the young David in the first Book of Samuel, appearing before Achish King of Gath feigning madness, so that he 'scrabbled on the doors of the gate and let his spittle fall down upon his beard', provoking Achish to the furious comment: 'Have I need of madmen, that ye have brought this fellow to play the madman in my presence?'[144] Or again the brilliant writer responsible for the Second Book of Samuel feels he has to give us some fascinating details about Solomon's officer Benaiah, son of Jehoiada, 'who had done many acts. He slew two lion-like men of Moab: he went down also and slew a lion in the midst of a pit in time of snow. And he slew an Egyptian, a goodly man: and the Egyptian had a spear in his hand; but he went down to him with a staff, and plucked the spear out of the Egyptian's hand, and slew him with his own spear.'[145]

This instinct was not merely or chiefly literary: it was historical. Israelite love of the past was so strong that they crammed their narratives with picturesque information even when the didactic purpose was unclear, or non-existent. The tales in the books of Judges and Samuel are not just short stories. They are history. Indeed, in the books of Samuel they are beginning to be great history. There is in Israelite–Jewish literature of this period none of the aimlessness of pagan myth and chronicle. The narrative is set down with an overwhelming purpose, to tell the story, both elevating and minatory, of a people's relationship with God, and because the purpose is so serious, the story must be accurate – that is, the writer must believe in it, in his heart. So it is history, and since it deals with the evolution of institutions, as well as war and conquest, it is peculiarly instructive history to us.

Indeed the Book of Judges, naïve though it is in some ways, is in another an essay on constitutional development, for it shows how the Israelites were obliged by harsh facts to modify their democratic theocracy to the extent of establishing limited kingship. Early in the book, Chapters 6–8, it tells the story of Gideon, another poor and lowly man, who 'threshed wheat by the winepress', and was raised up by God to be a 'mighty man of valour'. Gideon was originally a commander on a small scale, with a mere 300 men, but his eventual success was so great that he was, for the first time in Israel's history, offered the hereditary kingship: 'Then the men of Israel said unto Gideon, Rule thou over us, both thou, and thy son, and thy son's son also: for thou hast delivered us from the hand of Midian.' Gideon replied: 'I will not rule over you, neither shall my son rule over you: the Lord shall rule over you.' This good and humble man, in rejecting the crown, was stressing that Israel was still a theocracy.

Even so, some historians believe that the house of Gideon would none the less have become the royal line of Israel had not Gideon's son, Abimelech, developed into a monster and committed one of the most stupefying crimes in the entire Bible, slaughtering seventy of his father's male children.[146] That ruled out the tragic house of Gideon, but much of the rest of the Book of Judges shows by implication the unsatisfactory nature of the disunited tribal system, with the repeated moral: 'In those days there was no king in Israel and every man did what was right in his own eyes.' The story of Jephthah ends in a brief and violent episode of Israelite civil war. The last three chapters of the book narrate the atrocious rape–killing of the Levite's concubine in the Benjaminite town of Gibeah, which leads to a desperately cruel dispute between the Benjaminites and the other tribes, a sort of miniature Trojan War. And in the meantime the Philistine menace was increasing as the tribes of Israel fought among themselves. The way the facts are presented may be *ex post facto* royalist propaganda – as some scholars argue – but the facts themselves were plain enough. An external enemy brought the tribes together and Israel adopted a central system of command for war because it had no alternative.

The Philistines were a far more formidable opponent than the indigenous Canaanites whom the Israelites were in the process of dispossessing or turning into helots. Indeed, there are recurrent hints in the Bible that the Israelites had feelings of guilt about taking the Canaanites' land,[147] a curious adumbration of Israeli twinges about homeless Palestinian Arabs in the late twentieth century. The Israelites, however, hid any remorse in the belief that the conquest was a pious act: it is 'because of the wickedness of these nations that the Lord is driving them out before you'.[148] The Philistines, by contrast, were themselves aggressors; no room for doubts there. They formed part of the most predatory race of the Late Bronze Age, the so-called Peoples of the Sea, who wrecked what was left of Minoan civilization in Crete and came close to taking over Egypt. When the great nineteenth-dynasty pharaoh, Rameses III, drove them out of the Nile area, in the battles magnificently portrayed at Karnak, these *Pulesti* turned north-east and established themselves on the coast which still carries their name, Palestine. The five great cities they built there, Ascalon, Ashdod, Ekron, Gath and Gaza, have not been systematically excavated and there is still a lot to be learned about their culture. But they were unquestionably warlike. They already had iron weapons. They were organized with great discipline under a feudal–military aristocracy. Around 1050 BC, having exterminated the coastal Canaanites, they began a large-scale movement against the interior hill-lands, now mainly occupied by Israelites. They seem to have conquered most of Judah, in the south, but nothing east of Jordan or in the northern Galilee. The tribe of Benjamin suffered most from them, and spearheaded the resistance.[149]

The period beginning with the national campaign against the Philistines is exceptionally rich in documentation. By this time the Israelites had developed a passion for writing history. Most of this material has disappeared for ever. The Book of Judges gives tantalizing references to lost chronicles. We also hear of the 'Book of the Chronicles of the Kings of Israel', the 'Books of the Chronicles of the Kings of Judah', 'The Book of the Acts of Solomon' and many other works. But those that survive, especially the two books of Samuel and the two books of Kings, are history on the grand scale, among the greatest works of all antiquity. They incorporate in places material from the royal archives, such as lists of government officials, provincial governors and even the menus of the royal kitchens.[150] From these times it is possible to establish synchronisms between the king-lists given in the Bible and non-Biblical sources such as the Egyptian pharaoh canons and Assyrian *limmu* or eponym lists. These enable us to make accurate datings. In the early monarchical period the margin of error may be ten years or so, but later we get virtually absolute dates. Thus we can be fairly sure that Saul was killed about 1005 BC, that David reigned until *c.* 966, and that Solomon died in either 926 or 925 BC.

Moreover, the Biblical records give us astonishingly vivid portraits of the principal actors in the national drama, portraits which rival and even surpass those we find in the finest Greek historians more than half a millennium later. These characters are placed firmly in a consistent ethical setting. But there is not merely good and evil in these historical moralities; there is every shade of conduct, and above all pathos, intense sadness, human love in all its complexity – emotions never before set down in words by man. There is too a veneration for abstract institutions, a sense of national choices and constitutional issues.

What emerges from the record is that though the Israelites turned to kingship in response to the threat of annihilation by Philistine power, they did so with great reluctance, and through the medium of an earlier institution, the prophetship. Abraham had been a prophet; Moses was the greatest of the prophets. It was the oldest office the Israelites had, and in their eyes an essential one since in a theocracy like theirs the medium through whom God issues his commands, the prophet, held a central place in society. The origins of the word, *nabhi*, are obscure; it may have meant 'one who is called' or 'one who bubbles forth'. An important text in Samuel says, 'He that is now called a *nabhi* was previously called a *roeh*' (seer). Prophets were certainly judged by their ability to predict. Such men were found everywhere in the ancient Near East. One of the great strands of ancient Egyptian history, from the early third millennium onward, is the role of oracles and prophecies. From Egypt it spread to the Phoenicians and thus to the Greeks. According to Plato's *Phaedrus*, human reasoning was not necessary for prophecy since a man possessed by a god was a mere agent: his state was known as 'enthusiasm' or divine madness. The Israelite prophets likewise acted as mediums. In a state of trance or frenzy they related their divine visions in a sing-song chant, at times a scream. These states could be induced by music. Samuel describes the process himself: 'thou shalt meet a company of prophets coming down from the high place with a psaltery, and a tabret, and a pipe, and a harp, before them; and they shall prophesy'.[151] Elisha, too, asked for music: 'But now bring me a minstrel. And it came to pass, when the minstrel played, that the hand of the Lord came upon him.'[152] But the prophets also used, and sometimes abused, incense, narcotics and alcohol, as Isaiah points out: 'The priest and the prophet have erred through strong drink, they have swallowed up of wine, they are out of the way through strong drink; they err in vision, they stumble in judgment.'[153]

In Israelite society, however, the prophet was much more than a man who went into ecstasy and tried to predict the future. They performed all kinds of spiritual functions. They were religious judges, like Moses and Deborah. They formed colleges attached to shrines, like the one at Shiloh, where the tiny Samuel was deposited by his mother Hannah. There, he 'ministered before the Lord, being a child, girded with a linen ephod' – just like a priest, in fact. His mother brought him a new little priestly coat every year, 'when she came up with her husband to offer the yearly sacrifice'.[154] So at many shrines priests and guilds of prophets worked side by side, and there was no necessary conflict between them. But almost from the beginning the prophets set more store on the content as opposed to the forms of religion, thus inaugurating one of the great themes of Jewish, and indeed world, history. As Samuel put it himself: 'Behold, to obey is better than sacrifice, and to hearken than the fat of rams.'[155] They stood for the puritanical and fundamentalist elements in the religion, as opposed to the empty ceremonies and endless sacrifices of the priests. But just as the priests tended to slip into mechanistic religion, so the prophets might drift into sectarianism. Indeed Samuel, like Samson, belonged to the sect of the Nazarites, wild-looking men with uncut hair and few clothes. These sects might diverge into heresy or even into an entirely new religion. The Nazarites had much in common with the ultra-strict and ferocious Rechabites, who engaged in massacres of backsliders when opportunity offered. Such sects were the most extreme monotheists and iconoclasts. They tended to drift into semi-nomad life on the fringe of the desert, a featureless place conducive to strict monotheism. It was from such a background that the greatest of all Jewish sectarian heresies was to spring – Islam.[156]

There were, then, multitudes of prophets, many of them false ones as the Bible frequently stresses. To be influential, a prophet had to avoid the extremes of sectarianism and remain in touch with the mainstream of Israelite life. His greatest single function was to act as intermediary between God and people, and to do that he must mingle with the masses. When Samuel matured, he acted as a judge, travelling all over the country.[157] When the powerful Philistine forces struck at the heart of the Israelite settlements, inflicting humiliating defeats, even capturing the Ark itself and (it seems) destroying the Shiloh shrine, it was natural that the people should turn to Samuel and that he should play the critical role in deciding whether, and if so how, the Israelites in their desperation should embrace kingship.

The First Book of Samuel gives us exciting glimpses into the anxious constitutional debates which took place on the issue. There was an obvious candidate, the Benjaminite guerrilla captain Saul, typical of the charismatic Israelite leaders who sprang from nothing by their own energy and divine favour. But Saul was a southerner and lacked the diplomatic skills to conciliate the northerners, whose whole-hearted support he never obtained. His dark, saturnine character is

brilliantly portrayed in the Bible: an unpredictable oriental potentate–bandit, alternating between sudden generosity and unbridled
rage, a manic-depressive perhaps, always brave and clearly gifted but
often hovering on the brink of madness and sometimes slipping over it.
Samuel was right to hesitate before anointing this man. He also
reminded the people that they had never had a king – one function of
the prophets was to deliver popular history lectures – and that, being a
theocracy, for Israel to choose rule by king was to reject rule by God,
and thus sinful.[158] He outlined the nation's constitutional history 'and
wrote it in a book and laid it up before the Lord' – that is, deposited it
at a shrine.[159] He was willing to anoint Saul as a charismatic leader or
nagid, by pouring oil on his head, but hesitated to make him *melek* or
hereditary king, which implied the right to summon the tribal levy.[160]
He warned the people of all the disadvantages of monarchy –
professional armies, punitive taxation, forced labour. He seems to
have changed his mind several times about the precise powers Saul
should have. But in the end Saul's early victories and his striking
appearance – he was exceptionally tall and handsome – made the
popular will irresistible, and Samuel reluctantly complied, pleading
divine guidance: 'And the Lord said to Samuel, Hearken unto their
voice, and make him a King.'[161]

   This early constitutional experiment in kingship ended in disaster. A
year after Saul's coronation, the great Philistine army came up through
the Plain of Esdraelon and destroyed the new royal army at Mount
Gilboa, Saul and his son Jonathan being killed. Saul obviously lacked
the temperament to unite the country behind him but the real reason
for his failure was absence of the requisite military background. He
was no more than a small-scale resistance-leader and though, as king,
he began to recruit a mercenary army, it was clearly beyond his skill to
handle large regular forces. But even before the final disaster Saul had
lost the support of the clergy and the confidence of Samuel. In Chapter
15 of the First Book of Samuel there is a vivid and heartbreaking scene
in which the old prophet turns on the king for acts of religious
disobedience over the spoils of war; the king, abashed, admits his sin
but begs Samuel to give him his public countenance in front of the
people. Samuel does so, but in his anger and frustration he turns on a
wretched royal prisoner, Agag King of the Amalekites, who 'came unto
him delicately', pleading 'Surely the bitterness of death is past?' But
Samuel 'hewed Agag in pieces' on the altar. There had always been a
fanatical streak in Samuel, especially against the Amalekites, whose
extermination he demanded.[162] He refused to see King Saul again.
Nevertheless, the record adds, when Saul was killed Samuel mourned

for him; 'and the Lord repented that he had made Saul king over Israel'.

Among the mercenaries Saul had recruited was David; it was his policy: 'When Saul saw any strong man, or any valiant man, he took him unto him.'[163] But the Bible text, as it stands, confuses two distinct layers of David's military career. He was originally a shepherd, descended from the humble and enchanting Ruth the Moabitess. When first picked to serve, he knew nothing of arms. He girded on sword and armour 'and tried in vain to go for he was not used to them'.[164] He used a more primitive weapon, the sling, to achieve his first great exploit, the killing of the Philistine strongman, Goliath. But another version has David brought to Saul's attention because he is 'cunning in playing, and a mighty valiant man, and a man of war, and prudent in matters, and a comely person'.[165] The truth seems to be that David served Saul at different periods but his professional military training came as a mercenary under the Philistines themselves. He learned their methods of warfare, including the use of their new iron weapons, and he flourished to the point where King Achish of Gath awarded him a feudal fiefdom. He might have identified himself wholly with the Philistines but in the end he chose the throne of Judah. Partly as a Philistine commander, partly as an opposition leader to the blundering Saul, he built up a group of professional knights and soldiers who swore fealty to him, were attached to him personally and expected to be rewarded with land. This was the force which enabled him to become King of Judah after Saul's death. He then waited for dissensions to break out in the northern kingdom, Israel, and the murder of Saul's successor there, Ishbaal. At this point the elders of Israel offered him the throne of the north by constitutional covenant. It is important to grasp that David's kingdom was not, initially at least, a co-ordinated nation, but two separate national entities each of which had a separate contract with him personally.[166]

David became the most successful and popular king Israel ever had, the archetype king and ruler, so that for more than 2,000 years after his death Jews saw his reign as a golden age. At the time, however, his rule was always precarious. His most dependable forces were not Israelites at all but his personal guards of foreign mercenaries, the Cherethites and Pelethites. His power rested on a professional army, whose officers had to be rewarded by gifts of land they could turn into feudal fiefs to support their men. But to donate the land he had first to take it, and this could not always be done by conquest. Hence the series of revolts and conspiracies against his rule, the most serious of which was led by his own son Absalom. The tribes were still separatist by instinct. They resented the cost of David's campaigns, perhaps still more the centralizing tendencies he accelerated, and the apparatus of oriental kingship he introduced – a chancellery and secretariat, a harem, the *corvée*, an elaborate court. These rural folk felt they had no share in the new-style state and echoed the anguished cry of Sheba, the Benjaminite who 'blew a trumpet and said: We have no part in David, neither have we inheritance in the son of Jesse: every man to his tents, O Israel.'[167] All these revolts were put down, thanks to David's military machine; but the reign of forty years was never untroubled, and harem intrigues over the succession – inseparable from monarchical polygamy – continued to the end.[168]

David was none the less a great king, and for three reasons. First he conflated the regal and the sacerdotal role in a way which was never possible for Saul. Samuel had no immediate successor and much of his spiritual authority devolved on David. David, despite his occasional wickedness, was evidently a man of deep religious feeling. Like his son and heir, Solomon, he had many gifts, including a strong artistic imagination. The tradition that he was a musician, a poet and psalmist is too strong to be rejected. The Bible records that he took a personal part in ritual dancing. He seems to have transformed a throne created by brutal military necessity into a glittering institution which combined religious sanction, oriental luxury and new standards of culture. Conservative rustic chiefs might not like it but the popular masses found it exciting and satisfying.

Secondly, David's position as king–priest seemed to have received divine blessing since his purely military achievements were unrivalled. He decisively defeated the Philistines and pinned them permanently into a narrow coastal strip. Saul had done much to reduce the remaining Canaanite enclaves within the area of Israelite settlement, but David completed the process. He then moved east, south and north, establishing his authority over Ammon, Moab, Edom, Aram-Zobar and even Aram-Damascus in the far north-east. His military successes were rounded off by diplomatic alliances and dynastic marriages. In a sense this burgeoning little Israelite empire was dependent on an accident of history. The empire to the south, Egypt, had receded; the empires to the east, of Assyria and Babylon, had not yet matured. In this vacuum, David's kingdom flourished. But his own capacity and experience, his width of knowledge, his travels and his grasp of economic factors also made the expansions possible. He saw the significance of establishing his authority over the great regional trade-routes, and he opened up economic and cultural contacts with the rich city–kingdom of Tyre. He was an internationalist whereas earlier Israelite leaders had all been narrow regionalists.

Thirdly, David established a national and religious capital which was also his personal conquest. The Israelites had never been able to take Jerusalem in over 200 years, though it was the most strategically important city of the interior: 'And as for the Jebusites, the inhabitants of Jerusalem, the children of Judah could not drive them out: but the Jebusites dwell with the children of Judah unto this day.' Jerusalem controlled the main north–south route in the interior; more, it was the natural junction between north and south. The failure to take it was one of the most important reasons why two separate groupings of the Israelites emerged – what later became known as the Kingdom of Israel in the north, and the Kingdom of Judah in the south. By taking Jerusalem, David believed he could weld the two halves into one, and it is clear that the siege was a deliberate political as well as a military act. Only 'the King and his men' – the professional household troops, not the tribal levies – were used, thus ensuring that David could claim that the city was a personal conquest. It was, in fact, known forever after as 'the City of David'. He took the place by a great stroke of daring, of which his general, Joab, was the hero. The Old City of Jerusalem which we know today is built on three valleys, the Hinnom (west), Kedron (east) and Tyropoeon (central), which merge to the south into the Brook of Kedron. The much smaller Jebusite city covered merely the eastern ridge, the only one which had a reliable water supply from the Gihon Spring. Thanks to the excavations of Kathleen Kenyon, and the Second Book of Samuel, we know exactly what happened at David's siege. The Jebusites, like the citizens of other Palestine cities at this time, such as Gezer, Gibeon and Megiddo, had constructed a secret tunnel connecting the interior of the city to the spring, so that they were assured of water even in a siege. They thought this device their strength, and so confident were they of defying David that they staged a magic ritual-parade of the blind, lame and other deformed people, to enrage the Israelites. But it proved their weakness, for the king knew of the tunnel and called for volunteers: 'And David said on that day, Whosoever getteth up to the gutter, and smiteth the Jebusites, and the lame and the blind, that are hated of David's soul, he shall be chief and captain.'[169] Joab and his men performed this exploit, climbing up the water tunnel and so getting inside the walls and taking the city by surprise.[170]

David's subsequent behaviour in Jerusalem confirms the view that it was of great political importance to him. He did not massacre the inhabitants, or expel them. On the contrary he seems to have been anxious to turn them into faithful personal adherents of his. He repaired the walls and the terracing or Millo, occupied the citadel, or

Zion as it was called, built a barracks for his 'mighty men', a palace for himself, and purchased from the last ruler of the city the land on which a central shrine for the entire Israelite people could be erected. He then brought the Ark, which was the most precious religious relic the Israelites possessed and the symbol of their unity, and placed it in his own city under the protection of his throne and personal army. All these acts were to strengthen his personal position and to identify the national religion, the entire people, and the crown with himself and his line.

But what he did not do was as important as what he did do. David seems to have been much more conscious of the nature of the Israelite religion and community than either Saul or any of his own successors. Like Gideon, he grasped that it was indeed a theocracy and not a normal state. Hence the king could never be an absolute ruler on the usual oriental pattern. Nor, indeed, could the state, however governed, be absolute either. It was inherent in Israelite law even at this stage that, although everyone had responsibilities and duties to society as a whole, society – or its representative, the king, or the state – could under no circumstances possess unlimited authority over the individual. Only God could do that. The Jews, unlike the Greeks and later the Romans, did not recognize such concepts as city, state, community as abstracts with legal personalities and rights and privileges. You could commit sins against man, and of course against God; and these sins were crimes; but there was no such thing as a crime/sin against the state.[171]

This raises a central dilemma about Israelite, later Judaic, religion and its relationship with temporal power. The dilemma can be stated quite simply: could the two institutions coexist, without one fatally weakening the other? If the demands of religion were enforced, the state would have too little power to function. On the other hand, if the state were allowed to evolve normally, according to its nature, it would absorb part of the essence of the religion to itself, and sterilize it. Each had an inherent tendency to be parasitical upon the other. If the Israelites tried to survive simply as a religious community, without a state, they would sooner or later be attacked, scattered and absorbed into the local paganisms. Thus the worship of Yahweh would succumb to external assault. That, of course, was what nearly happened during the Philistine invasion, and would have happened had the Israelites not turned to the secular salvation of kingship and a united state. On the other hand, if kingship and state became permanent, their inevitable characteristics and needs would encroach upon the religion, and the worship of Yahweh would succumb to internal corruption. The dilemma was unresolved throughout the First and Second Commonwealths; it remains unresolved in Israel today.

One solution was for the Israelites to adopt kingship and the state only in times of great peril, as during the Philistine invasion. The evidence suggests that David would have liked to adopt this, but came to think it impractical. To defend his people and their faith, to make both secure from their external foes, he had not only to create a kingdom–state but immobilize its surrounding peoples. This meant he had to found and consolidate the House of David, with Jerusalem its capital and central shrine. But he plainly did not regard his kingship as normal. He understood the religion of Yahweh; he saw himself as a religious man; he had an additional role as a prophet–priest and often performed as one in his music, writings and dancings. It is significant that he established hereditary kingship without endorsing primo-geniture. Three of his elder sons, who might have succeeded, Absalom, Amnon and Adonijah, all broke with him and died violently. In his old age, David designated his successor. The son he chose, Solomon, was not an active general but a scholar–judge, in the Mosaic tradition, the only one of the sons capable of discharging the religious duties of kingship which David evidently felt essential to preserve the Israelite constitutional balance.

It was also significant that David, while transferring the Ark to Jerusalem to give his capital's status religious sanction, did not build a grandiose temple, associated with his crown and royal line, to house it. The Ark was a humble piece of religious furniture which originally contained the covenant itself. It was dear to the Israelites, reminding them of their lowly origins, and standing for the pristine orthodoxy and purity of their theocratic creed. The Bible account gives later justifications for David's failure to build a temple for it: God would not allow him, as he was above all a warrior, a 'man of blood'; it was also said that he was too busy making war.[172] The first excuse is certainly false for war and the Israelite religion were closely associated. The priests had special war-calls for their trumpets; the Ark could be, and sometimes was, carried on to the battlefield as a war-emblem; David's wars were in the highest degree blessed by divine approval.[173] The second excuse is more plausible, but David reigned in Jerusalem thirty-three years, many of which were peaceful, and if he had wanted to build a temple he would have given it high precedence among his extensive building activities there. The likelihood is that he did not wish to change the nature and balance within the Israelite religion, and he felt that a central royal temple would do exactly that.

In the old days, the Ark had been the physical focus of Israelite worship. It was a symbol of theocratic democracy. Once they settled in Canaan, the Israelites gave thanks and sacrificed at 'high places', open altars on hills and mountains; or at more elaborate historic shrines, where roofed buildings or temples were erected. We know of a dozen or so: Shiloh, Dan, Bethel, Gilgal, Mizpah, Bethlehem, Hebron, and five smaller ones. Their location followed the spinal core of the country from north to south. They ensured some element of decentralization to the Israelite cult, as well as continuity with the past – for all these temple–shrines had important associations for those who worshipped at them. It is likely that David, anxious as he was to ensure sufficient centralization of the community to provide its effective defence, did not wish to emasculate still further its democratic base. Hence his unwillingness to imitate the other kingly despots of his age and turn Israel into a royal temple–state. Hence also, one suspects, his death-bed charge to his designated heir, the learned Solomon, to follow the Mosaic law in its purity: 'And keep the charge of the Lord thy God, to walk in his ways, to keep his statutes, and his commandments, and his judgments and his testimonies, as it is written in the law of Moses.' That, he added, was the only way the throne would survive – by ensuring that the law in its plenitude and strictness balanced the demands of the new state.[174] Later generations sensed the depth of David's religious impulse, which illuminated his statesmanship. That is perhaps the final reason why they venerated his memory, and wished a return to his rule; and it is no accident that he occupies more space than any other sovereign in the Old Testament.

But David's heir, Solomon, was of a totally different stamp. Where David was passionate, rash, wilful, sinful but repentant, conscious of sin, ultimately pure in heart and God-fearing, Solomon was a secular person: a man of his world and age to the bottom of his heart, if he had a heart. The psalms which are attributed to David in the Bible are essentially spiritual in tone and content; they are close to the core of the religion of Yahweh. On the other hand, the Biblical literature associated with Solomon, the wise sayings and the voluptuous poetry of the 'Song of Solomon', though fine of their kind, are much closer to the other ancient Near Eastern writings of the period; they lack Israelite–Jewish transcendentalism and God-awareness.

What Solomon became was a Near Eastern monarch of outstanding skill. But his reputation for wisdom was based on a willingness to be ruthless. Though co-opted as king during his father's lifetime, when David's death made him sole ruler he marked the change of regime and direction by eliminating all his father's former ministers, some by murder. He also made a critical change in military policy. In describing the revolt of Absalom against David, the Second Book of Samuel distinguishes between the old tribal levies or 'the men of Israel', who supported the son, and the mercenaries, or 'servants of David', who naturally defended the king.[175] It was these same 'servants' who ensured Solomon's sole succession and enabled him to eliminate his opponents right at the beginning of his reign. David, while building up a mercenary army, had still used the 'men of Judah', or the tribal levy of the south, as the core of his main army. But the tribal levies of the north, or 'men of Israel', remained neutral or hostile to the crown, and Solomon decided to abolish them altogether.

Instead, he introduced the *corvée* or forced labour, which was applied to Canaanite areas and to the northern part of the kingdom – Judah itself being exempt. As a form of national service, forced labour was less honourable than serving in the levy, and more arduous; therefore, more resented. Solomon employed it on a huge scale for his building programmes. The First Book of Kings, using government records, says that there were 80,000 men in the quarries, led and watched by 3,300 officers, 70,000 men hauling the stones to the sites, and 30,000 men, sent in rotating batches of 10,000 each, who went to the Lebanon to cut timber for beams.[176] Construction work included the enlargement and glorification of David's rather elementary scheme to turn Jerusalem into a national–religious royal centre. But it also involved building three new royal fortress-cities in various parts of the country: 'And this is the reason of the levy [forced labour] which King Solomon raised: for to build the house of the Lord, and his own house, and Millo, and the wall of Jerusalem, and Hazor and Megiddo and Gezer.'[177]

These last three cities, strategically sited, were virtually rebuilt by Solomon from scratch, using Israelites for the heavy labour, but imported masons for the skilled work. Excavation shows an altogether higher level of craftsmanship than the Israelites had yet demonstrated; it also reveals that the prime purpose of the cities was military – to provide bases for Solomon's new chariot army.[178] David had never possessed a chariot force, the mark of a major power at this period. Solomon had about 1,500 chariots and 4,000 horses in his various stables.[179] At Megiddo, strategically the most important of the lot, overlooking what was later to be known as the Plain of Armageddon, he built a high, defended royal quarter, with an immensely powerful gateway, and buildings which would house 150 chariots and 400 horses. Hazor, an abandoned city, was likewise given a royal quarter, gatehouse, walls and huge stables. Gezer, a city he acquired by dowry, and which controlled the route to Egypt, he transformed into another royal chariot-city.[180] The very existence of these heavily defended royal quarters, rising above the ordinary houses of the city, was an affront to the Israelite theocratic democracy. Solomon needed his carefully disposed chariot forces to protect his trade routes and defend the realm from external assault. But it is clear that their purpose was also to maintain internal order, which they did with great efficiency, for the tribes had no chariots.

For his ambitious programmes, Solomon needed not only labour but money. So he taxed the tribes too. David had prepared the way for this by holding a census. But he had been ferociously criticized for this, as contrary to the Israelite religion, and he had recognized his sin. The episode was characteristic of his hesitation and ambivalence in building up the state at the expense of the faith. Solomon had no such scruples. On the basis of the census returns he divided the country into twelve tax districts and imposed a further levy to provide supplies for his chariot-cities and other royal depots.[181] But the resources of the kingdom were not enough. So Solomon rationalized his father's conquests, retreating from Damascus, which was too expensive to defend, and yielding other territories in the north-west to Hiram, King of Tyre, whom he made his firm ally, in return for skilled craftsmen and supplies. But he also expanded commerce, trading extensively on his own account through 'king's merchants', and encouraging traders both domestic and foreign to use his routes, so he could tax them.

The economy of the Near East was now entering fully into the Iron Age – we find the first iron blades used for ploughing about this time – and the world was becoming richer. Solomon ensured by his activities that his royal house received a princely share of this new prosperity. He expanded trade by marrying daughters of all the neighbouring princes, with the slogan 'trade follows the bride'. He 'made affinity with Pharaoh King of Egypt' by marrying his daughter – that is how he obtained Gezer. The Bible tells us of other matrimonial alliances, saying he 'loved many strange women together with the daughter of Pharaoh, women of the Moabites, Ammonites, Edomites, Zidonians and Hittites'.[182] His diplomacy and his trade were intertwined. The visit of the Queen of Sheba, who came from South Arabia, was concerned with trade, for Solomon controlled the Arabian trade, chiefly in myrrh, frankincense and spices. Josephus tells us that Solomon held riddle-contests with Hiram of Tyre, another great trading monarch. This was a not unusual form of diplomatic exchange in the early Iron Age, involving heavy cash forfeits – sometimes cities – and was part of the bartering process. Solomon and Hiram jointly ran a fleet of ships from Ezion-Geber in the south to Ophir, their name for East Africa. The two kings dealt in rare beasts and birds, sandalwood and ivory. In addition, Solomon was an arms-merchant. He bought horses from Cilicia which he sold to Egypt in return for chariots, which he then resold to kingdoms to the north of him. Solomon, in fact, was the arms-supplier for a considerable part of the Near East. Near his port at Ezion-Geber, the American archaeologist Nelson Glueck found the copper refinery he built, on the island of Hirbet el-Kheleifeh, where the high prevailing winds worked the flues of primitive blast-furnaces. This refined not only copper but iron, and produced finished articles.[183]

Much of the wealth Solomon derived from trade and taxes he poured into the royal capital. He built a sumptuous royal palace, with a great hypostyle hall on the lines of pharaoh's palaces at Memphis, Luxor and elsewhere, its cedarwood roof supported by forty-five enormous wooden pillars, what the Bible calls 'the house of the forest of Lebanon'. A separate palace was built for his chief wife, the Egyptian, since she kept her own pagan faith: 'My wife shall not dwell in the house of David King of Israel, because the places are holy, whereunto the Ark of the Lord hath come.'[184] Palace and royal quarter, barracks and inner fortifications were close to a new sacred quarter, or Temple, the whole being accommodated by extending the city of David 250 yards to the east.

There is now nothing visible left of Solomon's Jerusalem, since it was either submerged beneath the enormous Temple building which Herod the Great later erected, or quarried away by the Romans.[185] We are dependent entirely on literary sources, Chapters 6–7 of the First Book of Kings, for our description of Solomon's Temple. But the details thus supplied show that it was similar to Late Bronze Age Canaanite temples at Lachish and Beth Sh'an, and a somewhat later, ninth century BC, temple excavated at Tel Tainet in Syria. Like these, Solomon's had three rooms, each 33 feet wide, on an axis: the Ulam or porch, 16 feet long, the Hekal or holy room, 66 feet long, and the Holy of Holies, a square of 33 feet, which was kept entirely dark like the inner sanctum in an Egyptian temple.

This building was put up and equipped in a manner quite alien to the Israelites. Phoenician masons dressed the stone ashlars. Hiram of Tyre also sent an expert in bronze, a namesake, to cast the temple's ceremonial vessels. These included a 'basin on wheels', a bronze laver on a stand, similar to pagan ones found at Megiddo and in Cyprus, and the great 'molten sea', containing 2,000 baths of water, used by the priests for their pre-sacrificial lustrations, which stood on twelve bronze oxen. Two bronze pillars, Boaz and Jachin, each nearly 40 feet high, perhaps corresponding to the standing monoliths of the Canaanite high places, protected a gold-covered altar with ten gold candlesticks. The screen of the Holy of Holies was also of hanging gold chains. Cedar lined the floor and walls. The Holy of Holies, with its protective wooden Cherubim, covered in gold, was built to contain the venerated cult-relics of the ancient religion of Yahweh: the Ark of the covenant, first and foremost, and (according to Talmud tradition) the staff of Moses, Aaron's rod, the manna-jar, and the pillow on which Jacob's head rested when he had his ladder-dream.[186] But by the time Jerusalem fell in 587 BC, all these things had long since disappeared, and one must doubt whether they were ever there in the first place.

What is clear is that Solomon's Temple, in its size and magnificence, and in its location within the fortified walls of a royal upper city or acropolis, had very little to do with the pure religion of Yahweh which Moses brought out of the wilderness. The Jews later came to see Solomon's Temple as an essential part of the early faith, but that is not how it must have appeared at the time to pious men beyond the royal circle. Like the *corvée*, the tax-districts, the chariots, it was new, and in many ways simply copied from the more advanced pagan cultures of the Mediterranean coast or the Nile Valley. Was not Solomon embracing paganism, along with his foreign wives, his centralized monarchy and his ruthless ways with the old tribes? Was not his Temple an idolatrous place where objects were worshipped? The Ark itself must have looked out of place in its magnificent surroundings. It was just a wooden chest, 4 feet long, 2 feet 6 inches deep, carried on poles passing through rings on each side. Inside it were the Tablets of the Law. In strict Israelite belief, the Ark was simply a repository of God's commandments. It was not a cult-object to be worshipped. Yet they were confused on this point, just as they were confused in their belief that God, though unrepresentable, had made man in his image. One of the old, primitive temples at Dan actually had a statue of God.[187] Though the Ark was built to carry the tablets, the Israelites seem to have attached divine powers to God's words, so in a sense they believed the deity lived in the Ark. They related portions of the wilderness years accordingly: 'And it came to pass, when the Ark set forward, that Moses said, Rise up, Lord, and let thine enemies be scattered; and let them that hate thee flee before thee. And when it rested, he said: Return, O Lord, unto the many thousands of Israel.'[188]

Solomon took advantage of this confusion to push forward his religious reform in the direction of royal absolutism, in which the king controlled the sole shrine where God could be effectively worshipped.

In Chapter 8 of the First Book of Kings, Solomon emphasized that God was in the Temple: 'I have surely built thee an house to dwell in, a settled place for thee to abide in for ever.' But Solomon was not a pure pagan, as this would imply, for if so he would not have bothered to exclude his pagan wife from the sacred area. He understood the theology of his religion, for he asked: 'But will indeed God dwell on the earth? Behold the heaven and heaven of heavens cannot contain thee; how much less this house that I have builded?' He effected a compromise between his state needs, and his understanding of Israelite monotheism, by supposing not a physical but a symbolic presence of the Almighty: 'That thine eyes may be open towards this house night and day, even towards the place of which thou hast said, My name shall be there.' This was the way in which later generations fitted the Temple into the faith, the presence of the name of God alone in the Holy of Holies generating a powerful divine radiation, called the *shekhinah*, which destroyed any unauthorized person who approached it.

But, at the time, the notion of a central, royal temple was objectionable to many Israelite purists. They formed the first of the many separatist sects the religion of Yahweh was to breed, the Rechabites.[189] Many northerners, too, resented the concentration of the religion in Jerusalem and its royal Temple, for the priesthood which served it soon put forward absolutist demands, claiming that only their ceremonies were valid, and that the older shrines and temples, the high places, and the altars venerated since patriarchal times, were nests of heterodoxy and wickedness. These assertions ultimately prevailed and became Biblical orthodoxy. But at the time they met resistance in the north.

This hostility to Solomon's religious changes combined with his absolutist ways and exactions to make the united kingdom his father had constructed untenable in the long run. Solomon's craft and success held it together, but there were signs of strain even during his last years. To Israelites for whom the past was very real, the forced-labour system was particularly odious because it reminded them of the Egyptian servitude. Their freedom and their religion were inseparable in their minds. By concentrating the cult in Jerusalem, Solomon downgraded northern shrines such as Shechem, associated with Abraham, and Bethel, with Jacob. To the northerners, then, Solomon and his line were increasingly seen as spiritual destroyers as well as secular oppressors.

Hence when Solomon died in 925/6 BC, the northerners refused his successor, Rehoboam, a united coronation in Jerusalem, and insisted he go north to Shechem to be crowned their king. Men who had fled to exile under Solomon, such as Jeroboam, returned, and demanded constitutional rule, and in particular the lifting of the forced-labour levies and the high taxes: 'Now therefore make thou the grievous service of thy father, and his heavy yoke which he put upon us, lighter, and we will serve thee.'[190] There seems to have been a full-scale political conference in Shechem, in which Rehoboam, after consulting his father's old advisers, rejected their conciliatory recommendations, and took a hard line, backed by his young knights, telling the northerners: 'My father made your yoke heavy, and I will add to your yoke: my father also chastised you with whips, and I will chastise you with scorpions.'[191]

This extraordinary misjudgment destroyed the united kingdom. Rehoboam had not the military means and skill to hold it together by force, the northerners broke off and reverted to their own royal house, and in an age of rising empires – the Babylonians followed by the Assyrians – both these small kingdoms, Judah in the south, Israel in the north, went to their doom separately.

Yet this process of decline spanned several centuries, and in the course of it the Israelite religious culture underwent important changes. In the first instance, it was the northern kingdom which flourished. It was more populous than the south, had more fertile land and was closer to the trading centres of the time. Free of the southern yoke, it grew richer and, paradoxically, followed the pattern of constitutional and religious development Solomon had found neces-sary and which – when imposed by southerners – it had rejected. Like the House of David, the northern House of Omri became centralist and imitated the political and cultic patterns of successful neighbour-ing states. Omri himself was a formidable king, whose exploits were sorrowfully recounted in a tablet to the Moabite God Chemosh, which was discovered in 1866 and is known as the Moabite Stone: 'Omri King of Israel . . . oppressed Moab many days because Chemosh was angry with his land. And his son succeeded him, and he also said I will oppress Moab.'

Omri, like Solomon, consolidated his power by judicious foreign marriages. He espoused his son Ahab to the King of Sidon's daughter Jezebel, thus linking his inland kingdom to the sea and its trade routes. Like Solomon, he was a great builder. On a hill at Samaria, from which the sea can be seen 20 miles away, he founded and built a new city: we can even date its foundation to approximately 875 BC. Like Solomon's royal cities, it had a fortified royal acropolis. Ahab too was a great builder. At Samaria he constructed what the Bible calls an 'ivory house', that is a palace with a throne-room lined with ivory carved in low-relief – a luxury which only the richest kings of the time possessed. When Samaria was excavated in 1931–5, pieces of these ivory decorations were found in the rubble. Ahab, like his father Omri, was a highly successful warrior–king, who reigned for twenty-five years and twice defeated the King of Damascus, until, as the Bible says, during a chariot fight 'a certain man drew a bow at a venture' and his arrow struck between the joints of Ahab's armour, and fatally wounded him.[192]

But the House of Omri, worldly and successful like Solomon, also aroused bitter social and moral resentment. Great fortunes and estates accumulated. The gap between rich and poor increased. The peasants got into debt, and when they could not pay were expropriated. This was against the spirit of the Mosaic law, though not strictly against its letter, since what it insists is that you must not remove a neighbour's landmarks.[193] The kings were opposed to the oppression of the poor by the elite, because they needed poor men for their armies and labour-gangs; but any actions they took were feeble. The priests, at Shechem, Bethel and other shrines, were salaried, closely identified with the royal house, preoccupied with ceremonials and sacrifices, and uninterested – so their critics claimed – in the distress of the poor. In these circumstances, the prophets re-emerged to voice the social conscience. Like Samuel, they were uneasy about the whole institution of monarchy, perceiving it as inherently incompatible with the democratic theocracy. Under the House of Omri, the prophetic tradition was suddenly reinvigorated in the north by the astonishing figure of Elijah. He came from an unidentified place called Tishbe, in Gilead east of the Jordan, right on the fringes of the desert. He was a Rechabite, a member of that ultra-austere, wild and fundamentalist sect, 'an hairy man, and girt with a girdle of leather about his loins'. Like nearly all Jewish heroes, he came from the poor and spoke for them. The tradition said he lived near the Jordan and was fed by the ravens.[194] No doubt he looked not unlike John the Baptist, a thousand years later. He worked miracles on behalf of the poor, and was most active in times of drought and famine, when the masses suffered.

But of course Elijah, like other strict worshippers of Yahweh, was critical of the House of Omri not just for social but above all for religious reasons. For Ahab neglected the cult of Yahweh and slipped into his wife's cult of Baal: 'But there was none like unto Ahab, which did sell himself to work wickedness in the sight of the Lord, whom Jezebel his wife stirred up. And he did very abominably in following idols.'[195] It was Jezebel, too, who tempted Ahab to possess himself of

Naboth's vineyard by an act of despotic power, Naboth being sent to his death, a crime against the whole ethos of the Israelite theocracy.

It is evident that Elijah could rouse a mass following, especially in time of hardship, when no rain fell. He was a formidable public preacher. Chapter 18 of the First Book of Kings describes the dramatic scene when he gathered an immense crowd of Israelites on Mount Carmel and challenged the priests of Baal and 'the prophets of the grove' – 'which eat at Jezebel's table' – to a rain-making contest. His aim was to settle the religion of the people once and for all, saying to the assembly: 'How long halt ye between two opinions? If the Lord be God, follow him; but if Baal, then follow him.' The priests of Baal went through all their rituals, cutting themselves with 'knives and lancets, till the blood gushed out upon them'; but nothing happened. Then Elijah built his altar and offered sacrifice to Yahweh, and immediately 'the fire of the Lord fell, and consumed the burnt sacrifice'. Then all the people 'fell flat on their faces and said: The Lord he is the God, the Lord he is the God.' Elijah and his mob took the pagan priests to the Kishon Brook 'and slew them there', and, after further prayer on the summit of Carmel, Elijah summoned up 'a little cloud out of the sea, like a man's hand'; soon, 'the heaven was black with clouds and winds, and there was a great rain'.

Despite this triumphant vindication, Elijah was unable himself to eradicate paganism, or destroy the House of Omri, though he predicted its downfall. He was a lone figure, a charismatic man capable of swaying a huge crowd but not one to build up a party or a court faction. He stood for the individual conscience, perhaps the first man in Jewish history to do so; God spoke to him not in the thunder of the Mosaic era, but in 'a still, small voice'. In his cursing of Ahab's line over the killing of Naboth, he upheld the principle that a king's behaviour should be no different from a private man's: it must be guided by moral principle. Politics was about right, not might. But Elijah, though the first prophetic leader of the opposition, was not a politician. Much of his life he was a hunted fugitive. His last days were spent in the wilderness. Chapter 2 of the Second Book of Kings tells how he anointed his successor, Elisha, before being swept up in a whirlwind and mounting to heaven in a chariot of fire, leaving behind, for his heir to don, his sacral mantle.

Elisha was of a different cast, however. The Bible narrative shows him performing remarkable acts: when mocked by 'little children' (or possibly teenage roughs) near Bethel, he summoned two she-bears from the wood, which tore to pieces no less than forty-two of the delinquents.[196] But Elisha did not operate alone. He created an organized following, a college of prophets, and he worked with elements in the secular establishment to obtain the religious reforms Elijah had demanded. Ahab had maintained and enlarged Solomon's chariot cities in the north. He and his successors had a large professional army, a source of both strength and weakness. Among the successful chariot generals was Jehu, son of Nimshi, who 'driveth furiously'. Elisha engaged in a religious–military conspiracy with Jehu, had him anointed the future king and thus set in motion one of the bloodiest coups in history.[197] Jehu had Jezebel thrown out of the window of her palace by her eunuchs, 'and some of her blood was sprinkled on the walls, and on the horses; and he trod her underfoot'. Ahab's seventy sons were decapitated and piled 'in two heaps at the entering-in of the gate'. Jehu massacred Ahab's entire royal house, 'and all his great men, and his kinsfolk, and his priests, until he left him none remaining'. He then assembled and slaughtered all the priests of Baal, 'And they brake down the image of Baal, and brake down the house of Baal, and made it a draught house unto this day.'[198]

This ferocious religious purge may have re-established the official, sole worship of Yahweh for a time, but it did not resolve the perennial conflict between the need to maintain religious orthodoxy – to keep the people together – and the need to conform to the world – to keep the state in existence. Jehu, as was foreseeable, was soon behaving in as arbitrary a manner as the House of Omri; indeed, virtually all the kings of Israel broke with the religious purists sooner or later. To preserve his power, a king, or so it seemed, had to do things that a true follower of Yahweh could not countenance. The episode of Naboth's vineyard was a case in point, a symbol of the spiritual–secular conflict. There is a famous passage in which God inspires Elijah to say to Ahab, 'Hast thou killed, and also taken possession?'; and Ahab answers, 'Hast thou found me, O mine enemy?'[199] Merely replacing Ahab's sons by Jehu and his sons did not solve the problem. It is restated, in a rather different form, in the eighth-century Book of Amos. This book is contemporary with Hesiod's *Works and Days* in post-Homeric Greece, and shows a similar concern for abstract justice, though in the case of Amos it is associated directly with the worship of Yahweh. He was a southerner from Judah, a dresser of sycamore trees, who came north to Israel to preach social justice. He was at pains to point out that he was not a prophet by birth and belonged to no college: just a simple working man who saw the truth. He protested about the elaborate ceremonies conducted by the priests at the northern shrine of Bethel, which he said were a mockery when the poor were downtrodden and starving. He has God saying: 'I hate, I despise your feast-days. . . . Take thou away from me the noise of thy songs; for I will not hear the melody of thy viols. But let judgment run down as waters, and righteousness as a mighty stream.'[200] Amaziah, the head priest of Bethel, objected strongly to Amos' activities. The shrine, he argued, was the king's chapel, part of the king's court; the duties of the priests were to uphold the state religion with due decorum, and it was not part of them to play politics and interfere in economic processes. He said to Amos: 'O thou seer, go, flee thee away into the land of Judah, and there eat bread, and prophesy there.' To the king, he complained that Amos had, in effect, raised a conspiracy against him in the royal precincts, adding – in a significant phrase – 'the land is not able to bear all his words'.[201]

The debate was, and indeed is, important. The later Jewish seers, and in their turn most Christian moral theologians, endorsed Amos' view. The Talmud laid down: 'The commandment of righteousness outweighs all the commandments put together.'[202] But the Talmudists did not have the responsibility of holding the state together; that was all in the past and they could now afford the luxury of moral absolutism. In Amaziah's day, however, a compromise between the secular and spiritual authorities was essential if the state was to survive at all. If prophets from the south were allowed to go around stirring up class warfare in the name of God, the community would be fatally weakened and at the mercy of its external enemies, who would wipe out the worship of Yahweh altogether. That was what he meant when he said that the land could not bear Amos' bitter words.

Throughout the ninth century the power of Assyria had been growing. The Black Obelisk of Shalmaneser shows that, even in Jehu's day, Israel had been forced to pay tribute. For a time Israel bought the Assyrians off, or formed coalitions of other small states to halt their advance. But in 745 BC the cruel Tiglath-pileser III ascended the Assyrian throne and turned his warlike race into a nation of imperialists. He inaugurated a policy of mass deportation in conquered territories. In 740 his annals record: 'As for Menahem [King of Israel] terror overwhelmed him . . . he fled and submitted to me . . . silver, coloured woollen garments, linen garments . . . I received as his tribute.' In 734 he broke through to the coast, then advanced down it to 'the Brook of Egypt'. All the elite, the rich, merchants, craftsmen, soldiers, were transported to Assyria and resettled there; in their place were established Chaldean and Aramaean tribesmen from Babylonia. Then Tiglath pushed inland. Stricken internally by religious and social divisions, the northern kingdom of Israel was in no condition to resist. In 733–4, Tiglath-pileser conquered Galilee and Transjordan, leaving only Samaria. Tiglath died in 727, but his successor, Shalmaneser V, took Samaria in the winter of 722–1 and the following year his successor, Sargon II, completed the destruction of the northern kingdom, removing the entire elite and sending in colonists: 'I besieged and captured Samaria,' Sargon records in the Annals of Khorsabad, 'carrying off 27,290 of the people who dwelt therein.' The Second Book of Kings echoes mournfully: 'So Israel was carried out of their own land to Assyria unto this day. . . . And the King of Assyria brought down men from Babylon, and from Cuthat, and from Ava, and from Hamath, and from Sepharvaim, and placed them in the cities of Samaria instead of the children of Israel: and they possessed Samaria and dwelt in the cities thereof.'[203] There is abundant confirmation of the catastrophe in the archaeological record. At Samaria, the royal quarter was totally destroyed. Megiddo was levelled and new, Assyrian-type buildings set up on the rubble. The walls of Hazor were torn down. Shechem disappeared completely. So did Tirzah.

Thus the first great mass tragedy in Jewish history took place. It was, too, a tragedy unrelieved by ultimate rebirth. The holocaust-dispersion of the northern people of Israel was final. In taking their last, forced journey into Assyria, the ten tribes of the north moved out of history and into myth. They lived in later Jewish legend, but in reality they were simply assimilated into the surrounding Aramaean population, losing their faith and their language; and the spread of Aramaic westwards, as the common language of the Assyrian empire, helped to conceal their evanescence. In Samaria, Israelite peasants and artisans remained, and intermarried with the new settlers. Chapter 17 of the Second Book of Kings, which records these melancholy events, says that while the exiled elite in Assyria still worshipped Yahweh, they sent back one of their priests to live in Bethel and instruct the leaderless people. But it adds: 'Howbeit every nation made gods of their own, and put them into the houses of the high places which the Samaritans had made,' and it then paints a fearful picture of the confused paganism into which the northern kingdom collapsed. The way in which the north had worshipped Yahweh had always been suspect in Judah. This doubt about northern orthodoxy reflected the division of the Israelites which took place at the time of the entry into Egypt, and which was never really healed after the Exodus and the conquest of Canaan. In the eyes of Jerusalem and its priests, the northerners had always mingled with the pagans. The fall and dispersal of the northern kingdom, and the intermarriage of the remnant with aliens, was used to deny the Samaritans their original Israelite heritage. From this point onwards, their claim to be part of the chosen people, and to inhabit the Promised Land in full righteousness of possession, was never again acknowledged by the Jews.

Yet the north left a legacy to the south, which was to provide the germ of the new phase of the religion of Yahweh, flowering in the south during the last days of old Jerusalem. When Samaria fell, some literate refugees escaped the deportations and came south, where they were received and resettled in Jerusalem. One of them brought with him the writings of an obscure prophet called Hosea, which were then put into shape by a southern hand.[204] Hosea had been prophesying and writing on the eve of the destruction of the northern kingdom. He was the first Israelite to perceive clearly that military and political failure was an inevitable punishment visited on the chosen people by God because of their paganism and moral failings. In a brilliantly written and often poetic text, he predicted the fall of Samaria. God would break in pieces their idols: 'For they have sown the wind, and they shall reap the whirlwind.' And to all the sinful worshippers of Yahweh he warns: 'Ye have ploughed wickedness, ye have reaped iniquity.'[205]

Hosea is a mysterious figure, and in some ways his writing is among the most impenetrable in the whole Bible. His tone is often dark and pessimistic. He had the power, which was to become characteristic of so many Jewish writers, to convey the sense of having suffered, yet to have retained an inextinguishable spark of hope. He may have been a reformed drinker and womanizer. He laments: 'Whoredom and wine and new wine take away the heart.'[206] Sexuality in particular arouses his intense loathing. He says that God told him to marry the whore Gomer, and have children by her – Gomer standing both for the ritual prostitutes of the pagan temples and for Israel herself, who left her true husband, Yahweh, to fornicate with Baal. He denounces all the institutions of the north: indeed he thinks the north should never have existed at all, since Israel and Judah were properly one. Political solutions were useless; Jehu's purge was wicked. The organized priesthood was a scandal: 'as troops of robbers wait for a man, so the company of priests murder in the way by consent: for they commit lewdness'. The colleges of prophets, at the royal shrines and elsewhere, were no better: 'the prophet also shall fall with thee in the night . . . the prophet is a fool, the spiritual man is mad'.[207]

So Israel with its existing institutions was doomed, and would be carried away into exile. But in the long run this did not matter. For God loved his people. He punished, but he forgave: 'he hath smited, and he will bind us up'. Then, in a strikingly prophetic phrase, he adds: 'in the third day he shall raise us up, and we shall live in his sight'.[208] What mattered was not material preparation, but a change in human hearts. It was love for God, the response to God's love for us, which would ensure Israel's redemption, and enable a purged and purified 'remnant' to carry the faith into the future.

This remarkable message, in which for the first time an Israelite thinker seems to envisage a religion of the heart, divorced from a particular state and organized society, was received in a Judah which was terrified by the collapse of its northern neighbour and feared a similar fate. Judah was poorer than the north, more rural, less dominated by military power-politics and closer to the roots of Yahweh-worship, though both the Bible narrative and the excavation of Jerusalem in 1961–7 provide evidence of backsliding into paganism. The ordinary people of the land, the *am ha-arez*, were important there. They made their first appearance in history in 840 BC, when they overthrew the despotic queen–widow Athaliah, who seized the throne and introduced Baal-worship into the Temple. The Second Book of Kings makes clear that, in the constitutional restoration which followed, the notion of the theocratic democracy was revived. For it was a man of religion, Jehoiada, who led the popular uprising, and he insisted that the people should be recognized as a political and constitutional force: 'And Jehoiada made a covenant between the Lord and the king and the people, that they should be the Lord's people; between the king also and the people.'[209] In no other country in the Near East at that time, or even in Greece for long after, could such a novel arrangement have been drawn up. Indeed, as the shadows of imperialism fell on Judah too, the *am ha-arez* was given the specific right to elect the king if the succession to the throne was in doubt.

When Israel fell, Hezekiah King of Judah, whose professional army was meagre and much inferior to the old chariot-army of the north, used the support of the *am ha-arez* to refortify Jerusalem by building a new wall on the western ridge: he 'set to work resolutely and built up all the wall that was broken down, and raised towers upon it, and outside it he built another wall'. He also prepared against an Assyrian siege by driving through the Siloam Tunnel, which took the water from the Gihon spring into a cistern cut into the rock, a channel then carrying the overflow into the Kedron Brook. The town had access to this vast cistern without besiegers being aware of the arrangement. This too is described in the Bible,[210] and was strikingly confirmed when the tunnel was explored in 1867–70. A contemporary inscription, recording the completion of the work in Hebrew, was found on the walls:

This is the story of the boring through: while [the tunnellers lifted] the pick, each towards his fellows, and whilst three cubits [yet remained] to be bored through, [there was heard] the voice of a man calling his fellow, for there was a split in the rock on the right hand and on [the left hand]. And of the day of the boring through, the tunnellers struck, each in the direction of his fellow, pick against pick. And the water started to flow from the source to the pool, twelve hundred cubits.[211]

Jerusalem did, in fact, survive a fierce siege, by the Assyrian king Sennacherib, in 701 BC. The instrument of salvation was not so much the new walls and cistern, as a violent outbreak of bubonic plague, carried by mice, which struck the Assyrian camp, to which the Greek historian Herodotus later referred. In the Second Book of Kings it is seen as miraculous: 'And it came to pass that night, that the angel of the Lord went out, and smote in the camp of the Assyrians an hundred fourscore and five thousand: and when they arose early in the morning behold, they were all dead corpses.'[212] The rulers of Judah also sought safety in various alliances, with small neighbouring states, and even with vast, feeble Egypt, 'the broken reed', on which, as the Assyrians sneered, 'if a man lean, it will go into his hand, and pierce it'.[213]

Increasingly, however, the rulers and peoples of Judah began to link their ultimate political and military fate with their current theology and moral behaviour. The notion seems to have spread that the people could only be saved by faith and works. But the concept of a religious solution for the national problem of survival – the very opposite of the idea which drove Israel into kingship at the time of the Philistine invasion – itself drove Judah in two divergent directions. How could Yahweh most effectively be appeased? The priests of the Jerusalem Temple argued that it could only be done by destroying, once and for all, the suspect cultic practices of the old high places and provincial temples, and concentrating worship solely in Jerusalem, where orthodoxy could be maintained in all its purity. The process was accelerated in 622 BC when, during repairs to the Temple, Hilkiah the high-priest found a book of ancient writings, perhaps the original text of the Pentateuch, perhaps just the Book of Deuteronomy, giving the covenant between God and Israel and culminating in the terrifying curses of Chapter 28. This discovery created panic, for it seemed to confirm Hosea's prophetic warnings and suggested that the fate of the north was about to be visited on the south. The king, Josiah, 'rent his clothes' and ordered a total reform of the cult. All images were destroyed, the high places closed down, pagan, heterodox and heretic priests were massacred, and the fundamentalist reform culminated in a solemn national celebration of the Passover, of a kind never before staged in Jerusalem.[214] Hence, by a curious paradox, the chief beneficiary of this return to the roots of the nation's religious past was the Jerusalem Temple, introduced as a quasi-pagan innovation by Solomon. The power of its priests increased sharply, and it became the national – or at any rate the official – arbiter of all religious truth.

But in this doom-laden period, a second and unofficial line of thought began to express itself. It pointed to salvation in quite a different direction, which was eventually found to be the true one. Hosea had written of the power of love and called for a change in men's hearts. A younger contemporary of his, a southerner, carried these ideas further. Isaiah lived at the time when the northern kingdom was under sentence of death. Unlike most of the heroic figures in the Bible, he was not born poor: according to the tradition of the Babylonian Talmud, he was the nephew of King Amaziah of Judah.[215] But his ideas were populist or democratic. He put no faith in armies and walls, kings and magnificent temples. His work marks the point at which the Israelite religion began to spiritualize itself, to move from a specific location in space and time on to the universalist plane. It is divided into two parts: Chapters 1 to 39 deal with his life and prophesyings in the period 740–700 BC; Chapters 44–66, or Deutero-Isaiah, date from much later, and the historical connection between the two is not clear, though the development of the ideas is logical enough.

Isaiah was not only the most remarkable of the prophets, he was by far the greatest writer in the Old Testament. He was evidently a magnificent preacher, but it is likely he set his words down in writing. They certainly achieved written form very early and remained among the most popular of all the holy writings: among the texts found at Qumran after the Second World War was a leather scroll, 23 feet long, giving the whole of Isaiah in fifty columns of Hebrew, the best preserved and longest ancient manuscript of the Bible we possess.[216] The early Jews loved his sparkling prose with its brilliant images, many of which have since passed into the literature of all civilized nations. But more important than the language was the thought: Isaiah was pushing humanity towards new moral discoveries.

All the themes of Isaiah are interrelated. Like Hosea, he is concerned to warn of catastrophe. 'Watchman, what of the night?' he asks, 'Watchman, what of the night?' Foolish men take no notice: they say: 'Let us eat and drink, for tomorrow we die.' Or they put their trust in fortifications and alliances. Instead they should obey the Lord's command: 'Set thy house in order.' This means a moral change of heart, an internal reform for both individuals and the community.

Social justice must be the aim. Men must cease to pursue wealth as the main aim in life: 'Woe unto them that join house to house, that lay field to field, till there be no place.' God will not tolerate the oppression of the weak. He demands: 'What mean ye that ye beat my people to pieces, and grind the faces of the poor, saith the Lord God of hosts.'[217]

Isaiah's second theme is repentance. Provided there is a change of heart, the Lord is always forgiving. 'Come now, and let us reason together, saith the Lord: though your sins be as scarlet, they shall be as white as snow.' What God wants from man is a recognition and a reciprocation of his holiness – 'Holy, holy, holy is the Lord of Hosts, the whole earth is full of his glory' – and Isaiah imagines the angels touching men's lips with a coal of fire to burn away sin. And when sinful man changes his heart, and seeks not wealth and power but holiness, Isaiah introduces his third theme: the idea of an age of peace, when men 'shall beat their swords into ploughshares, and their spears into pruning-hooks: nation shall not lift up sword against nation, neither shall they learn war any more.' In this age of peace, 'the desert shall rejoice, and blossom as the rose'.[218]

Isaiah, however, is not simply preaching a new system of ethics. Coming from an historically minded people, he sees the will of God, cause and effect, sin and repentance, proceeding in a definite linear direction. He provides a vision of the future, and it is a vision peopled with distinct personages. At this point he introduces his fourth theme: the idea not just of a collective turning from sin, but of a specific saviour-figure: 'Behold, a virgin shall conceive, and bear a son, and shall call his name Immanuel.' This special babe shall be an agent in the age of peace: 'The wolf also shall dwell with the lamb, and the leopard shall lie down with the kid; and the calf and the young lion and the fatling together; and a little child shall lead them.' But he will also be a great ruler: 'For unto us a child is born, unto us a son is given: and the government shall be upon his shoulder: and his name shall be called Wonderful, Counsellor, The mighty God, The everlasting Father, the Prince of Peace.'[219]

Isaiah not only wrote but preached in the Temple. He was not, however, talking of a religion of official cult, of endless sacrifices and priestly ceremonies, but of an ethical religion of the heart: he was reaching over the heads of the priests to the people. A strong talmudic tradition says that he was murdered in the reign of the idol-worshipping King Manasseh; but he was not welcome to the orthodox priesthood, the Temple establishment, either. Martyrdom was the theme beginning to emerge more and more insistently in Israelite writing. In the second part of Isaiah, a new character emerges, who seems to be linked to the saviour-figure of the first: the Suffering Servant, who carries the sins of the whole community and, by his sacrifice, purges them, and who also personifies and directs to a triumphant conclusion the mission of the nation.[220] The Suffering Servant echoes Isaiah's own voice and fate, and the two parts of the book have a unity even though as much as two centuries separate their written composition. What, as a whole, the Book of Isaiah does is to mark a notable maturing of the religion of Yahweh. It is now concerned with justice and with judgment: judgment of nations and judgment of the individual soul. In Deutero-Isaiah in particular, the stress is on the individual as the bearer of faith, outside the claims of tribe, race, nation. Not just Elijah, but each and all of us has the 'still, small voice' of conscience. It is all part of the discovery of the individual, a giant step forward in human self-knowledge. The Greeks would soon be pushing in the same direction, but the Israelites, or as we shall soon call them, the Jews, were the forerunners.

Moreover, unlike the Greeks, the Israelites, under the inspiration of Isaiah, were moving towards a pure monotheism. There are many passages in the earlier parts of the Bible where Yahweh is seen not so much as the sole God but as the most powerful one, who can act in other gods' territories.[221] In Deutero-Isaiah, however, the existence of other gods is denied, not just in practice but in ideological theory: 'I am the first, and I am the last; and beside me there is no God.'[222] Moreover, it is now stated clearly that God is universal, ubiquitous and omnipotent. God is the motivating force, and the sole motivating force, throughout history. He created the universe; he directs it; he will end it. Israel is part of his plan, but then so is everyone else. So if the Assyrians strike, they do so at his command; and if the Babylonians carry the nation off into exile, that is God's will too. The wilderness religion of Moses is beginning to mature into a sophisticated world faith, to which all humanity can turn for answers.[223]

That the message of Isaiah penetrated into the people's consciousness before the fall of Jerusalem we cannot doubt. But in the last decades before the catastrophe, his powerful voice was joined by another living one, less poetic but equally penetrating. We know more about Jeremiah than any other of the pre-Exilic writers because he dictated his sermons and autobiography to his scribal pupil, Baruch.[224] His life was closely interwoven with the tragic history of his country. He was a Benjaminite, of a priestly family, from a village just north-east of Jerusalem. He began preaching in 627, in the tradition of Hosea and to some extent of Isaiah. He saw the nation as woefully sinful, hastening to its doom: 'This people hath a revolting and a rebellious heart.' He had no time, like Hosea, for the religious establishment, whether priests, scribes, 'wise men' or temple prophets: 'The prophets prophesy falsely, and the priests bear rule by their means; and my people love to have it so: and what will ye do in the end thereof?'[225] He saw the great pro-Temple religious reform, under Josiah, as a total failure, and soon after the death of the king, in 609 BC, he went to the Temple and preached a furious sermon, saying so. As a result he was very nearly killed and forbidden to go near the Temple quarter. His own village, even his family, turned against him. He could not or would not marry. In his isolation and loneliness, he exhibits signs in his writings of paranoia, as we would call it: 'Cursed be the day wherein I was born,' he writes. And again: 'Why is my pain perpetual, my wound incurable?' He felt he was surrounded by enemies who 'devised devices against me', and that 'I was like a lamb or an ox that is brought to the slaughter.'[226] There was some truth in this: not only was Jeremiah forbidden to preach but his writings were burned.

This unpopularity was understandable. For at a time when the 'Foe from the North', as he put it, Nebuchadnezzar and his army, grew ever more menacing, and all in the kingdom were striving to find some way out of the disaster, Jeremiah appeared to be preaching defeatism. He said the people and their rulers were themselves the authors of their danger through their wickedness. The enemy was merely the instrument of God's wrath, and was thus bound to prevail. This seemed like black fatalism: hence the notion of the 'Jeremiad'. But what his contemporaries missed was the other part of his message, the reasons for hope. For Jeremiah was saying that the destruction of the kingdom did not matter. Israel was still the chosen of the Lord. It could perform the mission given to it by God just as well in exile and dispersal as within the confines of its petty nation-state. Israel's link with the Lord would survive defeat because it was intangible and therefore indestructible. Jeremiah was not preaching despair; on the contrary, he was preparing his fellow Israelites to meet despair, and overcome it. He was trying to teach them how to become Jews: to submit to conquering power and accommodate themselves to it, to make the best of adversity, and to cherish the long-term certainty of God's justice in their hearts.

The lesson was needed, for the end of the First Commonwealth was in sight. Three years before Jeremiah preached his Temple sermon, the Assyrian empire suddenly collapsed and the new power of Babylon moved into the vacuum it left. In 605 BC, Babylon won the decisive battle of Karchemish, destroying the army of Egypt, the 'broken reed'.

Jerusalem fell in 597 BC, the Babylonian Chronicle, now in the British Museum, noting: 'In the seventh year, in the month of Kislev, [Nebuchudnezzar] mustered his troops, and having marched to the land of Hatti, besieged the city of Judah, and on the second day of the month of Adar took the city and captured the king. He appointed therein a king of his own choice, received its heavy tribute and sent [them] to Babylon.' This gives us the exact date, 16 March. The Second Book of Kings adds that the King of Judah, Jehoiakim, was taken to Babylon with 'all Jerusalem, and all the princes, and all the mighty men of valour, ten thousand captives, and all the craftsmen and all the smiths'; none remained, except 'the poorest people of the land'. The gold vessels in the Temple were likewise 'cut in pieces' and carried off.[227]

Nor was this the end of Judah's sorrows. Under Zedekiah, the Israelite governor the Babylonians had appointed, and who had sworn fealty to them, the city rose up, and was again besieged. In 1935 the archaeologist J. L. Starkey excavated the gatehouse at Lachish and found there inscribed ostraca now known as the Lachish Letters. They date from the autumn of 589 BC, are dispatches from an outpost to a Lachish staff officer, and cover the last phase of Jerusalem's freedom. One has a reference to 'a prophet', perhaps Jeremiah himself. Another states that Jerusalem, Lachish and Azekah are the only Israelite enclaves left. In 587/6, Jerusalem's walls were breached and the starving city surrendered. In an appalling scene, Zedekiah's children were murdered in front of him, and when he had witnessed this dreadful sight, his eyes were put out, standard punishment for a vassal who broke his oath. The Temple was torn down, the walls demolished, the great city houses wrecked and the old town of Millo, dating back from before David's conquest, slid into the ravine.[228]

There was, however, one vital difference between the Babylonian conquest of Judah and the Assyrian descent on the north. The Babylonians were much less ruthless. They did not colonize. No strange tribes were moved in from the east, to cover the Promised Land with pagan shrines. The poor people, the am ha-arez, were left without leaders but they could cling to their religion after a fashion. Moreover, the Benjaminites, who seem to have submitted in 588 BC, were not exiled, and their cities of Gibeon, Mizpah and Bethel were left intact. All the same, there was a great scattering of the nation. It was a diaspora as well as an exile, for many fled north, to Samaria, or to Edom and Moab. Some went into Egypt. Among them was Jeremiah himself. He had behaved with great obstinacy and courage in the final days of Jerusalem, insisting that resistance was useless and that

Nebuchudnezzar was the agent of the Lord, sent to punish Judah for its wickedness. So they put him under arrest. After the fall of the city, he wished to remain there and share the life of the poor; but a group of the citizens dragged him with them and settled across the Egyptian border, where he continued, in great old age, to denounce the sins which had brought on the Lord's vengeance, and to put his faith in a 'remnant', a 'small number' who would see his words justified by history. There his voice faded into silence, the first Jew.[229]

PART TWO

Judaism

Among the first group of the elite forced into Babylonian exile in 597 BC was a senior and learned priest called Ezekiel. His wife had died during the last siege of the city, and he lived and died in lonely exile, on the Chebar Canal near Babylon.[1] Sitting on its banks, in bitterness and despair, he experienced a divine vision: 'a whirlwind came out of the north, a great cloud, and a fire enfolding itself, and a brightness was about it, and out of the midst thereof as the colour of amber, out of the midst of the fire'.[2] This was the first of a series of intense visual experiences, unique in the Bible for the violent colours and dazzling light which Ezekiel saw and set down, ransacking his vocabulary for words with which to describe them: the colours are of topaz, sapphires, rubies, the light is flashing and radiant, it sparkles and glitters and blinds and burns in its fiery heat. His long book is confused and confusing, with dream-like sequences and terrifying images, threats, curses and violence. He is one of the greatest writers in the Bible, and one of the most popular, in his own time and since. But he surrounds himself in mysteries and enigmas, almost against his will. Why, he asks, do I always have to talk in riddles?

Yet in essence this weird and passionate man had a firm and powerful message to deliver: the only salvation was through religious purity. States and empires and thrones did not matter in the long run. They would perish through God's power. What mattered was the creature God had created in his image: man. Ezekiel describes how God took him to a valley which was full of bones, and asked him: 'Son of Man, can these bones live?' Then, before his terrified gaze, the bones begin to rattle and shake and come together: God puts on them sinews, flesh and skin, and finally he breathes into them, 'and they lived, and stood upon their feet, an exceeding great army'.[3] The Christians were later to interpret this fearsome scene as an image of the Resurrection of the dead, but to Ezekiel and his audience it was a sign of the resurrection of Israel, though of an Israel closer to and more dependent on God then ever before, each man and woman created by God, each individually responsible to him, each committed from birth to the lifelong obedience of his laws. If Jeremiah was the first Jew, it was Ezekiel and his visions which gave the dynamic impulse to the formulation of Judaism.

The Exile necessarily meant a break with the tribal past. Indeed, ten of the tribes had already disappeared. Ezekiel insisted, like Hosea, Isaiah and Jeremiah, that the calamities which befell the Jews were the direct and inescapable result of sinful breach of the Law. But whereas earlier histories and prophecies had dwelt on the sense of collective guilt, and attributed to kings and leaders the wickedness which had brought down divine wrath on all, the exiled Jews now had no one to blame but their individual selves. God, wrote Ezekiel, no longer punished people collectively for the sin of a leader, or the present generation for the faults of their ancestors. 'As I live,' God insisted thunderously, the old Israelite saying, 'The fathers have eaten sour grapes and the children's teeth are set on edge', was no longer true. It was obsolete, to be discarded. 'Behold, all souls are mine,' God told Ezekiel, and each was individually responsible to him: 'the soul that sinneth, it shall die'.[4] The idea of the individual had always, of course, been present in Mosaic religion, since it was inherent in the belief that each man and woman was created in God's image. It had been powerfully reinforced by the sayings of Isaiah. With Ezekiel it became paramount, and thereafter individual accountability became of the very essence of the Jewish religion.

Many consequences flowed from this paramountcy. Between 734 and 581 BC there were six distinct deportations of the Israelites, and more fled voluntarily to Egypt and other parts of the Near East. From this time onwards, a majority of Jews would always live outside the Promised Land. Thus scattered, leaderless, without a state or any of the normal supportive apparatus provided by their own government, the Jews were forced to find alternative means to preserve their special identity. So they turned to their writings – their laws, and the records of their past. From this time we hear more of the scribes. Hitherto, they had simply been secretaries, like Baruch, writing down the words of the great. Now they became an important caste, setting down in writing oral traditions, copying precious scrolls brought from the ruined Temple, ordering, editing and rationalizing the Jewish archives. For a time indeed they were more important than the priests, who had no temple to underline their glory and indispensability. The exile was conducive to scribal effort. The Jews were reasonably treated

in Babylon. Tablets found near the Ishtar Gate of the ancient city list
rations doled out to captives, including 'Yauchin, king of the land of
Yahud' – this is Jehoiakim. Some of the Jews became merchants. The
first success stories of the diaspora were told. Mercantile wealth
financed the scribal effort, and the work of keeping the Jews in their
faith. If the individual was responsible for obeying the Law, he must
know what the Law is. So it must not merely be set down and copied,
but taught.

   Hence it was during the Exile that ordinary Jews were first
disciplined into the regular practice of their religion. Circumcision,
which distinguished them ineffaceably from the surrounding pagans,
was insisted upon rigorously, and the act became a ceremony and so
part of the Jewish life-cycle and liturgy. The concept of the Sabbath,
strongly reinforced by what they learned from Babylonian astronomy,
became the focus of the Jewish week, and 'Shabbetai' was the most
popular new name invented during the Exile. The Jewish year was
now for the first time punctuated by the regular feasts: Passover
celebrated the founding of the Jewish nation; Pentecost the giving of
the laws, that is the founding of their religion; Tabernacles, the
wanderings in the desert where nation and religion were brought
together; and, as the consciousness of individual responsibility sank
into their hearts, the Jews began to celebrate too the New Year in
memory of the creation, and the Day of Atonement in anticipation of
judgment. Again, Babylonian science and calendrical skills helped to
regularize and institutionalize this annual religious framework. It was
in exile that the rules of faith began to seem all-important: rules of
purity, of cleanliness, of diet. The laws were now studied, read aloud,
memorized. It is probably from this time that we get the Deuteronomic
injunction: 'These commandments which I give you this day are to be
kept in your heart; you shall repeat them to your sons, and speak of
them indoors and out of doors, when you lie down and when you rise.
Bind them as a sign on the hand and wear them as a phylactery on the
forehead; write them up on the doorposts of your homes and of your
gates.'[5] In exile the Jews, deprived of a state, became a nomocracy –
voluntarily submitting to rule by a Law which could only be enforced
by consent. Nothing like this had occurred before in history.

   The Exile was short in the sense that it lasted only half a century
after the final fall of Judah. Yet its creative force was overwhelming.
We come here to an important point about Jewish history. As we have
already noted, there is an inherent conflict between the religion and the
state of Israel. In religious terms, there have been four great formative
periods in Jewish history: under Abraham, under Moses, during and

shortly after the Exile, and after the destruction of the Second Temple. The first two produced the religion of Yahweh, the second two developed and refined it into Judaism itself. But in none of these periods did the Jews possess an independent state, though it is true that, during the Mosaic period, they were not actually ruled by anyone else.

Conversely, it is also notable that when the Israelites, and later the Jews, achieved settled and prosperous self-government, they found it extraordinarily difficult to keep their religion pure and incorrupt. The decay set in rapidly after the conquest of Joshua; it again appeared under Solomon, and was repeated in both northern and southern kingdoms, especially under rich and powerful kings and when times were good; exactly the same pattern would return again under the Hasmoneans and under such potentates as Herod the Great. In self-government and prosperity, the Jews always seemed drawn to neighbouring religions, whether Canaanite, Philistine–Phoenician or Greek. Only in adversity did they cling resolutely to their principles and develop their extraordinary powers of religious imagination, their originality, their clarity and their zeal. Perhaps, then, they were better off without a state of their own, more likely to obey the law and fear God when others had the duties and temptations of ruling them. Jeremiah was the first to perceive the possibility that powerlessness and goodness were somehow linked, and that alien rule could be preferable to self-rule. He comes close to the notion that the state itself was inherently evil.

These ideas had deep roots in Israelite history, going back to the Nazarites and Rechabites. They were inherent in Yahwehism itself, since God, not man, is the ruler. There are times when the Bible seems to suggest that the whole aim of righteousness is to overturn existing, man-made, order: 'Every valley shall be exalted, and every mountain and hill laid low.'[6] In Chapter 2 of the First Book of Samuel, his mother Hannah sings a triumphant hymn to subversion in the name of God, to divine revolution: 'He raiseth up the poor out of the dust, and lifteth up the beggar from the dunghill, to set them among princes';[7] and the Virgin Mary was later to echo the same theme in the Magnificat. The Jews were the yeast, producing decomposition of the existing order, the chemical agent of change in society – so how could they be order and society itself?[8]

From this point forward, therefore, we note the existence of an Exile and a diaspora mentality among the Jews. The Babylonian empire was soon replaced by the alliance of Persians and Medes created by Cyrus the Great, who had no wish whatever to keep the Jews in custody. But many of them, perhaps the majority, preferred to remain in Babylon, which became a great centre of Jewish culture for 1,500 years. Other Jewish communities settled in Egypt, not just across the border, as Jeremiah did, but as far down the Nile as the island of Elephantine, near the First Cataract: there, among other documents, a papyrus letter has survived in which the Jewish community request permission to rebuild their temple.[9] Even among those who did return to Judah, there was an exile-minded element, who took Jeremiah's view that there was a positive virtue in the Exile until the day of perfect purity dawned. They lived on the desert fringe and saw themselves as internal exiles, in what they called 'The Land of Damascus', a symbol of deportation, where Yahweh had his sanctuary; they waited for God's good time, when a star and a holy leader would take them back to Jerusalem. These exilics were descendants of the Rechabites and precursors of the Qumran sect.[10]

Indeed, it may be that the Persian king, Cyrus the Great, was himself the instigator of the Return. The faith of the Persian ruling class was ethical and universalistic, unlike the intolerant, narrow nationalism of the earlier imperial powers. Cyrus himself was a Zoroastrian, believing in one, eternal, beneficent being, 'Creator of all things through the holy spirit'.[11] Under Cyrus, the Persians developed a radically different imperial religious policy to the Assyrians and Babylonians. They were happy to respect the religious beliefs of subject peoples, provided these were compatible with acceptance of their own authority. Indeed Cyrus seems to have regarded it as a religious duty to reverse the wicked deportations and temple-destructions of his predecessors. In the Cyrus-cylinder, discovered in the palace ruins of Babylon in the nineteenth century and now in the British Museum, he stated his policy: 'I am Cyrus, the king of the world. . . . Marduk, the great god, rejoices at my pious acts. . . . I gathered all their people and led them back to their abodes . . . and the gods . . . at the order of Marduk, the great lord, I had them installed in joy in their sanctuaries. . . . May all the gods whom I have led back to their cities [pray daily] for the length of my days.'[12] According to Deutero-Isaiah, edited about this time, it was the Lord who command-ed this restoration by Cyrus, whom it calls 'the Lord's anointed'.[13] In the Book of Ezra the Scribe, recounting the return, Cyrus says to the Babylonian Jews: 'The Lord, the God of Heaven, has given me all the kingdoms of the earth, and he has charged me to build him a house at Jerusalem, which is in Judah. Whoever is among you of all his people, may his God be with him, and let him go up to Jerusalem, and rebuild the house of the Lord, the God of Israel.'[14]

Despite Cyrus' support and command, the first return in 538, under Shenazar, son of the former King Jehoiakim, was a failure, for the poor Jews who had been left behind, the *am ha-arez*, resisted it, and in conjunction with Samaritans, Edomites and Arabs, prevented the settlers building walls. A second effort, with the full backing of Cyrus' son Darius, was made in 520 BC, under an official leader Zeurubbabel, whose authority as a descendant of David was reinforced by his appointment as Persian Governor of Judah. The Bible records that 42,360 exiles returned with him, including a large number of priests and scribes. This was the entry on to the Jerusalem scene of the new Jewish orthodoxy, revolving round a single, centralized temple and its lawful worship. Work on the Temple began immediately. It was built in a more humble style than Solomon's, as Haggai 2:2 makes clear, though cedars from Lebanon were again used. The Samaritans and other Jews regarded as heretical were not allowed to take part in the work: 'You have nothing to do with us,' they were told.[15] Perhaps because of the exclusiveness of the returning exiles, their colony did not flourish. In 458 BC it was reinforced by a third wave, led by Ezra, a priest and scribe of great learning and authority, who tried and failed to sort out the legal problems caused by heterodoxy, intermarriage and disputed ownership of land. Finally, in 445 BC, Ezra was joined by a powerful contingent headed by a leading Jew and prominent Persian official called Nehemiah, who was given the governorship of Judah and the authority to build it into an independent political unit within the empire.[16]

This fourth wave at last succeeded in stabilizing the settlement, chiefly because Nehemiah, a man of action as well as a diplomat and statesman, rebuilt with commendable speed the walls of Jerusalem and so created a secure enclave from which the work of resettlement could be directed. He described how he did it in his memoirs, a brilliant example of Jewish historical writing. We are told of the first survey of the ruined walls in secret by night; the honours-list of those who took part and what they built; the desperate attempts of Arabs, Ammonites and others to prevent the work; its continuation under armed guard – 'For the builders, everyone had his sword girded by his side, and so builded'[17] – and the return into the city each night ('none of us put off our clothes, saving that everyone put them off for washing') and the triumphant finish. Nehemiah says the business was done in fifty-two days. The rebuilt city was smaller than Solomon's, it was poor and to begin with it was sparsely populated. 'The city is wide and large', wrote Nehemiah, 'but the people within it were few and no houses had been built.' But families, chosen by lot, were brought in from all over Judah. Nehemiah's energy and resourcefulness were to be an inspiration when Palestine was again resettled by Jewish activists in the twentieth century. But with the completion of his work, a sudden calm and a complete silence descends.

The years 400–200 BC are the lost centuries of Jewish history. There were no great events or calamities they chose to record. Perhaps they were happy. The Jews certainly seem to have liked the Persians the best of all their rulers. They never revolted against them; on the contrary, Jewish mercenaries helped the Persians to put down Egyptian rebellion. The Jews were free to practise their religion at home in Judah, or anywhere else in the Persian empire, and Jewish settlements were soon to be found over a vast area: an echo of this diaspora is the Book of Tobit, set in Media in about the fifth century BC. Another is the collection of 650 cuneiform business documents, written between 455 and 403 BC in the city of Nippur, near where Ezekiel lived: 8 per cent of the names in these texts are Jewish.[18] Two Jewish family archives have survived from the Elephantine colony, and cast light on life and religion there.[19] Most of the Jews in the diaspora we hear about seem to have done well and practised their religion faithfully. Moreover, it was the religion of the new orthodoxy: Judaism.

The two hundred lost years, indeed, though silent were not unproductive. They saw the emergence of the Old Testament more or less as we know it. This was made necessary by the nature of the new Judaic version of the Israelite faith which Nehemiah and Ezra established in rebuilt Jerusalem. Chapter 8 of the Book of Nehemiah describes how all the citizens assembled near the watergate to hear a series of readings from 'the book of the law of Moses'. They were conducted by Ezra the Scribe, standing 'upon a pulpit of wood, which they had made for the purpose'. In the light of the readings, which caused intense emotion, a new and solemn covenant was made, signed and pledged by everyone, men and women, their sons and daughters, who considered themselves orthodox, 'everyone having knowledge, and everyone having understanding'.[20]

In short, the new covenant, which may be said to have inaugurated Judaism officially and legally, was based not upon revelation or preaching but on a written text. That meant an official, authorized, accurate and verified version. And that, in turn, meant sorting through, selecting and editing the vast literature of history, politics and religion the Jews had already accumulated. They had been literate at a very early stage in their history. The Book of Judges tells us that when Gideon was in Succoth he grabbed hold of a young lad and questioned him about the place, and the lad wrote down for him the names of all the local landowners and elders, 'threescore and seventeen men'.[21] It is likely that most of the farmers could read a little.[22] In the towns, the level of literacy was high and a large number of people were authors of a kind, setting down tales they had heard or their own adventures and experiences, both spiritual and secular. Hundreds of prophets had their sayings put down. The number of histories and chronicles was immense. The people of Israel were not great craftsmen, or painters, or architects. But writing was their national habit, almost their obsession. They probably produced, in sheer quantity, the greatest literature of antiquity, of which the Old Testament is only a small fragment.

However, the Jews saw literature as a didactic activity, with a collective purpose. It was not an act of personal self-indulgence. Most of the books of the Bible are ascribed individual authorship, but the Jews themselves awarded communal sanction and authority to the books which met their approval. The core of their literature was always public, subject to social control. Josephus, in his apologia for the Jewish faith, *Contra Apionem*, describes this approach:

> With us it is not open to everybody to write the records. . . . The prophets alone had the privilege, obtaining the knowledge of the most remote and ancient history through the inspiration which they owed to God, and committing to writing a clear account of the events of their own time just as they occurred. . . . We do not possess myriads of inconsistent books, conflicting with one another. Our books, those which are justly accredited, are twenty-two in number, and contain the record of all time.[23]

By 'justly accredited', Josephus meant 'canonical'. The word canon is very ancient, the Sumerian for 'reed', whence it acquired its sense of straight or upright; to the Greeks it meant a rule, boundary or standard. The Jews were the first to apply it to religious texts. For them it meant divine pronouncements of unquestioned authority or divinely inspired prophetic writings. Hence each book, to be accepted in the canon, had to possess a recognized true prophet as its accredited author.[24] The canon began to emerge when the first five or Mosaic books, the Pentateuch, which later became known to Jews as the Torah, reached written form. In its most primitive version, the Pentateuch probably dates from the time of Samuel, but in the form we possess it the text is a compilation of five and possibly more elements: a southern source, referring to God as Yahweh, and going back to the original Mosaic writings; a northern source, calling God 'Elohim', also of great antiquity; Deuteronomy, or parts of it, the 'lost' book found in the Temple at the time of Joshua's reforms; and two separate, additional codes, known to scholars as the Priestly Code and the Holiness Code and both dating from times when religious worship had become more formalized and the priestly caste strictly disciplined.

The Pentateuch is not, therefore, a homogeneous work. But neither is it, as some scholars in the German critical tradition have argued, a deliberate falsification by post-Exilic priests, seeking to foist their self-interested religious beliefs on the people by attributing them to Moses and his age. We must not allow the academic prejudices bred by Hegelian ideology, anti-clericalism, anti-Semitism and nineteenth-century intellectual fashions to distort our view of these texts. All the internal evidence shows that those who set down and conflated these writings, and the scribes who copied them when the canon was assembled after the return from Exile, believed absolutely in the divine inspiration of the ancient texts and transcribed them with veneration and the highest possible standards of accuracy, including many passages which they manifestly did not understand. Indeed, the Pentateuch text twice gives solemn admonitions, from God himself, against tampering: 'Ye shall not add unto the word which I command you, neither shall you diminish aught from it.'[25]

All the evidence suggests that copyists, or scribes – the word in Hebrew is *sofer* – were highly professional and took their duties with great seriousness. The word is first used in the ancient Song of Deborah, and we soon hear of hereditary scribal corporations, what the First Book of Chronicles calls 'families of scribes'.[26] Their most honourable duty was to preserve the canon in all its holy integrity. They began with the Mosaic texts which, for convenience, were transcribed on to five separate scrolls: hence its name (though Pentateuch itself is Greek, as are the individual names of the books). To these were added the second division of the Bible, Prophets, in Hebrew *Nevi'im*. These in turn consist of 'Former Prophets' and 'Later Prophets'. The former consist of the mainly narrative and historical works, Joshua, Judges, Samuel and Kings, and the latter the writings of the prophetic orators, themselves divided into two sections, the three major prophets, Isaiah, Jeremiah and Ezekiel – the term signifying length, not importance – and the twelve minor ones, Hosea, Joel, Amos, Obadiah, Jonah, Micah, Nahum, Habakkuk, Zephaniah, Haggai, Zechariah and Malachi. Then there are the works of the third division, the *Ketuvim* or 'writings', often known as the Hagiographa. This consists of the Psalms, the Proverbs, the Book of Job, the Song of Songs, Ruth, Lamentations, Ecclesiastes, Esther, Daniel, Ezra, Nehemiah and the two books of Chronicles.

The tripartite division does not reflect a deliberate classification so much as historical development. As public readings became an integral part of Jewish services, so more texts were added, and the scribes duly copied them. The Pentateuch or Torah was canonized as early as 622 BC. Other books were added gradually, the process being complete by about 300 BC. Other than the Torah, we do not know the criteria by which the canon was compiled. But popular taste, as well as priestly and scholarly judgment, appears to have played a part. The five scrolls known as the Megillot, or Canticles, were read in public at the great feasts, the Song of Solomon at Passover, Ruth at Pentecost, Ecclesiastes at Tabernacles, Esther at Purim and Lamentations at the feast of the Destruction of Jerusalem. They became popular in consequence, and that is why they were included in the canon. Apart from its association with a great king, the Song of Solomon is evidently an anthology of love poems, and there is no intrinsic reason for its inclusion. Rabbinical tradition says that at the Council of Jamnia or Jabneh, in the early Christian era, when the canon was finally determined, the Rabbi Akiva said: 'For in all the world there is nothing to equal the day on which the Song of Songs was given to Israel, for all the writings are holy, but the Song of Songs is the Holy of Holies.' But he then added, as a warning: 'He who, for the sake of entertainment, sings the song as though it were a profane song, will have no place in the next world.'[27]

Inclusion in the canon was the only certain way of ensuring that a work of literature survived, for in antiquity, unless a manuscript was constantly recopied, it tended to vanish without trace within a generation or so. The families of the scribes, then, ensured the survival of the Bible texts for a thousand years or more, and in due course they were succeeded by families of *masoretes* or scribal scholars who specialized in the writing, spelling and accenting of Bible texts. It was they who produced the official Jewish canonical version, known as the Masoretic text.

There is, however, more than one canon, and therefore more than one ancient text. The Samaritans, having been cut off from Judah in the middle of the first millennium BC, preserved only the five Mosaic books, since they were not allowed to take part in the canonization of later writings, and therefore did not recognize them. Then there is the Septuagint, the Greek version of the Old Testament, which was compiled by members of the Jewish diaspora at Alexandria during the Hellenistic period. This included all the books of the Hebrew Bible, but grouped them differently, and it also included books of the Apocrypha and pseudepigraphs, such as 1 Esdras, the so-called Wisdom of Solomon, the Wisdom of Ben Sira or Ecclesiasticus, Judith,

Tobit, Baruch and the books of the Maccabees, all of them rejected by the Jews of Jerusalem as impure or dangerous. In addition, we now have the scrolls preserved and copied by the Qumran sect and found in caves near the Dead Sea.

The Dead Sea Scrolls testify, on the whole, to the accuracy with which the Bible was copied through the ages, though many mistakes and variations occurred. The Samaritans claimed that their text went back to Abishua, great-grandson of Aaron, and it is clearly very old and remarkably uncorrupt as a rule, though in places it reflects Samaritan, as opposed to Jewish, traditions. It differs from the Masoretic text of the Pentateuch in about 6,000 instances, and on these it agrees with the Septuagint version in about 1,900. There are also variations in the Masoretic texts. Of the earliest surviving texts, the Karaite Synagogue in Cairo has a codex, a bound book, of the prophets, which was copied in 895 AD by Ben Asher, head of one of the most famous Masoretic families. The complete Asher text, on which the family worked for five generations, was copied in about 1010 by a Masorete called Samuel ben Jacob, and this is now in Leningrad. Another famous Masoretic text, by the Ben Naphtali family, survives in a copy dated 1105, known as the Reuchlin Codex, and now in Karlsruhe. The earliest surviving Christian version is the fourth-century AD Codex Vaticanus in the Vatican, the incomplete fourth-century Codex Sinaiticus and the fifth-century Codex Alexandrinus, the last two both in the British Museum. There is also a Syriac version in a manuscript dated 464 AD. The oldest Biblical manuscripts of all, however, are those found among the Dead Sea Scrolls in 1947–8, which include Hebrew fragments of all the twenty-four books of the canon, except Esther, and the entire text of Isaiah, plus some fragments of the Septuagint.[28] It is quite possible that more early texts will be discovered, both in the Judaean Desert and in Egypt, and clearly the search for perfect texts will continue until the end of time.

The attention which the Bible has received, in the search for the true text, in exegesis, hermeneutics and commentary, exceeds by far that devoted to any other work of literature. Nor is this interest dispro-portionate, because it has been the most influential of all books. The Jews had two unique characteristics as ancient writers. They were the first to create consequential, substantial and interpretative history. It has been argued that they learned the art of history from the Hittites, another historically minded people, but it is obvious that they were fascinated by their past from very early times. They knew they were a special people who had not simply evolved from an unrecorded past but had been brought into existence, for certain definite purposes, by a specific series of divine acts. They saw it as their collective business to determine, record, comment and reflect upon these acts. No other people has ever shown, particularly at that remote time, so strong a compulsion to explore their origins. The Bible gives constant examples of the probing historical spirit: why, for instance, was there a heap of stones before the city gate at Ai? What was the meaning of the twelve stones at Gilgal?[29] This passion for aetiology, the quest for explanations, broadened into a more general habit of seeing the present and future in terms of the past. The Jews wanted to know about themselves and their destiny. They wanted to know about God and his intentions and wishes. Since God, in their theology, was the sole cause of all events – as Amos put it, 'Does evil befall a city unless Yahweh wills it?' – and thus the author of history, and since they were the chosen actors in his vast dramas, the record and study of historical events was the key to the understanding of both God and man.

Hence the Jews were above all historians, and the Bible is essentially a historical work from start to finish. The Jews developed the power to write terse and dramatic historical narrative half a millennium before the Greeks, and because they constantly added to their historical records they developed a deep sense of historical perspective which the Greeks never attained. In the portrayal of character, too, the Biblical historians achieved a degree of perception and portraiture which even the best Greek and Roman historians could never manage. There is nothing in Thucydides to equal the masterly presentation of King David, composed evidently by an eye-witness at his court. The Bible abounds in sharply etched characters, often minor figures brought into vivid focus by a single phrase. But the stress on the actors never obscures the steady progression of the great human–divine drama. The Jews, like all good historians, kept a balance between biography and narrative. Most of the books of the Bible have a historical framework, all related to the wider framework, which might be entitled 'A history of God in his relations to man'. But even those which do not have a clear historical intention, even the poetry, such as the Psalms, contain constant historical allusions, so that the march of destiny, proceeding inexorably from creation to 'the end of days', is always heard in the background.

Ancient Jewish history is both intensely divine and intensely humanist. History was made by God, operating independently or through man. The Jews were not interested and did not believe in impersonal forces. They were less curious about the physics of creation than any other literate race of antiquity. They turned their back on nature and discounted its manifestations except in so far as they reflected the divine–human drama. The notion of vast geographical or economic forces determining history was quite alien to them. There is much natural description in the Bible, some of astonishing beauty, but it is stage-scenery for the historical play, a mere backdrop for the characters. The Bible is vibrant because it is entirely about living creatures; and since God, though living, cannot be described or even imagined, the attention is directed relentlessly on man and woman.

Hence the second unique characteristic of ancient Jewish literature: the verbal presentation of the human personality in all its range and complexity. The Jews were the first race to find words to express the deepest human emotions, especially the feelings produced by bodily or mental suffering, anxiety, spiritual despair and desolation, and the remedies for these evils produced by human ingenuity – hope, resolution, confidence in divine assistance, the consciousness of innocence or righteousness, penitence, sorrow and humility. About forty-four of the short poems, or psalms, included in the 150 in the canonical Book of Psalms, fall into this category.[30] Some are masterpieces, which find echoes in hearts in all ages and places: Psalm 22 crying for help. Psalm 23 with its simple trust, 39 the epitome of unease, 51 pleading for mercy, 91 the great poem of assurance and comfort, 90, 103, 104 celebrating the power and majesty of the Creator and the bonds between God and man, and 130, 137 and 139 plumbing the depths of human misery and bringing messages of hope.

Jewish penetration of the human psyche found one expression in these passionate poems, but it was also reflected in vast quantities of popular philosophy, some of which made its way into the canon. Here the Jews were less singular, for proverbs and wise sayings were written down in the ancient Near East from the third millennium on, especially in Mesopotamia and Egypt, and some of this wisdom literature achieved international status. The Jews were certainly familiar with the famous Egyptian classic, *The Wisdom of Amenope*, since part of it was directly borrowed in the Book of Proverbs.[31] However, wisdom texts produced by the Jews are of an altogether higher standard than their precursors and models, being both more observant of human nature and more ethically consistent. Ecclesiastes, written by the Koheleth or 'convenor', is a scintillating work, quite without equal in the ancient world. Its cool, sceptical tone, verging at times towards cynicism, and contrasting so strongly with the passionate earnestness of the psalms, illustrates the extraordinary range of Jewish literature, with which the Greeks alone could compete.

Yet not even the Greeks produced a document – it is hard to know in what category to place it – so mysterious and harrowing as the Book of Job. This great essay in theodicy and the problem of evil has fascinated and baffled both scholars and ordinary people for more than two millennia. Carlyle called it 'one of the grandest things ever written with pen' and of all the books of the Bible it has most influenced other writers. But no one knows what it is, where it comes from or when it was written. There are over 100 words in it which occur nowhere else and it obviously raised insuperable difficulties for the ancient translators and scribes. Some scholars think it comes from Edom – but we know very little about the Edomite tongue. Others have suggested Haran, near Damascus. There are slight parallels in Babylonian literature. As long ago as the fourth century AD, the Christian scholar Theodore of Mopsuestia argued that it derived from Greek drama. It has also been presented as a translation from the Arabic. The variety of origins and influences produced testify, in a paradoxical way, to its universality. For Job, after all, is asking the fundamental question which has puzzled all men, and especially those of strong faith: why does God do these terrible things to us? Job was a text for antiquity and it is a text for modernity, a text especially for that chosen and battered people, the Jews; a text, above all, for the Holocaust.[32]

Job is a formidable work of Hebrew literature. With the only exception of Isaiah, no work in the Bible is written at such a sustained level of powerful eloquence. That is befitting for its subject, the justice of God. As a work of moral theology, the book is a failure because the author, like everyone else, is baffled by the problem of theodicy. But in failing, he broadens the issue and poses certain questions about the universe and the way man ought to see it. Job is crammed with natural history in poetic form. It presents a fascinating catalogue of organic, cosmic and meteorological phenomena. In Chapter 28, for instance, there is an extraordinary description of mining in the ancient world. Through this image, a view is presented of the almost unlimited scientific and technological potential of the human race, and this is then contrasted with man's incorrigibly weak moral capacities. What the author of Job is saying is that there are two orders in creation – the physical and the moral order. To understand and master the physical order of the world is not enough: man must come to accept and abide by the moral order, and to do this he must acquire the secret of Wisdom, and this knowledge is something of an altogether different kind from, say, mining technology. Wisdom came to man, as Job dimly perceived, not by trying to penetrate God's reasoning and motives in inflicting pain, but only through obedience, the true foundation of the moral order: 'And he said to man: "Behold, the fear of the Lord, that is wisdom: and to depart from evil is understanding." '

The point was made again by Ben Sira in Chapter 24 of his poem about wisdom, the Ecclesiasticus, where he says that, after the Fall, God conceived a new plan and gave this secret of his a dwelling-place in Israel.[33] The Jews were to find wisdom through obedience to God, and teach humanity to do likewise. They were to overthrow the existing, physical, worldly order, and replace it by the moral order. Again, the point was echoed powerfully and paradoxically by the heretic Jew, St Paul, in the dramatic opening to his First Epistle to the Corinthians, when he quotes the Lord, 'I will destroy the wisdom of the wise, and will bring to nothing the understanding of the prudent'; and he adds, 'Because the foolishness of God is wiser than men; and the weakness of God is stronger than men . . . [therefore] God hath chosen the foolish things of the world to confound the wise; and God hath chosen the weak things of the world to confound the things which are mighty.'[34] Within the obscurity and confusion of Job, therefore, we have yet another statement of the divine role of the Jews to overturn the existing order and the worldly way of seeing things.

Job, then, was part of the Jewish philosophical mainstream: and that mainstream was now a powerful torrent. The transformation of Judaism into the first 'religion of the Book' took two centuries. Before 400 BC there is no hint of a canon. By 200 BC, it was there. Of course the canon was not yet complete and final. But it was beginning to solidify fast. This had several consequences. In the first place, additions were discouraged. Prophecy, and prophets, fell into disrepute. There is a reference in the First Book of Maccabees to 'the day when prophets ceased to appear'.[35] Those who tried to prophesy were dismissed as false. When Simon Maccabeus was made leader, his term of office was declared to be indefinite 'until a true prophet shall appear'. The Book of Zechariah has a tirade against prophets: 'if a man continues to prophesy, his parents, his own father and mother, will say to him: "You shall lie no longer, for you have spoken falsely in the name of the Lord".' Prophets were 'schooled in lust'.[36] The Jewish philosopher Ben Sira, writing a little after 200 BC, boasted, 'I will again pour out doctrine like prophecy and bequeath it to future generations.'[37] But the Jews did not add him to the canon; Daniel, writing a little later (c. 168–165 BC), was also excluded. Canonization also discouraged the writing of history. It did not kill the Jewish passion completely. There were some tremendous flare-ups to come – the Books of the Maccabees, the work of Josephus, for example. But the great dynamic was running down, and when the canon was finally sanctified early in the Christian era, Jewish history, one of the glories of antiquity, would cease for a millennium and a half.

But if one effect of canonization was to curb the creativity of Jewish sacred literature, another was enormously to increase the knowledge and impact of the approved texts on the Jewish population. The books, having been authorized and copiously reproduced and distributed, were now systematically taught. The Jews began to be a schooled people, as indeed their divine role as priests to the nations demanded. A new and quite revolutionary institution in the history of religion appeared: the synagogue – prototype of the church, the chapel and the mosque – where the Bible was systematically read and taught. Such places may have existed even before the Exile, as a result of Josiah's reform; they certainly matured during the Exile years, when the Jewish elite had no Temple; and on the Return, when all religious activity was rigorously centralized in the Jerusalem Temple, and provincial temples and high places finally disappeared, synagogues took over and taught the Temple orthodoxy which the canonical Bible encapsulated.[38]

This had another important consequence. With the sacred literature digested into a canon, and the canon systematically taught from a central focus, Judaism became far more homogeneous. And it was homogeneity with a pronounced puritanical and fundamentalist flavour. In the history of the Jews, the rigorists tend to win. It was Moses, the stern legal purist, who imposed his religion of Yahweh on the other tribal groups. It was the rigorists who again won at the time of Josiah's reform. It was rigorous Judah, not compromising Israel, which survived the assault of the empires; and it was the rigorist community of Babylon, returning from Exile, which imposed its will on all Jews, excluding many, forcing many others to conform. The canon and the synagogue became instruments of this rigour, and it was to win many more victories. The process, which occurs again and again in Jewish history, can be seen in two ways: as the pearl of purified Judaism emerging from the rotten oyster of the world and worldliness; or as the extremists imposing exclusivity and fanaticism on the rest.

But however it is seen, this rigorizing tendency in Judaism posed increasing problems both for the Jews themselves and for their neighbours. Under the benevolent rule of the Persians, who received nothing but praise in the Jewish texts, the Jews began to recover and flourish. Ezra says that 42,360 Jews, plus 7,337 male and female servants and 200 'singing men and singing women', returned from the Exile. The total population of refound Judah could not have been more than 70,000. Yet by the third century BC, the population of Jerusalem alone was 120,000.[39] With their strong religious sense and respect for law, the Jews were disciplined and hardworking. They spread into territories bordering on Judah, particularly Galilee, Transjordan and the coast. The diaspora widened steadily. The Jews made converts. They were beginning to be a proselytizing force. All the same, they were a small people in an age of empires, an uncompromising religious–cultural unit in a big, bruising world.

The problems began to manifest themselves from 332 BC, when Alexander of Macedon cracked the Persian empire like a rotten egg. This was the first true European invasion of Asia. In the third and most of the second millennia BC, the continental cleavage did not exist: the sea was a binding force for what was to a great extent a common international culture. But then followed the barbarian anarchy of the twelfth–eleventh centuries BC and a long Dark Age. When the world re-emerged into Iron Age civilization, the East–West division began to appear, and from the western side of it emerged one of the most powerful cultural forces the world has ever seen: the civilization of the *polis*, the Greek city-state.

The Greeks bred a continuing surplus population. They created a ubiquitous maritime commerce. They planted colonies throughout the Mediterranean. In Alexander's day they pushed into Asia and Africa, and his successors carved out of his empire sprawling kingdoms: Ptolemy in Egypt, Seleucus in Syria and Mesopotamia, and later Attalus in Anatolia. From 332 to 200 BC the Jews were ruled by the Ptolemies; thereafter by the Seleucids. Among the Jews, their new rulers inspired awe and terror. The Greeks had the fearsome and then-absolute weapon of the phalanx. They built increasingly powerful machines of war, towering siege-engines, huge warships, colossal forts. Daniel gives the Jewish image of Greek militarism: 'A fourth beast, dreadful and terrifying, and strong exceedingly; and it had great iron teeth: it devoured and brake in pieces, and stamped the residue with the feet of it.'[40] The Jews knew all about Greek militarism, for they served the Greeks as mercenaries, as they had served the Persians. Greek military training began in the gymnasium, the primary educational instrument of the *polis*. But that was not its only function. Its main purpose was to promote Greek culture, as were the other institutions with which each *polis* was equipped: the stadium, the theatre, the odeum, the lyceum, the agora. The Greeks were superb architects. They were sculptors, poets, musicians, playwrights, philosophers and debaters. They staged marvellous performances. They were excellent traders too. In their wake, the economy boomed; living standards rose. Ecclesiastes laments the craze for wealth under Greek rule. What good, he asks, ever came from piling up immense fortunes?[41] Most men, however, felt a lot of good would accrue, if the fortune were theirs. Greek economics and Greek culture both appealed strongly to the less sophisticated societies of the Near East, rather as nineteenth-century Asia and Africa found Western progress irresistible.

So the Greek colonists poured into western Asia, built their cities everywhere, and were joined by locals who wished to share their wealth and way of life. Syria and Palestine were areas of intense Greek settlement and rapid Hellenization of their existing inhabitants. The coast was soon completely Hellenized. The Greek rulers gave *polis*-style cities, such as Tyre, Sidon, Gaza, Straton's Tower, Byblos and Tripoli, generous freedoms and privileges, and these in turn set up satellite cities in the interior. There was one at Shechem, another at Marissa in the south, others at Philadelphia (Amman) and Gamal across the Jordan. Soon a ring of such cities, swarming with Greeks and semi-Greeks, surrounded Jewish Samaria and Judah, which were seen as mountainous, rural and backward. The Greek orbit had a number of such queer 'temple-states', antique survivors, anachronisms, soon to be swept away by the irresistible modern tide of Hellenic ideas and institutions.

How were the Jews to react to this cultural invasion, which was opportunity, temptation and threat all in one? The answer is that they reacted in different ways. Though the rigorizing tendency triumphed before, during and after the Exile, and sustained itself through the teaching of the canon, there was a countervailing force in the growing stress on the individual conscience we have already noted. Spiritual individualism bred disagreement, and it strengthened the sectarianism which had always been latent, and sometimes active, in Judaism. At one extreme, the coming of the Greeks pushed more fundamentalists into the desert, to join the absolutist groups who kept up the Rechabite and Nazarite traditions, and who regarded Jerusalem as already irredeemably corrupt. The earliest texts found in the Qumran community date from about 250 BC, when the noose of Greek cities around Judah first began to tighten. The idea was to retreat into the wilderness, recapture the pristine Mosaic enthusiasm, then launch back into the cities. Some, like the Essenes, thought this could be done peacefully, by the word, and they preached in villages on the edge of the desert: John the Baptist was later in this tradition. Others, like the Qumran community, put their trust in the sword: organized themselves for war, using a symbolic twelve-tribe structure, and were planning, when a sign brought their wilderness years to an end, to launch a Joshua-like invasion of the urban areas, rather like a guerrilla movement today.[42]

At the other extreme, there were many Jews, including pious ones, who hated isolationism and the fanatics it bred. They even contributed to the canon, in the shape of the Book of Jonah, which, despite its absurdities and confusions, is really a plea to extend toleration and friendship to foreigners. God ends the book by putting Jonah a rhetorical question: is it not right to be forgiving to Nineveh and its teeming people, 'that cannot discern between their right hand and their left' and whose only sin is ignorance?[43] This was an adumbration of Christ's, 'Forgive them father, for they know not what they do', and it was an invitation to take the Torah to the stranger, to proselytize. That, certainly, was the view of many, perhaps the majority, of observant Jews in the diaspora. These diaspora Jews learned Greek as a matter of routine to pursue their business. In due course they translated the Scriptures into Greek – the Septuagint – and this was the primary means by which converts, or 'Judaizers', were made. In Alexandria, for instance, the Greek gymnasium, originally set up to prevent the Greek colonists from becoming degenerate and embracing local languages and customs, was opened to resident non-Greeks (though not to Egyptians) and the Jews eagerly took advantage of this; later, the Jewish philosopher Philo took it for granted that sons of wealthy Jewish merchants would attend one.[44] They Hellenized their names, or used two sets, Hellenic names for journeys and business, Hebrew at religious services and at home.

The same tendency was at work in Palestine Judaism. The Hellenization of Hebrew–Aramaic Jewish names is reflected in inscriptions and graffiti. Many of the better-educated Jews found Greek culture profoundly attractive. The Koheleth, the writer of Ecclesiastes, shows himself torn between new foreign ideas and his inherited piety, between the critical spirit and conservatism. The impact of Hellenization on educated Jews was in many ways similar to the impact of the enlightenment on the eighteenth-century ghetto. It woke the Temple-state from its enchanted sleep. It was a destabilizing force spiritually and, above all, it was a secularizing, materialistic force.[45]

In Palestine, as in other Greek conquests, it was the upper classes, the rich, the senior priests, who were most tempted to ape their new rulers. It is a common experience of colonies everywhere. Acquiring Greek culture was a passport to first-class citizenship, as later would be baptism. There were some notable Jewish success stories. Just as Joseph had served pharaoh as his minister, so now clever, enterprising Jews rose high in the imperial bureaucracy. A second-century BC text, incorporated in Josephus' *Antiquities of the Jews*, tells how Joseph, son of the upper-class Tobias family (his mother was the high-priest's sister), went to the tax-farming auction held by the Ptolemies in Alexandria: 'Now it happened that at this time all the principal men and rulers went up out of the cities of Syria and Phoenicia to bid for their taxes; for every year the King sold them to the men of the greatest power in every city.' Joseph won by accusing his rivals of forming a cartel to lower the price; he held the contract for twenty-two years 'and brought the Jews from poverty and misery to a better way of life'. Joseph went further than his namesake of pharaoh's day. He developed into another archetype: the first Jewish banker.[46] As such he stood for the Hellenizing principle in second-century BC Judah.

Between the isolationists on the one hand and the Hellenizers on the other was a broad group of pious Jews in the tradition of Josiah, Ezekiel and Ezra. Many of them did not object to Greek rule in principle, any more than they had objected to the Persians, since they tended to accept Jeremiah's arguments that religion and piety flourished more when pagans had to conduct the corrupting business of government. They were quite willing to pay the conqueror's taxes provided they were left to practise their religion in peace. Such a policy was later explicitly advocated by the Pharisees, who sprang from this tradition. Up to a point, pious Jews were willing to learn from the Greeks and absorbed a great many more Hellenic ideas than they were prepared to admit. There had always been a rationalizing element in Mosaic legalism and theology, and this was almost unconsciously reinforced by Greek rationalism. That is how the Pharisees created the Oral Law, which was essentially rationalistic, to apply the archaic Mosaic law to the actual world of today. It is significant that their enemies the Sadducees, who stuck rigidly to the written law and would admit no casuistry, said that the logic of the Pharisees would lead to more respect for 'the book of Homer' (by which they meant Greek literature) than the 'holy scriptures'.[47]

However, any possibility of Greeks and Jews living together in reasonable comfort was destroyed by the rise of a Jewish reform party who wanted to force the pace of Hellenization. This reform movement, about which we know little since its history was written by its triumphant fundamentalist enemies, was strongest among the ruling class of Judah, already half-Hellenized themselves, who wanted to drag the little temple-state into the modern age. Their motives were primarily secular and economic. But among the reformers there were also religious intellectuals whose aims were more elevated – in some respects akin to the Christians of the first century AD. They wanted to improve Judaism, to push it further along the logical road it appeared to be travelling. <u>Universalism is implicit in monotheism</u>. Deutero-Isaiah had made it explicit. In universal monotheism, the Jews had a new and tremendous idea to give to the world. Now the Greeks also had a big, general idea on offer: universalist culture. Alexander had created his empire as an ideal: he wanted to fuse the races and he 'ordered all men to regard the world as their country . . . good men as their kin, bad men as foreigners'. Isocrates argued that 'the designation "Hellene" is no longer a matter of descent but of attitude'; he thought Greeks by education had better titles to citizenship than 'Greek by birth'.[48] Could not the Greek notion of the unified *oikumene*, world civilization, be married to the Jewish notion of the universal God?

That was the aim of the reformist intellectuals. They reread the historical scriptures and tried to deprovincialize them. Were not Abraham and Moses, these 'strangers and sojourners', really great citizens of the world? They embarked on the first Biblical criticism: the Law, as now written, was not very old and certainly did not go back to Moses. They argued that the original laws were far more universalistic. So the reform movement broadened into an attack on the Law, as it was bound to do. The reformers found the Torah full of fables and impossible demands and prohibitions. We know of their attacks from orthodox complaints and curses. Philo denounces those 'who express their displeasure with the statutes made by their forefathers and incessantly censure the law'; the seers added: 'Cursed be the man who rears a pig and cursed be those who instruct their sons in Greek wisdom.'[49] The reformers did not want to abolish the Law completely but to purge it of those elements which forbade participation in Greek culture – for instance, the ban on nudity, which kept pious Jews out of the gymnasium and stadium – and reduce it to its ethical core, so universalizing it. To promote their ultimate aim of a world religion, they wanted an immediate marriage between the Greek *polis* and the Jewish moral God.

Unfortunately this was a contradiction in terms. The Greeks were not monotheists but polytheists, and in Egypt they learned syncretism, that is the rationalization of innumerable overlapping deities by banging them together into synthetic polygods. One such mutant was Apollo–Helios–Hermes, the sun-god. They blended their own Dionysiac rites with the Egyptian Isis-cult. Their god of healing, Asclepios, was conflated with the Egyptian Imhotep. Zeus, the senior god, was the same as the Egyptian Ammon, the Persian Ahura-Mazda and, for all they cared, the Jewish Yahweh. That, needless to say, was not at all how pious Jews saw it. The truth, of course, was that the

Greek idea of deity was greatly inferior to the Jewish concept of limitless power. The Jews drew an absolute distinction between human and divine. The Greeks constantly elevated the human – they were Promethean – and lowered the divine. To them gods were not much more than revered and successful ancestors; most men sprang from gods. Hence it was not for them a great step to deify a monarch, and they began to do so as soon as they embraced the orient. Why should not a man of destiny undergo apotheosis? Aristotle, Alexander's tutor, argued in his *Politics*: 'If there exists in a state an individual so pre-eminent in virtue that neither the virtue nor the political capacity of all the other citizens is comparable with his ... such a man should be rated as a god among men.' Needless to say, such notions were totally unacceptable to Jews of any kind. Indeed, there was never any possibility of a conflation between Judaism and Greek religion as such; what the reformers wanted was for Judaism to universalize itself by pervading Greek culture; and that meant embracing the *polis*.

In 175 BC the Jewish reform movement found an enthusiastic but dangerous ally in the new Seleucid monarch, Antiochus Epiphanes. He was anxious to speed up the Hellenization of his dominions as a matter of general policy but also because he thought it would raise tax-revenues – and he was chronically short of money for his wars. He backed the reformers entirely and replaced the orthodox high-priest Onias III by Jason, whose name, a Hellenization of Joshua, proclaimed his party. Jason began the transformation of Jerusalem into a *polis*, renamed Antiochia, by constructing a gymnasium at the foot of the Temple Mount. The Second Book of Maccabees furiously records that the Temple priests 'ceased to show any interest in the services of the altar; scorning the Temple and neglecting the sacrifices, they would hurry to take part in the unlawful exercises on the training-ground'.[50] The next stage was the diversion of Temple funds away from the endless, expensive sacrifices, and towards such *polis* activities as international games and dramatic competitions. The high-priest controlled the public funds, since taxes were paid to him, and from him to the tax-farmers (they were all intermarried), and the Temple treasury thus acted as a state deposit bank for the population. The temptation for Antiochus was to put pressure on his Hellenizing allies who controlled the Temple to yield more and more cash to build triremes and war-engines; and he gave way to it. Thus the reformers became identified not only with the occupying power but with oppressive taxes. In 171 BC Antiochus found it necessary to replace Jason as high-priest with the still more pro-Greek Menelaus, and he reinforced Greek power in Jerusalem by building an acropolis–fortress dominating the Temple.[51]

In 167 the conflict came to a head with the publication of a decree which in effect abolished the Mosaic law as it stood, replacing it with secular law, and downgrading the Temple into an ecumenical place of worship. This meant introducing the statue of an interdenominational god whose Greek name, Olympian Zeus, the rigorist Jews scrambled into 'The Abomination of Desolation'. It is unlikely that Antiochus himself was the sponsor of this decree. He was not interested in Judaism and it was most unusual for a Greek government to stamp on a particular cult. The evidence suggests that the initiative came from the extreme Jewish reformers, led by Menelaus, who thought that such a drastic move was the only way to end, once and for all, the obscurantism and absurdity of the Law and Temple worship. It was not so much a desecration of the Temple by paganism as a display of militant rationalism, rather like the anti-Christian shows put on by republican deists in Revolutionary France. There is a rabbinical tale of how Miriam, who came from the same priestly family as Menelaus and had married a Seleucid officer, stormed into the Temple and 'struck against the corner of the altar with her sandal and said to it "Wolf, wolf, you have squandered the riches of Israel." '[52]

But both the Greeks and Menelaus himself overestimated his support. His activities in the Temple provoked an uproar. The priests were divided. The scribes sided with his orthodox opponents. So did most pious Jews or *hasidim*. There was one large category of Jews the reformers might have had on their side. This was the *am ha-arez*, the ordinary poor people of the land. They had been the principal victims when, after the return of the Judaic elite from Exile, Ezra had imposed religious rigour, with the full power of the Persian empire behind him. He had drawn a condescending distinction between the God-fearing, righteous 'people of the Exile', the *bnei hagolah*, and the *am ha-arez*, who were scarcely Jews at all, since in many cases, in his view, they were born of invalid marriages. He had not scrupled to punish them severely.[53] Since then, being mostly illiterate and ignorant of the Law, they had been treated as second-class citizens, or pushed out altogether. They would have been the first to benefit if the rigorists had lost and the Law had been rationalized. But how could the reformers, who were essentially a party of the well-to-do and the placemen, appeal over the heads of the rigorists to the common people? And how, in particular, could they hope to do so successfully when they were identified with high taxes, from which the poor suffered most? There were no answers to these questions, and so an opportunity to place universalism on a popular basis was missed.

Instead, Menelaus sought to impose reform from above, by state power. To make the decree effective, it was not enough to halt the old Temple sacrifices – that was welcome to many. The pious Jews had also to be forced to make symbolic sacrifices in the new way, on altars they regarded as pagan. The *hasidim* brushed aside the reformers' argument that these rituals signified the ubiquity of the one God, who could not be penned into a particular place of human fabrication; to the pious, there was no difference between the new universalism and the old Baal-worship, condemned so many times in their scriptures. So they refused to bow, and they were prepared to die for it. The reformers were forced to make martyrs, such as the ninety-year-old Eleazar, described as 'one of the principal scribes', who was beaten to death; or the seven brothers, whose gruesome slaughter is described in the Second Book of Maccabees. It is from this date, indeed, that the concept of religious martyrdom appears, and the writings of the Maccabees, in which the sufferings of the faithful were fed into the propaganda of religious purity and Jewish nationalism, contain the first martyrologies.

Hence it was not the reformers but the rigorists who were able to appeal to the deep-rooted Biblical instinct to overturn the existing order, and transform a religious dispute into a revolt against the occupying power. Like most anti-colonial struggles, it began not with an assault on the garrison but with the murder of a local supporter of the regime. In the town of Modin in the Judean foothills 6 miles east of Lydda, a Jewish reformer, who was superintending the new official ceremony, was slaughtered by Matthias Hasmon, head of an old priestly family from the Temple 'Watch of Jehoiarib'. The old man's five sons, led by Judas the Maccabee, or 'Hammer', then launched a guerrilla campaign against Seleucid garrisons and their Jewish supporters. In two years, 166–164 BC, they drove all the Greeks out of the area around Jerusalem. In the city itself they penned reformers and Seleucids alike in the Acra, and purged the Temple of its sacrileges, rededicating it to Yahweh at a solemn service in December 164 BC, an event the Jews still celebrate at the Feast of Hanukkah, or Purification.

The Seleucids, who had a multitude of troubles of their own, including the rising power of Rome, responded rather as modern colonial powers did in the mid-twentieth century, oscillating between fierce repression and increasing dollops of self-rule, to which the insurgent nationalists responded by demanding more. In 162 BC Epiphanes' son and successor, Antiochus V, turned on Menelaus, 'the man to blame for all the trouble', who had, in the words of Josephus, 'persuaded his father to compel the Jews to give up their traditional worship of God', and executed him.[54] The Hasmonean family responded in 161 BC by signing an alliance with Rome, in which they were treated as the ruling family of an independent state. In 152 BC the Seleucids abandoned their attempt to Hellenize Judah by force and recognized Jonathan, now head of the family, as high-priest, an office the Hasmoneans were to hold for 115 years. In 142 they virtually recognized Judaean independence by exempting it from taxation, so that Simon Maccabee, who had succeeded his brother as high-priest, became ethnarch and ruler: 'And the people of Israel began to engross their documents and contracts, "In the year one of Simon, great high-priest, military commissioner, and leader of the Jews".'[55] Thus Israel became independent again after 440 years, though it was not until the following year that the desperate reform Jews in the Acra were finally starved into surrender and expelled. Then the Hasmoneans entered the fortress, 'carrying palms, to the sound of harps, cymbals and zithers, chanting hymns and canticles, since a great enemy had been crushed and thrown out of Israel'.[56]

In this upsurge of nationalist sentiment, the religious issues had been pushed into the background. But the long struggle for independence from Greek universalism left an indelible mark on the Judaic character. There were thirty-four bitter and murderous years between the attack on the Law and the final expulsion of the reformers from the Acra. The zeal and intensity of the assault on the Law aroused a corresponding zeal for the Law, narrowing the vision of the Jewish leadership and pushing them ever more deeply into a Torah-centred religion.[57] With their failure, the reformers discredited the notion of reform itself, or even any discussion of the nature and direction of the Jewish religion. Such talk was henceforth denounced in all the official texts as nothing less than total apostasy and collaboration with the foreign oppression, so that it became difficult for moderates of any kind, or internationally minded preachers who looked beyond the narrow enclave of Orthodox Judaism, to get a hearing. The Hasmoneans spoke for a deeply reactionary spirit within Judaism. Their strength lay in atavism and superstition, drawn from the remote Israelite past of taboo and brutal physical intervention by the deity. Henceforth, any external tampering with the Temple and its sanctuaries instantly roused up a ferocious Jerusalem mob of religious extremists swollen by the excited rabble. The mob now became an important part of the Jerusalem scene, making the city, and so Judea as a whole, extremely difficult to govern by anyone – Greeks or Hellenizers, Romans or their tetrarchs, not least the Jews themselves.

Against this background of intellectual terror by the religious mob, the secular spirit and intellectual freedom which flourished in the Greek gymnasia and academies was banished from Jewish centres of learning. In their battle against Greek education, pious Jews began, from the end of the second century BC, to develop a national system of education. To the old scribal schools were gradually added a network of local schools where, in theory at least, all Jewish boys were taught the Torah.[58] This development was of great importance in the spread and consolidation of the synagogue, in the birth of Pharisaism as a movement rooted in popular education, and eventually in the rise of the rabbinate. The education provided in these schools was entirely religious, rejecting any form of knowledge outside the Law. But at least these schools taught the Law in a relatively humane spirit. They followed ancient traditions inspired by an obscure text in Deuteronomy, 'put it in their mouths',[59] that God had given Moses, in addition to the written Law, an Oral Law, by which learned elders could interpret and supplement the sacred commands. The practice of the Oral Law made it possible for the Mosaic code to be adapted to changing conditions and administered in a realistic manner.

By contrast, the Temple priests, dominated by the Sadducees, or descendants of Zadok, the great high-priest from Davidic times, insisted that all law must be written and unchanged. They had their own additional text, called the Book of Decrees, which laid down a system of punishment: who were to be stoned, who burned, who beheaded, who strangled. But this was written and sacred: they would not admit that oral teaching could subject the Law to a process of creative development. With their rigid adherence to the Mosaic inheritance, their concept of the Temple as the sole source and centre of Judaic government, and their own hereditary position in its functions, the Sadducees were naturally allies of the new Hasmonean high-priests, even though the latter had no strict title to this position by descent. The Sadducees soon became identified with Hasmonean rule in a rigid system of Temple administration, in which the hereditary high-priest performed the functions of a secular ruler, and a committee of elders, the Sanhedrin, discharged his religious–legal duties. To mark the supremacy of the Temple, Simon Maccabee not only smashed the walls of the Acra into rubble but went on (according to Josephus) 'to level the very hill on which the citadel had stood, so that the Temple might be higher than it'.

Simon was the last of the Maccabee brothers. The Maccabees were brave, desperate, fanatical, strong-minded and violent men. They saw themselves as reliving the Book of Joshua, reconquering the Promised Land from the pagans, with the Lord at their elbow. They lived by the sword and died by it in a spirit of ruthless piety. Most of them met violent ends. Simon was no exception, being treacherously murdered by the Ptolemies, along with two of his sons. Simon was a man of blood, but honourable in his fashion, not self-seeking. Despite his triumphant installation as high-priest and ethnarch, he retained the spirit of the religious guerrilla leader; he had the charisma of heroic piety.

Simon's third son, John Hyrcanus, who succeeded him and reigned 134–104 BC, was quite different: a ruler by birth. He issued his own coins, stamped 'Jehohanan the High-Priest and the Community of the Jews', and his son Alexander Jannaeus, 103–76 BC, actually called himself 'Jonathan the King' on his coinage. The recreation of the state and kingdom, originally and ostensibly on a basis of pure religious fundamentalism – the defence of the faith – rapidly revived all the inherent problems of the earlier monarchy, and in particular the irresolvable conflict between the aims and methods of the state and the nature of the Jewish religion. This conflict is reflected in the personal history of the Hasmoneans themselves, and the story of their rise and fall is a memorable study in hubris. They began as the avengers of martyrs; they ended as religious oppressors themselves. They came to power at the head of an eager guerrilla band; they ended surrounded by mercenaries. Their kingdom, founded in faith, dissolved in impiety.

John Hyrcanus was imbued with the fundamentalist notion that it was God's will he should restore the Davidic kingdom. He was the first Jew to seek military inspiration and geopolitical guidance from the ancient historical texts of the Bible, telescoping the books of Joshua and Samuel. He accepted as literal truth that the whole of Palestine was the divine inheritance of the Jewish nation, and that it was not merely his right but his duty to conquer it. To do this he created a modern army of mercenaries. Moreover, the conquest, like Joshua's, had to extirpate foreign cults and heterodox sects, and if necessary slaughter those who clung to them. John's army trampled down Samaria and razed the Samaritan temple on Mount Gerizim. He stormed, after a year's siege, the city of Samaria itself, and 'he demolished it entirely, and brought streams to it to drown it, for he dug ditches to turn it into floods and water-meadows; he even took away the very marks which showed a city had ever been there'.[60] In the same way he pillaged and burned the Greek city of Scythopolis. John's wars of fire and sword were marked by massacres of city populations whose only crime was that they were Greek-speaking. The province of Idumaea was conquered and the inhabitants of its two main cities, Adora and Marissa, were forcibly converted to Judaism or slaughtered if they refused.

Alexander Jannaeus, John's son, took this policy of expansion and forcible conversion still further. He invaded the territory of the Decapolis, the league of ten Greek-speaking cities grouped around the Jordan. He swept into Nabataea and took Petra, the 'rose-red city half as old as time'. He moved into the province of Gaulanitis. The Hasmoneans pushed north into the Galilee and Syria, west to the coast, south and east into the desert. Behind their frontiers they eliminated pockets of non-Jewish people by conversion, massacre or expulsion. The Jewish nation thus expanded vastly and rapidly in terms of territory and population, but in doing so it absorbed large numbers of people who, though nominally Jewish, were also half-Hellenized and in many cases were fundamentally pagans or even savages.

Moreover, in becoming rulers, kings and conquerors, the Hasmoneans suffered the corruptions of power. John Hyrcanus seems to have retained a reasonably high reputation in Jewish tradition. Josephus says he was considered by God 'worthy of the three greatest privileges: government of the nation, the dignity of the high-priesthood, and the gift of prophecy'.[61] But Alexander Jannaeus, according to the evidence we have, turned into a despot and a monster, and among his victims were the pious Jews from whom his family had once drawn its strength. Like any ruler in the Near East at this time, he was influenced by the predominant Greek modes and came to despise some of the most exotic, and to Greeks barbarous, aspects of the Yahweh cult. As high-priest, celebrating the Feast of Tabernacles in Jerusalem, he refused to perform the libation ceremony, according to ritual custom, and the pious Jews pelted him with lemons. 'At this,' Josephus wrote, 'he was in a rage, and slew of them about six thousand.' Alexander, in fact, found himself like his hated pre-decessors, Jason and Menelaus, facing an internal revolt of rigorists. Josephus says the civil war lasted six years and cost 50,000 Jewish lives.

It is from this time we first hear of the *Perushim* or Pharisees, 'those who separated themselves', a religious party which repudiated the royal religious establishment, with its high-priest, Sadducee aristo-crats and the Sanhedrin, and placed religious observance before Jewish nationalism. Rabbinic sources record the struggle between the monarch and this group, which was a social and economic as well as a religious clash.[62] As Josephus noted, 'the Sadducees draw their following only from the rich, and the people do not support them, whereas the Pharisees have popular allies'. He relates that at the end of the civil war, Alexander returned in triumph to Jerusalem, with many of his Jewish enemies among his captives and then 'did one of the most barbarous actions in the world . . . for as he was feasting with his concubines, in the sight of all the city, he ordered about eight hundred of them to be crucified, and while they were living he ordered the throats of their children and wives to be cut before their eyes'.[63] There is a reference to this sadistic episode in one of the Qumran scrolls: 'the lion of wrath . . . when he hangs men up alive'.

Hence, when Alexander died in 76 BC, after he had (according to Josephus) 'fallen into a distemper by hard drinking', the Jewish world was bitterly divided and, though much enlarged, included many half-Jews whose devotion to the Torah was selective and suspect. The Hasmonean state, like its prototype the Davidic kingdom, had flourished in an age between empires. It was able to expand in the period when the Seleucid system was in hopeless decay but before Rome had grown strong enough to replace the Greeks. By the time of Alexander's death, however, the advancing Roman empire was only just below the Jewish horizon. Rome had been an ally of the Jews when they were struggling against the old Greek empire, and it tolerated the existence, even the relative independence, of small and weak states. But an expansive-minded, irredentist Jewish kingdom, forcibly converting its neighbours to its own demanding and intolerant faith, was not acceptable to the Roman senate. Rome bided its time until the Jewish state was rendered vulnerable by internal divisions, as the Seleucid empire had been. Aware of this, Alexander's widow, Salome, who reigned for a time after him, tried to restore national unity by bringing the Pharisees into the Sanhedrin and making their Oral Law acceptable in royal justice. But she died in 67 BC and her sons fell out over the succession.

One of the claimants, Hyrcanus, had a powerful chief-minister, Antipater, an Idumean from a family which had been forcibly converted by the Hasmoneans. He was half-Jew, half-Hellenizer. For such men it was natural to come to terms with the new superpower Rome, which combined irresistible military technology with Greek culture. Antipater saw an arrangement with Rome, whereby his and other notable families flourished under Roman protection, as much preferable to civil war. So in 63 BC he came to terms with the Roman general Pompey and Judaea became a Roman client-state. Antipater's son, who became Herod the Great, firmly locked the Jews into the administrative system of the Roman empire.

The reign of Herod, who was effective ruler of Judaea and much else from 37 BC to his death four years before the Christian era, is an episode in Jewish history with which Jewish historians, no less than

Christian ones, have found it difficult to come to terms. Herod was both a Jew and an anti-Jew; an upholder and benefactor of Graeco-Roman civilization, and an oriental barbarian capable of unspeakable cruelties. He was a brilliant politician and in some ways a wise and far-seeing statesman, generous, constructive and highly efficient; but also naïve, superstitious, grotesquely self-indulgent and hovering on the brink of insanity – sometimes over it. He combines in one person the tragedy of Saul and the successful materialism of Solomon, who was clearly his idol; and it is a thousand pities there was no one close to him to record his character and career with the same brilliance as the author of the First Book of Kings.[64]

Herod came to prominence and notoriety during his father's time as Governor of Galilee. There, in the true spirit of Roman rule, he destroyed a band of semi-religious guerrillas, under a man called Hezekiah, and had the leaders executed, without any form of Jewish religious trial and solely on his authority. This was a capital offence under Jewish law, and Herod was arraigned before the Sanhedrin: only the presence of his guards, who overawed the court, prevented his conviction and sentence. Four years later, in 43 BC, Herod committed a similar religious crime by executing another fanatic Jew, Malichus, who had poisoned his father. Herod's family, of course, supported the Hasmonean faction headed by Hyrcanus II, and he himself married into the family by espousing Mariamne. But in 40 BC the rival faction, led by a nephew, Antigonus, seized Jerusalem with the help of the Parthians. Herod's brother Phasael, Governor of Jerusalem, was arrested and committed suicide in prison, and Hyrcanus was rendered ineligible as high-priest by mutilation, Antigonus himself biting off his uncle's ears.

Herod barely escaped with his life, but he made his way to Rome and put his case to the Senate. The senators responded by making him a puppet-king, with the formal title *rex socius et amicus populi Romani*, 'allied king and friend of the Roman people'. He then returned to the East at the head of a Roman army of 30,000 infantry and 6,000 cavalry, retook Jerusalem and installed a completely new regime. His policy was threefold. First, he used his great political and diplomatic gifts to ensure that he always had the backing of whoever was in power in Rome. When Mark Antony flourished he and Herod were friends and allies; when Antony fell, Herod quickly made peace with Octavius Caesar. In the imperial Augustan age, Herod was both the most loyal and reliable of Rome's oriental satellite kings, putting down pirates and bandits with ruthless efficiency and backing Rome in all her campaigns and quarrels. He was also the most richly rewarded, and with Rome's backing he extended the kingdom up to and even beyond its Hasmonean boundaries and ruled it with far greater security.

Secondly, he exterminated the Hasmoneans to the best of his ability. He handed Antigonus over to the Romans, who executed him. For his wife Mariamne, great-granddaughter of Alexander Jannaeus, he had, said Josephus, a jealous passion, and eventually he turned on her and all her kin. He had her brother, Aristobulus, drowned in a swimming bath in Jericho. He accused Mariamne herself of trying to poison him, convicted her before a court of his own family, and put her to death. He then indicted her mother, Alexandra, for high treason and she too was executed. Finally, he accused his own two sons by her of conspiracy to murder him, and they in turn were tried, convicted and judicially strangled. Josephus wrote: 'If ever a man was full of family affection, that man was Herod.' That was true so far as his own side of the family was concerned, for he founded cities named after his father, mother and brother. But towards the Hasmoneans, or anyone who had ancestral claims to his possessions – such as members of the House of David – he behaved with paranoid suspicion and reckless brutality. The story of the Massacre of the Innocents, albeit exaggerated, has a historical foundation in his own actions.

Herod's third policy was to emasculate the destructive power of rigorist Judaism by separating state and religion and by bringing the diaspora Jews into play. His first act on assuming power in Jerusalem in 37 BC was to execute forty-six leading members of the Sanhedrin who, in his own case and others, had sought to uphold the Mosaic law in secular matters. Henceforth, it became a religious court only. He did not even attempt to become high-priest himself and divorced it from the crown by turning it into an official post, appointing and dismissing high-priests as acts of his prerogative, and picking them mainly from the Egyptian and Babylonian diaspora.

Herod was historically minded, like most Jews, and it is clear that he modelled himself on Solomon. His aim was to perpetuate his memory by colossal buildings and endowments, by magnificent expenditure in the public interest, and by unprecedented charities. He was thus the archetype of yet another Jewish specimen, the acquisitive philanthropist. His life was devoted to getting and spending on a gigantic scale. Like Solomon, he both exploited his position on the trade routes to tax commerce and himself engaged in manufacturing. He rented the Cyprus copper mines from the Emperor Augustus, taking half their products. He farmed the taxes of a vast area, sharing the profits with Rome. Josephus says that his expenditure exceeded his means and he was therefore harsh to his subjects, and he certainly built up a huge personal fortune chiefly by confiscating the property of those he declared state enemies, notably the Hasmoneans of course. But the general level of Palestinian prosperity rose during his reign, thanks to external peace, internal order and expanding trade. The number of Jews, both born and converts, expanded everywhere, so that, according to one medieval tradition, there were at the time of the Claudian census in 48 AD some 6,944,000 Jews within the confines of the empire, plus what Josephus calls the 'myriads and myriads' in Babylonia and elsewhere beyond it. One calculation is that during the Herodian period there were about eight million Jews in the world, of whom 2,350,000 to 2,500,000 lived in Palestine, the Jews thus constituting about 10 per cent of the Roman empire.[65] This expanding nation and teeming diaspora were the sources of Herod's wealth and influence.

Indeed, it was Herod's consciousness of the rising tide of Jews and Judaism, his feelings of racial and religious pride, which lay at the roots of his policy. Rather like the Jewish Hellenizers before him, he saw himself as a heroic reformer, trying to drag an obstinate and conservative Near Eastern people into the enlightened circle of the modern world. Rome's power and new-found unity under its first emperor made possible a new era of international peace and universal trade, the foundations of an economic golden age in which Herod wanted his people to participate. To enable the Jews to take their rightful place in a better world, he had to destroy the debilitating elements of its past and in particular to rid Jewish society and religion of the selfish oligarchy of families which exploited both. He did this single-handed, and amid his paranoia and cruelty there was a strong element of idealism too.

Herod also wanted to show the world that Jews included many gifted and civilized people, capable of making an important contribution to the new, expansive spirit of Mediterranean world civilization. To do this he looked beyond Jerusalem, with its mobs and fanatics, to the Jews of the diaspora. Herod was a close friend of Augustus' leading general, Agrippa, and this friendship spread the special protection of Rome over the large, scattered and sometimes threatened Jewish communities in the Roman orbit. The diaspora Jews saw Herod as their best friend. He was also the most generous of patrons. He provided funds for synagogues, libraries, baths and charitable agencies, and encouraged others to do the same, so that it was in Herod's day that Jews first became famous for the miniature welfare states they set up among their communities in Alexandria,

Rome, Antioch, Babylon and elsewhere, providing for the sick and the poor, for widows and orphans, for visiting the imprisoned and burying the dead.

Herod was not so foolish as to make the Jews of the diaspora the sole recipients of his largesse. He was the benefactor of many multi-racial cities throughout the eastern part of the empire. He backed and financed all the institutions of Greek culture, not least the stadium, for he was an enthusiastic sportsman – a reckless hunter and horseman, a keen javelin-thrower and archer, a fervent spectator. By his money, his powers of organization and his energy, he single-handedly rescued the Olympic Games from decay and ensured they were held regularly and in honourable pomp – thus making his name revered in many small Greek islands and cities, which gave him the title of life-president. For civic and cultural purposes he gave large sums to Athens, Lycia, Pergamum and Sparta. He rebuilt the Temple of Apollo in Rhodes. He re-walled Byblos, built a forum in Tyre and another in Beirut, gave Laodicea an aqueduct, built theatres in Sidon and Damascus, gave gymnasia to Ptolomais and Tripoli and provided a fountain and baths in Ascalon. In Antioch, then the largest city in the Near East, he paved the main street, 2.5 miles long, providing colonnades the whole length to shelter its citizens from the rain, and finished this great work in polished marble. There were Jews living in nearly all these places and they basked in the reflected glory of their munificent brother-Yahwist.

Herod tried to pursue this generous and universalist policy in Palestine itself, embracing outcast or heterodox elements in his pan-Judaism. Samaria, the city John Hyrcanus had levelled and flooded, was rebuilt with his aid, and named Sebaste after the Greek name for his patron Augustus. He gave it a temple, walls and towers, and a colonnaded street. He built another temple, of Egyptian granite, at Baniyas on the coast. Also on the coast, on the site of Straton's Tower, he created a massive new city of Caesarea. According to Josephus, this involved designing an artificial harbour, 'bigger than the Piraeus' in Greece, which Herod's engineers enclosed by planting 'in 20 fathoms of water, blocks of stone which were mostly 50 feet long, ten broad and nine deep, sometimes even bigger'. This was the foundation of a giant breakwater 200 feet wide. The city, of 200 acres, had a theatre, market place and government building, all of limestone, with a fine amphitheatre where splendid games were held every four years. There, Herod set up a gigantic figure of Caesar not inferior, according to Josephus, to the Olympian Zeus, one of the seven Wonders of the Ancient World. This became the natural Roman administrative capital for Judaea when Herod's empire broke up at his death. Dotted about Palestine were Herod's fortresses and palaces. These included the Antonia (citadel works) in Jerusalem, erected on top of the Hasmonean fort of Baris, built by Jonathan the Maccabee; but, in true Herodian fashion, the new fort was bigger, stronger and more sumptuous. Others were the Herodium, Cypros near Jericho, called after his mother, Machaerus on the east side of the Dead Sea, and his villa–fortress cut out of the rock at Masada, with its spectacular view over the wilderness.

For Herod, building the Antonia fortress in Jerusalem was part of a political, almost a geopolitical, purpose. When he had first taken the city, in 37 BC, with the power of the legions, he had only with great difficulty persuaded his Roman allies not to expel all its inhabitants and pull it down, for they already took the view that it was an ungovernable place. Herod proposed to internationalize the city, to bring in new Jewry to redress the failings of the old, and to make the city the capital not just of Judaea but of the whole Jewish race. He saw the diaspora Jews as more enlightened than the Palestinians, more receptive to Greek and Roman ideas, and more likely to encourage forms of worship in Jerusalem compatible with the modern world. He appointed diaspora Jews to public offices in the capital and he wanted to bolster their authority by encouraging other diaspora Jews to come there regularly. In theory the Law demanded that Jews make pilgrimage to the Temple three times a year, for Passover, the Feast of Weeks and Tabernacles.[66] Herod decided to encourage this practice, especially from the diaspora, by providing Jerusalem with all the facilities of a modern Romano-Greek city and above all by rebuilding the Temple itself as a monument-spectacle worth coming to see. Herod was not merely a notable philanthropist; he was also an inspired propagandist and a great showman.

He set about his programme for Jerusalem, the world's most suspicious and edgy city, with system and forethought. The building of the Antonia gave him its physical mastery, and he strengthened his grip by erecting three powerful towers, the Phasael (later known as the 'Tower of David'), the Hippicus and the Mariamne (completed before he murdered his wife). Having done this, he felt it safe to build a theatre and an amphitheatre, though these were judiciously placed outside the Temple area. Then, in 22 BC, he summoned a national assembly and announced his life-work: the rebuilding of the Temple, on a magnificent scale, exceeding even the glory of Solomon's. The next two years were spent assembling and training a force of 10,000 workmen and 1,000 supervisory priests, who also worked as builder–craftsmen in the forbidden areas. These elaborate preparations were necessary to reassure the Jerusalem Jews that the destructive operation of tearing down the old Temple was the prelude to erecting a new and finer one.[67] Herod took extraordinary care not to offend the religious scruples of the rigorists: for instance, for the altar and its ramp, unhewn stones were used so that they would be untouched by iron. The creation of the Temple as a functional place of sacrifice took only eighteen months, during which time elaborate curtaining screened the sanctuary from profane gaze. But the vast building as a whole needed forty-six years to complete and craftsmen were still finishing the decorations not long before the Romans tore the whole thing down in 70 AD, leaving not one stone upon another.

We have descriptions of Herod's Temple in Josephus' *Antiquities of the Jews* and his *Jewish Wars*,[68] and in the Talmudic tractates *Middot*, *Tamid* and *Yoma*. These are supplemented by recent archaeology. To achieve the grandiose effects he desired, Herod doubled the area of the Temple Mount by building huge supporting walls and filling in the gaps with rubble. Around the vast forecourt thus created he erected porticos, and linked it all to the upper city by bridges. The sanctuary, at one end of the platform, was much higher and wider than Solomon's (100 as opposed to 60 cubits), but since Herod was not of a priestly family and could not therefore enter even the inner court, he spent little on the interior, and the Holy of Holies, though lined in gold, was bare. Instead, cash was spent profusely on the exterior, gates, fittings and decorations being covered in gold and silver plate. Josephus says the stone was 'exceptionally white', and the glitter of the stone and the gleam of the gold – reflected many miles away in the bright sun – was what made the Temple so striking to travellers seeing it from afar for the first time.

The prodigious platform, 35 acres in area and a mile in circumference, was more than twice the height as seen today from the bottom of the valley, for the lower courses of the great stone blocks are covered in the rubbish of centuries. Josephus says that some of these blocks were '45 cubits in length, 10 in height and 6 in breadth', finished by imported craftsmen to an unusually high standard. The top 40 feet of the platform covered vaulted corridors and above them, on the platform itself, were the cloisters, with hundreds of Corinthian pillars 27 feet high and so thick, says Josephus, that three men with arms extended could hardly encompass them. So high was the edifice, he says, that if you looked down from the cloisters you felt giddy.

Pilgrims from all over Palestine and the diaspora, converging on the city in hundreds of thousands for the great feasts, ascended the platform from the city by a vast staircase and the main bridge. The outer courtyard, within the walls, was open to everyone, and in its gates and cloisters money-changers swopped coins from all over the world for the 'Holy Shekels' used to pay Temple fees – it was these who attracted Jesus' fury – and doves were sold for sacrifices. Within this, a wall and gate with stone-carved warnings in Greek and Latin, forbidding non-Jews to proceed any further on pain of death, enclosed the Court of the Women, with special corners for Nazarites and lepers, and within this was the Court of the Israelites for male Jews. Each of the inner courts was raised up, and entered by steps, and a higher flight of steps led up to the sacrificial area or Court of the Priests, and the sanctuary within it.

Many thousands of priests, Levites, scribes and pious Jews worked in and around the Temple area. The priests were responsible for the rituals and ceremonies, the Levites were the choristers, musicians, cleaners and engineers. They were divided into twenty-four watches or shifts, and during the frantic activity of the big feasts were reinforced by men of priestly or Levitical birth from all over Palestine and the diaspora. The primary priestly duty was the care of the sanctuary. The Jews had taken from the Egyptians the notion of the perpetual altar-fire, and this meant keeping alight and constantly filling the many sanctuary lamps. Also from Egypt came the custom of regular incensing of the darkest and most secret parts. The Temple consumed 600 pounds of costly incense a year, made from a secret recipe by the priestly Avtina family, whose womenfolk were banned from using scent to avoid accusations of corruption. It was in fact made from ground-up sea-shells, Sodom salt, a special cyclamen, myrrh (camphor gum resin), frankincense (terebinth gum resin), cinnamon, cassiam, spikenard, saffron, gum balm and a mysterious substance called maalah ashan, which made the smoke rise impressively.

Then there were the normal sacrifices, two lambs at dawn each day and another two at sunset, with thirteen priests needed for each. Ordinary male Jews could not enter the sanctuary, of course, but its doors were kept open during the service so they could see. Each service ended with a ritual drinking of wine, the reading of scripture, and the singing of hymns and psalms. The choristers were accompanied by an orchestra of a double-pipe, twelve-stringed harp, ten-stringed lyre, and bronze cymbals, while both the silver trumpet and the *shofar* or ram's horn emitted blasts to mark stages in the liturgy. The sacrifice-rituals struck visitors as exotic, even barbarous, for most strangers came at feast-times when the quantities of sacrifices were enormous. At such times, the inner Temple was an awesome place – the screams and bellows of terrified cattle, blending with ritual cries and chants and tremendous blasts of horn and trumpet, and blood everywhere. The author of the Letter of Aristeas, an Alexandrine Jew who attended as a pilgrim, says he saw 700 priests performing the sacrifices, working in silence but handling the heavy carcasses with professional skill and putting them on exactly the right part of the altar.

Because of the huge number of animals, the slaughter, bloodying and carving up of the carcasses had to be done quickly; and to get rid of the copious quantities of blood, the platform was not solid but hollow, a gigantic cleansing system. It contained thirty-four cisterns, the largest, or Great Sea, holding over two million gallons. In winter, they stored the rainfall and in summer additional supplies were brought by aqueduct from the Pool of Siloam to the south. Innumerable pipes conveyed the water up to the platform surface, and a multitude of drains carried off the torrents of blood. Aristeas wrote: 'There are many openings for water at the base of the altar, invisible to all except those making the sacrifices, so that all the blood is collected in great quantities and washed away in the twinkling of an eye.'

The Temple was a struggling mass of people at festival time, and the gates had to be opened from midnight onwards. Only the high-priest could enter the Holy of Holies, once a year on the Day of Atonement, but for festivals its curtain was rolled up so that male Jewish pilgrims, peering through the sanctuary gates, could see inside it, and the holy vessels were brought out for inspection. Each pilgrim offered at least one individual sacrifice – hence the vast number of animals – and this privilege was open to gentiles also. Herod's Temple was world-famous and greatly esteemed, according to Josephus, and important gentiles offered sacrifices for pious reasons as well as to conciliate Jewish opinion. In 15 BC, for instance, Herod's friend Marcus Agrippa made the grand gesture of offering a hecatomb (100 beasts).[69]

The Temple was prodigiously wealthy, at any rate in between times of pillage. Foreign kings and statesmen from Artaxerxes to the Emperor Augustus presented it with vast quantities of golden vessels which were stored in special strong-rooms in its bowels. Jews from all over the diaspora poured money and plate into it, rather as they now contribute to Israel, and Josephus says that it became 'the general treasury of all Jewish wealth'. Hyrcanus, head of the rich tax-collecting Tobiad family, for instance, 'deposited there the entire wealth of their house'.[70] But the main regular source of income was a half-shekel tax on all male Jews over twenty years of age.

Herod was exceptionally generous to the Temple, for he paid for the entire new building work out of his own pocket. By downgrading the importance of the high-priest, who was a hated Sadducee, Herod automatically raised in importance his deputy, the *segan*, a Pharisee, who got control over all the regular Temple functions and ensured that even the Sadducee high-priests performed the liturgy in a Pharisaical manner. Since Herod was on reasonable terms with the Pharisees, he avoided conflict between the Temple and his government, as a rule. But this alliance broke down in his last months. As part of his decorative scheme, he set up a golden eagle over the main Temple entrance. The diaspora Jews were quite happy about this, but the pious Jews of the capital, Pharisees included, objected strongly, and a group of Torah students climbed up and smashed it to pieces. Herod was already sick, in his palace near Jericho, but he acted with characteristic energy and ruthlessness. The high-priest was removed from office. The students were identified, arrested, dragged down in chains to Jericho, tried in the Roman theatre there, and burned alive. With the smoke of this sacrifice to his wounded generosity and self-esteem still rising, Herod was taken by litter to the hot springs at Callirrhoe, where he died in spring 4 BC.

Herod's dispositions for his kingdom did not work because his legatees, his sons by his first, Nabatean wife Doris, were no good. Archelaus, to whom he left Judaea, had to be deposed by the Romans in 6 AD. Thereafter it was governed directly by Roman procurators from Caesarea, they being responsible in turn to the Roman legate in Antioch. The old king's grandson, Herod Agrippa, was able, and in 37 AD the Romans gave him Judaea. But he died in 44 AD, leaving Rome no choice but to impose direct rule again. The death of Herod the Great, then, effectively ended the last phase of stable Jewish rule in Palestine until the mid-twentieth century.

Instead there followed a period of great and rising tension. This was most unusual under Rome. The Romans ran a liberal empire. They respected local religious, social and even political institutions so far as this was consistent with their essential interests. It is true that the rare uprising was put down with great force and severity. But most of the Mediterranean and Near Eastern peoples prospered under Roman rule and judged it to be far preferable to anything else they were likely to get. This was the view of the six million or more Jews in the diaspora, who never gave the authorities any trouble, except once in Alexandria under the impact of events in Palestine. It is likely that even in the Jewish homeland many, perhaps most, Jews did not see the Romans as oppressors or enemies of religion. But a substantial minority in Palestine became irreconcilable to the *kittim* (Romans) and from time to time were prepared to risk the ferocious penalties which inexorably followed violent defiance. There was a rising, led by

Judas of Gamala, in 6 AD, in protest at the direct rule imposed after Herod the Great's death. There was another, for similar reasons, when direct rule was restored following the death of Herod Agrippa in 44 AD, led by a man called Theudas who marched down the Jordan Valley at the head of a mob. There was a third in the time of Procurator Felix (52–60 AD), when 4,000 people mustered on the Mount of Olives in the expectation that the walls of Jerusalem would fall, like Jericho's. Finally there were the great uprisings of 66 AD and 135 AD, which were on an enormous scale and convulsed the eastern empire. There is no parallel to this sequence of events in any other territory Rome ruled.

Why were the Jews so restless? It was not because they were a difficult, warlike, tribal and essentially backward society, like the Parthians, who gave the Romans constant trouble on the eastern fringe, rather as the Pathans and Afghans worried the British on the North-West Frontier of India. On the contrary: the real trouble with the Jews was that they were too advanced, too intellectually conscious to find alien rule acceptable. The Greeks had faced the same problem with Rome. They had solved it by submitting physically and taking the Romans over intellectually. Culturally, the Roman empire was Greek, especially in the East. Educated people spoke and thought in Greek, and Greek modes set the standards in art and architecture, drama, music and literature. So the Greeks never had any sense of cultural submission to Rome.

Therein lay the difficulty with the Jews. They had an older culture than the Greeks. They could not match the Greeks artistically and in some other ways, but their literature was in various fields superior. There were as many Jews as Greeks in the Roman empire, and a higher proportion of them were literate. Yet the Greeks, who controlled the cultural policies of the Roman empire, afforded no recognition at all to the Hebrew language and culture. It is a remarkable fact that the Greeks, who were so inquisitive about nature, and so quick to pick up foreign technology and artistic skills, were quite incurious about alien languages. They were in Egypt for a millennium but never bothered to learn anything except trading demotic; Pythagoras was apparently the only Greek scholar who understood hieroglyphics. They had exactly the same blindness towards Hebrew, Hebrew literature and Jewish religious philosophy. They ignored it and knew of it only from inaccurate hearsay. This culture-contempt on the Greek side, and the love–hate which some educated Jews had for Greek culture, were sources of constant tension.

In a way, the relationship between Greeks and Jews in antiquity was akin to the dealings between Jews and Germans in the nineteenth century and the early twentieth, though the comparison should not be pushed too far. Greeks and Jews had a great deal in common – their universalist notions, for example, their rationalism and empiricism, their awareness of the divine ordering of the cosmos, their feeling for ethics, their consuming interest in man himself – but in the event their differences, exacerbated by misunderstandings, proved more important.[71] Both Jews and Greeks claimed and thought they believed in freedom, but whereas with the Greeks it was an end in itself, realized in the free, self-governing community, choosing its own laws and gods, for the Jews it was no more than a means, preventing interference with religious duties divinely ordained and unalterable by man. The only circumstances in which the Jews could have become reconciled to Greek culture was if they had been able to take it over – as, in the form of Christianity, they eventually did.

Hence it is important to grasp that the apparent Jewish revolt against Rome was at bottom a clash between Jewish and Greek culture. Moreover, the clash arose from books. There were then only two great literatures, the Greek and the Jewish, for Latin texts, modelled on the Greek, were only just beginning to constitute a corpus. More and more people were literate, especially Greeks and Jews, who had elementary schools. Writers were emerging as personalities: we know the names of as many as 1,000 Hellenistic authors, and Jewish writers too were beginning to identify themselves. There were now great libraries, state as well as private – the one in Alexandria had over 700,000 rolls. Greek was the literature of international civilized society, but the Jews were far more assiduous at copying, circulating, reading and studying their own sacred texts.

Indeed, in many respects Hebrew literature was far more dynamic than Greek. Greek texts, from Homer onwards, were guides to virtue, decorum and modes of thought; but the Hebrew texts had a marked tendency to become plans for action. Moreover, this dynamic element was becoming more important. It was propagandist in intent, polemical in tone and thoroughly xenophobic, with particular animosity directed towards the Greeks. The stress on martyrdom, as a consequence of the Maccabee struggles, was notable. A typical work, by a Jew called Jason of Cyrene, originally in five volumes, survives in an epitome called the Second Book of Maccabees. Though employing all the rhetorical devices of Greek prose, it is an anti-Greek diatribe as well as an inflammatory martyrology.

Even more important than the martyr stories was the new literary device of apocalyptic, which from Maccabee times filled the vacuum in Jewish consciousness left by the decline of prophecy. The word means 'revelation'. Apocalyptic texts attempt to convey mysteries beyond the bounds of normal human knowledge or experience, often using the names of dead prophets to add authenticity. From the second century BC onwards, again under the stress of the Maccabee crisis, they concentrate overwhelmingly on eschatological themes: they carry the Jewish obsession with history into the future and predict what will happen at 'the end of days', when God winds up the historical period and mankind enters the era of summation. This moment will be characterized by great cosmic convulsions, the final battle of Armageddon and, as one of the Qumran scrolls puts it, 'the heavenly host will give forth in great voice, the foundations of the world will be shaken, and a war of the mighty ones of the heavens will spread throughout the world'.[72] These events are characterized by extreme violence, by absolute divisions between good (pious Jews) and evil (Greeks, later Romans) and by hints of imminence.

Of these works the most influential was the Book of Daniel, dating from early Hasmonean times, both because it found its way into the canon and because it became the prototype for many others. It uses historical examples, from Assyrian, Babylonian and Persian times, to whip up hatred against pagan imperialism in general, and Greek rule in particular, and it predicts the end of empire and the emergence of God's kingdom, possibly under a heroic liberator, a Son of Man. The book vibrates with xenophobia and invitations to martyrdom.

The apocalyptic books could be and were read at various levels of reality. To moderate-minded pious Jews, the majority in all probability, who had tended to accept, since the days of Jeremiah and Ezekiel, that their religion could be practised – was, perhaps, best practised – under a reasonably liberal foreign rule, Daniel promised not a restoration of the historic, physical kingdom, like David's, but a final event of an altogether different kind: resurrection and personal immortality. What particularly struck the Pharisees was the assertion at the conclusion of the Book of Daniel that, at the end of days, 'the people shall be delivered. . . . And many of them that sleep in the dust of the earth shall awake, some to everlasting life, and some to shame and everlasting contempt.'[73] This notion of Daniel's was reinforced by the so-called Ethiopic Book of Enoch, written early in the first century AD, which speaks of 'the last day' and the 'day of judgment', when the 'elect' would be favoured and come into their kingdom.

The idea of judgment at death and immortality on the basis of merit had been developed in Egypt more than a millennium before. It was not Jewish, because it was not in the Torah, and the Sadducees, who stuck to their texts, seemed to have denied the afterlife completely. But

NAIVE BUT COMMON

WRONG.

the idea was embryonic in Isaiah, and the Pharisees eagerly seized upon this aspect of apocalypse because it appealed to their strong sense of ethical justice. There might be no earthly answer to the problem of theodicy, as Job had shown; but if there were no justice in this world, there would certainly be justice in the next, when the righteous would be rewarded by the divine judge, and the wicked sentenced. The idea of a final judgment fitted neatly into the whole Judaic concept of the rule of law. It was because they taught this doctrine, together with a rationalistic approach to observing the Law, which made salvation feasible, that the Pharisees attracted such a following, especially among the pious poor, who knew from bitter experience the small likelihood of happiness this side of death.[74]

But if the Pharisees drew a distinction (as St Augustine was to do later) between the heavenly kingdom and the earthly one, others took apocalyptic more literally. They believed the kingdom of righteousness was physical, real, imminent and that they were bound to hasten its appearance. The most violent group were referred to by the Roman occupation forces as the Sicarii; they carried hidden daggers and used to assassinate Jewish collaborators, especially in the crowds at festival times. This was merely, however, the ultra-violent terrorist fringe of a movement who called themselves the Zealots. The name comes from the story of Phinehas in the Book of Numbers. He saved Israel from plague by slaying a wicked man and his wife with a javelin and was thus said to have been 'zealous for his God'.[75] According to Josephus, the movement was founded in 6 AD by Judah the Galilean, when he organized an uprising against Roman direct rule and taxation. He seems to have been a kind of early rabbi, and he taught the ancient doctrine that Jewish society was theocracy, acknowledging rule by none but God.

Josephus distinguishes between the Zealots, who preached and practised violence, and what he terms the other three principal sects, Pharisees, Sadducees and Essenes, who seemed to have accepted foreign rule in general.[76] But the fact that Judah's deputy, Zadok, was a Pharisee indicates that the lines could not be drawn sharply, and, as the first century AD progressed, more and more pious Jews, such as the Pharisees, seem to have accepted that violence was inevitable in certain circumstances.[77] However, this is an obscure area, for Josephus, who is our main authority, was an interested party. He regarded the term Zealot as an honourable title, and he withdrew it when he deemed their activities to be terroristic or anti-social. The legitimacy of terrorism when other forms of protest fail was as hotly debated then as it is today, and the precise part played by Zealots and Sicarii, who were active in every violent uprising of the century, is a subject of scholarly speculation.[77]

Even more controversy surrounds the various millenarian sects of the desert fringe, whom Josephus (as well as Philo and Pliny) grouped together as Essenes. There were, in fact, many different categories. The best known are the Qumran monks, because their Dead Sea monastery was excavated by G. L. Harding and Père de Vaux in 1951-6, and their numerous writings are being fully analysed and published. They lived in tents in summer, and in winter holed up in caves. They had elaborate plumbing arrangements in their central buildings for their ritual lustrations, and we have found their kitchen, bakery, dining-room and pottery shop, as well as a meeting room. The sect shows the importance of literature in these extremist groups, for there was an elaborate scriptorium and a large collection of books, put for safety in tall jars concealed in the nearby caves, when the community was menaced by the Romans in the rebellion of 66 AD. But it also illustrates the way in which literature fostered violence, for in addition to canonical texts with apocalyptic implications (such as Isaiah), the monks also produced eschatological writings of their own, of a revolutionary and indeed military kind. Their document, known to us as 'The War of the Children of Light Against the Children of Darkness', was not just vaguely apocalyptic but constituted a detailed training guide to a battle they believed imminent. Their camp was defensive in layout and provided with a watchtower, and indeed it seems to have been attacked and destroyed by the Romans when the 'end of days' came in 66-70 AD.[78]

However, the militant monks of Qumran were only one of many Essene-type communities. All were affected by apocalyptic, but not all were violent and a few were wholly pacific. Some were hermits dwelling in caves, like the Therapeutae, who came from Egypt, where desert communities had existed for at least 2,000 years. The Margherians, in Syria, were also monastic troglodytes. Other cave-monks were the baptist groups living near the Jordan, of which John the Baptist and his followers are the best known.

John the Baptist lived and worked for the most part in Galilee and the Peraea, territory which was now overwhelmingly Jewish but which had been annexed to Judaea by fire and sword – and often forcible conversion – in Maccabee times. It was an area both of fierce orthodoxy and diverse heterodoxy, and of religious and political ferment. Much of it had been devastated in the risings immediately after Herod's death and in 6 AD; and the great man's son, Herod Antipas, whom the Romans made governor, tried to rebuild it by planting new cities on Greek lines. Between 17 and 22 AD he created a new administrative centre at Tiberias on Lake Galilee, and to people it he forced Jews from the surrounding countryside to give up their farms and live there. He drafted in the poor and ex-slaves too. It thus became a curious anomaly: the only Greek city with a majority of Jews. Antipas attracted criticism for other reasons. His Judaism was suspect because he had a Samaritan mother; and he broke Mosaic law by marrying his brother's wife. It was John the Baptist's preaching against this sin which led to his imprisonment and execution.[79] According to Josephus, Antipas felt that the Baptist's following was growing so formidable that it was bound to end in revolt.

The Baptist was a believer in what the Jews called the Messiah. His mission centred on two books – Isaiah and Enoch. He was not a hermit, a separatist or an excluder. On the contrary: he preached to all Jews that the day of reckoning was coming. All must confess their sins, repent and receive baptism by water as a symbol of atonement, and so prepare themselves for the Last Judgment. His task was to respond to the injunction in Isaiah, 'Clear ye in the wilderness the way of the Lord',[80] and to proclaim the coming of the end of days and the advent of the Messiah, who would be the Son of Man as described by Enoch. According to the New Testament, the Baptist was related to Jesus of Nazareth, baptized him and identified him as the Son of Man; and it was shortly after the Baptist's execution that Jesus began his own mission. What was this mission, and who did Jesus think he was?

The Jewish doctrine of the Messiah had its origins in the belief that King David had been anointed by the Lord, so that he and his descendants would reign over Israel to the end of time and would exercise dominion over alien peoples.[81] After the fall of the kingdom, this belief had been transformed into a prophetic expectation that the rule of the House of David would be miraculously restored.[82] On top of this was grafted the Isaiac description of this future king as the dispenser of justice, and this was perhaps the most important element in the belief because Isaiah seems to have been the most widely read and admired, as it was certainly the most beautifully written, of all the Bible books. During the second and first centuries BC, this justice-dispensing reincarnation of the Davidic ruler fitted neatly into the notions, in the Book of Daniel, the Book of Enoch and other apocalyptic works, of an end of days and the Four Last Things – death, judgment, hell and heaven. It was at this comparatively late stage that the divinely chosen and charismatic figure was first called the Messiah or 'the anointed [king]'. The word was originally Hebrew, then Aramaic, and simply transliterated into Greek as *messias*; but the

meaning?
what?

Greek word for 'the anointed' is *christos*, and it is <u>significant that</u> it was the Greek, not the Hebraic, title which was attached to Jesus.

The messianic doctrine, being of complex and even contradictory origins, created great confusion in the minds of the Jews. But most of them seem to have assumed that the Messiah would be a political–military leader and that his coming would inaugurate a physical, earthly state. There is an important passage in the Acts of the Apostles describing how Gamaliel the Elder, grandson of Hillel, and at one time president of the Sanhedrin, dissuaded the Jewish authorities from punishing the early Christians, by arguing that the authenticity of their Messiah would be demonstrated by the success of their movement. There had been, he said, the case of Theudas, 'boasting himself to be somebody', but he had been killed, 'and all, as many as obeyed him, were scattered and brought to nought'. Then there had been Judas of Galilee, 'in the days of the taxing', and 'he also perished; and all, even as many as obeyed him, were dispersed'. The Christians, he said, should be left alone because, if their mission lacked divine sanction, 'it will come to nought'.[83]

The other Jewish elders were persuaded by Gamaliel's argument, for they too thought in terms of an uprising designed to alter the government. When Herod the Great heard that the Messiah or Christ was born, he reacted with violence as if to a threat to his dynasty. Any Jew who listened to a man making messianic claims would take it for granted he had some kind of political and military programme. The Roman government, the Jewish Sanhedrin, the Sadducees and even the Pharisees assumed that a Messiah would make changes in the existing order, of which they were all part. The poor people of Judaea and Galilee would also believe that a Messiah preaching fundamental changes would be talking not, or not only, in spiritual and meta-physical terms, but of the realities of power – government, taxes, justice.

Now it is obvious from the evidence we have that Jesus of Nazareth conformed to none of these messianic patterns. He was not a Jewish nationalist. On the contrary, he was a Jewish universalist. Like the Baptist, he was influenced by the teachings of the pacific elements of the Essenes. But like the Baptist he believed that the programme of repentance and rebirth should be carried to the multitude, as was foreseen in Chapter 53 of Isaiah. It was not the job of the teacher of righteousness to hide in the desert or in caves; or to sit in the seats of the mighty either, like the Sanhedrin. It was his mission to preach to all, and in a spirit of humility before God, who might demand the extremities of suffering. The person of whom Isaiah wrote had to be the 'tender plant', the 'despised and rejected of men', the 'man of sorrows', who would be 'wounded for our iniquities, bruised for our transgression', 'oppressed and afflicted and yet he opened not his mouth'. This 'suffering servant' of God would be 'taken from prison and from judgment', 'brought as a lamb to the slaughter', be buried with the wicked and 'numbered with the transgressors'. This Messiah was not a mob leader or democrat or guerrilla chieftain, let alone a future earthly king and world sovereign. He was, rather, a theologian and sacrificial victim, a teacher by his word and example, and by his life and death.[84]

If Jesus was a theologian, what was and whence came his theology? His background was the heterodox Judaism and increasing Hellenization of Galilee. His father, a carpenter, died before Jesus was baptized, in 28/29 AD. In the Greek New Testament Joseph bore a Hebrew name, but Jesus' mother was called Mary, a Greek form of Miriam. Two of Jesus' brothers, Judah and Simon, had Hebrew names but two others, James (in Hebrew Jacob) and Joses (in Hebrew Joseph), did not; and Jesus was the Greek form of the Hebrew Joshua. The family claimed descent from David, and it may have been predominantly conformist, since the New Testament hints at family tensions created by Jesus' teaching. After his death, however, the family accepted his mission. His brother James became head of the sect in Jerusalem and, after James' martyrdom by the Sadducees, Jesus' cousin Simon succeeded; the grandsons of his brother Judah were leaders of the Galilean Christian community in the reign of Trajan.

The evidence we possess shows that, though Jesus was influenced by Essene teaching and may have spent some time living with them, and though he was personally connected with the Baptist sect, he was in essentials one of the Hakamim, the pious Jews who moved in the world. He was closer to the Pharisees than to any other group. This statement is liable to be misleading, since Jesus openly criticized the Pharisees, especially for 'hypocrisy'. But on close examination, Jesus' condemnation is by no means so severe or so inclusive as the Gospel narrative in which it is enclosed implies; and in essence it is similar to criticisms levelled at the Pharisees by the Essenes, and by the later rabbinical sages, who drew a sharp distinction between the Hakamim, whom they saw as their forerunners, and the 'false Pharisees', whom they regarded as enemies of true Judaism.[85]

The truth seems to be that Jesus was part of a rapidly developing argument within the pious Jewish community, which included Pharisees of various tendencies. The aim of the Hakamic movement was to promote holiness and make it general. How was this to be done? The argument centred around two issues: the centrality and indispensability of the Temple, and the observance of the Law. On the first point, Jesus clearly sided with those who regarded the Temple as an obstacle to the general spread of holiness, since the concentration on the physical building, with its hierarchies, privileges (mostly hereditary) and wealth, was a form of separation from the people – a wall built against them. Jesus used the Temple as a preaching forum; but so had others who had opposed it, notably Isaiah and Jeremiah. The idea that the Jews could do without the Temple was not new. On the contrary, it was very old, and it could be argued that the true Jewish religion, long before the Temple was built, was universalistic and unlocated. Jesus, like many other pious Jews, saw holiness spreading to the whole people through the elementary schools and synagogues. But he went further than most of them by regarding the Temple as a source of evil and predicting its destruction, and by treating the Temple authorities and the whole central system of Judaic administration and law with silent contempt.[86]

On the second issue, the degree to which the Law must be obeyed, the original argument between the Sadducees, who admitted only the written Pentateuch, and the Pharisees, who taught the Oral Law, had by Jesus' time been supplemented by a further argument among the Hakamim and Pharisees. One school, led by Shammai the Elder (c. 50 BC–c. 30 AD), took a rigorist view especially on matters of cleanliness and uncleanliness, an explosive area since it militated strongly against the ability of ordinary, poor people to achieve holiness. The rigorism of the Shammai school, indeed, was eventually to take his descendants and followers out of the rabbinical–Judaic tradition altogether, and they vanished like the Sadducees themselves. On the other hand, there was the school of Hillel the Elder, Shammai's contemporary. He came from the diaspora and was later referred to as 'Hillel the Babylonian'.[87] He brought with him more humane and universalistic notions of Torah interpretation. To Shammai, the essence of the Torah lay in its detail; unless you got the detail exactly right, the system became meaningless and could not stand. To Hillel, the essence of the Torah was its spirit: if you got the spirit right, the detail could take care of itself. Tradition contrasted Shammai's anger and pedantry with Hillel's humility and humanity, but what was remembered best of all was Hillel's anxiety to make obeying the law possible for all Jews and for converts. To a pagan who said he would become a Jew if he could be taught the Torah while standing on one foot, Hillel is said to have replied, 'What is hateful to you, do not unto your neighbour: this is the entire Torah. All the rest is commentary – go and study it.'[88]

MORE
JUNK

?

Jesus was a member of Hillel's school, and may have sat under him, for Hillel had many pupils. He repeated this famous saying of Hillel's and it is possible that he used other *dicta*, for Hillel was a famous aphorist. But of course, taken literally, Hillel's saying about the Torah is false. Doing as you would be done by is not the entire Torah. The Torah is only in part an ethical code. It is also, and in its essence, a series of absolutist divine commands which cover a vast variety of activities many of which have no bearing at all on relations between men. It is not true that 'all the rest is commentary'. If it had been, other peoples, and the Greeks in particular, would have had far less difficulty in accepting it. 'All the rest', from circumcision, to diet, to the rules of contact and cleanliness, far from being commentary were injunctions of great antiquity which constituted the great barriers between the pious Jews and the rest of humanity. Therein lay the great obstacle, not merely in universalizing Judaism but even in making its practice possible for all Jews.

Jesus' teaching career saw him translate Hillel's aphorism into a system of moral theology and, in doing so, strip the law of all but its moral and ethical elements. It was not that Jesus was lax. Quite the contrary. In some respects he was stricter than many sages. He would not, for instance, admit divorce, a teaching which was later to become, and still remains today, enormously important. But, just as Jesus would not accept the Temple when it came between God and man's pursuit of holiness, so he dismissed the Law when it impeded, rather than assisted, the road to God.

Jesus' rigorism in taking Hillel's teaching to its logical conclusion led him to cease to be an orthodox sage in any sense which had meaning and, indeed, cease to be a Jew. He created a religion which was *sui generis*, and it is accurately called Christianity. He incorporated in his ethical Judaism an impressive composite of the eschatology he found in Isaiah, Daniel and Enoch, as well as what he found useful in the Essenes and the Baptist, so that he was able to present a clear perspective of death, judgment and the afterlife. And he offered this new theology to everyone within reach of his mission: pious Jews, the *am ha-arez*, the Samaritans, the unclean, the gentiles even. But, like many religious innovators, he had a public doctrine for the masses and a confidential one for his immediate followers. The latter centred on what would happen to him as a person, in life and in death, and therein lay his claim to be the Messiah – not just the Suffering Servant, but someone of far greater significance.

The more one examines the teachings and activities of Jesus, the more obvious it appears that they struck at Judaism in a number of fatal respects, which made his arrest and trial by the Jewish authorities inevitable. His hostility to the Temple was unacceptable even to liberal Pharisees, who accorded Temple worship some kind of centrality. His rejection of the Law was fundamental. Mark relates that, having 'called all the people unto him', Jesus stated solemnly: 'There is nothing from without a man, that entering into him can defile him: but the things which come out of him, those are they that defile the man.'[89] This was to deny the relevance and instrumentality of the Law in the process of salvation and justification. He was asserting that man could have a direct relationship with God, even if he were poor, ignorant and sinful; and, conversely, it was not man's obedience to the Torah which creates God's response, but the grace of God to men, at any rate those who have faith in him, which makes them keep his commandments.

To most learned Jews, this was false doctrine because Jesus was dismissing the Torah as irrelevant and insisting that, for the approaching Last Judgment, what was needed for salvation was not obedience to the Law but faith. If Jesus had stuck to the provinces no harm would have come to him. By arriving at Jerusalem with a following, and teaching openly, he invited arrest and trial, particularly in view of his attitude to the Temple – and it was on this that his enemies concentrated.[90] False teachers were normally banished to a remote district. But Jesus, by his behaviour at his trial, made himself liable to far more serious punishment. Chapter 17 of Deuteronomy, especially verses 8 to 12, appears to state that, in matters of legal and religious controversy, a full inquiry should be conducted and a majority verdict reached, and if any of those involved refuses to accept the decision, he shall be put to death. In a people as argumentative and strong-minded as the Jews, living under the rule of law, this provision, known as the offence of the 'rebellious elder', was considered essential to hold society together. Jesus was a learned man; that was why Judas, just before his arrest, called him 'rabbi'. Hence, when brought before the Sanhedrin – or whatever court it was – he appeared as a rebellious elder; and by refusing to plead, he put himself in contempt of court and so convicted himself of the crime by his silence. No doubt it was the Temple priests and the Shammaite Pharisees, as well as the Sadducees, who felt most menaced by Jesus' doctrine and wanted him put to death in accordance with scripture. But Jesus could not have been guilty of the crime, at any rate as it was later defined by Maimonides in his Judaic code. In any case it was not clear that the Jews had the right to carry out the death sentence. To dispose of these doubts, Jesus was sent to the Roman procurator Pilate as a state criminal. There was no evidence against him at all on this charge, other than the supposition

that men claiming to be the Messiah sooner or later rose in rebellion –
Messiah-claimants were usually packed off to the Roman authorities
if they became troublesome enough. So Pilate was reluctant to convict
but did so for political reasons. Hence Jesus was not stoned to death
under Jewish law, but crucified by Rome.[91] The circumstances
attending Jesus' trial or trials appear to be irregular, as described in the
New Testament gospels.[92] But then we possess little information
about other trials at this time, and all seem irregular.

What mattered was not the circumstance of his death but the fact
that he was widely and obstinately believed, by an expanding circle of
people, to have risen again. This gave enormous importance not just to
his moral and ethical teaching but to his claim to be the Suffering
Servant and his special eschatology. Jesus' immediate disciples
grasped the importance of his death and resurrection as a 'new
testament' or witness to God's plan, the basis on which every
individual could make a new covenant with God. But all they were
capable of doing to further this gospel was to repeat Jesus' sayings and
recount his life-story. The real evangelical work was carried out by
Paul of Tarsus, a diaspora Jew from Cilicia, whose family came from
Galilee, and who returned to Palestine and studied under Gamaliel the
Elder. He possessed the Pharisaic training to understand Jesus'
theology, and he began to explain it – once he was convinced that the
resurrection was a fact and Jesus' claims to be the Christ true. It is
often argued that Paul 'invented' Christianity by taking the ethical
teachings of Christ and investing them in a new theology which drew
on the intellectual concepts of the Hellenistic diaspora. His distinction
between 'the flesh' and 'the spirit' has been compared to Philo's
body–soul dichotomy.[93] It is also maintained that by 'Christ' Paul had
in mind something like Philo's 'logos'. But Philo was dealing in
abstractions. For Paul, Christ was a reality.[94] By body and soul, Philo
meant the internal struggle within man's nature. By spirit and flesh,
Paul was referring to the external world – man was flesh, the spirit was
God – or Christ.[95]

The truth seems to be that both Jesus and Paul had their roots in
Palestinian Judaism. Neither was introducing concepts from the
Hellenistic diaspora. Both were preaching a new theology, and it was
essentially the same theology. Jesus prophesied a new testament by the
shedding of his blood 'for many' and his resurrection.[96] Paul taught
that the prophecy had been accomplished, that the Christ had become
incarnate in Jesus, and that a New Covenant had thereby come into
existence and was offered to those who had faith in it.

Neither Jesus nor Paul denied the moral or ethical value of the Law.

They merely removed the essence of it from its historical context, which both saw as outmoded. It is a crude oversimplification to say that Paul preached salvation by grace as opposed to salvation by works (that is, keeping the Law). What Paul said was that good works were the condition of remaining eligible for the New Covenant, but they do not in themselves suffice for salvation, which is obtained by grace. Both Jesus and Paul were true Jews in that they saw religion as a historical procession of events. They ceased to be Jews when they added a new event. As Paul said, when Christ became incarnate in Jesus, the basis of the Torah was nullified. At one time, the original Jewish covenant was the means whereby grace was secured. That, said Paul, was no longer true. God's plan had changed. The mechanism of salvation was now the New Testament, faith in Christ. The covenantal promises to Abraham no longer applied to his present descendants, but to Christians: 'And if you are Christ's, then you are Abraham's offspring, heirs according to promise.'[97] What Jesus challenged, and Paul specifically denied, was the fundamental salvation-process of Judaism: the election, the covenant, the Law. They were inoperative, superseded, finished. A complex theological process can be summed up simply: Jesus invented Christianity, and Paul preached it.

Christ and the Christians thus took from Judaism its universalist potential and inheritance. Jesus Christ himself had sought to fulfil the divine mission as forecast: 'In thee shall all families of the earth be blessed.' Paul carried this gospel deep into diaspora Jewry and to the gentile communities who lived alongside it. He not only accepted the logic of Jesus' Palestinian universalism, and transformed it into a general universalism, but denied the existence of the old categories. The 'old man with his deeds', the former election and the Law, were 'put off'; the New Covenant, and its new elect, the 'new man', formed in God's image and limited by that alone, were 'put on'. Men were eligible for faith and grace solely by their human condition, 'Where there is neither Greek nor Jew, circumcision nor uncircumcision, Barbarian, Scythian, bond nor free: but Christ is all and in all.'[98]

Here, then, in a sense was the universalistic reform programme of the Hellenistic reformers of Seleucid times. But whereas Menelaus and his intellectual allies had sought to universalize from above, in alliance with power and wealth, armies and tax-collectors – and so had inevitably driven the bulk of the community, not least the poor, into the arms of the Torah rigorists – Jesus and Paul universalized from below. Jesus was a learned Jew who said that learning was not necessary, who took the spirit and not the letter as the essence of the Law and who thus embraced the unlearned, the ignorant, the despised, the *am ha-arez*, made them indeed his special constituency. Paul carried the message to those who were outside the law altogether. Indeed, unlike the Hellenizing reformers, he was able to draw upon an emotion deep in Judaism, deep in the ancient religion of Yahweh, a force which was almost the quintessence of the covenanting faith –the idea that God would overthrow the established order of the world, make the poor rich and the weak strong, prefer the innocent to the wise and elevate the lowly and humble. No Jew, not even Jesus, dwelt more eloquently on this theme than Paul. So the religion he preached was not only universalistic but revolutionary – a revolution, however, which was spiritualized and non-violent.

The portion of humanity ready and waiting for this message was enormous. The diaspora, through which Paul and others eagerly travelled, was vast. The Roman geographer Strabo said that the Jews were a power throughout the inhabited world. There were a million of them in Egypt alone. In Alexandria, perhaps the world's greatest city after Rome itself, they formed a majority in two out of five quarters. They were numerous in Cyrene and Berenice, in Pergamum, Miletus, Sardis, in Phrygian Apamea, Cyprus, Antioch, Damascus and Ephesus, and on both shores of the Black Sea. They had been in Rome for 200 years and now formed a substantial colony there; and from Rome they had spread all over urban Italy, and then into Gaul and Spain and across the sea into north-west Africa. Many of these diaspora Jews were pious to a fault and were to remain staunch observers of the Torah in its essential rigour. But others were waiting to be convinced that the essence of their faith could be kept, or even reinforced, by abandoning circumcision and the multitude of ancient Mosaic laws which made life in modern society so difficult. Still more ready for conversion were vast numbers of pious gentiles, close to the diaspora Jewish communities but hitherto separated from them precisely because they could not accept the rules which the Christians now said were unnecessary. So the slow spread of the new religion accelerated. Ethical monotheism was an idea whose time had come. It was a Jewish idea. But the Christians took it with them to the wider world, and so robbed the Jews of their birthright.

The bifurcation of Christianity and Judaism was a gradual process. To some extent it was determined by the actions of the Jews themselves. The consolidation of Judaism round the rigorous enforcement of Mosaic law, as a result of the crushing of the reform programme by the Maccabees, was the essential background to the origin and rise of Jewish Christianity. Equally, the drift of Jewish rigorism towards violence, and the head-on collision with the

Graeco–Roman world which inevitably followed in 66–70 AD, finally severed the Christian branch of Judaism from its Jewish trunk. The earliest followers of Jesus Christ in Jerusalem undoubtedly regarded themselves as Jews. Even Stephen, the most extreme of them, went no further than to resurrect some of the intellectual principles of the old reform programme. In the long speech of defence he made before the Sanhedrin, he echoed the reformers' view that God could not be localized in the Temple: 'the Most High dwelleth not in temples made with hands; as saith the prophet, Heaven is my throne and earth is my footstool: what house will ye build me saith the Lord: or what is the place of my rest? Hath not my hand made all these things?' But in his very next breath he called his accusers 'uncircumcised in heart and ears' – that is, bad Jews – and both his attack and his execution by stoning were made within the framework of Judaism.[99] Chapter 15 of the Acts of the Apostles makes it clear that during Paul's early mission the Jerusalem Christians included many Pharisees, who felt strongly that even gentile converts should be circumcised, and only with difficulty did Paul obtain exemption for his flock.[100] In Judaea, Jewish followers of Christ – as they would doubtless have called themselves – continued to be circumcised and to observe many aspects of the Mosaic law until the catastrophe of 66–70 AD.

Both the great Jewish revolts against Roman rule should be seen not just as risings by a colonized people, inspired by religious nationalism, but as a racial and cultural conflict between Jews and Greeks. The xenophobia and anti-Hellenism which was such a characteristic of Jewish literature from the second century BC onwards was fully reciprocated. It is anomalous to speak of anti-Semitism in antiquity since the term itself was not coined until 1879. Yet anti-Semitism in fact if not in name undoubtedly existed and became of increasing significance. From deep antiquity the 'children of Abraham' had been, and had seen themselves, as 'strangers and sojourners'. There were many such groups – the Habiri, which included the Israelites, were only one – and all were unpopular. But the specific hostility towards the Jews, which began to emerge in the second half of the first millennium BC, was a function of Jewish monotheism and its social consequences. The Jews could not, and did not, recognize the existence of other deities, or show respect for them. Even in 500 BC, the Jewish faith was very old and retained antique practices and taboos which had been abandoned elsewhere but which the Jews, under the impulse of their increasingly rigorous leadership, observed faithfully. Circumcision set them apart and was regarded by the Graeco–Roman world as barbarous and distasteful. But at least circumcision did not prevent social intercourse. The ancient Jewish laws of diet and cleanliness did. This, perhaps more than any other factor, focused hostility on Jewish communities. 'Strangeness', in a word, lay at the origin of anti-Semitism in antiquity: the Jews were not merely immigrants, but they kept themselves apart.[101]

Thus Hecataeus of Abdera, writing before the end of the fourth century BC – 150 years before the clash with the Seleucids – in many ways approved of the Jews and Judaism but he attacked their abnormal way of life, which he called 'an inhospitable and anti-human form of living'.[102] As Greek ideas about the one-ness of humanity spread, the Jewish tendency to treat non-Jews as ritually unclean, and to forbid marriage to them, was resented as being anti-humanitarian; the word 'misanthropic' was frequently used. It is notable that in Babylonia, where Greek ideas had not penetrated, the apartness of the large Jewish community was not resented – Josephus said that anti-Jewish feeling did not exist there.[103] The Greeks saw their *œcumene*, that is the civilized universe (as opposed to the *chaos* beyond it) where their ideas prevailed, as a multi-racial, multi-national society, and those who refused to accept it were enemies of man. In his great offensive against Mosaic Judaism, Antiochus Epiphanes swore to abrogate Jewish laws 'inimical to humanity', and he sacrificed swine over Jewish sacred books.[104] In 133 BC the Seleucid ruler Antiochus Sidetes was told by his advisers that Jerusalem should be destroyed and the Jewish people annihilated because they were the only people on earth who refused to associate with the rest of humanity.

Much of the anti-Semitic feeling which found its way into literature was a response to what was felt to be the aggressive Jewish presentation of their own religious history. In the third century BC, the Greek-speaking Egyptian priest Manetho wrote a history of his country, a few passages of which survive in Josephus' *Antiquities of the Jews*, attacking the Jewish account of the Exodus. Obviously he and other Egyptian intellectuals found it deeply offensive and responded in kind. He presented the Exodus not as a miraculous escape but as the expulsion of a leper colony and other polluted groups. Manetho reflected Greek notions of the Jews as misanthropic in his charge that Moses (whom he presents as Osarsiph, a renegade Egyptian priest) ordained that the Jews 'should have no connection with any save members of their own confederacy', but it is evident that Egyptian anti-Semitism antedated the Greek conquest of Egypt. From Manetho's time we can see emerging the first anti-Semitic slanders and inventions. Various Greek writers echoed and embroidered them in saying the Jews were specifically commanded by the Mosaic laws to show goodwill to no men, but especially to Greeks. The volume of criticism of the Jews was greatly increased by the establishment of the Hasmonean kingdom and its religious oppression of Greek–pagan cities. The Egyptian libels were circulated and the argument went that the Jews had no real claim on Palestine – they had always been homeless wanderers and their sojourn in Judaea was merely an episode. In reply, the Jews retorted that the land of Israel was God's gift to the Jews: Chapter 12 of the apocryphal Wisdom of Solomon, written in the first century BC, castigates its original inhabitants as infanticists, cannibals and murderers, guilty of unspeakable practices, a 'race accursed from the very beginning'.[105]

As in the modern age, fables about the Jews were somehow fabricated, then endlessly repeated. The statement that the Jews worshipped asses, and had an ass's head in their Temple, goes back at least as far as the second century BC. Apollonius Molon, the first to write an essay directed exclusively against Jews, used it, and it later figured in Posidonius, Democritus, Apion, Plutarch and Tacitus – the last repeating it, though he knew perfectly well that the Jews never worshipped images of any kind.[106] Another fable was that the Jews conducted secret human sacrifices in their Temple: that was why no one was allowed to enter it. They avoided pork because they were more liable to contract leprosy – an echo of Manetho's smear.

As in modern times, moreover, anti-Semitism was fuelled not just by vulgar rumour but by the deliberate propaganda of intellectuals. Certainly, in the first century AD anti-Jewish feeling, which grew steadily, was to a large extent the work of writers, most of them Greeks. The Romans, once allies of the Jews, initially accorded privileges to the Jewish communities in the big cities – the right not to work on the Sabbath, for example.[107] But with the foundation of the empire and the adoption of emperor-worship, relations deteriorated swiftly. The Jewish refusal to practise the formalities of state worship was seen not merely as characteristic of Jewish exclusiveness and incivility – the charges always brought against them by the Greeks – but as actively disloyal. Official Roman hostility was eagerly whipped up by Greek intellectuals. Alexandria, where the Jewish community was exceptionally large, and Graeco–Jewish feelings tense, was a centre of anti-Semitic propaganda. Lysimachus, head of the Alexandrian library, was a notable trouble-maker. It was following a disturbance there that the Emperor Claudius, while confirming Jewish rights, warned the Jews publicly that they must be more reasonable towards other people's religions.[108] An edict of his to Alexandria, written on papyrus, has survived. It tells the Jewish community there

that, if they prove intolerant, he will treat them as people who spread
'a general plague throughout the world' – another echo of
Manetho.[109] Anti-Semitic Greek intellectuals not only circulated
charges, like Apion, but systematically poisoned the minds of rulers.
For example, the Emperor Nero showed no personal hostility to the
Jews, and one talmudic tradition even presents him as a proselyte; but
his Greek tutor Chaeremon was a notable anti-Semite.

From the death of Nero the Great onwards, relations between the
Jews and Rome deteriorated steadily, the rule of his grandson in
Judaea being a brief halt on the downward spiral. The revolt might
indeed have come during the reign of Caligula (37–41 AD), who sought
to impose full-blooded emperor-worship, had it not been for his
merciful assassination. The rise of Jewish apocalyptic nationalism was
undoubtedly one factor, as Tacitus explicitly asserts: 'Most Jews were
convinced that it was written in the ancient priestly writings that in
those times the East would gain in might and those who came forth
from Judaea should possess the world.'[110] But equally important was
the growing Graeco–Jewish hatred. The Hellenized gentiles were the
elite of Palestine. They, rather than Jews, supplied the rich men and the
merchants. They constituted the local civil service and tax-collectors.
Most of the soldiers in the Roman garrisons were gentiles recruited
from Hellenized cities such as Caesarea and Samaritan Sebaste. Like
the Greeks of Alexandria, the Hellenes of Palestine were notorious for
their anti-Semitism: it was Greek-speakers from Jabneh and Ashkelon
who put Caligula up to his anti-Jewish measures.[111] Foolishly, Rome
insisted on drawing its Judaean procurators from Greek-speaking
gentile areas – the last, and most insensitive of them, Gessius Florus,
came from Greek Asia Minor. Roman rule in first-century AD Palestine
was clumsy and unsuccessful. It was also chronically insolvent, and
raids on the Temple treasury for allegedly unpaid taxes were a source
of outrage. There were numerous unpunished bands of brigands,
swollen by insolvents and political malcontents. Many of the farmers
were hopelessly in debt. In the towns with mixed Greek–Jewish
populations the atmosphere was often tense.

Indeed, the revolt itself began in 66 AD not in Jerusalem but in
Caesarea, following a Graeco–Jewish lawsuit, which the Greeks won.
They celebrated with a pogrom in the Jewish quarter, while the
Greek-speaking Roman garrison did nothing. The news caused uproar
in Jerusalem, and feelings were raised still further when Florus chose
that moment to take money from the Temple treasury. Fighting broke
out, the Roman troops looted the Upper Town, the Temple priests
suspended the sacrifices in honour of the people and emperor of Rome,

and furious argument broke out between moderate and militant Jews. Jerusalem was filling up with angry and vengeful Jewish refugees from other cities where the Greek majority had invaded the Jewish quarters and burnt their homes. This element turned the tide in favour of the extremists, and the Roman garrison was attacked and massacred. So the Great Revolt was a civil and racial war between Greeks and Jews. But it was also a civil war among Jews, because – as in the time of the Maccabees – the Jewish upper class, largely Hellenized, was identified with the sins of the Greeks. As the radical nationalists took over Jerusalem they turned on the rich. One of their first acts was to burn the Temple archives so that all records of debts would be destroyed.

The Great Revolt of 66 AD and the siege of Jerusalem constitute one of the most important and horrifying events in Jewish history. Unfortunately it is badly recorded. Tacitus left a long account of the war but only fragments survive. Rabbinic accounts are made up of anecdotes with no clear historical context, or of sheer fantasy. There is very little epigraphical or archaeological evidence.[112] Virtually our only authority for the war is Josephus, and he is tendentious, contradictory and thoroughly unreliable. The broad outline of events is as follows. After the massacre of the garrison in Jerusalem, the Roman legate in Syria, Cestius Gallus, assembled a large force in Acre and marched on the city. When he reached the outskirts he was dismayed by the strength of the Jewish resistance and ordered a retreat which turned into a rout. Rome then took charge and reacted with enormous force, no fewer than four legions, the v, x, xii and xv, being concentrated on Judaea, and one of the empire's most experienced generals, Titus Flavius Vespasian, being given the command. He took his time, leaving Jerusalem severely alone until he had cleared the coast and secured his communications, reduced most of the fortresses held by Jews and settled the countryside. In 69 AD Vespasian was proclaimed emperor, and at the end of the year he left for Rome, leaving his eldest son, the twenty-nine-year-old Titus, in charge of the final phase of the campaign, the siege and capture of Jerusalem, which lasted from April to September 70 AD.

Josephus took a prominent part in these events and left two different accounts of them. His *Jewish War*, describing the years 66–70 in detail, and preceded by a history of the Jews in Palestine from the Maccabees onwards, was largely written while Titus, who succeeded Vespasian, was still alive. Then, about twenty years later, Josephus finished his *Antiquities of the Jews*, giving the entire history from the Creation onwards (based mainly on the Bible), ending in 66, but including an autobiographical *Vita* as an appendix. There are many discrepancies between the *War* and the *Vita*.[113] Most historians of antiquity wrote from tendentious motives. The trouble with Josephus is that his motives changed between writing the two works. In his *Vita* he was responding, for instance, to an attack on his character by the Jewish writer Justus of Tiberias.[114] But the main reason for his change of viewpoint was that he was an example of a Jewish phenomenon which became very common over the centuries: a clever young man who, in his youth, accepted the modernity and sophistication of the day and then, late in middle age, returned to his Jewish roots. He began his writing career as a Roman apologist and ended it close to being a Jewish nationalist.

Hence, as a recent analyst of Josephus has observed, it is easy to destroy confidence in his account but almost impossible to replace it with a truthful one.[115] What light, then, does it throw on this tragic chapter in Jewish history? The overwhelming impression is that the Jews were throughout irreconcilably divided into many factions. The original massacre of the garrison was the work of a small minority. Only when Cestius Gallus was driven back and his force destroyed did the aristocratic element decide to raise troops, and even then it had mixed motives. Its object seems to have been to carry on government and await events. So bronze coins – shekels, half-shekels and small change – were minted. Josephus, a senior priest attached to the house of one of the aristocrats, Eleazar ben Ananias, was sent to Galilee with two other priests to prepare the population for the conflict. He found most of the population opposed to the war. The farmers hated the brigands (including the ultra-Jewish nationalists) and hated the cities too. They did not like the Romans either but were not anxious to fight them. Of the cities, Sephoris was pro-Roman; Tiberias was divided; Gabara favoured John of Giscala, one of the insurgent leaders. Josephus says he tried to unite the cities, the peasants and the brigands, but failed; the peasants would not join up and when conscripted soon deserted. So he retired on Herod's old fortress of Jotapata and, after a token resistance, surrendered to Vespasian. Thereafter he served the Romans, first as an interpreter at the siege of Jerusalem, later as a propagandist. He took the same line as Jeremiah at the first fall of Jerusalem: it was all God's will, and the Romans were His instruments; to fight the Romans was therefore not only foolish but wicked.[116]

Josephus was probably correct to see this long, savage and disastrous war as the work of small, malignant minorities on both sides. Later, he came to see the force of the Jewish demand for religious and political rights, to have some respect for the Maccabees, and to take pride and pleasure in Jewish particularism. Yet his original contention, that the resistance of Jerusalem was unconscionable, remains valid. Titus had 60,000 men and the latest siege equipment. He could rely on starvation and Jewish divisions to do their work. The defenders had about 25,000 fighters, split into groups: the Zealots, under Eleazar ben Simon, held the Antonia and the Temple; the extremist Simeon ben Giora and his Sicarii ran the upper city; and there were Idumeans and other partisans under John of Giscala. The mass of the citizens and refugees were the helpless prisoners of these militants. Josephus described the final stages of the siege in horrifying detail. The Romans had to fight all the way. They stormed the Antonia, then took the Temple, which was burned, then Herod's citadel a month later. The people were sold as slaves, or massacred, or saved to die in the arenas of Caesarea, Antioch and Rome. Simeon ben Giora was captured alive, taken to Rome for Titus' triumphal process, then executed in the Forum. Titus' arch still stands there, the Temple *menorah* he captured carved on its stone. He also preserved, in his palace, the curtain which screened the Holy of Holies and a copy of the scriptures – would that it had survived!

After the fall of Jerusalem, only three Jewish centres of resistance remained: Herodium, which was taken soon after; Machaerus, taken in 72 AD; and Masada, the spectacular, 1,300-foot high rock on the edge of the Judaean desert, which Herod had turned into a great fortress, 37–31 BC. It could only be approached by what Josephus called 'a snaky path'. It fell to the Jews in 66 by 'a stratagem', the hero of this episode being Menahem, son of the Zealot founder and executed revolutionary, Judah the Galilean.[117] But Menahem was murdered during one of the many struggles for power in Jerusalem and the Masada command devolved on his nephew Eleazar. When the Roman general Flavius Silva finally invested it at the end of 72 AD, there were 960 insurgents and refugees in the fortress, men, women and children. In 1963–5, the site was exhaustively excavated by Yigael Yadin with a huge force of archaeologists and thousands of volunteer helpers from all over the world. The details of the siege have been vividly recreated. Silva had the entire xth legion, plus auxiliaries, and countless Jewish prisoners of war as labourers. Taking the place was essentially a problem in military engineering of precisely the type in which Rome excelled. Its fall was inevitable and, when this became apparent, Eleazar forced or persuaded the remaining defenders to engage in an act of mass suicide. Josephus gives what purports to be his final speech. Two women, and their five children, survived by hiding in a cave. Scraps of clothing, sandals, bones, entire skeletons, baskets, fragments of personal belongings – storerooms left intact to prove to the Romans that the mass suicide had not been dictated by hunger – nationalist coins, armour-scales and arrows are mute witnesses of the siege. They testify to the hopeless valour of the defenders far more eloquently than Josephus' powerful description. Among the ostraca found are what appear to be the lots cast by the last ten survivors to determine who was to kill the other nine and then himself. Abundant evidence of services in the fort's synagogue and parts of fourteen scrolls of Biblical, sectarian and apocryphal books indicate that this was a God-fearing garrison of militants, profoundly influenced by the terrible power of Jewish literature.[118]

Jerusalem was left a ruined city by the siege, its Temple destroyed, the walls nothing but rubble. But the woeful experience of these seven bloody years did not end the Graeco–Jewish clash nor the capacity of religious sentiment to drive pious Jews, young and old, to violent defence of their faith, however hopeless. Anti-Semitic sentiment continued to spread. The fall of Jerusalem was cited as evidence that Jews were hated by God. Philostratus asserted in his *Vita Apollonii* that when Helen of Judaea offered Titus a victory wreath after he took the city he refused it on the grounds that there was no merit in vanquishing a people deserted by their own God. This sounds highly unlikely coming from a professional commander who had fought a hard war against a very determined enemy. But it is typical of the anti-Semitic propaganda which now appeared everywhere. Horace and Martial were muted in their criticisms but Tacitus summarized all the Greek smears. From about 100 AD onwards, the Jews were attacked even more fiercely for subverting the lower orders and introducing novel and destructive ideas – a charge which was to echo through the ages.[119] So there were constant troubles in the diaspora cities, especially in 115–17.

The last Jewish risings were precipitated by a wave of government hostility to the Jews under the Emperor Hadrian, who was in the East 128–32. Initially sympathetic to Judaism, he later swung into hostility, possibly under the influence of the Tacitus circle. He came to dislike oriental religions in general, and developed a particular loathing for circumcision, which he classified with castration, a form of self-mutilation forbidden on pain of death. Hadrian introduced pan-Hellenistic policies throughout the East and one of his projects was to create a new, pagan *polis* on the ruins of Jerusalem, with a Roman temple dedicated to Jupiter on Temple Mount.

Dio Cassius, the Roman historian who is our chief source for these years, says the Jews did not dare rise while Hadrian was in the East, though they armed secretly and built hidden fortifications. There were two legions stationed in the area. But as soon as Hadrian departed, the Jews of Judaea struck and, says Dio, 'the Jews in the entire world also rose and joined them and created a great deal of trouble for the Romans, secretly or openly, and even many gentile people came to their aid'.[120] The revolt lasted four years. Roman losses, says Dio, were heavy. Legions had to be concentrated in Palestine from all over the empire, including Britain and the Danube, so that eventually the Jews were facing no fewer than twelve. Once again the Roman methods were slow but systematic and sure, splitting up and isolating the rebel forces, starving outlying pockets into surrender, then gradually closing in on the remaining centres of resistance. The Jews occupied Jerusalem for a time but it had no walls and was not defensible. They held various fortresses and their tunnelling, as for instance at Herodium, has been excavated. They seem to have made their headquarters in what was then the town of Betar, in the Judaean hills south-west of the capital, and this final stronghold fell to the Romans in 135 AD.

The extent and the initial success of the revolt were made possible by the fact that on this occasion the Jews, or at least their militant elements, were united and under the leadership of a single strong personality. Simon bar Kokhba or Kosiva is one of the most enigmatic personalities in Jewish history, and his name or names alone have excited intense but inconclusive scholarly argument. The more enterprising Jewish rebels, like Judah of Galilee, called themselves the Messiah to attract wider support – the main reason the Romans were willing to crucify Jesus Christ. According to Bishop Eusebius, a hostile Christian source, Simon did make messianic claims and his name Kokhba or 'star' referred to the prophecy in Numbers 'there shall come a star out of Jacob and a sceptre shall rise out of Israel, and shall smite the corners of Moab and destroy all the children of Sheth'.[121] A rabbinic source says he was recognized as Messiah by the greatest scholar of the age, the rabbi Akiva ben Joseph (c. 50–135 AD).[122] Akiva is an interesting social case, for he came of very humble stock, the *am ha-arez*, with no tradition of literacy, and for a long time (as he says) hated scholarship and worked as a shepherd. In time he became prodigiously learned but he retained a passionate concern for the poor, and this may be why he joined the rebellion (if he did: the tradition has been disputed). But other rabbis did not follow him. According to the Jerusalem Talmud, when Akiva said of Simon, 'This is the King Messiah', Rabbi Johanan ben Torta replied: 'O Akiva, grass will sprout between your jaws and the Son of David will still not have come.'[123]

Simon did not call himself 'star' but 'Koseva' and the coins he issued make no mention of the Messiah and refer to him as 'Simon Nasi [prince] of Israel'. His chief spiritual adviser was not Akiva but his uncle, Eleazar of Modin, whose name also figures on some of his coins; but in the final stages of the revolt the two men quarrelled and Eleazar was murdered by his nephew.[124] From the fragments of evidence we have, it looks as if Simon got little support from learned Jews and in the end lost what he had. In the years 1952–61, archaeologists working in the Judaean desert found objects connected with the revolt in various locations, especially in what is termed 'the Cave of the Letters'. Many of these documents, in Hebrew, Aramaic and Greek, were written and signed on his behalf. These discoveries show that the men of the rebellion were orthodox Jews who took great trouble, despite desperate circumstances, to observe the Mosaic law – the Sabbath, the festivals, priestly and levitical dues for instance. But there is no evidence that Simon regarded himself as a Messiah, the anointed one or in any way a spiritual leader. The letters show him ruling an extensive territory, concerned with farm leases, agricultural supplies, the mobilization of the countryside to supply men and food for his war. He was in every respect a secular ruler, a *nasi* as he calls himself in his letters, harsh, practical, unbending, ruthless: 'I call Heaven to witness . . . I shall put you in chains'; 'if you will not do this you will be punished'; 'You are living well, eating and drinking off the property of the house of Israel, and care nothing about your brethren.'[125] The later rabbinic legends woven around the 'Son of a Star' seem to have no basis in fact. Simon was more of a prototype for a modern Zionist fighter: unromantic and professional, a man who lived and died a guerrilla and nationalist.

Simon was killed in Betar. Akiva was captured, imprisoned, finally tortured to death, the flesh torn from his body 'by iron combs'. Dio says that of the rebels 'very few were saved'. The Roman vengeance was awe-inspiring. Fifty forts where the rebels had put up resistance were destroyed and 985 towns, villages and agricultural settlements. Dio says 580,000 Jews died in the fighting 'and countless numbers of starvation, fire and the sword. Nearly the entire land of Judaea was laid waste.'[126] In the late fourth century, St Jerome reported from Bethlehem a tradition that, after the defeat, there were so many Jewish slaves for sale that the price dropped to less than a horse.

Hadrian relentlessly carried through to completion his plan to transform ruined Jerusalem into a Greek *polis*. He buried the hollows of the old city in rubble to level the site. Outside the limits he removed the debris to get at and excavate the rock below to provide the huge ashlars for the public buildings he set up on the levelled site. The new city was the first to be broadly on the plan of the present Old City of Jerusalem. The main road from the north entered through the present Damascus Gate; the main east gate was the one later known as St Stephen's Gate, spanned by a triumphal arch, whose ruins remain. The city he built was called Aelia Capitolina. Greek-speakers were moved in to populate it and the Jews were forbidden to enter on pain of death. This regulation may not have been strictly enforced, and in the mid-fourth century it was lifted under the pagan recidivist Emperor Julian. At any rate Jews contrived to visit a section of the old ruins, now known as the Wailing Wall, on the anniversary of the city's destruction. Jerome, in his Commentary on Zephaniah, gives a picture which is both moving and harsh:

On the day of the Destruction of Jerusalem, you see a sad people coming to visit, decrepit little women and old men encumbered with rags and years, showing both in their bodies and their dress the wrath of the Lord. A crowd of pitiable creatures assembles and under the gleaming gibbet of the Lord and his sparkling resurrection, and before a brilliant banner with a cross, waving from the Mount of Olives, they weep over the ruins of the Temple. And yet they are not worthy of pity.[127]

These two catastrophes, of 70 and 135 AD, effectively ended Jewish state history in antiquity. There were two immediate consequences of great historical significance. The first was the final separation of Judaism and Christianity. Paul, writing in the decade around 50 AD, had effectively repudiated the Mosaic law as the mechanism of justification and salvation, and in this (as we have seen) he was consistent with Jesus' teaching. At a meeting with the Jewish–Christian leaders in Jerusalem he had won the right to exempt his gentile converts from Jewish religious requirements. But none of this meant necessarily that Jews and Christians would come to regard their beliefs as mutually exclusive and their respective supporters as enemies of each other. The Gospel of Luke, written perhaps in the 60s, resembles in some ways the writings of Hellenistic Jews in the diaspora, directed at potential converts to Judaism. Luke's aim seems to have been to summarize and simplify the Law, which he saw as an enlightened body of Jewish customs – the ethics of a specific people. Piety was the same among Jews and gentiles: both were the means by which the soul was prepared to receive the gospel. The gentiles had their good customs too, and God did not discriminate against those who did not possess the Law, i.e. Jewish customs. Nor did God discriminate against Jews. Both categories were saved by means of faith and grace.[128]

The notion that gentiles and Jews could both subscribe to Christianity as a sort of super-religion could not survive the events of 66–70, which effectively destroyed the old Christian–Jewish church of Jerusalem.[129] Most of its members must have perished. The survivors scattered. Their tradition ceased in any way to be mainstream Christianity and survived merely as a lowly sect, the Ebionites, eventually declared heretical. In the vacuum thus created, Hellenistic Christianity flourished and became the whole. The effect was to concentrate Christian belief still more fiercely on Paul's presentation of Christ's death and resurrection as the mechanism of salvation – itself clearly foreshadowed in Jesus' teaching – and on the nature of this anointed saviour. What did Jesus claim to be? The term he himself used most often, and others used of him, was 'Son of Man'. It may have meant a great deal; or little or even nothing at all – just Jesus saying he was a man, or the man for his particular mission.[130] It can be argued that Jesus regarded himself as nothing more than a charismatic Jewish *hasid*.[131] But the notion that Jesus was divine, implicit in his resurrection and his foresight of this miracle, and in his subsequent epiphanies, was present from the very beginnings of Apostolic Christianity. Moreover, it was accompanied by the equally early belief that he had instituted the ceremony of the eucharist, in anticipation of his death and resurrection for the expiation of sin, in which his flesh and blood (the substance of the sacrifice) took the form of bread and wine. The emergence of the eucharist, 'the holy and perfect sacrifice', as the Christian substitute for all Jewish forms of sacrifice, confirmed the doctrine of Jesus' apotheosis. To the question Was Jesus God or man?, the Christians therefore answered: both. After 70 AD, their answer was unanimous and increasingly emphatic. This made a complete breach with Judaism inevitable. The Jews could accept the decentralization of the Temple: many had long done so, and soon all had to do so. They could accept a different view of the Law. What they could not accept was the removal of the absolute distinction they had always drawn between God and man, because that was the essence of Jewish theology, the belief that above all others separated them from the pagans. By removing that distinction, the Christians took themselves irrecoverably out of the Judaic faith.

Moreover, they did so in a way which made antagonism between the two forms of monotheism inevitable, irreconcilable and bitter. The Jews could not concede the divinity of Jesus as God-made-man without repudiating the central tenet of their belief. The Christians could not concede that Jesus was anything less than God without repudiating the essence and purpose of their movement. If Christ was not God, Christianity was nothing. If Christ was God, then Judaism was false. There could be absolutely no compromise on this point. Each faith was thus a threat to the other.

The quarrel was all the more bitter because, while differing on the essential, the two faiths agreed on virtually everything else. The Christians took from Judaism the Pentateuch (including its morals and ethics), the prophets and the wisdom books, and far more of the apocrypha than the Jews themselves were prepared to canonize. They took the liturgy, for even the eucharist had Jewish roots. They took the notion of the Sabbath day and feast-days, incense and burning lamps, psalms, hymns and choral music, vestments and prayers, priests and martyrs, the reading of the sacred books and the institution of the synagogue (transformed into the church). They took even the notion of clerical authority – which the Jews would soon modify – in the shape of the high-priest whom the Christians turned into patriarchs and popes. There is nothing in the early church, other than its Christology, which was not adumbrated in Judaism.

Not least, the Christians sprang from the Jewish literary tradition and therefore they inherited, among other things, Jewish sacred polemic. As we have seen, this was a legacy of the Maccabee martyrologies and a very important element in Judaic writing during the first century AD. The very earliest Christian writings assume the hostile tone with which Jewish sectarians addressed each other. Once the break between Christianity and Judaism became unbridgeable, the only form of discourse between them was polemical. The four gospels, which quickly became the Torah of Christianity, incorporated the Jewish polemic–sectarian tradition. Their language is very similar in this respect to some of the Dead Sea Scrolls, and like the scrolls should be seen as an inter-Jewish argument. The expression 'the Jews' appears five times each in the gospels of Matthew and Luke, six in Mark and seventy-one in John. This is not necessarily because John reached written form later and is therefore more hostile to Judaism. In its original form John may, indeed, have been the earliest of the gospels. In John 'the Jews' appears to mean many different things – the Sadducees, the Pharisees, or both together, the Temple police, the Jewish establishment, the Sanhedrin, the Jewish ruling class – but also the people. The most common meaning is 'the opponents of Jesus' teaching'.[132] John is simply heresy-polemic. When the Qumran monks write of 'the sons of Belial', they are referring to their opponents within Judaism and making exactly the same point as in John: 'You are of your father the devil.' Equally, the Qumran Damascus Document used 'Jews', 'land of Judah' and 'house of Judah' in exactly the same way as John, meaning their Jewish opponents who currently have the predominant voice.[133] The most offensive and damaging passage in the gospels is, in fact, in Matthew, sometimes cited as the most 'pro-Jewish' text in the New Testament. This occurs when, after Pilate washes his hands, 'the people' exclaim: 'His blood be upon us and on our children',[134] because this explicitly shows Jews accepting the death of Jesus as a burden to be borne by their progeny. The incident is given even more emphasis in the passion narrative of the apocryphal 'Gospel of Peter'.[135]

Alas, these professional religious polemics, these literary exercises in *odium theologicum*, were lifted out of their historical context and became the basis for a general Christian indictment of the Jewish people. Polemic should be avoided, Erasmus was later to observe, 'because the long war of words and writings ends in blows'. The collective guilt charge in Matthew, and the 'sons of the devil' charge in John, were linked together to form the core of a specifically Christian branch of anti-Semitism which was superimposed on and blended with the ancient and ramifying pagan anti-Semitic tradition to form in time a mighty engine of hatred.

The collapse of the Jewish–Christian church after 70 AD and the triumph of Hellenistic Christianity led the Jews, in turn, to castigate the Christians. Jewish daily prayers against heretics and opponents date from the Hellenistic reform programme of the second century BC – Ecclesiasticus, the wisdom-polemic by the rigorist Ben Sira (which the Sicarii had with them at Masada), asked God: 'Rouse your fury, pour out your rage, destroy the opponent, annihilate the enemy.'[136] The prayer against heretics, originally known as 'the Benediction to Him who humbles the arrogant', became part of the daily service, or Amidah, as the Twelfth Benediction. At one time it was specifically directed against the Sadducees. Under the rule of Raban Gamaliel II (*c.* 80–*c.* 115 AD), the Twelfth Benediction or *Birkat ha-Minim* ('Benediction concerning heretics') was recast to apply to Christians and this seems to have been the point at which the remaining Jewish followers of Christ were turned out of the synagogue. By the 132 rising, Christians and Jews were seen as open opponents or even enemies. Indeed Christian communities in Palestine petitioned the Roman authorities to be given separate religious status to Jews, and the Christian writer Justin Martyr (*c.* 100–*c.* 165), who lived in Neapolis (Nablus), reported that the followers of Simon bar Kokhba massacred Christian as well as Greek communities. It is from this period that anti-Christian polemic begins to appear in Jewish Bible commentaries.

The second consequence of the final failure of state Judaism was a profound change in the nature and scope of Jewish activities. From 70 AD, and still more so after 135 AD, Judaism ceased to be a national religion in any physical and visible sense, and the Jews were depatriated. Instead, both Jewry and Judaism became coextensive with the study and observance of the Torah. It is difficult to fit Jewish history into any general taxonomy of national and religious develop-ment because it is a unique phenomenon. Indeed, the historian of the Jews is constantly faced with the problem of categorizing a process of which there is no other example anywhere. The concentration of Judaism and the Jewish nation on the Torah had proceeded steadily since the last phase of the Davidic kingdom. The reforms of Josiah, the Exile, the Return from Exile, the work of Ezra, the triumph of the Maccabees, the rise of Pharisaism, the synagogue, the schools, the rabbis – all these developments in turn had first established, then progressively consolidated, the absolute dominance of the Torah in Jewish religious and social life. It had, in so doing, emasculated the other institutions of Judaism and Jewry. After 135, its rule became complete because there was nothing else left. The rigorists, partly by design, partly by the catastrophes they had provoked, had driven everything else out.

Was this providential or not? In the short-term perspective of the second century AD, the Jews appeared to have been a powerful national and religious group which had courted ruin, and achieved it. During most of the first century, the Jews not only constituted a tenth of the empire, and a much higher proportion in certain big cities, but were expanding. They had the transcendent new idea of the age: ethical monotheism. They were almost all literate. They had the only welfare system that existed. They made converts in all social groups, including the highest. One or more of the Flavian emperors might easily have become a Jew, just as Constantine was to become a Christian 250 years later. Josephus was entitled to boast: 'There is not one city, Greek or barbarian, nor a single nation where the custom of the seventh day, on which we rest from all work, and the fasts and the lighting of candles are not observed ... and as God permeates the universe, so the Law has found its way into the hearts of all men.' A century later, the whole process had been reversed. Jerusalem was no longer a Jewish city at all. Alexandria, once 40 per cent Jewish, lost its Jewish voice completely. The huge casualty figures cited by such authors as Josephus, Tacitus and Dio for the two revolts (Tacitus said 1,197,000 Jews were killed or sold as slaves in the 66–70 struggle alone) may be exaggerated but it is clear that the Jewish population of Palestine fell rapidly at this time. In the diaspora, the expanding Christian communities not only purloined the best Jewish theological and social ideas, and so the role of 'light to the gentiles', but made increasing inroads into the Jewish masses themselves, diaspora Jews forming one of the chief sources of Christian converts.[137]

Not only did the Jewish population fall dramatically, in both the homeland and the diaspora, but there was an equally dramatic narrowing of the Jewish horizon. In the age of Herod the Great, the Jews were beginning to take a prominent part in the cultural and economic life of the new empire. A man like Philo Judaeus (c. 30 BC– c. 45 AD), a member of one of the richest and most cosmopolitan diaspora families in Alexandria, brought up on the Septuagint, speaking and writing beautiful Greek, at home in all Greek literature, a historian and diplomat, and a major secular philosopher in his own right, was at the same time a pious Jew and a voluminous commentator both on the books of the Pentateuch and on the whole corpus of Jewish law.[138] Philo embodied the best tradition of Jewish rationalism. Christian scholars were later to be deeply indebted to him for their understanding of the Old Testament, especially in an allegorical sense. Philo's presentation of the spirit of Judaism is profound, original and creative, and the fact that he seems to have known no Hebrew indicates the extent to which enlightened Jews, by the beginning of the Christian era, had made themselves a part of international civilization and secular culture without forfeiting anything essential of their faith. By the mid-second century however, a man of Philo's breadth of outlook could not have been accommodated within the Jewish community. It had ceased to write history. It no longer engaged in speculative philosophy of any kind. All its traditional forms – wisdom, poetry, psalmody, allegory, historical novellae, apocalyptic – had been abandoned. It was engaged, with passionate concentration and sincerity, on a solitary form of literary work: commentary on the religious law. And it continued this task, oblivious of its richer past, unaware of any intellectual ferment in the world outside, for hundreds of years.

Yet the turning in upon itself of Judaism, the logical culmination of seven centuries of increasing rigorism, was probably the condition of its very survival, and the survival of the Jewish people as a distinct entity. The Jews did not simply vanish from the historical record, as did so many peoples in the great convulsive population movements of late antiquity. They did not lose their identity in the emergent Dark Age communities – like Romans and Hellenes, Gauls and Celts or, indeed, like the millions of diaspora Jews who became Christians. Judaism and the Jewish remnant were preserved in the amber of the Torah. Nor was this preservation and survival an inexplicable freak of history. The Jews survived because the period of intense introspection enabled their intellectual leaders to enlarge the Torah into a system of moral theology and community law of extraordinary coherence, logical consistency and social strength. Having lost the Kingdom of Israel, the Jews turned the Torah into a fortress of the mind and spirit, in which they could dwell in safety and even in content.

This great enterprise in social metaphysics began humbly enough in the aftermath of the fall of Jerusalem in 70 AD. The hereditary priestly families, and the traditional Jewish upper class as a whole, perished in the ruin of the city. Henceforth the Jews formed themselves into a cathedocracy: they were ruled from the teacher's chair. This had always been inherent in Judaism – for were not prophets instruments through whom God taught his people? But now it became explicit. Tradition says that the Pharisaic rabbi, Johanan ben Zakkai, the deputy head of the Sanhedrin, was smuggled out of besieged Jerusalem in a coffin. He had opposed the revolt and spoke for the long-established element in Judaism who believed that God and the faith were better served without the burden and corruption of the state. He obtained permission from the Roman authorities to set up a centre for the regulation of the Jewish religion at Jabneh (Jamnia), near the coast west of Jerusalem. There the Sanhedrin and the state were buried, and in their place a synod of rabbis met, in a vineyard near a dovecote, or in the upper chamber of a house. The rabbi and the synagogue became the normative institutions of Judaism, which from now on was essentially a congregationalist faith. The academy at Jabneh made the annual calculations of the Jewish calendar. It completed the canonization of the Bible. It ruled that, despite the fall of the Temple, certain ceremonies, such as the solemn eating of the Passover meal, were to be regularly enacted. It established the form of community prayers and laid down rules for fasting and pilgrimage. The new spirit of Judaism was in marked reaction to the violent exaltation of the zealots and nationalists. 'Do not hurry to tear down the altars of the gentiles', the Rabbi Jonathan was remembered as saying, 'lest you be forced to rebuild them with your own hands.' Or again: 'If you are planting trees, and someone tells you the Messiah has come, put the sapling in first, then go and welcome the Messiah.'[139] At Jabneh, the sword was forgotten, the pen ruled. The system was a self-perpetuating oligarchy,

the academy selecting or 'ordaining' new rabbis on the basis of
learning and merit. But authority tended to be vested in families
distinguished for their scholarship. In due course the progeny of Rabbi
Jonathan were ousted by Rabbi Gamaliel II, son of the man who had
taught St Paul. He was recognized by the Romans as *nasi* or patriarch.

These scholars, as a body, declined to join the Bar Kokhba revolt.
But, of course, it affected them. Scholars often had to meet secretly.
Jabneh itself became untenable, and after the revolt was crushed the
rabbinical authorities transferred themselves to the town of Usha in
western Galilee. Most rabbis were poor. They worked, usually with
their hands. Constructing the Jewish history of these times is difficult,
for the Jews themselves had ceased to write it, and the biographical
and other information recorded emerges incidentally and without
anchorage in chronology from passages in the halakhah or legal
rulings, or in the aggadah stories and legends. Jewish academic society
was not always homogeneous and self-contained. One of the greatest
Jabneh scholars, Elisha ben Avuyah, became a heretic. But one of his
pupils, the Rabbi Meir, best of the second-century scholars, may have
been a convert. Women played their part. Meir's wife Bruria made
herself into a leading halakhic authority. At times the Jews were
harassed or even persecuted by the imperial authorities. Sometimes
they were left alone. At times they worked in harmony with Rome.
Their leaders received grants of imperial lands and were permitted to
exercise wide judicial powers. The Christian scholar Origen (185–
254) says the *nasi* even imposed death-sentences. He certainly had the
right to collect taxes. The Rabbi Judah Ha-Nasi, or Judah the Prince,
who lived in the second half of the second century and the beginning of
the third, was a rich man attended by guards, who ruled the Jewish
community both of Galilee and of the south almost like a secular
potentate. Almost, but not quite: he spent his wealth on supporting
scholars, the ablest of whom ate at the top table in his hall; he
exempted scholarly men from taxation, at the expense of the workers;
and in times of scarcity he fed scholars, but not the unlettered, from his
food reserves. Even his maidservant, it is said, knew Hebrew and could
explain the meaning of rare words. Judah was an intellectual elitist of
the most uncompromising kind. He used to say, grimly: 'It is the
unlearned who bring trouble into the world.'[140]

Dynasties of scholars existed even in the period of the Second
Commonwealth, when they are classified as zugot or 'pairs'. There
were five pairs of the leading scholars, the last being the famous Hillel,
Christ's teacher, and his opponent Shammai. Their descendants and
followers, and other scholars who joined the elite, are known as the

tannaim. Hillel's grandson, Gamaliel the Elder, was the first of six generations, Judah Ha-Nasi the last. The next generation, beginning with Rabbi Hiya Rabbah about 220 AD, inaugurated the age of the amoraim, which lasted five generations in Judaea, up to the end of the fourth century, and eight generations in Babylon, up to the end of the fifth. There had, of course, been large Jewish communities in Babylon and its surroundings since the Exile. Contact was continuous since Babylonian Jewry accepted the calendar calculations from the Jerusalem authorities, and later from Jabneh. Babylonian Jews also came to Jerusalem on pilgrimage when this was possible. Pharisee or rabbinical Judaism came to Babylonia as a direct result of the Bar Kokhba revolt, when refugee scholars fleeing from Judaea established academies in what was then the territory of the Parthians. These schools were centralized at Sura, south of what is now Baghdad, and at Pumbedita to the west, where they flourished until the eleventh century. The location of the western academies in Palestine varied. In Judah Ha-Nasi's time he concentrated all scholarship at Bet Shearim, but after his death there were important academies at Caesarea, Tiberias and Lydda.

The physical traces of this period of Jewish history are not impressive. Jewish archaeologists have not, of course, been able to explore sites in Iraq. The Jewish settlement at Sura had vanished completely as long ago as the 1170s, when the Jewish traveller Benjamin of Tudela visited the spot; the town, he wrote, was in ruins. By contrast he found a sizeable community at Pumbedita, but that is the last we hear of it. On the other hand, excavations in 1932 uncovered, at the Roman caravan city of Dura Europus on the Euphrates, the remains of a synagogue dated 245 AD, with inscriptions in Aramaic, Greek and Pahlevi-Parthian. The Jewish colony there dated back, it appears, to the destruction and exile of the Northern Kingdom, but had been reinforced by more orthodox Jews after the revolts of 66–70 and 132–35. Even so it was a heterodox community, as perhaps were many at that time. The architecture was Hellenistic, as one would expect, but the surprise lay in some thirty painted panels (now in the Damascus National Museum), which illustrate the messianic theme of the Return, the restoration and salvation. There are images of the patriarchs, of Moses and the Exodus, of the loss of the Ark and its return, of David and Esther. Scholars relate these paintings to the illustrated Bibles which are believed to have existed in the second and third centuries AD, and which indicate that Christian art too had a Jewish origin. Evidently the rule on images was not then strictly observed, at any rate in all Jewish circles.[141]

A number of synagogues and tombs from the time of the sages have survived in Palestine. At Tiberias on the Lake of Galilee, the fourth-century synagogue also has human and animal images on its mosaic floor, and signs of the zodiac too. On the hill near the town is the tomb of the martyr, Rabbi Akiva, and that of Johanan ben Zakkai; two miles down the lake, Rabbi Meir has his tomb. At Capernaum, where the centurion whose servant Jesus healed built a synagogue, its second–third-century successor was excavated between 1905 and 1926, and carvings discovered of the *shofar* and *menorah*, the manna-pot, the palm tree and the shield of King David. Three synagogues have been unearthed in Syria and in northern Israel, and just off the Nazareth–Haifa road is Judah Ha-Nasi's academic centre of Bet Shearim, with its synagogue, catacombs and cemetery – the last crowded with figurative art and concealing, somewhere, the tomb of Judah himself.[142]

But the chief memorials to this age of collective and individual scholarship are the Jewish holy writings themselves. Jewish sacred scholarship should be seen as a series of layers, each dependent on its predecessor. The first is the Pentateuch itself, which was essentially complete before the Exile, though some editing clearly went on after the Return. This is the basic body of written Jewish law, on which all else rests. Then come the books of the prophets, the psalms and wisdom literature, canonization of which was completed, as we have seen, under Rabbi Johanan ben Zakkai, between 70 and 132 AD. To this were added various non-canonical works essential to the study of Jewish religion and history: the Greek translation of the Bible, or Septuagint; the works of Josephus; the Apocrypha and various papyri.

The next layer or stage was the sorting out and writing of Oral Law, which had been accumulating for centuries. This was a practice termed Mishnah, meaning to repeat or study, since it was originally memorized and recapitulated. Mishnah consisted of three elements: the midrash, that is the method of interpreting the Pentateuch to make clear points of law; the halakhah, plural halakhot, the body of generally accepted legal decisions on particular points; and the aggadah or homilies, including anecdotes and legends used to convey understanding of the law to the ordinary people. Gradually, over many generations, these interpretations, rulings and illustrations found written form. After the Bar Kokhba revolt, and culminating in the work of Rabbi Judah Ha-Nasi and his school at the end of the second century AD, this material was edited into a book called the Mishnah, the epitome of 'repetition'. It has six orders, each divided into a variable number of tractates. The first is *Zera'im*, with eleven tractates, dealing with benedictions, offerings and titles. *Mo'ed*, with twelve tractates, covers the Sabbath and feasts. *Nashim* (seven tractates) deals with marriage and divorce. *Nezikin* (ten) covers civil wrongs or torts, judges, punishments and witnesses. *Kodashim* (eleven) deals with sacrifices and sacrileges, overlapping somewhat with the first order. Finally, *Tohorot* (twelve) covers uncleanliness and rituals.[143] In addition to the Mishnah, there is a collection of sayings and rulings by the tannaim, four times larger in bulk, known as the Tosefta. The exact provenance, date and composition of the Tosefta – and its precise relationship to the Mishnah – have been subjects of unresolved scholarly dispute for over a thousand years.[144]

Of course, immediately the Mishnah was complete, further generations of scholars – who were, it should be remembered, determining legal theory in the light of actual cases – began to comment upon it. By this time, since the rabbinic methods had spread to Babylonia, there were two centres of commentary, in Eretz Israel and in the Babylonian academies. Both produced volumes of Talmud, a word meaning 'study' or 'learning', which were compiled by the various generations of the amoraim. The Jerusalem Talmud, more correctly called the Talmud of the West, was completed by the end of the fourth century AD, and the Babylonian Talmud a century later. Each has folios of commentary dealing with the tractates of the Mishnah. This formed the third layer.

Thereafter further layers were added: *Perushim*, or commentaries, on both the Talmuds, of which the outstanding example was Rashi's on the Babylonian Talmud in the eleventh century; and *Hiddushim* or *novellae*, which compare and reconcile different sources, so producing new rulings or halakhot, the classic *novellae* being composed on the Babylonian Talmud in the twelfth–thirteenth centuries. There was another layer of *responsa prudentium* (*She'elot u-Teshuvot*) or written answers by leading scholars to questions put to them. The last of the layers consisted of attempts to simplify and codify this enormous mass of material, by such outstanding scholars as Isaac Alfasi, Maimonides, Jacob ben Asher and Joseph Caro, from the eleventh to the sixteenth centuries. From the fifth to the eleventh centuries, which is known as the age of the *gaons* or *geonim*, scholars worked to produce collective rulings and compilations bearing the authority of academies. Later, in what is known as the rabbinic age, rulings were decentralized and individual scholars dominated the evolution of the Law. As an epilogue, from the sixteenth to the end of the eighteenth century, came the age of the aharonim or later scholars.

During all this time, Jewish communities, spread throughout the

Near East and Mediterranean, and eventually through most of central and eastern Europe, settled most of their legal problems through their own religious courts, so this multi-layered body of writings constituted not just a work of continuing research into the true meaning of the Bible, but a living body of communal law, dealing with actual cases and real people. Seen in Western terms, it was natural law, the law of the Bible, the code of Justinian, the canon law, the English common law, the European civil law, the parliamentary statutes, the American Constitution and the Napoleonic Code all rolled into one. Only in the nineteenth century, by which time many Jews had been emancipated and had ceased to live in judicial autonomy, did the study of Jewish halakhah begin to become academic – and even then it continued to govern Jewish marriage law in advanced societies and many other aspects of life in the backward areas.

There is, then, no system in the history of the world which has sought for so long to combine moral and ethical teaching with the practical exercise of civil and criminal jurisprudence. It always had many drawbacks. That was why the Jewish Christians could achieve universalism only by breaking away from it. Eventually, in the Age of Enlightenment, it came to be seen as irredeemably backward, even positively abhorrent by many educated Jews, as well as by non-Jewish society. But it had many remarkable strengths too, and it gave to the Jews a moral and social world-view which is civilized and practical and proved extremely durable.

The notion of human life being sacred, because created in God's image, was the central precept of Jewish ethics, and as we have seen it determined the provisions of Jewish criminal codes from the earliest times. But the sages and their successors worked out the implications of this doctrine in ingenious detail. Everything came from God, and man merely had the temporal use of these gifts: thus he must, for instance, farm the land industriously and with a view to its use by future generations. But these gifts included man's own body. Hillel the Elder taught that man therefore had a duty to keep his body fit and healthy. Philo, like many influenced by Greek notions, separated the body and soul in moral terms and even referred to the body as an emotional, irrational 'plotter' against the rational soul. But mainstream, rabbinical Judaism rejected a body–soul dichotomy, just as it rejected the good powers/evil powers of gnosticism. Body and soul, it taught, were one and jointly responsible for sin, therefore jointly punishable. This became an important distinction between Christianity and Judaism. The Christian idea that, by weakening the body through mortification and fasting, you strengthened the soul, was anathema to Jews. They

had ascetic sects as late as the first century AD, but once rabbinical
Judaism established its dominance, the Jews turned their backs forever
on monasticism, hermitry and asceticism. Public fasts might be
commanded as symbols of public atonement, but private fasts were
sinful and forbidden. Abstaining from wine, as the Nazarites did, was
sinful, for it was rejecting the gifts God has provided for man's
necessities. Vegetarianism was rarely encouraged. Nor – another
important distinction from Christianity – was celibacy. The rabbinic
attitude was: 'Do the prohibitions of the Torah not suffice for thee that
thou addest others for thyself?' In all things, the body made in God's
image must behave, and be treated, with moderation. Over a whole
range of human behaviour, the Jewish watchword was continence or
temperance, not abstinence.[145]

Since man belonged to God, suicide was a sacrilege, and it was sinful
to risk one's life unnecessarily. For a people now without the
protection of a state, and in constant danger of persecution, there were
important issues here, which became paramount during the Holocaust
two millennia later. The sages ruled that a man had no right to save his
life by causing the death of another. He was not required to sacrifice
his life to save another either. During the Hadrian persecution, the
sages at Lydda ruled that a Jew, in order to save his life, could violate
any commandment save three: those against idolatry, adultery–incest,
and murder. When it came to human life, quantitative factors did not
signify. An individual, if innocent, might not be sacrificed for the lives
of a group. It was an important principle of the Mishnah that each
man is a symbol of all humanity, and whoever destroys one man
destroys, in a sense, the principle of life, just as, if he saves one man, he
rescues humanity.[146] Rabbi Akiva seems to have thought that to kill
was to 'renounce the Likeness', that is leave the human race. Philo
called murder the greatest of sacrileges, as well as by far the most
serious criminal act. 'Ransom', wrote Maimonides, 'is never acceptable, even if the murderer is ready to pay all the money in the world,
and even if the plaintiff agrees to let the murderer go free. For the life of
the murdered person is . . . the possession of the Holy One blessed be
He.'[147]

As God owns all and everyone, he is an injured party in all offences
against fellow men. A sin against God is serious but a sin against a
fellow man is more serious since it is against God too. God is 'the
Invisible Third'. Hence if God is the only witness to a transaction, false
denial of it is more wicked than if there is a written transaction; open
robbery is less wicked than secret theft since he who perpetrates the
latter shows he has more respect for the earthly power of man than the
divine vengeance of God.[148]

As men are all equally made in God's image, they have equal rights in any fundamental sense. It is no accident that slavery among the Jews disappeared during the Second Commonwealth, coinciding with the rise of Pharisaism, because the Pharisees insisted that, as God was the true judge in a court of law, all were equal there: king, high-priest, free man, slave. This was one of their prime differences with the Sadducees. The Pharisees rejected the view that a master was responsible for the actions of his slaves, as well as his livestock, since a slave, like all men, had a mind of his own. That gave him status in the court, and once he had legal status, slavery could not work. The Pharisees, when they controlled the Sanhedrin, also insisted that the king was answerable to it, and must stand in its presence – one source of the bitter conflicts between the Sanhedrin and both the Hasmoneans and Herod. These violent kings might and did overawe the court in practice but the theory remained and triumphed completely when Jewish halakhic practice was being collected into the Mishnah, so that equality before the law became an unassailable Jewish axiom. There was a conflict here with the notion of the Jewish king being 'the Lord's anointed', which later Christian theorists used to evolve the doctrine of divine-right kingship. But the Jews never accepted the legal implications of anointing. All David's acts of arbitrary power were roundly condemned in the Bible and Ahab's getting possession of Naboth's vineyard is presented as a monstrous crime. These were reasons why kingship did not mix with Judaism: the Jews wanted a king with all the duties and none of the rights of kingship. In their hearts, indeed, many never believed in anointing but in election, which appeared to precede it. In favour of elective kings, judges or other authorities, Philo quoted Deuteronomy: 'Thou shalt establish a ruler over thyself, not a foreigner but from thy brethren.'[149] Josephus took Gideon's view that God and no one else ruled but that, if kings were felt necessary, they must be of Jewish race and subject to the Law.

The truth is, the real rulers of the Jewish community, as was natural in a society under divine law, were the courts. One stresses the court, not the judge, since one of the most important axioms was that men could not constitute solitary judges: 'Judge not alone, for none may judge alone save One.'[150] The verdict went with the majority and in capital cases a majority of at least two was required. The same majority principle applied to the interpretation of the Torah. One reason why Judaism clung together over the centuries was its adherence to majority decisions and the great severity with which it punished those who refused to submit to them once they were fairly reached. At the same time, submissive dissentients had the right to have their views recorded, an important practice established by the Mishnah. In courts and scholarly bodies, co-option rather than election applied, since learning was a necessity and only the learned could judge – Jewish society was the first to construct a franchise by educational qualification – but in practice, 'We do not appoint an officer of the community unless we first consult with it.'[151] Not only the courts but the Law had an underlying democratic basis. A body not unlike the later Anglo-Saxon jury was used to ascertain what the practice in a particular community was, so that legal decisions might take this into account. The principle that the Law must be acceptable to the community as a whole was implicit in Judaic jurisprudence and sometimes explicit: 'Any decree which the court imposes on the community and which the majority of the community does not accept, has no force.'[152]

Man was seen both as an individual, with rights, and as member of a community, with obligations. No system of justice in history has made more persistent and on the whole successful efforts to reconcile individual and social roles – another reason why the Jews were able to keep their cohesion in the face of otherwise intolerable pressures. Society required that there should be equality before the law – the greatest of all possible safeguards for the individual – but society, especially one under constant persecution, had its own priorities within that general equality. A remarkable series of rulings by the sages runs:

The saving of a man's life takes priority over a woman's. . . . The covering of a woman's nakedness takes priority over a man's. A woman's ransom has priority over a man's. A man in danger of being forcibly sodomized has priority over a woman in danger of rape. The priest takes priority over the Levite, the Levite over the Israelite, the Israelite over the bastard, the bastard over the *natin*,* the *natin* over the proselyte, the proselyte over the slave. . . . But if the bastard is learned in the Law and the high-priest is ignorant of the Law, the bastard has priority over the high-priest.[153]

A scholar was more valuable to society than, say, one of the *am ha-arez*, an ignorant fellow. The scholar therefore was entitled to sit when before the court. But if the other party to the suit was of the *am ha-arez*, the principle of individual equality demanded that he sit too. The sages were the first jurisprudents to accord all men the right to their dignity. They ruled: 'If a man wounds his fellow man he becomes thereby culpable on five counts: injury, pain, healing, loss of time and indignity inflicted.' But loss of dignity was assessed hierarchically in terms of social standing in the community.[154]

* From *nathin*, gibeonite descendant.

Man was not only equal before the Law, he was physically free. The sages and rabbis were extraordinarily reluctant to use imprisonment as a punishment (as opposed to a restraint before trial), and the notion of man's basic right to roam freely was very deep in Judaism, another reason why it was the first society of antiquity to reject slavery. But if a man was free physically, he was certainly not free morally. On the contrary, he had all kinds of duties to the community, not least the duty of obedience to its duly constituted authorities. Jewish law has no mercy on the rebel, whose punishment might be death. In late antiquity, each Jewish community was ruled in effect congregationally, with a governing board of seven, which fixed wages, prices, weights and measures, and bye-laws, and had powers to punish offenders. The obligation to pay communal taxes was religious as well as social. Moreover, philanthropy was an obligation too, since the word *zedakah* meant both charity and righteousness. The Jewish welfare state in antiquity, the prototype of all others, was not voluntary; a man had to contribute to the common fund in proportion to his means, and this duty could be enforced by the courts. Maimonides even ruled that a Jew who evaded contributing according to wealth should be regarded as a rebel and punished accordingly. Other communal obligations included respect for privacy, the need to be neighbourly (i.e. to give neighbours first refusal of adjoining land put up for sale), and strict injunctions against noise, smells, vandalism and pollution.[155]

Communal obligations need to be understood within the assumptions of Jewish theology. The sages taught that a Jew should not regard these social duties as burdens but as yet more ways in which men showed their love for God and righteousness. The Jews are sometimes accused of not understanding freedom as well as the Greeks, but the truth is that they understood it better, grasping the point that the only true freedom is a good conscience – a concept St Paul carried from Judaism into Christianity. The Jews thought sinfulness and virtue were collective as well as individual. The Bible showed repeatedly that a city, a community, a nation, earned both merit and retribution by its acts. The Torah bound the Jews together as one body and one soul.[156] Just as the individual man benefited from the worth of his community, so he was obliged to contribute to it. Hillel the Elder laid down: 'Separate not thyself from the community and trust not in thyself until the day of thy death.' Even a liberal like Maimonides warned that a Jew who held aloof from the community, albeit God-fearing in other ways, would have no share in the next world.

Implicit in the Bible is the holistic notion that one man's sin, however small, affects the entire world, however imperceptibly, and vice versa. Judaism never allowed the principle of individual guilt and judgment, however important, to override completely the more primitive principle of collective judgment, and by running the two in tandem it produced a sophisticated and enduring doctrine of social responsibility which is one of its greatest contributions to humanity. The wicked are the shame of all, the saints are our pride and joy. In one of his most moving passages, Philo writes:

Every wise man is ransom for the fool, who would not last an hour did not the wise preserve him by compassion and forethought. The wise are like physicians, fighting the infirmities of the sick. . . . So when I hear that a wise man has died, my heart is sorrowful. Not for him, of course, for he lived in joy and died in honour. No – it is for the survivors that I mourn. Without the strong protecting arm which brought them safety, they are abandoned to the miseries which are their desert, and which they will soon feel, unless Providence should raise up some new protector to replace the old one.[157]

A wise man must give of his wisdom to the community, just as a rich man must give of his wealth. So it is a sin not to serve when required. Prayer for others is a duty. 'Whoever is able to plead God's mercy for his fellows and does not do so is a sinner.' Every Jew is a surety for every other Jew. If he sees a fellow sinning, he must remonstrate and if possible prevent it – otherwise he sins too. The community is responsible for the man who does wrong publicly. A Jew must always bear witness and protest against evil, especially great public sins of the powerful crying to God for vengeance. But precisely because the duty to protest against another's sin is so important, false and malicious accusations are particularly abhorrent. To destroy a man's reputation wilfully and unjustly is one of the worst of sins. The 'witch hunt' is a great collective evil.

The Torah and its superstructure of commentaries formed a moral theology as well as a practical system of civil and criminal law. Hence though it was very specific and legalistic on particular points, it always sought to reinforce the temporal authority of the courts by appeals to spiritual factors and sanctions. The notion of strict justice was never enough. The Jews were the first to introduce the concept of repentance and atonement, which became a primary Christian theme also. The Bible repeatedly refers to the 'change of heart' – 'Turn ye even to me with all your heart,' as the Book of Joel puts it, and 'Rend your hearts and not your garments.' In the Book of Ezekiel the injunction is 'Make ye a new heart.' The Law and the courts sought to go beyond restitution to bring about reconciliation between the contending parties. The aim was always to keep the Jewish community cohesive. So the Law and the rulings of the sages were designed to be positive in promoting harmony, and preventative in removing possible sources of friction. It was more important to promote peace than to do nominal justice. In doubtful cases it was the custom of the sages to quote the saying in Proverbs about wisdom: 'Her ways are ways of pleasantness and all her paths are peace.'[158]

The idea of peace as a positive state, a noble ideal which is also a workable human condition, is another Jewish invention. It is one of the great motifs of the Bible, especially of its finest book, Isaiah. The Mishnah laid down: 'Three things sustain the existence of the world – justice, truth and peace,' and the closing words of the whole work are: 'God did not bestow any greater blessing on Israel than peace, for it is written: "The Lord will give strength to his people, the Lord will bless his people with peace." '[159] The sages argued that one of the great functions of scholarship was to use the Law to promote peace, between husband and wife, parents and children, and then in the wider world of the community and the nation. A prayer for peace was one of the chief benedictions and was said by pious Jews three times a day. The sages quoted Isaiah, 'How beautiful upon the mountains are the feet of him that bringeth good tidings, that publisheth peace,'[160] and they claimed that the first action of the Messiah would be to declare peace.

One of the most important developments in the history of the Jews, one of the ways in which Judaism differed most strongly from primitive Israelite religion, was this growing stress on peace. After 135 AD, in effect, Judaism renounced even righteous violence – as it implicitly renounced the state – and put its trust in peace. Jewish valour and heroism was pushed into the background as a sustaining national theme; Jewish irenicism came to the foreground. To countless generations of Jews, what happened at Jabneh, where the scholar finally took over from the warrior, was far more significant than what happened at Masada. The lost fortress, indeed, was virtually forgotten until, in the lurid flames of the twentieth-century Holocaust, it became a national myth, displacing the myth of Jabneh.

The concentration on external peace and internal harmony, and the study of the means whereby both could be promoted, were essential for a vulnerable people without the protection of the state, and were clearly one of the main objects of Torah commentary. In this it was brilliantly – one might almost say miraculously – successful. The Torah became a great cohesive source. No people have ever been better served by their public law and doctrine. From the second century AD onwards, the sectarianism which had been such a feature of the Second Commonwealth virtually disappeared, at any rate to our view, and all the old parties were subsumed in rabbinical Judaism. Torah study remained an arena of fierce argument, but it took place within a consensus sustained by the majority principle. The absence of the state was a huge blessing.

Equally important, however, was another characteristic of Judaism: the relative absence of dogmatic theology. Almost from the beginning, Christianity found itself in grave difficulties over dogma, because of its origins. It believed in one God, but its monotheism was qualified by the divinity of Christ. To solve this problem it evolved the dogma of the two natures of Christ, and the dogma of the Trinity – three persons in one God. These devices in turn created more problems, and from the second century onwards produced innumerable heresies, which convulsed and divided Christianity throughout the Dark Ages. The New Testament, with its enigmatic pronouncements by Jesus, and its Pauline obscurities – especially in the Epistle to the Romans – became a minefield. Thus the institution of the Petrine church, with its axiom of central authority, led to endless controversy and a final breach between Rome and Byzantium in the eleventh century. The precise meaning of the eucharist split the Roman trunk still further in the sixteenth. The production of dogmatic theology – that is, what the church should teach about God, the sacraments and itself – became the main preoccupation of the professional Christian intelligentsia, and remains so to this day, so that at the end of the twentieth century Anglican bishops are still arguing among themselves about the Virgin Birth.

The Jews escaped this calvary. Their view of God is very simple and clear. Some Jewish scholars argue that there is, in fact, a lot of dogma in Judaism. That is true in the sense that there are many negative prohibitions – chiefly against idolatry. But the Jews usually avoided the positive dogmas which the vanity of theologians tends to create and which are the source of so much trouble. They never adopted, for instance, the idea of Original Sin. Of all the ancient peoples, the Jews were perhaps the least interested in death, and this saved them a host of problems. It is true that belief in resurrection and the afterlife was the main distinguishing mark of Pharisaism, and thus a fundament of rabbinic Judaism. Indeed the first definite statement of dogma in the whole of Judaism, in the Mishnah, deals with this: 'All Israel share in the world to come except the one who says resurrection has no origin in the Law.'[161] But the Jews had a way of concentrating on life and pushing death – and its dogmas – into the background. Predestination,

single and double, purgatory, indulgences, prayers for the dead and
the intercession of the saints – these vexatious sources of Christian
discord caused Jews little or no trouble.

It is significant, indeed, that whereas the Christians started to
produce credal formulations very early in the history of the church, the
earliest Jewish creed, listing ten articles of faith, was formulated by
Saadiah Gaon (882–942), by which time the Jewish religion was more
than 2,500 years old. Not until much later did Maimonides' thirteen
articles become a definitive statement of faith, and there is no evidence
it was ever actually discussed and endorsed by any authoritative body.
The original thirteen-point formulation, given in Maimonides' commentary on the Tenth Chapter of the Mishnah, on the Tractate
Sanhedrin, lists the following articles of faith: the existence of a perfect
Being, the author of all creation; God's unity; his incorporeality; his
pre-existence; worship without intermediary; belief in the truth of
prophecy; the uniqueness of Moses; the Torah in its entirety is divinely
given; the Torah is unchangeable; God is omniscient; He punishes and
rewards in the afterlife; the coming of the Messiah; the resurrection.
This credo, reformulated as the *Ani Ma'amin* ('I believe'), is printed in
the Jewish prayer-book. It has given rise to little controversy. Indeed,
credal formulation has not been an important preoccupation of Jewish
scholars. Judaism is not so much about doctrine – that is taken for
granted – as behaviour; the code matters more than the creed.

The lasting achievement, then, of the sages was to transform the
Torah into a universal, timeless, comprehensive and coherent guide to
every aspect of human conduct. Next to monotheism itself, the Torah
became the essence of the Jewish faith. Even in the first century,
Josephus had been able to write, with only a pardonable degree of
exaggeration, that whereas most races did not know much about their
laws until they found themselves in conflict with them, 'should any one
of our nation be asked about our laws, he will repeat them as readily as
his own name. The result of our thorough education in our laws from
the very dawn of intelligence is that they are, as it were, engraved on
our souls. Hence to break them is rare, and no one can evade
punishment by the excuse of ignorance.'[162] This position was reinforced in the age of the academies and sages, so that knowing God
through the Law became the summation of Judaism. It made Judaism
inward-looking, but it gave it the strength to survive in a hostile world.

The hostility varied, in place and time, but it tended to increase. The
most fortunate Jews, in the Dark Ages, lived in Babylonia, under
exilarchs. These princes, more powerful and secular than the
Palestinian *nasi*, claimed direct Davidic descent from the kings of

Judah, and lived with some ceremony in their palaces. Indeed in Parthian times, the exilarch was in effect a senior official of the state. The rabbis stood in his presence and, if favoured, dined at his table and taught in his courtyard. With the coming of the Sassanid dynasty, early in the third century, and their revival of the national religion of Zoroaster, religious pressure on the Jewish communities increased. The power of the exilarch declined and, as it did so, the influence of the scholars rose. At the academy of Sura in the third century AD there were as many as 1,200 scholars, and these numbers increased during the slack months of the farming year. Having escaped the appalling consequences of the Jewish revolts against Rome, the Babylonian communities produced higher standards of scholarship. In any case, Babylonian Jewry had always regarded itself as the repository of the strictest Jewish tradition, and the purest blood. The Babylonian Talmud asserted: 'All countries are dough compared to the [yeast of the] land of Israel, and Israel is dough compared to Babylonia.'[163] It is true that Babylonia depended on the West for calendrical decisions, and a chain of signal-beacons connected the academies to Jerusalem to receive them. But the Babylonian Talmud is more detailed than its Jerusalem counterpart – neither survives complete – and was for long regarded as more authoritative. It was the main source of instruction for Jews everywhere (Palestine alone excepted) throughout the Middle Ages.

Yet Babylonia was not safe for Jews. There are many accounts of persecutions and martyrs under the Sassanids, but the documentary evidence is scarce and unreliable. In 455, Tazdigar III abolished the Sabbath by decree, and (according to a letter of Rabbi Sherira Gaon) 'the rabbis proclaimed a fast, and the Holy One, blessed be He, sent a crocodile unto him in the night, which swallowed him as he lay on his couch, and the decree was invalidated'. But Sherira, head of the Pumbedita academy, flourished c. 906–1006, and was writing 450 years after the event. Jewish tradition terms Tazdigar's son and heir Firuz the Evil, and accuses him of martyring the exilarch. After he died, there was a period of anarchy, in which the Jewish exilarch Mar Zutra II (c. 496–520) with 400 warriors succeeded in setting up an independent state, with a capital at Mahoza; but after seven years, its immorality led to a Persian victory, and the exilarch was beheaded and crucified. There was another outbreak of persecution in 579–80. But some Persian monarchs favoured the Jews and it is significant that when the Persians invaded Palestine and occupied Jerusalem in 624, the local Jews received them warmly.[164]

Nor is this surprising, for in Palestine and the western diaspora the position of the Jews was much harder. In 313 the Emperor Constantine had become a Christian catechumen and ended state persecution. There followed a brief period of general toleration. From the 340s, however, Christianity began to assume some of the characteristics of a state church. The first edicts against pagan worship date from this time. There was a brief pagan reaction under the Emperor Julian in the 360s, followed by a harsh and systematic campaign to eradicate paganism altogether. Christianity was now a mass religion. In the eastern Mediterranean it was often a mob religion too. Popular religious leaders held vast torchlight meetings, at which angry slogans were shouted: 'To the gallows with the Iscariot!', 'Ibas has corrupted the true doctrine of Cyril!', 'Down with the Judophile!' These mobs were initially raised to threaten participants in church councils. But they were easily set to work smashing idols and burning pagan temples. It was only a matter of time before they turned on the Jews too. Christianity became the norm throughout the Roman empire in the late fourth century and paganism began to disappear. As it did so, the Jews became conspicuous – a large, well-organized, comparatively wealthy minority, well educated and highly religious, rejecting Christianity not out of ignorance but from obstinacy. They became, for Christianity, a 'problem', to be 'solved'. They were unpopular with the mob, which believed that Jews had helped the authorities when the emperors persecuted Christians. They had greeted with relief the pagan revival under Julian, who is known in Jewish tradition not as the Apostate but as 'Julian the Hellene'. During the 380s, under the Emperor Theodosius I, religious uniformity became the official policy of the empire, and a mass of statutes and regulations began to rain down on heretics, pagans and nonconformists of all kinds. At the same time, Christian mob attacks on synagogues became common. This was contrary to the public policy of the empire, since the Jews were a valuable and respectable element in society, who gave consistent support to duly constituted authority. In 388, a Christian mob, instigated by the local bishop, burned down the synagogue at Callinicum on the Euphrates. Theodosius I decided to make this a test-case and ordered it rebuilt at Christian expense. He was hotly denounced by the most influential of all the Christian prelates, Bishop Ambrose of Milan. He warned Theodosius in a letter that the royal order was highly damaging to the church's prestige: 'What is more important,' he asked, 'the parade of discipline or the cause of religion? The maintenance of civil law is secondary to religious interest.' He preached a sermon in front of the emperor putting this argument, and the royal command was shamefacedly withdrawn.[165]

and refused Wine
Communion!

During the late-fourth and fifth centuries, Jews living in Christian societies had most of their communal rights and all their privileges withdrawn. They were excluded from state office and the army. Proselytism and intermarriage with Christians was punishable by death. It was never the aim of responsible Christian leaders to extirpate Judaism by force. St Augustine (354–430), the most influential of all the Latin theologians, argued that the Jews, by their mere existence, were part of God's design, since they were witnesses to the truth of Christianity, their failure and humiliation symbolizing the triumph of church over synagogue. The policy of the church, therefore, was to allow small Jewish communities to survive in conditions of degradation and impotence. The Greek church, however, inheriting the whole corpus of pagan Hellenistic anti-Semitism, was more emotionally hostile. Early in the fifth century, the leading Greek theologian John Chrysostom (354–407) delivered eight 'Sermons Against the Jews' at Antioch, and these became the pattern for anti-Jewish tirades, making the fullest possible use (and misuse) of key passages in the gospels of St Matthew and John. Thus a specifically Christian anti-Semitism, presenting the Jews as murderers of Christ, was grafted on to the seething mass of pagan smears and rumours, and Jewish communities were now at risk in every Christian city.

In Palestine, from the early decades of the fourth century, Jerusalem and the other sites associated with Jesus were Christianized, and churches and monasteries established. Small Jewish communities survived, especially in Galilee, where the Talmud of the West was completed around the time of St Jerome (342–420), who established his own private monastic circle in Jerusalem and testified to the poverty and misery of the Jews. Shortly after his death, a band of Syrian monks under the fanatic Barsauma conducted a series of pogroms against Jewish Palestine, burning synagogues and entire villages. During the Dark Ages, indeed, Palestine became increasingly impoverished and depopulated as a result of religious conflict. Pelagianism, Arianism and later the Monophysite controversies divided the Christians themselves. Each tendency persecuted the other with ferocious zeal when it captured state power. In the fourth century, the Samaritans enjoyed a revival: at least eight new synagogues were built at this time. But their increase attracted the hostile attention of the Byzantine authorities. In 438 the Emperor Theodosius II applied the anti-Jewish statutes to them. Some forty-five years later they staged a rebellion, massacred Christian communities and burned churches. Byzantine armies put them down, and in the repression they lost their ancient sanctuary on Mount Gerizim, which became a basilica of the Blessed Virgin. Under the Emperor Justinian (527–65), a ruler of still stricter orthodoxy, who allowed citizenship only to the baptized, and hounded even Christians if they would not submit to the decisions of the Council of Chalcedon – as well as everyone else – the Samaritans rose again. The vengeance which followed was so bloody that they were virtually destroyed as a nation and a faith. The Jews lay low at this time and certainly gave the Samaritans no help. But in the first half of the seventh century, the Emperors Phocas and Heraclius, under pressure from monkish fanatics, who warned them their empire would be destroyed by the circumcised, tried to impose baptism on the Jews by force.

The Byzantine empire, enfeebled by its multitudinous religious disputes, invited invasion. It came first in 611 when the Persians broke into Palestine, taking Jerusalem three years later after a twenty-day siege. The Jews were accused of assisting them. But if, as the Christians alleged, the Persians had given, in return, a promise to restore the city to the Jews, they certainly did not keep their word. In any case, Heraclius retook the city in 629 and a massacre of Jews followed. But this was the last act of Greek power in Palestine. The same year, Mohammed completed the conquest of Mecca. The Byzantines were decisively defeated at the battle of the Yarmuk in 636, and within four years the Moslems occupied all Palestine and most of Syria too. Chalcedonians and Monophysites, Nestorians and Copts, Seleucians and Armenians, Latins and Greeks, Samaritans and Jews, were all collectively submerged beneath the flood of Islam.

Like Christianity, Islam was originally a heterodox movement within Judaism which diverged to the point where it became a separate religion, and then rapidly developed its own dynamic and characteristics. The Jewish presence in Arabia is very ancient. In the south, in what is now Yemen, Jewish trading interests date back to the first century BC, but in the north or Hijaz, it goes back very much further. One Arab historical legend says that Jewish settlement in Medina occurred under King David, and another puts it back to Moses. Babylonian inscriptions discovered in 1956 suggest that Jewish religious communities were introduced into the Hijaz in the sixth century BC, and they may have been there even before.[166] But the first definite confirmation, in the form of Jewish names in tomb inscriptions and graffiti, does not go back further than the first century BC. At all events, during the early Christian era, Judaism spread in north Arabia and some tribes became wholly Jewish. There is evidence that Jewish poets flourished in the region of Medina in the fourth century AD, and it is even possible that a Jewish-ruled state existed there at this time. According to Arab sources, about twenty tribes in and around Medina were Jewish.

These settled oasis tribes were traders as much as pastoralists, and Islam was from the start a semi-urban trader's religion rather than a desert one. But the desert was important, because Jews living on its fringes, or moving to it to escape the corruptions of city life, such as the Nazarites, had always practised a more rigorous form of Judaism and, in particular, had been uncompromising in their monotheism. That was what attracted Mohammed. The influence of Christianity, which would not have been strictly monotheistic in his eyes, was very slight, at any rate at this early stage. What he seems to have wished to do was to destroy the polytheistic paganism of the oasis culture by giving the Arabs Jewish ethical monotheism in a language they could understand and in terms adapted to their ways. He accepted the Jewish God and their prophets, the idea of fixed law embodied in scripture – the Koran being an Arabic substitute for the Bible – and the addition of an Oral Law applied in religious courts. Like the Jews, the Moslems were originally reluctant to commit Oral Law to writing. Like the Jews, they eventually did so. Like the Jews, they developed the practice of submitting points of law to their rabbis or muftis, soliciting a *responsum*, and the earliest *responsa* seem to have consciously adopted a Judaic formula. Like the Jews, the Moslems accepted strict and elaborate codes covering diet, ritual purity and cleanliness.

Mohammed's development of a separate religion began when he realized that the Jews of Medina were not prepared to accept his arbitrarily contrived Arab version of Judaism. Had Mohammed possessed the skill and patience to work out an Arab halakhah, the result might have been different. But it is unlikely. One of the strongest characteristics of Judaism is the willingness of Jewish communities to exist in distant areas without the need for acculturalization. At all events, Mohammed was rebuffed, and he thereafter gave a deliberate new thrust to Islamic monotheism. He altered the nature of the Sabbath and changed it to Friday. He changed the orientation of prayers from Jerusalem to Mecca. He redated the principal feast. Most important of all, he declared that most of the Jewish dietary laws were simply a punishment for their past misdeeds, and so abolished them, though he retained the prohibitions on pork, blood and carcasses, and some of the slaughtering rules. All these changes made it quite impossible to bring about a merging of Jewish and Islamic communities, however much they might agree on ethical or dogmatic fundamentals; but, in addition, Islam soon developed a dogmatic dynamism of its own, and theological debate – leading to violent sectarianism – soon began to play a central role in Islam, as in Christianity.

Above all, Islam quickly created a theory and practice of forcible conversion, as the Jews had done in the time of Joshua, David and the Hasmoneans, but which rabbinic Judaism had implicitly and conclusively renounced. It spread with astonishing speed, to engulf the Near East, the whole of the southern Mediterranean, Spain and vast areas of Asia. By the early eighth century, the Jewish communities, which still retained precarious footholds in the Greek and Latin worlds, found themselves cocooned in a vast Islamic theocracy, which they had in a sense spawned and renounced, and which now held the key to their very survival. But, by now, they had developed their own life-support system, the Talmud, and its unique formula for self-government – the cathedocracy.

PART THREE

Cathedocracy

In the year 1168 an exceptionally observant Jewish traveller from Spain – probably a gem-merchant – visited the great Byzantine capital city of Constantinople. We know virtually nothing about Benjamin of Tudela save that he wrote a *Book of Travels* about his extensive journeys around the northern Mediterranean and the Middle East in the years 1159–72. It is the most sensible, óbjective and reliable of all travel books written during the Middle Ages, was published as early as 1556, thereafter translated into almost all European languages, and became a primary source-book for scholars of the period.[1]

Benjamin made careful notes on the conditions of Jewish communities wherever he stopped, but he seems to have spent more time in Constantinople than anywhere else, and his description of this great city, then by far the largest in the world, is particularly full. He found that there were about 2,500 Jews there, divided into two distinct communities. The majority, 2,000, were Jews in the rabbinical tradition, who accepted the Mishnah, the Talmud and the whole multi-layered superstructure of commentary. The remaining 500 were Karaites, who followed the Pentateuch alone, rejecting the Oral Law and everything which flowed from it. They had organized themselves as a distinct body since the eighth century and throughout the diaspora they were regarded by rabbinic Jews with such hostility that, says Benjamin, a high fence divided the two sections of the Jewish quarter.

Benjamin wrote that the Jews were 'craftsmen in silk' and merchants of all kinds. They included 'many rich men'. But none was allowed by law to ride a horse, 'except for Rabbi Solomon the Egyptian, who is the King's doctor. Through him, the Jews find much relief in their oppression – for they live under heavy oppressions.' Under the Justinian code, and subsequent statutes, the Jews of Byzantium, unlike pagans and heretics, enjoyed legal status. In theory at least, Jewish synagogues were legally protected places of worship.

The state also recognized Jewish courts of law, and its magistrates enforced their decisions between Jews. Jews who went about their lawful business were supposed to be safe, since the law specifically forbade anti-Semitic acts and stated that 'the Jew is not to be trampled upon for being Jewish and not to suffer contumely for his religion . . . the law forbids private revenge'.[2] None the less, the Jews were second-class citizens; scarcely citizens at all, in fact. They lost their right to serve in government posts completely in 425, though they were forced to serve as decurions on city councils, as this cost money. The Jews were not allowed to build any new synagogues. They had to shift the date of their Passover so that it always took place after the Christian Easter. It was an offence for Jews to insist that their scriptures be read in Hebrew even in their own communities. The law made it as easy as possible to convert Jews, though the baptismal formula contained a statement by each Jewish convert that he had not been induced by fear or hope of gain. Any Jew caught molesting a convert was burned alive, and a converted Jew who reverted to his faith was treated as a heretic.[3]

Yet Benjamin suggests that popular hostility towards the Jews was as much occupational as religious: 'Most of the hatred towards them comes because of the tanners who pour out their dirty water outside their houses and thus defile the Jewish quarter. For this the Greeks hate the Jews, whether good or bad, and hold them under a heavy yoke. They strike them in the streets and give them hard employment.' All the same, concluded Benjamin, 'the Jews are rich, kind and charitable. They observe the commandments of the scriptures and cheerfully bear the yoke of their oppression.'[4]

Benjamin of Tudela travelled through north-eastern Spain, Barcelona, Provence, and then by way of Marseilles, Gerona and Pisa to Rome. He visited Salerno, Amalfi and other south Italian towns, then crossed via Corfu to Greece, and, after seeing Constantinople, passed through the Aegean to Cyprus, then via Antioch into Palestine, and through Aleppo and Mosul into Babylonia and Persia. He visited Cairo and Alexandria, returning to Spain via Sicily. He noted Jewish conditions and occupations carefully, and though he describes one Jewish agricultural colony at Crisa on Mount Parnassus, the picture he gives is of an overwhelmingly urban people – glassworkers in Aleppo, silkweavers in Thebes, tanners in Constantinople, dyers in Brindisi, merchants and dealers everywhere.

Some Jews had always been town-dwellers, but in the Dark Ages they became almost exclusively so. Their European settlements, nearly all in towns, were very ancient. The First Book of Maccabees gives a list of Jewish colonies scattered through the Mediterranean. As the historian Cecil Roth put it, culturally the Jews could be termed the first Europeans.[5] In the early Roman empire, there were distinctive Jewish communities as far north as Lyons, Bonn and Cologne, and as far west as Cadiz and Toledo. During the Dark Ages, they spread further north and east – into the Baltic and Poland, and down into the Ukraine. Yet though the Jews were widely scattered, they were not numerous. From being about eight million at the time of Christ, including 10 per cent of the Roman empire, they had fallen by the tenth century to between one million and one and a half million. Of course the population of all the former Roman territories fell during this period, but Jewish losses were proportionately much higher than the population as a whole. Under Tiberius, for instance, there were 50,000 to 60,000 Jews in Rome alone, out of a total population of one million, plus forty other Jewish settlements in Italy. In the late empire, the number of Italian Jews collapsed, and even by 1638 there were no more than 25,000 in total, only 0.2 per cent of the population. These losses were only partly due to general economic and demographic factors. In all areas, and at all periods, Jews were being assimilated and blending into the surrounding populace.[6]

Yet the social importance of the Jews, especially in Dark Age Europe, was much greater than their tiny numbers suggest. Wherever towns survived, or urban communities sprang up, Jews would sooner or later establish themselves. The near destruction of Palestinian Jewry in the second century AD turned the survivors of Jewish rural communities into marginal town-dwellers. After the Arab conquest in the seventh century, the large Jewish agricultural communities in Babylonia were progressively wrecked by high taxation, so that there too the Jews drifted into towns and became craftsmen, tradesmen and dealers. Everywhere these urban Jews, the vast majority literate and numerate, managed to settle, unless penal laws or physical violence made it impossible.

Indeed in Europe, the Jews played a critically important role in Dark Age urban life. The evidence is hard to come by but much can be gleaned from the *responsa* literature. In many ways the Jews were the only real link between the cities of Roman antiquity and the emerging town communes of the early Middle Ages – indeed, it has been argued that the very word commune is a translation of the Hebrew *kahal*.[7] The Jews carried with them certain basic skills: the ability to compute exchange-rates, to write a business letter and, perhaps even more important, the ability to get it delivered along their wide-spun family and religious networks. Despite its many inconvenient prohibitions, their religion was undoubtedly a help to them in their economic life. The ancient Israelite religion had always supplied a strong motivation to work hard. As it matured into Judaism, the stress on work became greater. With the rise of rabbinic Judaism after 70 AD, its economic impact increased. Historians have frequently noticed, at different periods and in diverse societies, that the weakening of clericalism tends to strengthen economic dynamism. During the second century AD, clericalism virtually disappeared from Jewish societies. The Temple priests, the Sadducees, the teeming servitors of a state-supported religion all vanished. The rabbis, who replaced the clerics, were not a parasitic caste. It is true that some scholars were supported by the community, but even scholars were encouraged to acquire a trade. Rabbis as a whole were specifically enjoined to do so. Indeed rabbis were often the most assiduous and efficient traders. The routes by which they communicated their decisions and *responsa* were trading routes too. Rabbinical Judaism was a gospel of work because it demanded that Jews make the fullest possible use of God's gifts. It required the fit and able to be industrious and fruitful not least so they could fulfil their philanthropic duties. Its intellectual approach pushed in the same direction. Economic progress is the product of rationalization. Rabbinical Judaism is essentially a method whereby ancient laws are adapted to modern and differing conditions by a process of rationalization. The Jews were the first great rationalizers in world history. This had all kinds of consequences as we shall see, but one of its earliest, in a worldly sense, was to turn Jews into methodical, problem-solving businessmen. A great deal of Jewish legal scholarship in the Dark and Middle Ages was devoted to making business dealings fair, honest and efficient.

One of the great problems was usury, or rather lending money at interest. This was a problem the Jews had created for themselves, and for the two great religions which spring from Judaism. Most early religious systems in the ancient Near East, and the secular codes arising from them, did not forbid usury. These societies regarded inanimate matter as alive, like plants, animals and people, and capable of reproducing itself. Hence if you lent 'food money', or monetary tokens of any kind, it was legitimate to charge interest.[8] Food money in the shape of olives, dates, seeds or animals was lent out as early as c. 5000 BC, if not earlier. Cuneiform documents show that loans for fixed amounts in the form of bills of exchange were known from at least the time of Hammurabi – the usual creditors being temples and royal officials. Babylonian cuneiform records indicate interest-rates of 10–25 per cent for silver, 20–35 per cent for cereals. Among the

Mesopotamians, Hittites, Phoenicians and Egyptians, interest was legal and often fixed by the state. But the Jews took a different view of the matter. Exodus 22:25 laid down: 'If thou lend money to any of my people that is poor by thee, thou shalt not be to him as an usurer, neither shalt thou lay upon him usury.' This is evidently a very early text. If Jewish law had been drawn up during the more sophisticated times of the kingdom, interest would not have been forbidden. But the Torah was the Torah, valid for eternity. The Exodus text was reinforced by Leviticus 25:36: 'Take thou no usury of [thy brother], or increase'; and clarified by Deuteronomy 23:24: 'Unto a stranger thou mayest lend upon usury; but unto thy brother thou shalt not lend upon usury.'

The Jews were thus burdened with a religious law which forbade them to lend at interest among themselves, but permitted it towards strangers. The provision seems to have been designed to protect and keep together a poor community whose chief aim was collective survival. Lending therefore came under philanthropy – but you were not obliged to be charitable towards those you did not know or care for. Interest was thus synonymous with hostility. As a settled community in Palestine, of course, the Jews needed to borrow money from each other like anyone else. The Biblical record shows that the law was constantly evaded.[9] The papyri from the Jewish community in Elephantine tell the same tale. Yet the religious authorities tried to enforce the law strictly. They laid down that not only the principals to a usurious transaction but any accessory committed a sin. Concealed interest was wrong too. Rent-free premises supplied by the borrowers, gifts, useful information – all these were termed 'the dust of interest' and banned; talmudic rulings show amazing efforts over the years to block loopholes created by cunning usurers or desperate would-be borrowers.[10]

At the same time, the talmudic casuists tried hard to make possible fair business dealings which in their view did not violate the Torah. These included an increased price for repayment, business partnerships which paid the lender a salary, or gave him a share of the profits, or devices which allowed a lender to lend money to a non-Jew who in turn lent it to a Jew. But Jewish courts which detected a clear interest-transaction could fine the creditor; debts which included capital and interest were declared unenforceable, and moneylenders as such were forbidden to bear witness in court and threatened with hell.[11]

However, the more strictly and intelligently the law was enforced and obeyed, the more calamitous it was for the Jews in their relations with the rest of the world. For, in a situation where the Jews were small, scattered communities in a gentile universe, it not merely permitted Jews to serve as moneylenders to non-Jews but in a sense positively encouraged them to do so. It is true that some Jewish authorities recognized this danger and fought against it. Philo, who understood perfectly well why a primitive law-code differentiated between brothers and strangers, argued that the prohibition of usury extended to anyone of the same nation and citizenship, irrespective of religion.[12] One ruling said that if possible interest-free loans should be made to Jews and gentiles alike, though the Jews should have priority. Another praised a man who would not take interest from a foreigner. A third disapproved of charging foreigners interest and said it was lawful only when a Jew could live in no other way.[13]

On the other hand, some authorities stressed the difference between Jews and non-Jews. A midrash on the Deuteronomy text, probably written by the nationalistic Rabbi Akiva, seemed to say that Jews were obliged to charge interest to foreigners. The fourteenth-century French Jew Levi ben Gershom agreed: it was a positive commandment to burden the gentile with interest 'because one should not benefit an idolator . . . and cause him as much damage as possible without deviating from righteousness'; others took this line. But the most common justification was economic necessity:

If we nowadays allow interest to be taken from non-Jews it is because there is no end of the yoke and the burden kings and ministers impose upon us, and everything we take is the minimum for our subsistence; and anyhow we are condemned to live in the midst of the nations and cannot earn our living in any other manner except by money dealings with them; therefore the taking of interest is not to be prohibited.[14]

This was the most dangerous argument of all because financial oppression of Jews tended to occur in areas where they were most disliked, and if Jews reacted by concentrating on moneylending to gentiles, the unpopularity – and so, of course, the pressure – would increase. Thus the Jews became an element in a vicious circle. The Christians, on the basis of the Biblical rulings, condemned interest-taking absolutely, and from 1179 those who practised it were excommunicated. But the Christians also imposed the harshest financial burdens on the Jews. The Jews reacted by engaging in the one business where Christian laws actually discriminated in their favour, and so became identified with the hated trade of moneylending. Rabbi Joseph Colon, who knew both France and Italy in the second half of the fifteenth century, wrote that the Jews of both countries hardly engaged in any other profession.[15]

In the Arab–Moslem territories, which in the early Middle Ages included most of Spain, all of North Africa, and the Near East south of Anatolia, the Jewish condition was easier as a rule. Islamic law to non-Moslems was based on the arrangements Mohammed made with the Jewish tribes of the Hijaz. When they refused to acknowledge his prophetic mission, he applied the principle of what he called the *jihad*. This divides the world into the *dar al-Islam*, the peaceful territory of Islam, where the law reigns, and the *dar al-Harb*, the 'territory of war', controlled temporarily by non-Moslems. The *jihad* is the necessary and permanent state of war waged against the *dar al-Harb*, which can only end when the entire world submits to Islam. Mohammed waged *jihad* against the Jews of Medina, beat them, decapitated their menfolk (save one, who converted) in the public square, and divided their women, children, animals and property among his followers. Other Jewish tribes were treated rather more leniently, but at Mohammed's discretion, since God gave him absolute rights over the infidel, rather as Yahweh permitted Joshua to deal with Canaanite cities as he saw fit. Mohammed, however, sometimes found it politic to make a treaty, or *dhimma*, with his beaten foes, under which he spared their lives and permitted them to continue to cultivate their oases, provided they gave him half the proceeds. The *dhimma* eventually took a more sophisticated form, the *dhimmi*, or one who submitted, receiving the right to his life, the practice of his religion, even protection, in return for special taxes – the *kharaj* or land-tax to the ruler, the *jizya* or poll-tax, higher commercial and travel taxes than the believers in the population, and special taxes at the ruler's pleasure. Moreover, the status of the *dhimmi* was always at risk, since the *dhimma* merely suspended the conqueror's natural right to kill the conquered and confiscate his property; hence it could be revoked unilaterally whenever the Moslem ruler wished.[16]

In theory, then, the status of Jewish *dhimmi* under Moslem rule was worse than under the Christians, since their right to practise their religion, and even their right to live, might be arbitrarily removed at any time. In practice, however, the Arab warriors who conquered half the civilized world so rapidly in the seventh and eighth centuries had no wish to exterminate literate and industrious Jewish communities who provided them with reliable tax incomes and served them in innumerable ways. Jews, along with Christian *dhimmis*, constituted a large proportion of the administrative intelligentsia of the vast new Arab territories. The Arab Moslems were slow to develop any religious animus against the Jews. In Moslem eyes, the Jews had sinned by rejecting Mohammed's claims, but they had not crucified him.

Jewish monotheism was as pure as Islam's. The Jews had no offensive dogmas. Their laws on diet and cleanliness were in many ways similar. There is, then, very little anti-Jewish polemic in Islamic religious writing. Nor had the Arabs inherited the vast pagan–Greek corpus of anti-Semitism, on which to superimpose their own variety. Finally, Judaism, unlike Christianity, never constituted a political and military threat to Islam, as did the Byzantine East and later the Latin West. For all these reasons the Jews found it easier to live and prosper in Islamic territories. Sometimes they flourished. In Iraq, in addition to the great academies, the Jews constituted a wealthy quarter of the new city of Baghdad which the Abbasid dynasty founded in 762 as their capital. The Jews provided court doctors and officials. They learned spoken and written Arabic, first as a demotic trading device, then as a language of scholarship, even sacred commentary. The Jewish masses spoke Arabic, as they had once learned to speak Aramaic, though some knowledge of Hebrew was treasured in almost all Jewish families.

Throughout the Arab world, the Jews were traders. From the eighth to the early eleventh century, Islam constituted the main international economy and the Jews supplied one of its chief networks. From the East they imported silks, spices and other scarce goods. From the West they brought back pagan slaves, taken by Christians and called 'Canaanites' by the Jews, who were sold in Islam: in 825 Archbishop Agobard of Lyons claimed that the slave trade was run by Jews. Both Moslem sources and Jewish *responsa* show that, at this time, Jewish merchants were operating in India and China, where most of the luxuries originated. From the tenth century, especially in Baghdad, the Jews served as bankers to Moslem courts. They accepted deposits from Jewish traders, then lent large sums to the caliph. Granted the vulnerability of the Jewish *dhimmis*, this was a risky trade. There was no shame in a Moslem sovereign repudiating his debts or even decapitating his creditors – as sometimes happened – but it was more convenient to keep the bankers in being. Some of the profits from the banks went to support the academies, which the heads of the banking houses quietly manipulated behind the scenes. Jews were very influential at court. Their exilarch was honoured by the Arabs, who addressed him as 'Our Lord, the Son of David'. When Benjamin of Tudela came to Baghdad in 1170, he found, he said, 40,000 Jews living there in security, with twenty-eight synagogues and ten *yeshivot* or places of study.

Another centre of Jewish prosperity was Kairouan in Tunisia, founded in 670 and capital of the Aghlabid, Fatimid and Zirid dynasties in succession. The city may originally have been settled by the transfer of Jewish, as well as Christian–Copt, families from Egypt, for throughout the Dark and early Middle Ages Jewish tradesmen and merchants made by far the most efficient urban colonists in both the Mediterranean area and north and west Europe. In the eighth century, an academy was founded there by disgruntled scholars from Babylonia, and for the next 250 years Kairouan was one of the great centres of Jewish scholarship. It was also an important link in East–West trade, and here again successful Jewish merchants made a rich academic life possible. Jews also supplied the court with doctors, astronomers and officials.

From the eighth to the eleventh centuries, however, the most successful area of Jewish settlement was Spain. Jewish communities had prospered here under the Roman empire and to some extent under the Byzantine rule, but under the Visigoth kings a church–state policy of systematic anti-Semitism was pursued. A succession of royal ecclesiastical councils at Toledo, brushing aside orthodox Christian policy, either decreed the forcible baptism of the Jews or forbade circumcision, Jewish rites and observance of the Sabbath and festivals. Throughout the seventh century, Jews were flogged, executed, had their property confiscated, were subjected to ruinous taxes, forbidden to trade and, at times, dragged to the baptismal font. Many were obliged to accept Christianity but continued privately to observe the Jewish laws. Thus the secret Jew, later called the *marrano*, emerged into history – the source of endless anxiety for Spain, for Spanish Christianity, and for Spanish Judaism.[17]

Hence when the Moslems invaded Spain in 711, the Jews helped them to overrun it, often garrisoning captured cities behind the advancing Arab armies. This happened in Córdoba, Granada, Toledo and Seville, where large and wealthy Jewish communities were soon established. Indeed later Arab geographers refer to Granada, as well as Lucena and Tarragona, as 'Jewish cities'. Córdoba became the capital of the Ummayid dynasty, who made themselves caliphs, and treated the Jews with extraordinary favour and tolerance. Here, as in Baghdad and Kairouan, the Jews were not only craftsmen and traders but doctors. During the reign of the great Ummayid caliph Abd al-Rahman III (912–61), his Jewish court doctor, Hisdai ibn Shaprut, brought to the city Jewish scholars, philosophers, poets and scientists, and made it the leading centre of Jewish culture in the world. There were substantial and well-to-do Jewish communities in no fewer than forty-four towns in Ummayid Spain, many with their own *yeshiva*. The rapport the educated Jewish community established with the liberal caliphs recalled the age of Cyrus and brought to Spanish Jewry a gracious, productive and satisfying way of life the Jews were not, perhaps, to find anywhere else until the nineteenth century.

But it was not without menace. The dynamic of Islamic politics was the conflict of the great religious dynasties exacerbated by doctrinal disputes over rigour and purity. The richer and more liberal a Moslem dynasty, the more vulnerable it became to the envy and fanaticism of a fundamentalist sect. If it fell, the Jews under its aegis were immediately exposed to the evil logic of their *dhimmi* status. The primitive Berber Moslems took Córdoba in 1013. The Ummayids disappeared. Prominent Jews were assassinated. At Granada there was a general massacre of Jews. The Christian armies were pushing southwards, and under pressure from them the Moslems put their trust in fierce and zealous warriors rather than leisured patrons of culture. In the closing decades of the eleventh century, another Berber dynasty, the Almo-ravids, became dominant in southern Spain. They were violent and unpredictable. They threatened the large and rich Jewish community of Lucena with forcible conversion, then settled for a huge ransom. The Jews were adroit at turning away Moslems by judicious bribes and negotiations. They had much to offer each successive wave of conquerors in terms of financial, medical and diplomatic skills. They served the new masters as tax-farmers and advisers, as well as doctors. But from this time onwards, Jews were sometimes safer in Spain under Christian rulers. It was the same story in Asia Minor, where the Byzantines might offer Jewish communities more security than they could find as *dhimmis*.

Early in the twelfth century a new wave of Moslem fundamentalism arose in the Atlas Mountains, creating a dynasty of zealots, the Almohads. Their aim was to stamp out Islamic corruption and back-sliding. But in the process they extinguished Christian communities which had existed in north-west Africa for nearly a millennium. Jews too were given a choice between conversion and death. The Almohads carried their fanaticism into Spain from the year 1146. Synagogues and *yeshivot* were shut down. As under the Visigoth Christians, Jews converted at sword-point often practised their religion secretly and were distrusted by the Moslems. They were forced to wear a special blue tunic with absurdly wide sleeves and, instead of a turban, a long blue cap in the shape of a donkey's packsaddle. If they were spared this garb, and a special sign of infamy called the *shikla*, their clothes, though normal in cut, had to be yellow in colour. They were forbidden to trade except on a small scale. The splendid Jewish settlements of southern Spain did not survive this persecution, at least in any of their old dignity and grandeur. Many Jews fled north into Christian territory. Others moved into Africa in search of more tolerant Moslem rulers.

Among the refugees was a young and brilliant scholar called Moses ben Maimon, better known as Maimonides or to Jews as Rambam from the acronym Rabbi Moses ben Maimon. He was born in Córdoba on 30 March 1135, the son of a scholar. When the Almohads took the city he was just thirteen, a prodigy already possessed of astonishing learning. He and his family wandered in Spain, possibly in Provence also, and finally settled in Fez in 1160. Five years later, a revival of forced conversion led them to move again, first by sea to Acre, from whence Maimonides made a tour of the Holy Places, then to Egypt, where they settled in Fustat, the Old City of Cairo. There Maimonides gradually acquired a world-wide reputation both as a doctor and as a scholar–philosopher. He was recognized as head of the Fustat community in 1177, was appointed court physician in 1185 and became, in the words of one Moslem chronicler, 'very great in wisdom, learning and rank'. His scholarly output was of immense variety and impressive both in quantity and quality. He was supported by his trading brother, David, who dealt chiefly in jewels, and after David's death he traded on his own account or lived by his medical fees. When he died on 13 December 1204, his remains were, on his instructions, taken to Tiberias, where his grave is still a place of pilgrimage for pious Jews.

Maimonides is worth examining in detail not only because of his intrinsic importance but because no one illustrates better the paramount importance of scholarship in medieval Jewish society. He was both the archetype and the greatest of the cathedrocrats. Ruling and knowledge were intimately associated in rabbinical Judaism. Of course by knowledge was meant, essentially, knowledge of the Torah. The Torah was not just a book about God. It pre-existed creation, in the same way as God did. In fact, it was the blueprint of creation.[18] Rabbi Akiva thought it was 'the instrument of creation', as though God read out of it like a magician reading from his book. Simeon ben Lakish said it preceded the world by 2,000 years while Elizer ben Yose taught that it had lain in God's bosom for 974 generations before God used it to create the universe. Some sages believed it had been offered simultaneously to seventy different nations in seventy languages, but all had refused. Israel alone had accepted it. Hence it was in a peculiar sense not just the Law and religion but the wisdom of Israel and the key to the ruling of Jews. Philo called it the ideal law of the philosophers, as Moses was the ideal lawgiver. Torah, he wrote in his book on Moses, was 'stamped with the seals of nature' and 'the most perfect picture of the cosmic polity'.[19] It followed that the greater the knowledge of Torah, the greater the right to rule, especially over Jews.

Ideally, then, every public personality ought to be a distinguished scholar, and every scholar should help to rule. The Jews never took the view – beloved of the Anglo-Saxon mind – that intellectual capacity, a passion for books and reading, somehow debilitated a man for office. On the contrary. Nor did they see Torah scholarship, as outsiders tended to do, as dry, academic, remote from real life. They saw it as promoting precisely the kind of wisdom needed to rule men, while also inculcating the virtues of humility and piety which prevented the corruptions of power. They quoted Proverbs: 'Counsel is mine, and sound wisdom: I am understanding; I have strength.'[20]

The problem, as Jews saw it, was how to combine study with the exercise of government. When, during the Hadrian persecution, the sages of Lydda met to debate the most pressing problems facing their imperilled community, one of those at the head of their list was: 'Is studying more important or doing?' After hearing arguments they voted unanimously for Rabbi Akiva's view that study must come first since 'studying leads to doing'. In terms of spiritual merit, acquiring wisdom through study and exercising it to serve communal needs were ruled equally deserving. But the sages said that if a widow or an orphan came to a sage for advice, and he replied that he was too busy studying to give it, God would be angry and say, 'I impute to you as if you had destroyed the world.' A scholar who buried his nose in his book was accused of 'causing the destruction of the world' – because the Jews believed that the world without applied wisdom would fall to pieces. A Levite might retire from active life at fifty and do nothing but study, but a leading scholar had to be available till death. Philo wrote earnestly of the conflicting claims of study and public service. His life was a case in point because, in addition to his prolific writings, he had to serve as a communal leader and went on at least one embassy to Rome. Such a noted scholar, especially one with his wide reputation, had an endless stream of callers seeking advice. Fortunately, Philo could serve the duties of ruling with his brother, one of the richest men in the diaspora, whom Josephus refers to as Alabarch.[21]

The notion of two brothers helping each other to resolve the conflicting claims of study and commentary, on the one hand, and judicial administration and other public duties on the other, is one reason why the Jewish cathedocracy was usually a family affair. Scholastic dynasties sprang originally from scribal lines and were already a feature of Jewish life in the second century BC. In some

Jewish societies they lasted until the First World War – and even beyond it.

In Babylonia, the exilarch had to come from the family of David, but all the men of importance in the academies and *yeshivot* were chosen from an acknowledged group of academic families. The phrase, 'not of the scholarly families, being of the merchants', was dismissive – even though the merchant's cash kept the academies going. In Babylonia, the *gaon* or head of each academy came from one of six families, and in Palestine he had to be descended from Hillel, Ezra the Scribe, or David himself. An outsider of colossal learning could be accepted, but this was rare. Within the hierarchical grades of the academy, too, birth was usually decisive. By origin, of course, the major or ecumenical academies were not so much places where the young were instructed, as councils – the term *yeshivah* is the Hebrew version of *synhedrion* or Sanhedrin. In fact, during the early Middle Ages they were still called 'Grand Sanhedrin' in official Torah documents. The Palestine academy also referred to itself as 'The Righteous Corporation'. They were places where scholars sat together to produce authoritative rulings – academy, parliament, supreme court in one.

A scholar from one of the Babylonian academies, writing in Egypt just before Maimonides' time, described the hierarchy of learning as follows. The ordinary Jewish literate masses learned the five books of Moses and the prayer-book, which also contained material on the Oral Law, the Sabbath and feasts. Scholars in addition must have mastered the rest of the Bible as well as 'ordinances' and codified law. The doctors knew all this, plus the Mishnah, the Talmud and the commentaries. A scholar could give a sermon, write an expository epistle and serve as an assistant judge. But only a doctor, with the title of Member of the Academy, understood the sources of Law and the literature expounding them, and could deliver a learned judgment.[22]

Doctors and senior scholars constituted the academy. In Babylonia, the governing triumvirate was the *gaon*, the president of the court, who acted as his deputy, and the scribe, who wrote down the judgments. The body of the academy sat facing the *gaon*, in seven rows. Each row had ten places, and the most distinguished scholar in each row was called the *rosh ha-seder*, head of the row. Every member of the academy had a fixed seat in order of precedence, which was originally determined by birth. But he could be promoted or demoted, according to performance, and his stipend varied accordingly. For most of them, however, belonging to the academy was not a full-time job. They served the community as officials, or earned their living by crafts and trade. The full academy gathered twice a year for a month each, at the end of summer and the end of winter. The plenary session, or *kallah*, which took place in the early spring, discussed and pronounced rulings on questions sent from abroad, so that the answers could be carried off by merchants who set out immediately after Passover. Both plenaries also included teaching sessions, at which the *gaon* himself expounded sections of the Talmud to 2,000 squatting students, his interpreter or *turgeman* (a term which survives as dragoman) acting as his loudspeaker. There were various grades of teachers, the lowest being the 'repeaters', often blind from birth, who had been trained to repeat by heart immense passages of the scriptures with the exact cantillation, or punctuation-pauses and stresses. A doctor puzzled by a disputed text might summon a repeater to sing it out correctly. A great deal of this public learning was by heart, conducted in noisy choruses. This was the method pursued by Moslem universities, such as Cairo's al-Azhar, until a generation ago. Until recently, indeed, Jewish schoolboys in Morocco could recite by heart lengthy legal rulings in a mixture of Hebrew and Aramaic, and even today Yemeni Jews possess an oral repetitive tradition which has enabled them to conserve the exact pronunciation of the ancient text, long since lost by European Jews.[23]

The Babylonian academies, with their hereditary ranks of carefully graded sages, had absorbed much of the atmosphere and obsequious ceremonial of the oriental court. They took their cue from the exilarch, who was, as it were, the executive arm of the academies. The Hebrew chronicler Joseph ben Isaac Sambari (1640–1703), quoting a tenth-century tradition, has this description of the *nasi*:

He has extensive dominion over all the Jewish communities by authority of the Commander of the Faithful. Jews and gentiles alike rise before him and greet him. Whoever does not rise before him receives one hundred lashes, for so the caliph has ordered. Whenever he goes to have an audience with the caliph, he is accompanied by Jewish and Moslem horsemen who ride in front calling out in Arabic, 'Make way for Our Lord, the Son of David'. He himself is mounted, and wears an embroidered silk robe and a large turban. From it hangs a white scarf with a chain on it. When he gets to the caliph's court, the royal eunuchs come forth to greet him and run ahead of him until he reaches the throne-room. A servant precedes the *nasi* carrying a purse of gold which he distributes in honour of the caliph. Before the caliph, the *nasi* prostrates himself, then stands, to show he is humble as a slave. Then the caliph makes a sign to his eunuchs to seat the *nasi* on the chair closest to him on the left side and solicits his petition. When the *nasi* presents his petition he again stands, blesses the caliph, and departs. He levies on the merchants a fixed annual tax, as well as the gifts they bring him from the ends of the earth. This is the custom they follow in Babylonia.[24]

The academic *gaons* and their senior doctors demanded similar treatment. They were addressed with sonorous titles and gave elaborate blessings and curses. They formed a hereditary sacral–academic nobility, not unlike the mandarins in China.

In the Dark Ages, this Babylonian cathedocracy was also a hereditary judiciary, the final court of appeal for the entire diaspora. Strictly speaking it had no physical power of enforcement – no army, none but a local police. But it had the power of excommunication, an impressive, even terrifying, ceremony, which went back at least to the age of Ezra. It had the authority of its learning too. In practice, however, the power of the Babylonian cathedocrats lasted only so long as the vast Moslem empire stuck together. As the territorial sway of the Baghdad caliph contracted, so did theirs. Local centres of authoritative scholarship sprang up in Spain and North Africa around emigrant scholars from the old academies. Around 1060, for instance, Cairo became a halakhic centre, thanks to the arrival of Nahrai ben Nissim from Kairouan and Judah ha-Kohen ben Joseph, the famous Rav. In the next generation their authority went to a scholar from Spain, Isaac ben Samuel, 'in whose hands', according to a contemporary document, 'authority over all of Egypt reposes'. Such men usually claimed gaonic descent from one of the great academies. They were often, in addition, successful traders, or related to such. But a leading academic family did not retain its prestige, however rich it might be, unless it could produce a regular quota of distinguished scholars. For in practice a Jewish community could not govern itself unless it had the benefit of regular halakhic rulings which were accepted as authoritative precisely because they came from men of unchallengeable learning. In short, as one historian has put it, to acquire authority, family mattered and commercial success was useful, but scholarship was essential.[25]

Maimonides had all three. In one of his works, his commentary on the Mishnah, he listed seven generations of his forefathers. Most Jews could do the same, and the practice has been preserved to this day in many Yemeni Jewish families, even very poor ones. The point of these memorial lists was to display the academic ancestors, and they usually began with a scholar of distinction. Women were not listed, but their genealogies were, if distinguished enough. Thus in the case of Maimonides' father-in-law, his mother's lineage was listed back through fourteen generations, while only six of his father's was given, albeit quite impressive. Fame could be won in various ways, but scholarship was the talisman. The faith the Jews had in learning was unshakeable. A notation survives from Maimonides' time: 'This document must be correct, for the father of its writer was the son of the daughter of the head of the *yeshivah*.'[26] Maimonides himself could be quite content with his lineage: those seven generations had included four important scholar–judges.

He also came from a family able to sustain itself, and support its scholar-members, by skilful trading. As a rule, our knowledge of individual Jews and even of whole Jewish societies, from the second century AD to early modern times, is fragmentary. The Jews had stopped writing history, and their disturbed, wandering and often persecuted existence meant that few documents survived. As it happens, however, we know a lot about Maimonides and his background in twelfth-century Egyptian Jewry. All synagogues contained a room called a genizah. This room was used to store old ritual objects and prayer-books which were no longer usable but which, under Jewish law, could not be destroyed because they contained God's name. In some cases these semi-sacred dumps also contained masses of documents, including secular ones. Damp and rot made them unreadable in a generation or two. But Egypt, with its amazingly dry climate, is famous among scholars for its propensity to preserve fragments of paper and papyrus going back to the first millennium BC and beyond. At Fustat, Maimonides worshipped and taught at the Ezra Synagogue, built in 882 on the ruins of a Coptic church sold to the Jews. Its genizah was in the attic, and there vast quantities of medieval documents remained virtually undisturbed until the end of the nineteenth century, when the great Jewish scholar Solomon Schechter began their systematic recovery. About 100,000 pages went to the Cambridge University Library, and another 100,000 pages or more are deposited in academic centres across the world. The information they reveal is almost inexhaustible. The great scholar S. D. Goitein has already used them to brilliant effect to recreate the eleventh- and twelfth-century society which formed the background to Maimonides' work and ideas.[27]

The Cairo genizah contains at least 1,200 complete business letters, which show that Egyptian Jews, including Maimonides' younger brother David, travelled immense distances and handled a remarkable variety of products. Dyes were a Jewish trading speciality, but they also concentrated on textiles, medicaments, precious stones and metals, and perfumes. The immediate trading area was Upper and Lower Egypt, the Palestine coast and Damascus in Syria. One big Fustat trader, Moses ben Jacob, who dealt in dried fruit, paper, oil, herbs and coins, ranged this region so frequently he was known as 'the Commuter'. But a note in the handwriting of Maimonides' son

Abraham shows that Fustat traders went as far as Malaysia, and he also handled the case of a man who died in Sumatra. The scale too could be impressive: the great eleventh-century merchant Joseph ibn Awkal handled one shipment of 180 bales, and his network allowed him to act as official agent of the two big Babylonian academies, carrying their rulings throughout the Jewish world. Thus a small Jewish community in the Indies could keep in touch, even if a decision took a long time – Cairo to Sumatra was four months.[28]

David Maimonides was on such a long trip when he perished. A letter from him to his elder brother survives, recounting various misfortunes in Upper Egypt, from whence he was travelling direct to the Red Sea to take ship to India. After that: silence. Maimonides wrote:

The greatest misfortune that has befallen me during my entire life, worse than anything else, was the death of the saint (may his memory be blest), who drowned on the Indian Sea, carrying much money belonging to me, to him and to others, and leaving me with a little daughter and his widow. On the day I received that terrible news I fell ill and remained in bed about a year, suffering from a sore boil, fever and depression, and was almost given up. About eight years have since passed but I am still mourning and unable to accept consolation. And how should I console myself? He grew up at my knee, he was my brother, my student, he traded in the markets and earned and I could safely sit at home. He was well versed in the Talmud and the Bible, and knew [Hebrew] grammar well, and my joy in life was to look at him. . . . Whenever I see his handwriting or one of his letters my heart turns upside down and all my grief returns again. In short, 'I shall go down to the nether world to my son in mourning.'[29]

This letter is very characteristic, in its warmth of heart and melancholy. We can dismiss Maimonides' assertion that he spent a year in bed. He was prone to stress his ailments and physical weaknesses, but he was in fact a hyperactive man with a prodigious output of work. We do not know what this greatest of medieval Jews looked like: the portrait used for the first volume of his collected works published in 1744 – though endlessly reproduced since – is pure invention. But his letters and books, and the material found in the genizah, tell us a good deal about him. He was part of the great twelfth-century pre-Renaissance which marked the first real emergence from the Dark Ages and which affected Jewry as well as the Arabic world and Christian Europe. He was cosmopolitan. He wrote in Arabic but he was familiar with other tongues and usually answered his correspondents in their own language. All his life he was an omnivorous reader. He claims in one letter to have read every known treatise on astronomy, and in another that there is nothing in idolatry with which he is not familiar.[30]

Maimonides' capacity to absorb masses of difficult material, sacred and secular, was developed very early in life. So was his determination to re-present it to the Jewish world in orderly and rational form. He was not yet sixteen when he finished his *Treatise on Logic*. Then, in 1158, followed his astronomical *Treatise on the Calendar*. When he was twenty-two he began his first major work, his *Commentary on the Mishna*, completing it at Fustat in 1168. This was the equivalent of the *summae* of the Christian schoolmen and included a vast amount of secular material, on animals, plants, flowers and natural history, as well as human psychology. Much of it was written when he and his family were trying to find a safe place to live: 'I was driven from one end of the world to the other,' he notes, '. . . God knows that I have explained some chapters whilst on my wanderings, and others on board ship.'[31] Thereafter he turned to the major task of codifying talmudic law, the *Mishneh Torah*, in fourteen volumes, which took him ten years and was finished in 1180. By this time the death of David had forced him to take up the practice of medicine. He was also an active judge, and in due course became head of the Egyptian Jewish community, though never with the official title of *nagid*. A great many people from all over the Jewish world consulted him by letter, and over 400 of his Hebrew *responsa* have been printed. But he found time in 1185 to begin his most famous and remarkable work, his three-book *Guide of the Perplexed*, explaining the fundamental theology and philosophy of Judaism, which he finished in about 1190.

Maimonides took his medical career with great seriousness, and in the non-Jewish world it was his chief claim to fame. He wrote extensively on diet, drugs and treatment: ten of his medical works survive and there may be more. He also lectured on physiology and therapeutics, as well as Judaic religion and law. He doctored Saladin's vizier, Al-Fadi al-Baisami, who paid him an annual salary, and later Saladin's son, who became sultan in 1198. He was invited, but declined, to become court doctor to 'the Frankish King' (either Richard Lionheart of England or Amalric King of Jerusalem). The Arabic sources make it clear that he was regarded as one of the world's leading doctors, with a particular skill in treating psychosomatic cases. An Arabic verse circulated: 'Galen's medicine is only for the body, but that of [Maimonides] is for both body and soul.'[32]

He led a life of heroic industry and public service, for he visited patients in the big public hospitals as well as receiving them at home. To his favourite pupil, Joseph ibn Aknin, he wrote:

I have acquired a high reputation among the great, such as the chief kadi, the emirs, the house of Al-Fadr and other city nobles, who do not pay much. The ordinary people find it too far to come and see me in Fustat, so I have to spend my days visiting the sick in Cairo and when I get home I am too tired to pursue my studies in the medical books – you know the amount of time a conscientious man needs in our art to check his sources, so that he can be sure all his statements can be supported by argument and proper authority.

To another correspondent, Samuel ibn Tibbon, he wrote in 1199:

I dwell in Fustat and the sultan in Cairo itself and the distance between the two places is a double Sabbath-day journey [i.e. 1.5 miles]. My duties to the sultan are heavy. I must visit him early every morning. If he feels ill, or any of his children or harem are sick, I do not leave Cairo but spend the greater part of the day in the palace. If some of the court officials are ill I am there the whole day ... even if there is nothing, I do not get back to Fustat until afternoon. Then I am tired and hungry and find the courtyard of my house full of people, high and low, gentiles, theologians and judges, waiting for my return. I dismount, wash my hands and beg them to wait while I eat, my only meal of the twenty-four hours. Then I attend to the patients. They are queueing up until nightfall, sometimes till 2 a.m. I talk to them lying on my back because I am weak. When night falls I am sometimes too weary to speak. So no Israelites can have a private talk with me except on the Sabbath. Then they all come to me after the services, and I advise them what to do during the coming week. Afterwards, they study a little till noon, then depart. Some of them come back and study again until the evening prayers. This is my routine.[33]

The year after this was written, Maimonides found it impossible to continue visiting the sultan in person, instead issuing written instructions to his physicians. But he continued to hold his medical, judicial and theological court until his death in 1204, in his seventieth year.

Maimonides' life was devoted wholeheartedly to the service of the Jewish community and, to a more limited extent, to the human community as a whole. This was in accord with the central social tenet of Judaism. Yet helping the Fustat community – or even the wider gentile community of Cairo – was not enough. Maimonides was conscious of possessing great intellectual powers; and, equally important, the energy and concentration needed to put those powers to huge productive use. The Jews had been created to leaven the dough of humanity, to enlighten the gentiles. They did not have state power, or military force, or wide territories. But they had brains. The intellect, and the reasoning process, were their weapons. The scholar thus had outstanding status in their society, and so peculiar responsibilities; the leading scholar had the most exacting duties it was possible to imagine

– he must take the lead in turning a savage and irrational world into a reasonable one, conforming to the divine and perfect intellect.

The Jewish rationalization process had begun by the introduction of monotheism and by linking it to ethics. This was primarily the work of Moses. It was typical of Maimonides that he not only gave Moses a unique role – he was the only prophet, he argued, who had communicated directly with God – but saw him as a great intellectual ordering force, creating law out of chaos. Clearly, it was the continuing function of the Jews to push forward the frontiers of reason, always adding more territory to God's kingdom of the mind. Philo, who was a precursor of Maimonides in many ways, saw the object of Jewish scholarship in the same way. It was a protective shield for the Jews in the first place – for they were the 'race of suppliants' who interceded with God on behalf of humanity – and in the second it was the means whereby a terrifyingly irrational world could be civilized. Philo took a sombre view of the unreformed human condition. He had lived through an appalling pogrom in Alexandria, which he described in his historical works, *In Flaccum* and the fragmentary *Legatio in Gaium*. Lack of reason could turn men into monsters, worse than animals. Anti-Semitism was a kind of paradigm of human evil because it was not only irrational in itself but a rejection of God, the epitome of folly. But Jewish intellectuals, by their writings, could fight folly. That was why, in his *De Vita Mosis*, he tried to present Jewish rationality to a gentile readership and why, in his *Legum Allegoriarum*, he sought to rationalize, by the use of allegory, some of the more bizarre elements of the Pentateuch for Jewish readers.[34]

Maimonides stood half-way between Philo and the modern world. Like Philo, he had no illusions about humanity in its godless, irrational state. He had no direct knowledge of Christian persecution, but he had bitter, first-hand experience of Islamic savagery, and even in his tranquil haven of Fustat, his correspondents – in the Yemen, for instance – reminded him that atrocities were constantly being perpetrated against Jews; his letter to the Yemenis reflects his profound contempt for Islam as an answer to the world's unreason.[35] Unlike Philo, he did not have the benefit of the broad panoply of Greek rationalism available in the great Alexandrine library. But Aristotelianism was being spread again by Arab intermediaries – Avicenna (980–1035) and Maimonides' older Spanish contemporary, Averroes (1126–98). Moreover, he was the beneficiary of a thousand years of Judaic commentary, much of which was another form of rationalism.

Then too, Maimonides was a rationalist by temperament. Like

Philo, his writings exude caution, moderation and distrust of enthusiasm. He was always anxious to avoid rows, and *odium theologicum* most of all: 'Even when men insult me I do not mind, but answer politely with friendly words, or remain silent.' He was a little vain but certainly not proud: 'I do not maintain that I never make mistakes. On the contrary, when I discover one, or if I am convicted of error by others, I am ready to change anything in my writings, in my ways and even in my nature.' In a famous letter of reply to the comments on his *Mishneh Torah* by the scholars of southern France, he admits errors, says he has already made some corrections and will insert others, and insists they are quite right to challenge his work: 'Do not humble yourselves. You may not be my teachers but you are my equals and friends and all your questions were worth raising.'[36] He was an elitist, of course. He said he would rather please one intelligent man than ten thousand fools. But he was also tolerant: he thought all pious men would be saved, whatever their faith. He was wonderfully urbane, irenic, calm, judicious. Above all, he was a scientist, looking for truth, confident it would prevail in the end.

Maimonides had a clear view of what the truthful and rational – and therefore divine – society would be like. It would not consist of physical or material satisfaction. Ultimate happiness lay in the immortal existence of the human intellect contemplating God.[37] In the last chapter of the *Mishneh Torah* he describes messianic society: 'His rule will be firmly established and then the wise will be free for the study of the Law and its wisdom and in those days there will be no hunger or war, no hatred or rivalry . . . and no toil on earth but for the knowledge of the Lord alone.' The guarantor of perfect society is divine law. A good state, by definition, is one under the rule of law; the ideal state is under divine law.[38]

That, of course, had to await the coming of the Messiah, and Maimonides, being the cautious scientist, was the last man to raise eschatological visions. In the meantime, however, good societies could be produced by law. In his *Guide of the Perplexed*, he sets out his intensely rationalistic view of the Torah: 'The law as a whole aims at two things – the welfare of the soul and the welfare of the body.' The first consists in developing the human intellect, the second in improving men's political relations with each other. The Law does this by setting down true opinions, which raise the intellect, and by producing norms to govern human behaviour. The two interact. The more stable and peaceful we make our society, the more time and energy men have for improving their minds, so that in turn they have the intellectual capacity to effect further social improvements. So it goes on – a virtuous circle, instead of the vicious circle of societies which have no law.[39] One is tempted to guess that Maimonides saw the age of the Messiah coming, not out of the blue, in a sudden clap of thunder, but as a result of progressing, unmiraculous improvements in human rationality.

Hence, the best way to improve the human condition in general – and ensure the survival of the Jewish vanguard in particular – was to spread knowledge of the Law, because the Law stood for reason and progress. Maimonides was an elitist but he thought in terms of an ever-expanding elite. Every man could be a scholar according to his lights. This was not impossible in an intensely bookish society. It was a Jewish axiom: 'One should sell all he possesses and buy books, for as the sages put it, "He who increases books, increases wisdom." ' A man who lent his books, particularly to the poor, earned merit with God. 'If a man has two sons, one of whom dislikes lending his books, while the other is eager, a man should leave all his library to the second, even if he be younger,' wrote one of Maimonides' contemporaries, Judah of Regensburg. Pious Jews saw heaven as a vast library, with the Archangel Metatron as the librarian: the books in the shelves there pressed themselves together to make room for a newcomer. Maimonides disapproved of this anthropomorphic nonsense but he agreed with the notion of the world to come being an abstract version of a heavenly academy. He would have agreed, too, with Judah's practical injunctions that a man should never kneel on a big folio to fasten its clasps, or use pens as bookmarks, or employ the books themselves as missiles or instruments to chastise scholars – and with his splendid maxim: 'A man should have regard to the honour of his books.'[40] Temperate in all things save learning, Maimonides had a passion for books, which he wished all Jews to share.

'All Jews' included women and working men. Maimonides said that it was not required of a woman to study, but she earned merit if she did so. Every man should study according to his capacity: thus, a clever artisan could devote three hours to his trade, leaving nine for the Torah – 'three in studying the written law, three in the Oral Law, and three reflecting on how to deduce one rule from another'. This little analysis, which he termed 'the beginning of learning', gives some indication of his standards of industry.[41]

However, it was little use bidding the Jewish people to study without at the same time doing everything possible to make that study productive. Convinced as he was that reason and the Law were the only real defences a Jew had, and the only means whereby the world could become a more civilized place, Maimonides was also painfully aware that the Law itself, after a thousand years of legal accretions and unco-ordinated commentary, was in an appalling state of confusion and penetrated by grossly irrational elements. His lifework then was twofold: to reduce the Law to order, and to re-present it on a thoroughly rational basis. To achieve the first, he wrote his Mishnah commentary, which for the first time made clear the underlying principles of mishnaic legislation, and he codified talmudic law, with the object, as he put it, to make it quick and easy to find a decision 'in the sea of the Torah'. Maimonides observed: 'You either write a commentary or a code – each is a distinct task in itself.' Being an intellectual giant, he did both. He wrote with a sense of urgency, against a background (as he saw it) of danger to the Jews: 'In times of persecution like the present,' he said, 'people lack the mental equanimity to devote themselves to intricate studies, and nearly every one finds serious difficulties in deriving a clear-cut decision from the works of the earlier codifiers, where the arrangement is as un-systematic as in the Talmud itself. Still fewer persons are able to deduce the law directly from the talmudic sources.' What he produced was clear, orderly, concise and uncluttered by endless source-listing. It was not, as he hoped, definitive. Like every other attempt to say the last word on the Law, it merely detonated another huge avalanche of tomes – in 1893, a list (itself incomplete) was compiled of 220 major commentaries on Maimonides' Code.[42] But it was highly effective: a Spanish contemporary said judges opposed the work precisely because it enabled laymen to check their decisions. That was exactly what Maimonides wanted – for the Law, the sword and armour of the Jews, to become the working property of all of them.

At every stage in the code and commentary, he was rationalizing. But in addition he wrote his *Guide of the Perplexed* to show that Jewish beliefs were not just a set of arbitrary assertions imposed by divine command and rabbinical authority, but could be deduced and proved by reason too. Here he was following in the steps of Saadiah ben Joseph (882–942), the famous and controversial *gaon* of the Sura academy, the first Jewish philosopher since Philo to try to place Judaism on a rational basis. Maimonides did not agree with every-thing in Saadiah Gaon's *Book of Beliefs and Opinions*, but it encouraged him to marry Jewish faith and philosophy. Avicenna and Averroes had performed the same task for Islam and Thomas Aquinas was soon to do it for Christianity. But Maimonides was the greatest rationalist of them all. On the key issue of prophecy, for instance, he used metaphor, analogy and parable to explain the prophets' com-munications with God and their miracles as 'natural'. He had a theory of divine emanations, which the prophets tapped. The so-called angels who helped to produce the vision were the imaginative faculty of the prophet; he used the word cherub to signify the intellect.[43]

However, there was a point at which Maimonides' rationalism stopped. He felt he had to differentiate between Moses and the other prophets. He dismissed them as amphibolous or analogical, but Moses 'did not, like the other prophets, prophesy by means of parables'; he actually spoke to God 'as a presence to another presence, without an intermediary'. He tried to explain away Moses' uniqueness by arguing that the highest possible degree of perfection natural to the human species must be reached in one individual – and Moses was the man. What in effect Maimonides was doing was to reduce the area of irrationality in Judaism but not to eliminate it: he isolated certain core areas of belief which reason could not explain – though he was reluctant to admit it. He would, however, concede that certain issues were almost beyond man's powers of reason. On the apparent conflict between free will and predestination, he quoted Ecclesiastes – 'exceeding deep, who can find it out?'[44] – and in his writings there are passages which favour both absolute freedom of the will to obey or disobey the Law, and strict determinism. He attacked astrologers, for rendering the Law futile. On the other hand, the first of his thirteen principles of faith is: 'God alone performed, performs and will perform all actions.'[45] It is possible to point to other contradictions in his vast body of work though there are surprisingly few of them.

What Maimonides was trying to do was to strengthen the faith by stripping it of superstition and buttressing what remained by reason. But of course in doing so he introduced and popularized a critical approach to its mysteries which would eventually tempt men much further. Reason, once let out of the bottle of pure faith, develops a life and will of its own. Maimonides was a great harbinger of the Jewish future; indeed, of the human future. His *Guide of the Perplexed* continued to shift Jewish minds for centuries – not always in the direction he wished. In a sense, he played the same role in Judaism as Erasmus in Christianity: he laid dangerous eggs which hatched later. To the science of medicine he brought the Judaic doctrine of the oneness of body and soul, mind and matter, which gave him important insights into the sickness of the psyche, thus foreshadowing Freud. To theology he brought a confidence in the compatibility of faith and reason which fitted his own calm and majestic mind but which was in due course to carry Spinoza outside Judaism completely.

There were many learned Jews at the time who feared the direction in which Maimonides was taking Judaism. In Provence, where

Christianity was torn apart by the Albigensian heresy and where the new agency of the Dominican Inquisition was being forged to impose orthodoxy, many rabbis wanted the Judaic authorities to adopt a similar approach. They detested Maimonides' allegorical explanation of the Bible and wanted his books banned. In 1232 the Dominicans, intervening in this internal Jewish dispute, actually burned them. But this, of course, spurred the rationalists into a counter-attack. 'The hearts of the people', wrote the followers of Maimonides, 'cannot be turned away from philosophy and the books devoted to it so long as they have a soul in their bodies . . . they intend to fight for the honour of the Great Rabbi and his books, and will dedicate their money, their offspring and their spirits to his holy doctrines so long as the breath of life is in their nostrils.'[46]

Despite this flourishing of verbal fists, few actual blows were struck. In theory Jewish law was severe on heterodoxy – if two Jews testified they saw a third worshipping an image, he could be sentenced to death – but in practice, being a cathedocracy, not an autocracy, it allowed for varying views over a surprisingly wide area. Even a man declared to be a heretic incurred no physical punishment unless he systematically sought to convert others to his views. Hence rationalism and super-stition continued to coexist in uneasy harmony, sometimes in the same person.

Bearing in mind the misery and fear in which Jews were often forced to live, the persistence of irrationalism was not surprising. Maimo-nides saw intellect and reason as the Jew's best weapons, and they were – for the self-confident elite. For the mass of ordinary Jews, tales of miracles past, hope of those to come, were a surer comfort in time of trouble. Jewish sacred literature catered for both needs, for alongside its intellectually satisfying commentarial method was the sprawling mass of aggadic stories, the *piyyut* or poetry, and endless weird superstitions children learned at their mother's knee. The more the Jews were persecuted and economically depressed, the more they turned to sacred fairy tales. 'At one time', a midrash notes, 'when money was not scarce, people longed to hear Mishnah, halakhah and Talmud. Nowadays money is scarce and, worse, people sicken under their slavery, and all they want to hear are blessings and conso-lation.'[47]

The Jews suffered severely, under both Islam and Christianity. It might be true, as one of Abelard's pupils enviously observed, 'A Jew, however poor, if he has ten sons, will put them all to letters, not for gain as the Christians do, but for the understanding of God's law – and not only his sons but his daughters too.'[48] But the kind of Judaic rationalism Maimonides advocated was really possible only for the upper class, and remained largely its property. As the genizah documents show, the folk religion he detested and denounced flourished under his nose in Fustat. Jews practised both white and black magic. They did fire-tricks, made birds cease to fly, then fly again, conjured up both good and evil spirits in ceremonies which sometimes lasted the entire night, then held fumigation sessions to get rid of them. They went into trances. They held seances. There were abracadabra spells for protection on journeys, ridding a house of lice, making women or men fall in love, or 'swearing in of the angels'. There were even secret manuals, written in Judaeo-Arabic, purporting to guide Jews to the secret tomb-treasures of the ancient Egyptians.[49]

Such an irrational approach to religion was not confined to the Jewish masses, however. It appealed also to the upper classes, among whom it took the form of mysticism. Maimonides' own wife was an emotional believer who came from a long line of pietist–mystics. His son and heir, Abraham, took after his mother rather than his father. Though he seems to have been devoted to his father's memory and zealously defended his views, his own *magnum opus*, a gigantic tome called *The Complete Guide for the Pious*, presents pietism or *hasidut* as a way of life, a counter-science to rationalism.[50] He became known as the *rosh kol ha-hasidim*, the 'head of all the pietists', and attracted letters and disciples from all over the Jewish world. These *dévots* fasted all day and stood in prayer all night. Abraham even admired the Moslem mystics, or *sufis*, and said they were worthier disciples of the prophets of Israel than the Jews of his day.[51] This would have angered his father, who wanted to ban the works of Jewish mystics, let alone Moslem ones.

Unfortunately for the rationalists, mysticism had deep roots in Judaism; indeed, it might be said to have roots in Yahweh-worship. The notion that, in addition to the written law of the Pentateuch given by God to Moses, God had also given him Oral Law was convenient to the religious authorities. But it was also exceedingly dangerous for it led to the belief there was a mass of special knowledge about God, handed down orally and secretly, which only the privileged few were permitted to learn. In the Talmud the word 'kabbalah' simply means 'received [doctrine]' or 'tradition' – the latter part of the Bible, after the Pentateuch and the oral teaching. However, it gradually came to mean esoteric teaching, enabling the privileged few either to make direct communion with God or to acquire knowledge of God through non-rational means. Chapter 8 of Proverbs and Chapter 28 of the Book of Job, which treat by metaphor and analogy of wisdom as a creative living force, giving the key to God and the universe, seem to lend authority to the idea. In later ages, whenever a rationalist Jew tried to stamp on mysticism, he found its exponents could always quote the Bible at him.

Still more so could they quote the Talmud, because by that stage Judaism had picked up a multitude of esoteric elements. Some scholars argue that they were acquired from Persia, during the Exile; others, more plausibly, that they came from Greek gnosticism. Gnosticism, or the lore of secret knowledge-systems, is an extremely insidious parasitic growth, which attaches itself like a poisonous ivy to the healthy trunk of a major religion. In Christianity, the early church fathers had to fight desperately to prevent it from smothering the faith. It attacked Judaism too, especially in the diaspora. Philo, in *De Vita Contemplativa*, wrote of a sect called The Worshippers of God, who had developed the theory of the Torah as a living body, a typically gnostic idea.[52] It penetrated circles in Palestine who were normally most resistant to Greek ideas – the Pharisees, the Essenes, the Qumran sect, and later the tannaim and amoraim. Josephus says the Essenes had a magic literature. Its first real efflorescence was in apocalyptic.

These books, whose real authors concealed their identities behind the names of Enoch, Moses, Noah, Baruch and other great historical figures, were xenophobic, nationalist and inflammatory, as we have seen; they were the angry, bitter refuge of an oppressed people calling down cataracts and hurricanes on their heavily armed enemies. They wrote of angels, devils, hell, heaven, firestorms and the end of time, when Greeks and Romans would be smitten. These texts dealt in secret knowledge, denied to all except the most trustworthy and zealous Jews – it was typical of the fierce Qumran monks that they had the Book of Enoch in both Hebrew and Aramaic – and hidden sources of power, which could be conjured up to overwhelm the *kittim* and other hated opponents of God. Chapter 14 of the Book of Enoch, dealing with the mysteries of the Throne, lying on its chariot – itself suggested by Chapter 1 of Ezekiel – led to the emergence of a whole school of *Merkabah* (chariot) mystics. They unloaded on credulous Jews masses of information about the angels who 'stood before the chariot', the descent of fire from above, and the ascent of the pious soul to the chariot through ecstasy. Unlike Torah-teaching, which was publicly conducted in noisy chanting, chariot-knowledge was imparted covertly, in a whisper, to specially chosen pupils who had to display some specified ethical qualities, possess certain facial characteristics and have palms which satisfied the chiromancers. Expositors of the lore were sometimes surrounded by fire, or a nimbus, or went into trances.

They entered paradise miraculously, like Elijah – one 'looked and died', another 'looked and was smitten', a third 'ascended in peace and descended in peace'.[53] Aspirants to the ecstatic state placed their heads between their knees and recited songs about the Throne of Glory or early sacred poems.

In addition to the practical magic of direct communion with God through mystical states, the esoteric books from the first century onwards poured forth a torrent of information about the deity and paradise. Since the Torah was holy, letters were holy; so were numbers; if the key were found, secret knowledge could be obtained. One key was Psalms 147:5: 'Great is our Lord, and of great power', which was used to give the dimensions of divinity – using the letter–figure code as 236 multiplied by 10,000 celestial leagues to provide the basic measurements of head and limbs, and their secret names. These secret names for God – Adiriron, Zavodiel, Akhtriel, Tazash, Zoharariel, for instance – were important because they formed passwords allowing the celestial doorkeepers to let the ascending soul into the fantastic series of eight palaces which led up to paradise. Eight was a magic number pinched from the Greek gnostics, and the chariot, the power and emanation of God, was the equivalent of the Greek aeon. But twenty-two, the letters of the Hebrew alphabet, was a magic number also, since creation itself was enacted through combinations of Hebrew letters and, when discovered, these codings revealed the secrets of the universe.

The sages were both fascinated and repelled by this egregious superstition. The anthropomorphism of God's bodily measurements went against the basic Judaic teaching that God is non-created and unknowable. The sages advised Jews to keep their eyes firmly fixed on the law and not to probe dangerous mysteries: 'Whosoever ponders on four things it were better for him if he had never been born – what is above, what is below, what is before time, what will be hereafter.' But they then proceeded to do just that themselves; and, being elitists, they tended to fall in with the idea of special knowledge conveyed to the elect: 'The story of creation should not be expounded before two persons, and the chapter on the chariot before even one person, unless he is a sage and already has an independent understanding of the matter.' That was the Talmud; indeed the Talmud and other holy writings contained a good deal of this suspect material.

Hence rationalists like Maimonides were embarrassed, indeed exasperated, by much of what they found in the Talmud. There was, for instance, the *Shi'ur Qoma* or 'Measure of the Divine Body', which interpreted the Song of Solomon as a divine allegory of God's love for

Israel and gives astounding detailed dimensions for God's limbs, as well as their secret names. The Karaites, who rejected talmudic Judaism completely, sneered at this text and used it to attack the rabbis. They claimed that it measured God's face down to the tip of his nose as 5,000 ells. This was an invention; but there was material in the book equally bad. Moslems, too, used it to attack the Jews and justify persecution. One later commentator tried to explain it away by saying the figures were actually the dimensions of the universe. Maimonides' distaste at having to deal with the text can be imagined. At first he took refuge in the phrase: 'It would take a hundred pages to discuss the topic.' Then he crossed it out – the manuscript of his Mishnah commentary in which this occurs survives. Later, he persuaded himself that the whole thing was the work 'of one of the Byzantine preachers, nothing else', and denounced it as a forgery.[54]

The rationalism for which Maimonides stood was, in part, a reaction to the growth of esoteric literature and its penetration of Jewish intellectual life. And rationalism did have some effect. In the twelfth and thirteenth centuries it forced the leading mystics, at any rate those with a claim to intellectual respectability, to refine their literature and corpus of belief, purge it of its magical dross and the gnostic clutter of centuries, and turn it into a coherent system. The higher kabbalah, as we might call it, began to emerge in Provençal France in the second half of the twelfth century. It was drawn from many elements. One was poetry, and especially the poems of the great Spanish lyricist Judah Halevi (1075–1141), whose 800 known poems include 350 *piyyutim*. Halevi was a religious Zionist, an unusual thing to be at that time, and his most famous group of thirty-four lyrics are termed *Poems of Zion*. He thought that life in Spain, however comfortable it might be between bursts of persecution, was slavery compared to the true Jewish existence in Palestine, and he eventually went there. He saw the Jews as a tragic and injured people, and he called his one philosophical work, an apologia for Judaism, a book 'in defence of the despised faith'. It was an attack on Aristotelian rationality as well as Christianity and Islam, and he took the view strongly that, for suffering humanity, and the cruelly treated Jews in particular, deductive reasoning, however desirable in a perfect world, was no substitute for direct experience of God.[55] This was a hard point for even a highly educated, wealthy Jew to answer in time of persecution, and there is no doubt that mysticism appealed more strongly whenever the Christian or Islamic net tightened round the Jews.

The Provençal mystics also drew on neo-Platonism and developed imposing philosophic theories of their own – even Maimonides was forced to admit that some of them were learned. One, Abraham ben David, or Rabad, wrote a scholarly work attacking Maimonides' *Mishneh Torah*. Abraham's son, Isaac the Blind (*c.* 1160–1235), created something approaching a coherent system of kabbalah, based on the ten *sefirot* or attributes of God, and the theory that all creation was, and is, a mere linguistic development, the materialization of divine speech. This uses the neo-Platonist concept of the *logos* (as in the opening of St John's Gospel) but recasts it in terms of Torah study and prayer. From Narbonne, where Isaac lived, mystical kabbalah spread south across the Pyrenees to Gerona, Burgos and Toledo. Its standing was immeasurably improved by the patronage of the great rabbi Moses ben Nahman, known as Nahmanides or Ramban (1194–1270), who became a convert to the system in youth and later rose to be the leading judicial authority in Spain.

Nahmanides produced at least fifty works, mostly Talmud and halakhic commentary, and in his old age he wrote a famous commentary on the Torah. None is specifically kabbalistic but there are throughout hints of the system, especially in the Bible commentary, and the effect was to carry the kabbalah into the mainstream of orthodox Jewish scholarship, above all in Spain. Nahmanides made it possible for the kabbalists to pose as the conservatives, tracing the origin of their ideas back to the Bible and Talmud, and upholding the best and most ancient Jewish traditions. It was the rationalists who were the innovators, bringing to the study of the Torah the pagan ideas of the ancient Greeks. In this respect, the campaign against the works of Maimonides could be described as the last squeak of the anti-Hellenists.

Nahmanides himself never joined the witch-hunt against rationalism – on the contrary, he opposed it – but he made it possible for the kabbalists to escape similar charges of heresy, which in fact would have been much better grounded. For kabbalah not only introduced gnostic concepts which were totally alien to the ethical monotheism of the Bible, it was in a sense a completely different religion: pantheism. Both its cosmogony – its account of how creation was conceived in God's words – and its theory of divine emanations led to the logical deduction that all things contain a divine element. In the 1280s, a leading Spanish kabbalist, Moses ben Shem Tov of Guadalajara, produced a *summa* of kabbalistic lore, the *Sefer-ha-Zohar*, generally known as the *Zohar*, which became the best-known treatise on the subject. Much of this work is explicitly pantheist: it insists repeatedly that God 'is everything' and everything is united in Him, 'as is known to the mystics'. But if God is in everything, and everything is in God, how can God be a single, specific being, non-created and absolutely separate from creation, as orthodox Judaism had always emphatically insisted? There is no answer to this question, except the plain one that *Zohar*-kabbalah is heresy of the most pernicious kind. Yet it is a fact that this kind of mystic pantheism exercises a curious appeal to very clever people whose customary approach to thought is soberly rational. By a remarkable paradox, the current of speculation which was to carry Spinoza out of Judaism brought him to pantheism too, so that he was the end-product both of the rationalism of Maimonides and the anti-rationalism of his opponents.

But that was for the future: in medieval Jewry, with its wide dispersal of religious authority, these rival currents were able to coexist. In a harsh world, the poor looked to superstition and folk religion for comfort; the rich, if they had the strength of mind, to rationalism, if not, to mystic kabbalah. Judaism had too many external enemies to want to risk its internal harmony by imposing a uniformity no one really wanted. Indeed, one can see medieval Judaism as essentially a system designed to hold Jewish communities together in the face of many perils: economic disaster, plague, arbitrary rule, above all the assault of two great imperialist religions.

The state, whether Christian or Islamic, was not as a rule the main enemy. Often, indeed, it was the best friend. The Jews were staunchly loyal to duly constituted authority, for religious reasons and from plain self-interest: they were a minority dependent on the ruler for protection. Geniza documents of 1127–31 show that Jews said regular public prayers for Islamic rulers 200 years before the text surfaced in the Jewish prayer-book. In contrast to Moslem sources of the same period, the geniza reveals no criticism of authority. The rulers responded. They regarded Jews as an exceptionally law-abiding and wealth-producing element in the community. The stronger authority was, the more likely the Jews were to be safe. Trouble came, in both Christian and Moslem lands, during waves of religious enthusiasm, when fundamentalist priests overawed the ruler or, worse still, turned him into a zealous convert.

The Jews could never be sure when these moments would come. They prepared against them. They had renounced resistance by force in the second century, and did not resume it until the twentieth in Palestine. But there were other methods. One was for their ablest members to adopt professions which made them useful to the host communities but also kept them mobile. In Islam this was not usually difficult. Able Jews became doctors. Islamic rulers made daily use of their services; so did humble people if they could, consulting them even for minor complaints such as constipation and diarrhoea, as prescriptions which survive in the geniza show. In Egypt there was a Jewish doctor in every town and often in every village in areas of Jewish settlement. Jewish doctors were popular. They attended the big public hospitals and often had small private ones of their own. They could go anywhere, have access to anybody. So they were nearly always the leaders of the Jewish community. The first family of Egyptian *nagids* were all doctors. Medicine was the profession not only of Maimonides but of his son, probably his grandson, and his great-grandson. The al-Amman family were doctors for eight generations, and in one of them the father and all five sons were in the profession. So, occasionally, were daughters, at any rate as oculists. Judah Halevi was a doctor. So was Nahmanides. These medical families also traded in related products: drugs, opium, medical herbs, perfumes, scientific books. The trading networks thus developed enabled a medical family to switch from one country to another whenever persecution threatened. Jewish doctors were welcome everywhere except in phases of religious frenzy – when, of course, they were frequently accused of poisoning.[56]

Keeping family corporations together was the best Jewish defence. The extended family was far more important than the nuclear family. The genizah sources show that primary loyalty went to fathers, sons, brothers, sisters, not spouses. Letters between brothers and sisters were much commoner than between husbands and wives. A woman's proverb went: 'A husband I can get, children I can bear, but a noble brother – where can I find him?'[57] Wills show that when a man died without children, his estate went to his brother, or the closest member of the 'House of the Father', not the wife, who got only her own dowry. As one will put it, 'the balance of the estate returns to my father's house'.[58]

To keep the family strong, marriage was in effect compulsory for men, and for women of child-bearing age; the genizah documents reveal no word for a spinster. It was a great economic and social strength of Judaism, as opposed to Islam, that it rejected polygamy. The Pentateuch did not actually prohibit it, but Proverbs 31:10–31 appeared to uphold monogamy and it was the rule from post-Exilic times; from the age of Rabbi Gershom (960–1028), bigamy and polygamy were punished by the severest type of excommunication in European Jewry.[59] Bigamy led to excommunication in Egypt too, though in the case of compulsory levirate marriage, Maimonides sanctioned bigamy provided the wives were equally treated – 'one

night with this one, one night with that'.[60] A male became adult at
thirteen, when he could make up a quorum for the services and put on
phylacteries, and from the early thirteenth century this point was marked
by the bar-mitzvah, meaning he had come under the yoke of the
commandments.[61] Then he was married as soon as convenient –
Maimonides was most unusual in not marrying until he was past thirty.

Marriage was a social and business transaction designed to keep
society cohesive, so the contract or *ketubbah* was read out at the
ceremony and it was drawn up, like a partnership agreement, to avoid
disputes or make dissolution uncontentious. Here is a Karaite contract
dated 26 January 1028:

> I, Hezekiah, the bridegroom, will provide her with clothing, roof and food,
> supply her with all her needs and wishes according to my ability and to the
> extent I can afford. I will conduct myself towards her with truth and sincerity,
> with love and affection, I will not grieve and oppress her and will let her have
> food, clothes and marital relations to the extent habitual among Jewish
> men. . . . Sarna the bride heard the words of Hezekiah and agreed to marry
> him and be his wife and companion in purity, holiness and fear of God, to
> listen to his words, to honour and hold him dear, to be his helper and to do in
> his house what a virtuous Jewish woman is expected to do, to conduct herself
> towards him with love and consideration, to be under his rule, and her desire
> will be toward him.[62]

The Bible said 'God . . . hateth putting away' (i.e. divorce),[63] but it
was part of the strength of the extended, as opposed to nuclear, family
system that divorce was easy provided the contract was properly
drawn up. Genizah sources show it was commoner in Egypt than
among European or American Jewish families until the second half of
the twentieth century.[64] In divorce the Mishnah favoured the man: 'A
wife is divorced irrespective of her will, but the husband is divorced
only when he is willing.'[65] Jewish women were of less account in
Moslem Afro-Asia than in Christian Europe, but genizah records hint
that they were often more powerful than their formal rights suggested.
If they were beaten they could go to the courts, and sometimes a
husband had to seek court protection from a dominant wife. Many
letters make it clear that wives handled their husband's business affairs
when he was trading abroad. Women agents and brokers were
common. One woman who figures in the records was in fact
nicknamed 'The Broker', ran a business partnership, got herself
expelled from a synagogue but figured on a public subscription-list,
and died rich.[66]

Women also played a role in the educational system, which was the
real cement of the Jewish world. They had their own all-female classes

– usually taught by blind scholars. Female Bible-teachers were common. A woman might also run a school, though this was rare. But the main educational effort was entrusted to men supported by the community. In fact the Jewish legal definition of a town as opposed to a village was that it had at least ten *batlanim*, 'persons who do not work', foregoing private profit to study on behalf of the community. At the end of the eleventh century there were twenty-nine in Fustat, fourteen in Cairo, including the *rayyis* or head of the Jews (under the Fatimids), the *rabbenu* (master), who was the chief scholar and religious authority, two judges, five *yeshivah* scholars, three *ravs* or masters, six cantors, one teacher and five beadles.[67]

The community revolved around the school–synagogue complex. Cairo–Fustat was regarded as lax, even luxurious. Maimonides, who hated music, disapproved of the singing of *piyyutim* during services but the people loved them and he ruled that it would cause too much bitterness to have them stopped. His son Abraham deplored the use of huge cushions and reclining pillows in synagogue, but here again the popular will prevailed. But even in lax Fustat, there were three services daily and four on the Sabbath.[68] Sabbath and dietary laws were kept in all their rigour. Jewish law was strict, and this caused a constant, though largely unrecorded, leakage into the host communities, but it was the discipline which also kept the Jews together and their heads high. Sabbath (root-verb *shabath*) meant to cease. All work was forbidden, Exodus specifically prohibiting kindling a fire and the Mishnah listing thirty-nine categories of labour used in making it. The Oral Law principle of erecting 'fences round the law', to prevent even accidental breaches, spread the area of prohibition still further. Thus, as you could not break a branch to kindle a fire, you could not ride a horse even if it did not belong to you (animals you owned had to be rested on the Sabbath), since you might have to break a branch to use as a whip. Since Jeremiah 17:21 forbade carrying burdens on the Sabbath, the Mishnah devoted two chapters to the quantitative minimums, and a vast amount of commentary discussed the difference between a private place in which some carrying was allowed, and a public one. Since Exodus 16:29 forbade a man to 'go out of his place on the seventh day', there was a huge volume of commentary on walks.[69]

Paid public officials supervised these prohibitions. They played an even more important role in the dietary laws. As food was part of religion and eating a communion with God, the material had not only to come from a permitted species but a blessing pronounced during the killing, which had to be done in regulated form. Animals and fowl had to have their oesophagus and windpipe cut with a knife run three times over finger and three over nail to ensure it was unblemished and sharp. After slaughter, the meat was examined for signs of disease, especially of the lungs, and then veins containing blood picked out, together with prohibited fat and sinews in the hindpart. The *shohet* or official ritual slaughterer was appointed by the rabbis, and a genizah letter shows they examined him under three heads, religiosity, good conduct and scholarship – a good example, as Goitein has observed, of the tendency of Jewish crafts to ascend into the academic realm.[70] After he had done his work, which included the removal of all blood, a guard ensured it was untouched until ready for cooking, at which point it was soaked in water for thirty minutes and salted for an hour to ensure no blood was left. The guard also supervised milking and cheese-making, which was governed by purity rules. To be kosher, an egg had to be unmarked by blood, have one round, one oval end, and its yolk surrounded by white. As the Bible prohibited seething a kid in its mother's milk, commentators interpreted this as forbidding eating meat and milk foods together, unless each is in a proportion to the other of more than sixty to one. That in turn led to the use of two sets of cooking and serving dishes.[71]

Communal slaughtering thus helped to solidify the Jewish parish. Moreover, though a poor Jew might have to be strict in what he ate, he knew he would never want for food, since he could receive every Friday enough money (or equivalent) to cover fourteen meals for his family. From Temple times, the *kuppah* or collecting box was a pivot around which the Jewish welfare-community revolved, Maimonides stating: 'We have never seen or heard of a Jewish community which does not have a *kuppah*.'[72] There were three trustees, solid citizens, for each *kuppah* and, charity being mandatory in Jewish law, they had power to seize goods from non-contributors. There were carefully graded forms of welfare-provision, each with its own fund and administrators: clothes, schools for the poor, dowries for poor girls, Passover food and wine for the poor, orphans, the aged, the sick, burials of the poor, and prisoners and refugees. The notion of 'from each according to his ability, to each according to his need' was one the Jews adopted before the birth of Christ and always practised even when the community as a whole was distressed. A solvent Jew had to give to the *kuppah* once he had resided in the community a month; to the soup-kitchen fund after three, the clothing fund after six and the burial fund after nine.[73] But as helping the poor was one way of showing gratitude to God, a substitute for the old Temple sacrifices, a pious Jew gave more than the mandatory minimum, and long, elaborately written lists of contributors were hung up in the synagogue at Fustat – for God to see, as well as men. The Jews hated welfare dependence. They quoted the Bible: 'You must help the poor man in proportion to his needs', but added, 'you are not obliged to make him rich.'[74] The Bible, Mishnah, Talmud, the commentaries were full of injunctions to work, to achieve independence. The grace after meals pleaded: 'We beseech you, O God of our fathers, that you cause us not to be in need of the gifts of flesh and blood . . . but make us only dependent on your hand, which is full, open, holy and ample, so that we may not be ashamed.' The sages commanded: 'Flay a carcass in the market-place if necessary, receive thy wages and do not say "I am a great man, and it is beneath my dignity to do such a thing." '[75]

Yet the genizah documents, such as lists of recipients and donors, show that in practice welfare had to be distributed on a large scale. At the time Maimonides arrived in Fustat (c. 1150–60), of 3,300 Jews, 500 were breadwinners and there were 130 households on charity; in the period 1140–1237, there was an average of one relief recipient for every four donors.[76] Poverty was often inescapable. In 1201–2, for instance, famine and plague cut Fustat's population in half, leaving widows and children destitute. The genizah documents show that the *jizya* or poll-tax, the worst aspect of Moslem rule, was the real terror of the poor, enforced with great ferocity and relentlessness, relatives being held responsible for defaulters and travellers being forced to show tax-clearance certificates before leaving.

Always, in the background, there was the menace of anti-Semitism. It is described in the genizah documents by the word *sinuth*, hatred. The worst actual persecution occurred under the fanatical or mad Fatimid caliph al-Hakim, early in the eleventh century, who turned first on the Christians, then on the Jews. Another zealot-ruler was Saladin's nephew al-Malik, who called himself caliph of the Yemen (1196–1201); a letter of August 1198 from the Yemen relates how the Jews were summoned to the ruler's audience-hall and forcibly converted: 'Thus all apostacized. Some of the pious, who [then] defected from Islam, were beheaded.' Parts of Islam were much worse than others for Jews. Morocco was fanatical. So was northern Syria. Anti-*dhimmi* regulations, such as sumptuary laws, were often strictly enforced to gouge a financial settlement out of the Jewish community. A genizah document of 1121 describes decrees in Baghdad forcing Jews to wear:

two yellow badges, one on the headgear and one on the neck. Furthermore, each Jew must hang round his neck a piece of lead weighing [3 grammes] with the word *dhimmi* on it. He also has to wear a belt round his waist. The women have to wear one red and one black shoe and have a small bell on their necks or shoes. . . . The vizier appointed brutal Moslem men to supervise the Jewish males and brutal Moslem women to watch over the females and hurt them with curses and humiliations. . . . The Moslems were mocking the Jews and the mob and the youths were beating them up in all the streets of Baghdad.[77]

During most of this period Egypt was a relatively safe place for Jews, though Alexandria retained its long tradition of anti-Semitism dating from Hellenistic times. The writer of one genizah letter, describing an anti-Semitic outbreak there when a Jewish elder was falsely accused of rape, added: 'anti-Semitism is continually taking on new forms and everyone in the town has become a kind of police inspector over the Jews to express their *sinuth*'.[78] But in Fustat and Cairo, the genizah papers show that Jews, Christians and Moslems lived mingled together and went into common business partnerships. Goitein concludes that the evidence does not support the view that in Egypt, at least, anti-Semitism was endemic or serious. But then Egypt under the Fatimids and Ayyubids was a refuge for persecuted Jews (and others) from all over the world.

If the treatment of the Jews under Islam varied, from place to place and from time to time, it was always bad under Byzantine rule. In Latin Christendom, it was tolerable until the preaching of the First Crusade in 1095; thereafter the position of the Jews deteriorated almost everywhere. As in Islam, the powers-that-be always favoured Jews, other things being equal. They were the best of all urban colonists, had useful trading networks, possessed rare skills, accumulated wealth quickly and were easy to tax. They flourished under the Carolingians. The Emperor Louis the Pious, around 825, gave them a number of charters as inducements to settle. The letters of Agobard of Lyons show that they not only enjoyed imperial protection but were allowed to build synagogues. There was periodic trouble – persecutions in France in 1007, for instance; forced conversions in Mainz in 1012. But on the whole Jewish communities did well and spread, especially throughout the Rhine basin, and from the Lower Rhine to England after 1066. As late as 1084 the ruling Bishop of Speyer gave them a charter of privileges, including a defensive wall round their quarter, as an inducement to settle in his city; and in 1090, the Emperor Henry IV renewed this charter and gave them a new one in Worms.

Yet there was a growing ambivalence in the official attitude to Jews. The secular lords tended to treat the Jews as personal property, to be farmed; not only their incomes but, in case of necessity, their capital too were there to be plundered. The ecclesiastical lords, as the rulers of cities, appreciated the economic value of the Jewish presence; as churchmen they abhorred it. Pope Gregory the Great (reigned 590–604) protected the Jews of Rome; but at the same time he created the ideology of a Christian anti-Judaism which was to lead directly to physical attacks on Jews. What he argued, in effect, was that the Jews were not blind to the claims of Christianity. They knew Jesus was the Messiah, was the son of God. But they had rejected Him, and continued to reject Him because their hearts were corrupt. And it had always been thus – the evidence against the Jews was all there in the Bible, which they had written themselves.[79] Therein, of course, lay a terrible problem for the Jews. One of their greatest gifts was the critical faculty. They had always had it. It was the source of their rationality, one of the factors which brought them to monotheism in the first place, for their critical sense would not allow them to accept the follies of polytheism. But they were not only critical; they were, perhaps above all, self-critical. And they were, or at any rate had been in ancient times, superb historians. They saw the truth, sometimes the ugly truth, about themselves, and they told it in the Bible. Whereas other peoples produced their national epics to endorse and bolster their self-esteem, the Jews wanted to discover what had gone wrong with their history, as well as what had gone right. That is why the Bible is littered with passages in which the Jews are presented as a sinful people, often too wicked or obstinate to accept God's law, though they know it. The Jews, in fact, produced the evidence for their own prosecution.

Christian apologists did not, on the whole, believe that Jews should be punished for the crime of their ancestors in killing Christ. They made a different point. Jewish contemporaries of Jesus had witnessed his miracles, seen the prophecies fulfilled and had refused to acknowledge him because he was poor and humble. That was their sin. But every generation of Jews ever since had shown the same spirit of obstinacy, as in the Bible. They were constantly concealing the truth, tampering with it, or suppressing the evidence. St Jerome accused them of cutting out references to the Trinity in the prophets. There were clues in Ezra and Nehemiah which, said St Justin, they had taken out. The old rabbis who compiled the Talmud knew the truth and even put it in the record in hidden form – that was one reason Christian debaters tried to use it for their arguments. Even the Jewish historian, Josephus, had written the truth about Jesus (it was in fact an obvious interpolation when the manuscript chain was under Christian control), but the Jews set their faces against it. It was not ignorance. It was malice. Here is a comment from the twelfth-century historian Gerald of Wales:

even the testimony of their historian, whose books they have in Hebrew and consider authentic, they will not accept about Christ. But Master Robert, the Prior of St Frideswide at Oxford, whom we have seen and was old and trustworthy . . . was skilled in the scriptures and knew Hebrew. He sent to diverse towns and cities of England in which Jews have dwellings, from whom he collected many Josephuses written in Hebrew . . . and in two of them he found this testimony about Christ written fully and at length, but as if recently scratched out; but in all the rest removed earlier, as if never there. And when this was shown to the Jews of Oxford summoned for that purpose, they were convicted, and confused at this fraudulent malice and bad faith towards Christ.[80]

The tragedy of this Christian line of argument was that it led directly to a new kind of anti-Semitism. That the Jews could *know* the truth of Christianity and still reject it seemed such extraordinary behaviour that it could scarcely be human. Hence the notion that the Jews were quite different to ordinary people, an idea reinforced by their laws about food, slaughtering, cooking and circumcision. There were stories that the Jews had concealed tails, suffered from a bloody flux, had a peculiar smell – which instantly disappeared when they were baptized. This in turn led to reports that Jews served the devil – which explained everything – and communed with him at secret, vicious ceremonies.

An accumulation of anti-Jewish feeling seems to have built up for some time before the preaching of the First Crusade at Clermont-Ferrand in 1095 unleashed it. The wave of crusading fervour had been provoked by countless stories of Christians being ill treated in the Holy Land. The Moslems were the chief villains of these tales, but Jews were often included as treacherous auxiliaries. It was an age of Christian fundamentalism, which produced a reformed papacy and rigorist orders like the Cistercians. Many believed the end of the world and the Second Coming were imminent. Men wanted to win themselves grace and remission of sin urgently. The assembling of a mass of armed men in north-west Europe provided opportunities for all kinds of anti-nomian behaviour and produced a breakdown in normal order. Men sold up to pay their crusading expenses. Or they borrowed money. They expected debts to be cancelled. The Jews, one of the few groups with working capital – ready cash – were in an exposed position. It is worth noting that even fervent crusaders did not attack the Jews in their own neighbourhoods, whose inhabitants they knew to be ordinary people like themselves. But once on the march, they readily turned on the Jews of other cities. Then the Christian townspeople, caught up in the frenzy and the lust for loot, would sometimes join in.

Local rulers were taken by surprise at the sudden fury and lost control.

We have an account of the massacres by the twelfth-century Jewish chronicler Rabbi Solomon ben Samson.[81] They began in Rouen in France and in the spring of 1096 spread to the Rhineland cities. As the crusading host, often no better than a mob, gathered, any Jewish community on its line of march was in jeopardy. The Bishop of Speyer stopped the rioting quickly by using force and hanging the ringleaders: 'For he was a righteous man among the gentiles, and the Ever-Present brought about the merit of our deliverance through him.'[82] The Archbishop of Cologne did the same. But at Mainz the Archbishop had to flee for his own life. The Jews tried to fight but were overcome. The males were massacred or forcibly converted. Children were slaughtered to prevent them being brought up Christians, and the women, holed up in the archbishop's castle, committed mass suicide – over 1,000 perished in all. The ancient, rich and populous Jewish communities of the Rhineland were destroyed, most Jews being killed or dragged to the fonts. Others, dismayed by the sudden, inexplicable hatred of fellow townsmen, scattered. They had learned that protective charters were no more use than (as they put it) 'parchment for covering jars'.

The anti-Semitic ideology and folklore which helped to detonate the first crusader riots proved to be simply the plinth on which a vast superstructure of hostile myth and rumour was built. In 1144 there occurred an ominous incident at Norwich in East Anglia, then the richest and most populous area in England. There had been few if any Jews in Anglo-Saxon England. They came, along with many other Flemish immigrants, in the wake of William the Conqueror's invasion. Half of them settled in London, but Jewish communities sprang up in York, Winchester, Lincoln, Canterbury, Northampton and Oxford. There were no Jewish quarters, but usually two Jewish streets, one for well-to-do Jews, the other for the poor: thus in Oxford, near St Aldates, there was Great Jewry Street and Little Jewry Lane.[83] Jews built themselves good houses, often of stone for security. Indeed at Lincoln two twelfth-century Jews' houses (one perhaps used as a synagogue) survive, among the earliest in England to do so.[84] Norwich, which was settled by Rhineland Jews, did not have a large community: 200 at most, out of a total Jewish population in England which, at its maximum, was not more than 5,000. But its activities have been thoroughly explored by the researches of V. D. Lipman.[85] In Norwich the Jews lived near the market-place and castle (for safety), but were interspersed with Christians. Their chief activity was moneylending on the security of lands and rents. They were also pawnbrokers. Some English Jews were doctors.[86] As in some other towns of the seventeen settled by Jews in England, there was one outstandingly rich family, the Jurnets. They can be traced through five generations. They had business partners in London, travelled, operated on a national scale and handled very large sums. Their big stone house in King Street was set apart from those of the other Jews. They patronized Talmud scholars and some were scholars in their own right.[87]

In 1144 this little community was the centre of an appalling accusation. On 20 March, shortly before Easter and Passover, a boy called William, son of a substantial farmer and apprenticed to a skinner, disappeared. He was last seen going into a Jew's house. Two days later, on the Wednesday of Holy Week, his body was found east of the city in Thorpe Wood, 'dressed in his jacket and shoes with his head shaved and punctured with countless stabs'. Our knowledge of the details comes primarily from a hagiography, *The Life and Miracles of St William of Norwich*, compiled by Thomas of Monmouth, a monk of Norwich Priory, shortly afterwards.[88] According to Thomas, the boy's mother Elvira and a local priest called Godwin accused the Norwich Jews of murder, saying the crime was a re-enactment of Christ's passion. Later, Christian maidservants working in a Jewish house said the boy was seized after synagogue service, gagged, tied with cords, his head pierced with thorns, then bound as if on a cross, his left hand and foot nailed, his side pierced and scalding water poured over his body – they claimed they saw this through a chink in the door. A group of Jews were accused of the sacrilege before an ecclesiastical court. But the local sheriff claimed they were king's property, refused to let them stand trial, and hustled them to safety in Norwich Castle.

At this point the first miracles connected with the boy's body began to take place. Initially the local church authorities, like the secular ones, were hostile to the whole story. But two years later a monk who favoured the cult was appointed Bishop of Norwich and it is significant that his formal election in the priory was made the occasion for an anti-Jewish demonstration. The same year Eleazir, a local Jewish moneylender, was murdered by the servants of one Sir Simon de Nover, who owed him money. Slowly the legend expanded. The ritual murder of a Christ-substitute at Easter fitted the official view that the Jews knew the truth but rejected it. Then it was pointed out that the day the murder was discovered, 22 March, was the second day of the Jewish Passover. For this the Jews, as was well known, made special unleavened bread. One anti-Semitic tale was that all Jews suffered from haemorrhoids ever since they had called out to Pilate, 'His blood be upon us and upon our children!' They had been told by their sages that they could be cured only through 'the blood of Christ' – that is, by embracing Christianity – but they took the advice literally. To get the necessary blood, with which to make their curative Passover bread, they had to kill a Christ-substitute every year. One Theobald of Cambridge, a convert from Judaism, married this tale to the murder of William and alleged that a congress of Jews in Spain picked out by lot, every year, the town where the ritual murder must take place and that in 1144 the lot fell on Norwich.[89] Thus from this one crime flowed two distinct, but intermingled, accusations against the Jews – the ritual murder charge and the blood libel.[90]

This episode was particularly devastating to Jewish security because William, by the very nature of his ritual death, acquired an element of Christ's sanctity and power to work miracles. So they flowed – and each was a further proof of Jewish malice. Canonization, not yet centrally controlled by Rome, was conferred by popular clamour. And, since the body of a saint of this exciting type brought wealth to the church which owned it, by attracting pilgrims, gifts and endowments, accusations of ritual murder tended to be made whenever a child was killed in suspicious circumstances near a settlement of Jews – at Gloucester in 1168, Bury St Edmunds in 1181 and Bristol in 1183. The preaching of a new crusade always brought anti-Semitic sentiment to the boil. The Third Crusade, launched 1189–90, in which England figured largely because Richard the Lionheart led it, whipped up mob fury already aroused by the ritual murder charges. A deputation of wealthy Jews attending Richard's coronation in 1189 was attacked by the crowd, followed by an assault on London's Jewry. With the approach of Easter the next year, pogroms broke out, the most serious being at York, where the wealthy Jewish community was massacred, despite taking refuge in the castle. Norwich, of course, was one victim, a chronicler recording: 'Many of those who were hastening to go to Jerusalem determined first to rise against the Jews. . . . So on 6 February all the Jews who were found in their own houses in Norwich were slaughtered; some had taken refuge in the castle.'[91]

This was another milestone in the destruction of Latin Jewry. The rise of organized heresy in the twelfth century led an increasingly authoritarian and triumphalist papacy to look with suspicion on any non-orthodox form of religious activity, not least on Judaism. The greatest of the medieval centralizers, Innocent III (pope 1198–1216), enacted a series of anti-Jewish decrees at the Fourth Lateran Council,

1216, and gave his sanction to the creation of two preaching orders, the Dominicans and Franciscans, specifically charged with consolidating the orthodox faith in the cities. The Dominicans were further mandated to put down heresy by inquiring into doubtful practices, interrogating and trying suspects, and handing over to the secular power for punishment those found guilty.

As an additional manifestation of Christology, Innocent launched a new cult of the eucharist. This in turn created yet another layer of anti-Semitism. In 1243, near Berlin, the Jews were accused of stealing a consecrated host and using it for their own evil purposes. This practice too fitted into the Christian view that the Jews knew the truth but fought against it. They did indeed believe that the host was Christ's body: that was why they stole it and tortured it, making it relive Christ's sufferings, just as they stole Christian boys and murdered them in fiendish rituals. As with all conspiracy theories, once the first imaginative jump is made, the rest follows with intoxicating logic. After 1243, cases of host-stealing were reported all over Latin Europe. They came to light, according to court cases, because the host in its agony produced miracles: it rose into the air, provoked earthquakes, changed into butterflies which healed cripples, gave forth angels and doves or – most commonly of all – screamed in pain or cried like a child.[92]

No plausible evidence to justify any of these slanders has ever been produced. Some accusations may have been the result of a genuine misunderstanding. For instance, in 1230 Jews were accused of forcibly circumcising a five-year-old boy in Norwich. Jews were imprisoned and fined when the case finally came to court in 1234, and it seems to have provoked a violent attack on Norwich Jews by citizens the following year. Around 1240 several Jews were hanged in connection with this case. The most likely explanation is that members of the same Jewish family were reclaiming the son of a convert.[93] But most charges against Jews were pure inventions, and whenever a genuine ecclesiastical inquiry was held, its findings always exonerated the Jewish community.[94]

The slanders must, of course, be seen against the background of Jewish moneylending. It affected a very wide social spectrum. Evidence from thirteenth-century Perpignan in the south of France shows that villagers formed 65 per cent of the borrowers, though they borrowed only 43 per cent of the total sums; townsmen were 30 and 41 per cent; knights and nobles 2 and 9; clergy 1 and 5 per cent.[95] The pattern in England was much the same. Large religious houses and the higher nobility used the Jews but on a comparatively small scale. The big borrowers in both countries were the needy rural gentry – the class most likely to lead a wave of anti-Semitic activism. A squire with name and prestige but no money, and about to lose his lands, was just the man to whip up a mob. The whole of history teaches that money-lending leads to trouble in rural societies. A Jewish betrothal contract from thirteenth-century England shows that money lent at interest was expected to bring in not less than 12.5 per cent a year.[96] This does not seem much by medieval standards. Unfortunately, as Lipman points out, lenders had very complex transactions among themselves, often forming syndicates, with layers of borrowing; and all activities were complicated by Judaic rulings, efforts to evade them, Christian rulings, and efforts to evade them too. The net effect was to raise the ultimate rate of interest the borrower had to pay and above all to produce a legal situation of such density that accusations of robbery were almost bound to ensue in the event of any dispute. Internal Jewish as well as Christian courts handled these matters. The records show: 'Judas, Jew of Bristol, owes two ounces of gold for an inquisition made in a chapter of the Jews whether a Jew ought to take usury from a Jew'; or again Abraham ben Joshua of York told the 'Justices of the Jews' that 'a Jew may take usury by a Christian hand, and if it seems unjust to his opponent, let him go before the masters of his law in chapter and implead him there, because matters of this sort touching his law ought not to be corrected elsewhere'.[97] A city merchant could understand these things but not a rustic knight.

Kings in theory, and often in practice, stood to benefit enormously from a large and busy Jewish community. In twelfth-century England, the Angevin kings undoubtedly did well out of rich Jewish lenders. There was a special Exchequer of the Jews, which ran chests in each town with a Jewish community. Each chest was run by two Jews and two Christians, who kept a record of all debt-bonds. At headquarters there was one Jewish as well as Christian judges, and a rabbi to advise.[98] The king in effect took a cut of all Jewish business transactions, and he needed to know who owed what Jew which money. When Aaron of Lincoln, the most successful Jewish financier in medieval England, died in 1186, a special exchequer was set up to deal with his estate. By one of those ironies which glitter through all Jewish history, Aaron had financed the vast expansion programme of the ultra-rigorist Cistercian order by lending them the then-colossal sum of 6,400 marks in return for mortgages. The king inherited his debts, though some were resold to his son Elias.[99]

If windfalls like this had occurred more often, the kings of England would certainly have kept the Jewish communities in being. But

Aaron's prosperity antedated the great anti-Semitic outbreaks of the 1190s, which destroyed the community in York and other places.[100] Thereafter it became steadily more difficult for English Jews to make money. The anti-Jewish code of the Lateran Council in 1215 added to their burden. In England the Archbishop of Canterbury, Stephen Langton, one of the architects of Magna Carta, which itself had an anti-Jewish clause, tried to organize a boycott of Jewish business. The Jews were in economic decline in England throughout the thirteenth century. Aaron of York, who told the chronicler Matthew Paris he had paid the king over 30,000 marks, died impoverished in 1268.[101]

Under Edward I, a former crusader and a hammer of the Celts with an insatiable need for cash, the decline accelerated. To some extent the Jews' role as lenders to the great had been taken over by the Knights Templar of Jerusalem and their European Commanderies, the first real Christian bankers. The Jews had been pushed downmarket into small-scale lending, coin-changing and pawnbroking. For Edward, it was no longer profitable enough to milk the Jews systematically; he was tempted to go in for the kill and a quick seizure of their assets. In 1275 he passed an anti-Jewish statute, making usury illegal; the crime was later linked to blasphemy, a yet more serious offence. In 1278 groups of Jews were arrested throughout the country. Many were taken to the Tower of London. One chronicler says 300 were hanged. Their property went to the crown and the sum realized tempted Edward to go further. The next stage was to accuse Jews of habitual coin-clipping. A dozen were hanged in Norwich for this offence. Finally, in the late 1280s, Edward found he needed a large sum in cash to ransom his cousin Charles of Salerno. He confiscated the property of his Gascony Jews, expelling them completely in 1289. The next year, alleging widespread evasion of the law against usury, he threw them out of England too, grabbing all of their assets. The richest Jew in Norwich yielded £300. Jews in eleven different towns produced a total of £9,100, of which eighteen families provided about £6,000. It was a disappointing haul, but by this time the Jewish community had shrunk to only half its maximum size – there were only 2,500 left to expel.[102]

By this time medieval Christian governments saw themselves as confronted with a 'Jewish problem', to which expulsion was a 'final solution'. It had been tried before: in part of the Rhineland in 1012, in France in 1182, in upper Bavaria in 1276. The device worked in England, more or less, because of the Channel barrier, but in Continental Europe, with its thousands of straggling lordships, expulsion was difficult to enforce. None the less, governments were under constant ideological pressure to take anti-Jewish measures.

Innocent III had argued in his Lateran decrees that, because of their unscrupulous use of money power, the Jews had reversed the natural order – the free Christian had become the servant of the Jewish slave – and government must restore nature by imposing disabilities.[103] So governments tried. From the twelfth century onwards, Jews became less useful to princes. Their trading and money-handling skills had been acquired by Christians. The age was a notable one for founding new towns, but the Jews were no longer needed as urban colonists – the Christians could do that for themselves. So authority looked less benignly on the Jewish presence which, thanks to the blood and ritual murder libels, became a source of frequent rioting They also, quite genuinely, began to fear the Jewish contribution to the spread of disturbing ideas. In the later Middle Ages, heresy was often linked to radicalism. Heretics occasionally had contact with learned Jews, who discussed scriptural texts with them and lent them books. The Jews always had books, often ones regarded by authority as subversive. When the church seized them, the Jews would ransom their books, like slaves. When their York community was massacred in 1190, they managed to get their books to Cologne, to be sold to the Jews there.[104]

In theory, the Jews were banned from universities, both by Christian law and by their own. But they congregated in university cities. Students, as always, were in the van of anti-Semitism. At Turin they had the right, on the first fall of snow of the winter, to pelt the Jews with snowballs unless they paid a ransom of twenty-five ducats; at Mantua the 'fine' was sweets and writing-paper, at Padua a fat capon. At Pisa, on the feast of St Catherine, the students put the fattest Jew they could find on the scales and 'fined' the community his weight in sweets. At Bologna the Jews had to provide a student banquet. Where there was a medical school, Jews had to provide corpses, or pay money, and this sometimes led to desecration of Jewish cemeteries.[105] All this indicates that Jews were an accepted, if unpopular, part of the university community. They often taught there. In 1300, for instance, Jacob ben Machir became dean of the Montpellier medical school. In the early fifteenth century, Master Elias Sabot taught medicine at Pavia (and was summoned to England to treat the ailing Henry IV). Converted Jews were prominent on the campus throughout Christendom. Sometimes, as we shall see, converts became scourges of their former co-religionists; more often, especially if forced, they constituted a critical, questing, disturbing element within the intelligentsia. The church was by no means wide of the mark when it identified Jewish influences in the Albigensian movement or the Hussites in fifteenth-century Bohemia. Jews were active in the two forces which finally broke the church's monopoly, the Renaissance and Reformation. They were the fermenting yeast. The populist accusations hurled against Jews in the Middle Ages were all, without exception, fantasy. But the claim that they were intellectually subversive had an element of truth. The point was made by the Viennese–Jewish novelist, Jakob Wasserman, in his famous autobiography, *Mein Weg als Deutscher und Jude*:

> The unfortunate fact is that one cannot dispute the truth that the persecutors, promoted agents and volunteers alike, had something to go on. Every iconoclastic incident, every convulsion, every social challenge has seen, and still sees, Jews in the front line. Wherever a peremptory demand for a clean sweep is made, wherever the idea of governmental metamorphosis is to be translated into action with frenzied zeal, Jews have been and still are the leaders.[106]

The medieval Latin state did not permit them the luxury of leadership, but it could not wholly deny them the role of mentor.

Hence, during the second half of the Middle Ages, churchmen devised instruments to counter what they saw as Jewish subversion. Foremost among them were the friars. Dominicans and Franciscans came to dominate university life in the thirteenth century, and they also captured important bishoprics. They supervised every aspect of Jewish life in Latin countries. They took the view that Augustine's relatively tolerant attitude, whereby the Jews were preserved as 'witnesses' and allowed to practise their faith, was no longer tenable; they wanted to remove all Jewish rights.[107] In 1236 Pope Gregory IX was persuaded to condemn the Talmud and this proved in effect, though not in intention, a decisive shift from Augustinian tolerance.[108] The friars did not begin as anti-Semites. St Francis had no animosity towards Jews, and St Dominic, according to testimony at his canonization process, was 'loving to all, the rich, the poor, the Jews, the gentiles'.[109] At first they concentrated on strictly theological issues and even tried to discourage ritual murder charges.

But the friars were coarsened by the urban environment on which they concentrated. They were aggressive proselytizers, to lapsed Christians, to the heterodox, not least to Jews. They held 'missions' in the towns, at which they beat the drum of orthodoxy and zealotry and stirred up rigorist enthusiam. They tended to open their friaries in or near the Jewish quarter, as bases for harassment. The Jews learned to fear them more than any other Christian group. They saw them as the incarnation of the scourge threatened by Moses in Deuteronomy 32:22, 'those which are not a people'.[110] Their policy gradually became to convert the Jews or get them out. In England, the Franciscans were behind a royal decree which removed the right of Jews to buy urban freeholds and they may have been an element in securing their expulsion.[111] Soon they turned to outright anti-Semitism. In 1247 two Franciscans helped to circulate a blood libel at Valréas which led to a bloody pogrom. In 1288, following a blood libel in Troyes, Dominicans and Franciscans united to provoke a massacre of local Jews.

Even in Italy, where attitudes to Jews were fairly tolerant even in the later Middle Ages, the Franciscans were a baneful force. There, the municipalities allowed Jews to open banks under regulation and in return for lump sums or an annual tax. The Jews survived because their interest-rates, at 15–20 per cent, undercut Christian ones. The Franciscans specialized in urban and mercantile problems and took a particular interest in moneylending. They kept close watch over the Jews and hounded them unmercifully at the slightest breach of the rules. The Franciscans preached love but it did not apply to the Jews as people: 'In respect of abstract and general love,' the Friar Bernardino of Siena laid down, 'we are permitted to love them. However, there can be no concrete love towards them.'[112] The Franciscans organized boycotts and set up 'piety funds' to undercut the Jews and drive them out of business; then they could raise a clamour for their expulsion. Some Franciscan anti-Semites, like John of Capistrano, ranged over a huge area, on both sides of the Alps, his preaching to mass open-air congregations often leading to pogroms. His disciple Bernardino de Fletre, a third-generation Franciscan agitator, conducted a mission at Trent in 1475 which produced accusations that the Jews had murdered a two-year-old boy. In the uproar that followed, the entire Jewish community was arrested, many tortured and executed, the rest expelled.

Throughout Europe, the onset of the Black Death, which spread northwards from the Mediterranean, added another universal layer to the anti-Semitic superstructure. Its causes were not understood, and its unprecedented impact – it killed between a half and a quarter of the population – inspired the belief that it was a *pestis manufacta*, a disease spread by human malice. Inquiry focused on the Jews, especially after terrified Jews confessed under torture. In September 1348 in the Castle of Chillon on Lake Geneva, Jews admitted that the plague was the work of one John of Savoy, who had been told by the rabbis: 'See, I give you a little package, half a span in size, which contains a preparation of poison and venom in a narrow, stitched leathern bag. This you are to distribute among the wells, the cisterns and the springs about Venice and in the other places where you go.'[113] The fantasy spread rapidly, especially as more Jews confessed under torture – in Freiburg, for instance, a Jew admitted that the motive was 'because you Christians have destroyed so many Jews . . . and also because we too want to be lords, for you have lorded long enough'. Everywhere Jews were accused of poisoning wells. On 26 September 1248 Pope Clement VI issued a bull in Avignon contradicting the allegation and blaming it on the devil: he argued that the Jews were suffering as badly as any other element in the community. The Emperor Charles IV, King Peter IV of Aragon and other rulers put out similar statements. Nevertheless, the greatest wave of anti-Semitism since 1096 engulfed over 300 Jewish communities, especially in Germany, Austria, France and Spain. According to Jewish sources, 6,000 died in Mainz and 2,000 in Strasbourg.[114] Charles IV found he had to issue pardons to cities which murdered their Jews: 'Forgiveness is [granted] for every transgression involving the slaying and destruction of Jews which has been committed without the positive knowledge of the leading citizens, or in their ignorance, or in any other fashion whatever.' This pardon dates from 1350, by which time it was generally known that the Jews were not responsible. Unfortunately, once anti-Semitism spread, it stuck; once a neighbourhood learned to go for local Jews violently, the likelihood was that it would happen again. The Black Death set precedents everywhere, especially in German-speaking countries.

In the early Middle Ages, and even as late as the early fourteenth century, Spain was the safest Latin territory for Jews. For a long time it was a place where Jews and Christians were more likely to meet in debate than come to blows. Not that the notion of Christian and Jewish experts meeting in scholarly battle was Spanish. Thanks to the work of Hyam Maccoby the complex story of the debates is now better understood.[115] The process of public debate began at Paris in 1240 as a direct result of Pope Gregory IX's ban on the Talmud. In his letter to the princes of Europe, he asked them to seize all the condemned books on the first Saturday in Lent, 'while the Jews are gathered in the synagogue', and place the haul 'in the custody of our dear sons, the Dominican and Franciscan friars'.[116] Louis IX, a crusader and anti-Semite, was the only monarch to co-operate with Gregory's campaign. The 1240 confrontation was not, therefore, a debate – Louis once said that the best way to argue with a Jew was to plunge a sword in him – so much as a trial of the Talmud, the prosecutor being Nicholas Donin, a former Jew, now a zealous Franciscan, who had incited Gregory to launch the campaign in the first place. The Jewish spokesman, Rabbi Jehiel, was in effect the witness for the defence, and the 'debate' consisted of his interrogation. As Donin knew the Talmud well, he was able to take the Rabbi through all the passages in the Talmud – only a tiny proportion of the whole – to which Christians might or did object: those insulting Christ (i.e. describing Jesus in Hell drowned in boiling excrement) or blaspheming God the Father (showing him weeping or out-argued) or forbidding Jews to mix with Christians. On the last point, Jehiel was able to show that it was Christian law which really prevented intercourse, though it is true that most Jews in their hearts regarded the Latins as barbarians. Jehiel insisted: 'We sell cattle to Christians, we have partnership with Christians, we allow ourselves to be alone with them, we give our children Christian wet-nurses, and we teach Torah to Christians – for there are now many Christian priests who can read Hebrew books.'[117] However, the books were duly burned in 1242. Official policy admitted that the Talmud was not heretical as a whole but rather contained blasphemous passages – thus being liable to censorship rather than destruction. The points made by Donin quickly became routine ammunition for clerical anti-Semitism.[118]

In Spain, at any rate for a time, the debates were more genuine and covered a wide area. Were cathedrals better than the Temple? Should priests/rabbis marry? 'Why are more of the gentiles white and handsome whilst most of the Jews are black and ugly?', to which the Jews replied that Christian women had sexual intercourse during menstruation, so passing on the redness of blood to their children's complexion, and also that when gentiles had sex 'they are surrounded by beautiful paintings and give birth to their likeness'.[119] It was the Spanish, or rather King James I of Aragon, who staged by far the best of the debates, at Barcelona on 20–31 July 1263. The idea again came from an ex-Jew, Pablo Christiani (many Jewish converts chose the name Paul), and he was backed by Raymund de Penaforte, head of the Dominican Inquisition in Aragon and Master of the Order, and Peter de Janua, general of the Spanish Franciscans. The Jews had a sole spokesman, but the best: Nahmanides, learned, fluent, well-born, self-confident. He agreed to come to Barcelona to take part because he knew King James, who employed many Jews as officials, was well-disposed and anyway guaranteed him complete liberty of speech. James was a vast man, with many mistresses and illegitimate children, who had angered the Pope by repudiating his first wife and who did not hesitate to tear out the tongue of the Bishop of Gerona. He ignored papal demands to get rid of his Jewish bureaucrats.

The exact course of the debate is not clear, since the Christian and Jewish accounts of it conflict. The Christian version shows Nahmanides caught in inconsistencies, defeated in argument, reduced to silence and finally fleeing in disorder. Nahmanides' own account is clearer and much better presented. The Christian attack was designed to show, from aggadic and homiletical passages in the Talmud, that the Messiah had indeed appeared, that he was both human and divine and had died to save mankind, and that in consequence Judaism had lost its *raison d'être*. Nahmanides replied by contesting the meaning attributed to these passages, denying that Jews were obliged to accept the aggadah and insisting that the doctrine of the Messiah was not of paramount importance for Jews. He counter-attacked by arguing that the belief in Jesus had proved disastrous. Rome, once master of the world, had declined the moment it accepted Christianity 'and now the followers of Mohammed have greater territories than they'. Moreover, he added, 'from the time of Jesus until the present the world has been filled with violence and injustice, and the Christians have shed more blood than all other peoples'. On the Incarnation, he said: 'The doctrine in which you believe, the foundation of your faith, cannot be accepted by reason, nature affords no grounds for it, nor have the prophets ever expressed it.' He told the king that only life-long indoctrination could persuade a rational person that God was born from a human womb, lived on earth, was executed and then 'returned to his original place'.[120] According to the Jewish account, the Christian clergy, aware that the debate was going against them, made sure the proceedings ended without a conclusion. The following Sabbath, the king attended the synagogue, made a speech, heard a reply from Nahmanides, and sent him home with a purse of 300 *solidos*.

The likelihood is that both the conflicting accounts presented what each side would have liked to have said, rather than what it did say.[121] Some Jewish scholars have argued that Nahmanides' version is a work of propaganda, and disingenuous too, since in his own writings he placed much more weight on aggadic interpretations than he admitted in the debate. According to this view, Pablo was well aware of the internal Jewish conflict between rationalists and anti-rationalists; the agenda of the debate was cleverly drawn up to exploit this and catch Nahmanides in contradictions or force him to deny previous views.[122] But as Maccoby points out, much of the debate was at cross-purposes. There was such a variety of views about the Messiah in Judaism that it was almost impossible to be heretical on the subject.[123] Judaism was about the Law and its observance; Christianity was about dogmatic theology. A Jew might be in trouble over a fine point of Sabbath observance which a Christian found ridiculous. On the other hand, a

Christian might be burned alive for holding a view of God which all Jews would see as a matter of legitimate opinion and controversy. Barcelona showed the difficulty Christians and Jews had in debating honestly the central point which divided their faiths because they could not agree what that point was.

Jews had learned from long experience to recognize the signs of impending peril. Nahmanides was reluctant to take part in the debate: the fact that it was being held at all was ominous. Such debates had nothing to offer Jews. But they were important to the Christian clergy, both as propaganda exercises for their own zealots and as fishing expeditions to discover Jewish dialectical weaknesses or vulnerable points they had not known existed. The year after the dispute, Raymund de Penaforte was head of a commission which examined the Talmud for blasphemy, and in 1265 took part in the trial of Nahmanides for publishing his account of the debate. He was convicted and, though only lightly punished by the king, decided to leave Spain for good and went to Palestine. Thus a great pillar of Spanish Judaism was removed.

In Nahmanides' day the Jews in Spain could still with reason regard themselves as the intellectually superior community. Their skills were still extremely useful, if not quite indispensable, to Christian rulers. But the Christians were catching up fast, and by the end of the thirteenth century they had absorbed Aristotelianism themselves, had written their own *summae*, and in trade and administration were a match for anything the Jews could provide. During the fourteenth century the Jews, even in Spain, were in steady relative decline. Their economic position was eroded by anti-Semitic laws. Their numbers were depleted by forcible conversion. For the first time, moreover, it seemed to make sense for an ambitious and clever Jew to accept baptism willingly: he was joining a wider, progressive culture. The Jewish remnant took refuge in kabbalah, aggadic stories, superstition and poetry. It was the triumph of irrationality. The works of Maimonides and other rationalists were not exactly burned, but they became marginal. In the aftermath of the Black Death and the countless atrocities inflicted on Jews, it became the fashion in orthodox circles to blame rationalism and other sins against God for these calamities.

So Judaism, which in the eleventh and twelfth centuries had been in the intellectual forefront, turned in on itself. Maimonides had included belief in the Messiah as a Jewish article of faith but he had always deplored apocalyptic and messianism as the 'myth of the rabble'. 'Do not think', he wrote in his *Mishneh Torah*, 'that the

Messiah will have to work signs and miracles. . . . the Torah with all its laws and ordinances is everlastingly valid and nothing will be added to it or taken away from it.' There would be 'no departure from the normal course of things or any change in the ordained order' – any suggestions to the contrary in the Bible were mere 'figures of speech'.[124] With the increasing misery of Jewish communities, apocalyptic and messianism began to revive. Angels and devils multiplied. So did scruples and weird devotions. The Rabbi Jacob ben Yakar used to clean a space before the Ark with his beard; Rabbi Shalom in Austria ate meat dishes in one room and dairy food in another, and insisted that gentiles who brought him water wear white robes. There was a widespread belief that piety would hasten the Messiah and so shatter the legions of oppressors. The Jews launched an internal witchhunt against informers, who were cursed every Sabbath and sometimes executed if caught. They remained remarkably tolerant in some ways: in smaller communities, a Jew who felt he had been wronged could make what was termed 'an authorized scandal' by interrupting prayers or Torah-readings. But increasing resort was made to excommunications. There were degrees of punishment: *nazifah*, a mere seven-day exclusion; *niddui*, isolation from the community; *herem*, a still more drastic form of expulsion, which might mean intervention by Christian royal officers and seizure of the offender's assets. Maimonides had listed the twenty-four offences which the sages said deserved *niddui*, ranging from insulting a scholar (even after he was dead) to keeping dangerous dogs. But as the Middle Ages progressed, punishments became more complex and severe and, under the influence of Christian procedures, excommunication itself developed into a dramatic and fearful ceremony. A severe *herem* was pronounced in the synagogue before the open Ark or while holding a Torah scroll, to the sound of the *shofar*; when the sentence was pronounced, the guilty man was anathematized and cursed, while all the candles were extinguished.

But internal discipline could not stop the haemorrhage of converts as the Christian pressure increased. Even by the close of the thirteenth century, the Christian kings of Aragon were being reported to Rome by their own bishops for favouring Jews, or not containing them vigorously enough. In 1282 the crown prince, the Infante Sancho, rebelling against his father, played the anti-Semitic card to rally the clergy to his side.[125] Jews were progressively eased out of the royal service. After the Black Death disturbances, the whole position of the Jews in Spain began to deteriorate quite rapidly, as the blood libels and other anti-Semitic tales got a grip on the people. In Seville, for instance, there were anti-Semitic riots in 1378 and a positive explosion in 1391.

These riots are often blamed on the great Dominican preacher Vicente Ferrer (c. 1350–1419), afterwards canonized. But his role was much more subtle, and more sinister from the Jew's point of view. Indeed he helped to develop a pattern of anti-Semitism which was to reverberate thunderously in the twentieth century. It is true that his public preachings were often associated with anti-Semitic hysteria and outrages. But he did not encourage rioting; on the contrary – he deplored it. He publicly condemned the 1391 riots. He thought it wicked and un-Christian that the mob should take the law into its own hands. Instead, it was the duty of the state to act, and proceed lawfully. The riots showed clearly that the Jews posed a 'problem' to society to which a 'solution' must be found. Hence Ferrer and his clerical colleagues were responsible for a series of anti-Jewish policies approved by the Spanish-favoured antipope Benedict XIII, and for the selection as King of Aragon of Ferdinand I, who began to implement them. The war against the Jews was taken out of the hands of the mob and made the official business of church and government.[126]

It was against this background that the last of the great Jewish–Christian debates took place at Tortosa in 1413–14. It was not a genuine debate, more a public show – even a show-trial. Ferrer did not officially participate but he acted behind the scenes. His aim seems to have been to whip up popular enthusiasm for Christianity as the sole valid religion; to demolish the claims of Judaism in a big public spectacle; and then, with church, state and populace behind him, and the Jews demoralized, to effect a mass conversion. The Jewish leaders wanted to have nothing to do with it. But in many cases the rabbis had no choice but to attend. The antipope, whom Ferrer was later to disown, presided. Ferdinand, the king Ferrer had made, controlled the political framework. Some seventy seats were provided for cardinals, bishops and other grandees. Benedict announced right at the beginning that it was not proposed to hold a discussion between equal parties but to prove the truth of Christianity from talmudic sources. It was, in effect, the trial of the Jewish religion. The prosecuting counsel was Joshua Lorki, one of Ferrer's converts, renamed Gerónimo de Sante Fé. There were about twenty Jewish participants, including the leading philosopher and apologist Joseph Albo, who later wrote a famous treatise on Jewish religious principles, the *Sefer ha-Ikkarim*, or *Book of Principles*. But they were given none of the freedom Nahmanides seems to have enjoyed at Barcelona. They were under threat from Gerónimo right at the start, both for 'Jewish obstinacy' and, ingeniously, for heresy against their own religion, which would have put them in the power of the Inquisition.[127]

The ground covered was chiefly the familiar one of proving Jesus the Messiah from Jewish sources, though Original Sin and the causes of the Exile were also discussed, and many technical questions on Jewish texts were raised on the Christian side. The Christians were by now very well briefed for this kind of exercise and Gerónimo was both learned and clever. A total of sixty-nine sessions were held, over twenty-one months, and while the rabbis were in Tortosa, Ferrer and his friars were moving through their leaderless communities, making converts. In some cases the converts were brought to Tortosa for display and to provide a triumphant counterpoint to the Christian propaganda within the disputation. Rabbi Astruk ha-Levi protested vigorously as the debates dragged on:

We are away from our homes. Our resources are diminished and are almost entirely gone. In our absence great damage has occurred to our communities. We do not know the fate of our wives and children. We have inadequate maintenance here and even lack food. We have been put to extraordinary expenses. Why should people suffering from such woes be held accountable for their arguments, when contending with Gerónimo and others who are in the greatest prosperity and luxury?[128]

Rabbi Astruk contended that a point was reached when no further purpose was served by repeating the old arguments – it was a matter of what each man believed. What did a stage-managed debate against a background of hostility prove? 'A Christian living in the land of the Saracens', he said, 'may be defeated by the arguments of a pagan or a Saracen but it does not follow that his faith has been refuted.'[129] During the later stages of the dispute, the Jews claimed they did not understand the questions and tried, whenever possible, to preserve a dignified silence.

None the less, Tortosa was a propaganda defeat for Judaism and to some extent an intellectual one too. For the first time in Spain, the Jews could be seen as forming enclaves of obscurantism and irrational backwardness, amid a superior culture. This, as much as the legal and economic pressure, and the fear generated by the high-pressure conversion drives of the friars, produced a stampede of converts. So to a great extent Ferrer succeeded in his object. Alas, converting Jews did not solve 'the Jewish problem'. What it did, as the Spanish authorities rapidly discovered, was to present it in a new and far less tractable form. For the problem now became racial as well as religious. The church had always presented the Jews as a spiritual danger. Since the twelfth century, popular superstition had presented them as a social and physical danger too. But at least Jews, as such, were an open and public danger: they were known, they lived in recognizable communities, they were forced to bear distinguishing marks and dress. But when they became converts, *conversos*, or as the populace called them *marranos*, a term of abuse derived from the Spanish word for 'swine',[130] they became a hidden danger. Spanish townsfolk knew that many, perhaps most, of the converts were reluctant. They ceased formally to be Jews from fear, or to gain advantage. As Jews they suffered from severe legal disabilities. As *conversos* they had the same economic rights, in theory, as other Christians. A *marrano* was thus much more unpopular than a practising Jew because he was an interloper in trade and craft, an economic threat; and, since he was probably a secret Jew, he was a hypocrite and a hidden subversive too.

The faithful rabbis warned what would happen. Rabbi Yitzhak Arama told converts: 'You will find no rest among the gentiles, and your life will hang in the balance.' Of the *anusim* (forcible converts) he prophesied: 'One third burnt by fire, one third flying hither to hide and those who remain living in deadly fear.'[131] Rabbi Yehuda ibn Verga saw the *anusim* as three pairs of turtle doves: the first pair would remain in Spain and be 'plucked', would lose their property, be slaughtered or burned; the second pair would be plucked too – would lose their goods – but would save their bodies by fleeing when bad times came; the third pair, who 'will be the first to flee', would save both body and goods.[132]

This pessimistic view was soon confirmed by events. A Spanish Jew found he could not evade anti-Semitic hostility by converting. If he moved to another town, as many did, his Christianity became even more suspect. His Christian persecutor changed tactics. With conversion, anti-Semitism became racial rather than religious, but the anti-Semites found, as their successors were to do in Nazi Germany, that it was exceedingly difficult to identify and isolate Jews by racial criteria. They were forced back, as the Nazis were to be, on the old religious ones. In fifteenth-century Spain, a Jew could not be persecuted on religious grounds, because he was born a Jew, or his parents were; it had to be shown that he was still practising Judaism secretly in some form. The Castilian king Alfonso VII is alleged to have ruled that 'No *converso* of Jewish origin be allowed to hold public office or enjoy any benefice in Toledo and its area of jurisdiction, since they are suspected in their fidelity to Christ.'[133]

How could this suspicion be proved? In Ciudad Real, where the plight of the *conversos* has been examined in detail by the historian Haim Beinart, the first accusation that a 'New Christian' was secretly taking part in *mitzvot* dated from 1430. The ex-Jews were usually hard-working, anxious to get on, often clever; they rose in wealth and in the public service, and the trouble developed *pari passu*. In the 1440s, the first anti-*conversos* riots broke out in Toledo. In 1449 in Ciudad Real they lasted a fortnight. The *conversos* fought back, organized an armed band of 300, killed an Old Christian; in the struggle twenty-two were murdered and many houses burned. In 1453, Constantinople fell to the Turks and Byzantium, the old enemy of the Jews, was no more; many Jews believed that the Messiah would now come, and some *conversos* felt they could soon revert to their old religion.[134] They even proposed to go to Turkey and live openly as Jews. There were riots in Ciudad Real in 1464, 1467 and 1474, the last particularly severe, perhaps engineered by a semi-professional group of anti-Semites who moved into a city, putting up at friendly religious houses. In 1474 the *conversos* of Ciudad Real lost houses and furniture, their flocks in the suburbs, their shops and stock in the city. Any list of debtors found by the rioters was destroyed – an invariable practice. The frightened *conversos* fled to the protection of the *corregidor* or governor in the citadel, but (states the official deposition), 'The rioters stormed it, destroyed the central tower, killing many; the *corregidor* and many of the *conversos* were expelled; the town was closed to them and none permitted to re-enter.'[135] Some fled to the protection of a kind nobleman at Palma, near Córdoba, where they remained three years.

Riots against converts led to the same sequence of events as riots against Jews. The state was terrified of riots as a symptom of popular unrest. It could not prevent the riots, or even punish them adequately, so it sought to remove the cause by attacking the *conversos*. This was not difficult. Many were indeed secret Jews. A contemporary Jewish account says that those who fled to Palma observed *mitzvot* in public, kept Sabbath and festivals, fasted and prayed on Yom Kippur, observed Passover and celebrated other feasts 'no less than the Jews and no worse than them'. One Franciscan fanatic, Alfonso de Espina, a *converso* himself, or the son of one, compiled a volume, *Fortalitium Fidei*, listing (among other things), twenty-five 'transgressions' by which treacherous *conversos* could be identified. These included not only secret Jewish practices but, perhaps more easily noted, evidence of bad Christianity: avoiding the sacraments, working on Sundays, avoiding making the sign of the cross, never mentioning Jesus or Mary, or perfunctory attendance at mass. To these he added all the crimes (such as stealing the host) popularly ascribed to Jews, together with some new ones, such as 'holding philosophical discussions'.

Again we see fear of the Jew, especially in his concealed form as a *converso*, fomenting disorder, dissent and doubt in society.

Fra Alfonso was the ideologue of the next phase of anti-Semitism. Having shown that it was indeed possible to identify the secret Jew not on a racial but on a religious basis, he advocated the solution: isolation and segregation. The populace should shun suspect *conversos* and the state should interpose physical barriers between them and the true Christian population. At the same time, church and state alike should combine to search out and destroy those among the *conversos* who, by practising Judaism, were legally heretics. He described in great detail the methods and punishments to be used, based on the old thirteenth-century Inquisition. But he hinted that a new kind, suited to Spain's peculiar national needs, ought to be set up.[136]

In due course the state adopted all Fra Alfonso's programme. Segregation was decreed by the Cortes at Toledo in 1480. At the same time a special Spanish inquisition was being created. The first inquisitors, including the vicar-general of the Dominicans, were appointed to operate a central inquiry for Andalucia, run from Seville. It began work in January 1481 and in the next eight years burned over 700 at the stake there. Some sources put the figure as high as 2,000.[137] During the same year the national inquisition replaced the traditional papal one in Aragon, and from February 1483 the entire organization was put under central control, its effective master being a Dominican prior, Tomás de Torquemada. In less than twelve years the Inquisition condemned about 13,000 *conversos*, men and women, for the secret practice of Judaism. The Inquisition sought all kinds of victims, but secret Jews were among the chief ones. In its whole existence it numbered a total of about 341,000 victims. Of these, more than 32,000 were killed by burning, 17,659 burned in effigy and 291,000 given lesser punishments. The great majority of those killed, some 20,226, suffered before 1540 under the first five inquisitors-general, and most of them were of Jewish origin. But the *auto-da-fé* continued to claim victims until 1790.[138]

Prior Torquemada had become confessor to Queen Isabella of Castile in 1469, the year she married King Ferdinand of Aragon, leading to the unification of the two kingdoms in 1479. The anti-Jewish policy was to some extent a personal creation of these two monarchs. The Inquisition they set up had many opponents, internal and external. One was the queen's secretary, Fernando del Pulgar, himself a *converso*. In a letter addressed to the primate, Cardinal-Archbishop Pedro Gonzales de Mendoza of Toledo, and intended for publication, he complained of the segregation edicts which prevented converts from living in Guipuzcoa and intermarrying with its people or learning the trade of mason; he admitted some converts reverted, but pointed out that in Andalucia there were, for instance, 10,000 young women *conversos* who had never left their parents' homes and simply followed their fathers' ways – to burn them all was extremely cruel and would simply force them to flee. To which associates of Torquemada replied that it was better to burn some innocents than allow heresy to spread: 'Better for a man to enter heaven with one eye than go to hell with both.' The only result was the demotion of Pulgar from royal secretary to royal chronicler.[139]

The papacy, too, objected to the Inquisition, partly because it was a royal and national instrument outside papal power, partly because it clearly offended natural justice. Sixtus IV in April 1482 demanded that Rome be given the right to hear appeals, that the accused should be told the names of hostile witnesses, and that in any event personal enemies and former servants should be disqualified as such, that repentant heretics should be allowed to confess and receive absolution instead of facing trial, and that they should be given the right to choose their counsel. Ferdinand flatly declined to do any of these things and in his reply insisted that it was essential he should appoint inquisitors, because when the system was run solely by the church, heresy had flourished. Popes continued to object, to little avail.[140]

Both Ferdinand and Isabella claimed they were acting purely from orthodox and Catholic zeal. Both hotly rejected the charge, made by their enemies at the time and by historians since, that they wanted to confiscate the property of convicted heretics. Writing to her agents in Rome, Isabella protested that she had never touched 'a single maravedi' of confiscated property – that part of the money had been made into a dowry-fund for children of the Inquisition's victims – and that whoever claimed she had acted for love of money was a liar: she boasted that, from her passionate devotion to the faith, she had caused the ruin of royal towns, emptied them of their inhabitants and desolated whole regions.[141] Ferdinand, too, stressed the losses to the royal revenue, but said all the factors had been weighed carefully before the decision to launch the Inquisition on a national campaign was taken and that they had 'set the service of our Lord God above our own service . . . [and] in preference to any other consideration'.[142] The truth seems to be that both monarchs were driven by a mixture of religious and financial motives and also, more importantly, by the desire to impose a centralizing, emotional unity on their disparate and divided territories. But, most of all, they were caught up in the sinister, impersonal logic of anti-Semitism itself. The historical record shows, time and again, that it develops a power and momentum of its own.

Haim Beinart's study of Ciudad Real reveals a pitiful pattern of human degradation. The object of concealing the names of hostile witnesses was to avoid family blood-feuds, but it gave the Inquisition its most evil aspect, particularly since many informers were motivated by malice, especially against rich or prominent men. Thus Juan Gonzales Pintado, who had been secretary to two kings, had naturally made enemies: he was burned alive for it. Still more wretched was the testimony of husbands against wives, and vice versa, sons against fathers, brothers against sisters. One of the worst informers was Fernan Falcon who testified in the posthumous trial of his own father, who seems to have been head of the local crypto-Jewish community: 'All that is stated against him in the arraignment is true, and more yet – enough to fill over an entire sheet of paper.' Falcon was a witness in all the Ciudad Real trials, 1483–5, his favourite descriptive phrase about an accused being 'a Jew in every way'. Of one, Carolina de Zamora, he said 'that he would see to it that they burned her even if he had to do thirty rounds in hell'; in fact the most damning witness against her was her own son, a monk, who swore to see her burned – though she got off with a flogging. Many of the women accused turned out to be learned as well as pious. Leonor Gonzales managed to escape to Portugal. The court gave her son, Juan de la Sierra, authority to go to Portugal and persuade her to return. He did so, she came back, was tried, convicted and burned alive. Some did escape. Others attempted it and were caught. The richest *converso* of the city, Sancho de Ciudad, bought a boat and sailed with his family for Valencia, but the winds drove them back, they were caught and all were burned in Toledo. Successful evaders were tried and burned in effigy. If a man was convicted posthumously, his remains were dug up and burned too – a symbol of what was supposedly happening to him in hell.[143]

A few got off. But usually the evidence was overwhelming. In Ciudad Real, in this period, it was only necessary to resort to torture twice. Many of those convicted were clearly strict Jews. One woman was trapped because she was seen lighting a candle on Sabbath eve to avoid kindling the next day; another because she declined to drink from the same cup as one who had eaten pork; a strict compliance with the laws of ritual slaughtering brought many to the stake. Not all got death sentences. A *converso* who abjured might get a term of imprisonment – possibly life – which could be commuted to a fine if he was rich. But he had to wear a sackcloth garment with two yellow crosses for at least a year, sometimes for ever, and if he failed to do so could be branded *relapso* and burned. He also had a special obligation to inform the Inquisition, failing which he was branded a 'rebel against the church', and burned. The list of positive and negative penalties imposed on such a man was enormous: he was banned from all benefices and offices down to town-crier, could not practise as a doctor, lawyer or notary, bear arms, receive moneys or goods, carve stone, own a tavern, ride a horse or travel by cart or carriage, wear gold, silver, pearls, jewels of any kind, silk and brocade, or grow a beard.[144] These prohibitions were inherited by the children, females to the first generation, males to the second.[145]

This ferocious persecution lasted twelve years in its initial impulse and spread to every Jewish community in Spain. The misery and loss was appalling but all the results served to do was to reveal the magnitude of the 'Jewish problem' in the eyes of authority. It coincided with the final phase of the conquest of the old Moorish kingdom of Granada, the *reyos catholicos* entering the fallen city triumphantly on 2 January 1492. The débâcle added yet more Jewish communities, as well as Moslem ones, to the Spanish state. Dealing with the Jews, open or secret, was now almost the principal activity of the government. All the gaols were full. Tens of thousands were under house arrest and often starving. Despairing of ending contact between *conversos* and Jews by the conventional means of inquisitorial investigation, egged on by rapacious followers anxious to loot, the *reyos* determined on a gigantic act of will to produce a 'final solution'. On 31 March they signed an Edict of Expulsion, promulgated a month later, physically driving from Spain any Jew who would not accept immediate conversion.

There were then about 200,000 Jews still in the kingdom. It is an indication of the demoralized state of the Jewish community, and also of the attachment Jews nevertheless felt for Spain, the country where they had enjoyed most comfort and security in the past, that very large numbers, including the senior rabbi and most of the leading families, chose to be baptized. About 100,000 trudged across the frontier into Portugal, from which in turn they were expelled four years later. About 50,000 went across the straits into North Africa, or by ship to Turkey. By the end of July 1492 the expulsion was an accomplished fact.

The destruction of Spanish Jewry was the most momentous event in Jewish history since the mid-second century AD. There had been Jews in Spain from early classical times, perhaps even since Solomon's day, and the community had developed marked characteristics. In the Dark and early Middle Ages, dispersed Jews tended to fall into two main groups: those in touch with the Babylonian academies and those linked to Palestine. There were two such communities, each with its synagogue, in Maimonides' Fustat (and a third synagogue for the Karaites). From the fourteenth century, however, it is more accurate to speak of Spanish or Sephardi Jews – the term is a corruption of an old name for Spain – and Ashkenazi or German Jews radiating from the Rhineland.[146] The Sephardis created their own Judaeo-Spanish language, Ladino or Judezmo, once written in rabbinic cursive script, as opposed to the modern (originally Ashkenazi) Hebrew cursive. They were learned, literary, rich, immensely proud of their lineage, worldly-wise, often pleasure-loving and not over-strict, following the liberal codification of Joseph Caro. They were a bridgehead of the Latin world in Arab culture and vice versa, and transmitters of classical science and philosophy. Sephardis were brilliant craftsmen in precious metals and stones, mathematicians, makers of precision instruments, accurate maps and navigational tables.

Now this large and gifted community was dispersed all over the Mediterranean and Moslem world and, from Portugal, in a second Sephardi diaspora, to France and north-west Europe. Many embraced Christianity and made their mark therein. Christopher Columbus, for instance, was legally Genoese but did not write Italian, and may have come from a Spanish family of Jewish origin. The name Colon was common among Jews living in Italy. He boasted of his connections with King David, liked Jewish and *marrano* society, was influenced by Jewish superstitions, and his patrons at the Aragonese court were mainly New Christians. He used the tables drawn up by Abraham Zacuto and the instruments perfected by Joseph Vecinho. Even his interpreter, Luis de Torres, was Jewish – though baptized just before they sailed for America. Thus Jews, having lost Spain in the old world, helped to recreate it in the new.[147] Sephardis went to France, too, and characteristic of their impact there was the glittering but urbane Michel de Montaigne, whose mother Antoinette Louppes was a direct descendant of Spanish Jews.[148] What Spain lost, others gained; and in the long run the Sephardi diaspora was to prove exceedingly creative and of critical importance in Jewish development. But at the time it seemed an unrelieved disaster for the Jews.

Nor was it the only one. At the close of the European Middle Ages – the Jewish Middle Ages were not to end until the last decades of the eighteenth century – the Jews had ceased to make, at any rate for the time being, a primary contribution to the European economy and culture. They had become dispensable, and were being ejected in consequence. The Spanish expulsions were preceded by many in Germany and Italy. Jews were expelled from Vienna and Linz in 1421, from Cologne in 1424, Augsburg in 1439, Bavaria in 1442 (and again in 1450) and from the crown cities of Moravia in 1454. They were thrown out of Perugia in 1485, Vicenza in 1486, Parma in 1488, Milan and Lucca in 1489 and, with the fall of the philosemitic Medicis, from Florence and all Tuscany in 1494. By the end of the decade they had been turned out of the Kingdom of Navarre too.

One expulsion provoked another, as refugees streamed into cities which already housed more Jews than their rulers now wanted. In Italy their only function at the end of the fifteenth century was pawn-broking and making small loans to the poor. Even in backward Rome the role of the Jewish bankers was declining.[149] Christian bankers and craftsmen got the Jews banned as soon as their guilds were powerful enough. In Italy, in Provence and in Germany, the Jews had been virtually eliminated from large-scale trade and industry by the year 1500. So they moved into the less developed territories further east – first into Austria, Bohemia, Moravia, Silesia, then on into Poland, to Warsaw and Cracow, Lwov, Brest-Litovsk and into Lithuania. The demographic axis of Ashkenazi Jewry shifted itself several hundred miles into east-central and eastern Europe. There was trouble here, too – there were anti-Jewish riots in Poland in 1348–9, in 1407 and in 1494; they were expelled from both Cracow and Lithuania the following year. All these movements and expulsions were interlinked. But because the Jews were needed more in the east, they managed to cling on; by the year 1500 Poland was regarded as the safest country in Europe for Jews, and it soon became the Ashkenazi heartland.

The degradation and impoverishment of the Jews in Europe, the fact that their contribution to the economy and culture had become marginal by the end of the Middle Ages, might have been expected to erode if not demolish the wall of hatred which had been built around them. But that did not happen. Like other forms of irrational conduct, anti-semitism did not respond to the laws of economics. On the contrary: like some vicious organism, it bred new mutations of itself. In Germany in particular it began to develop its own repulsive iconography – the *Judensau*.

The medieval mind delighted in reducing all aspects of the universe to imagery. The conflict between Christianity and Judaism had formed part of the vast panorama of life which swarmed, for instance, over the walls of the cathedrals. But the sculptors had represented it in purely theological terms. The favourite pair of images, often rendered with striking grace, was the triumphant church and the sorrowing syna-gogue. The medieval sculptor did not deal in anti-Semitic themes; he never portrayed the Jew as a usurer, a diabolical creature who poisoned wells, murdered Christian youth or tortured the host.

There were, however, other images used for Jews in the graphic arts: the golden calf, the owl, the scorpion. In Germany, towards the end of the medieval period, a new one began to emerge: the sow. The motif was not originally conceived as a polemical one, but it gradually came to symbolize all unclean persons, sinners, heretics, above all Jews.[150] It seems to have been confined almost exclusively to areas affected by German culture; but there, it became the commonest of all motifs for the Jew, and one of the most potent and enduring of abusive stereotypes.[151] It assumed an infinite variety of repellent forms. Jews were portrayed venerating the sow, sucking its teats, embracing its hindquarters, devouring its excrement. It offered rich opportunities to the coarser type of popular artist, presented with a target where none of the usual rules of taste and decorum applied and where the crudest obscenity was not merely acceptable but positively meritorious. Indeed, it is clear that the gross indecency of the image was the prime reason for its popularity over 600 years. With the invention of printing, it proliferated rapidly and became ubiquitous in Germany. It appeared not only in books but in countless prints, in etchings, in oils and watercolours, on the handles of walking-sticks, in faience and on china. Its endless repetition helped on a process which in Germany was to become of great and tragic importance: the dehumanization of the Jew. The notion that the Jew knew the truth but rejected it, preferring to work with the forces of darkness – and therefore could not be human in the sense that Christians were – was already well established. The Jew's unnatural and inhuman relations with the *Judensau* drove it ever more firmly into the German popular mind. And if a particular category of person was not human, it could effectively be excluded from society. That, indeed, was what was already happening. For the walls of hatred, far from disappearing, were being replaced by real ones, as the European ghetto made its appearance.

PART FOUR

Ghetto

The great Sephardi diaspora, from Spain in 1492, from Portugal in 1497, set Jews in motion everywhere, for the arrival of refugees in large numbers usually led to further expulsions. Many Jews, reduced to near destitution, denied entrance to cities from which Jews had already been banned, took to peddling. It is no coincidence that the legend of the Wandering Jew assumed mature form about this time. The story of a Jew who had struck Christ on his *via dolorosa*, and so been condemned to wander until the Second Coming, first appeared in a Bolognese chronicle in 1223; Roger of Wendover recorded it five years later in his *Flowers of History*. But it was in the early decades of the sixteenth century that the Wanderer became Ahasuerus, the Jewish archetype pedlar, old, bearded, ragged, sad, a harbinger of calamity.[1] The Bishop of Schleswig claimed he saw him in a church in Hamburg in 1542, and as the hundred or more folktale versions circulated in print, he was seen repeatedly: at Lübeck in 1603, Paris in 1604, Brussels in 1640, Leipzig in 1642, Munich 1721, London in 1818. He became the subject of a vast literature. There were, of course, innumerable, genuine wandering Jews: it was the Jewish predicament in the Renaissance and after, to become again 'strangers and sojourners', like Abraham.

One such wanderer was Solomon ibn Verga (*c.* 1450–*c.* 1525), a native of Malaga, thrown out of Spain, then Portugal, who came to Italy in 1506 and wandered there. We do not know where, if anywhere, he finally settled; but he spent some time in Rome. There he wrote a book called *Shevet Yehuda*, the Rod of Judah, asking, in effect, Why do men hate Jews? This essay has some claim to be called the first work of Jewish history since Josephus' *Antiquities* 1,400 years before, for Ibn Verga describes no less than sixty-four persecutions of Jews. In writing it he signalled the first sign, albeit a faint one, of a return of Jewish historical self-consciousness.

pun on Gen. 49:10.

It was evidence of the pitiful Jewish predicament in Christian Europe that Ibn Verga could not get his book published in his lifetime, and it was first printed about 1554 in Turkey. But, all the same, Ibn Verga was a man of the Renaissance, a rationalist, a sceptic, an independent mind. He was strongly critical of the Talmud, he mocked Maimonides, he parodied the views of Judah Halevi. Using the form of imaginary dialogues, he derided much Jewish scholarship. If the Jews were downtrodden, it was to a great extent their own fault. They were proud but at the same time too passive and trustful in God; hopeful and over-obedient, they neglected both political and military science and so were 'twice naked'. Neither Jews nor Christians would recognize the case for rival beliefs; both countenanced superstition and legends. If the Christians were intolerant, the Jews were un-accommodating. He pointed out that, as a rule, 'the kings of Spain and France, the nobility, the learned and all the men of dignity were friendly to the Jews'; prejudice came chiefly from the ignorant, uneducated poor. 'I have never seen a man of reason hate the Jews', he has a wise man say, 'and there is none who hates them except the common people. For this there is a reason – the Jew is arrogant and always seeks to rule; you would never think that they are exiles and slaves driven from people to people. Rather, they seek to show themselves lords and masters. Therefore the masses envy them.'[2] Why did not the Jews try to break down prejudice by behaving more modestly and humbly, and by preaching religious tolerance and understanding?[3]

Ibn Verga wrote in Hebrew and was clearly addressing himself to an educated Jewish readership, who would know the justice of his criticisms. So we must attach some weight to his charges. But the evidence we have does not suggest that overbearing arrogance was usually the reason why Jews were attacked. The usual cause of trouble was an influx of strange Jews, pushing numbers in the established Jewish community beyond a critical point. In Venice, for instance, which had been a major trading state since the tenth century, and which was a natural place for Jews to settle, they had met some resistance. In the thirteenth century they were corralled on the island of Spinalunga, the Giudecca; at other times they were forced to live on the mainland at Mestre. They had to wear a circular yellow badge, then a yellow hat, then a red hat. But there were always Jews there. They did well. They made important contributions to the Venetian economy, not least by paying special taxes. They had a charter or *condotta*, repeatedly confirmed.

In May 1509 the forces of the League of Cambrai defeated the

Venetian army at Agnadello, and there was a panic flight from the *terra firma* to the main islands. The refugees included over 5,000 Jews, many of them immigrants from Spain and Portugal. Two years later, an agitation for their expulsion began, touched off by sermons from the friars. It culminated in 1515–16 in a decision by the state to confine the entire Jewish community to a segregated area of the city. The spot chosen was a former canon foundry, known as the *ghetto nuovo*, in the part of the central islands furthest removed from the Piazza San Marco. The new foundry was formed into an island by canals, equipped with high walls, all windows facing outward bricked up, and two gates set up manned by four Christian watchmen; six other watchmen were to man two patrol boats, and all ten were to be paid for by the Jewish community, which was also instructed to take out a perpetual lease of the property at one-third above the going rate.[4]

The concept of a separate quarter for Jews was not new. It went back to antiquity. Most major Islamic cities had one. In Dark Age Europe the Jews had often demanded segregation and high walls as a condition for settling in a town. But they objected strongly to the Venetian proposal. It was plainly designed to secure the maximum economic advantage from a Jewish presence (including special taxes) while ensuring Jews had the minimum social contacts with the rest of the population. They were, in effect, permitted to do their business by day, at an inconvenient distance, and locked in at night. But Venice insisted, and in fact the system probably prevented subsequent proposals, to expel the Jews altogether, from being accepted. The original *ghetto nuovo* accommodated Italian Jews chiefly of German origin. In 1541 Jews of the Levant were moved into the nearby old foundry or *ghetto vecchio*. Finally in 1633 the area was further enlarged by adding the *ghetto novissimo* to house western Jews.[5] At this time (1632) there were 2,412 Jews in the ghetto out of a total Venetian population of 98,244. With the extra space the ghetto was able to house nearly 5,000 Jews by 1655.[6] To live thus enclosed, the Jews paid not only ordinary taxes and custom dues, but a special annual tax of 10,000 ducats a year and forced levies, during the first century of the ghetto, of at least 60,000 ducats, totalling not less than 250,000 ducats in all.[7]

Why did the Jews submit so patiently to this kind of oppression? In a book about the Jews of Venice, Simhah Luzzatto (1583–1663), who served them as rabbi for fifty-seven years, argued that Jewish passivity, which so irritated Ibn Verga, was a matter of faith: 'For they believe that any recognizable change which relates to them . . . derives from a higher cause and not human effort.'[8] Many Jews were disturbed at the time by the failure of the huge and once wealthy and powerful Spanish community to offer any resistance to their cruel expulsion. Some pointed to the contrast with Jewish bellicosity in antiquity; why could not Jews be more like their ancestor, Mordecai? They quoted the Book of Esther: 'And all the king's servants that were in the king's gate bowed and reverenced Haman. . . . But Mordecai bowed not, nor did he do reverence.'[9] But the same text – a favourite among Jews, then and now – offered alternative guidance. Had not Esther, on Mordecai's advice, concealed her Jewishness? She 'had not showed her people nor her kindred', as many *marranos* pointed out. The concealed, secret Jew, as well as the passive Jew, was as old as the Bible. Then, too, there was Naaman who 'bowed in the House of Rimmon'. Yet Jews were aware that the Book of Esther contained a warning, for the evil Haman had proposed a general massacre of the Jews to King Ahasuerus. Rabbi Joseph ibn Yahya, in his commentary on Esther published in Bologna in 1538, pointed out that Haman's reasoning – the Jews being 'scattered abroad and dispersed among the people' made them incapable of resistance – applied equally well to the Jews of his day.[10]

The truth is that Jewish communities accepted oppression, and second-class status, provided it had definite rules which were not constantly and arbitrarily changed without warning. What they hated most was uncertainty. The ghetto offered security and even comfort of a kind. It made the observance of the law easier in many ways, by concentrating and isolating Jews. If segregation, as the church claimed, safeguarded Christians from evil Jewish contacts, equally it protected Jews from secularity. The law-code of Joseph Caro (1488–1575), which became the authoritative halakhic text for many generations of orthodox Jews, might have been designed for the self-containment and introspection which the ghetto produced.

Within the ghetto, Jews were able to pursue an intense, if separate, cultural life. But there were many inter-faith contacts. Around the time the ghetto was created, the Christian printer Daniel Bomberg set up a Hebrew printing-press in Venice. Christians, Jews and converts collaborated in producing a magnificent edition of the two Talmuds (1520–3), whose pagination has become standard ever since. The Jewish typesetters and proof-readers were dispensed from wearing the yellow hat. Other Hebrew printing shops appeared. Not only religious classics but contemporary Jewish works thus got into print. Caro's popular condensation of his great code, the *Shulhan Arukh*, was published in Venice, and in 1574 it appeared there in a pocket edition, 'so that', the title-page states, 'it can be carried in one's bosom and may be referred to at any time and any place, while resting or travelling'.[11]

Despite the exactions of the state, the Venetian community flourished. It was divided into three nations, the Penentines from Spain, the Levantines who were Turkish subjects, and the Natione Tedesca or Jews of German origin, the oldest, largest and least wealthy section. They alone were allowed to practise moneylending, and they spoke Italian. But they were not granted Venetian citizenship; even at the end of the eighteenth century the law laid down that 'the Jews of Venice and of the state or any other Jew cannot claim nor enjoy any right of citizenship'.[12] Shakespeare was correct in making this point in *The Merchant of Venice*. He was also plausible in having Jessica say that her father Shylock's house was full of treasures. Successful Jewish moneylenders often accumulated quantities of unredeemed pledges, especially jewels. Local sumptuary laws were enacted to prevent them wearing such spoil; indeed the Jews drew up their own sumptuary prohibitions, to avert 'the envy and hatred of the gentiles, who fix their gaze upon us'.[13]

Despite the restrictive garb, however, there was no lack of gaiety in the Venetian ghetto. A contemporary described the Rejoicing of the Law ceremonies:

A sort of half-carnival is held on this evening, for many maidens and brides mask themselves, so as not to be recognized, and visit all the synagogues. They are thronged at this period by Christian ladies and gentlemen out of curiosity. . . . There are present all nations, Spaniards, Levantines, Portuguese, Germans, Greeks, Italians and others, and each sings according to his own usage. Since they do not use instruments, some clap their hands above their head, some smite their thighs, some imitate the castanets with their fingers, some pretend to play the guitar by scraping their doublets. In short they so act with these noises, jumpings and dancings, with strange contortions of their faces, mouths, arms and all other members, that it appears to be carnival mimicry.[14]

The absence of musical instruments was entirely due to opposition by the rabbis. Many of them objected to art music of any kind on the grounds that it involved excessive repetition of the sacred words of the prayers, and especially of God's name – they argued, not very convincingly, that it might lead the simple to believe there were two or more Gods. (In sixteenth- and seventeenth-century England, the Puritans put forward similar arguments against polyphonic music, insisting on no more than one note for each syllable of the prayer.) In Senigallia, near Ancona, the record has survived of a furious row between the local rabbi and the *maestro di capella*, Mordecai della Rocca – the rabbi insisting, with the help of voluminous citations from the Talmud and kabbalistic sources, that music existed simply to bring out the meaning of the text, all else being 'mere buffoonery'.[15] None the less, the Venetian ghetto certainly had an academy of music early in the seventeenth century. Cecil Roth's studies of Renaissance Venice Jewry show that there were frequent complaints from rigorists about the luxury and worldliness of ghetto life, and the preference for Italian over Hebrew, so that a clamour arose for prayers in the vernacular. Jews wrote plays and works on mathematics, astronomy and economics, all in Italian. They also produced ingenious arguments for taking gondolas on the Sabbath.[16] They had their own schools in the ghetto, but they were allowed to attend the medical school at nearby Padua, and take degrees there. Many rabbis would have liked the walls of the ghetto higher.

Indeed, though relations between Jews and the world outside tend to constitute the stuff of history, for most of the time Jews were more concerned by their own internal affairs, which were sometimes stormy. At the time the Venetian ghetto was being set up, Italian Jewry was convulsed by attempts to bring to book Immanuel ben Noah Raphael da Norsa, a rich man who ruled the Ferrara community like a tyrant, with his own tame rabbi, David Piazzighettone, to produce rulings on his behalf. He used to say: 'Here I sit in my city in the midst of my people, and whoever has any claim against me let him come here to sue me.' Christians as well as Jews bowed before him, it was said. His activities came to light when Abraham da Finzi, who claimed Norsa had defrauded him of 5,000 gold florins, a ruby and an emerald, took him before the rabbinical court in Bologna. Norsa's son, claiming his father was away, refused to accept the writ, saying 'Get away, you *fresca di merda.*' The tame rabbi also refused service, exclaiming: 'What have I to do with you, *putto di Haman?*' The case went before half a dozen rabbinical courts all over Italy, and although most sided against Norsa, he had a doughty champion in Abraham Mintz, whose father Rabbi Judah Mintz had been head of the Padua *yeshivah* for forty-seven years, and who was later rabbi of Mantua. Rival letters and summonses were torn up; rabbis were threatened with the pillory and with being dragged into Christian courts. Each rabbinical group abused the other for lack of family and learning; each boasted of its own genealogies and scholarly prowess, and the argument was envenomed by the Sephardi–Ashkenazi divide. Mintz accused Rabbi Abraham Cohen of Bologna of being 'a smooth-tongued Sephardi . . . the Satan in the case'. Cohen retorted: 'You call my forefathers quarrelsome priests. . . . I am proud of that name [Sephardi] for we Sephardim sanctified the divine name before the whole world, I among them, and passed through the greatest temptations. . . . You are a wretch, worthless, a liar and swindler. . . . You ignorant, stupid, silly, senseless fool.' He said Mintz had always made his living by robbery and embezzlement, 'known from one end of the world to the other as a villain and mocker'. It was said, too, that Mintz had succeeded his father only because he played the *shofar* well. In the end more than fifty rabbis, some from outside Italy, were involved and Norsa had to yield. The case against him looks black, but then the account that has survived was compiled by his rabbinical opponents; rabbis on both sides were linked by networks of marriages and the legal–doctrinal points were complicated by dynastic feuds going back generations.[17]

The Norsa case gives the impression of a vigorous group of Italian Jewish communities, well capable of defending themselves. Jews tended to thrive on their ability, like anyone else. There were some remarkable Jewish success-stories in sixteenth-century Italy. There was, for instance, the polymath Abraham Colorni, born in Mantua in 1540, who achieved an astonishing reputation as an engineer in the service of the Dukes of Ferrara. Like Leonardo da Vinci he specialized in military gear, designing mines, explosives, pontoons, collapsible boats, folding siege-ladders and forts. He manufactured an early machine-gun, producing 2,000 arquebuses which could each fire ten shots from a single priming. But he was also a distinguished mathematician, compiling tables and developing a new mirror-method for measuring distances. He was a brilliant escapologist. He wrote on secret writing and denounced the art of chiromancy. Not least, he was a notable conjuror, specializing in card-tricks. Not surprisingly, he was invited to the dazzling Prague court of Rudolph II, the wizard–emperor.[18]

At the other end of the spectrum, however, were the wretched Jews who fell victims of the wide-ranging if intermittent war between Christians and Turks in the Mediterranean, and were sold into slavery. It was Jewish policy to keep on good terms with both sides. Jews fleeing from Spain and Portugal in the 1490s were well received in Constantinople and in return helped to create a local arms-industry. They reinforced an existing Jewish community in Ottoman Salonika until it became one of the largest in the world, over 20,000 Jews living in the city by 1553. There were Jewish traders throughout the Levant, the Aegean and the Adriatic, and at times the Jews of Venice, thanks to their connections in the Balkans and further east, were able to dominate a great portion of the city's eastern trade. Jews operated from other Italian ports especially Ancona, Leghorn (Livorno), Naples and Genoa. There were very few commercial ships which did not have a Jewish businessman on board. But all such were at risk from Ottoman and Christian warships and privateers. Jews were particularly valued as captives since it was believed, usually correctly, that even if they were themselves poor a Jewish community somewhere could be persuaded to ransom them.

If a Jew was taken by Turks from a Christian ship, his release was usually negotiated from Constantinople. In Venice, the Jewish Levantine and Portuguese congregations set up a special organization for redeeming Jewish captives taken by Christians from Turkish ships. Jewish merchants paid a special tax on all goods to support it, which acted as a form of insurance since they were likely victims. The chief predators were the Knights of St John, who turned their base in Malta into the last European centre of the slave-trade. They always had their eye on Jews and took them even from Christian ships on the grounds that they were Ottoman subjects. The knights kept their captives in a slave-barracks and sold them off periodically to speculators, who paid a price for Jews above the going rate; it was assumed all Jews were rich and would be ransomed. The Venetian Jews maintained an agent in Malta who noted the arrival of Jewish captives and arranged their release if funds were available. The Christian owners exploited the Jewish relief-system to demand exorbitant prices. One Judah Surnago, aged seventy-five, was shut up naked in a cellar for two months so that he was blind and unable to stand. The owner said he would pluck out his beard and eyelashes and load him with chains unless the Jewish agent paid 200 ducats. This was done, but the agent refused to pay 600 ducats for Aaron Afia of Rhodes, who was also ill treated by his speculator owner, pointing out that if the poor man died in captivity, the owner would lose his capital. This happened in the case of Joseph Levy, beaten by the owner to stimulate a higher price, who died under the lash.[19]

This odious business went on for 300 years. In 1663, the old Cromwellian Philip Skippon described the Maltese slave-prison and noted: 'Jews, Moors and Turks are made slaves here and are publicly sold in the market. . . . The Jews are distinguished from the rest by a little piece of yellow cloth on their hats or caps, etc. We saw a rich Jew who was taken about a year before and sold in the market for 400 scudi the morning we visited the prison. Supposing himself free, by reason of a passport he held from Venice, he struck the merchant that bought him. Whereupon he was presently sent hither, his beard and hair shaven off, a great chain clapp'd on his legs, and bastinadoed with 50 blows.'[20] As late as 1768 the Jewish community in London sent £80 to help ransom a batch of Jewish slaves in Malta, and it was another thirty years before Napoleon ended the trade.

Because of their Ottoman connections, following the Spanish dispersal, the Jews were regarded by many Italians as enemies. That was a collateral reason for the ghetto system of segregation. They were popularly supposed, for instance, to have tried to help the Turks take Malta during the great siege of 1565. But the principal factor affecting Jewish destinies in sixteenth-century Europe was the Reformation. In the long run, the rise of Protestantism was of huge benefit to the Jews. It broke up the monolithic unity of Latin Europe. It meant that it was no longer possible for Christians even to aspire to a single-faith society. Thus it ended the exposed isolation of the Jews as the only nonconformist group. In large parts of Europe it brought about the destruction of the friars, the Jews' most hated enemies, and the end of such institutions as clerical celibacy and monasticism, both of which worked heavily against Jewish interests.

The Reformation, building on the work of Renaissance scholars, also brought renewed interest in Hebrew studies and the Old Testament in particular. Many Catholic apologists blamed the Jews, and still more *marranos*, for aiding and inspiring Protestant thinkers. The Jews themselves circulated tales about powerful Christians, such as even the King of Spain, being descended from *marranos* and secretly working for Christian destruction; their chroniclers attributed the rise of Protestantism in Navarre, for example, to the *marrano* factor. But there is not much actual evidence that the interest of the Reformers in the Old Testament made them pro-Jewish as such. Such Christian Hebraists as Pico della Mirandola (1463–94), Johannes Reuchlin (1455–1522), Sebastian Münster, Professor of Hebrew at Basel after 1528, and Philip Melanchthon (1497–1560) were as strongly opposed to Judaism as any Dominican, though Melanchthon, for instance, criticized the blood libel and other anti-Semitic excesses. They rejected the Mishnah and the Talmud and indeed all Jewish commentary except parts of the kabbalah. Erasmus, the most important of them all, rejected the kabbalah too and considered Jewish scholarship exceedingly dangerous – more destructive of faith than the obscurantism of the medieval schoolmen: 'Nothing more adverse and inimical to Christ can be found than this plague.'[21] He wrote to the Cologne inquisitor: 'Who is there among us who does not hate this race of men? . . . If it is Christian to hate the Jews, here we are all Christians in profusion.'[22]

It is true that, right at the beginning, the Jews welcomed the Reformation, because it divided their enemies. True also that Luther, in particular, turned to the Jews for support in his new construing of the Bible and his rejection of papal claims. In his 1523 pamphlet, *Das*

Jesus Christus ein geborener Jude sei, he argued that there was now no reason at all why they should not embrace Christ, and foolishly looked forward to a voluntary mass conversion. When the Jews retorted that the Talmud conveyed an even better understanding of the Bible than his own, and reciprocated the invitation to convert, Luther first attacked them for their obstinacy (1526), then in 1543 turned on them in fury. His pamphlet *Von den Juden und ihren Lügen* ('On the Jews and their Lies'), published in Wittenberg, may be termed the first work of modern anti-Semitism, and a giant step forward on the road to the Holocaust. 'First', he urged, 'their synagogues should be set on fire, and whatever is left should be buried in dirt so that no one may ever be able to see a stone or cinder of it.' Jewish prayer-books should be destroyed and rabbis forbidden to preach. Then the Jewish people should be dealt with, their homes 'smashed and destroyed' and their inmates 'put under one roof or in a stable like gypsies, to teach them they are not master in our land'. Jews should be banned from the roads and markets, their property seized and then these 'poisonous envenomed worms' should be drafted into forced labour and made to earn their bread 'by the sweat of their noses'. In the last resort they should be simply kicked out 'for all time'.[23] In his tirade against Jews, Luther concentrated on their role as moneylenders and insisted that their wealth did not belong to them since it had been 'extorted usuriously from us'. The usurer, Luther argued,

is a double-dyed thief and murderer. . . . Whoever eats up, rots and steals the nourishment of another, that man commits as great a murder (so far as in him lies) as he who starves a man or does him in. Such does a usurer, and sits there safe on his stool when he ought rather to be hanging on the gallows, and be eaten by as many ravens as he has stolen guilders. . . . Therefore is there on earth no greater enemy of man, after the Devil, than a gripe-money and usurer, for he wants to be God over all men. . . . Usury is a great, huge monster, like a werewolf. . . . And since we break on the wheel and behead highwaymen, murderers and housebreakers, how much more ought we to break on the wheel and kill . . . hunt down, curse and behead all usurers!

Luther was not content with verbal abuse. Even before he wrote his anti-Semitic pamphlet, he got Jews expelled from Saxony in 1537, and in the 1540s he drove them from many German towns; he tried unsuccessfully to get the elector to expel them from Brandenburg in 1543. His followers continued to agitate against Jews there: they sacked the Berlin synagogue in 1572 and the following year finally got their way, the Jews being banned from the entire country. Jean Calvin, on the other hand, was more well disposed towards Jews, partly because he tended to agree with them on the question of lending at interest; he reported Jewish arguments objectively in his writings and was even accused, by his Lutheran enemies, of being a Judaizer.[24] None the less, Jews were expelled from Calvinist cities and the Calvinist Palatinate.[25]

Because of Protestant hostility, the Jews were driven into the arms of the emperor. Charles V, when wearing his Spanish hat, was no friend. He got the papacy to set up an inquisition in Portugal in 1543, threw many *marranos* out of Lisbon seven years later, expelled the Jews from Naples in 1541 and turned them out of some of his territories in Flanders. But in Germany he found the Jews useful allies and at the diets of Augsburg (1530), Speyer (1544) and Regensburg (1546) his protection prevented their expulsion. The Catholic prince–bishops also found the Jews a useful ally against their Protestant burghers, even if they were not prepared to admit it in public. Hence at the Peace of Augsburg, it was agreed to omit the ecclesiastical states from its central provision, *cuius regio, eius religio* (religion follows the faith of the prince), and this allowed Jews to remain in Germany. Josel of Rosheim, senior rabbi in Alsace, who acted as the Jewish spokesman in this tense period, denounced Luther as a 'ruffian' and called Emperor Charles 'an angel of the Lord'; the Jews prayed for the success of the imperial army in their synagogues, and supplied it with money and provisions – thus setting a new and important Jewish survival-pattern.[26]

None the less, the Counter-Reformation, when it came, dealt harshly with the Jews as well as the Protestants. Traditionally the popes, like other princes, had used and protected Jews. There had been 50,000 Jews in Italy even before the Spanish expulsions, and the number was quickly swollen by refugees. The influx caused trouble, as in Venice, but on the whole papal policy remained benign. Paul III (1534–49) even encouraged the settlement of Jews expelled from Naples (1541) and six years later accepted *marranos* too, promising them protection from the Inquisition. His successor Julius III renewed the guarantees. In May 1555, however, Cardinal Caraffa, Grand Inquisitor and scourge of Jews, dissidents and heretics, became pope as Paul IV and immediately reversed the policy. Not only in Ancona but in many other Italian cities, papal and other, Christians and Jews were mixing freely, and he took Erasmus' view that the influence of Judaism was a mortal threat to faith. Two months after his election, with the Bull *Cum nimis absurdam* he applied the Venetian solution in Rome, where the city's Jews were driven on to the left bank of the Tiber and surrounded by a wall. In Ancona, at the same time, he carried out a purge of *marranos*, burning twenty-five of them in public. The ghetto was quickly extended to all cities in the papal states and from 1562 the word became the official term used in anti-Jewish laws. There were great bonfires of Hebrew books, not only in Rome and Bologna but in Florence. Pius v (1566–72) was even fiercer, his Bull *Hebraeorum Gens* (1569) expelling Jewish communities, some of which had had a continuous existence since antiquity. Later popes varied, but it remained papal policy to ghetto Jews in the papal states and to put pressure on other rulers to do likewise. Thus the ghetto was introduced in Tuscany in 1570–1, in Padua 1601–3, in Verona in 1599 and in Mantua in 1601–3. The Dukes of Ferrara refused to comply, but they agreed to stop Jews printing books.[27] In the end, Leghorn was the only city which did not create a ghetto of some kind.

The papacy was not the only institution to turn on the Jews. The strongest monarchies, which traditionally had been the keenest and most effective protectors of Jewish communities, were also the most vehement against heresy. In large parts of Europe, the Counter-Reformation was a great wave of reaction to the disturbing ideas circulated in the first half of the century, a return to sobriety and order, led from the top but with wide popular backing. It was a drive against racialism, subversion and innovation of every kind. The Jews were seen as a generally disturbing element, especially in the form of *marranos*. These forced converts and their descendants, cut off from the discipline of Jewish orthodoxy, tended to turn to anything, including Anabaptism, which was what authority hated most of all – it was a generic term for religious insubordination. Many *marranos* evolved weird mixtures of Christian and Jewish beliefs. They were sceptics, sneering at the Virgin Mary and the saints, laughing at images and pious practices. They set up their individual judgment against authority of every kind. *Marranos* were regarded as potential traitors to the state as well as heretics – authority could instance the useful hate-figure of João Miguez, Duke of Naxos, the most powerful of all the ex-Christian Jews, who advised the sultan himself.

The Counter-Reformation, both clerical and secular, was most suspicious of immigrants, of whom the *marranos* were one element. Authority learned from experience that movement meant trouble. It did not mind so much the old-established Jews. It was the newcomers who brought dangerous ideas. This fear operated at many levels. The Bakers' Guild of Venice publicly denounced their immigrant journeymen: 'They follow in the footsteps of the Lutherans and, boasting of having flung once most Christian Germany into confusion . . . are now sparing no effort to ruin the bakers' guild here.' At the top Charles v's ambassador to Venice warned the republic that, by failing to stamp out heresy it would invoke 'the enmity of princes for the sake of winning the friendship of peoples . . . for they wish no vassal to give obedience to his prince and they seek to destroy all dominion and to make peoples free'.[28] Pius v's nuncio in Venice, Giovanni Antonio Facchinetti, did not hesitate to attribute Venice's military failures in her war against the Turks to her culpable failure to root out Jews and heretics: it was God himself, rather than the Turks, who was now making war on the republic, and its rulers should ask themselves the question: 'Why should the majesty of God think itself offended by this state?'[29] Authority loved the Jew as a wealth-creator; hated him as an ideas-monger.

Yet the two activities were different faces of the same human coin. Experience showed that the Jew on the move, who was most likely to bring unsettling ideas, was also the most likely to introduce new, or more efficient, ways of adding to a nation's wealth. History is continually teaching us that the very fact of displacement and resettlement has an invigorating effect on ideas and ways of doing things, and so turns the emigrant into a more efficient economic animal. As far back as the eighth and seventh centuries BC, impoverished Greek herdsmen and olive-growers, leaving their ancient soil, blossomed into successful merchant–colonists throughout the Mediterranean. In the nineteenth century, clansmen who had starved in the Highlands, wretched bog-Irish from Clare and Kerry, semi-serfs from Poland, landless peasants from the Mezzogiorno, transformed themselves into enterprising citizens in Ontario and New Zealand, in Boston, New York and Chicago, in the Midwest, Argentina and New South Wales. In our own day we have constantly seen the almost miraculous effect of movement as mainland Chinese settle in Taiwan and Hong Kong, Vietnamese come to California and Australia, and Cubans to Florida.

The Reformation, Counter-Reformation and the Wars of Religion stamped on the European anthill and sent industrious little communities scurrying in all directions. Sometimes, to escape harassment and persecution, they moved two or three times before achieving permanent settlement. Almost invariably, the final host-areas prospered. It used to be argued, by Max Weber and R. H. Tawney, that modern capitalism was the product of religious notions, variously termed the 'Protestant ethic' and the Calvinist 'salvation panic', both inculcating a spirit of hard work and accumulation. But there are many insuperable objections to this theory, and it now seems more likely that displacement, rather than sectarian belief, was the common factor. The dynamic impulse to national economies, especially in

England and the Netherlands, and later in North America and Germany, was provided not only by Calvinists, but by Lutherans, Catholics from north Italy and, not least, by Jews.[30]

What these moving communities shared was not theology but an unwillingness to live under the state regimentation of religious and moral ideas at the behest of clerical establishments. All of them repudiated clerical hierarchies, favouring religious government by the congregation and the private conscience. In all these respects the Jews were the most characteristic of the various denominations of emigrants. They had repudiated clericalism ever since the destruction of the Second Temple. They had adopted congregationalism long before any Protestant sect. Their communities chose their own rabbis, and this devolved form of authority was made workable by an absence of dogmatic theology and a spirit of intellectual tolerance. Above all, they were expert settlers. They had been moving all their history. Strangers and sojourners from their earliest origins, they had, over many generations and in an endless variety of different situations, perfected many immigrant arts, especially skill in concentrating their wealth so that it could be switched quickly from a point of danger to an area of resettlement. Their trades and crafts, their folk-culture and their laws combined to assist their creative mobility.

That was one reason why new Jewish arrivals, whatever their misfortunes, always seemed to have access to working capital. And that, in turn, made them generally welcome. As one Jewish apologist, Manasseh ben Israel, put it in the mid-seventeenth century:

Hence it may be seen that God hath not left us; for if one persecutes us, another receives us civilly and courteously; and if this prince treats us ill, another treats us well; if one banisheth us out of his country, another invites us with a thousand privileges; as divers princes of Italy have done, the most eminent King of Denmark, and the mighty Duke of Savoy in Nissa. And do we not see that those Republics do flourish and much increase in trade who admit the Israelites?[31]

In addition to their general propensities, the Jews had particular contributions to make to the spirit of economic innovation and enterprise. In the Middle Ages, as we have seen, their urban, trading and financial skills were gradually acquired by the surrounding Christian communities; then the Jews had outlived their social and economic usefulness and were often told to go, or discriminated against. They might then move into a less developed area where their skills were still needed. But the alternative was to develop new methods, and the Jews were adept at this too. They kept one jump ahead of the competition, either by raising the efficiency of existing methods, and so lowering rates and prices, or by inaugurating new ones. It was when they moved into a new area that their innovatory spirit was most in evidence, usually because that was the moment for a new generation to take over. Equally important, the Jews were quick to respond to entirely new phenomena and situations. Their religion taught them to rationalize. Capitalism, at all its stages of development, has advanced by rationalizing and so improving the chaos of existing methods. The Jews could do this because, while intensely conservative (as a rule) within their own narrow and isolated world, they had no share in or emotional commitment to society as a whole and so could watch its old traditions, methods and institutions being demolished without a pang – could, indeed, play a leading role in the process of destruction. They were thus natural capitalist entrepreneurs.

This relative freedom to follow the logic of reason which their outsider status gave the Jews was nowhere better demonstrated than in their attitude to money. One of the greatest contributions the Jews made to human progress was to force European culture to come to terms with money and its power. Human societies have always shown an extraordinary unwillingness to demystify money and see it for what it is – a commodity like any other, whose value is relative. They tend, indeed, to attach absolute values to all commodities – failing to see that the value of a thing varies in time and space – and particularly to money because it has a fixed apparent value. They also invest money with special moral overtones. Why did St Paul lay down, and countless millions thoughtlessly repeat, 'The love of money is the root of all evil'? Why not the love of land or of flocks or horses; or houses or paintings? Or, most of all, the love of power? There is no ascertainable reason why money should be viewed with such opprobrium. Moreover, the moral distinction between money and all other commodities spread over into the notion of investment, making it extraordinarily difficult to construct an ethical framework for saving and economic development. Men bred cattle with honour; they sowed grain and reaped it worthily. But if they made money work for them they were parasites and lived on 'unearned increment', as it came to be termed.

The Jews were initially as much victims of this fallacy as anyone else. Indeed, they invented it. But their technique of religious rationalization, and their predicament as unwilling traders in money, eventually made them willing to face the problem, and resolve it. As we have seen, they began by working out a double standard for money dealings with Jews and gentiles. Some elements of this remain even today: many Jewish banks in Israel (and elsewhere) display notices insisting

that loans between Jews will observe the religious laws. From the end
of the fifteenth century, however, Jewish rationalizers attempted to
strip money of its magic. In a dispute at Ferrara in 1500, Rabbi
Abraham Farissol of Avignon, using a familiar (and somewhat
dishonest) argument of innovators, insisted that things had changed
since Biblical times and that money had become a mere commodity:

This has brought into being a new situation and new obligations. [It is
natural to give something for nothing to a pauper, for pity's sake but] in other
cases when a man needs something of which his comrade has plenty . . . he
purchases it at a price. Hence . . . the established practice of paying for the
hire of houses and workers . . . all of whom have their price. . . . For if nature
and wisdom were to demand that aid be given to everyone who needs it so as
to satisfy his wants, and that money be loaned without interest to those who
need money, then nature would also require that if anyone needs a house or a
horse or work to be provided for him, they should all be supplied without
payment.[32]

Farissol felt that an agreed system of prices, wages and interest was
socially beneficial since it helped to regulate amicably economic
relationships in an ordered society. To earn an income from
possession of money was no more, nor less, opprobrious than earning
it from possessing land, or any other commodity; 'it follows in
accordance with practice and nature that he who benefits from the
money of his comrade is duty bound to pay something back'. About
the same time, Isaac Abrabanel produced a similar line of defence in
his commentary on the Deuteronomy text, first published in 1551:
'There is nothing unworthy about interest . . . because it is proper that
people should make a profit out of their money, wine and corn, and if
someone wants money from someone else . . . why should a farmer
[who] received wheat to sow his field not give the lender 10 per cent if
he is successful, as he usually should be? This is an ordinary business
transaction, and correct.' An interest-free transaction, he added, was
reserved for someone to whom we owe especial kindness, such as
indeed a needy co-religionist.[33]

The willingness to face the idea of money squarely, to deal with it
honestly and rationally, had deep roots in both Biblical and rabbinical
Judaism. Judaism did not polarize piety and prosperity. It praised the
poor, it deplored avarice, but it also constantly suggested links
between the good things of life and moral worthiness. There is a
beautiful passage in Deuteronomy in which Moses stresses the bounty
which God will bestow on those who keep his law: 'And he will love
thee, and bless thee, and multiply thee: he will also bless the fruit of thy
womb, and the fruit of thy land, thy corn and thy wine, and thine oil,

the increase of thy kine and the flocks of thy sheep, in the land which he swore unto thy fathers to give thee.'[34] Israel itself shall be wealthy: 'thou shalt lend unto many nations, but thou shalt not borrow'.[35] 'They that seek the Lord', said the Psalms, 'shall not want any good thing.'[36] The Psalms and Proverbs, the Wisdom of Solomon, Ecclesiastes, the book of Ben Sira were full of such sentiments. The Talmud echoed them: 'In time of scarcity a man learns to value wealth best.' 'Seven characteristics are there which are "comely to the righteous and comely to the world". One of them is riches.' Jewish halakhah had always dealt directly with actual and not just theoretical business problems, on the assumption that properly conducted trading was not only wholly compatible with strict morality but positively virtuous since it made possible the good works and systematic charity around which the Jewish community revolved. The cathedocracy had ruled and written realistically about trade because many of its members engaged in it. Men like Maimonides and Nahmanides had never made the assumption, so characteristic of the Christian intelligentsia, that there is an absolute distinction between book-reading and book-writing on the one hand, and book-keeping on the other. Rabbinical Judaism said things about business which all sensible men know to be true and just, but which convention normally excludes from the realm of religious discourse.

That being so, the Jews were well prepared to take advantage of the growth in the world economy which marked the sixteenth century; indeed, in view of their exclusion from the Spanish peninsula, and their treatment in Reformation and Counter-Reformation Europe, they had no alternative but to push the diaspora further and seek new outlets for their business skills. To the West, Columbus' voyages were not the only ones which had a Jewish and *marrano* background in finance and technology. Expelled Jews went to the Americas as the earliest traders. They set up factories. In St Thomas, for instance, they became the first large-scale plantation-owners. Spanish laws forbidding Jews to emigrate to the colonies proved ineffective and in 1577 were repealed. Jews and *marranos* were particularly active in settling Brazil; the first governor-general, Thomas de Souza, sent out in 1549, was certainly of Jewish origin. They owned most of the sugar plantations. They controlled the trade in precious and semi-precious stones. Jews expelled from Brazil in 1654 helped to create the sugar industry in Barbados and Jamaica. The new British colonies in the West welcomed them. The Governor of Jamaica, rejecting a petition for their expulsion in 1671, wrote that 'he was of opinion that his Majesty could not have more profitable subjects than the Jews and the

Hollanders; they had great stocks and correspondence'. The government in Surinam pronounced: 'We have found that the Hebrew nation . . . have . . . proved themselves useful and beneficial to the colony.'[37]

To the East, the Jews had been active in the Russian border territories, especially on the shores of the Black Sea, since Hellenistic times at least. Indeed, legends connect the arrival of Jews in Armenia and Georgia with the Ten Lost Tribes of the despoiled northern kingdom of Israel. In the first half of the eighth century, the Kingdom of the Khazars had been converted to Judaism. From early medieval times Jews had been active over a vast swathe of territory in southern Euro-Asia, both as traders and as proselytizers. In the 1470s, in the rapidly expanding Principality of Moscow, Jewish activities brought into existence a semi-secret sect which the authorities termed the Judaizers, and ferocious efforts were made to stamp it out. Tsar Ivan IV Vasilievich, 'Ivan the Terrible' (1530–84), ordered Jews who refused to embrace Christianity to be drowned, and Jews were officially excluded from Russian territory until the partition of Poland in the late eighteenth century.

The Russian barrier to further eastern penetration led to intensive Jewish settlement in Poland, Lithuania and the Ukraine. As in western Europe in the Dark and early Middle Ages, the Jews served as a key element in a vast colonization process, marked by a rapid expansion in the agricultural and trading economy, and a phenomenal increase in population. In about 1500 there were only 20,000–30,000 Jews living in Poland, out of a total population of five million. By 1575, while the total population had risen to seven million, the number of Jews had jumped to 150,000, and thereafter the rise was still more rapid. In 1503 the Polish monarchy appointed Rabbi Jacob Polak 'Rabbi of Poland', and the emergence of a chief rabbinate, backed by the crown, allowed the development of a form of self-government which the Jews had not known since the end of the exilarchate. From 1551 the chief rabbi was elected by the Jews themselves. This was, to be sure, oligarchic rather than democratic rule. The rabbinate had wide powers over law and finances, appointing judges and a great variety of other officials. When he shared his powers with local councils, only between 1 and 5 per cent of Jewish householders had the right to vote.[38] The royal purpose in devolving power on the Jews was, of course, self-interested. There was a great deal of Polish hostility to the Jews. In Cracow, for instance, where the local merchant class was strong, Jews were usually kept out. The kings found they could make money out of the Jews by selling to certain cities and towns, such as Warsaw, the privilege *de non tolerandis Judaeis*. But they could make even more by allowing Jewish communities to grow up, and milking them. The rabbinate and local Jewish councils were primarily tax-raising agencies. Only 30 per cent of what they raised went on welfare and official salaries; all the rest was handed over to the crown in return for protection.

The association of the rabbinate with communal finance and so with the business affairs of those who had to provide it led the eastern or Ashkenazi Jews to go even further than the early-sixteenth-century Italians in giving halakhic approval to new methods of credit-finance. Polish Jews operating near the frontiers of civilization had links with Jewish family firms in the Netherlands and Germany. A new kind of credit instrument, the *mamram*, emerged and got rabbinical approval. In 1607 Jewish communities in Poland and Lithuania were also authorized to use *heter iskah*, an inter-Jewish borrowing system which allowed one Jew to finance another in return for a percentage. This rationalization of the law eventually led even conservative authorities, like the famous Rabbi Judah Loew, the Maharal of Prague, to sanction lending at interest.

With easy access to credit, Jewish pioneer settlers played a leading part in developing eastern Poland, the interior of Lithuania, and the Ukraine, especially from the 1560s onwards. The population of western Europe was expanding fast. It needed to import growing quantities of grain. Ambitious Polish landowners, anxious to meet the need, went into partnership with Jewish entrepreneurs to create new wheat-growing areas to supply the market, take the grain down-river to the Baltic ports, and then ship it west. The Polish magnates – Radziwills, Sovieskis, Zamojkis, Ostrogskis, Lubomirskis – owned or conquered the land. The ports were run by German Lutherans. The Dutch Calvinists owned most of the ships. But the Jews did the rest. They not only managed the estates but in some cases held the deeds as pledges in return for working capital. Sometimes they leased the estates themselves. They ran the tolls. They built and ran mills and distilleries. They owned the river boats, taking out the wheat and bringing back in return wine, cloth and luxury goods, which they sold in their shops. They were in soap, glazing, tanning and furs. They created entire villages and townships (*shtetls*), where they lived in the centre, while peasants (Catholics in Poland and Lithuania, Orthodox in the Ukraine) occupied the suburbs.

Before 1569 when the Union of Brest-Litovsk made the Polish settlement of the Ukraine possible, there were only twenty-four Jewish settlements there with 4,000 inhabitants; by 1648 there were 115, with a numbered population of 51,325, the total being much greater.

Most of these places were owned by Polish nobles, absentee-landlords, the Jews acting as middlemen and intermediaries with the peasants – a role fraught with future danger. Often Jews were effectively the magnates too. At the end of the sixteenth century Israel of Zloczew, for instance, leased an entire region of hundreds of square miles from a consortium of nobles to whom he paid the enormous annual sum of 4,500 zlotys. He sub-let tolls, taverns and mills to his poorer relatives.[39] Jews from all over Europe arrived to take part in this colonizing process. In many settlements they constituted the majority of the inhabitants, so that for the first time outside Palestine they dominated the local culture. But they were important at every level of society and administration. They farmed the taxes and the customs. They advised government. And every Polish magnate had a Jewish counsellor in his castle, keeping the books, writing letters, running the economic show.

Indeed, by the end of the sixteenth century, there were few men of importance in east-central Europe who 'knew not Joseph'. One great Jewish archetype had come into his own at last. By the last quarter of the century, the ideological thrust of the Counter-Reformation had spent itself. Philip II of Spain was the last of the committed princes, acting in close concert with the papacy. In his old age, in the spirit of Paul IV, he turned the Jews out of his Duchy of Milan (1597). But other princes backed the Catholic cause, or indeed the Protestant one, from reasons of self-interest. Or they became *politiques*, and compromised. The power and influence of the church declined; the authority of the state increased. The most influential legal and political writers – Montaigne, Jean Bodin, Lipsius, Francis Bacon – advocated a secular view of public policy. Nations should not be disturbed and divided by religious broils. It was the function of the state to achieve reasonable settlements and promote unity and prosperity. In this new atmosphere of toleration and *realpolitik*, sophisticated Jews were welcomed on their merits.[40]

Thus the Republic of Venice, from 1577 onwards, authorized the Dalmatian *marrano*, Daniel Rodriguez, to create the new port of Spalato (Split), as part of a new policy, in which Jews played a notable part, of re-routing trade down the Balkan rivers.[41] The Duke of Tuscany gave the Jews of Leghorn a charter. The Duke of Savoy acted to create Jewish settlements in Nice and Turin. The kings of France issued letters of protection to Jewish merchants. Henri IV even played cards with one, Manoel de Pimentel, whom he called 'the king of the Gamblers'. In Amsterdam, the Calvinist authorities did not inquire into the religious views of *marranos*, or of Sephardi Jews who arrived in the 1590s, or indeed of Ashkenazi settlers who moved in from about 1620. They held their services, at first in private. They ran a Torah school from 1616, printed their own books from the 1620s. To the Dutch, they were a useful and well-behaved addition to the mercantile community.[42] In Frankfurt, the community became so prosperous that general rabbinical synods were held there in 1562, 1582 and 1603.

German-speaking towns and principalities which had expelled Jews earlier in the century readmitted them. The Habsburg Emperor Maximilian II allowed the Jews to return to Bohemia and in 1577 his successor, Rudolph II, gave them a charter of privileges. The old Jewish community of Vienna was reconstituted and in Prague, where Rudolph had set up his court, there were 3,000 Jews by the end of the century. Famous teaching rabbis like the Maharal, Ephraim Solomon ben Aaron of Luntschits and Isaiah ben Abraham ha-Levi Horowitz lived in the Jewish quarter alongside merchant princes like Jacob Bassevi von Treuenberg, Mordecai Zemah Cohen and Marcus Meisel. Rudolph had a famous interview with the Maharal in his palace, and he patronized gifted Jews of all kinds, from astronomers to jewel-smiths. But he found Jews most useful of all as financiers. He made Meisel into the first 'court Jew' – a type which was to dominate government finance in much of central Europe for 150 years, and remained of some significance until 1914.

The great Jewish strength lay in the ability to take quick advantage of new opportunities; to recognize an unprecedented situation when it arose and devise methods of handling it. Christians had long learned how to deal with conventional financial problems, but they were conservative and slow to react to novelty. Towards the close of the sixteenth century, the principal novelty was the ever-growing scale and cost of war. Meisel supplied Rudolph, a leading collector, with *objets d'art* and scientific instruments but his main function was to help finance the war against Turkey. In return the emperor allowed him to loan money not only against actual pledges, such as jewellery, but against promissory notes and lands. The relationship between the two men – the clever, devout Jew and the selfish, self-indulgent Habsburg – was inevitably exploitative on both sides. When Meisel died in 1601, leaving over half a million florins, the state seized his estate on the grounds that his transactions, despite imperial permission, were illegal. But Meisel, no doubt foreseeing this, had already spent vast sums on the Prague community. He built a synagogue, to which Rudolph gave the privileges of denying entrance to the police, displaying the star of David and tax immunity; he endowed a Jewish cemetery; he set up a hospital; he even paved the streets of the Jewish quarter. He financed Jewish communities in Poland, and contributed to the entire range of Jewish funds, including those in Palestine. The epitaph on his Prague tombstone (which survives) is doubtless the truth: 'None of his contemporaries was truly his equal in deeds of charity.'[43] In effect, it paid the leading members of the Jewish community to be exploited by the crown, provided it was the only one and protected them from other predators.

During this period at least the Habsburgs kept their part of the bargain. When the Frankfurt mob, led by Vincent Fettmilch, stormed the Jewish quarter in Frankfurt in 1614, expelling the Jews and plundering their houses, the Emperor Matthias declared the insurgents rebels and outlaws and hanged their leaders two years later. The Jews were restored to their homes, with imperial ceremony and new privileges, a highly satisfactory event which they celebrated annually thereafter as 'The Purim of Vincent'. In turn, the Jews helped the Habsburgs. In 1618 the Thirty Years War broke out in Germany and during its opening phase the Habsburgs came close to destruction. It was the Jews, especially the financier Jacob Bassevi of Prague, who kept them in the saddle. Hence when the tide turned at the Battle of the White Mountain, and the imperial armies recaptured the city (1620), the Jewish quarter was the only one they did not pillage. The Emperor Ferdinand II himself presented Bassevi with two of the finest confiscated Protestant houses.

This terrible conflict, which brought ruin to Germany, pushed the Jews to the very centre of the European economy. Huge armies had to be kept in the field for years at a time, and often right through the winter. The Jewish food-supply network in eastern Europe enabled them to provide the food and fodder. They set up foundries and powder-mills and scoured Europe and the east for arms. Above all, they raised ready money, often by finding novel ways of exploiting sluggish imperial assets. It was Bassevi who in 1622 set up a consortium, with Prince Liechtenstein and the imperial general Wallenstein, which leased the imperial silver mint. The emperor got a huge sum to finance the war, and Bassevi and his colleagues recuperated it by debasing the coinage. Bassevi was called *Judenfürst* (princely Jew) by his community; he was raised to the imperial peerage. On the other hand, his property was confiscated in 1631 and when he died in 1634, soon after his protector Wallenstein was assassinated, all his privileges were revoked. The life of a Jewish war-financier was vulnerable. But when had the life of any Jew not been vulnerable?

When war came, especially the new kind of total war inaugurated by Wallenstein and Gustavus Adolphus, the need to win it – or just to survive – took precedence over ideology, religion, race and tradition. The Jews, with their extraordinary capacity to get their hands on scarce supplies and raise cash in a bleak and hostile world, soon made themselves indispensable to all sides. When the Swedes reversed the Catholic tide, and most of German Jewry fell under Lutheran rule, they began by penalizing the Jews with forced loans. But within a year, Jews were operating as principal contractors to the Swedish army. As with the Habsburgs, they supplied food, munitions and, above all, horses. Moreover, the Lutheran commanders found, as had the Catholic Habsburgs, that as the Jews were second-class citizens and often a persecuted minority, they were content to be paid in credit, protection and privileges – the last enabling them to make the cash for themselves. In due course, as more and more European powers intervened in the struggle, the Jews of the Rhineland and Alsace, of Bohemia and Vienna, supplied them all. In Emmerich, occupied by Dutch troops, Solomon Gomperz became rich by selling them food and tobacco. In Alsace, the Jews sold Cardinal Richelieu's army horses and fodder. All these services brought privileged status in return. Richelieu, who controlled the entire maritime effort of France, gave the Portuguese *marranos* special status in the ports, though it was obvious they were Jews, not Christians. In 1636 Ferdinand II issued orders to his commanders that the Jews of Worms were not to be subjected to forced loans or billeting, or harassed in any way. In fact it was rare for either side to conscript Jews for service. Not only the imperialist commanders but the Swedes and Lutherans too strictly forbade any looting of Jewish quarters. Hence it is a curious fact that, during the Thirty Years War, for the first time in their history, the Jews were treated better, rather than worse, than the population as a whole. While Germany underwent the worst harrowing in its history, the Jews survived and even prospered. As the historian Jonathan Israel has put it: 'There is not a scrap of evidence to show that central European Jewry declined at all in size during the Thirty Years War.'[44]

In the closing stages of the war, court Jews were acting as provision-contractors for entire armies, though the first actual contracts for them to do so date only from the 1650s. Moreover, they were found to be just as useful in peacetime as in war. They became a permanent part of the absolutist princely state, raising the money for the gigantic baroque palaces and planned capital cities which were its hallmarks, and launching the mercantilist economic policies which kept it afloat. Jewish loans financed the great Karlskirche in Vienna and the splendid Schönbrunn Palace of the Habsburgs. Some Jews acted as virtual chief ministers to German princes, helping them to effect the concentration of political and economic power in the palace from which the Jews, as well as sovereigns, benefited. There were a score or more famous dynasties of court Jews. Three generations of the Gomperz family served the prince–bishops of Munster, five the Hohenzollerns. The Behrends served the court of Hanover, the Lehmanns Saxony. From another professional court family, the Fuersts, Samuel Fuerst was court Jew to successive Dukes of Schleswig-Holstein, Jeremiah Fuerst to the Duke of Mecklenburg and Israel Fuerst to the court of Holstein-Gottorp. The Goldschmidts served several German princes and the Danish royal family too. Indeed, German Jews, both Sephardi and Ashkenazi, were active at Scandinavian courts: the de Lima and the de Casseres families served the Danes, the de Sampaios the Swedes. The Kings of Poland employed the Lehmanns and the Abensurs, the Kings of Portugal the da Costas, the Kings of Spain the Bocarros.[45]

Jewish skill in raising and deploying huge sums of cash played a decisive role in two of the greatest military confrontations of the second half of the seventeenth century: the Habsburgs' successful resistance to the advance of Turkey into Europe and their subsequent counter-offensive; and the great coalition which halted Louis XIV's attempt to dominate the Continent. Samuel Oppenheimer (1630–1703) played the leading role in both. He was Imperial War Purveyor to the Austrian monarchy during the 1673–9 struggle against France, and in Austria's struggle against Turkey from 1682 he got the sole contract to supply her armies. He produced the uniforms and rations for the troops, paid their wages, supplied and fed their horses, ran the hospitals for their wounded and even built rafts to transport guns, horses and men down the river-systems. It was he, as much as anyone else, who saved Vienna during the frantic siege of 1683 when the emperor fled; it was he who played a decisive role in the siege and capture of Budapest (1686) and Belgrade (1689–98). In 1688 Oppenheimer was called on to equip and pay the armies raised to resist Louis XIV's invasion of the Palatinate, so that for some years he was running the finances of a two-front war, marshalling the resources of a vast network of Jewish financial families, throughout Germany and the Netherlands, to raise the cash.

Court Jews had all kinds of titles – *Hoffaktor, Hofjude, Hof-provediteur, Hofagent, Kabinettfaktor, Kommenzienrat, General-provediteur* and many others; the great Oppenheimer seems to have been called *Oberhoffaktor* in peace and *Oberkriegsfaktor* in war.

They enjoyed great privileges: easy access to the sovereign, the right to travel anywhere, any time they liked; exemption from the Jewish courts and usually from local courts too, instead coming under the jurisdiction of the princely court, the *Hofgericht*. They constituted a distinct class not only in general but in Jewish society: it became rare for court Jews to marry any other kind. Thus virtually all of them were interrelated. These alliances did not always work. Oppenheimer's nephew, Samson Wertheimer, became his greatest rival and enemy. But as a rule it was the family links which made the Jewish system for raising and transferring vast sums so efficient.

Moreover, the family principle tended to reinforce the Jewish principle in the lives of these men who straddled two worlds. The court Jew was tempted to assimilate to the glittering aristocratic societies he served. Some were awarded the right to have coats of arms, in addition to their official titles. They were allowed to wear swords or carry pistols; to ride on horseback and keep carriages; they and their womenfolk could dress as they pleased. Most important of all, they could live as and where they wanted. They could buy a house outside the Jewish quarter or even in a town where Jews were banned – thus Oppenheimer won the right to live in Vienna not only for himself but for an estimated one hundred families related to or dependent on him. But few of these men, at any rate in the seventeenth century, were keen actually to break away from the Jewish community. Although their way of life might be remote from the ghetto, they served their fellow Jews with their money and their negotiating power. They knew that the family network and the Jewish embrace was their only refuge in time of trouble. They could not trust the Christian law. The Christian mob was always ready to spring. Princes were usually volatile and faithless. Even if one were loyal, he might die and then a court Jew's enemies would fall on him like wolves.

Oppenheimer's experience was instructive. No one ever rendered greater services to the Habsburgs. Yet when the Peace of Nijmegen (1679) left him owed 200,000 florins, the Austrian Treasury refused to pay and even a personal appeal to the emperor secured only part-repayment. In 1692, by which time he was owed 700,000 florins, the Treasury brought false charges against him and he was forced to buy his freedom by producing half a million. Two years later he was owed the colossal sum of five million, and this later rose still higher. Yet during the brief peace, 1698–1702, when there was less need for his services, the mob was allowed to attack and plunder his house in Vienna. The authorities eventually acted and hanged two of the rioters, but when the old man died in 1703 the state repudiated his debts. As Oppenheimer had himself borrowed hugely to finance his loans, this gave Europe a taste of its first modern financial crisis, and the Habsburgs had to go cap in hand to the old man's competitor, Wertheimer, to get out of the mess they had created. But the heirs were never paid and the estate had to be auctioned off sixty years later.[46]

Another member of the family, Joseph Oppenheimer (c. 1698–1738), who tried to assist the new Duke of Württemberg from 1733 to establish an authoritarian state based upon ducal control of the economy, was a tragic victim when the duke died suddenly four years later. Oppenheimer was arrested the same day, charged with subverting the rights of the community and embezzling its revenues, convicted and hanged. His body was publicly exhibited in an iron cage. The rise and fall of Oppenheimer, also known as Süss or 'Jud' (Jew) Süss, acted as a warning to Jews who put their trust in gentiles and was later the subject of a famous novel by Leon Feuchtwanger.

It was significant that Oppenheimer, who had virtually ceased to be a Jew during his prosperity, returned to strict orthodoxy during his imprisonment, refused baptism as a condition of reprieve, and died confessing his faith. A contemporary print shows him clean-shaved. Some other court Jews shaved their beards but most refused. An Elector of Saxony, who employed some twenty Jewish families around his court, offered 5,000 thalers to one patriarch to shave his beard. But the man refused and the elector, in his fury, called for scissors and cut it off himself. Samson Wertheimer not only kept his beard but dressed (as the courtiers said) 'like a Pole'. Most court Jews, while marrying only among themselves, served their local Jewish communities, often acting as *shtadlan* (official negotiator). The great Samuel Oppenheimer had agents roaming through Hungary, Slovakia and the Balkans, ransoming poor Jews captured in the Austro-Turkish wars, and resettling them in secure communities. The Jew at court, however wealthy or powerful, knew he was never really safe and he did not have to look far to find Jews who were in desperate trouble.

In 1648–9, the Jews of south-eastern Poland and the Ukraine were struck by catastrophe. This episode was of great importance in Jewish history for several reasons, as we shall see, but its immediate impact was to remind Jews everywhere of the fragility of their position and the power and fury of the forces which could strike them without warning. The Thirty Years War had put growing pressure on the food-exporting resources of Poland. It was because of their Polish networks that Jewish contractors to the various armies had been so successful in supplying them. But the chief beneficiaries had been the Polish landlords; and the chief losers had been the Polish and

Ukrainian peasants, who had seen an ever increasing proportion of the crops they raised marketed and sold at huge profit to the ravenous armies. Under the Arenda system, whereby the Polish nobility leased not only land but all fixed assets such as mills, breweries, distilleries, inns and tolls to Jews, in return for fixed payments, the Jews had flourished and their population had grown rapidly. But the system was inherently unstable and unjust. The landlords, absentee and often spendthrift, put continual pressure on the Jews by raising the price each time a lease was renewed; the Jews in turn put pressure on the peasants.

In the Ukraine the injustice was particularly resented since both sets of oppressors, Catholic nobles and Jewish middlemen, were of a different religion to the Orthodox peasantry. Some Jewish leaders were sensitive to the wrongs of the peasants and aware of the danger to the Jews. At a council of rabbis and communal leaders held at Volhynia in 1602, Jewish lessees were begged, for instance, to allow the peasants off work on the Sabbath and Jewish holidays as a sign of goodwill: 'Let not [the Jews] be ungrateful to the Giver of bounty, the very bounty given; let the name of the Lord be glorified through them.'[47] But many Jews were not in a position to exercise benevolence, being sub- and sub-sub-lessees, forced to grind the peasants in order to pay their own rents. They put their trust in cannon. Jews and Poles alike fortified the towns; synagogues were built with embrasures and had guns mounted on the roof.

The Ukrainian peasants finally rose in the late spring of 1648, led by a petty aristocrat called Bogdan Chmielnicki, with the help of Dnieper Cossacks and Tartars from the Crimea. His rising was fundamentally aimed at Polish rule and the Catholic church, and many Polish nobles and clergy were among the victims. But the principal animus was directed against Jews, with whom peasants had had the most contact, and when it came to the point the Poles always abandoned their Jewish allies to save themselves. Thousands of Jews from the villages and *shtetls* scrambled for safety to the big fortified towns, which turned into death-traps for them. At Tulchin the Polish troops handed over the Jews to the Cossacks in exchange for their own lives; at Tarnopol, the garrison refused to let the Jews in at all. At Bar, the fortress fell and all the Jews were massacred. There was another fierce slaughter at Narol. At Nemirov, the Cossacks got into the fortress by dressing as Poles, 'and they killed about 6,000 souls in the town', according to the Jewish chronicle; 'they drowned several hundreds in the water and by all kinds of cruel torments'. In the synagogue they used the ritual knives to kill Jews, then burned the building down, tore up the sacred books and trampled them underfoot, and used the leather covers for sandals.

We do not know exactly how many Jews died. The Jewish chronicles say 100,000 were killed and 300 communities destroyed. One modern historian believes most of the Jews escaped and that the massacres were 'less a major turning-point in the history of Polish Jewry than a brutal but relatively short interruption in its steady growth and expansion'.[48] The chroniclers' figures are certainly exaggerated, but the tales of the refugees had a profound emotional effect not only on Polish Jews but on Jewish communities everywhere.[49]

As in earlier periods, the effect of calamity was to reinforce the irrational and apocalyptic elements in Judaism and in particular to make Jews hypersensitive to signs of a messianic deliverance. The rationalist optimism of the twelfth century reflected in the works of Maimonides had largely disappeared by the end of the fourteenth century, as Jewish communities almost everywhere came under pressure. Among the Jewish upper classes, kabbalistic mysticism strengthened its grip. The destruction and scattering of the great Spanish community from the 1490s reinforced the trend towards irrationalism in two specific ways. First, it democratized the kabbalah. From being an esoteric science taught orally among an educated elite, or through secretly circulated manuscripts, it became public property. Large numbers of manuscripts containing portions of the *Zohar* or kabbalistic anthologies circulated in Jewish communities everywhere. The rise of the Jewish press had a loudspeaker effect. In 1558–60, two complete versions of the *Zohar* were printed competitively in Cremona and Mantua. Further printings followed all over the Jewish diaspora, in Leghorn and Constantinople, in Smyrna, Salonika, and especially in Germany and Poland.[50] In its popular versions, the kabbalah mixed with the folk-superstitions and vulgarized aggadic tales which had always constituted a great part of the everyday religion of ordinary Jews. After a generation or two, it was impossible to separate one tradition from the other: they merged in a glutinous mass of magic–mystic lore.

Secondly, the Spanish expulsions made the kabbalah itself dynamic by adding an eschatological element concentrated on the notion of Zion and the coming of the Messiah. The kabbalah and its growing volume of superstitious accretions ceased to be just a mystic way of knowing God and became an historical force, a means to accelerate Israel's redemption. It moved to the very centre of Judaistic belief and took on some of the characteristics of a mass movement.

The process was assisted by the drift of exiled Jews to Palestine and the growth of a school of kabbalistic studies at Safed in northern Galilee. Its first notable scholar was David ben Solomon ibn abi Zimra, who moved to Safed from Egypt, and was known as Radbaz. Moses ben Jacob Cordovero, or Remak (1522–70), provided the first complete and systematic theology of the kabbalah. But the real genius of the new movement was Isaac ben Solomon Luria (1534–72), known as ha-Ari, the Lion. His father was an Ashkenazi from east-central Europe who went to Jerusalem and married a Sephardi girl. So in the transmission of kabbalistic culture, Luria acted as a bridge between the two communities. He himself was brought up in Egypt by an uncle who was a tax-farmer. He went into trade, specializing in pepper and corn. Luria was a splendid example of the Jewish tradition that business is not incompatible with the intellectual life, or even the most intense mystical speculation. He traded and studied all his life. It was a sign of the democratization of the kabbalah that he absorbed its legends as a child. But as a young man he became expert in orthodox, non-mystic halakhah. One of his gifts was to reconcile and move easily between the two. He wrote very little. His only known book is a commentary on the 'Book of Concealment' in the *Zohar*. He only moved to Safed towards the end of his life, after spending the years 1569–70 pondering the *Zohar* on an island in the Nile. But once in Safed he had a mesmerizing effect on the wide circle of pupils he gathered round him. They memorized his teaching and later wrote it down (like the philosopher Wittgenstein's pupils in the 1930s). He radiated not only holiness but power and authority. Some thought he might be the Messiah himself. He seemed to understand the language of birds. He often talked to the prophets. He would walk around Safed with his pupils, pointing out from intuitive knowledge the unidentified graves of holy men. Then he would get back to the export–import trade. He made up his last set of accounts only three days before he died. His early death produced tales that he had ascended to heaven, and miracle-stories quickly attached themselves to his name.[51]

Luria won his initial influence by teaching his pupils how to achieve intense states of meditation by concentrating entirely on the letters of the Divine Names. Like most kabbalists, he believed that the actual letters of the Torah, and the numbers which they symbolized, offered means of direct access to God. It is a very potent brew once swallowed. However, Luria also had a cosmic theory which had an immediate direct bearing on belief in the Messiah, and which remains the most influential of all Jewish mystical ideas. The kabbalah listed the various layers of the cosmos. Luria postulated the thought that Jewish miseries were a symptom of the breakdown of the cosmos. Its shattered husks, or *klippot*, which are evil, none the less contain tiny sparks, *tikkim*, of the divine light. This imprisoned light is the Exile of the Jews. Even the divine *Shekinah* itself is part of the trapped light, subject to evil influences. The Jewish people have a dual significance in this broken cosmos, both as symbols and as active agents. As symbols, the injuries inflicted on them by the gentiles show how evil hurts the light. But as agents they have the task of restoring the cosmos. By the strictest observance of the Law, they can release the sparks of light trapped in the cosmic husks. When this restitution has been made, the Exile of the Light will end, the Messiah will come and Redemption will take place.

The attractiveness of this theory to ordinary Jews was that it enabled them to believe they had some hand in their destiny. In antiquity they had fought the gentiles and evil – and lost. In the Middle Ages they had accepted passively the wrongs inflicted on them – and nothing had happened; their predicament had grown worse. Now they were told, in effect, that they were potent actors in a cosmic drama, for the greater the catastrophes which involved the Jews, the more certain they could be that the drama was reaching crisis. By their very piety, they could accelerate and resolve the crisis, generating a great wave of prayer and devotion on which the Messiah would sweep in to triumph.

All the same, the spread of kabbalistic messianism among the Jewish masses took more than a century. One of the reasons why Maimonides was so opposed to active speculation about the Messiah, and sought to present the Messianic Age itself in rational, almost humdrum terms as a time when all Jews would take to intense scholarship, was that he feared that what he termed 'the rabble'[52] would be swept by a wave of excitement into hailing a false Messiah, and then lapse into demoralized disillusionment. His apprehensions proved justified. The 1492 expulsions were seen as the birthpangs of the Messiah. In 1500–2 in north Italy Rabbi Asher Lemlein preached an imminent Coming. Messiahs of a sort duly appeared. In 1523 a plausible young man, probably a Falasha Jew from Ethiopia, arrived in Venice. One of his tales was that he was descended from King David. Another was that his father was a certain King Solomon, and his brother King Joseph, ruler of the Lost Tribes of Reuben, Gad and half-Manasseh. Hence he was known as David Reubeni. He took in many Jews and, for a time, some Christian princes. But he ended up in a Spanish prison. His tales inspired another claimant, Solomon Molcho, to proclaim himself the Messiah at Rome in 1530. He was burned alive two years later.[53]

These fiascos – and there were others – discouraged learned men from using kabbalistic method to discern signs of Redemption. Joseph Caro, who went to Safed, deliberately ignored the kabbalah in both the academic and the popular versions of his code, and he did nothing to increase messianic speculation. But he also wrote a mystical diary, in which a miraculous mentor or *maggid* – the personified Mishnah – makes an appearance.[54] Most rabbis were cool towards messianism, since it was not at all clear what part, if any, the rabbi would play in the Messianic Age. Luria's greatest pupil, Hayyim Vital (1542–1620), certainly made no effort to bring his master's theory to the masses. He spent the latter part of his long life concealing most of the lessons Luria taught him. However, in his *Book of Visions*, which he compiled 1610–12, an autobiographical work recording nearly half a century of dreams, he makes it clear that he believed Luria was worthy to have become the Messiah and that he himself might be called. One dream recounts: 'I heard a voice saying out loud: "The Messiah is coming and the Messiah stands before me." He blew the horn and thousands and tens of thousands from Israel were gathered to him. He said to us: "Come with me and you shall see the avenging of the destruction of the Temple." '[55] Moreover, by the 1630s most of Luria's teaching, as revised by Vital and the Master's other leading pupil, Joseph ibn Tabul, was in print and widely read.

From Safed, Lurianic kabbalah spread gradually to Jewish communities in Turkey, the Balkans and eastern Europe. In Poland, where Jewish printing presses existed in Lublin and elsewhere, its impact was strong and wide. By the end of the sixteenth century, it was regarded there as a normative part of Judaism. Rabbi Joel Sirkes ruled in a *responsum* that 'he who raises objections to the science of the kabbalah' was 'liable to excommunication'. During the first half of the seventeenth century, in the teeming Jewish *shtetls* and ghetto-quarters of Poland, Lithuania and the Ukraine, this form of Judaism, ranging from highbrow mysticism and ascetic piety at one end of the spectrum, to idiot superstition at the other, became the essential religion of the community.

Much of the superstition in the ghetto was very old. Though the Bible itself was remarkably free, on the whole, of angel–devil material, it began to penetrate Judaism during the early rabbinic period and acquired official status in the aggadah. The miraculous tales told about Luria had circulated about the early sages too. Hillel, like Luria, could understand what the birds were saying to each other – and all the animals, and even the trees and clouds. The sages dealt in moral fables of all kinds. It was said that Hillel's pupil, Johanan ben Zakkai, 'knew the parables of laundrymen and fox fables'. The Rabbi Meir was reckoned to have known 300 fox fables. It was the sages who let the devils into Judaism. The difficulty was, of course, that despite the Bible's condemnation of sorcery (e.g. 'Thou shalt not tolerate a sorceress' – Exodus 22:18), and despite the Judaic belief that all actions were willed by God alone, ruling out any kind of dualism, some relics of ancient black and white magic lingered on in the texts and were given a kind of inferred sanction. Thus the bells worn on the robes of the high-priest were designed to combat devils. So, it could be argued, were phylacteries, one of the most honoured devices of responsible Jewish piety. There were not many devils in the Bible, but they did exist: Mevet the death-god, Lilith the child-stealer (sometimes an owl), Reshev the plague-god, Dever, another sickness-god, Belial, a sort of devil-commander, Satan, leader of the anti-God forces, Azazel, the scapegoat-god of the wilderness.[56] So the invasion of Judaism by devils over the period 150 BC to 300 AD had some precedents. Needless to say, Hillel could understand devil language too. Devils varied greatly, though according to Isaac of Acre they all lacked thumbs. Some, like Satan and Belial, were formidable, serious. Some were evil or unclean spirits, called *ru'ah tezazit* in the Talmud. They entered an individual, possessed him, spoke through the mouth. Kabbalistic literature written by Luria's disciples was full of stories about these disgusting creatures, which in the ghettos of Ashkenazi Jewry, especially in Poland, came to be known as *dybbuks*. The literature also taught how they could be exorcised by a learned, holy man, or *ba'al shem*, who redeemed the possessed soul by using one of Luria's 'sparks'. There were also poltergeist-devils, called *kesilim* or *lezim*, who threw things and, for instance, hit people who left holy books open. There were she-devils also, in addition to Lilith, one of them being the Queen of Sheba. Ghetto Jews believed it was dangerous to drink water at the change of the seasons because that was when devil-women dropped evil menstrual blood in wells and streams.

To combat these devils, an army of angels came into existence. These too had Biblical sanction in some cases. Angels like Michael, Gabriel, Raphael and Metatron had special alphabets, derived from ancient cuneiform writing or obsolete Hebraic scripts, the letters often containing small circles which looked like eyes. These letters were put on amulets and other charms to magic away devils. Or they could be driven off by pronouncing special combinations of letters. One such was the name of the devil in Aramaic, which was given as *abracadabra*; another was *shabriri*, after the devil of blindness.[57] Letter combination magic, performed by using the secret names of God and the angels in special formulae, was known as 'Practical Kabbalah'. In theory only men of great sanctity could, let alone should, exercise this white magic. In practice, protective charms were mass produced and circulated freely in the ghetto. There was also black magic, invoked by manipulating 'the unholy names'. According to the *Zohar*, the sources of this forbidden magic were the leaves of the Tree of Knowledge in the Book of Genesis. The fallen angels Azael and Aza taught it to sorcerers who journeyed to the Mountains of Darkness to study. Virtuous kabbalists had a right to acquire such arts but only for theoretical purposes. In practice, harmful spells were also cast in the ghetto.

The most stupendous piece of magic was the creation of a *golem*, an artificial man into which a *ba'al shem*, or Master of the Name, could breathe life by pronouncing one of the secret divine names according to a special formula. The idea derives from the creation story of Adam, but the actual word occurs only once in the Bible, in a mysterious passage in the Psalms.[58] However, talmudic legends accumulated around the *golem*. Jeremiah was said to have made one. Another was made by Ben Sira. From the fifteenth to the seventeenth centuries the notion gathered force, so that the ability to make a *golem* was attributed to any man of outstanding sanctity and kabbalistic knowledge. The *golem* was brought to life to perform a variety of tasks, including defending Jews from their gentile enemies. In theory, a *golem* came to life when God's secret name, with the letters arranged in the correct order, was put into its mouth; it was deactivated by reversing the name. But a *golem* occasionally got out of hand and ran amok – thereby generating a new layer of terror-tales.

Devils, angels, *golems* and other mysterious figures constituted the basic population of ghetto folklore, leading to countless superstitious practices. They gave life in the ghetto an extraordinary density, which was at one and the same time frightening and comforting, and always vivid, rich, exciting. Some of the customs current in the sixteenth and seventeenth centuries surfaced in a work published in London in 1738 called *The Book of Religion, Ceremonies and Prayers of the Jews*, supposedly by Gamaliel ben Pedahzur, actually written by an apostate, Abraham Mears. It related that evil spirits were to be found in whirls of dust and rubbish-heaps. Bad ghosts could harm a person in the dark but only if he was by himself. If two were present, the ghost could appear but do no harm; if three, it could do nothing. A torch had the same effect. Witches could do harm if they found discarded pottery or eggshells which had not been pounded into bits; or green vegetable tops tied together in a bunch. Much of the lore concerned funerals and weddings. Thus, if you wished to ask forgiveness of a dead man you had wronged, you stood at the foot of the coffin and took the man's big toe in your hand while praying for his pardon; if the nose bled violently, pardon was refused. To break a glass at a wedding-feast was to ward off bad luck. 'The Bachelors', wrote the author, 'generally strive to carry off a bit of the broken pipkin, believing it likely to promote their being married soon after.' Superstition blended imperceptibly into folk-medicine:

There are some women among them that pretend to cure all Distempers, which they believe to proceed from an evil Eye, by the Sympathy of Fumigation: some part of the Garment worn by the Patient is sent to the said Doctoress, which she holds over some certain smoking stuff of her own Composure, muttering some few words over the Garment, under the Operation, and that Garment being return'd in a few minutes to the Patient, to wear immediately, never fails of giving Relief, unless their Ailment has been of too long Standing before the old Woman smoak'd them. The usual Price for smoaking of a Child's Cap, is a shilling. A woman's Petticoat, two shillings. A Man's Pair of Breeches, half a crown. NB, the *Spanish Jews* pay more because the *Smoakers* are *German*.[59]

Ghetto folklore centred around devils and sin, especially the first sin, the transmigration of souls and, not least, the Messiah. Belief in the Messiah was the summation and climax of all the ghetto's trust in the supernatural because it had the highest sanction of orthodox Jewish religion. The most learned and rational-minded rabbi and the worldliest merchant trusted in the Messiah's coming as fervently as the semi-literate wife of a humble milkman. The Messiah was linked to tales of the Lost Tribes since it was widely assumed that, in order to achieve the restoration of a godly kingdom on earth, the Messiah would summon the tribes from their remote exile and they would march, a mighty army, to place him on King David's throne. It was not a ghetto story-teller but the great Mishnah commentator Obadiah ben Abraham Yare of Bertinoro who described (1489), on the authority of 'reliable Moslem merchants', how a 'fifty-day journey through the desert' brought one to 'the great Sambatyon River'. There 'the children of Israel live like a thread . . . saintly and pure like angels: there are no sinners among them. On the outer side of the Sambatyon River there are Children of Israel as numerous as the sands of the seashore, kings and lords, but they are not as saintly or pure as those living on the inner side of the river.'[60] These teeming millions would form the legions of the Messiah's conquering host.

History shows repeatedly that what helps to spread a religious idea fastest is a clear and practical description of the mechanics of salvation. That is precisely what Lurianic kabbalah provided: a description of how ordinary Jews, by their prayers and piety, could precipitate the Messianic Age. It was among the generation born in the 1630s that Luria's ideas spread most widely and rapidly, in both sophisticated and vulgar form. The great historian Gershom Scholem, who spent his life studying the impact of kabbalistic mysticism on Jewish society, stressed the universality of the belief among Jewish communities, around the mid-seventeenth century, that the world was on the brink of great events.[61] The series of catastrophes which overtook Ashkenazi Jewry in eastern Europe from 1648 onwards, culminating in the Swedish War of the late 1650s, constituted a potent factor in raising messianic hopes. The greater the distress, the more urgently was deliverance awaited. In the 1650s and 1660s, there were many thousands of refugees to be accommodated in Jewish communities everywhere, and fund-raising activities for their support helped to generate the ferment of expectation. But messianic hopes, thanks to Lurianic doctrine, were high even in remote communities, like Morocco, where little was known of the Polish disasters. The wave of excitement mounted especially in Salonika and the Balkans, in Constantinople and throughout Turkey, in Palestine and Egypt; but it was felt too in hard-bitten trading centres like Leghorn, Amsterdam and Hamburg. It swept along rich and poor, learned and ignorant, communities which were in danger and those which felt themselves safe. By the 1660s, the feeling that the Lurianic process was virtually complete, and the Messiah waiting in the wings, united hundreds of Jewish communities scattered over two continents. On this point popular superstition and learned mysticism were at one.

On 31 May 1665, as if on cue, the Messiah appeared and was proclaimed as such in Gaza. He was called Shabbetai Zevi (1626–76). But the man behind his appearance, the master-mind, chief theorist and impresario of the whole phenomenon, was a local resident, one Abraham Nathan ben Elisha Hayyim Ashkenazi, known as Nathan of Gaza (c. 1643–80). This young man was learned, brilliant, inventive and resourceful. He had been born in Jerusalem, son of a respected rabbinical scholar and kabbalist; had married the daughter of a wealthy Gaza merchant and gone to live there; and in 1664 he had taken up the intensive study of Lurianic kabbalah. He quickly mastered Lurianic techniques of meditation and ecstasy-inducement. By early 1665 he was experiencing prolonged visions. But it is significant that he was already modifying Lurianic concepts to suit the particular projection of the Messiah he was conceiving in his mind. Nathan was an outstanding example of a highly imaginative and dangerous Jewish archetype which was to become of world importance when the Jewish intellect became secularized. He could construct a system of explanations and predictions of phenomena which was both highly plausible and at the same time sufficiently imprecise and flexible to accommodate new – and often highly inconvenient – events when they occurred. And he had the gift of presenting his protean-type theory, with its built-in capacity to absorb phenomena by a process of osmosis, with tremendous conviction and aplomb. Marx and Freud were to exploit a similar capacity.

oh ho...

While still in Jerusalem, Nathan had come across Shabbetai Zevi, who was about eighteen years his senior, and a well-known eccentric. He had paid Zevi little attention. After he had absorbed Lurianic kabbalah, however, and developed – at any rate to his own satisfaction – visionary and prophetic powers, Nathan recalled the Zevi case and drew him into his system. Zevi was in every way Nathan's inferior: less learned, less intelligent, less inventive; but he had the necessary ingredient for a Messiah-subject: self-absorption. He was born in Smyrna, now an expanding trading-centre, where his father was an agent for Dutch and English firms. Both his brothers became successful merchants. He was bookish, went through a rabbinic training, graduated at eighteen, and then studied the kabbalah. He had the characteristics of what would later be called a manic-depressive. Periods of exaltation and hyperactivity were abruptly succeeded by spasms of intense gloom. These are common enough among mystics of all religions, and are seen as God's work – God 'illuminates', then 'hides His face'. Thus the abrupt transformations do not necessarily detract from the subject's reputation for sanctity. Unfortunately for Zevi, during his manic phases he had a tendency to break the law and blaspheme. He pronounced the forbidden name of God. He conflated three feasts and celebrated them simultaneously. He went through a mystic marriage with the Torah under a wedding canopy. The 1648 massacres inspired him to proclaim himself the Messiah. Like many mystics, he wanted to do and legitimize forbidden things. Thus he invoked a benediction to 'Him who allows the forbidden'. During the 1650s he was expelled in turn from Smyrna, Salonika and Constantinople. At times his state of mind was placid and normal, and he even sought treatment for what he saw were diabolical fantasies. But then the bad urges would return. He had been married and divorced twice, neither union being consummated. In 1664, while in a manic state in Cairo, he contracted a third marriage with a girl called Sarah, a refugee from the massacres, whose reputation was dubious. But there was prophetic precedent for this too: had not Hosea married a whore? In the following winter, however, he again decided to seek help in exorcising his demons. Having heard that a young kabbalist called

Nathan was experiencing remarkable visions, he went there in the spring of 1665.

By the time the two men came together, in April, Nathan had already experienced his vision in which the Messiah-claimant he remembered from Jerusalem figured prominently. So when Zevi actually turned up in his house, seeking help, Nathan judged the event providential. Far from exorcising Zevi's demons, Nathan concentrated his formidable powers of argument and invention on persuading Zevi that his messianic claims were authentic and must be pursued. Then and thereafter Nathan proved extraordinarily adept at fitting Zevi's biography and characteristics into the patterns of canonical and apocryphal texts, and Lurianic theory – especially as amended by himself. So he hailed Zevi as the Messiah, and Zevi, convinced again, promptly went into another manic phase. With the zealous Nathan at his side, he made his claim public, and this time it was accepted. He was soon riding around Gaza on horseback, in kingly state, and appointing ambassadors to summon all the tribes of Israel.

The difference between Zevi and previous, sixteenth-century Messiahs was that his candidature was conceived and presented not only against a background of Orthodox learning, which both he and his impresario possessed, but also in specific terms of Lurianic science with which the whole of Jewry was now familiar. The time was right; the intellectual mood was right. Nathan the Prophet, the 'holy lamp', burned with conviction and radiated exact knowledge. Zevi the Messiah dispensed charm and regal condescension. The combination worked brilliantly in Gaza, where the rabbis joined in the acclamation. It was less successful in Jerusalem, where many rabbis (including Nathan's old teacher) rejected the claims and eventually had the new messiah expelled. But the Jerusalem authorities were none the less anxious to hedge their bets. They did not send out letters to Jewish communities warning them about an imposture. There and elsewhere sceptical rabbis usually judged it best to hold their peace. The majority of rabbis everywhere were taken in. Later, after the bubble had burst, many insisted they had opposed Zevi's pretensions. But, as Scholem has shown, the documents tell a different story.

Hence in 1665 and for most of 1666 there was no authoritative pronouncement against the new Messiah. The skilfully worded letters announcing the events, which Nathan wrote or drafted, and which were dispatched to Jewish communities over the world, went unanswered. Of course, most Jews expected the coming of the Messiah to be attended by miracles. But there was good authority – Maimonides no less – to say that this would not happen. Moreover, Nathan anticipated an absence of miracles by cleverly adapting Lurianic theory. Since, he argued, the Messiah had been summoned by Jewish prayers and piety, it followed logically that pure, trusting faith was alone requisite to sustain his mission. So neither he nor his prophet was required to perform miracles. In fact Nathan's precaution was unnecessary. Miracles were duly performed – though always somewhere else. This followed spontaneously from the Jewish custom of spreading news of disaster and triumph in long, excited letters, often based on rumours. Thus Constantinople wrote to Leghorn recounting wonders occurring in Cairo. News of miracles in Salonika was passed from Rome to Hamburg, and then on to Poland. The first announcement most western Jews received did not concern Zevi at all but the Ten Lost Tribes, who were variously said to be assembling in Persia or the Sahara, and marching on Mecca – or Constantinople.

In September 1665 Nathan sent out a long letter outlining the Messiah's programme. His work, said Nathan, had now superseded the Lurianic system and opened a new phase in history. He had the power to justify all sinners himself. First he would take the crown of Turkey, and make the sultan his servant. Next he would go to the River Sambatyon to gather the tribes and marry Rebecca, the thirteen-year-old daughter of Moses, who had come back to life again. During his absence the Turks might rebel and cause tribulations for Jews. Hence it was necessary for all Jews to do penance immediately. Meanwhile Zevi himself had begun a triumphal northwards progress, first to Aleppo, then to Smyrna and on to Constantinople, and it was now that mass hysteria began to break out. Zevi increased it by reverting to his old manic habits. He 'pronounced the Ineffable Name, ate [forbidden] fats and did other things against the Lord and his Law, even pressing others to do likewise', according to a contemporary account.[62] If a rabbi protested, the vast crowd which now accompanied Zevi everywhere was liable to attack the critic's house. In Smyrna, Zevi himself took an axe to the door of the Sephardi synagogue, which refused to recognize him, and forced his way in. Once inside, he denounced the unbelieving rabbis as unclean animals, took a holy scroll into his arms and sang a Spanish love-song, announced the date of the Redemption for 18 June 1666, proclaimed the imminent deposition of the Turkish sultan, and distributed the kingdoms of the world among his immediate followers. When one of the critical rabbis present asked him for proofs, Zevi excommunicated him on the spot, and led the mob in pronouncing the forbidden name as proof of their faith in him. He then 'liberated' Jewish womenfolk by freeing them from the curse of Eve, and dispatched messengers to Constantinople to prepare for his arrival, leaving for the city by boat on 30 December 1665.

Throughout the winter of 1665–6, and for most of the following year, the Jewish world was in ferment. Responding to Nathan's calls to penance – his exhortations were printed in vast numbers in Frankfurt, Prague, Mantua, Constantinople and Amsterdam – Jews prayed, fasted and took constant ritual baths. They lay down naked in the snow. They scourged themselves. Many sold all their possessions and went on pilgrimage to the Holy Land, hoping to see the Messiah there. Some believed they would be transported on clouds. Others bought passages. Abraham Pereira, reputedly the richest Jew in Amsterdam, left with his household for Palestine, though his ship got no further than Leghorn. Poems were written, books printed and dated 'the first year of the renewal of the prophecy and the kingdom'. Public processions were organized. Some of the excitement was generated by Christian millenarians, who also believed that 1666 was a magic year. There were riots in various Polish cities, and in May the crown forbade any further Jewish demonstrations. The Jewish fervour also set off reactions, some sympathetic, some hostile, in the Islamic world, and the Turkish authorities became alarmed.

Hence when Zevi's ship reached Turkish waters in February 1666, it was promptly detained and the Messiah taken ashore in chains. He was held in honourable captivity, however, and allowed to receive visitors. Nathan, in the first of his rationalizations of events to fit his theory, explained that the Messiah's imprisonment was no more than symbolic and outward and reflected his inward struggle with the evil forces which prevented the divine sparks from shining forth. Zevi maintained his pretensions in the fortress at Gallipoli, where he was held, and apparently sent away delegations of Jews quite happy. An inquiry from the community in Venice elicited a reassuring response from the Constantinople Jews, carefully disguised as a trade report: 'We looked into the matter and examined the merchandise of Rabbi Israel, for his goods are displayed here under our very eyes. We have come to the conclusion that they are very valuable . . . but we must wait until the day of the great fair comes.'[63] But the day, scheduled for the summer of 1666, passed. Early in September Zevi was visited by a Polish kabbalist Nehemiah ha-Cohen, who may have been a Turkish plant, or possibly a rival Messiah. He cross-questioned Zevi about his claims, found his answers unsatisfactory and denounced him to the Turks as an impostor. On 15 September Zevi was brought before the council, or divan, in Constantinople, in the presence of the sultan, who listened hidden in a latticed alcove. Zevi denied ever having made messianic claims. He was then given the choice between converting to Islam or death. At the urging of the sultan's doctor, an apostate Jew, he took the turban, assumed the name of Aziz Mehmed Effendi and the title 'Keeper of the Palace Gates' and accepted a government pension of 150 piastres a day.

What happened after the Messiah's apostasy was almost as instructive as the mission itself. The euphoria in the Jewish world collapsed abruptly as the news got out, though many refused to believe it at first. Rabbis and communal leaders, both those who had accepted the claims and the few who had denied them, closed ranks to impose a total silence on the affair. It was argued that any post-mortem would be to challenge the divine, inscrutable wisdom which allowed the fiasco to happen. There was also grave concern that the Turks would start a witch-hunt against Jewish leaders who acquiesced in what, after all, would have been a revolt against Ottoman rule. So every official effort was made to rewrite, or unwrite, history and pretend the affair had never happened. Communal records referring to it were destroyed.

Nathan of Gaza, on the other hand, merely enlarged his theory again to fit the new facts. The apostasy was transformed into a necessary paradox or dialectical contradiction. Far from being a betrayal, it was in fact the beginning of a new mission to release the Lurianic sparks which were distributed among the gentiles and in particular in Islam. While the Jews were restoring the sparks scattered among themselves – that was the easy part – the Messiah had the far more difficult task of gathering in the sparks in the alien world. Only he could do it, and it meant descending into the realm of evil. In appearance he was submitting to it, but in reality he was a Trojan Horse in the enemy's camp. Warming to his task, Nathan pointed out that Zevi had always done strange things. This was merely the strangest – to embrace the shame of apostasy as the final sacrifice before revealing the full glory of his messianic triumph. The notion of hidden meanings was familiar to students of kabbalah. Once the idea of the pretend-apostasy was accepted, everything else – including Zevi's subsequent actions under Turkish supervision – confirmed the new theory, for which Nathan quickly provided massive documentation in Biblical, talmudic and kabbalistic texts. Nathan visited Zevi several times and the two men were able to align Nathan's explanations with Zevi's behaviour. His manic phases recurred from time to time, and during them he sometimes reasserted his messianic claims. He also engaged in wild sexual antics, to the point where his enemies in

Constantinople, both Jewish and Moslem, combined to persuade or bribe the sultan – who rather liked Zevi – to exile him to Albania, where he died in 1676. Even his death, however, did not stump Nathan, who declared it a mere 'occultation': Zevi had ascended into heaven and been absorbed into the 'supernal lights.'

Nathan himself died four years later in 1680. But by the time he too disappeared he had elaborated a flexible theory which accommodated not only all Zevi's actions but any other disconcerting events which might occur in the future. There were not, he argued, one set of lights, as Luria and other kabbalists had believed, but two: a thoughtful set (good) and a thoughtless set (indifferent but liable to be bad). Creation proceeds by a dialectic between the two sets of lights, in which the Messiah-figure plays a unique part, quite different from that of ordinary souls, which often demands heroic sacrifices from him, including taking on to himself the appearance of evil to purify others. The theory made sense whether Zevi reappeared, sent a substitute or stayed silent and invisible. In this alternative or heretical system of kabbalah, Nathan worked out his dialectic in enormous detail and with copious imagery.

As a result, the Shabbatean movement, sometimes openly, sometimes in secret, not only survived the débâcle of the apostasy but continued in existence for over a century. Most rabbis came to hate it not only because Nathan's theory in its final form was plainly heretical but also because when predicted reappearances of Zevi failed to happen – as in 1700 and 1706 – many disappointed Shabbateans converted to Christianity or Islam. But some rabbis were occult Shabbateans themselves, and there were few people in the non-rationalist stream of Judaism to whom Nathan's rubbery ideas did not exercise some appeal. The movement survived splits, nonconformist deviations of its own and eventually produced a breakaway religion founded by a reincarnation of Zevi called Jacob Frank (1726–91).

Frank was born Jacob ben Judah Leib, the son of a Polish merchant and part-time rabbi. He himself became a cloth-dealer. He had little learning and called himself a *prostak* or simple man. None the less, while trading in the Balkans, he was initiated into secret Shabbatean rites, by followers of the extreme wing of the movement. He became a prophet and eventually claimed quasi-divine status as the possessor of Zevi's soul. When he returned to Poland, while posing as an orthodox Sephardi Jew – hence his name Frank, the Ashkenazi Yiddish term for a Sephardi – he secretly conducted Shabbatean services as head of an underground movement within Judaism. He and his followers also indulged in sexual practices forbidden by the Torah. Indeed, following the convenient dialectic established by Nathan of Gaza, they distinguished between the ordinary Torah of halakhah, which they ignored, and claimed the right to follow only the 'higher' or 'spiritual' Torah forms, the 'Torah of Emanation'.

In 1756 Frank was excommunicated by a rabbinical court at Brody, and to escape arrest he fled to Turkey where he found it useful to embrace Islam. The Orthodox Jews then appealed to the Polish Catholic authorities for help in dispersing the sect. But the Frankists also turned to the Catholics, on the grounds that they rejected the Talmud and therefore had more in common with Rome. The bishops, delighted, organized a public disputation and forced the rabbis as well as the Frankists to attend. It took place in June 1757 and the presiding prelate, Bishop Dembowski, pronounced in favour of the Frankists and ordered copies of the Talmud to be burned in the city square of Kamieniec. Alas for the bishop, he died suddenly during the conflagration. The rabbis took this as a divine sign of approval, and resumed their persecution of the Frankists with new fervour. In retaliation, Frank took his following into Catholicism, being baptized in 1759. He even assisted the Catholics in investigating blood libels. But he also collected twelve 'sisters', who served as his concubines, practised various enormities, and found himself in prison. He then turned to the Russian Orthodox Church.

While embracing Judaism, Islam, Roman Catholicism and Orthodoxy, Frank continued to follow Nathan's expanded religious theories. He created a new Trinity, of the 'Good God', 'Big Brother' and 'She', the last an amalgam of the *Shekinah* and the Virgin Mary, and eventually propounded the notion that the messianic idea could be pursued equally well in all the main religions or, for that matter, in the secular enlightenment or freemasonry. Thus the kabbalah, which began in unspecific, formless gnosticism in late antiquity, returned to unspecific, formless gnosticism in the late eighteenth century.

It is significant that Frank, in order to achieve some kind of legal cover for his sect, had to affect adherence to both Christianity and Islam. The contrast with the activities of his contemporary, Samuel Jacob Hayyim Falk (*c.* 1710–82), is instructive. Falk, born in Galicia, was another kabbalist and adventurer, though far more learned than Frank. He too came in conflict with the law. In Westphalia he narrowly escaped burning as a wizard. The Archbishop of Cologne expelled him from his territories. In 1742 he came to England, and there he seems to have pursued his religious destiny without hindrance. He ran a private synagogue from a house in Wellclose Square, London. On old London Bridge he maintained a kabbalistic laboratory, where he practised alchemy. He was said to have saved the Great Synagogue from fire by putting magical inscriptions on the doorposts. In his time he was known as 'the Ba'al Shem of London'.[64]

That a Jew like Falk could live his life in freedom under English law was a fact of immense importance in Jewish history. It meant that, for the first time since the days of the liberal Roman empire, there was one country where Jews could enjoy something approximating to normal citizenship. How did this come about? To understand this great turning-point, we must return again to the fateful year 1648. The great slaughter of Jews which took place then, beginning eight years of desperate troubles for the Jews of eastern Europe, was by far the worst outbreak of anti-Semitism since the First Crusade. Hitherto, the trend of Jewish emigration had been eastward, for hundreds of years. Now the trend was reversed. Though the teeming Ashkenazi community in eastern Europe continued to grow in numbers, and to a limited extent in prosperity, it never looked really safe again. For security, the more enterprising Jews began to turn their gaze to the West. Thus 1648 was a sombre milestone on the long road which led eventually to the Holocaust. But 1648, with its slaughter and distress, was also – thanks to a series of coincidences which some might call providential – the first in a remarkable chain of events which led to the creation of an independent Jewish state.

The agent in this new development was a distinguished Jewish scholar from Amsterdam, Manasseh ben Israel (1604–57). He had been born a *marrano* in Madeira and baptized Manoel Dias Soeiro. But after his father escaped from an auto-da-fé in Lisbon and came to the Netherlands, the family resumed its Jewish identity and Manasseh became a talmudic prodigy, writing his first book at seventeen.[65] He was concerned throughout his life to present a favourable image of Judaism to the gentile world and win acceptance. Many of his books were written for Christian readers. He tried to demonstrate that Christianity and Judaism had more in common than most people supposed, and he achieved a high reputation among Christian fundamentalists. When the first refugees from the 1648 massacres began to reach western Europe, Manasseh and other Amsterdam Jews feared the consequences for the community of a large influx of distressed Ashkenazis. Their own position in Holland was ambiguous. They had no rights of citizenship. They were not admitted to the guilds. The Dutch government did not interfere with the practice of their faith, provided it was done quietly, and in fact the community, especially in Amsterdam, was thriving. But all this could be jeopardized by the refugees. Indeed in Hamburg the arrival of large numbers led to a temporary expulsion of all Jews in 1649. Manasseh therefore proposed a radical solution: why should not England be opened up as a country of refuge for Jewish immigrants?

Since Edward I had expelled the English Jews in 1290, it was widely believed there was an absolute legal ban on Jews residing there. In fact a few Jews lived there throughout the centuries of supposed exclusion, especially as doctors and traders.[66] One Jew, Sir Edward Brampton, alias Duarte Brandão, was Governor of Guernsey under Richard III. Another, Dr Roderigo Lopez, had been Elizabeth I's doctor and the victim of a notorious anti-Semitic witch-hunt and treason trial in 1593–4.[67] At the time when the Ukrainian massacres took place, one of the five merchants contracted to supply corn to the English army was a Jew, Antonio Fernandez Carvajal, who had come to London in 1630, and was said to import £100,000 of silver annually. All the same, Jews were not officially admitted.

Manasseh perceived that the defeat of the English royalists and the execution of the king in 1649 offered a unique opportunity for the Jews to gain entry to England. The king's Puritan opponents, now effectively running the country, had always represented the philo-semitic tradition there. The Bible was their guide to current events. They invoked the Prophet Amos to condemn Star Chamber. They adduced the case of Naboth's Vineyard as a prefiguration of Ship Money. The Puritan common lawyer, Sir Henry Finch, had published in 1621 *The World's Great Restauration, or Calling of the Jews* – a work the crown had condemned for *lèse-majesté*.[68] Many believed that the Second Coming was imminent. But both Deuteronomy 28:64 and Daniel 12:7 suggested this could not happen until the scattering of the Jews was complete, 'from the one end of the earth even unto the other'. Hence, until Jews were scattered in England too, the millennium would be delayed. This was a notion Manasseh shared with English fundamentalists, since Kezeh ha-Arez, the 'end of the earth', was the medieval Hebrew term for England, and he believed the acceptance of Jews in England would hasten the Messiah's coming. He opened his campaign in the winter of 1648–9 with a book entitled *An Apology for the Honourable Nation of the Jews*, which he signed 'Edward Nicholas'. He followed this in 1650 with a far more important work, *Spes Israelis*, translated as *The Hope of Israel*, in which he advanced the millenarian argument. The first Anglo-Dutch War postponed more practical measures, but in September 1655 Manasseh came to London himself. He presented a petition to Oliver Cromwell, the Lord Protector, requesting that the laws forbidding the Jews entry be repealed and that they be granted admission on terms to be laid down by the government.[69]

What followed was a characteristic English muddle, which is worth examining in detail because it proved of such critical importance in the whole of Jewish history. Cromwell received Manasseh's petition favourably and referred it to the Council. On 12 November 1655 the Council appointed a sub-committee to examine the matter and seek expert legal advice. On 4 December a conference was held in Whitehall attended by twenty-five lawyers, including the Chief Justice, Sir John Glynne, and the Chief Baron of the Exchequer, William Steele. To the surprise of the politicians they announced that there was no law whatever which prevented Jews coming to England. Edward's 1290 expulsion was an act of royal prerogative which affected only the individuals concerned. Somewhat illogically, the sub-committee then got down to discussing the conditions on which Jews were to be admitted. But it could not agree. The Jews had enemies among the Commonwealth men, as well as friends. After four sessions, Cromwell dismissed it on 18 December. Manasseh, bitterly disappointed, went back to Amsterdam the following year, believing he had failed.

But he had, in fact, misunderstood the way the English did things. They preferred a pragmatic to a clear-cut ideological solution. If an agreement had been drawn up, giving a special legal status to Jewish immigrants, they would necessarily have been branded as second-class citizens. When the monarchy was restored in 1660, Charles II would quite possibly have repudiated the deal, or renegotiated it with harsher terms. In either case the Jewish question would have become a public issue, raising anti-Semitic hackles. As it was, the matter was resolved pragmatically, without a specific treaty. While Manasseh was still in London, a man called Antonio Rodrigues Robles, a *marrano* legally, though in fact a Jew, was being proceeded against in court as a Spanish alien, England and Spain being at war. Some twenty *marrano* families decided, in March 1656, to resolve the matter by openly confessing their Judaism, declaring themselves refugees from the Spanish Inquisition, and petitioning the Council for the right to practise their religion in private. On 16 May the Council ordered the proceedings against Robles quashed, and at a further meeting on 25 June it seemingly granted the petition, though the minutes for that day were later mysteriously removed. At any rate, on 4 August there arrived from Amsterdam 'a scroll of the Law of fine parchment, with its binder and mantle of yellow velvet, a red damask cloth for the reading desk and a spice-box lined with red taffeta', and the London Jews went ahead with leasing a building in Creechurch Lane for their first synagogue.

Hence, by a sort of tacit conspiracy, the question of the special status for the Jews was dropped. As there was no statute stopping them from coming, they came. As the Council said they could practise their religion, they practised it. When the Conventical Act, aimed at Nonconformists, was passed in 1664, the Jews, led by their new rabbi, Jacob Sasportas, took their anxieties to Charles II, who told them, 'laughing and spitting', not to worry; and later the Privy Council put it in writing that Jews could 'promise themselves the effects of the same favour as formerly they have had, so long as they demean themselves peaceably and quietly, with due obedience to His Majesty's laws and without scandal to his government'.

Thus the English Jews, by an act of omission, as it were, became full citizens, subject to no more disabilities than those inherent in their own unwillingness, like Catholics and Nonconformists, to belong to the Church of England or, in their particular case, to swear Christian oaths. Over the next generation, various judicial rulings established the right of Jews to plead and give evidence in the courts, and to have their religious susceptibilities recognized for this purpose. It is true that, like other non-Anglicans, they were barred from many offices and from parliament. But there were no legal restraints, as such, on their economic activities. Indeed discrimination arose chiefly within the Jewish community. Its dominant Sephardi element still felt insecure and deplored any influx of poor Ashkenazi Jews, especially if the community had to support them. It ruled in 1678–9 that German Jews could not be allowed to hold office, vote at meetings or read the scrolls. But this ruling was found to be against Jewish law and had to be modified. So far as the English courts were concerned, the Jews seem to have received justice and protection from the start, English judges in general being well disposed to hard-working, law-abiding citizens who did not disturb the king's peace. Indeed in 1732 a judgment gave Jews, in effect, legal protection against generic libels which might endanger life. Hence almost by accident England became the first place in which it was possible for a modern Jewish community to emerge.

The consequences in America were still more important. In 1654 the French privateer *St Catherine* brought twenty-three Jewish refugees from Recife in Brazil to the Dutch colonial town of New Amsterdam. As in Amsterdam itself, the position of Jews under Dutch colonial rule was uncertain: Calvinists, though better disposed than Lutherans, could also be oppressive and anti-Semitic. The Governor of New Amsterdam, Peter Stuyvesant, protested to the Dutch West India Company against this settlement of what he termed 'a deceitful race' whose 'abominable religion' worshipped 'the feet of Mammon'. The

Jews were allowed to stay but they were not accorded any rights and company and governor united to forbid them to build a synagogue. But any ambiguities were resolved in 1664 when the town fell to the English and became New York. Thereafter the Jews enjoyed not only the advantages of English citizenship but the additional religious freedoms the colonists in the New World had taken for themselves.

Richard Nicholls, New York's first English governor, stressed the right to freedom of worship when he proclaimed in 1665: 'No person shall be molested, fined or imprisoned for differing in judgment in matters of religion, who profess Christianity.' The omission of any reference to Judaism seems to have been an oversight. The English wanted colonists, especially those with mercantile skills and good trading contacts. The next governor, Edmund Andros, made no reference to Christianity when he promised equal treatment and protection to law-abiding persons 'of what religion soever'. As in England, the issue of Jewishness was not raised. Jews simply came, built houses, enjoyed equal rights and, it seems, voted in the earliest elections; they held offices too.[70]

They began to settle in other areas, notably the Delaware Valley and Rhode Island, which Roger Williams had founded as a libertarian colony where no religious bars whatever applied. Some difficulties arose when Jews wished to have their own cemetery in New York. But in 1677 one was opened in Newport, RI – later the subject of one of Longfellow's finest poems – and New York got its own five years later. In 1730 the Shearith Israel Congregation in New York consecrated its first synagogue, and a particularly fine new one was built at Newport in 1763, today a national shrine. Under the English Navigation Acts, trade within colonies and the mother country was limited to English citizens; and when the imperial parliament enacted the Naturalization Act for the North American colonies, the Jews were allowed to acquire citizenship on a par with Christian settlers, two provisions being dropped to allow for Jewish scruples. Hence the Swede Peter Kalm, visiting New York in 1740, recorded that Jews 'enjoy all the privileges common to the other inhabitants of this town and province'.[71] It was the same in Philadelphia, where an important Jewish colony began to grow up from the 1730s onwards.

Thus was born American Jewry. It was, from the start, unlike any Jewry elsewhere. In Europe and Afro-Asia, where religious barriers were universal in some form, the Jews always had to negotiate or have imposed upon them a special status. This obliged them to form specific and usually legally defined communities, wherever they settled. To a greater or lesser extent, all these Jewish communities were self-governing, even though the actual condition of the Jews might be miserable and perilous. In Poland, under the monarchy, the Jews enjoyed a kind of home rule, governing themselves through the Councils of the Lands, which their wealthier members elected. They were taxed more heavily than the surrounding Poles and had no real right of self-defence, but otherwise they ran their own affairs. To a less pronounced extent this was true of every Jewish settlement in Continental Europe. The Jews always ran their own schools, courts, hospitals and social services. They appointed and paid their own officials, rabbis, judges, slaughterers, circumcisers, schoolteachers, bakers and cleaners. They had their own shops. Wherever they were, the Jews formed tiny states within states. This was the ghetto system, and it applied even in places like Amsterdam where no legal ghettoing existed.

In North America it was quite different, even before the United States attained independence. With the virtual absence of religious-determined law, there was no reason why Jews should operate a separate legal system, except on matters which could be seen as merely internal religious discipline. Since all religious groups had virtually equal rights, there was no point in any constituting itself into a separate community. All could participate in a common society. Hence from the start, the Jews in America were not organized on communal but on congregational lines, like the other churches. In Europe, the synagogue was merely one organ of the all-embracing Jewish community. In North America it was the only governing body in Jewish life. American Jews did not belong to 'the Jewish community', as they did in Europe. They belonged to a particular synagogue. It might be Sephardi or Ashkenazi; or, of the latter, it might be German, English, Holland, Polish, all of them differing on small ritual points. Protestant groups were divided on comparable lines. Hence a Jew went to 'his' synagogue, just as a Protestant went to 'his' church. In other respects, both Jew and Protestant were part of the general citizenry, in which they merged as secular units. Thus for the first time Jews, without in any way renouncing their religion, began to achieve integration.

This was of enormous long-term consequence when the Jewish population of North America began to expand rapidly.[72] For it meant that Jewry was no longer a dualism: Erez Israel and the diaspora. The Jewish presence in the world formed, rather, a tripod of forces: Israel, the diaspora, American Jewry, which was quite different in kind to any other diaspora settlement and proved, in the end, the Third Force which enabled the Zionist state to come into existence.

This was in the future, but even in the early modern period the acceptance of the Jews in the Anglo-Saxon area of power began to have a growing impact on the role Jews played in the economy, giving it a permanency and stability it had never possessed before. At various times, in antiquity, in the Dark and early Middle Ages, in the seventeenth century, the Jews had been brilliant traders and entrepreneurs, and often extremely successful ones. But Jewish economic power was ultra-vulnerable, with little security in law. In both Christendom and Islam Jewish fortunes were liable to arbitrary seizure at any time. One might say that the Nazi assault on Jewish business, 1933–9, or the confiscations of Jewish property by Arab states in 1948–50, were merely the last and most comprehensive of such economic attacks on the Jews. As a result, during the period up to the mid-seventeenth century, Jewish fortunes were transitory or at best migratory, and the Jewish contribution to the growth of an international, entrepreneurial economy was correspondingly restricted. The Jews had always been skilful at using and transferring capital. But once they were established in Anglo-Saxon society, the security they then enjoyed in law enabled them to accumulate it too. Confidence in their rights led Jews to expand the scope of their activities. Trading, especially in articles of small volume and high value, such as jewels, easily concealed and whisked from place to place, no longer constituted almost the sole economic occupation in which Jews found it safe to engage.

The pattern can be seen changing in eighteenth-century America. At the beginning of the century, the Jews there were almost entirely concentrated in the overseas trading sector, dealing in jewels, coral, textiles, slaves, cocoa and ginger. In 1701 in New York, though only 1 per cent of the population, they formed 12 per cent of the overseas trading community. By 1776, this proportion had fallen to only 1 per cent, as the Jews, feeling increasingly settled, secure and accepted, turned their backs on the sea – their traditional escape-route – and began to look inland, to developing the continent. They became settlers themselves, and sold guns, rum, wine, ironware, glass, furs and provisions.

In Europe, the financial means which held together the great coalition against Louis XIV, and eventually broke his military dominance of Europe – as it was to do Napoleon's – was largely assembled by Jews. William of Orange, later William III of England, who led the coalition from 1672 to 1702, was financed and provisioned by a group of Dutch Sephardi Jews operating chiefly from The Hague. The two leading *providiteurs general*, as William had them called, were

Antonio Alvarez Machado and Jacob Pereira. As we have seen, such men, however useful they might be to Continental princes, had to operate in a climate of financial and personal insecurity. It required intense pressure from William and the Austrian emperor, for instance, to secure Machado or his agents admission into a city like Cologne. England, by contrast, was a far more secure base from which to operate. In 1688 the Lopez Suasso family advanced William two million gulden to finance his invasion of England, Suasso telling him: 'If you are fortunate, I know you will pay me back. If you are unlucky, I agree to lose them.'[73] Once William was safely installed many Jewish financiers moved to London, led by Pereira's son Isaac, who became commissary-general there, being paid the enormous sum of £95,000 for shipping and supplies during the year September 1690 to August 1691.[74]

In London the Jews became a founding element in the financial market of the City which grew up in William's day. The element of anti-Jewish blackmail, which dominated Jewish–state relations on the Continent, was not wholly absent to begin with. The Earl of Shrewsbury, as secretary of state, wrote to the Lord Mayor in February 1690: 'Taking into consideration that the Jews residing in London carry on, under favour of the government, so advantageous a trade', their 'offer only of £12,000' was 'below what His Majesty expected of them'; it ought, he added, to be doubled to £20,000 or even raised to £30,000; and 'His Majesty believes that, upon second thoughts', they will 'come to new resolutions'.[75] But the English government did not confiscate Jewish fortunes or rob Jews by oppressive lawsuits. Solomon de Medina, chief London agent for the Hague consortium, was never brought to book for his many misdeeds – he admitted he bribed the Duke of Marlborough, the allied captain-general, £6,000 a year during the years 1707–11. William III had dined with him in Richmond in 1699 and knighted him the following year, and if Solomon ended up practically bankrupt, that was due to his own miscalculations, not to anti-Semitic fury.[76]

Whereas in central Europe the pillaging of an Oppenheimer could produce financial crisis, the London Jews, secure in their property, were able to help the state to avoid them. The Menasseh Lopes family under Queen Anne, the Gideons and the Salvadors under the first three Georges, played notable roles in maintaining the stability of London financial markets. They avoided the South Sea Bubble. When the Jacobite rising of 1745 panicked the City, Samson Gideon (1699–1762) raised £1,700,000 to help the government restore calm. At his death he left over £500,000, which went to his heir, not the government – though the Gideons moved into the House of Lords and out of Judaism.[77]

It was the unconscious collective instinct of the Jews both to depersonalize finance and to rationalize the general economic process. Any property known to be Jewish, or clearly identifiable as such, was always at risk in medieval and early modern times, especially in the Mediterranean, which was then the chief international trading area. As the Spanish navy and the Knights of Malta treated Jewish-chartered ships and goods as legitimate booty, fictitious Christian names were used in the paperwork of international transactions, including marine insurance. These developed into impersonal for-mulae. As well as developing letters of credit, the Jews invented bearer-bonds, another impersonal way of moving money. For an underprivileged community whose property was always under threat, and who might be forced to move at short notice, the emergence of reliable, impersonal paper money, whether bills of exchange or, above all, valid banknotes, was an enormous blessing.

Hence the whole thrust of Jewish activity in the early modern period was to refine these devices and bring them into universal use. They strongly supported the emergence of the institutions which promoted paper values: the central banks, led by the Bank of England (1694) with its statutory right to issue notes, and the stock exchanges. Jews dominated the Amsterdam stock exchange, where they held large quantities of stock from both the West and East India Companies, and were the first to run a large-scale trade in securities. In London they set the same pattern a generation later in the 1690s. Joseph de la Vega, an Amsterdam Jew (though a nominal Protestant) wrote the earliest account of stock exchange business in 1688, and Jews were probably the first professional stock jobbers and brokers in England: in 1697, out of one hundred brokers on the London exchange, twenty were Jews or aliens. In due course, Jews helped to create the New York stock exchange in 1792.

Next to the development of credit itself, the invention and still more the popularization of paper securities were probably the biggest single contribution the Jews made to the wealth-creation process. Jews hastened the use of securities just as much in areas where they felt safe as in areas where they were vulnerable, for they saw the entire world as a single market. Here, too, the global perspective which the diaspora gave them turned them into pioneers. For a race without a country, the world was a home. The further the market stretched, the greater were the opportunities. For people who had been trading regularly from Cairo to China in the tenth century, the opening up of the Atlantic,

Indian and Pacific oceans to commerce in the eighteenth century was no great challenge. The first wholesale trader in Australia was a Montefiore. The Sassoons built the first textile mills and factories in Bombay. Benjamin Norden and Samuel Marks started up industry in Cape Colony. The Jews were in the whaling trade at both poles. More important than these specific pioneering efforts was the Jewish drive to create world markets for the staple articles of modern commerce – wheat, wool, flax, textiles, spirits, sugar, tobacco. The Jews went into new areas. They took big risks. They dealt in a wide variety of goods. They held big stocks.

Jewish financial and trading activities in the eighteenth century became so widely diffused that economic historians have sometimes been tempted to regard them as the primary force in creating the modern capitalist system. In 1911 the German sociologist Werner Sombart published a remarkable book, *Die Juden und das Wirtschaftsleben*, in which he argued that Jewish traders and manufacturers, excluded from the guilds, developed a destructive antipathy to the fundamentals of medieval commerce. These were primitive and unprogressive: the desire for 'just' (and fixed) wages and prices, for an equitable system in which shares of the market were agreed and unchanging, profits and livelihoods modest but guaranteed, and limits placed on production. Excluded from the system, Sombart argued, the Jews broke it up and replaced it with modern capitalism, in which competition was unlimited and pleasing the customer was the only law.[78] Sombart's work was later discredited because it was used by the Nazis to justify their distinction between Jewish commercial cosmopolitanism and German national culture; and Sombart himself, in *Deutscher Sozialismus* (1934), endorsed the Nazi policy of excluding Jews from German economic life. Sombart's thesis contained an element of truth but the conclusions he reached were exaggerated. Like Max Weber's attempt to attribute the spirit of capitalism to Calvinist ethics, it left out inconvenient facts. Sombart ignored the powerful mystical element in Judaism. He refused to recognize, as did Weber, that wherever these religious systems, including Judaism, were at their most powerful and authoritarian, commerce did not flourish. Jewish businessmen, like Calvinist ones, tended to operate most successfully when they had left their traditional religious environment and had moved to fresh pastures.

But if Jews formed only one of the elements in creating the modern commercial system, it was certainly an influential one. They rationalized what had previously been a comfortable, traditional and often obscurantist process. Their influence was exercised in five principal ways. First they favoured innovation. The stock market was a case in point. This was an efficient and rational way of raising capital and allocating it to the most productive purposes. Traditional mercantile interests, unable to distinguish between the market's occasional excesses and its fundamental validity, objected. In 1733, Sir John Barnard MP introduced, with all-party support, a Bill to make illegal 'the infamous practice of stockjobbing'. *Postlethwayt's Universal Dictionary of Trade and Commerce* (1757) condemns 'those mountebanks we very properly call stockbrokers'. Stockjobbing was 'a public grievance', 'scandalous to the nation'. Many of these accusations were dealt with by the Portuguese Jew Joseph de Pinto in his *Traité du crédit et de la circulation* (1771). In general, financial innovations which Jews pioneered in the eighteenth century, and which aroused much criticism then, became acceptable in the nineteenth.

Secondly, Jews were in the vanguard in stressing the importance of the selling function. Here again, there was much traditional opposition. Daniel Defoe's *Complete English Tradesman* (fifth edition 1745), for instance, condemned elaborate window-dressing as immoral. *Postlethwayt's Dictionary* commented on the 'recent innovation' of advertising (1751): 'however mean and disgraceful it was looked upon a few years since, by people of reputation in trade, to apply to the public by advertisements in the papers, at present it seems to be esteemed quite otherwise, persons of great credit in trade experiencing it to be the best . . . method of conveying whatever they have to offer to knowledge of the whole kingdom'. A Paris ordinance of 1761 actually forbade traders 'to run after one another trying to find customers' or 'distribute handbills calling attention to their wares'. Jews were among the leaders in display, advertising and promotion.

Thirdly, they aimed for the widest possible market. They appreciated the importance of economies of scale. As in banking and moneylending during the Middle Ages, they were willing to accept much smaller profits in return for a larger turnover. They accordingly – and this was their fourth main contribution – strove hard to reduce prices. They were much more willing than established traders to make an inferior, cheaper product and sell to a popular market. They were not alone in this. Sir Josiah Child, in his *Discourse on Trade* (fourth edition 1752) pointed out: 'If we intend to have the trade of the world, we must imitate the Dutch, who make the worst as well as the best of all manufactures, that we may be in a capacity of serving all markets and all humours.' The ability of Jews to undercut aroused much comment, fury and accusations that they cheated or traded in smuggled or confiscated goods. In fact it was usually another case of rationalization. Jews were prepared to trade in remnants. They found uses for waste-products. They accepted cheaper raw materials, or devised substitutes and synthetics. They sold inferior goods to the poor because that was all the poor could afford. They effected further economies of scale by opening general stores selling a wide variety of products under the same roof. This angered traditional traders, who specialized, particularly when Jews attracted custom through what we would now call 'loss leaders'. Above all, Jews were more inclined than others in commerce to accept that the consumer was the ultimate arbiter of trade, and that businesses flourished by serving consumer interests rather than guild interests. The customer was always right. The market was the final judge. These axioms were not necessarily coined by Jews or exclusively observed by Jews, but Jews were quicker than most to apply them.

Finally, Jews were exceptionally adept at gathering and making use of commercial intelligence. As the market became the dominant factor in all kinds of trading, and as it expanded into a series of global systems, news became of prime importance. This was perhaps the biggest single factor in Jewish trading and financial success. By the time of the Industrial Revolution, they had been operating family trading networks, over a growing area, for the best part of two millennia. They had always been passionate letter-writers. From Leghorn, Prague, Vienna, Frankfurt, Hamburg, Amsterdam, and later from Bordeaux, London, New York and Philadelphia – and between all these centres – they ran sensitive and speedy information systems which enabled them to respond rapidly to political and military events and to the changing demands of regional, national and world markets. Such families as the Lopez or Mendes of Bordeaux, the Carceres of Hamburg, the Sassoons of Baghdad, the Pereiras, the D'Acostas, the Coneglianos and the Alhadibs, operating from branches in many cities, were among the best-informed people in the world, long before the Rothschilds set up their own commercial diaspora. Traditional, medieval-style commerce tended to suffer from what has been termed the 'physical fallacy', that goods and commodities have a fixed and absolute value. In fact value varies in space and time. The larger the market, the longer the distances, the greater the variations. Getting the right goods in the right place at the right time is the essence of commercial success. It always had been. But in the eighteenth century, the increasing size and scale of the market made it of paramount importance. It enhanced the significance of strategic decision-making in business. Decisions, naturally, reflect the quality of the information available in reaching them. That was where the Jewish networks scored.

For all these reasons, then, Jews made a contribution to the creation of modern capitalism quite disproportionate to their numbers. It would have occurred without them. In some areas they were weak or absent. They played very little direct part, for instance, in the early stages of the Industrial Revolution in Britain. In some fields – raising large-scale capital – they were notably strong. In general, they brought to the eighteenth-century economic system a powerful spirit of rationalization, a belief that existing ways of doing things were never good enough, and that better, easier, cheaper and quicker ways could and must be found. There was nothing mysterious about Jewish commerce; nothing dishonest either; simply reason.

The rationalizing process was at work within Jewish society too, though at first more diffidently and fearfully. There is a paradox that, at one and the same time, the ghetto bred mercantile innovation and religious conservatism. The Jews in the early modern period were curiously dualistic. They often saw the world outside with clearer eyes than it saw itself; but when the Jews turned inward, on themselves, their eyes misted over, their vision became opaque. In the twelfth century Maimonides had tried hard to align Judaism with natural reason. That effort faltered and went underground in the fourteenth century. The ghetto helped to keep it there. It strengthened traditional authority. It discouraged speculation. It made the penalities of communal disapproval much more severe, since a Jew could not leave the ghetto without sacrificing his faith entirely. But of course it could not kill the rationalizing spirit altogether because that was inherent in Judaism and in the halakhic method. Even in the ghetto, Judaism remained a cathedocracy, a society ruled by learned men. Where scholars exist, controversies will erupt and ideas circulate.

The ghettos were depositories of books too. The Jews set up presses everywhere. Despite frequent raids by hostile religious authorities, they accumulated impressive libraries. One member of the Oppenheimer family, David, who was Chief Rabbi of Prague 1702–36, set out to acquire all the Hebrew books ever printed. Having inherited a fortune from his uncle Samuel, he was a very rich man; certainly no radical. Christians accused him of using his powers of excommunication to get choice treasures. In fact he had to keep his library in Hamburg to escape the Inquisition in Catholic Bohemia. His collection, which now forms the basis of the Bodleian *hebraica* in Oxford, once encompassed over 7,000 volumes and 1,000 manuscripts. Rabbi Oppenheimer got a ruling from the Emperor Charles VI in 1722 giving him sole control over Jewish studies in Prague. But the library he spent his life assembling was itself an inevitable breeding-ground for intellectual subversion.[79]

All the same, the spirit of rationalism within the Judaic world was slow to develop, partly because Jews with new ideas hesitated to challenge tradition, partly because such challenges were liable to meet crushing disapproval. Experience suggests that the most effective way to change conservative religious modes is to adopt the historical approach. Maimonides, while adumbrating modern techniques of Biblical criticism, never used historical criteria as such. It was one of his few intellectual weaknesses that he regarded non-messianic history as 'of no practical benefit but purely a waste of time'.[80] His disapproval was no doubt a collateral reason why the Jews were so slow to return to historical writing. But they did come to it again in the end, in the second half of the sixteenth century. After Ibn Verga's pioneer if naïve book, Azariah dei Rossi (c. 1511–78), a Mantuan, at last produced a genuine book of Jewish history, the Me'or Eynayim (Light of the Eyes) in 1573. Using gentile sources and critical techniques developed by Christians during the Renaissance, he subjected the writings of the sages to rational analysis. His manner was apologetic and diffident and he clearly took no pleasure in pointing out where the wise old men had erred. But his work on the Hebrew calendar none the less destroyed the traditional basis of messianic calculations and cast doubt on much else.[81]

Rossi's work aroused intense resentment among Orthodox learned Jews. The great codifier Joseph Caro, the most influential scholar of his time, died just before he could sign a decree ordering the book to be burned. The Rabbi Judah Loew, the famous Maharal of Prague, the dominant figure in the next generation, was just as critical of Rossi's book. He thought that Rossi's sceptical investigations into talmudic legends and Jewish history would undermine authority and destroy belief. Rossi, in his view, had failed to distinguish between two totally different forms of intellectual process, the divine and the natural. It was absurd to use methods suitable for investigation of the natural world to try to understand the workings of divine providence. Now this was to repudiate Maimonides completely, in one sense. Yet the Maharal was not really an obscurantist and irrationalist; he straddled many trends in Judaism.[82] His opposition to Rossi, whose book was banned to Jewish students without special rabbinical permission, indicates the strength of the opposition any intellectual innovator had to face.

This power of orthodoxy was dramatically demonstrated in the tragic case of Baruch (or Benedict) de Spinoza (1632–77) of Amsterdam. Spinoza is usually approached as a central figure in the history of philosophy, as indeed he was. But his importance in Jewish (and Christian) history is still more crucial, and in some ways baneful: he set in motion chains of events which still influence us today. By birth he was the son of a Sephardi refugee who became a successful Dutch merchant. By trade he was a scholar (he probably studied under Manasseh ben Israel) and a grinder of optical lenses. By temperament he was a melancholic and ascetic. He was slender, swarthy, with long, curling hair and large, dark, lustrous eyes. He ate practically nothing except porridge with a little butter and gruel mixed with raisins: 'It is incredible', wrote his early biographer, the Lutheran pastor Colerus who lodged in the same house, 'with how little in the shape of meat or drink he appears to have been satisfied.'[83]

By intellectual descent, Spinoza was a follower of Maimonides. But some of his views on the origins of the Pentateuch seem to have derived from veiled hints in the writings of the older rationalist Abraham ibn Ezra (1089–1164). He was a precocious youth in what was then (the 1650s) perhaps the most intellectually radical city in the world, and at an early age he became part of a circle of free thinkers from various religions: the ex-Jesuit Franciscus van den Enden, a former *marrano*, Juan de Prado, a notorious schoolteacher, Daniel de Ribera, and various Socinians, anti-Trinitarians and anti-clericals. A generation earlier, the Jew Uriel da Costa had been expelled from the Amsterdam community not once but twice for denying the immortality of the soul. In 1655, when Spinoza was twenty-three, *Praedamnitiae*, a sensational book by an ex-Calvinist, Isaac La Peyrère, which had been banned everywhere, was published in Amsterdam, and Spinoza undoubtedly read it. La Peyrère was certainly not an atheist; he was, rather, a *marrano* messianist, an enthusiastic kabbalist, part of the wave that was to carry Shabbetai Zevi to fame a decade later. But his work had the tendency to treat the Bible not as revelation but as a secular history to be critically examined. It seems to have reinforced in Spinoza's mind doubts already aroused by Ibn Ezra and Maimonides. At all events, the year after it appeared Spinoza and De Prado were hauled before the Jewish authorities. De Prado apologized; Spinoza was excommunicated publicly.

The actual rabbinical pronouncement, dated 27 July 1656 and signed by Rabbi Saul Levi Morteira and others, has survived. It reads:

The chiefs of the council make known to you that, having long known of evil opinions and acts of Baruch de Spinoza, they have endeavoured by

various means and promises to turn him from evil ways. Not being able to
find any remedy, but on the contrary receiving every day more information
about the abominable heresies practised and taught by him and about the
monstrous acts committed by him, having this from many trustworthy
witnesses who have deposed and borne witness on all this in the presence of
the said Spinoza, who has been convicted; all this having been examined in
the presence of the rabbis, the council decided, with the advice of the rabbis,
that the said Spinoza should be excommunicated and cut off from the Nation
of Israel.

Then followed the anathema and cursing:

With the judgment of the angels, and the sentence of the saints, we
anathematize, execrate, curse and cast out Baruch de Spinoza ... pronouncing against him the anathema wherewith Joshua anathematized
Jericho, the malediction wherewith Elisha cursed the children, and all the
maledictions written in the book of the Law. Let him be accursed by day and
accursed by night; accursed in his lying down and his rising up, in going out
and in coming in. May the Lord never more pardon or acknowledge him!
May the wrath and displeasure of the Lord burn against this man henceforth,
load him with all the curses written in the book of the Law, and raze out his
name from under the sky. ... Hereby, then, are all admonished that none
hold converse with him by word of mouth, or communication by writing,
that no one do him any service, abide under the same roof with him, approach
within four cubits' length of him, or read any document dictated by him or
written by his hand.[84]

During the reading of this curse, 'the wailing and protracted note of a
great horn was heard to fall in from time to time; the lights, seen
burning brightly at the beginning of the ceremony, were extinguished
one by one as it proceeded, till at the end the last went out, symbolizing
the extinction of the spiritual life of the excommunicated man, and the
congregation was left in total darkness'.[85]
Spinoza, aged twenty-four, was then expelled from his father's
house, and shortly after from Amsterdam too. He claimed that an
attempt to kill him had been made one night when he was returning
from the theatre: he used to show the coat with the dagger-hole. When
his father died, his rapacious sisters tried to deprive him of his
inheritance. He went to law to establish his rights but, having done so,
withdrew all claims except to one bed with its hangings. He finally
settled in The Hague, where he lived by his lens-work. He had a small
pension from the state, and an annuity left by a friend. He turned
down other offers of help and refused a professorship at Heidelberg.
He lived the austere life of a poor scholar, as he probably would have
done had he remained orthodox; but he did not marry. He was the

reverse of a Bohemian, dressing with great sobriety, and insisting: 'It is not a disorderly and slovenly carriage which makes us sages; rather, affected indifference to personal appearance is evidence of a poor spirit in which true wisdom could find no fit dwelling place and science only meet with disorder and disarray.'[86] He died, aged forty-four, of a form of tuberculosis, and his estate was so small that his sister Rebecca refused to administer it.

The origin and substance of Spinoza's quarrel with the Jewish authorities is not entirely clear. He was accused of denying the existence of angels, the immortality of the soul and the divine inspiration of the Torah. But an *apologia* for his views, which he wrote in Spanish soon after the *herem*, has not survived. However, in 1670 he published, unsigned, his *Tractatus Theologico-Politicus*, in which he set out his principles of Biblical criticism. Therein lay his essential heterodoxy. He argued that the Bible should be approached in a scientific spirit and investigated like any natural phenomenon. In the case of the Bible, the approach had to be historical. One began by analysing the Hebrew language. Then one proceeded to analyse and classify the expression in each of the books of the Bible. The next stage was to examine the historical context:

the life, the conduct, and the pursuits of the author of each book, who he was, what was the occasion and the epoch of his writing, whom did he write for and in what language . . . [then] the history of each book: how it was first received, into whose hands it fell, how many different versions there were of it, by whose advice was it received into the Canon, and lastly how all the books now universally accepted as sacred were united into a single whole.

Spinoza proceeded to apply his analysis, discussing which parts of the Pentateuch were actually written by Moses, the roll of Ezra, the compilation of the canon, the provenance of such books as Job and Daniel, and the dating of the works as a whole and its individual parts. In effect, he rejected the traditional view of the origin and authenticity of the Bible almost completely, providing alternative explanations from its internal evidence. He thus began the process of Biblical criticism which, over the next 250 years, was to demolish educated belief in the literal truth of the Bible and to reduce it to the status of an imperfect historical record.[87] His work and influence were to inflict grievous and irreparable damage on the self-confidence and internal cohesion of Christianity. They also, as we shall shortly see, raised new, long-term and deadly problems for the Jewish community.

Spinoza was the first major example of the sheer destructive power of Jewish rationalism once it escaped the restraints of the traditional community. During his lifetime and for long after, he was treated as an atheist by all the main religious bodies. His works were banned everywhere – though everywhere they survived and were constantly reprinted. In 1671 he sent a letter to the Jewish leader Orobio de Castro denying that he was an atheist and refuting the charge that the *Tractatus* was an anti-religious book. But his *Ethics*, published after his death, showed that he was a pantheist of a peculiarly thorough-going type. Strange as it may seem to us, some forms of pantheism were evidently regarded as compatible with Judaism in the seventeenth century. Kabbalah, then regarded as acceptable by many Jews, was pantheistic in tendency; the *Zohar* has many passages which suggest that God is everything and everything is God. Twenty years after Spinoza died, the London Sephardi rabbi David Nieto (1654–1728) got into serious trouble for producing a work in Spanish, *On Divine Providence*, which identified nature with God. The dispute was referred to the great Talmudic scholar Zevi Ashkenazi of Amsterdam, who ruled that Nieto's argument was not merely acceptably Judaic but almost commonplace among some Jewish thinkers.[88]

The trouble with Spinoza's pantheism, however, was that he pushed it to the point where it was impossible to make valid distinctions between it and atheism. He himself insisted he had not said that the material world, as we see it and treat it, was God. He states in his *Ethics* that 'We easily conceive the whole of nature to be one individual,' because one individual can be part of a larger one, *ad infinitum*. But he does not see God as a person. He states in terms that to credit God with such attributes as 'will' or 'intellect' would be like asking Sirius to bark, just because we call it the Dog Star. In fact he only retains the word God at all for historical and sentimental reasons. Identifying God with the whole of reality, he has to agree with the atheist when the latter insists that reality cannot be divided into a part which is God and one which is non-God – both of them deny an effective contrast.[89] But if God cannot be isolated from anything else, it is impossible to say He 'exists' in any sense an ordinary person can grasp. Spinoza was saying: 'There is no God in the sense we have always understood the word.' To most people that is atheism. The German mathematician and philosopher Gottfried Wilhelm von Leibniz (1646–1716) knew Spinoza well and was certainly in a position to penetrate his mind on this matter. He was a careerist, and he has often been accused of cowardice in seeking to distance himself from Spinoza's work as it attracted opprobrium. But he correctly summed up Spinoza's position in the religious spectrum thus: 'He was truly an atheist in that he did not acknowledge any Providence which distributes good fortune and bad according to what is just.'[90]

Spinoza's work represents the hypertrophy of one aspect of the Jewish spirit: its tendency not just to rationalize but to intellectualize. He was one of those who thought it might be possible to resolve all disputes and conflicts of opinion and reach human perfection by a process of logic. He believed the problems of ethics could be solved by geometrical-type proofs. He was thus in the tradition of Maimonides, who argued that perfect worldly peace could be achieved through reason – that was how he thought the Messianic Age would come. But Maimonides imagined this state being reached when the Law was fully observed in all its noble rationality. It would be achieved on the basis of Revelation, through the Torah. Spinoza, however, did not believe in Revelation and wanted to scrap the Torah. He thought the end could be achieved by pure intellect.

That led him into a posture of anti-humanism. He sought to give man what he called 'all the remedies against the emotions'. To a limited extent this is attractive. Spinoza wanted to overcome passion. He certainly practised what he preached. He never in his life became angry, despite much provocation, or lost his temper. He was self-disciplined, self-denying to the point of heroism. All sin was due to ignorance, he argued; miseries have to be understood, seen in relation to their causes, and as part of the whole order of nature. Once this is grasped, one does not yield to sorrow, hatred, the desire for revenge. 'Hatred is increased by being reciprocated; on the other hand, it can be destroyed by love. Hatred which is completely vanquished by love is transformed into love; and love is thereupon greater than if hate had not preceded it.' But Spinoza's 'love' is a peculiar thing. All is predetermined. He does not believe in free will. So hope and fear are bad; so are humility and repentance. 'He who repents of an action is doubly wretched or infirm.' Whatever happens is God's will. The wise man tries to see the world as God sees it. Only ignorance makes us think we can alter the future. Once we grasp this we can free ourselves from fear; thus freed, we meditate not on death, but on life. When we understand ourselves and our feelings, from which passion has been removed, we can love God. But this is not person-to-person love, of course, since God is not a person but everything; and love is not a passion, but understanding. God, or rather 'God', has no passions or pleasures or pains; loves and hates no one. So 'he who loves God cannot endeavour that God should love him in return'. Or again: 'the intellectual love of the mind towards God is part of the infinite love wherewith God loves himself'.[91]

It is not hard to see why Spinoza appeals to a certain cerebral but heartless type of philosopher, like Bertrand Russell; or why other people find him bloodless, even repellent. Among contemporaries Spinoza, like Hobbes – from whom he acquired a certain chilly rigour – inspired genuine fear. It might have been better if he had felt free to abandon the use of code-words like 'God' altogether, and written plainly. His influence on other key European writers was incalculable. He fascinated both French intellectuals, such as Voltaire, and the Germans, such as Lessing, who remarked: 'There is no other philosophy than the philosophy of Spinoza.' But so far as the Jews themselves were concerned, he simply mined out one vein of inquiry: he carried the rationalist tradition of Maimonides not so much to its logical conclusion as out of Judaism altogether.

There remained the irrationalist tradition. It had triumphed in the fourteenth century. Its kabbalah had been received into normative Judaism. It had received a stunning blow with the apostasy of Shabbetai Zevi. Shabbeteanism had gone underground. The antics of Jacob Frank showed that this tradition, too, could take the enthusiastic and the obstinate out of Judaism. The huge emotional energy and fervour which had powered the messianic movement in the 1660s remained. Was there no way it could be allowed to express itself and yet at the same time remain harnessed – if only loosely – to the Judaic chariot?

In the eighteenth century the problem was not confined to Judaism. The scientific revolution that preceded the industrial one was already under way by 1700. Newton's theory of a mechanical cosmos, governed by iron mathematical laws, had triumphed. At the top of society, scepticism was spreading. Established religious leaders were cool, urbane, worldly, inclined to tolerance because they did not care deeply about fine points of doctrine for which their predecessors had killed and been killed. But the masses, whose lives were hard, needed more. Men arose to give it to them. In Germany there was the Pietist Movement. In England there were the Wesley Brothers and their Methodism. In America there was the first Great Awakening. In eastern Europe, where more than half of all the Jews now lived, there was hasidism.

Pious fervour among the Jewish masses of Poland was not just a religious force. It had radical undertones. Jewish society was authoritarian and often oppressive. It was run by an intermarried oligarchy of rich merchants and lawyer–rabbis. The system of councils gave this elite formidable powers and the franchise which elected it was narrow. The oligarchy was not closed, for education offered a ladder of ascent.

In theory even the poor had full access to it. The cathedocracy was, of necessity, a meritocracy too. Yet most of the poor remained, and felt, powerless. They were nothing in synagogue. They might petition against a rabbi; but no notice was taken if his family background was right. On the contrary: many local ordinances punished all those 'who gossip and jest about the deeds of the town notables'. The spirit of oppression was felt not just communally, but within families. The ghetto was a patriarchy as well. A father was entitled to use force to teach Torah to a son once he was twelve. After he was thirteen, the Deuteronomic Law of the Rebellious Son applied. In theory a defiant son could be taken before the elders, convicted and stoned to death; he could be scourged even on the first offence. The Talmud said no such case had ever occurred, but the shadow of the Law lay over the son. A daughter could be contracted into marriage by her father while she was still a minor. In theory she could reject the husband when she became *bogeret*, at twelve and a half, but this rarely happened. Children were taught that honouring parents was equivalent to honouring God.[92] In short, there was an excessive amount of subordination in the ghetto.

But it is one of the glories of the Jews that they do not meekly submit to their own appointed authorities. The Jew is the eternal protestant. And Jewish tradition, albeit often reluctantly, gives the protestor a place. It also allows a holy man to operate outside the standard religious structure. We have already come across the *ba'al shem*, the Master of the Divine Name. This type went back to the days of the Babylonian *geonim*. From the sixteenth century there were numbers of them in Ashkenazi Jewry, performing practical kabbalah. A few were genuine scholars. Most wrote amulets or performed folk-medicine cures, by means of special prayers, incantations, herbs and bits of animals. They specialized in mental disorders and casting out *dybbuks*.

In about 1736 one of these men, Israel ben Eliezer, later known as the Ba'al Shem Tov (*c.* 1700–60), or the Besht, from the initials, felt the call. He was an orphan, born in Okop in backward Podolia. At various times he had helped in the ritual slaughterhouse, worked in the claypits of the Carpathian mountains, served as a synagogue watchman and a sexton, and kept an inn. Portraits usually show him with a pipe in hand or mouth. He was a man of the people. He was quite outside the line of apostolic succession of rabbis, which in theory could be traced back to Moses. He had little learning. No authentic work of his has survived. Letters bearing his signature may be forged. His homilies were put down in writing by disciples. He worked outside the synagogue system and never seems to have preached there. But, like John Wesley, he travelled around the country. He wrote amulets. He cured and purged men of their evil spirits, did in fact all the things an ordinary holy man would do. But in addition he had genuine charisma: men and women felt themselves capable of higher aspirations, or purer behaviour, in his presence. This impression of intense, though homely, sanctity was reinforced by his cures, which were often spectacular, by his dreams in which he correctly foretold events, by his mystical states and by the miracles attributed to him.[93]

All this made him an influential individual. As he became known, he held his court, like a famous rabbi, and people came to see him from long distances. What made him the founder of a movement, however, was his creativity. He was responsible for two new institutions. The first was his revival of the ancient concept of the *zaddik*, or superior human being – superior because of his special capacity to adhere to God. The idea was as old as Noah. But the Ba'al Shem Tov gave him a special role. With the apostasy of Shabbetai Zevi, messianism had become discredited. The Besht had no time for Frankism or any messianic sect which moved away from Jewish monotheism. As he put it, 'The *Shekinah* wails and says that as long as a limb is attached to the body there is hope of a cure. But when it is severed it cannot be restored, and every Jew is a limb of the *Shekinah*.' So he had no intention of travelling down the road to severance. But he recognized that the vanished Messiah had left a hole in Jewish hearts. He filled it by reviving the *zaddik*, who (he taught) descends from the heights, rather like God's grace and mercy. The *zaddik*, in Ba'al Shem Tov's teaching, was not a messiah, but not quite an ordinary human being either – somewhere between the two. Moreover, since the *zaddik* did not claim a messianic role, there could be many of them. Thus a new kind of religious personality arose, to perpetuate and spread the movement.

Secondly, he invented a revolutionary form of popular prayer. This was important because it enabled ordinary, humble Jews to contribute. The great strength of Lurianic kabbalah had been the feeling among the masses that they could hasten the coming of the Messiah by their prayers and piety. The Ba'al Shem Tov achieved a similar element of popular participation by the new theory of prayer which he and his successors taught. He stressed that prayer was not so much a human activity as a supernatural act, in which man breaks down the barriers of his natural existence and reaches into the divine world. How does man do this? He takes the prayer-book and concentrates all his mind on the letters. He does not read, he wills. As he does so, their actual shapes dissolve and – this is a typical kabbalistic idea – the divine attributes concealed in the letters become spiritually visible. It is like seeing through a transparent object. The Besht called it 'entering into the letters of the prayers' or the 'heavenly halls' – a man knew he was worthy when he 'passed into the halls of the prayers'.[94]

The Besht taught that, in order to enter in, the man has to annihilate his personality and become nothing. He thus creates a vacuum, which is filled up by a sort of supernal being, who acts and speaks for him. When the words of the prayer-book blur and merge into a single point, the transformation occurs, the man ceases human activity and, instead of the man sending up his words, they are sent down into his mouth. The mouth continues to speak but the spirit supplies the thoughts. The Besht said: 'I let the mouth speak whatever it wants to say.'[95] His successor, leader in the second generation of Hasidism, Dov Baer, explained that the spiritual power which made this divine possession possible arose because the Torah and God were actually one, and divine energy, as it were, was stored up in the letters of the book. A successful act of contemplative prayer released this power. Dov Baer used another simile: 'When a man studies or prays, the word should be uttered with full strength, like the ejaculation of a drop of semen from his whole body, when his [entire] strength is present in that drop.'[96]

Hence hasidic ceremonies became very noisy affairs. They scorned the synagogue. They had their own *shtiblekh*, or prayer houses, where they assembled in their rustic clothes and broad fur hats. Some smoked or drank if they felt like it. When they prayed, often at the top of their voices, they swayed and clapped their hands. They sang a tune called a *niggun* and danced to it. They had their own special prayers, a mixture of Polish Ashkenazi and Luriac Sephardi. They were poor, rough people. They shocked the Jewish establishment, particularly when their practices spread all over Poland and into Lithuania. They were quickly accused of secret Shabbeteanism. There were angry calls for their suppression.

In Elijah ben Solomon Zalman (1720–97), the *gaon* of Vilna, the early hasidics found a dedicated enemy. The *gaon*, even by the standards of Jewish infant prodigies, was a spectacular child. He had delivered a homily in the Vilna synagogue at the age of six. His secular as well as his religious knowledge was awesome. When marriage at eighteen brought him independent means, he purchased a small house outside Vilna and concentrated entirely on study. His sons said he never slept more than two hours a day, nor more than half an hour at a time. To eliminate distractions, he closed the shutters even in daytime and studied by candlelight. To stop himself falling asleep, he cut off the heating and put his feet in a bowl of cold water. As his power and influence in Vilna grew, so his devotion to study intensified. He did not despise kabbalah, but everything had to be subordinated to the demands of the halakhah. He regarded hasidism as an outrage. Its claims to ecstasy, miracles and visions were, he said, all lies and delusions. The idea of the *zaddik* was idolatry, worship of human beings. Most of all, its theory of prayer was a substitute for, an affront to, scholarship – the be-all and end-all of Judaism. He was the cathedocracy personified, and when asked his opinion about what should be done to the *hasidim*, he replied: persecute them.[97] Fortunately for the orthodox, the *hasidim* had started to use unorthodox knives for the *shehitah* or ritual slaughter. The first *herem* was proclaimed against them in 1772. Their books were publicly burned. There was another *herem* in 1781, stating: 'They must leave our communities with their wives and children . . . and they should not be given a night's lodging. Their *shehitah* is forbidden. It is forbidden to do business with them, to intermarry with them, or assist at their burial.' The *gaon* wrote: 'it is the duty of every believing Jew to repudiate and pursue them with all manner of afflictions and subdue them, because they have sin in their hearts and are a sore on the body of Israel'.[98]

But the *hasidim* replied with their own excommunications. They issued pamphlets to defend themselves. In Lithuania, and Vilna in particular, the *gaon* created an enclave of halakhic orthodoxy and scholarship, before departing to end his days in Erez Israel. But elsewhere hasidism established itself permanently as an important and seemingly necessary part of Judaism. It spread west into Germany and thence into the world. The orthodox attempt to destroy it failed. Indeed it was soon abandoned, as both scholars and enthusiasts united in the face of a new and common enemy – the Jewish enlightenment or haskalah.

Although the haskalah was a specific episode in Jewish history, and the *maskil* or enlightened Jew is a special type peculiar to Judaism, the Jewish enlightenment is nevertheless part of the general European enlightenment. But it is, more particularly, linked to the enlightenment in Germany, and this for a very good reason. The movement in both France and Germany was concerned to examine and readjust man's attitude to God. But whereas in France its tendency was to repudiate or downgrade God, and tame religion, in Germany it sought genuinely to reach a new understanding of and accommodation with the religious spirit in man. The French enlightenment was brilliant but fundamentally frivolous; the German was serious, sincere and creative. Hence it was to the German version that enlightened Jews felt attracted, which influenced them most, and to which they in turn made a substantial contribution.[99] For perhaps the first time Jews in Germany began to feel a distinct affinity with German culture, and thus sowed in their hearts the seeds of a monstrous delusion.

To intellectuals in Christian society, the question posed by the enlightenment was really: how large a part, if any, should God play in an increasingly secular culture? To Jews, the question was rather: what part, if any, should secular knowledge play in the culture of God? They were still enfolded in the medieval vision of a total religious society. It is true that Maimonides had argued strongly in favour of admitting secular science and had demonstrated how completely it could be reconciled to the Torah. But his argument had failed to convince most Jews. Even a relatively moderate man like the Maharal of Prague had attacked Rossi precisely for bringing secular criteria to bear on religious matters.[100] A few Jews, for instance, attended the medical school in Padua. But they turned their back on the world outside the Torah the moment they re-entered the ghetto in the evening, as indeed did Jewish men of business. Of course many went out into the world never to return; but that had always happened. What the awesome example of Spinoza had shown, to the satisfaction of most Jews, was that a man could not drink at the well of gentile knowledge without deadly risk of poisoning his Judaic life. So the ghetto remained not merely a social but an intellectual universe on its own.

By the mid-eighteenth century the results were pitifully apparent to all. As long ago as the Tortosa dispute, early in the fifteenth century, the Jewish intelligentsia had been made to seem backward and obscurantist. Now, more than 300 years later, the Jews appeared to educated Christians – or even uneducated ones – figures of contempt and derision, dressed in funny clothes, imprisoned in ancient and ludicrous superstitions, as remote and isolated from modern society as one of their lost tribes. The gentiles knew nothing, and cared less, about Jewish scholarship. Like the ancient Greeks before them, they were not even aware it existed. For Christian Europe there had always been a 'Jewish problem'. In the Middle Ages it had been: how to prevent this subversive minority from contaminating religious truth and social order? No fear of that now. For gentile intellectuals, at least, the problem was now rather: how, in common humanity, to rescue this pathetic people from their ignorance and darkness.

In 1749 the young Protestant dramatist Gotthold Lessing put on a one-act play, *Die Juden*, which for almost the first time in European literature presented a Jew as a refined, rational human being. It was a gesture of tolerance, warmly reciprocated by Lessing's exact contemporary, a Dessau Jew called Moses Mendelssohn (1729–86). The two men met and became friends, and the brilliant playwright introduced the Jew into literary society. Mendelssohn suffered from curvature of the spine, which made him retiring, patient, modest. But he had formidable energy. He had been well educated by the local rabbi, trained as a bookkeeper and remained a merchant all his life. But his powers of reading were impressive and he acquired a great range of secular knowledge. With Lessing's help he began to publish his philosophical writings. Frederick the Great gave him 'right of residence' in Berlin. His conversation was much admired and he became a figure in the salons.[101] He was ten years younger than the *gaon*, nearly thirty years younger than the Besht, but seemed divided from both by centuries. The fiery Talmud scholar; the mystic–enthusiast; the urbane rationalist – the whole of modern Jewry was to be written round these three archetypes!

Initially Mendelssohn laid no claim to a specific Jewish stake in the enlightenment; he simply wanted to enjoy it. But he was driven to publicize his Jewish convictions by the ignorance and disparagement of Judaism he encountered everywhere in the gentile world. The traditional gentile world said: keep the Jews under or expel them. The enlightened gentile world said: how can we best assist these poor Jews to stop being Jewish? Mendelssohn replied: let us share a common culture, but allow us Jews to remain Jewish. In 1767 he published *Phaedon*, an inquiry into the immortality of the soul modelled on the Platonic dialogue. At a time when cultured Germans still usually wrote in Latin or French, and Jews in Hebrew or Yiddish, Mendelssohn followed Lessing in striving to make German the language of intellectual discourse and to exploit its magnificent resources. He wrote it with great elegance and decked his text with classical, rather than Biblical, allusions – the mark of the *maskil*. The book was well received in the gentile world, but in a manner Mendelssohn found distressing. Even his own French translator condescendingly declared (1772) that it was a remarkable work considering it was written by one 'born and raised in a nation which stagnates in vulgar ignorance'.[102] A clever young Swiss pastor, Johan Caspar Lavater, praised its accomplishments and wrote that the author was obviously ready for conversion – he challenged Mendelssohn to defend his Judaism in public.

Thus Mendelssohn was driven, despite himself, into a rationalist defence of Judaism; or, more precisely, into a demonstration of how Jews, while remaining attached to the essentials of their faith, could become part of a general European culture. His work took many forms. He translated the Pentateuch into German. He tried to foster the study of Hebrew among German Jews, as opposed to Yiddish, which he deplored as the dialect of vulgar immorality. As his prestige increased, he found himself fighting the battles of local Jewish communities against gentile authority. He opposed the expulsion of the Jews from Dresden and new anti-Semitic laws in Switzerland. He refuted in detail the common accusation that Jewish prayers were anti-Christian. For the benefit of secular authority, he explained the Jewish laws of matrimony and oaths. But while on the one hand he presented Judaism to the outside world in its best possible light, he sought on the other to encourage changes to rid it of its unacceptable face. He detested the institution of the *herem*, especially in the light of the witch-hunt against Shabbeteans which took place in Altona in the 1750s. He took the view that whereas the state was a compulsory society, based on social contract, all churches were voluntary, based on conviction. A man should not be compelled to belong to one, nor expelled from one against his will.[103] He thought it best to end separate Jewish jurisdiction and opposed those gentile liberals who wanted the state to give backing to Jewish courts. He called for the end of all persecution and discrimination against Jews, and said he believed this would come as reason triumphed. But equally he thought that Jews must abandon those habits and practices which limited reasonable human freedom and particularly freedom of thought.

Mendelssohn was walking a tightrope. He was terrified of treading down Spinoza's road and became upset if comparisons were made. He was scared of bringing down Christian wrath if, in his public controversies, his defence of Judaism involved unacceptable criticism of Christianity. In arguing with Lavater he pointed out that it was dangerous to dispute with the creed of the overwhelming majority, adding: 'I am a member of an oppressed people.' In fact he believed that Christianity was far more irrational than Judaism. At all times he was anxious to defend the bridge with the enlightenment while keeping in contact with the bulk of believing Jews. So he sometimes tried to be all things to all men. It is difficult to present a summary of his views without making them seem confused. He followed Maimonides in arguing that the truths of religion could be proved by reason. But whereas Maimonides wanted rational truth reinforced by Revelation, Mendelssohn wanted Revelation dispensed with. Judaism was not revealed religion but revealed law: it was a historical fact that Moses received the Law at Sinai, and that Law was the means whereby the Jewish people achieved spiritual happiness. The truth did not need miracles to validate it. 'A wise man', he wrote, 'whom the arguments of true philosophy have convinced of the existence of a supreme deity, is much more impressed by a natural event, whose connections with the whole he can partly discern, than by a miracle' (notebook entry, 16 March 1753).[104] However, to prove the existence of God Mendelssohn relied on the old metaphysics: the *a priori* or ontological proof and the *a posteriori* or cosmological. Both were demolished, in the general opinion, by Kant's *Critique of Pure Reason* (1781), published in Mendelssohn's last decade.

As an apologist for Jewish religion, then, Mendelssohn was not very successful. The truth is, there was much of it in which he simply did not believe: the idea of the chosen people, the mission to humanity, the Promised Land. He seems to have thought that Judaism was an appropriate creed for a particular people, which should be privately practised in as rational a manner as possible. The idea that the whole of a culture could be contained in the Torah was to him absurd. The Jew should worship at home and then, when he went out into the world, participate in the general European culture. But the logic of this was that each Jew would belong to the culture of the people among whom he happened to live. So Jewry, which had kept its global unity for 1,500 years despite appalling ill-treatment, would gradually dissolve, except as a private, confessional faith. That was why the great modern apologist for Judaism, Yechezkel Kaufmann (1889–1963), called Mendelssohn 'the Jewish Luther' – he cut the faith and the people apart.[105]

But Mendelssohn does not seem to have appreciated the logic of his rejection of Torah-culture. The idea that the Jews, absorbed into 'the culture of the nations', would gradually lose belief in a Jewish God too, would have distressed him. It is true he argued that Judaism and Christianity could come together, if the latter were stripped of its irrationalities. But he hated the idea of Jews converting to Christianity in order to emancipate themselves. He encouraged the Prussian official, Christian Wilhelm von Dohm, to publish his well-meaning but condescending plea for Jewish liberties, *On the Improvement of the Jews as Citizens* (1781), but found its tone unsatisfactory. In effect, Dohm was saying: the Jews are very objectionable people but not intrinsically bad; no worse, anyway, than Christian ill-treatment and their own superstitious religion have made them. The Jews had 'an exaggerated tendency [to seek] gain in every way, a love of usury'. These 'defects' were aggravated 'by their self-imposed segregation owing to their religious precepts as well as rabbinical sophistry'. From these followed 'the breaking of the laws of the state restricting trade, the import and export of prohibited wares, the forgery of money and precious metals'. Dohm advocated state reforms 'by which they can be cured of this corruption so as to become better people and more useful citizens'.[106] But the implication, of course, was that Jewish religion would have to undergo radical changes too.

Hence Mendelssohn found it necessary to clarify his attitude to the Jews' role in society in *Jerusalem, or upon Religious Power and Judaism* (1783). He defended Judaism as an undogmatic religion. It gave a man precepts, a code of living, but did not seek to control his thoughts. 'Faith accepts no commands,' he wrote, 'it accepts only what comes to it by way of reasoned conviction.' To be happy, men needed to seek and find truth. Truth had therefore to be accessible to people of all races and creeds. Judaism was not the only agent by which God revealed the truth. All men, Jews included, must be allowed to seek it: 'Let every man who does not disturb the public welfare, who obeys the law, acts righteously towards you and his fellow man, be allowed to speak as he thinks, to pray to God after his own fashion or after that of his fathers, and to seek eternal salvation where he thinks he may find it.' This was a formula for securing civilized treatment of Jews, but it was not Judaism. In fact in religious terms it was a formula for natural religion and natural ethics, to which of course the Jews would make a contribution, but nothing more. Gone, irrecoverably, was the thunder of Moses.

Moreover, if the Jews, by accepting the enlightenment, were to forfeit the particular claims of Judaism, it was by no means certain that they would get a quiet life in return. The country which came closest to Mendelssohn's ideal was the United States, where the notions of the enlightenment rested on a solid basis of English parliamentarianism and tolerant religious pluralism. The very year Mendelssohn was writing *Jerusalem*, Thomas Jefferson, in *Notes on Virginia* (1782), argued that the existence of a variety of sensible, ethical religions was the best guarantee of material and spiritual progress, and of human freedom. Mendelssohn's dualistic solution to 'the Jewish problem', later succinctly described by the poet Judah Leib Gordon as 'a Jew in his tent and a man abroad', fitted very well into American ideas of religion. Like the population as a whole, a majority of American Jews supported the independence movement, though some were loyalist and some neutral. Others were prominent in the struggle. At the public feast given in Philadelphia in 1789 to celebrate the new constitution, there was a special table where the food conformed to Jewish dietary laws.[107]

The Jews had something to celebrate. In the light of their history, they stood to gain more from the new American constitution than any other group – the separation of church and state, general liberty of conscience and not least the end of all religious tests in appointments. The constitution worked, too, in giving liberties to the Jews, though feet were dragged in some states. In Protestant North Carolina the last Jewish disabilities, admittedly minor ones, did not vanish until 1868. But the Jew felt free in the United States; even better, he felt valued. The fact that he practised his faith assiduously and was a staunch member of synagogue, far from being a handicap, as in Europe, was a ticket to respectability in the United States, where all conventional forms of piety were esteemed as pillars of society. Jews did not find a new Zion in America, but at last they found a permanent resting-place and a home.

In Europe, the enlightenment brought them hopes which proved illusions, and opportunities which turned into a new set of problems. In some areas the rule of reason did not operate at all. By the three partitions of Poland (1772, 1793, 1795), the Russian empire, which had hitherto refused to admit Jews at all, acquired a million of them as a result of its territorial greed. It now gave them rights of residence but only within a Pale of Settlement, where their numbers, poverty and disabilities all increased rapidly. In Italy, too, at any rate in the papal states, the position of the Jews also deteriorated under the anti-Semitic pope Pius VI (1775–99) whose Edict on the Jews, published right at the start of his long reign, led directly to forced baptisms. Jews were obliged by law to listen to contemptuous and insulting sermons, and if some sort of baptismal ceremony had been performed over a Jewish child – perhaps in secret by a Catholic maidservant – the church could claim possession later. The person was then taken to the House of Catechumens, where his consent was required (if an adult), and he might give it just to get out. Ferrara, once liberal to Jews, was now worse than Rome. As late as 1817 the little daughter of Angelo Ancona was forcibly taken away from her parents by armed men employed by the archbishop's tribunal, on the grounds that five years before, aged two months, she had been privately baptized by her nurse, later dismissed for dishonesty. The case led to a reign of terror in the Ferrara ghetto.[108]

States which considered themselves more enlightened were only marginally better. The Empress Maria Theresa of Austria actually expelled the Jews from Prague as late as 1744–5, though they were readmitted three years later. Frederick the Great, despite his supposed personal support for the enlightenment, enacted a Jewish law in 1750 which distinguished between 'ordinary' and 'extraordinary' Jews. The latter had no hereditary rights of residence and even the former's descended only to one child. Jews had to pay 'protection' taxes and fines in lieu of military services and had to make compulsory purchases of state products. They were confined to a limited range of trades and professions. The first genuine reforms in central Europe were introduced by Maria Theresa's son, Joseph II, from 1781 onwards, and even they were a mixed blessing. He abolished the special poll-tax and yellow badge, the ban on Jews attending universities and some trade restrictions. On the other hand, he prohibited Yiddish and Hebrew in business and public records, scrapped rabbinical jurisdictions and introduced military service for Jews. Jews were still under residence restrictions in Vienna and other places, and their new rights were often denied by hostile bureaucrats.

Indeed, the impact of these Jew-reforms, *Judenreformen*, and Edicts of Toleration, *Toleranzpatent*, was often spoilt by the spirit in which they were administered by bitterly hostile petty officials who feared that Jews would soon be after their jobs. For instance, an Austrian law of 1787 compelled Jews to adopt German-sounding first and family names. While Sephardi Jews had long since adopted the Spanish practice of family names, the Ashkenazis had been very conservative, still following the antique custom of using their personal, plus father's personal, name, and in the Hebrew–Yiddish form – Yaakov ben Yitzhak, for example. Hebrew-sounding names were now usually forbidden and the bureaucrats produced lists of 'acceptable' names. Bribes were necessary to secure 'nice' family names, derived from flowers or precious stones: Lilienthal, Edelstein, Diamant, Saphir, Rosenthal. Two very expensive names were Kluger (wise) and Fröhlich (happy). Most Jews were brutally lumped by bored officials into four categories and named accordingly: Weiss (white), Schwartz (black), Gross (big) and Klein (little). Many poorer Jews had unpleasant names foisted on them by malignant clerks: Glagenstrick (gallow's rope), Eselkopf (donkey's head), Taschengregger (pickpocket), Schmalz (grease), Borgenicht (don't borrow), for example. Jews of priestly or levitical descent, who could claim names like Cohen, Kahn, Katz, Levi, were forced to Germanize them: Katzman, Cohnstein, Aronstein, Levinthal and so on. A large group were given places of origin: Brody, Epstein, Ginzberg, Landau, Shapiro (Speyer), Dreyfus (Trier), Horowitz and Posner.[109] The pain of this humiliating procedure was not lessened by the knowledge that the government's main object in imposing it was to make Jews easier to tax and conscript.

The internal contradictions of the so-called enlightened despots were perfectly illustrated by Jewish policy during the last years of the *ancien régime* in France. In January 1784 Louis XVI abolished the poll-tax on Jews; six months later, the Jews of Alsace were subjected to a 'reform' which curbed the rights of Jews to lend money and trade in cattle and grain, forced them to seek crown permission before marrying, and ordered a census so that those without residence qualification could be expelled.[110] This directly reflected anti-Jewish feeling in eastern France, where Ashkenazi Jews were now very numerous and much hated at a popular level.

The ambivalence was by no means wholly resolved by the outbreak of the French Revolution. In theory the Revolution was to make all men, including Jews, equal. In return Jews must abandon any separatism. The tone was set by Stanilas Comte de Clermont-Tonnerre who, in the first debate on the 'Jewish question', 28 September 1789, argued that 'there cannot be a nation within a nation'. Hence: 'The Jews should be denied everything as a nation but granted everything as individuals.' That was all very well, but it was the voice of the enlightened elite. The voice of the people could be rather different. Jean-François Rewbell, the left-wing radical deputy from Alsace, fought bitterly against equal rights for the Jews there, on behalf of 'a numerous, industrious and honest class of my unfortunate compatriots' who were being 'oppressed and ground down by these cruel hordes of Africans who have infested my region'. It was only after tremendous resistance that the National Assembly voted a decree of complete emancipation for Jews (27 September 1791), to which was added a sinister rider that the government was to supervise debts owed to Jews in eastern France.[111]

Nevertheless, the deed was done. French Jews were now free and the clock could never be turned back completely. Moreover, emancipation in some form took place wherever the French were able to carry the revolutionary spirit with their arms. The ghettos and Jewish closed quarters were broken into in papal Avignon (1791), Nice (1792) and the Rhineland (1792–3). The spread of the revolution to the Netherlands, and the founding of the Batavian Republic, led to Jews being granted full and formal rights by law there (1796). In 1796–8 Napoleon Bonaparte liberated many of the Italian ghettos, French troops, young Jews and local enthusiasts tearing down the crumbling old walls with their bare hands.

For the first time a new archetype, who had always existed in embryonic form, began to emerge from the shadows: the revolutionary Jew. Clericalists in Italy swore enmity to 'Gauls, Jacobins and

Jews'. In 1793–4 Jewish Jacobins set up a revolutionary regime in Saint-Esprit, the Jewish suburb of Bayonne. Once again, as during the Reformation, traditionalists saw a sinister link between the Torah and subversion. The subversive Jew appeared in many guises, often as brutal caricature, occasionally as farce. In England it was personified in the eccentric figure of Lord George Gordon, the former Protestant fanatic whose mob had terrorized London in 1780. Three years later he turned to Judaism. The Rabbi David Schiff, of the Great Synagogue in Duke's Place, turned him down. So he went to the Hambro Synagogue, which accepted him. The poorer Jews, reported Dr Watson (who figures as Gashford in Dickens's novel of the riots, *Barnaby Rudge*), 'regarded him as a second Moses and fondly hoped he was designed by Providence to lead them back to their fathers' land'.[112] In January 1788 Gordon was sentenced to two years in Newgate for publishing a libel on the Queen of France. He was given comfortable quarters, in the name of the Hon. Israel bar Abraham Gordon, and hung on his walls the Ten Commandments in Hebrew, his bag containing phylacteries and the *tallit*. 'It was more like the study of a recluse in a private house than a prison,' said John Wesley, one of his innumerable illustrious visitors, who included the royal dukes, York and Clarence. He had a Jewish maidservant–mistress, Polly Levi, kept a magnificent table, never dined with less than six guests and sometimes to the music of a band. As he refused to give security for good behaviour, the court kept him in prison throughout the early stages of the French Revolution, which he welcomed noisily, playing radical dirges on his bagpipes and entertaining subversives such as Horne Tooke. Edmund Burke, in his *Reflections on the Revolution in France*, proposed a swop to the new Paris regime: 'Send us your popish archbishop of Paris and we will send you our Protestant rabbi.' A few hours after Marie Antoinette had been guillotined in Paris, Gordon died in his cell, shouting the revolutionary song, '*Ça Ira – les aristocrates à la lanterne!*'[113]

One of Bonaparte's earliest moves as First Consul was to ban this song. As part of the same attempt to unite the age of reason with the requirements of order he tried hard to bring the Jews into society not as potential or actual subversives but as solid citizens. During his years of triumph, other monarchs followed in his wake, the most important being Prussia, which on 11 March 1812 recognized Jews already resident as full citizens and abolished all disabilities and special taxes. There was a consensus, at any rate among most educated Jews, that France had done more for them than any other nation, and this feeling persisted for a century, until it was shattered by the Dreyfus case.

But Jews sensibly declined to identify their interests with French imperialism. English Jews were rightly worried by the wave of xenophobia which the Revolutionary Terror inspired and which produced the Aliens Act of 1793. The Wardens of the Portuguese Synagogue in London ordered the rabbi to preach a sermon insisting on the duty of Jews to show their devotion to king and constitution. Rabbi Solomon Hirschell's thanksgiving sermon on the victory of Trafalgar was the first from the Great Synagogue to be published. It breathed, wrote the *Gentleman's Magazine,* 'a strain of true piety, a great loyalty and universal benevolence'.[114] The Jews flocked to join the London volunteers. Reviewing them in Hyde Park, George III exclaimed, characteristically, on what he called 'the large number of animal names, like Wolf, Bear, Lion – what, what!' At the other end of Europe, in Russia, the *hasidim* did not want French-style enlightenment and riches. As one rabbi said: 'If Bonaparte wins, the wealthy among Israel would increase and the greatness of Israel would be raised, but they would leave and take the heart of Israel far from the Father in Heaven.'[115]

Jews were abundantly justified in viewing radical attitudes to them with grave suspicion. There was a worm in the apple which the revolutionary goddess proffered them. The events of 1789 were a product of the French enlightenment, which was strongly anti-clerical and, at bottom, hostile to religion as such. This posed a problem. Much was permitted to clever writers in eighteenth-century France, but direct attacks on the Catholic Church were dangerous. It was at this point that they found Spinoza's work particularly useful. Concerned to develop a rationalist approach to Biblical truth, he had inevitably exposed the superstitions and obscurantism of rabbinical religion. He had pointed the way to a radical critique of Christianity too, but in doing so he had assembled the materials for an indictment of Judaism. The French *philosophes* were willing to follow him in the first, but they found it safer to do so by concentrating on the second. Thus they turned on its head the old Augustinian argument that Judaism was a witness to the truth of Christianity. It was, rather, a witness to its inventions, superstitions and sheer lies. They saw Judaism as Christianity taken to the point of caricature, and it was on this ugly travesty that they concentrated. Here, they insisted, was an example of the distorted effects that the enslavement of religion can produce on a people.

In the *Dictionnaire philosophique* (1756), Voltaire argued that it was absurd for modern European society to take its fundamental laws and beliefs from the Jews: 'Their residence in Babylon and Alexandria, which allowed individuals to acquire wisdom and knowledge, only trained the people as a whole in the art of usury . . . they are a totally ignorant nation who for many years have combined contemptible miserliness and the most revolting superstition with a violent hatred of all those nations which have tolerated them.' 'Nevertheless,' he added in a condescending afterthought, 'they should not be burned at the stake.'[116] Diderot, editor of the *Encyclopédie*, was less abusive but in his article *Juifs (philosophie des)* he concluded that the Jews bore 'all the defects peculiar to an ignorant and superstitious nation'. The Baron d'Holbach went much further. In a variety of books, especially his *L'Esprit du Judaisme* (1770), he portrayed Moses as the author of a cruel and bloodthirsty system which had corrupted Christian society too but had turned the Jews into 'the enemies of the human race. . . . The Jews have always displayed contempt for the clearest dictates of morality and the law of nations. . . . They were ordered to be cruel, inhuman, intolerant, thieves, traitors and betrayers of trust. All these are regarded as deeds pleasing to God.'[117] On the basis of this anti-religious analysis, D'Holbach heaped all the common social and business complaints against the Jews.

Hence the French enlightenment, while helping Jewish aspirations in the short term, left them with a sombre legacy. For these French writers, above all Voltaire, were widely read throughout Europe – and imitated. It was not long before the first German idealists, like Fichte, were taking up the same theme. The works of Voltaire and his colleagues were the title-deeds, the foundation documents, of the modern European intelligentsia, and it was a tragedy for the Jews that they contained a virulently anti-Semitic clause. Thus yet another layer was added to the historical accumulation of anti-Jewish polemic. On top of the pagan plinth and the Christian main storey there was now placed a secular superstructure. In a sense this was the most serious of all, for it ensured that hatred of the Jews, so long kept alive by Christian fanaticism, would now survive the decline of the religious spirit.

Moreover, the new secular anti-Semitism almost immediately developed two distinct themes, mutually exclusive in theory but in practice forming a diabolical counterpoint. On the one hand, follow-ing Voltaire, the rising European left began to see the Jews as obscurantist opponents to all human progress. On the other, the forces of conservatism and tradition, resenting the benefits the Jews derived from the collapse of the ancient order, began to portray the Jews as the allies and instigators of anarchy. Both could not be true. Neither was true. But both were believed. The second myth was unwittingly aided by Napoleon's well-intentioned attempts to solve the 'Jewish problem' himself. In May 1806 he issued a decree convening an Assembly of

Jewish Notables from all over the French empire (which included the Rhineland) and the Kingdom of Italy. The idea was to create a permanent relationship between the new state and the Jews on the lines of those Napoleon had already concluded with the Catholics and the Protestants. The 111-strong body, elected by Jewish community leaders, met from July 1806 to April 1807, and provided answers to twelve questions the authorities put to it, concerning marriage-laws, Jewish attitudes to the state, internal organization, and usury. On the basis of these answers, Napoleon replaced the old communal organization with what were termed consistories, as part of a general Jewish statute which regulated the conduct of those now seen, not as Jews, but as 'French citizens of the Mosaic faith'.[118]

By the standards of the day, this was progress, of a sort. Unfortunately, Napoleon supplemented this secular body by convening a parallel meeting of rabbis and learned laymen, to advise the Assembly on technical points of Torah and halakhah. The response of the more traditional elements of Judaism was poor. They did not recognize Napoleon's right to invent such a tribunal, let alone summon it. None the less, the rabbis and scholars met, February–March 1807, in considerable splendour and with suitable ceremony. The body was dubbed the Sanhedrin.[119] It attracted infinitely more attention than the serious, secular gathering, and lingered in the European memory long after Napoleon's Jewish policy had been forgotten. On the right of the political spectrum, already violently suspicious of Jewish activities because of their real or supposed radical purpose, the meeting of the fake Sanhedrin – a body which had not existed for a millennium and a half – set up powerful conspiratorial chemistry. Was this not merely an open and sanctified gathering of a conclave which convened secretly all the time? Memories stirred of the secret international Jewish assemblies which had supposedly met to pick the town selected each year for the ritual murder. Thus a new conspiracy theory appeared, launched the same year by the Abbé Barruel in his book *Mémoire pour servir à l'histoire du jacobinisme*. It adumbrated most of the fantasies later set forth in myths about the 'Elders of Zion' and their secret plots. The Sanhedrin also attracted the attention of the new secret police organizations which the autocracies of central and eastern Europe were creating to counter the radical threat, now seen as a permanent challenge to traditional order. And it was from the *milieu* of the secret police that the *Protocols of the Elders of Zion* was eventually to emerge.

Hence when the ghetto walls fell, and the Jews walked out into freedom, they found they were entering a new, less tangible but equally hostile ghetto of suspicion. They had exchanged ancient disabilities for modern anti-Semitism.

PART FIVE

Emancipation

On 31 July 1817 a precocious twelve-year-old boy, Benjamin Disraeli, was baptized into the Anglican Church, at St Andrew's, Holborn, by the Rev. Mr Thimbleby. This was the culmination of a quarrel between the boy's father, Issac D'Israeli and the Bevis Marks Synagogue, on an important point of Jewish principle. In Judaism, as we have noted, service to the community was not an option or a privilege, but an obligation. In 1813 the well-to-do Mr D'Israeli had been elected a warden or parnas, in strict accord with the laws of the Bevis Marks congregation. He was indignant. He had always paid his dues and considered himself a Jew. Indeed, as an antiquarian author he had actually written an essay called *The Genius of Judaism*. But his major work, by contrast, was a five-volume life of King Charles the Martyr. He had a low opinion both of Judaism and of Jews. In his book *Curiosities of Literature* (1791) he had described the Talmud as 'a complete system of the barbarous learning of the Jews'. He thought the Jews had 'no men of genius or talents to lose. I can count all their men of genius on my fingers. Ten centuries have not produced ten great men.'[1] So he wrote to the Chamber of Elders that he was a man 'of retired habits of life', who had 'always lived out of the sphere of your observation'; and that such a person as himself could on no account perform 'permanent duties always repulsive to his feelings'.[2] He was fined £40, but the matter was allowed to lapse. Three years later it was resumed, and this time D'Israeli withdrew from Judaism completely and had his children baptized. The breach was significant for the son, for Britain, and much else. For Jews were not legally admitted to parliament until 1858, and without his baptism Disraeli could never have become Prime Minister.

Seven years after Disraeli's baptism, on 26 August 1824, a similar event took place in the German town of Trier, this time involving the six-year-old Karl Heinrich Marx, as he was now renamed. This

family apostasy was more serious. Marx's grandfather was rabbi in
Trier until his death in 1789; his uncle was still the rabbi. His mother
came from a long line of famous rabbis and scholars, going back to
Meier Katzellenbogen, a sixteenth-century rector of the talmudic
college in Padua.[3] But Marx's father, Heinrich, was a child of the
enlightenment, a student of Voltaire and Rousseau. He was also an
ambitious lawyer. Trier was now in Prussia, where Jews had been
emancipated since the edict of 11 March 1812. In theory it was still in
force, despite Napoleon's defeat. In reality it was evaded. Thus, Jews
could train in law, but not practise it. So Heinrich Marx became a
Christian and, in due course, rose to be dean of the Trier bar. Karl
Marx, instead of going to the *yeshiva*, attended Trier High School,
then in charge of a headmaster later sacked for his liberalism. His
baptism proved to be even more significant to the world than
Disraeli's.

Conversion to Christianity was one way in which Jews reacted to
the age of emancipation. Traditionally baptism had been an escape
from persecution, and emancipation should have made it unnecessary.
In fact, from the end of the eighteenth century it became more
common. It was no longer a dramatic act of treason, a change from
one world to another. With the decline of the part all religion played in
society, conversion might be less of a religious act than a secular one; it
might be quite cynical. Heinrich Heine (1797–1856), who had himself
baptized the year after Karl Marx, referred to the act contemptuously
as 'an entrance-ticket to European society'. During the nineteenth
century, in east-central Europe, at least 250,000 Jews bought their
tickets.[4] The German historian Theodor Mommsen, who was a great
friend of the Jews, pointed out that Christianity was not so much a
name for a religion as 'the only word expressing the character of
today's international civilization in which numerous millions all over
the many-nationed globe feel themselves united'.[5] A man felt he had to
become a Christian in the nineteenth century in the same way he felt he
had to learn English in the twentieth. It applied to countless non-white
natives as well as Jews.

For a Jew, everywhere except in the United States, remaining a Jew
was a material sacrifice. The Austrian novelist and newspaper editor
Karl Emil Franzos (1848–1904) said that it took Jews different ways:
'One Jew can't bring himself to make the sacrifice and gets baptized. A
second makes it, but in his heart regards his Judaism as a misfortune
and comes to hate it. A third, just because the sacrifice has been so
heavy, starts to grow closer to his Judaism.'[6] The rewards of baptism
could be considerable. In England, from the mid-eighteenth century

onward, it removed the last obstacles preventing a Jew from getting to the top. The millionaire Samson Gideon was prepared to make the sacrifice himself but not to impose it on his son. Accordingly he was able to get Samson Gideon Junior made a baronet while he was still at Eton, and in due course the boy became an MP and an Irish peer. Sir Manasseh Lopez accepted baptism and became an MP; so did David Ricardo; a third ex-Jewish MP, Ralph Bernal, rose to be Chairman of Committees (Deputy Speaker).

On the Continent, Judaism remained an obstacle not just to a political career but to many forms of economic activity. Even Napoleon had imposed (1806) some legal restrictions on Jews. They lapsed in 1815 and the restored Bourbons, to their credit, did not renew them; but not until 1831, when Jews were granted equal rights with Christians, did they feel legally secure, and the old Jewish oath lasted another fifteen years. The articles of the German Confederation (1815) deprived Jews of many of the rights they had been granted in Napoleon's time, especially in Bremen and Lübeck, where they were banned altogether for a time, Hamburg, Frankfurt and Mecklenburg. In Prussia Jews remained subject to poll-tax, the Jewish annual tax, a registration levy and a 'lodging increment'. They could not own land or exercise a trade or profession. They were confined to 'authorized emergency business' which the guilds would not touch, or money-lending. There was a further Prussian reform in 1847, and the following year the revolution produced a list of 'Fundamental Rights of the German People', establishing civil rights on a non-religious basis, which were included in the constitutions of the majority of German states. Yet residence restrictions on Jews remained in most of them until the 1860s. In Austria, overall legal emancipation did not come until 1867. In Italy, the fall of Napoleon put the clock back for Jews nearly everywhere, and it took another generation to restore the rights first gained in the 1790s. Not until 1848 did permanent emancipation come in Tuscany and Sardinia, followed by Modena, Lombardy and Romagna (1859), Umbria (1860), Sicily and Naples (1861), Venice (1866) and Rome (1870). This is a bald summary of a long and complicated process, involving many setbacks, retractions and exceptions. Hence even in western Europe, the process begun in 1789–91 in France took eighty years to complete purely in a nominal legal sense. Further east, especially in Russia and Rumania, Jewish disabilities remained severe.

These delays and uncertainties explain why so many Jews took their ticket to society through baptism. But there were other solutions to the 'problem' of being a Jew in the nineteenth century. To many Jews, the ideal one had been found by the Rothschilds. They became the most illustrious exponents of the new phenomenon of eighteenth-century finance, the private bank. Such private finance houses were founded by many Jews, chiefly descendants of court Jews. But the Rothschilds alone escaped both baptism and failure. They were a remarkable family because they contrived to do four difficult and often incompatible things simultaneously: to acquire immense wealth quickly and honestly; to distribute it widely while retaining the confidence of many governments; to continue to earn huge profits, and to spend them, without arousing popular antagonism; and to remain Jewish in law and, for the most part, in spirit too. No Jews ever made more money, spent it more self-indulgently, or remained more popular.

Yet the Rothschilds are elusive. There is no book about them which is both revealing and accurate.[7] Libraries of nonsense have been written about them. For this the family is largely to blame. A woman who planned to write a book entitled *Lies About the Rothschilds* abandoned it, saying: 'It was relatively easy to spot the lies, but it proved impossible to find out the truth.'[8] The family was highly secretive. That was understandable. They were private bankers. They had confidential relations with several governments as well as innumerable powerful individuals. They were Jews, and therefore particularly vulnerable to destructive litigation. They kept no more documentation than was necessary. They systematically destroyed their papers, for all kinds of personal as well as business reasons. They were particularly concerned that no details of their lives should be used to promote anti-Semitism. So their deaths were followed by holocausts of private papers even larger and more drastic than those of Queen Victoria's family. Their latest historian, Miriam Rothschild, believes there was a further reason. They kept no muniment room. They were not interested in their history. They were respectful towards their ancestors, as a matter of good form, and prudently thought about tomorrow. But they lived for the present and did not care deeply about past or future.[9]

All the same, the salient facts about the Rothschilds are clear enough. They were a product of the Napoleonic Wars, just as the first phase of large-scale Jewish finance was a product of the Thirty Years War, and for the same reason: in wartime, Jewish creativity comes to the fore and gentile prejudice goes to the rear. In all essentials, the family fortune was created by Nathan Mayer Rothschild in London. What happened was this. Until the beginning of the revolutionary wars in France, in the mid-1790s, European merchant banking was dominated by non-Jews: the Barings of London, the Hopes of

Amsterdam and the Gebrüder Bethmann of Frankfurt. The war quickly expanded the money-raising market and so opened room for newcomers.[10] Among them was a German–Jewish group – Oppenheims, Rothschilds, Heines, Mendelssohns. The Rothschild name derived from the sixteenth-century red shield on their house in the Frankfurt ghetto. The family patriarch, Mayer Amschel (1744–1812), was a money-changer who also traded in antiques and old coins. He branched into textiles, which meant a British connection, and from selling old coins to William IX, Elector of Hesse-Cassel, he became his main financial agent. The elector had made himself very rich by supplying mercenaries to the British army. So that was another English connection.

In 1797 Mayer Amschel sent his son Nathan to England to attend to his affairs there. Nathan went to Manchester, the centre of the first phase of the Industrial Revolution and of what was rapidly becoming a world trade in cotton manufactures. He did not make cottons himself but bought them from small spinners, sent them out for printing, and then sold the finished product to Continental buyers direct, by-passing the fairs. He thus pioneered a path later trodden by other Jewish textile families: the Behrens in Leeds, for example, and the Rothensteins in Bradford.[11] Nathan's direct-selling method involved giving three months' credit, and that in turn meant access to the London money market. He had already 'studied' there under his father's connection, Levi Barent Cohen, and married Cohen's daughter Hannah. In 1803 he transferred his operations to London, in time to enter the government loan business as the war expanded. The British government needed to sell £20 million of loan stock every year. The market could not absorb this amount directly, so portions of it were sold to contractors who found customers. Nathan Rothschild, who had already established a good reputation for his bills of exchange in the textile trade, participated in these contractor syndicates and at the same time acted as an acceptance house for international bills of exchange.[12] He had one enviable advantage in getting working capital. After the disastrous Battle of Jena in 1806, the Elector of Hesse-Cassel sent his fortune to Nathan in London for investment in British securities, and Nathan built up his own resources while serving William IX's interests too. Thus Nathan's reputation in the City was established. But he also excelled in the traditional Jewish skill of transferring bullion quickly and safely under trying conditions. In the six years 1811–15, Rothschild and the British Commissary-in-Chief, John Herries, contrived to get £42.5 million in gold safely to the British army in Spain, of which more than half was handled by Nathan himself or by his younger brother James, operating from France.[13] By the time of Waterloo, the Rothschild capital was £136,000, of which Nathan in London had £90,000.[14]

James's operations in Paris from 1811 marked the expansion of the family network. A third brother, Salomon Mayer, founded a Vienna branch in 1816, and a fourth, Karl Mayer, set one up in Naples in 1821. The eldest son, Amschel Mayer, ran the Frankfurt branch after the old patriarch died in 1812. This network was ideally suited to the new era of peacetime finance which opened in 1815. Raising the vast sums needed to pay the armies had brought into existence an international finance system based on paper and credit, and governments now found they could use it for all kinds of purposes. In the decade 1815–25 more securities were floated than in the whole of the preceding century, and Nathan Rothschild gradually succeeded Barings as the principal house as well as London's top financial authority. He did not deal with volatile Latin American regimes but mainly with solid European autocracies – Austria, Russia, Prussia, known as the Holy Alliance; he raised an enormous sum for them in 1822. He handled seven of the twenty-six foreign government loans raised in London, 1818–32, and one jointly, making a total of £21 million or 39 per cent of the whole.[15]

In Vienna, the Rothschilds sold bonds for the Habsburgs, advised Metternich and built the first Austrian railway. The first French railways were built by Rothschild Frères in Paris, who also raised money, in turn for Bourbons, Orleanists and Bonapartes, and financed the new king of Belgium. In Frankfurt they floated issues on behalf of a dozen German thrones. In Naples, they raised money for the government there, for Sardinia, Sicily and the papal states. The combined Rothschild capital rose steadily, to £1.77 million in 1818, to £4.3 million in 1828, to £34.35 million in 1875, of which the London house controlled £6.9 million.[16] The wide spread of the network's contacts made the money-power the firm could actually deploy very much greater. They exploited to the full the traditional Jewish flair for news-gathering and transmission. Jews by mid-century were already turning from banks to wire-services. Paul Julius Reuter (1816–99), whose name was originally Israel Beer Josaphat, left his uncle's bank in Göttingen to set up the world's greatest news-agency in 1848. Adolf Opper, or as he called himself Adolphe Opper de Blowitz (1825–1903), made himself, as The Times Paris correspondent, the centre of Europe's finest personal news-network with private telegraph lines when necessary. But no newspaper has ever been better served with key financial news than the Rothschilds. As late as the 1930s, their couriers were still recruited in the Folkestone area, descendants of the sailors who took cutters carrying dispatches across the Channel in the age of Waterloo.[17]

Unlike the old court Jews, the new kind of international firm the Rothschilds created was impervious to local attack. In 1819, as if to demonstrate that newly acquired Jewish rights were illusory so far, anti-Semitic violence broke out in many parts of Germany. These 'Hep Hep' riots as they were called (perhaps after a crusader war-cry, or more likely after a goat-drover's call from Franconia) included an assault on the Rothschild house in Frankfurt. It made no difference. Nor did a further attack during the 1848 revolution. The money was no longer there. It was paper, circulating through the world. The Rothschilds completed a process the Jews had been working on for centuries: how to immunize their lawful property from despoiling violence. Henceforth their real wealth was beyond the reach of the mob, almost beyond the reach of greedy monarchs.

Nathan Mayer Rothschild, the financial genius who made the firm's fortunes, died in 1836 in Frankfurt, while attending the marriage of his eldest son Lionel to Charlotte, daughter of his brother Karl, head of the Naples branch. The Rothschilds nearly always married each other: when they spoke of 'marrying out' they did not mean out of Jewry but out of the family. The object of intermarriage was to keep dowries within the firm; though it was said that wives' settlements were usually shares the men wanted to unload, such as South American railway stock.[18] The Lionel–Charlotte wedding was celebrated at the old family houses in the Judengasse, where the eighty-four-year-old matriarch, born Gudule Schnappers, who had produced nineteen children, still lived: she was to survive another decade. Nathan's death was a matter of considerable importance: the carrier-pigeon dispatched to London with news of it was shot down over Brighton and was said to have borne the cryptic message, '*Il est mort.*'[19] But his branch, N. M. Rothschild, heart of the firm's power, continued to grow in strength, as was natural: London was the financial centre of the world, Rothschilds its most reliable pillar. Thus, in the sixteen years 1860–75, foreign governments raised over £700 million in London. Of the fifty banks involved, ten were Jewish, including such important names as Hambro, Samuel Montagu and Helbert Wagg.[20] Rothschilds, however, played the biggest and most varied role of all fifty.

Inevitably, such financial pull brought political influence as well. It was the young Disraeli who first argued that Jews and Tories were natural allies, pointing out that the critical City of London elections of

June 1841 and October 1843 had both been decided by Jewish votes: in the second, he noted, the Rothschilds brought out the Jews to win the seat for the anti-Corn Law Liberal even on a Saturday![21] Lionel, as head of the family, won the City seat himself in 1847 (though he could not take his place in parliament until disabilities were finally removed in 1858), and the Tory leader, Lord George Bentinck, pointed out in a letter to J. W. Croker the significance of the vote: 'The City of London having elected Lionel Rothschild one of her representatives, it is such a pronunciation of public opinion that I do not think the party, as a party, would do themselves any good by taking up the question against the Jews. It is like [County] Clare electing O'Connell, or Yorkshire Wilberforce. Clare settled the Catholic question, Yorkshire the slave trade and now the City of London has settled the Jew question.'[22]

But the Rothschilds wisely did not try to force this issue, or any other. They knew time was on their side and were prepared to wait for it. They hated to make undue use of their financial power or to be seen exercising it at any time. Collectively, the Rothschilds always favoured peace, as one would expect; individually, the branches tended to back the policy aims of their respective countries, as one would also expect.[23] In Britain, where they had most power if they chose to exercise it, a recent sifting of the evidence shows they rarely if ever took the initiative in pushing government.[24] In moments of doubt over foreign affairs, it was their custom to ask government what ministers wanted them to do, as for instance during the 1884 Egyptian crisis.

They took, in fact, a very English line of deprecating money as such – they always referred to it as 'tin' – and using it, rather, to build up a social position. They created two palatial ghettos, one urban, the other rural. The urban one was at the bottom corner of Piccadilly, where it joins Park Lane. Old Nathan began the process in 1825, when he stopped living 'over the shop' in 2 New Court, St Swithin's Lane in the City, and bought 107 Piccadilly from Mrs Coutts, the banker's widow. Other members of the family, English and Continental, followed him. His son Lionel built 148 Piccadilly, next to Apsley House, in the 1860s, providing it with the finest ballroom in London: the housewarming was combined with the marriage of his daughter Evelina to her cousin Ferdinand of Vienna; Disraeli proposed the toast to the bride's health. Ferdinand himself bought 143 Piccadilly, and that too had a famous ballroom, all in white. Next door, at 142, was his sister Alice. At the back, Leopold de Rothschild bought 5 Hamilton Place. Round the corner, at 1 Seamore Place, was Alfred de Rothschild, the famous dandy. Hannah Rothschild, the heiress who married Lord Rosebery, took over the original 107.[25]

For a country house, old Nathan paid £20,000 for Gunnersbury, near Acton, in 1835. But that was a false start. The rural ghetto began when his widow bought a house near Mentmore in the Vale of Aylesbury, Buckinghamshire. Gradually they all settled in this part of Bucks, spreading into nearby Hertfordshire. Baron Mayer Rothschild built Mentmore Towers, modelled on Wollaton. Sir Anthony de Rothschild moved into Aston Clinton. In 1873 Lionel bought Tring, in Hertfordshire, for £250,000. He also had a 1,400-acre estate at Halton, later owned by Alfred de Rothschild. Then there was Leopold de Rothschild's house Ascott, at Wing near Leighton Buzzard. In the 1870s Baron Ferdinand built Waddesdon, and he had other houses at Leighton Buzzard and Upper Winchendon. His sister Alice had Eythrop Priory. So the Vale of Aylesbury became Rothschild country. They owned 30,000 acres there and represented it in parliament from 1865 to 1923.

The rural headquarters was Tring, extended by Lionel's son and heir Nathan to an estate of 15,000 acres. He became the 1st Lord Rothschild and Lord-Lieutenant of Buckinghamshire. In the true Jewish tradition, he turned Tring into a miniature welfare state. He supplied the locals with water and electricity, a fire service, a reading-room, allotments, a health service, even a cemetery for their dogs; for employees there were holiday camps, a pension scheme, apprentice-ships, an unemployment plan, hampers and parties. The estate engaged in stock-breeding, sylviculture, sheep trials and conservation experiments.[26]

Lord Rothschild's father, Lionel, had taken charge of many government loans, to finance Irish famine relief, fight the Crimean War, buy the khedive's Suez Canal shares; he was very close to Disraeli, much closer than either found it convenient to admit, both in the City and in public life. He was felt to be disinterested because it was known he had forgone a £2 million profit rather than float a £100 million loan for the anti-Semitic Russian government.[27] He was on excellent terms with Gladstone and his Foreign Secretary, Lord Granville. But he got on equally well with the Tories. He transformed Lord Randolph Churchill from a conventional slanger of Jewish 'vested interests' into a notable philosemite. He turned round A. J. Balfour too, making him into perhaps the most effective British friend the Jews ever had. He was the unofficial spokesman for the City from his father's death in 1879 to his own in 1915. In her account of him, his great-niece Miriam Rothschild reflects that in world-wide terms he probably had a greater influence than any Jew since antiquity.[28] 'I should like to know', asked Lloyd George rhetorically in his 1909

Limehouse speech, 'is Lord Rothschild the dictator of this country?' He was nothing of the sort: merely beneficently powerful. In 1915 on his death-bed in 148 Piccadilly, he was visited by Lord Haldane (temporarily in charge of the Foreign Office) who asked him to stop a neutral ship taking gold to Germany. He said: 'That is a very simple matter,' and scribbled an instruction on the back of an envelope.[29]

Rothschild was popular because his princely acts of charity were not just wise and systematic but eccentric. Children who waved to his carriage were liable to experience a shower of glittering half-sovereigns. His wife Emma denounced this as 'insensitive and insulting', but he replied that children took a different view and he was right – an old woman at Tring told Miriam Rothschild she remembered such an incident for the rest of her life. The Rothschilds were generally liked in England not just because they ran highly successful racing stables but because 'they never pulled their horses'. So ordinary folk did not mind if Lady Rothschild's chef, Grosstephen Senior, probably the world's best, ran a fishmonger's bill alone of £5,000 a year. Rothschild gave the East End cabbies he used a brace of pheasants each at Christmas, and when he died the costermongers put black crêpe on their barrows. The *Pall Mall Gazette* wrote: 'It is owing to the life of Lord Rothschild that Great Britain has escaped those collections of race feeling . . . with which so many other countries have been embarrassed during the last generation. He was at once a Prince in Israel and an Englishman of whom all England could be proud.'

It was Disraeli who first perceived that the Rothschild approach, with its unaffected rejoicing in Jewish capacity, including skill in making money – to be spent equally joyfully – had a lot to be said for it. Early in his career he was enjoying the Gunnersbury hospitality, writing to his sister Hannah (1843): 'I got well waited on by our old friend Amy, who brought me some capital turtle, which otherwise I would have missed.'[30] Disraeli thought the Rothschilds were an immense asset to the Jewish race, to be boosted to the full at every opportunity. He published his novel *Coningsby* in 1844, the same year in which Marx, as we shall see, took a viciously destructive view of the 'Jewish problem'. The all-seeing mentor of the tale is Sidonia, the Jewish superman, whom Disraeli let it be known was based on Lionel Rothschild. This was a very flattering portrait. But then Disraeli was always concerned to exaggerate Rothschild wisdom and foresight, just as he made mysteries and dramas of their activities. It was he himself who sensationalized the purchase of the khedive's shares in 1876 and he was responsible for much of the absurd, but in Disraeli's eyes valuable and creative, mythology which grew up around the family.

Of course Disraeli would have freely admitted that presenting Rothschild success as a magic fairy-tale could only work in a country like England where the political and social climate was hospitable. From 1826, when all restrictions were lifted, Jews were free to come to Britain from anywhere without hindrance. Once in, and naturalized, their position was summed up by Lord Chancellor Brougham in 1833: 'His Majesty's subjects professing the Jewish religion were born to all the rights, immunities and privileges of His Majesty's other subjects, except in so far as positive enactments of law deprived them of those rights, immunities and privileges.'[31] These restrictions did indeed exist, and Jews usually found out about them through test-cases. But once a difficulty had been discovered and agitated about, parliament, or the appropriate body, usually acted to give the Jew equality. Thus in 1833, the year of Brougham's pronouncement, Jews were admitted to practise at the bar. Thirteen years later, a statute resolved in their favour the vexed question of whether Jews could own freehold land.

Moreover, from an early date, Britain had been prepared not just to welcome and accept Jews, but to help them abroad. The first time occurred in 1745, when Maria Theresa expelled Jews from Prague; her ally, George II, protested through diplomatic channels. In 1814 Lord Castlereagh, Foreign Secretary, instructed his envoy, the Earl of Clancarty, to 'encourage the general adoption of a system of toleration with respect to individuals of the Jewish persuasion throughout Germany'. No doubt with the Rothschilds in mind, he made special efforts on behalf of the Frankfurt community. Britain also helped the Jews at the Congress of Aix-la-Chapelle.[32]

Lord Palmerston was very active on behalf of the Jews, both on general grounds of policy and because his stepfather-in-law, Lord Shaftesbury, believed strongly that the return of the Jews to Jerusalem would hasten the Second Coming.[33] Between 1827 and 1839, largely through British efforts, the population of Jerusalem rose from 550 to 5,500 and in all Palestine it topped 10,000 – the real beginning of the Jewish return to the Promised Land. In 1838 Palmerston appointed the first western vice-consul in Jerusalem, W. T. Young, and told him 'to afford protection to the Jews generally'.[34] Two years later he wrote to Lord Ponsonby, British ambassador in Constantinople, instructing him to put pressure on the Turks to allow Jews from Europe to return to Palestine. He was to argue that hard-working Jewish settlers backed by Rothschild money 'would tend greatly to increase the resources of the Turkish Empire, and to promote the progress of civilization therein'. 'Palmerston', noted Shaftesbury, 'has already been chosen by

God to be an instrument of good to His ancient people'; the letter to Ponsonby was 'a prelude to the Antitype of the Decree of Cyrus'.

Palmerston was also instrumental in helping wealthy western Jews to come to the rescue of their beleaguered co-religionists. In February 1840 the murder of a Capuchin friar (and his servant) in Damascus abruptly and horrifyingly resuscitated the medieval blood libel. The local Capuchins promptly claimed that the two men had been killed by the Jews for their blood, in preparation for Passover. Both the Turkish governor and the French consul, officially charged with protecting the Christian community, believed the accusation and conducted a brutal investigation on this basis. A Jewish barber, Solomon Negrin, confessed under torture and accused other Jews. Two of them died under torture, one converted to Islam to escape it, and others provided information, leading to more arrests of Jews. The atrocities culminated in the seizure of sixty-three Jewish children, to be held as hostages until their mothers revealed the hiding-place of the blood.[35]

One of the arrested Jews was an Austrian citizen, and this led to the great powers taking a direct interest in the affair. In London, Palmerston's help was invoked by Sir Moses Montefiore (1784–1885), the president of the Board of Deputies, which represented British Jews. Montefiore, who was actually born in Leghorn, had been one of the twelve 'Jew brokers' of the City of London, and through his marriage to Judith Cohen had become brother-in-law to Nathan Rothschild, for whom he acted as stockbroker. He retired from business in 1824 in order to devote his life to oppressed Jews everywhere. He was perhaps the last of the *shtadtlanim*, prominent Jews whose social standing enabled them to intercede with persecuting governments. He was a friend of Queen Victoria, who as a girl stayed at his 'marine residence' in Ramsgate, and later knighted him; he was probably responsible for her marked Judophilia. With Palmerston's help, Montefiore organized a delegation of western Jews, including the famous French lawyer Adolphe Crémieux (1796–1880), and went to see the ruler of Syria, Mohammed Ali, in Alexandria. Montefiore and his colleagues not only secured the release of the Jewish captives, in August 1840, but persuaded the Sultan of Turkey to issue a *firman* forbidding the circulation of blood libels or the arrest of Jews on such a basis. The success of this mission led to many others in which Montefiore, who lived to be over a hundred, worked with the Foreign Office to help Jewish victims of injustice.[36] But the British government also intervened on its own account: in 1854, on behalf of Swiss Jews; in 1856, on behalf of Jews in the Balkans, the Foreign Office instructing the British envoy in Bucharest, 'The peculiar position of the

Jews places them under the protection of the civilized world'; and at
the Congress of Berlin in 1876, where Disraeli fought for equality of
religious rights.[37]

Disraeli, however, had never been satisfied with advancing the claim
of the Jews to justice. He believed that the Jews, by their virtues and
their glorious past, were entitled to special esteem, and he devoted his
tremendous audacity and imagination to securing it for them. Brought
up a Christian, his interest in his race was fired by a grand tour of the
Mediterranean and the Holy Land in 1830–1. He was fascinated by
the rise of successful Jews throughout Syria, despite all their handi-
caps, the Rothschilds of the East as he called them. Much of the
material he gathered he later used in his novels. He noted that the
pashas preferred to use Jewish financial experts, as they could be easily
persecuted if necessary: 'They kept their accounts in Hebrew written
in a calligraphy so obscure as to be barely decipherable,' and he later
portrayed one as Adam Besso in *Tancred*.[38] Jerusalem he loved best of
all, and in the same novel, published in 1847, he reproduced his vivid
impressions of fifteen years before. It was his own favourite among his
novels and has been aptly termed 'a fictional version of the Victorian
spiritual autobiography'.[39]

Disraeli never took the defensive line that Jews were no worse than
other men. He thought they were better. He said he despised 'that
pernicious doctrine of modern times, the natural equality of man'.
One modern historian has seen him as essentially a *marrano*, and there
is a lot to be said for this analysis.[40] He epitomized the incipient
arrogance, pride and romance of the Sephardis, which he conferred on
the Jews as a whole. The self-destructive Ashkenazi tendency to see
Jewish sufferings in Biblical fashion as the merited consequence of
Jewish sins meant absolutely nothing to him. He took the Sephardi
view that Israel, being the heart of the human body, had been unfairly
made to shoulder the burden of the wickedness of mankind.[41] Once
liberated, Jewish gifts would shine forth to astonish the world. They
were essentially racial gifts. 'All is race,' says his superman Sidonia,
'there is no other truth.'

Thus Disraeli preached the innate superiority of certain races long
before the social Darwinists made it fashionable, or Hitler notorious.
He was descended, he says in *Contarini Fleming*, 'in a direct line from
one of the oldest races in the world, from that rigidly separate and
unmixed Bedouin race who had developed a high civilization at a time
when the inhabitants of England were going half naked and eating
acorns in the woods'.[42] 'Sidonia', he wrote in *Coningsby*, 'and his
brethren could claim a distinction which the Saxon and the Greek, and

the rest of the Caucasian nations, have forfeited. The Hebrew is an unmixed race.' This was a privilege the Hebrews shared with the desert Arabs, who were 'only Jews on horseback'. Disraeli thought that Moses was 'in every respect a man of the complete Caucasian model, and almost as perfect as Adam when he had just been finished and placed in Eden' (*Tancred*). He thought 'the decay of a race is an inevitable necessity, unless it lives in deserts and never mixes its blood', like the Bedouin. Jewish purity had been saved by persecution, by constant movement and migration:

the Mosaic Arabs [i.e. the Jews] are the most ancient, if not the only, unmixed blood that dwells in cities! An unmixed race of a first-rate organization are the aristocracy of nature. . . . To the unpolluted current of their Caucasian structure and to the segregating genius of their great lawgiver, Sidonia ascribed the fact that they had not been long ago absorbed among those mixed races, who presume to persecute them, but periodically wear away and disappear, while their victims still flourish in all the primeval vigour of the pure Asian breed. [*Coningsby*]

He reiterates the point in the same novel: 'No penal laws, no physical tortures work. Where mixed persecuting races disappear, the pure persecuted race remains.'

What, then, of Disraeli's Christianity? His brilliant gift for paradox supplied an answer to that one too. 'I am', he loved to remark, 'the missing page between the Old Testament and the New.' He took great satisfaction in both blaming the Christians for not recognizing the virtues of Judaism, and blaming the Jews for not grasping that Christianity was 'completed Judaism'. In his 1849 preface to *Coningsby* he stated: 'In vindicating the sovereign right of the Church of Christ to be the perpetual regenerator of man, the writer thought the time had arrived when some attempt should be made to do justice to the race which had founded Christianity.' The Jews had produced Moses, Solomon and Christ, 'the greatest of legislators, the greatest of administrators, and the greatest of reformers – what race, extinct or living, can produce three men such as these?' Equally, however, he thought it absurd that Jews should accept 'only the first part of the Jewish religion'. A note, from around 1863, survives in his papers at Hughenden:

I look upon the Church as the only Jewish institution remaining – I know no other. . . . If it were not for the Church, I don't see why the Jews should be known. The Church was founded by Jews, and has been faithful to its origin. It secures their history and their literature being known to all . . . publicly reads its history, and keeps alive the memory of its public characters, and has diffused its poetry throughout the world. The Jews owe everything to the Church. . . . The history of the Jews is development or it is nothing.[43]

Disraeli thought it illogical that Tories should oppose the Bill to allow professing Jews to sit in parliament, since Sephardi beliefs in tradition, in hierarchical authority, in the need for the religious spirit to inform all secular life, were essentially Tory ones. He noted in his *Life of Lord George Bentinck* that when the Jew Bill came up in 1847, only four Tories voted for it – himself, Bentinck, Thomas Baring and Milnes Gaskell, and they 'almost monopolized the speaking talent on their side of the House'. It was Bentinck's speech on this occasion, in favour of Jewish rights, which led to his ousting as leader of the Tories in the Commons. So, by one of those paradoxes in which Disraeli delighted, the Tories, by punishing Bentinck for speaking up for the Jews, eventually ended up with Disraeli himself as their leader. But that, Disraeli felt, was right: he believed in a combination of aristocracy and meritocracy, and the Jews were supreme meritocrats. Disraeli not only pointed with pride to the achievements of acknowledged Jews, he detected Jewish genius everywhere. The first Jesuits had been Jews. Napoleon's best marshals, Soult and Massena (he called him Manasseh), were Jews. Mozart was a Jew.

Disraeli's philosemitic propaganda would not have worked on the Continent. The Jews of Europe would not in any case have followed him in the wilder paths of his imagination. Nevertheless, there was in the early nineteenth century a determined attempt by learned Jews to counter the presentation of Judaism as a survival of medieval obscurantism, and to replace the repulsive image of the professing Jew, fashioned by Voltaire on a Spinozan basis, by an intellectually attractive one. The first requisite was to erect some kind of bridge between the best of rabbinical scholarship and the world of secular learning. The assumption of Spinoza, and those who had been influenced by him, was that the closer one studied Judaism, the more objectionable it became. Mendelssohn had never been able to refute this widespread impression: he simply did not know enough about traditional Jewish culture. Some of his more radical followers had no desire to do so. Men like Napthali Herz Homberg and Hartwig Wessely, while strongly favouring the study of Hebrew, wanted to renounce traditional Jewish religious education, scrap the Torah and the Talmud, and embrace a form of natural religion.

But among the second generation of the *maskilim* there were those who were both enlightened and learned in Judaism, faithful to their creed yet skilled in secular methodology. Isaac Marcus Jost (1793–1860), a schoolmaster from central Germany, produced a nine-volume history of the Israelites which was a half-way house between the traditional Jewish and the modern secular approach. As such it was the first work of its kind to impress the gentile public. More important, however, was the dogged, plodding, highly industrious Leopold Zunz (1794–1886), who devoted the whole of an immensely long life to the refurbishment of the old-style Jewish learning and its presentation in a modern, 'scientific' spirit.

Zunz and his friends of the immediate post-Napoleonic period called their work the *Wissenschaft des Judentums*, the Science of Judaism. They started with ambitious éclat in 1819, immediately after the Hep Hep riots had shown how fragile was the acceptance of Jews even in modern-minded Germany. They set up a Society for Jewish Culture and Science, whose object was to investigate the nature of Judaism by modern scientific methods and demonstrate the universal value of Jewish knowledge. They had an institute, which gave lectures on Jewish thought and history, and a magazine. They started from the assumption that the Jews had once made formidable contributions to the general culture, but then had lapsed into narrow religious antiquarianism. Now Jewish scholarship should come to life again. 'The Jews must once again show their mettle as doughty fellow workers in the common task of mankind,' wrote one of the founders, Immanuel Wolf, in the first issue of their *Zeitschrift*. 'They must raise themselves and their principle to the level of a science . . . if one day a bond is to join the whole of humanity, then it is the bond of science, the bond of pure reason.'[44]

This was all very fine, but it was open to a number of serious objections. The first was practical. In 1819 German Jews were only half-emancipated. To what extent could you pursue a life of secular study and remain a Jew? One of the most enthusiastic founders of the society was Eduard Gans (1798–1839), a brilliant young lecturer in historical jurisprudence. He got a lectureship at Berlin University and his courses were spectacularly successful. But his path to further advancement in his academic career was firmly blocked by his Judaism. Others found themselves in the same predicament. The 'bond of pure reason' did not yet exist, and for most of them the sacrifice to Judaism was too much. The Society was dissolved in May 1824. The following year Gans underwent baptism and proceeded to a professorship and fame. Several prominent members took the same course. Many Orthodox Jews, who had viewed the entire project with suspicion from the start, nodded their heads sagely: that was where secularization always led, to the extinction of faith.

Zunz himself plodded on. He translated an enormous amount of

Jewish literature, especially the midrashim and liturgical poetry. He elaborated a philosophy of Jewish history. He contributed to encyclo-paedias. He visited all the great libraries in search of material, and found himself barred from the Vatican Library. But his work raised a second objection to 'Jewish science': was it not contrary to the true spirit of Judaism? What he really envisaged was an encyclopaedia of Jewish intellectual history. In this, Jewish literature, for instance, would be presented alongside the other great literatures of the world, a giant among peers. He said he wanted to emancipate Jewish writing from the theologians and 'rise to the historical viewpoint'.[45] But what did this historical viewpoint involve? In practice it involved accepting, as Zunz did accept, that the history of the Jews, the main theme of their literature, was merely an element in world history. Like everyone else in Germany, Zunz was influenced by Hegelian ideas of progression from lower to higher forms, and inevitably applied this dialectic to Judaism. There had been only one period in Jewish history, he said, when their inner spirit and their external form had matched, and they had become the centre of world history, and that was under the ancient commonwealth. Thereafter they were delivered into the hands of other nations. Their internal history became a history of ideas, their external history a long tale of suffering. Zunz thought that a kind of Hegelian climax of world history would eventually occur in which all historical development would come together – that was what he understood by the Messianic Age. When that happened, the Talmud and all it stood for would become irrelevant. In the meantime the Jews had to show, by their new science of history, that they had contributed to this fulfilment; they had the job of ensuring that the distilled legacy of Jewish ideas became part of the common property of enlightened mankind.[46]

That was in some ways a most attractive prospect. But it was not Judaism. The pious Jew – and there could be no other – did not admit the existence of two kinds of knowledge, sacred and secular. There was only one. Moreover, there was only one legitimate purpose in acquiring it: to discover the exact will of God, in order to obey it. Hence the 'science of Judaism', as a dislocated academic discipline, was contrary to Jewish belief. Worse, it was the exact reversal of the true Jewish attitude to studying. As the Rabbi Hiyya put it in the fourth century AD: 'If a man learns the Law without intending to fulfil the Law, it were better for him had he never been born.'[47] A real Jew did not see Jewish history as a self-contained bit of world history, on a parallel with that of other peoples. To them, Jewish history *was* history. They believed that, without Israel, there would have been no world and therefore no history. God had created many worlds and destroyed them as unsatisfactory. He made the present one for the Torah, and so it gave him pleasure. But if Israel, when offered by him the Torah, had rejected it – and some talmudic scholars thought it nearly had done – then the world would have simply reverted to its previous formless state. Hence the destruction of the Second Temple and the end of the Bar Kokhba revolt were episodes not in Jewish, but in total history, with God saying (according to the tannaim): 'Woe to the children on account of whose sins I have destroyed my house, burned my temple and exiled them among the peoples of the world.'[48] The Jews had ceased to write history from then on because there was no history, as they conceived it, to write. It had stopped. History would be resumed with the coming of the Messiah. All that had happened in the meantime would be quickly forgotten, rather like, as the Rabbi Nathan put it, a princess–bride forgets the storms of her sea-voyage once she arrives in the country of the king she is to marry.

Hence, though Zunz's 'scientific' presentation of Jewish history and learning as a contribution to the world stock might make some impression on gentile society, it involved almost by definition a severance from a great part of Judaism. It was subjected to devastating, and in religious terms unanswerable, criticism by Rabbi Samson Raphael Hirsch (1808–88), the brilliant spokesman of nineteenth-century Orthodoxy. This Hamburg Jew who served as rabbi in Frankfurt for thirty-seven years was not an obscurantist. To begin with, he wrote beautiful German. His presentation of the Jewish faith, designed for young people, which was published under the title *Nineteen Letters on Judaism* (1836), was immensely effective. He had no objection to secular education; quite the contrary. He used to quote the Rabbi Gamaliel that both Torah knowledge and worldly knowledge were proper objects of study. The ideal 'man of Israel', he said, was 'an enlightened Jew who observes the precepts'.[49] Nevertheless, there was all the difference in the world, he argued, between Jews making use of secular knowledge and secular knowledge absorbing Judaism. Israel was not a secular community but a divine one. So any science dealing with the Jews as a community was a form of theology, and necessarily so. The history of what Jews do, and what happens to them, cannot be part of secular history as such because it is the unfolding of God's will and rightly therefore part of Revelation. General culture and Jewish culture are not in conflict: they are quite different. By confusing the two, you can only damage Judaism. If you merge Jewish with secular history, you desacralize it and kill the living idea which is its theme.

In a bitter and forceful passage, Hirsch explained what this would mean:

Moses and Hesiod, David and Sappho, Deborah and Tyrtaeus, Isaiah and Homer, Delphi and Jerusalem, Pythian tripod and Cherubin-sanctuary, prophets and oracles, psalms and elegy – for us, they all lie peacefully in one box, they all rest peacefully in one grave, they all have one and the same human origin, they all have one and the same significance – human, transitory and belonging to the past. All the clouds have dispersed. The tears and sighs of our fathers no longer fill our hearts but our *libraries*. The warmly pulsating hearts of our fathers have become our national *literature*, their fervent breath of life has become the dust of our bookshelves. . . . Do these departed spirits rejoice in the literary gratitude of our present generation? Whom do they recognize as their true heirs? Those who repeated their prayers but forgot their names, or those who forget their prayers but remember their names?[50]

Later in the century, the point was to be made still more decisively by Nietzsche: once it became possible to study scientifically the history of a religion, he said, it is already dead.

Yet if the logic of Hirsch's criticism was followed, Jews would in effect be back where they started before the enlightenment. They would constantly be forced to make distinctions between two types of knowledge. It would not so much be Gordon's dichotomy of 'A man in his town and a Jew in his tent' as 'secular knowledge for business (or pleasure), Jewish knowledge for true understanding'. That would be a fatal barrier to Jews ever becoming accepted as a legitimate part of the general community. Was it not possible to reach some kind of half-way house?

The effort was made by a Galician Jew, Nachman Krochmal (1785–1840), who was part of the original *Wissenschaft* movement, but did not share its view that the intellectual integration of the Jews could be easily accomplished. He was a kind of Hegelian too, but rather more influenced by Maimonidean rationalism. Indeed, he sought to update the *Guide of the Perplexed*, though he was very diffident about publishing the results. In the end, his manuscript was worked on by Zunz himself and printed posthumously in 1851. Krochmal believed that the Jewish enlighteners and the unreconstructed Orthodox were alike unacceptable. The first devitalized Judaism, the second made it repellent; both, in nineteenth-century conditions, produced apostasy. The trouble was that neither type of Jew had a sense of Jewish history. The enlighteners thought it was just something you learned as a child, then went on to secular, 'adult' history when you grew up. The Orthodox Jews ignored history altogether – as he put it, 'there is no early or late in the Torah'. What he proposed was to create a Jewish philosophy of history. He took the Hegelian theory of growth, as Marx was soon to do, but instead of turning it on its head, he Judaized it. He divided Jewish history into three cycles: growth, maturity, then decline-and-fall. This was to show how 'when the days of disintegration and destruction were fulfilled, there was always renewed in us a new spirit and new life; and if we fell, how we arose and were encouraged and the Lord our God did not abandon us'. This was clearly far from being just secular history. It was not wholly unlike the old medieval wheel-of-fortune style of history, or the cycles of growth and decay to be popularized by Arnold Toynbee in the mid-twentieth century. But Krochmal introduced a Hegelian element by adding an upward progression through all these cycles – the process of human awareness from its roots in pure nature to its ultimate identification with pure spirit. All national histories showed this in some degree, but whereas other peoples were transitory, the Jews were eternal because they had a special relationship with the Absolute Spirit (i.e. God). Hence 'The history of Judaism is thus properly the history of the education of consciousness' – with a beginning, a middle and an end.[51]

Unfortunately, Krochmal could not satisfy Orthodox Jews with his philosophy of history since he could not, or did not, fit the Messianic Age into his scheme, unless it was seen in some vague metaphorical sense. Still less could his work appeal to the gentile. With Heinrich Graetz (1817–91), on the other hand, the Jews at last produced a historian, and on a massive scale too, who could not only be read and believed by enlightened Jews, but read – and to some extent accepted – by gentiles too. Between 1856 and 1876 he published an eleven-volume *History of the Jews* which is one of the great monuments of nineteenth-century historical writing. In various condensed forms it appeared all over the world and in numerous translations, and it is still of considerable value today.[52] But in structure the work is Judaic rather than secular: it tells Jewish history primarily in terms of the Torah and Torah study. Moreover, his historical dynamic is religious too. In his view, the Jews were emphatically not a people like any other. They were part of a unique politico-religious organic entity, 'whose soul is the Torah and whose body is the Holy Land'. The Jewish archetype had a central, and dramatic, part to play in the history of the world. In a brilliant passage introducing volume four of his work, Graetz presented the Jew of historical–divine destiny: 'On the one hand enslaved Judah with his wanderer's staff in hand, the pilgrim's bundle on his back, his grim features turned heavenwards, surrounded by dungeon walls, instruments of torture and the glow of branding irons; on the other, the same figure with a questing look in the transfigured features, in a study filled with a vast library in all the languages of man . . . a slave with a thinker's pride'.[53] Graetz made use of a vast number of sources in many languages, but his vision of the Jew was rooted in Deutero-Isaiah, and especially in the 'Suffering Servant'. The Jews, he argued, had always been 'powerful and productive in religious and moral truths for the salvation of mankind'. Judaism was (by divine providence) self-created. In that respect it was unlike any other great religion. Its 'sparks' had ignited Christianity. Its 'seeds' had brought forth the fruits of Islam. From its insights could be traced the origins both of scholastic philosophy and Protestantism.[54] Moreover, the destiny of the Jews was continuing. Graetz did not see the Messiah as a person but as a collective. The Jews were a messianic people. Like Hegel he believed in the concept of a perfect state, and he saw the final Jewish task as preparing a religious state constitution, which would somehow inaugurate a golden age.

This summary does not do justice to Graetz; but then it is not easy to do justice to him because his views about what exactly it was the Jews would accomplish changed substantially, as his enthusiasm for a 'Jewish solution' to the world's problems waxed and waned. Sometimes he seemed to think Jews would provide actual world leadership. At others it was to be merely ethical example. But in either event he presented the Jews as a superior people. He was not a Zionist. But he was certainly a Jewish nationalist of a kind, and he put forward Jewish claims not, like Disraeli, in an attractive spirit of romantic paradox, but in a tone of voice which even other Jews found aggressive, and which was bound to repel gentiles, especially Germans. So Graetz's work, though of permanent importance in Jewish historical studies, did not supply an answer either to the problem of bridging Judaism and the secular world. As history it was useful; as a philosophy it was not in the end acceptable to any group. Indeed, German nationalists were not the only ones to be offended. Graetz seems to have known little about Jewish mysticism. For the kabbalah and the *hasidim* he had nothing but contempt. Contemporary students of haskalah were dismissed as 'fossilized Polish Talmudists'. He called Yiddish ridiculous. Hence he could have no real message for the great masses of eastern Jewry. But he did not satisfy the enlightened Orthodox either. He began as a disciple of Hirsch. As a young man in 1836, his faith had been saved by reading the Rabbi's *Nineteen Letters*. He saw his own beliefs as essentially Jewish. But Hirsch rejected his work as 'superficial and fantastical'. Was there no pleasing anyone? It seemed so.

If no satisfactory solution could be found to the problem of how to relate Jewish to secular culture, was it possible to bring the practice of Jewish religion into harmony with the modern world? That too was attempted. Reform Judaism, as it came to be called, was the product of the second decade of the nineteenth century when the first full effects of emancipation and enlightenment were felt on Jewish communities. Like every other effort to bring Judaism into a new relationship with the world, it was primarily a German initiative. The first experiments were conducted at Seesen in 1810, at Berlin in 1815, then in Hamburg, where a Reform Temple was opened in 1818. These took place against a background of what contemporaries saw as Protestant Triumphalism. The Protestant nations appeared to be doing well everywhere. Protestant Prussia was becoming the most powerful and efficient state in Germany. Protestant Britain was the first industrial power, the conqueror of Napoleon, the centre of the richest commercial empire the world had ever seen. The United States, also Protestant, was the rising power in the West. Was not this link between the reformed Christian faith and prosperity evidence of divine favour – or at least a valuable lesson in religious sociology? Many political writers in Catholic countries, especially France, voiced their fears that Protestantism was taking over the world, and their anxiety that Catholicism should adopt the most socially useful Protestant characteristics. But which? Attention focussed on the outward and visible signs of a religion: its services. Most Protestant services were solemn but seemly, impressive in their simplicity, marked by readings in the vernacular and well-argued sermons. Catholicism, by contrast, retained the embarrassing religiosity of the medieval world, indeed of antiquity: incense, lamps and candles, fantastic vestments, relics and statues, a liturgical language which few understood. All this, it was argued, needed to be changed. But these calls for reform went unheeded within the Catholic Church itself, where authority was centralized and severely imposed. Besides, the traditional mode of Catholicism had its own powerful defenders, such as Chateaubriand, whose *Le Génie du Christianisme* (1802) laid the basis for a new Catholic populism. In England, the Protestant citadel, the Oxford Movement was soon to turn to Rome for guidance, not vice versa. The truth is, Catholicism did not on the whole suffer from any inferiority complex, at any rate in the countries which mattered, where it was the overwhelming majority religion. So the changes were delayed for 150 years, to the 1960s, when Rome too would be in manifest disarray.

It was a different matter for the Jews, especially in Germany and other 'advanced' countries. Enlightened Jews were ashamed of their traditional services: the dead weight of the past, the lack of intellectual content, the noisy and unseemly manner in which Orthodox Jews prayed. In Protestant countries, for Christians to visit a synagogue was quite fashionable, and provoked contempt and pity. Hence Reform Judaism was, in the first place, an attempt to remove the taint of ridicule from Jewish forms of worship. The object was to induce a seemly religious state of mind. The watchwords were *Erbauung* (edification) and *Andacht* (devotion). Christian-style sermons were introduced. The reformer Joseph Wolf (1762–1826), teacher and community secretary at Dessau, and a devoted admirer of Mendelssohn, took the best German Protestant orators as his models. The Jews learned to preach in this style quickly, as they learned all novelties quickly. Soon, sermons at the Berlin Temple were so good that Protestant pastors, in turn, came to listen and learn. Hints were exchanged.[55] Organ music, another powerful feature of German Protestantism, was introduced, and choral singing in the European mode.

Then, in 1819, the same year as the Society for Jewish Science was founded, the Hamburg Temple introduced a new prayer-book, and the aesthetic changes spread to more fundamental matters. If liturgical habits could be discarded because they were embarrassing, why not absurd and inconvenient doctrines? The mention of the Messiah was dropped; so was a return to the Holy Land. The idea was to purify and re-energize Judaism in the same spirit as Luther's reformation.[56] But there was an important difference, alas. Luther was not constantly looking over his shoulder at what other people were doing, and copying them. For better or for worse, he was animated by his own crude and powerful inner impulse: 'I can do no other,' as he put it. He was *sui generis* and his new form of Christianity, with its specific doctrines and its special liturgical modes, was a genuine and original creation. Reform Judaism was animated less by overwhelming conviction than by social tidy-mindedness and the desire to be more genteel. Its spirit was not religious but secular. It was well meaning but an artificial construct, like so many idealistic schemes of the nineteenth century, from Comte's Positivism to Esperanto.

It might have been a different matter if the movement had produced one of the religious exotics of which eastern European hasidic Jewry was so prolific. But Reform waited in vain for a Luther. The best it could produce was Rabbi Abraham Geiger (1810–74), who effectively led the movement successively in Breslau, Frankfurt and Berlin.[57] He was energetic, pious, learned and sensible. Too sensible perhaps. He lacked the self-regarding audacity and willingness to destroy which the religious revolutionary needs. In a private letter he wrote in 1836, he spoke of the need to abolish all the institutions of Judaism and rebuild them on a new basic. But this was not what he felt able to do in practice. He opposed prayers in Hebrew, but would not eliminate it from the services. He thought circumcision 'a barbaric act of blood-letting', but opposed its abolition. He sanctioned some breaches of the Sabbath prohibitions, but he would not scrap the Sabbath principle entirely and adopt the Christian Sunday. He omitted passages on the Return to Zion and other references to what he regarded as outdated historical conditions, but he could not bring himself to surrender the principle of the Mosaic law. He tried to extract from the vast, accumulated mass of Judaic belief what he called the religious–universal element. That in his view involved dropping the automatic assumption of solidarity with Jews everywhere – he thus refused to take an active role in the protest over the Damascus atrocities. But as he grew older, like so many well-educated Jews before and since, he began to feel the pull of traditional Judaism more and more, so that his enthusiasm for change abated.

The Reformers might have had more impact if they had been able to erect a clearly defined platform of belief and practice, and stick to it. But Geiger was not the only one who failed to find a final resting-point of faith. The leading reformers differed among themselves. Rabbi Samuel Holdheim (1806–60), who came from Poznan, but ended up as head of a new Reform congregation in Berlin, started as a moderate reformer – he merely wished to end cantillated reading of the Torah. Gradually he became an extremist. Geiger believed in 'progressive revelation', whereby the practice of Judaism had to be changed periodically as God's will was made manifest. Holdheim wanted to abolish Temple and ceremonial Judaism altogether, immediately. Most of the Talmud had to go too: 'In the talmudic age, the Talmud was right. In my age, I am right.' He saw traditional Judaism as an obstacle to Jews becoming part of a universal brotherhood of man, which to him represented the messianic era. So he argued that the uncircumcised could still be Jews. He thought a man's professional duties came before strict observance of the Sabbath. Indeed, in Berlin he not only radically transformed the services but eventually held them on a Sunday. When he died there was even a row about whether he could be buried in the rabbis' part of the cemetery.

Holdheim's version of reform was not the only alternative to Geiger's. In Frankfurt, an anti-circumcision group appeared. In London a Reform movement accepted the Bible, as God's work, and rejected the Talmud, as man's. As Reform spread abroad, it appeared in more and more guises. Some groups retained links with Orthodox Jews. Others broke off completely. Rabbinical conferences were held, to no great purpose. New prayer-books were issued, and provoked fresh controversies. In one version or another Reform Judaism clearly provided a satisfactory expression of the religious spirit for many thousands of educated Jews. In England, for instance, both a rather traditional-minded Reform Judaism, and eventually a more radical sub-group, Liberal Judaism, became firmly established. In America, as we shall see, the Reform, in both its conservative and liberal versions, became an important element in what was to become the third leg of the Jewish world tripod.

But what Reform did not do, any more than the 'Science of Judaism', was to solve the Jewish problem. It did not normalize the Jews because it never spoke for more than a minority. It was, in essence, an alternative to baptism and complete assimilation, among Jews whose faith, or at any rate whose piety, was strong enough to keep them attached to their religion in some form, but not strong enough to defy the world. By the end of the 1840s, it was obvious that it was not going to take over Judaism, even in enlightened Germany. By the end of the century, it had acquired enough institutional supports to keep going, at any rate in some countries, but its creative force was spent. The traditionalist writer John Lehmann noted in 1905: 'Today, when complete apathy has overtaken the neologue circles, it is hardly possible to imagine that there were once people who regarded it as their life's task, and who were determined with their whole heart and their whole soul to reform Judaism, and who each considered himself as a miniature Luther, Zwingli or Calvin.'[58]

One reason why Jews who wished to participate fully in the modern world without losing their Judaism failed to achieve a workable formula was that they could not agree on a language in which to express it. There were, at this stage, three possible alternatives. One was the ancient hieratic language of Judaism, Hebrew. A second was the language of their own country, whatever it might be. The third was the demotic language which most Jews actually spoke, Yiddish. Or possibly there might be a combination of all three. The men of the Jewish enlightenment wanted to resurrect Hebrew. Indeed, the very word Haskalah, with which they chose to identify themselves, was the Hebrew word for understanding or reason: they used it to signify their commitment to reason, as opposed to revelation, as the source of truth. They produced educational works in Hebrew. They ran a Hebrew publication. But there were a number of reasons why their project lacked dynamism. Few of them wrote much Hebrew themselves – Mendelssohn, their leader, very little. They chose Hebrew not because they wanted to express themselves in it: for that, they much preferred German. Nor did they venerate it for religious reasons. They saw it, rather, as being intellectually respectable, the Jewish equivalent of the Latin and Greek which was the ancient cultural heritage of Christian Europe. The age saw the dawn of modern philological studies. Everywhere in Europe, experts were compiling grammars, putting local tongues into written form and endowing them with rules and syntax – Finnish, Hungarian, Rumanian, Irish, Basque, Catalan were being promoted from local patois to the status of a 'modern language'. The *maskils* wanted to subject Hebrew to this process. Logically, of course, they should have picked Yiddish, a tongue which Jews actually spoke. But the *maskils* regarded it with abhorrence. They dismissed it as nothing more than a corrupt form of German. It stood for everything they most deplored about the ghetto and unregenerated Judaism: poverty, ignorance, superstition, vice. The only people who studied Yiddish scientifically, they argued, were the police, who needed to know thieves' slang.

So the *maskils* revived Hebrew. But they did not know what to write in it. Their biggest project was a hybrid presentation of the Bible, using German words in Hebrew characters. This was quite a success. Many thousands of Jews, particularly of the older generation, who had had no access to secular schools, used it to acquire literary German. But this led to less Hebrew, not more. Once Jews read German, and acquired secular culture, their interest in Hebrew declined, or vanished; many even lost their Judaism. Even those who retained their faith found less use for Hebrew as services and prayer-books began to use the vernacular.

There was, indeed, a living if tenuous Hebrew tradition in literature. But the *maskils* found that distasteful too, for ideological reasons. Great medieval scholars like Maimonides had written in Arabic. But the practice of writing in Hebrew also survived in Moslem Spain, and thence it re-emerged in Renaissance Italy. Some Italian Jews continued to write beautiful Hebrew throughout the seventeenth century. Then the tradition acquired a genius: Moses Hayyim Luzzatto (1707–46). This remarkable man came from one of the oldest and most distinguished families of Italian Jewry in Padua. He was a prodigy and had the best teachers, as well as access to the great university. He learned secular science, the classics, modern Italian, in addition to the entire range of Judaic studies. Luzzatto had the unusual capacity of being able to write abstruse material in high academic style, and also to propound complex matters in simple fashion to a popular audience.

He could also express himself in various languages, ancient and modern. One of his works is in Aramaic, the language in which the *Zohar* was originally written. But his customary mode of address was Hebrew. He turned out a great deal of Hebrew poetry, some religious, which has not survived, some secular, in honour of his friends. He produced three Hebrew verse dramas. Above all, he wrote an ethical work, *Mesillat Yesharim*, or *The Path of the Upright*, which in the late eighteenth and most of the nineteenth century was the most influential of all Hebrew books, and the most widely read, in the Jewries of eastern Europe.[59] Was not he the ideal progenitor of a Hebrew revival? Not for enlightened German Jews. On the contrary: he symbolized what they wished to repudiate and eliminate.

For Luzzatto was a kabbalist and a mystic. Worse: he may well have been a secret Shabbatean, or something very like it. He had acquired, as he admitted himself, a taste for the fatally insinuating writings of Nathan of Gaza, with their ability to explain anything once you had made the first irrational leap. In Padua, he seems to have drawn around him a group of clever young men who dabbled in dangerous thoughts. The Venetian rabbis had his house searched and found evidence of magic. To escape controversy, he went to Amsterdam. There, too, he was forbidden to practise kabbalah. So he finally went to the Holy Land, where the plague got him in Acre.[60] Being named Moses, married to a girl called Zipporah, he seems to have reached the conclusion that he was the reincarnation of Moses and his wife. Many Jews in the East agreed; or at least treated him as a saint. No enlightened German Jew could accept that sort of thing. And, even if his personal claims were brushed aside, the contents of his ethics were also unacceptable to *maskils*. In his *Path of the Upright* and a further work, *Da'ath Tevunot* or *Discerning Knowledge*, he produced a brilliant recapitulation of the history of God's purpose in the world and the role of the Jews, the covenant and the diaspora. He showed exactly why the Jews were in the world today, and what they had to do to justify themselves. His summary of the purpose of life was uncompromising:

> The essence of the existence of a human being in this world is that he should fulfil commandments, perform worship and resist temptation. It is unfitting that worldly happiness should mean anything more to him than a mere aid or support in the sense that satisfaction and peace of mind allow him to devote his heart to this service that is incumbent upon him; and it is fitting that the whole of his attention should be devoted only to the Creator – blessed be He – and that he should have no other purpose in any of his actions, whether small or great, except to draw near to Him – blessed be He – and to break down all the partitions separating him from his Owner.[61]

Here was a man, writing in Hebrew, propounding a coherent, if rigorous, philosophy which inspired millions of Jews and continues to be a living tradition in Judaism even today. But it was anathema to the enlightened. Far from using Hebrew to beckon the ex-ghetto Jews into the modern world, and bid them take a decent and honourable place there, it did exactly the opposite. It told the Jew to about-face, and turn his gaze to God – as pious Jews had always done. So the living Hebrew tradition, such as it was, could not be fitted into the master-plan of the enlightenment. Their scheme to run Hebrew in tandem with German thus made no progress. Jews simply learned German, and assimilated themselves. The *maskils* were not to foresee that Hebrew would indeed make a formidable re-entry into Jewish life – but as the instrument of Zionism, a form of Judaism which was as abhorrent to them as mystic messianism.

Ironically enough, the Jewish language which made most, and entirely spontaneous, progress in the nineteenth century was Yiddish. It is a pity that the *maskils*, whose ability to speak and write German was the certificate of their enlightened status, knew so little about it. It was not just a criminal *argot*. It was much more than a corrupt form of German. To pious Jews it was a 'temporary' language in that it was non-divine, non-historical (in Jewish terms). Once history got going again, as the Messianic Age approached, Jews would presumably revert to Hebrew, the language of the Torah, in which in any case important matters such as ritual, scholarship and often communal administration were conducted. But for a temporary language, Yiddish was old, almost as old as some European tongues. Jews first began to develop it from the German dialects spoken in the cities when they pushed up from France and Italy into German-speaking Lotharingia. Old Yiddish (1250–1500) marked the first contact of German-speaking Jews with Slavic Jews speaking a dialect called Knaanic. During the 200 years 1500–1700, Middle Yiddish emerged, becoming progressively more Slavic and dialectic. Finally, modern Yiddish developed during the eighteenth century. Its literary form was completely transformed in the half-century 1810–60, in the cities of the east European diaspora, as Yiddish newspapers and magazines proliferated, and a secular Yiddish book-trade flourished. Philologists and grammarians tidied it up. By 1908 it was sophisticated enough for its proponents to hold a world Yiddish conference in Czernowitz. As the Jewish population of eastern Europe grew, more people spoke, read and wrote it. By the end of the 1930s it was the primary tongue of about eleven million people.

Yiddish was a rich, living language, the chattering tongue of an urban tribe. It had the limitations of its origins. There were very few Yiddish words for animals or birds. It had virtually no military vocabulary. Such defects were made up from German, Polish, Russian. Yiddish was particularly good at borrowing: from Arabic, from Hebrew–Aramaic, from anything which came its way. On the other hand it contributed: to Hebrew, to English–American. Its chief virtue, however, lay in its internal subtlety, particularly in its characterization of human types and emotions.[62] It was the language of street wisdom, of the clever underdog; of pathos, resignation, suffering, which it palliated by humour, intense irony and superstition. Isaac Bashevis Singer, its greatest practitioner, pointed out that it is the only language never spoken by men in power.

Yiddish was the natural tongue for a revived Jewish nation because it was widely spoken and living; and in the second half of the nineteenth century it began, quite rapidly, to produce a major literature of stories, poems, plays and novels. But there were many reasons why it could not fulfil its appointed destiny. Its role was riddled with paradoxes. Many rabbis saw it as the language of women, who were not clever or educated enough to study in Hebrew. The German maskils, on the other hand, linked it with Orthodoxy, because its use encouraged backwardness, superstition and irrationality. Among the large Jewish community of Hungary, for instance, the local language was used for everyday life, and Yiddish was the language of religious instruction, into which Jewish boys had to render the Hebrew and Aramaic texts – so it was associated with the uncorrupted Orthodox. In the Russian Pale, however, and Austrian Galicia, it was often the language of secularization. In the second half of the nineteenth century, almost every sizeable Jewish community in eastern Europe had a circle of atheists and radicals, whose language of dissent was Yiddish and who read Yiddish books and periodicals which catered to their views. Yet even in the East, where Yiddish was the majority Jewish tongue, it had no monopoly of worldliness. For the political radicals increasingly turned to German, then to Russian. The non-political secularizers usually, in true maskil fashion, accorded a superior status to Hebrew. The point was made by Nahum Slouschz, who translated Zola, Flaubert and de Maupassant into Hebrew:

While the emancipated Jew of the Occident replaced Hebrew by the vernacular of his adopted country; while the rabbis were distrustful of whatever was not religion; and rich patrons refused to support a literature which had not the entrée to good society – while these held aloof, the maskil, the 'intellectual', of the small provincial town, the Polish mehabber [author], despised and unknown, often a martyr to his convictions, who devoted himself heart, soul and might to maintaining honourably the literary traditions of Hebrew – he alone remained faithful to what had been the true mission of the Bible language since its beginnings.[63]

That was doubtless true. But there were many Yiddish writers who could make an equally heroic–pathetic case for themselves, with at least as strong a claim to be upholding the Jewish spirit.

In short, during the early decades of the nineteenth century, the Jewish linguistic outlook and future was confused, for reasons which had their roots deep in history and faith. This linguistic confusion was merely one part of a much wider cultural confusion. And this cultural confusion sprang, in turn, from a growing religious confusion among Jews themselves, which can be summed up in one sentence: was Judaism a part of life, or the whole of it? If it was only a part, then a compromise with modernity was possible. But in that case the Jews might simply fade into the majority societies around them. If it was the whole, then they had merely replaced the ghetto of stone with the ghetto of intellect. So in that case, too, most Jews would choose to escape from the prison, and be lost to the Law for ever. All the compromises we have examined collapsed before the majestic logic of this stark choice.

Hence the central fact of the Jewish predicament in the first half of the nineteenth century was the absence of an agreed programme or a united leadership. Where other oppressed and insurgent peoples could concentrate their energy on marching behind the banners of nationalism and independence, the Jews were rebels without a cause. Or rather, they knew what they were rebelling against – both the hostile society in which they were implanted, which gave them full citizenship grudgingly if at all, and the suffocating embrace of ghetto Judaism – but they did not know what they were rebelling *for*. None the less, though inchoate, the Jewish rebellion was real. And the individual rebels, though lacking a common objective, were formidable. Collectively, they constituted a huge force for good and evil. So far we have looked at only one side of the problem of emancipation: how could Jews liberated from the ghetto adjust to society? But the other side was equally important: how could society adjust to liberated Jews?

The problem was gigantic because for 1,500 years Jewish society had been designed to produce intellectuals. It is true they were sacerdotal intellectuals, in the service of the god Torah. But they had all the characteristics of the intellectual: a tendency to pursue ideas at the expense of people; endlessly sharpened critical faculties; great destructive as well as creative power. Jewish society was geared to support them. The community rabbi was designated in his writ of appointment 'Lord of the Place'. He received the chief honour, as the spiritual descendant of Moses himself. He was the local model of the ideal Jew. He was the charismatic sage. He spent his life absorbing abstruse material and then regurgitating it in accordance with his opinions. He expected to be, and was, supported by the wealth of the local oligarchs. The Jews subsidized their culture many hundreds of years before the practice became a function of the Western welfare state. Rich merchants married sages' daughters; the brilliant *yeshiva* student was found a wealthy bride so he could study more. The system whereby sages and merchants ran the community in tandem thus redistributed rather than reinforced wealth. It also ensured the production of large numbers of highly intelligent people who were given every opportunity to pursue ideas. Quite suddenly, around the year 1800, this ancient and highly efficient social machine for the production of intellectuals began to shift its output. Instead of pouring all its products into the closed circuit of rabbinical studies, where they remained completely isolated from general society, it unleashed a significant and ever-growing proportion of them into secular life. This was an event of shattering importance in world history.

Heinrich Heine (1797–1856) was the archetype of the new phenomenon. He was born in Düsseldorf of a mercantile family. Fifty years before he would have become, without question, a rabbi and talmudic scholar, no doubt of distinction. Instead he was a product of the revolutionary whirlwind. By the age of sixteen, without leaving his place of birth, he had undergone six changes of nationality. His family was half-emancipated. His mother, Piera van Geldern, had secular ambitions for him. When Napoleon's armies advanced, she saw her son as a courtier, a marshal, a politician or governor; when the French retreated, he was transformed into a millionaire businessman.[64] She saw that he got very little Jewish education, sending him to the Roman Catholic lycée. Heine lacked personal, religious, racial and national identity. His Jewish name was Hayyim. As a boy he was called Harry. Later he called himself Heinrich, but he signed his work H. Heine and hated the 'H' to be spelled out.[65] As a boy he had lived under the Napoleonic creation, the Grand Duchy of Berg, so he claimed his spirit was French. But the most important book of his childhood was the great Lutheran Bible, than which there is nothing more German. He moved to Paris in 1831 and did not return to Germany (except for two short visits). But he never applied for French citizenship, though eligible. He wrote all his works in German. He thought the Germans, though often evil, more profound; the French lived on the surface. Their poetry was 'perfumed curds'.[66]

Heine's ambiguities about his Judaism would fill, and indeed have filled, many books.[67] He did not learn to read Hebrew properly. He hated being a Jew. He wrote of 'the three evil maladies, poverty, pain and Jewishness'. In 1822 he was briefly associated with the Society for Jewish Science, but he had nothing to contribute. He did not believe in Judaism as such and saw it as an anti-human force. He wrote the next year: 'That I will be enthusiastic for the rights of the Jews and their civil equality, that I admit, and in bad times, which are inevitable, the Germanic mob will hear my voice so that it resounds in German beerhalls and palaces. But the born enemy of all positive religion will never champion that religion which first developed the fault-finding with human beings which now causes us so much pain.'[68] But if he rejected talmudic Judaism, he despised the new Reform version. The Reformers were 'chiropodists' who had 'tried to cure the body of Judaism from its nasty skin growth by bleeding, and by their clumsiness and spidery bandages of rationalism, Israel must bleed to death. . . . we no longer have the strength to wear a beard, to fast, to hate and to endure out of hate; that is the motive of our Reform.' The whole exercise, he said scornfully, was to turn 'a little Protestant Christianity into a Jewish company. They make a tallis out of the wool of the Lamb of God, and a vest out of the feathers of the Holy Ghost, and underpants out of Christian love, and they will go bankrupt and their successors will be called: God, Christ & Co.'[69]

But if Heine disliked both Orthodox and Reform Jews, he disliked the *maskils* perhaps even more. He saw them as careerists heading for baptism. He noted that four out of six of Mendelssohn's children converted. His daughter Dorothea's second husband was Friedrich Schlegel; she became a Catholic reactionary. His grandson Felix became the leading composer of Christian music. It may not have been Heine who said, 'The most Jewish thing Mendelssohn ever did was to become a Christian.' But he certainly remarked: 'If I had the luck of being the grandson of Moses Mendelssohn, I would surely not use my talent to set the pissing of the Lamb to music.'[70] When Eduard Gans converted, Heine denounced him as a 'scoundrel', guilty of 'felony', of 'treason', worse than Burke (in Heine's view the arch-traitor who betrayed the cause of revolution). He marked Gans's baptism by a bitter poem, *An einen Abtrunnigen*, 'To an Apostate'.

Yet Heine himself had become a Protestant only a few months before, three days after he took his doctorate. His reasons were entirely worldly. By a law of August 1822, Jews had been excluded from state academic posts – a ruling aimed specifically at Gans. Ten years later Heine defended his Protestantism as his 'Protest against injustice', his 'warlike enthusiasm which made me take part in the struggles of this militant church'. But this was nonsense, for he also argued that the spirit of Protestantism was not really religious at all: 'The blooming flesh in Titian's paintings – that is all Protestantism. The loins of his Venus are much more fundamental theses than those the German monk stuck on the church door of Wittenberg.' And at the time of his baptism, he wrote to his friend Moses Moser: 'I should not like it if you saw my baptism in a favourable light. I can assure you, if our laws allowed the stealing of silver spoons, I would not have done it.'[71] His saying that baptism was 'the entrance-ticket to European culture' became notorious.[72]

Why, then, did Heine abuse Gans for what he did himself? There is no satisfactory explanation. Heine suffered from a destructive emotion which was soon to be commonplace among emancipated and apostate Jews: a peculiar form of self-hatred. He attacked himself in Gans. Later in life he used to say he regretted his baptism. It had, he said, done him no good materially. But he refused to allow himself to be presented publicly as a Jew. In 1835, lying, he said he had never set foot in a synagogue. It was his desire to repudiate his Jewishness, as well as his Jewish self-hatred, which prompted his many anti-Semitic remarks. A particular target was the Rothschild family. He blamed them for raising loans for the reactionary great powers. That, at any rate, was his respectable reason for attacking them. But his most venomous remarks were reserved for Baron James de Rothschild and his wife, who showed him great kindness in Paris. He said he had seen a stockbroker bowing to the Baron's chamber-pot. He called him 'Herr von Shylock in Paris'. He said, 'There is only one God – Mammon. And Rothschild is his prophet.' He said there was no more need for the Talmud, once the Jews' defence against Rome, since every quarter-day the papal nuncio had to bring Baron James the interest on his loan. None of this stopped him getting a lot of money out of the Rothschilds, or boasting that his relations with them were (as he put it) *famillionaire*.[73]

Heine, in fact, expected wealthy Jews to maintain him, even though he was not a rabbinical student but a secular intellectual. His father had been a hopeless failure at business; his own efforts, such as they were, did him little good. So he was perpetually dependent on his uncle, Solomon Heine, a Hamburg banker who became one of the richest men in Europe. Heine was always in need of money, however much he got. He even stooped to accept an annual secret pension of

4,800 francs from the Louis-Philippe government. But usually he pestered Uncle Solomon, none too politely: 'The best thing about you', he wrote to him in 1836, 'is that you bear my name.' The uncle was sceptical about Heine's deserts, remarking: 'If he had learned anything, he wouldn't need to write books.' He thought his nephew was a bit of a *schnorrer*, a professional Jewish beggar. But, faithful to the ancient tradition, he paid up. When he died in 1844 he left Heine a legacy, but on condition the poet did not attack him or his family. The sum was less than Heine had hoped for, so he engaged in a long-drawn-out row over the will with Solomon's son.[74]

This was the personal background to Heine's astonishing genius. In the 1820s he superseded Byron as Europe's most widely acclaimed poet. The turning-point came with his *Buch der Lieder* (1827), which contained such famous lyrics as his 'Lorelei' and 'Auf Flügeln des Gesanges' ('On Wings of Song'). The Germans came to recognize him as their greatest man of letters since Goethe. When he settled in Paris, he was hailed as a hero of European culture. His prose was as brilliant, and as popular, as his poetry. He produced scintillating travel books. He virtually established a new genre of French literature, the short essay or *feuilleton*. Much of his energy was wasted on furious quarrels and character-assassination, in which his self-hatred (or whatever it was) found an outlet, and which were so extravagant that they usually aroused sympathy for the victim. But his fame continued to spread. He contracted a venereal infection of the spine, which confined him to a sofa for his last decade. But his final poems were better than ever. Moreover, his lyrics were perfectly adapted to the new German art-song, now sweeping Europe and North America, so that all the leading composers, from Schubert and Schumann onwards, set him to music. There was no escaping Heine, then or ever since, especially for Germans, in whom he stirred irresistible responses. His works were used as German school textbooks even in his lifetime.

Many Germans found it hard to admit that this Jew had such a perfect German ear. They tried to convict him of 'Jewish superficiality', as opposed to true German profundity. The charge could not be made to stick. It was so manifestly untrue. It was as though a superfine talent had been building up in the ghetto over many secret generations, acquiring an ever more powerful genetic coding, and then had suddenly emerged to find the German language of the early nineteenth century its perfect instrument. The point had now been established: the Jew and the German had a special intellectual relationship. The German Jew was a new phenomenon of European culture. For German anti-Semites, this posed an almost unbearable emotional problem, epitomized in Heine. They could not deny his genius; they found its expression in German intolerable. His ghostly presence, right at the centre of German literature, drove the Nazis to incoherent rage and childish vandalism. They suppressed all his books. But they could not erase his poems from the anthologies and were forced to reprint them with what every schoolboy knew was a lie: 'By an Unknown Author'. They seized a statue of him, once owned by the Empress Elisabeth of Austria, and used it for target-practice. In 1941, on Hitler's personal orders, his grave in the Montmartre cemetery was destroyed. It made no difference. In the last forty years, Heine's work has been more widely and furiously debated, especially by Germans, than that of any other figure in their literature.

Heine had been banned in his lifetime too, at the insistence of Metternich – not as a Jew, but as a subversive. Therein lay another paradox, and a typical Jewish paradox. From emancipation onwards, the Jews were blamed both for seeking to ingratiate themselves with established society, enter it and dominate it; and, at the same time, for trying to destroy it utterly. Both charges had an element of truth. The Heine family was a case in point. Next to the Rothschilds themselves, who collected titles from half-a-dozen kingdoms and empires, the Heines were the most upwardly mobile family in Europe. Heine's brother Gustav was knighted and made Baron von Heine-Geldern. His brother Maximilian married into the Tsarist aristocracy and was styled von Heine. His sister's son became a Baron von Embden. Her daughter married an Italian prince. One of Heine's close relatives became a Princesse Murat, another married the reigning Prince of Monaco.[75] But Heine himself was both the prototype and the archetype of a new figure in European literature: the Jewish radical man of letters, using his skill, reputation and popularity to undermine the intellectual self-confidence of established order.

The notion of Heine as a lifelong radical needs severe qualification. Privately, at least, he always distinguished between the grim political progressives, and literary ones like himself. He hated their puritanism. He wrote to one of them: 'You demand simple dress, abstemious habits and unseasonable pleasures; we, on the other hand, demand nectar and ambrosia, purple cloaks, sumptuous aromas, voluptuousness and luxury, laughing nymph-dances, music and comedies.'[76] Privately, again, his conservatism increased with age. He wrote to Gustav Kolb in 1841: 'I have a great fear of the atrociousness of proletarian rule, and I confess to you that out of fear I have become a conservative.' When his long final illness confined him to what he called 'my mattress-grave', he returned to Judaism of a kind. Indeed, he insisted, quite untruthfully: 'I have made no secret of my Judaism, to which I have not returned since I never left it' (1850). His latest and greatest poems, *Romanzero* (1851) and *Vermischte Schriften* (1854), mark a return to religious themes, sometimes with a Judaic cast of thought. Like thousands of brilliant Jews before, and since, he came to associate the Hellenic spirit of intellectual adventure with health and strength, while age and pain turned him to the simplicities of faith. 'I am no longer', he wrote to a friend, 'a zestful, well-nourished Hellene, smiling down on gloomy Nazarenes. I am now only a mortally ill Jew, an emaciated image of misery, an unhappy man.' Or again: 'Sickened by atheistic philosophy, I have returned to the humble faith of the ordinary man.'[77]

Nevertheless, the public persona of Heine was overwhelmingly radical, and to a great extent remained so. For generations of European intellectuals, his life and work was a poem to freedom. For Jews in particular, he presented the French progressive tradition as the true story of human advance, which all gifted young men and women should seek, each in their time, to push forward another league or two. He came close to a public declaration of faith when he wrote:

Freedom is the new religion, the religion of our time. If Christ is not the god of this new religion, he is nevertheless a high priest of it, and his name gleams beatifically into the hearts of the apostles. But the French are the chosen people of the new religion, their language records the first gospels and dogmas. Paris is the New Jerusalem, the Rhine is the Jordan that separates the consecrated land of freedom from the land of the Philistines.

For a time Heine even became, or fancied he did, a disciple of Saint-Simon. There was a streak of the hippy, the 'flower-person', in Heine: 'the part of flowers and nightingales is closely allied to the revolution', he wrote, quoting Saint-Simon's dictum: 'The future is ours.' Heine never committed himself to a specific theory of revolutionary social-ism. But in Paris he associated with many trying to devise one. They were often of Jewish origin.

One such was the young Karl Marx, who came to Paris in 1843. He had been editor of the radical Cologne newspaper *Rheinische Zeitung*, which the Jewish socialist Moses Hess (1812–75) had helped to found in 1843. It lasted only fifteen months before the Prussian government killed it, and Marx joined Hess in Parisian exile. But the two socialists had little in common. Hess was a true Jew, whose radicalism took the form of Jewish nationalism and eventually of Zionism. Marx, by contrast, had no Jewish education at all and never sought to acquire any. In Paris he and Heine became friends. They wrote poetry together. Heine saved the life of Marx's baby Jennie, when she had convulsions. A few letters between them survive, and there must have been more.[78] Heine's jibe about religion as a 'spiritual opium' was the source of Marx's phrase 'the opium of the people'. But the notion that Heine was the John the Baptist to Christ's Marx, fashionable in German scholarship of the 1960s, is absurd. A huge temperamental gulf yawned between them. According to Arnold Ruge, Marx would say to Heine: 'Give up those everlasting laments about love and show the lyric poets how it should be done – with the lash.'[79] But it was precisely the lash Heine feared: 'The [socialist] future', he wrote, 'smells of knouts, of blood, of godlessness and very many beatings'; 'it is only with dread and horror that I think of the time when those dark iconoclasts will come to power'. He repudiated 'my obdurate friend Marx', one of the 'godless self-gods'.

What the two men had most in common was their extraordinary capacity for hatred, expressed in venomous attacks not just on enemies but (perhaps especially) on friends and benefactors. This was part of the self-hatred they shared as apostate Jews. Marx had it to an even greater extent than Heine. He tried to shut Judaism out of his life. Whereas Heine was deeply disturbed by the 1840 Damascus atrocities, Marx deliberately prevented himself from showing the smallest concern for any of the injustice inflicted on Jews throughout his lifetime.[80] Despite Marx's ignorance of Judaism as such, there can be no doubt about his Jewishness. Like Heine and everyone else, his notion of progress was profoundly influenced by Hegel, but his sense of history as a positive and dynamic force in human society, governed by iron laws, an atheist's Torah, is profoundly Jewish. His Communist millennium is deeply rooted in Jewish apocalyptic and messianism. His notion of rule was that of the cathedocrat. Control of the revolution would be in the hands of the elite intelligentsia, who had studied the texts, understood the laws of history. They would form what he called the 'management', the directorate. The proletariat, 'the men without substance', were merely the means, whose duty was to obey – like Ezra the Scribe, he saw them as ignorant of the law, the mere 'people of the land'.

Marx's methodology, too, was wholly rabbinical. All his conclusions were derived solely from books. He never set foot in a factory and rejected Engels' offer to take him to one. Like the *gaon* of Vilna, he locked himself up with his texts and solved the mysteries of the universe in his study. As he put it, 'I am a machine condemned to devour books.'[81] He called his work 'scientific' but it was no more scientific than theology. His temperament was religious, and he was quite incapable of conducting objective, empirical research. He simply went through any likely material to furnish 'proof' of conclusions he had already reached in his head, and which were as dogmatic as any rabbi's or kabbalist's. His methods were well summarized by Karl Jaspers:

The style of Marx's writings is not that of the investigator . . . he does not quote examples or adduce facts which run counter to his own theory but only those which clearly support or confirm that which he considers the ultimate truth. The whole approach is one of vindication, not investigation, but it is vindication of something proclaimed as the perfect truth with the conviction not of the scientist but of the believer.[82]

Stripped of its spurious documentation, Marx's theory of how history, class and production operate, and will develop, is not essentially different from Lurianic kabbalah's theory of the Messianic Age, especially as amended by Nathan of Gaza, to the point where it can accommodate any awkward facts whatever. In short, it is not a scientific theory at all, but a piece of clever Jewish superstition.

Finally, Marx was the eternal rabbinical student in his attitude to money. He expected it to be provided to finance his studies, first by his family, then by Engels, the merchant, as his endless bullying *schnorrer*-letters testify. But the studies, as with so many learned rabbis, were never finished. After the publication of volume one of *Capital*, he could never put the rest together, leaving his papers in total confusion, from which Engels assembled volumes two and three. So the great commentary on the Law of History ended in muddle and doubt. What happened when the Messiah came, when 'the expropriators are expropriated'? Marx could not say; he did not know. But he prophesied the Messiah-revolution all the same: in 1849, in August 1850, in 1851, in 1852, 'between November 1852 and February 1853', in 1854, in 1857, in 1858, in 1859.[83] His later work, like Nathan of Gaza's, was to a great extent an explanation for the non-arrival.

Marx was not merely a Jewish thinker, he was also an anti-Jewish thinker. Therein lies the paradox, which has a tragically important bearing both on the history of Marxist development and on its consummation in the Soviet Union and its progeny. The roots of Marx's anti-Semitism went deep. We have already seen the part anti-Jewish polemic played in the works of enlightenment writers like Voltaire. This tradition passed into two streams. One was the German 'idealist' stream, going through Goethe, Fichte, Hegel and Bauer, in each of whom the anti-Jewish elements became more pronounced.

The other was the French 'socialist' stream. This linked the Jews to the Industrial Revolution and the vast increase in commerce and material-ism which marked the beginning of the nineteenth century. In a book published in 1808, François Fourier identified commerce as 'the source of all evil' and the Jews as 'the incarnation of commerce'.[84] Pierre-Joseph Proudhon went further, accusing the Jews of 'having rendered the bourgeoisie, high and low, similar to them, all over Europe'. Jews were an 'unsociable race, obstinate, infernal . . . the enemy of mankind. We should send this race back to Asia, or exterminate it.'[85] Fourier's follower, Alphonse Toussenel, edited the anti-Semitic journal *Phalange* and in 1845 produced the first full-scale attack on the Jews as a network of commercial conspirators against humanity, *Les Juifs: rois de l'époque: histoire de la féodalité financière*. This became a primary source-book for anti-Semitic literature, in many languages, for the next four decades.

Marx absorbed both streams, adding to the turbid waters the outpourings of his own anguish. In his discussion of revolutionary Jews, the historian Robert Wistrich sees the self-hatred of some of them as reflecting the fury of very clever members of an under-privileged minority denied the position and recognition in society which their talents merited. Enlightenment thinkers, both French and German, argued that the objectionable features of Judaism had to be erased before the Jew could be free: Jews who were discriminated against accepted this, and thus often directed their rage more towards the unregenerated Jew than those who persecuted them both.[86] The self-hatred focussed on the ghetto Jew, who was of course the anti-Semitic archetype. Heine, who really knew very little about how most Jews actually lived, used all the standard anti-Semitic clichés when in self-hating mood. Marx, who knew even less, borrowed his abuse straight from the gentile student café. And both used the ghetto caricature to belabour educated and baptized Jews like themselves, especially fellow progressives. One of Heine's most vicious and almost incomprehensible attacks was unleashed on Ludwig Börne (1786–1837), born Lob Baruch, a baptized Jewish radical writer whose background and views were similar to his own.[87] Marx seems to have picked up this habit from Heine.[88] Thus, while himself attempting, whenever possible, to conceal his Jewish origins, he constantly attacked Jewish opponents for this very failing. Why, he asked, did Joseph Moses Levy, owner of the London *Daily Telegraph* and a baptized Jew, seek 'to be numbered among the Anglo-Saxon race . . . for Mother Nature has written his pedigree in absurd block letters right in the middle of his face'.[89]

Marx's most flagrant exercise in self-hatred, however, was directed at his fellow socialist Ferdinand Lassalle (1825–64), a Breslau Jew who changed his name from Lasal in honour of the French revolutionary hero and went on to become the founder of German socialism as a mass movement. His practical achievements in the cause were much more considerable than Marx's own. Despite or perhaps because of this he was made the object of extraordinary vituperation in Marx's correspondence with Engels. Marx called him 'Baron Itzig', the 'Jewish Nigger'. He saw him as a Polish Jew and (as he put it), 'The Jews of Poland are the dirtiest of all races.'[90] Engels wrote to Marx, 7 March 1856: '[Lassalle] is a real Jew from the Slav frontier and he has always been willing to exploit party affairs for private purposes. It is revolting to see how he is always trying to push his way into the aristocratic world. He is a greasy Jew disguised under brilliantine and flashy jewels.'[91] In attacking Lassalle's Jewishness, and sneering at his syphilis, Marx did not scruple to use the oldest of all anti-Semitic smears. Thus he wrote to Engels, 10 May 1861: 'A propos Lasalle–Lazarus. Lepsius in his great work on Egypt has proved that the exodus of the Jews from Egypt was nothing but the history which Manetho narrates of the expulsion of the "leprous people" from Egypt. At the head of these lepers was an Egyptian priest, Moses. Lazarus, the leper, is therefore the archetype of the Jew, and Lassalle is the typical leper.'[92] Or again, 30 July 1862: 'It is now perfectly clear to me that, as the shape of his head and the growth of his hair indicates, he is descended from the Negroes who joined in Moses' flight from Egypt (unless his mother or grandmother on the father's side was crossed with a nigger). This union of Jew and German on a Negro base was bound to produce an extraordinary hybrid.'[93]

Marx's personal anti-Semitism, however disagreeable in itself, might have played no greater part in his lifework than it did in Heine's, had it not been part of a systematic and theoretical anti-Semitism in which Marx, quite unlike Heine, profoundly believed. In fact it is true to say that Marx's theory of communism was the end-product of his theoretical anti-Semitism. Spinoza had first shown how a critique of Judaism could be used to reach radical conclusions about the world. His example had been followed by the French enlightenment, though their treatment of Judaism was far more hostile, and racial, in tone. Among radical German writers, the idea that solving the 'Jewish problem' might provide a key to solving the problems of humanity was much discussed. In the 1820s and 1830s, this was the route the much abused Ludwig Börne had taken towards socialism.[94] In 1843 Bruno Bauer, the anti-Semitic leader of the Hegelian left, published an essay demanding that the Jews abandon Judaism completely and transform their plea for equal rights into a general campaign for human liberation both from religion and from state tyranny.[95]

Marx replied to Bauer's work in two essays published in the *Deutsch-Francösische Jahrbucher* in 1844, the same year Disraeli published *Tancred*. They are called 'On the Jewish Question'.[96] Marx accepted completely the savagely anti-Semitic context of Bauer's argument, which he said was written 'with boldness, perception, wit and thoroughness in language that is as precise as it is vigorous and meaningful'. He quoted with approval Bauer's maliciously exaggerated assertion that 'the Jew determines the fate of the whole [Austrian] empire by his money power . . . [and] decides the destiny of Europe'. Where he differed was in rejecting Bauer's belief that the anti-social nature of the Jew was religious in origin and could be remedied by tearing the Jew away from his religion. In Marx's view, the evil was social and economic. 'Let us', he wrote, 'consider the real Jew. Not the *Sabbath Jew* . . . but the *everyday Jew*.' What, he asked, was 'the profane basis of Judaism? *Practical* need, *self-interest*. What is the worldly cult of the Jew? *Huckstering*. What is his worldly god? *Money*.'[97] The Jews had gradually conveyed this 'practical' religion to all society:

Money is the jealous God of Israel, besides which no other god may exist. Money abases all the gods of mankind and changes them into commodities. Money is the self-sufficient *value* of all things. It has, therefore, deprived the whole world, both the human world and nature, of their own proper value. Money is the alienated essence of man's work and existence: this essence dominates him and he worships it. The god of the Jews has been secularized and has become the god of this world.[98]

The Jews, Marx continued, were turning Christians into replicas of themselves, so that the once staunchly Christian New Englanders, for example, were now the slaves of Mammon. Using his money-power, the Jew had emancipated himself and had gone on to enslave Christianity. The Jew-corrupted Christian 'is convinced he has no other destiny here below than to become richer than his neighbours' and 'the world is a stock exchange'. Marx argued that the contradiction between the Jew's theoretical lack of political rights and 'the effective political power of the Jew' is the contradiction between politics and 'the power of money in general'. Political power supposedly overrides money; in fact 'it has become its bondsman'. Hence: 'It is from its own entrails that civil society ceaselessly engenders the Jew.'[99]

Marx's solution, therefore, is not like Bauer's, religious, but economic. The money-Jew had become the 'universal *anti-social* element of the present time'. To 'make the Jew impossible' it was necessary to abolish the 'preconditions' and the 'very possibility' of the kind of money activities for which he was notorious. Once the economic framework was changed, Jewish 'religious consciousness would evaporate like some insipid vapour in the real, life-giving air of society'. Abolish the Jewish attitude to money, and both the Jew and his religion, and the corrupt version of Christianity he had imposed on the world, would simply disappear: 'In the final analysis, the *emancipation* of the Jews is the emancipation of mankind from Judaism.' Or again: 'In emancipating itself from *hucksterism* and *money*, and thus from real and practical Judaism, our age would emancipate itself.'[100]

Marx's two essays on the Jews thus contain, in embryonic form, the essence of his theory of human regeneration: by economic changes, and especially by abolishing private property and the personal pursuit of money, you could transform not merely the relationship between the Jew and society but all human relationships and the human personality itself. His form of anti-Semitism became a dress-rehearsal for Marxism as such. Later in the century August Bebel, the German Social Democrat, would coin the phrase, much used by Lenin: 'Anti-Semitism is the socialism of fools.' Behind this revealing epigram was the crude argument: we all know that Jewish money-men, who never soil their hands with toil, exploit the poor workers and peasants. But only a fool blames the Jews alone. The mature man, the socialist, has grasped the point that the Jews are only symptoms of the disease, not the disease itself. The disease is the religion of money, and its modern form is capitalism. Workers and peasants are exploited not just by the Jews but by the entire bourgeois–capitalist class – and it is the class as a whole, not just its Jewish element, which must be destroyed.

Hence the militant socialism Marx adopted in the later 1840s was an extended and transmuted form of his earlier anti-Semitism. His mature theory was a superstition, and the most dangerous kind of superstition, belief in a conspiracy of evil. But whereas originally it was based on the oldest form of conspiracy-theory, anti-Semitism, in the late 1840s and 1850s this was not so much abandoned as extended to embrace a world conspiracy theory of the entire bourgeois class. Marx retained the original superstition that the making of money through trade and finance is essentially a parasitical and anti-social activity, but he now placed it on a basis not of race and religion, but of class. The enlargement does not, of course, improve the validity of the theory. It merely makes it more dangerous, if put into practice, because it expands its scope and multiplies the number of those to be treated as conspirators and so victims. Marx was no longer concerned with specific Jewish witches to be hunted but with generalized human witches. The theory remained irrational but acquired a more sophisticated appearance, making it highly attractive to educated radicals. To reverse Bebel's saying, if anti-Semitism is the socialism of fools, socialism became the anti-Semitism of intellectuals. An intellectual like Lenin, who clearly perceived the irrationality of the Russian anti-Semitic pogrom, and would have been ashamed to conduct one, nevertheless fully accepted its spirit once the target was expanded into the whole capitalist class – and went on to conduct pogroms on an infinitely greater scale, killing hundreds of thousands on the basis not of individual guilt but merely of membership of a condemned group.

Once Marx had generalized his anti-Semitism into his theory of capital, his interest in the Jews was pushed into the background. Occasionally, as on a palimpsest, it reappears in the pages of *Capital*. Thus: 'The capitalist knows that all commodities, however scurvy they may look, or however badly they may smell, are in faith and in truth money, inwardly circumcised Jews.'[101] More important was the general retention of the aggressive emotional tone so characteristic of anti-Semitism. The archetype Jew was replaced by the archetype capitalist, but the caricature features were essentially the same. Take, for instance, Marx's presentation of the capitalist monster himself:

Only in so far as the capitalist is personified capital has he a historical value. . . . Fanatically bent upon the exploitation of value, he relentlessly drives human beings to production for production's sake . . . he shares with the miser the passion for wealth as wealth. But that which in the miser assumes the aspect of mania, is in the capitalist the effect of the social mechanism in which he is only a driving wheel . . . his actions are a mere function of the capital which, through his instrumentality, is endowed with will and consciousness, so that his own private consumption must be regarded by him as a robbery perpetrated upon accumulation.[102]

Could such a weird personification of humanity ever have existed? But then, when had the anti-Semitic archetype Jew actually existed in real life? That Marx still, in his emotions, confused Jew and capitalist is suggested by the footnote he appended to the passage just quoted. He referred to the usurer, terming him 'the old-fashioned but perennially renewed form of the capitalist'. Marx knew that in the minds of most of his readers the usurer was the Jew – as Toussenel put it, the terms usurer and Jew were interchangeable. Most of the footnote consisted of Luther's violent polemic against the usurer already reproduced on page 242. That Marx should quote this brutal exhortation to kill from an anti-Semitic writer, in a work purporting to be scientific, is suggestive both of Marx's own violence and of the emotional irrationality which expressed it, first as anti-Semitism and then as economic theory.

However, Marx's paradoxical combination of Jewishness and anti-Semitism did not prevent his works from appealing to the growing Jewish intelligentsia. Quite the contrary. For many emancipated Jews, especially in eastern Europe, *Capital* became a new kind of Torah. Granted the initial leap of faith in both cases, Marxism had the logical strength of the halakhah and its stress upon abstract interpretation of events was highly congenial to clever Jews whose ancestors had spent a lifetime in talmudic studies or who themselves had started in the *yeshivah* – and then escaped. Throughout the century, the number of Jews of rabbinical type, from scholarly or merchant families, who turned their back on religion, increased steadily. By the end of it, Orthodox Jewry, despite the vast increase in the Jewish population almost everywhere, was becoming conscious of the haemorrhage. Ancient Jewish communities of Bohemia and Moravia, celebrated for their scholarship and spiritual leaders, found they had to import rabbis from more backward parts.

Most of the 'missing rabbis' seemed to have become radicals, and turned on their Judaism and Jewishness with contempt and anger. They turned on their parents' class too, for a high proportion came from wealthy homes. Marx's father had been a lawyer, Lassalle's a silk merchant; Victor Adler, the pioneer Austrian Social Democrat, was the son of a real-estate speculator, Otto Bauer, the Austrian Socialist leader, of a textile magnate, Adolf Braun, the German Socialist leader, of an industrialist, Paul Singer, another leading German socialist, of a clothing manufacturer, Karl Hochberg of a Frankfurt banker. There were many other examples. Their break with the past, with family and community, often combined with self-hatred, promoted among them a spirit of negation and destruction, of iconoclasm, almost at times of nihilism – an urge to overthrow institutions and values of all kinds – which gentile conservatives were beginning to identify, by the end of the nineteenth century, as a peculiarly Jewish social and cultural disease.

There were four principal reasons why Jews, once they began to take part in general politics, moved overwhelmingly first to the liberal and then to the left end of the spectrum. In the first place there was the Biblical tradition of social criticism, what might be termed the Amos Syndrome. From the earliest times there had always been articulate

Jews determined to expose the injustices of society, to voice the bitterness and needs of the poor, and to call on authority to make redress. Then too there was the talmudic tradition of communal provision, which itself had Biblical origins, and which adumbrated modern forms of state collectivism. Jews who became socialists in the nineteenth century and who attacked the unequal distribution of wealth produced by liberal, *laissez-faire* capitalism were expressing in contemporary language Jewish principles which were 3,000 years old and which had become part of the instincts of the people.

But was it not true, as Disraeli claimed, that Jews also had a high regard for authority, hierarchy and traditional order? It was true, but subject to important qualifications. Jews, as we have seen, had never accorded absolute power to any human agency. Rule resided in the Torah and the vicarious authority accorded to man was limited, temporary and recoverable. Judaism could never have evolved, as Latin Christianity did, the theory of the divine right of kings. Jews had the strongest regard for the rule of law, so long as it was ethically based, and they could and did become devoted adherents of constitutionally based systems, as in the United States and Britain. To that extent Disraeli was correct in arguing that Jews were often natural Tories. But they were also natural enemies to authority which was arbitrary and tyrannical, illogical or outmoded. When Marx wrote, 'Thus we find every tyrant backed by a Jew, as is every pope by a Jesuit. In truth, the cravings of oppressors would be hopeless and the practicability of war out of the question, if there were not an army of Jesuits to smother thought and a handful of Jews to ransack pockets,'[103] he was wrong. Rothschild loans to absolute monarchies were geared not to reinforce tyranny but to abate it, especially in securing better treatment for Jews (in which, of course, Marx was not interested). Jewish money power in the nineteenth century, in so far as it had any overall political policy, tended to be irenic and constitutionalist. 'Peace, retrenchment and reform', Gladstone's famous Liberal slogan, was also the axiom of the Rothschilds.

Moreover there was one important respect in which Disraeli misunderstood the impact of the Jews. He tended to see the Jewish archetype as a Sephardi. The Sephardis indeed had a strong regard for ancient historical institutions, and thus conformed to his image of the Jew. But the Ashkenazis, whom he chose to ignore in his argument, were far more restless, innovatory, critical and even subversive. They were also becoming far more numerous.

Here we come to the second force pushing emancipated Jews to the left: demography. In the period 1800–80, roughly Disraeli's lifetime, the Sephardi percentage of Jewry as a whole fell from 20 to 10 per cent. Most of them were concentrated in the Afro-Asian Mediterranean area, where standards of hygiene remained primitive throughout the nineteenth century. In Algiers, for instance, where Maurice Eisenbeth carried out a detailed analysis of the Jewish population, he found it rose from a maximum of 5,000 in the sixteenth century to a peak of 10,000–20,000 in about 1700, falling to 5,000 again by 1818.[104] In Africa and Asia as a whole the number of Jews did rise, 1800–80, but only from 500,000 to 750,000. In Europe, during the same period, the total leapt from two million to seven million. The Jews, and the Ashkenazi in particular, were benefiting from the prime fact of modern times, the demographic revolution, which hit Europe first. But they did better than the European average. They married younger. Marriages between boys of fifteen to eighteen with girls of fourteen to sixteen were quite common. Nearly all Jewish girls married and tended to produce children soon after puberty. They tended to look after their children well, and with the help of communal welfare facilities, Jewish infantile death rates fell more quickly than the European average. Jewish marriages remained more stable. Jews lived longer. A survey of Frankfurt in 1855, for instance, shows Jewish life-spans averaged forty-eight years nine months, non-Jews thirty-six years eleven months.[105] The discrepancy was even more marked in eastern Europe. In European Russia, the Jewish death rate, at 14.2 per 1,000 per year, was even lower than that of the well-to-do Protestant minority, and less than half that of the Orthodox majority (31.8). As a result, during the period of most rapid growth, 1880–1914, the number of Jews increased by an average of 2 per cent a year, well above the European mean, raising the total number of Jews from 7.5 million to over thirteen million.

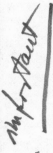

These 'new' Jews were overwhelmingly Ashkenazis, concentrated in big cities. In 1800 it was rare to come across a Jewish city community of more than 10,000 – there were only three or four in the world. By 1880 Warsaw had 125,000 Jews, and there were over 50,000 in Vienna, Budapest, Odessa and Berlin. There were about this number in New York too, and from this time North America drained off a huge proportion of the European Jewish population increase. All the same, their numbers continued to grow. By 1914 there were eight million Jews in the two great empires of east-central Europe, Russia and Austria, nearly all of them in towns and cities. In short, Jewish demography reflected, but in an exaggerated form, both the European population revolution and its urbanization. Just as the teeming ghetto, in its day, force-fed Jewish popular religion, so now the crowded industrial quarters of the new or expanded towns, where traditional Jewish life was struggling to survive, bred an intense secular Jewish radicalism.

The third reason was that the Jewish sense of injustice was never allowed to sleep. Just as, in the sixteenth and seventeenth centuries, Jewish antennae everywhere were ever alert to pick up murmurs of a messiah, so in the nineteenth century an act of injustice to Jews anywhere stirred emotions in the growing Jewish urban centres. There were now hundreds of Jewish newspapers which related these outrages, and virtually all Jews could read. Among the secularized intelligentsia, there was no longer any disposition to attribute the sufferings of the race to sins, ancient or modern. The Damascus blood libel of 1840 was an important milestone in the radicalization of the Jews. The fifteen-year-old Lassalle noted in his diary, 21 May 1840: 'Even the Christians marvel at our sluggish blood, that we do not rise, that we do not rather perish on the battlefield than by torture. . . . Is there a revolution anywhere which could be more just than if the Jews were to rebel, set fire to every quarter of Damascus, blow up the powder magazine and meet death with their persecutors? Cowardly people, you deserve no better fate.'[106] Such events fed a determination among young secularized Jews to combat injustice not just towards Jews but to mankind, and to take advantage of the growing political opportunities to end them for ever. Lassalle went on to create the first major German trade union federation and to found German social democracy. Countless other young Jews took the same path.

There was no lack of stimulus. For instance, on the night of 23–24 June 1858, a six-year-old Jewish boy, Edgardo Mortara, living with his family in Bologna, was seized by the papal police and taken to the House of Catechumens in Rome. A Christian servant testified that five years before, thinking the child was dying, she had baptized him. Under the law of the papal states, the police and the church were within their rights, and the parents had no remedy. There was a world-wide chorus of protest, not merely from Jews but from Christian clerics and statesmen, but Pope Pius IX refused to give way and the boy remained in Catholic hands.[107] This unredressed outrage led directly to the foundation, in 1860, of the French Alliance Israélite Universelle, to 'defend the civil rights and religious freedom of the Jews', as well as other specifically Jewish organizations elsewhere. But, still more, it fed the Jewish secular hatred of absolutism everywhere.

It was in Tsarist Russia, however, that ill-treatment of the Jews was most systematic and embittering. Indeed the Tsarist regime epito-mized for radicals everywhere the most evil and entrenched aspects of autocracy. For Jews, who viewed it with peculiar loathing, it was the fourth, and probably the most important, of the factors driving them leftwards. Hence the Russian treatment of the Jews, horrifying in itself, constitutes one of the important facts of modern world history and must be examined in some detail. It must first be grasped that the Tsarist regime from the very start viewed the Jews with implacable hostility. Whereas other autocracies, in Austria, Prussia, even in Rome, had preserved an ambivalent attitude, protecting, using, exploiting and milking the Jews, as well as persecuting them from time to time, the Russians always treated Jews as unacceptable aliens. Until the partitions of Poland, 1772–95, they had more or less succeeded in keeping Jews out of their territories. The moment their greed for Polish land brought them a large Jewish population, the regime began to refer to it as 'the Jewish problem', to be 'solved', either by assimilation or by expulsion.

What the Russians did was to engage in the first modern exercise in social engineering, treating human beings (in this case the Jews) as earth or concrete, to be shovelled around. Firstly they confined Jews to what was called the Pale of Settlement, which took its final form in 1812, and which consisted of twenty-five western provinces stretching from the Baltic to the Black Sea. Jews could not travel, let alone live, outside the Pale except with special legal authority. Next, a series of statutes, beginning in 1804, determined where the Jews could live inside the Pale and what they could do there. The most damaging rule was that Jews could not live or work in villages, or sell alcohol to peasants. This destroyed the livelihood of a third of the Jewish population, who held village leases or ran village inns (another third were in trade, and most of the rest craftsmen). In theory the object was to push the Jews into 'productive labour' on the land. But there was little or no land available, and the real aim was to drive Jews into accepting baptism, or getting out altogether. In practice it led to Jewish impoverishment and a steady stream of poor Jews into the Pale towns.

The next turn of the screw came in 1827, when Nicholas I, one of the most savage of the autocrats, issued the 'Cantonist Decrees', which conscripted all male Jews from twelve to twenty-five, placing the younger boys in canton-schools at the military depots, where they were liable to be forced into baptism, sometimes by whole units. The government was also anxious to destroy the Jewish schools. The authorities tried repeatedly to force Jewish children into state schools where the languages of instruction were Russian, Polish and German only, the object again being to promote baptism. In 1840 a Committee for the Jews was formed to promote the 'moral education' of what was treated publicly as an undesirable, semi-criminal community. Jewish religious books were censored or destroyed. Only two Jewish presses were permitted, in Vilna and Kiev – and Jews were expelled from the latter town completely three years later. The government was quite cunning at dividing Jewish communities, and setting *maskils* against Orthodox. In 1841, for example, they put the *maskil* Max Lilienthal (1815–82) in charge of the new state Jewish schools, which were in effect anti-Talmud establishments designed, as the Orthodox claimed, to offer their children to 'the Moloch of the Haskalah'. But he found the bitter battle which ensued too much for him and slipped out of the country four years later, to emigrate to America. The government also forbade Jews to wear traditional garments such as the skullcap and kapota. It divided them into 'useful Jews' and 'useless Jews', subjecting the latter group to triple conscription quotas.

Gradually, over the century, an enormous mass of legislation discriminating against Jews, and regulating their activities, accumu-lated. Some of it was never properly enforced. Much of it was frustrated by bribery. Rich parents could buy Jewish children to take the place of their own in state schools or in the army. They could pay to buy legal certificates entitling them to travel, to live in cities, to engage in forbidden occupations. The attempt to 'solve' the Jewish problem created, or rather immensely aggravated, another one: corruption of the Tsarist bureaucracy, which became incorrigible and rotted the heart of the state.[108] Moreover, government policy was never con-sistent for long. It oscillated between liberalism and repression. In 1856 the new Tsar, Alexander II, introduced a liberal phase, granting certain rights to Jews if they were long-service soldiers, university graduates or 'useful' merchants. That phase ended with the Polish revolt of 1863 and his attempted assassination. There was another liberal phase in the 1870s, again brought to an end by an attempt on his life – this time a successful one. Thereafter the position of Jews in Russia deteriorated sharply.

In the last half-century of imperial Russia, the official Jewish regulations formed an enormous monument to human cruelty, stupidity and futility. *Gimpelson's Statutes Concerning the Jews (1914–15)*, the last annotated collection, ran to nearly 1,000 pages.[109] A summary of the position, compiled by the English historian Lucien Wolf, established the following facts.[110] The Jews formed one-24th of the Russian population. Some 95 per cent of them were confined to the Pale, one-23rd part of the empire, and of these the vast majority were trapped in the Pale towns and *shtetls*, forming one-2,000th part of the territory. A Jew's passport stated he was a Jew and where he might reside. Even in the Pale, most areas were banned to Jews, but 'legal' parts were constantly being eroded. Jews were banned from Sebastopol and Kiev. The Don territory was suddenly taken out of the Pale, then the Caucasian Kuban and Terek; then the Yalta health resort, a consumptive Jewish student being expelled in the middle of his treatment when the decree took effect. Jews wishing to use the Caucasian mineral springs had to pass an exam conducted by an army officer. Some resorts were 'open' but had quotas: thus only twenty Jewish families were allowed into Darnitza in any one season. Other Pale resorts were banned to Jews under any circumstances.

There were privileged categories of Jews permitted to travel or even reside outside the Pale – discharged soldiers, graduates, 'useful merchants' and 'mechanics, distillers, brewers and artisans while pursuing their calling'. But they needed special papers, which were very difficult to obtain and had to be renewed constantly. All these categories tended to be whittled down, especially after 1881. Thus, ex-soldiers were suddenly limited to those serving before 1874. Merchants were abruptly forbidden to bring clerks or servants with them. Struck from the category of privileged artisans were tobacco-workers, piano-tuners, butchers, goloshes-menders, bricklayers, carpenters, plasterers and gardeners. There were particularly severe restrictions on women workers, except for prostitutes. (A prostitute who ceased to ply for hire was quickly spotted by the police and sent back to the ghetto.)[111] A Jewish midwife privileged to practise outside the Pale could not have her children with her unless her husband was also a 'privileged person'.

Students who took their degrees abroad, because of anti-Jewish quota restrictions at Russian universities, were not entitled to privileged status. In the Caucasus, so-called 'Mountain Jews', who claimed their forefathers were deported there by Nebuchadnezzar in 597 BC, had rights of residence; on the other hand, they could not go anywhere else. Jews privileged to live outside the Pale were not allowed to have even a son or a daughter sleep in their houses, unless they too were privileged. In fact privileged Jews faced an additional set of restrictions outside the Pale, and if they broke the rules were fined on the first offence, banished on the second. The law on all these points was exceptionally complex and subject to endless changes by votes of the senate, ministry circulars, rulings by the local authorities or arbitrary decisions by officials high and low.

Enforcing these constantly changing codes was a nightmare for all concerned except the corrupt policeman or bureaucrat. Visitors from the West were shocked to see troops of frightened Jews being driven through the streets by police posses in the early hours of the morning, the result of *oblavas* or night raids. The police were entitled to break into a house during the night using any force necessary and demand documentary proof of residence rights of everyone, irrespective of age or sex. Anyone unable to produce it instantly was taken to the police station. Jews were constantly humiliated in front of gentile neighbours, thus keeping alive the view that they were different, sub-human, and perpetuating the pogrom instinct. Even in first-class hotels, police stopped and questioned people on suspicion of 'Jewish physiognomy'. They were quite capable of banning distinguished foreigners, Oscar Straus, the American ambassador to Constantinople, being one victim. Jewish pianists were allowed to compete for the International Rubinstein Prize in St Petersburg, but only on condition that they did not spend the night in the city.

Occasionally, the police organized massive 'Jew Hunts'. In Baku, police surrounded the stock exchange, arrested every Jew and took them to the police station where each was forced to prove his right of residence. In Smolensky district, at Pochinok, mounted police in 1909 surrounded the entire town but flushed out only ten 'illegals'; they had a big hunt through the woods and found seventy-four more.[112] The Law of Settlement corrupted the entire police force, which milked the Jews. When business was slack, police chiefs would encourage Christians to draw up petitions calling for expulsions on the grounds that Jews were 'causing local discontent'. Then poor Jews would be thrown out and rich ones 'tapped'. The poor, returning to the Pale, became a growing social problem. In Odessa, for instance, over 30 per cent were dependent on Jewish charities.

The residence laws, however, were only the beginning of the Jews' troubles. The government demanded fixed quotas of Jewish conscripts from the local communities. But these took no account of emigration. Jews should have provided no more than 4.13 per cent of recruits. The government demanded 6.2 per cent. Some 5.7 per cent were actually produced, and this led to official complaints about the 'Jewish deficit' – provoking, in turn, anti-Semitic clamour that Jews evaded conscription. In fact they furnished between 20 and 35 per cent more than their fair share.[113] From 1886 families were held legally responsible for non-service of conscripts and fined heavily; there was no possibility of successful evasion without massive bribes. But if the state forced Jews to soldier, it circumscribed narrowly how they did it. Jews were banned from the guards, the navy, the frontier or quarantine service, the gendarmerie, the commissariat and clerical grades. In 1887 they were banned from all military schools and army examinations, so effectively excluded from becoming officers. In 1888 they were banned from army dispensaries, in 1889 from military bands.

All Jews whatever were banned from any kind of state service in Moscow and St Petersburg. In theory, a Jew holding an MA or doctorate was eligible for certain posts elsewhere but, reported Wolf, 'without undergoing the rite of baptism it is well nigh impossible for a Jew to fulfil all the conditions preliminary to employment by the state'.[114] There was not a single Jewish teacher in the state system. There was no Jewish university professor and only a handful of lecturers. There were no Jews in the Justice Department, no examining magistrates, only one judge (appointed during the last 'liberal' period). Ministry circulars forbade the appointment of Jews as police inspectors: they were to be used only as spies or informers. Jews formed the majority of the urban population in six main regions and in many towns they were in a big majority, but they were not allowed to vote in municipal elections or stand for office; in the Pale government could 'appoint' them, up to one-tenth of the total. Jews were excluded from juries, from the boards of asylums or orphanages. From 1880 they were forbidden to practise as notaries, and from 1890 as barristers and solicitors, without special permission – Wolf reported none had been given for fifteen years. They were forbidden to buy, rent or manage land beyond the immediate precincts of the Pale towns and *shtetls*. They could not even buy land for cemeteries. As with military service, Jews were accused of being unwilling to work the land, but in practice the regulations made this impossible, and wrecked the few Jewish agricultural colonies which had been established. Moreover, the fear that Jews would evade property laws by third-party transactions led to a mass of additional regulations covering partnerships and joint-stock companies. Hence many companies excluded Jews even as shareholders, and the fact was marked on share-certificates. Jews were excluded by law from the mining industries, and a further set of regulations attempted to keep them from dealing in gold, oil, coal and other minerals.

Next to the residence qualifications the anti-Semitic laws most hated by Jews governed education. Jews were excluded completely from such top training institutions as the St Petersburg Institute of Civil Engineers, the Army Medical College, the St Petersburg Electrical Institute, the Moscow Agricultural College, the St Petersburg Theatrical School, the Kharkov Veterinary Institute and the various colleges of mines. Their attendance at secondary and high schools was governed by the quota system or *numerus clausus*. They could occupy up to 10 per cent of such places in the Pale, only 5 per cent outside and only 3 per cent in Moscow and St Petersburg. The 25,000 *chedarim* schools, with 300,000 pupils, were forbidden to teach Russian, to stop children getting a secondary education. As a result of these measures, the number of Jews in the higher schools fell dramatically, and parents fought desperately to get their children in, often bribing the gentile headmasters, who had a fixed scale of charges.

The anti-Jewish codes of Tsarist Russia thus succeeded, chiefly, in corrupting every element in the state service. They were an extraordinary amalgamation of past and future – they looked back to the medieval ghetto and forward to the Soviet slave-state. What they did not do was 'solve' the Jewish problem. Indeed, by radicalizing the Jews, they ended, it could be said, in solving the Tsarist problem. Despite all the restrictions, some Jews continued to prosper. Discrimination was purely religious and by getting themselves baptized Jews could evade it completely, at any rate in theory. In Russian music, for instance, Anton Rubinstein (1829–94) and his brother Nikolay (1835–81), whose parents had converted, ran the Petersburg and Moscow Conservatoires for many years and dominated the musical scene during the great age of the Russian symphony and opera. Even non-Christian Jews contrived to flourish in a rapidly expanding economy, being strongly represented in brewing, tobacco, leather, textiles, grain, banks, shipping, railways and – despite the bans – oil and mining.[115]

Hence the government code did nothing to reduce anti-Semitism. Quite the contrary. While baptized and smart Jews did well, the code impoverished or criminalized others, so ethnic Russians ended by both envying and despising the race, accusing Jews of being, at one and the same time, perfumed and filthy, profiteers and beggars, greedy and starving, unscrupulous and stupid, useless and too 'useful' by half. Russian anti-Semitism had all kinds of ingredients. The Tsarist regime persecuted other minorities besides the Jews but it was skilful at setting them off one against another, and in particular in inciting Poles, Letts, Ukrainians and Cossacks to go for the Jews. Indeed, Russia was the only country in Europe, at this time, where anti-Semitism was the official policy of the government. It took innumerable forms, from organizing pogroms to forging and publishing the *Protocols of the Elders of Zion*.

The object of the government was to reduce the Jewish population as quickly and as drastically as possible. A glimpse of the mentality of the Tsarist regime can be found in the diaries of Theodor Herzl, who interviewed several ministers in St Petersburg in 1903 to solicit help

Good.

for his Zionist programme. The Finance Minister, Count Serge Witte, by Tsarist standards a liberal, told him:

One has to admit that the Jews provide enough reasons for hostility. There is a characteristic arrogance about them. Most Jews however are poor, and because they are poor they are filthy and make a repulsive impression. They also engage in all sorts of ugly pursuits, like pimping and usury. So you see it is hard for friends of the Jews to come to their defence. And yet I am a friend of the Jews.

(Herzl commented: 'If so, we certainly do not need enemies.') Witte complained of the large number of Jews in the revolutionary movement. Herzl: 'To what circumstances do you attribute this?' Witte: 'I believe it is the fault of our government. The Jews are too oppressed. I used to say to the late Tsar, Alexander III, "Majesty, if it were possible to drown the six or seven million Jews in the Black Sea, I would be absolutely in favour of that. But if it is not possible, one must let them live." What, then, do you want from the Russian government?' Herzl: 'Certain encouragements.' Witte: 'But the Jews *are* given encouragements – to emigrate. Kicks in the behind, for example.'[116]

The first modern Russian pogrom came in 1871 in Odessa. It was instigated chiefly by Greek merchants. There was an ethnic element in most of the disturbances of the 1870s, Slav nationalists being particularly violent in their anti-Semitism. But after the murder of Alexander II in 1881, the state took over, and the 'kicks in the behind' followed in rapid succession. The major pogroms which began on 29 April 1881 were incited, condoned or organized by the Minister of the Interior, Ignatiev, an enthusiastic Slavophile. They spread over one hundred centres, lasted nearly a year, and in some cases involved huge mobs. Not only the government but the police and innumerable ethnic groups were involved. The far left joined in. The revolutionary Narodnaya Volya party incited the Ukrainians to kill the Jews in August 1881 under the slogan: 'Rise against the Tsar of the *pans* [nobles] and the *zhids* [Jews].'[117] Great liberal writers like Turgenev and Tolstoi remained silent. The pogroms were followed by a mass of anti-Semitic legislation, known as the May Laws. Indeed, the pogroms were used to justify the legislation, the argument running: mob attacks on the Jews, while deplorable in themselves, indicate the extent of popular indignation against this anti-social minority; therefore its activities must be restricted. Of course the government inspired and permitted the mob action in the first place, and the whole aim of the regime was to bolster its crumbling popularity by attacking an easy target. The Nazis were to use exactly the same technique of violence-led legislation. Hence the thirty years 1881–1911 were a long calendar of anti-Jewish actions: 1882, May Laws; 1886–9, restrictions of Jewish entry to the professions and reduction of the Pale area; 1891, over 10,000 Jews expelled from Moscow; 1893–5, huge expulsions from non-Pale areas; 1894–6, introduction of the spirits monopoly, an economic catastrophe for the Jews; from 1903, a series of vicious pogroms, in which Jews were not merely robbed but killed. At Kishinev in 1905 fifty Jews were murdered and 500 injured. In Odessa, a four-day pogrom in 1905 killed more than 400 Jews. In Bialystok, the police and the army joined in the pogroms of 1906. From 1908 to 1911 there were more large-scale expulsions.

Hence from 1881, this vicious, mounting and cumulatively over-whelming pressure on Russian Jewry produced the inevitable con-sequence – a panic flight of Jews from Russia westwards. Thus 1881 was the most important year in Jewish history since 1648, indeed since the expulsion of the Jews from Spain in 1492. Its consequences were so wide, and fundamental, that it must be judged a key year in world history too. The first big rush to get out came in 1881–2. Thereafter Jews left at an average of 50,000–60,000 a year. With the Moscow expulsions, 110,000 Russian Jews left in 1891 and 137,000 in 1892. In the pogrom year 1905–6, over 200,000 Jews left. The exodus was by no means confined to Russia. Between 1881 and 1914 more than 350,000 Jews left Austrian Galicia. More Jews emigrated from Rumania, where they were also under pressure. The net result was not to reduce the Jewish population of eastern Europe. In 1914 there were still five and a half million Jews in Russia and two and a half million in the Austrian empire. What the movement did was to take the natural population increase, some two and a half million, and transfer it elsewhere. Therein lay momentous effects, both for the Jews and for the world. We must now examine them in turn.

Of these emigrants, more than two million went to the United States alone, and the most obvious and visible consequence, therefore, was the creation of a mass American urban Jewry. This was a completely new phenomenon, which in time changed the whole balance of Jewish power and influence in the world, and it came quite suddenly. The original Jewish settlement in America was small and slow to expand. As late as 1820 there were only about 4,000 Jews in the United States, and only seven of the original thirteen states recognized them politically. The slow growth of the community is hard to understand. As we have seen, there were few legal barriers to Jewish advancement. North Carolina denied public office to all non-Protestants, and in

1809 a Jew, Jacob Henry, made a speech which became famous, asserting his inalienable right to sit in the state's House of Commons – the House took his part. Maryland had a ban on non-Christians holding office or practising law. From 1797, another Jew, Solomon Etting, campaigned persistently to have this barrier removed. He finally succeeded in 1826 and was immediately elected to the Baltimore City Council. There was some trouble over the Sabbath–Sunday conflict. In 1816 Abraham Wolf was convicted in Pennsylvania for 'having done and performed worldly employment on the Lord's Day, commonly called Sunday'; he appealed and lost. But all this seemed of minor importance compared with the fundamental issues and horrific injustices which wracked the Jews in the Old World. Dedicating a new synagogue in Savannah, Georgia, in 1820, the physician Jacob de la Motta preached a grateful sermon: 'On what spot in this habitable Globe does an Israelite enjoy more blessings, more privileges, or is more elevated in the sphere of preferment, and most conspicuously dignified in respectable stations? . . . Have we not ample cause to exult?'[118]

There were 6,000 Jews in America when Etting won in 1826; 15,000 at the time of the Damascus affair in 1840; 150,000 on the eve of the Civil War. Old settlements like Newport or Norfolk did not grow. Jewish arrivals, overwhelmingly German-speaking, from Bavaria, north Germany and German–Jewish parts of Poland, Bohemia and Hungary, were poor, orderly, hard-working; many began as pedlars, then graduated to keeping shops or founding small businesses. They settled in Albany, Syracuse, Buffalo and Rochester in New York State; in Chicago and Detroit, Cleveland and Milwaukee. For a time Cincinnati was the second largest Jewish centre to New York. St Louis, Minneapolis, Louisville and New Orleans also became Jewish centres. About 10,000 Jews went to California in the 1840s gold rushes. By the Civil War, New York had a Jewish community of 40,000 with Philadelphia next in size. A sure sign of the security Jews enjoyed in America was that their communities there positively encouraged more Jews to join them. Emigrants were spurred by enthusiastic letters from relatives, word-of-mouth tales, success-stories printed by Jews in local German papers. Thus, *Das Füllhorn* of Bamberg wrote in 1836:

A Jewish journey-man baker from Bavaria who was ready and willing to work, who travelled through Germany and the neighbouring countries for ten years and obtained work only rarely, so that he could not even earn his bread in this way, migrated to North America last summer. Now he has written home to his parents that he has found a place as a journey-man in the house of a baker at Petersburg immediately after his arrival and that he receives 40 florins wages a month in addition to free board, laundry and room. Blessed land of freedom and prosperity![119]

In America Jews found they could conform to the pattern of the new life without difficulty. Like American Protestants, they became congregational, setting up multitudes of synagogues to suit their varying religious tastes. They became self-conscious during the Damascus protest, which brought them together as a national body for the first time. But mostly they continued to go their own ways. Like other ethnic or religious groups, they founded a few Utopian or agricultural colonies. Like other groups they produced pioneers and eccentrics. A US shipmaster complained to Washington about the vice-consul in St Thomas's, ending: 'PS. This N. Levy is a Jew and lives with a Black Woman and frequently Walks the Streets with her arm in arm to the mortification of all the Americans who are under the painful necessity of witnessing the Same'; but Consul Levy was not removed.[120]

A more interesting case was that of Mordecai Noah, the first Jew to have diplomatic status, whom James Monroe removed as US Consul in Tunis in 1815 on the grounds that 'the Religion which you profess [is] an obstacle to the exercise of your consular functions'. Noah did not take this lying down and wrote a pamphlet about it. He was the first American Jew to emerge as a larger-than-life figure. A hundred years later he would certainly have become a movie mogul. As it was he was born in Philadelphia in 1785, son of a bankrupt pedlar. He was in turn a gilder, carver, clerk in the US Treasury, politician, editor of the Charleston *City Gazette*, then after his spell in Tunis (where he was accused of misappropriating funds), editor of the New York *National Advocate*, High Sheriff of New York and in 1824 grand sachem of Tammany Hall.

A year later he announced an ambitious scheme to found 'a City of Refuge for the Jews' on an island in the Niagara River opposite Buffalo. To support the project he wrote to the Rothschilds and other Jewish bankers, to rabbis and chief rabbis throughout the world, and proposed to levy 'a capitation tax of three shekels in silver, *per annum*, or one Spanish dollar' on each Jew throughout the world, 'to be collected by the treasurers of the different congregations'. In a public proclamation he announced that the new settlement, 'a Commercial City', would provide Jews from all over the world with 'that peace, comfort and happiness which have been denied them through the intolerance and misgovernment of former ages'. Among these he included 'The Karaite and Samaritan Jews, together with the black Jews of

India and Africa, and likewise those in Cochin, China and the sect on the coast of Malabar'; and he added: 'The Indians of the American continent . . . being in all probability the descendants of the Lost Tribes of Israel, which were carried captive by the King of Assyria, means will be adopted to make them sensible of their condition and finally reunite them with their brethren, the chosen people.' Noah wore a 'fine silk gown', with a gold chain round his neck, and described himself as 'citizen of the United States, late Consul of the said State to the City and Kingdom of Tunis, High Sheriff of New York, Counsellor at Law and, by the Grace of God, Governor and Judge of Israel'. He was mocked by rival newspaper editors and the Jewish press in Europe, and nothing much came of his plan. But he went on to create the Native American Party (precursor of the Know Nothings), organize Jewish protest against the Damascus atrocities, and support the Texas revolt of 1836, and ended a judge.[121]

It was part of the Americanness of the Jewish settlers that they were divided on every issue. Noah, for instance, was a Northern anti-abolitionist. In the South, American Jews were Southerners. They owned slaves. Jacob Jacobs, a Charleston auctioneer, directed in his will: 'Item, I give and devise unto my said dearly beloved Wife Katey Jacobs during her widowhood and no longer all those my Negro and other slaves named Toby, Scipio, Jack, Jenny with her three children Peter, John and Eve, and Flora with her two children Rachel and Lucy and all the other slaves that I may be possessed of, at the time of my death.' A Southern Jew, insulted in his religion and honour, reacted in Southern fashion. In 1832, Philip Minis, of a leading Jewish family in Savannah, was abused in Luddington's Bar Room by a member of the Georgia legislature, James J. Stark, who told him he was 'a damned Jew', a 'damned Israelite' and that 'he ought to be pissed upon'. There were negotiations over an apology, and then over a duel, and in the end Minis shot Stark dead in the public bar of the City Hotel, when Stark drew his pistol. He was tried for manslaughter but acquitted – to the satisfaction of Southern duellists.[122]

Given the identification of American Jews with the particular part of the US landscape they inhabited, it is not surprising that during the Civil War they split with the nation, according to their states. Some 7,000 Jews served the North, 3,000 the South. When they did react communally, and that rarely happened, it was in response to specific challenges to their rights. There was a famous instance during the War, on 17 December 1862, when General Ulysses S. Grant, in the Tennessee, issued an order reading: 'The Jews as a class, violating every regulation of trade established by the Treasury Department, and

also Departmental orders, are hereby expelled from the Department.'
The hostile response was immediate and overwhelming, and not only
from Jews; on Lincoln's instructions Grant revoked the order, 6
January 1863.

American Jewry during these years took its tone from the German–
Jewish enlightenment. It was liberal, optimistic, sober, rational,
patriotic, unostentatious and highly respectable. Jewish immigrants
tended to speak English with German accents but their children went
to public schools (and Jewish schools on Sunday) and merged wholly
into local society. From the 1840s onward Reform Judaism spread
rapidly in America, under the impulse of such progressive rabbis as
David Einhorn, Samuel Hirsch, Isaac Mayer Wise and Samuel Adler.
Leading American Jews were not interested in the Messiah or Zion;
the road to Redemption, as they saw it, was to spread the message of
ethical monotheism throughout the world. That accorded exactly
with the general tone of American religion. There was a more
conservative trend, especially in Philadelphia, which became perhaps
the leading centre of the Jewish religion. There, Rabbi Isaac Leeser
(1806–68), from Westphalia, a man of prodigious energy, produced
the first Jewish translation of the Bible into English, completed English
translations of the Ashkenazi and Sephardi prayer-books, founded the
first successful Jewish newspaper, *The Occident* (1843), and later the
first Jewish Publication Society in America, and produced a mass of
American Jewish textbooks for the schools.[123] But during the
'German' phase of American Jewry, Reform Judaism became
dominant.

Reform was the mode of Judaism most likely to appeal to the highly
successful businessmen who were now beginning to emerge as major
figures on the American scene. Such were the banker Joseph Seligman
(1820–80), to whom President Grant offered the Treasury, and Jacob
Henry Schiff (1847–1920), who became head of Kuhn, Loeb & Co. in
1885. As with the Thirty Years War and the Napoleonic Wars, the
Civil War brought out the organizational and financial skills of many
Jewish bankers, contractors and clothing-suppliers, and from the
1860s onwards the Jews were a power in American business,
especially in New York. Their massive philanthropy provided Judaism
with a well-endowed institutional framework, and inevitably this had
a strong liberal orientation. The Union of American Hebrew Congregations was established in 1873, Hebrew Union College two years
later, the Central Conference of American Rabbis in 1889. The
Pittsburg Platform (1885), drawn up by Rabbi Kaufmann Kohler,
which rejected all Torah laws 'such as are not adapted to the views and

habits of modern civilization', became the standard creed of Reform
Judaism until 1937. It rejected the old rules on diet, purity and dress,
asserted that Jews were 'no longer a nation, but a religious community', denied the resurrection, heaven and hell, dismissed a return
to Zion, and presented messianism as the struggle for truth, justice and
righteousness in modern society – in which it would participate
alongside other religions and people of goodwill generally.[124]

Hence at the time of the great emigration, American Jewry seemed
fated to remain yet another strand of the worthy fabric of New World
religiosity, wearing and fading imperceptibly into the whole. The
panic set in motion by the 1881 disaster changed that prospect
irrevocably. In the decade 1881–92, Jews were arriving in the US at the
rate of 19,000 a year; in the decade 1892–1903, the average jumped to
37,000 a year; and in the twelve years 1903–14 it averaged 76,000.
These two million refugee Jews had very little in common with the
quarter-million genteel, Reformist, well-heeled, American-minded
and increasingly apprehensive established Jews who greeted them.
They were overwhelmingly Yiddish-speaking, Orthodox or hasidic,
wild-eyed and frightened, superstitious and desperately poor. For the
first time, American Jewry began to fear new arrivals, especially in
such staggering numbers. They rightly judged that an anti-Semitic
reaction was inevitable.

Hitherto, mainstream Protestant America, like England before it,
had been papist-baiting rather than Jew-baiting. But since the Civil
War, when the Jews had been perceived as war-profiteers, anti-
Semitism had become noticeable. In 1876, a hotel on the New Jersey
coast announced publicly in the newspapers that it would not admit
Jews. The next year Joseph Seligman himself was refused admission to
the leading hotel in the resort of Saratoga. Jewish businessmen then
bought several Saratoga hotels, and as a result, throughout the New
York area, resort hotels split into those which would, and those which
would not, accommodate Jews. The habit spread to masonic lodges
and country clubs, and some schools and colleges began to adopt a
numerus clausus, on Russian lines.

The mass arrival of poor Ashkenazi Jews in New York naturally
force-fed the growth of this new anti-Semitic sub-culture. But,
infinitely more important, the immigrants gave the kiss of life to
American Jewry. They transformed it from an exercise in gentility,
doomed to mortify, into a vibrant creature of an entirely new kind – a
free people, cradled in a tolerant republic, but shouting their faith and
their nature from the rooftops of a city they turned into the greatest
Jewish metropolis in the world. Here was a true City of Refuge, and

more than that – the nucleus of a power which in time would exert itself effectively on behalf of Jews throughout the world.

The wealthy Jews of New York did not yet grasp the opportunities the flight from Europe would create. If, like so many events in Jewish history – like the massacres of 1648, for example – it could eventually be interpreted as part of a providential plan, bringing triumph from tragedy, that was not how they saw it at the time. To do them justice, they stifled their apprehensions and did all in their power to welcome and absorb the eastern masses. But some were more perceptive. Among those who worked for the Jewish immigrant relief agency set up on Ward Island was the young poetess Emma Lazarus (1849–87). Her talent had been detected and cultivated by Emerson. She burned with romantic zeal for Jewish culture, ancient and modern. She translated the great medieval poet Judah Halevi. She translated Heine. She saluted Longfellow's moving poem on Newport Cemetery but deplored its dismissive ending: 'And the dead nations never rise again.' It was not true! The Jews would rise again! She came of an old and wealthy Sephardi family, but she saw in the poor Ashkenazi Jews pushing their way through US immigration with their bundles the elements of a future army which would rebuild Jerusalem in America, or in Israel – perhaps in both. She defended them against anti-Semitic smears in the magazine *New Century* (1882). She grasped, perhaps better than anyone else in America at that time, the true significance of the American idea and the American reality to the persecuted poor of Europe. When the Statue of Liberty was raised at the entrance to New York harbour, her sonnet, 'The New Colossus', gave Liberty an immortal voice:

> Give me your tired, your poor,
> Your huddled masses yearning to breathe free,
> The wretched refuse of your teeming shore.
> Send these, the homeless, tempest-toss't to me.
> I lift my lamp beside the golden door.

In particular, Emma Lazarus understood the meaning of America for world Jewry. Would not in time the huddled masses stand upright, grow strong and stretch a powerful hand from the New World back to the Old? Her poem, 'The Banner of a Jew', is Zionist. Her 'An Epistle to the Hebrews' (1882–3) foresees a revival of Jewish civilization through mutual action from America and the Holy Land. In the wretched refuse of Ashkenazi Jewry accumulating in the New York slums she saw not only life but hope.[125]

There was certainly life, in daunting abundance. When the new

arrivals flooded into New York, the fashionable German-type synagogues moved uptown on Manhattan. The refugees crowded into the
Lower East Side, into one and a half square miles bounded by the
Bowery, Third Avenue, Catherine Street, 14th Street and the East
River. Here, by 1910, 540,000 Jews were crammed into what were
called Dumbbell Tenements, their shape determined by a 1879
municipal regulation which required airshafts. They were five to eight
storeys high, 25 feet wide, 100 feet deep, each floor with fourteen
rooms, only one of which got any light. The heart of New York Jewry
was the ultra-dense Tenth Ward, where 74,401 people lived in 1,196
tenements spread over forty-six blocks (1893). This meant a density of
701.9 people an acre. Here too was the source of the 'needle trades', in
which most of the immigrants were employed, cutting and sewing
ready-made clothes, working a seventy-hour week, twelve to a tiny
room. Already by 1888 234 out of 241 New York clothing firms were
Jewish; by 1913 it was New York's biggest industry, 16,552 factories,
nearly all Jewish, employing 312,245 people.

Was this sweated labour? It was. It was also the great engine of
upward mobility. The refugees arrived frightened and submissive. A
Yiddish newspaper noted (1884): 'In the philanthropic institutions of
our aristocratic German Jews you see beautiful offices, desks, all
decorated, but strict and severe faces. Every poor man is questioned
like a criminal, is looked down upon; every unfortunate suffers self-
degradation and shivers like a leaf, just as if he was standing before a
Russian official.'[126] Twenty years later, the submissive spirit had
gone. An entire Jewish-led labour movement had been created and
established its power through four dramatic strikes. By their needles,
too, the eastern Jews pushed their way into independence and respect.
The average stay of Jewish immigrants in the Lower East Side was
only fifteen years. Then they moved on, first to Harlem (once a
wealthy German–Jewish quarter), then to the Bronx and Washington
Heights, then to Coney Island, Flatbush, Boro Park and the Eastern
Parkway. Their children went to colleges and universities; vast
numbers became doctors and lawyers. Others became small businessmen; then big businessmen. Across America, one-time Jewish pedlars
had created mail-order firms, epitomized by Julius Rosenwald's Sears,
Roebuck. In New York, Jews moved from small stores and workshops
to vast department stores. The family of Benjamin Bloomingdale from
Bavaria, who opened a dry-goods store in 1872, had 1,000 employees in
their East Side shop by 1888. The Altman Brothers had 1,600 in their
store. Isidor and Nathan Straus took over R. H. Macy. Other family
groups created Gimbels, Sterns and, in Brooklyn, Abraham & Straus.

By the 1900s, with a million Yiddish-speakers, New York had the world's largest Yiddish press, selling 600,000 copies daily, and with four major titles: *Warheit* (radical and nationalist), *Jewish Morning Journal* (Orthodox and conservative), *Forward* (socialist), *Tageblat* (Orthodox and Zionist). But Jews soon dominated the New York printed word in English too. Arthur Hays Sulzberger and Arthur Ochs ran the *New York Times*, Dorothy Schiff and J. David Stern the *New York Post*; and in time great Jewish publishing houses emerged – Horace Liveright created Liveright & Boni, George Oppenheim and Harold Guinzburg created Viking Press, Richard Leo Simon and Lincoln Schuster made Simon & Schuster, Bennett Cerf developed Random House and Alfred Knopf founded Alfred A. Knopf. By this time Manhattan and Brooklyn each had Jewish settlements of over 600,000. In the Bronx Jews were 38 per cent of the total population; in New York as a whole Jews made up 29 per cent, by far the largest ethnic group. With 1,640,000 Jews (1920), New York was easily the biggest Jewish (and Yiddish) city on earth. In 1880, American Jewry was just over a quarter of a million out of a nation of fifty million; forty years later, in a nation of 115 million, it had jumped to 4.5 million, an eighteen-fold increase.

There was no possibility of this immense Jewry simply merging into its American background. It was the epitome and summation of all Jewry and contained in its ranks some of the most passionate exponents of Judaism in its most rigorous form. In 1880 some 90 per cent of America's 200-plus synagogues were Reform institutions. But their dominance was untenable as the new arrivals made their voice and power heard. In 1883 there was a notorious scene at the first graduation dinner at the Hebrew Union College, the main, Reform-controlled rabbinical seminary in the US. Shrimp and other non-kosher food was served. There was uproar, and many distinguished rabbis walked out in outrage and disgust. Thereafter a rapid realignment of American Jewry took place. In 1886 the Conservatives founded their own Jewish Theological Seminary. The Orthodox also formed an institutional framework. Even by 1890, 316 out of 533 US congregations were Orthodox. In time, a threefold structure emerged, with the Conservatives in the lead, the Orthodox second and Reform a mere third. By 1910 the spread of varieties of American Judaism was enormous. The wealthier Reform synagogues had preachers in Anglican-style robes, English services, mixed seating, choirs and organs. Rabbi Judah Magnes, of the fashionable Temple Emanu-El, proudly told his New York congregation that year: 'A prominent Christian lawyer of another city has told me that he entered this building at the beginning of a service on Sunday morning and did not discover that he was in a synagogue until a chance remark of the preacher betrayed it.'[127] But within five miles it was possible to find Jewish congregations where the Maharal of Prague, the Ba'al Shem Tov or the Vilna Gaon would, each in turn, have felt equally at home. By that time too, American Jewry represented every strand of secular Judaism. It was not yet in a position to point overwhelmingly in a particular direction, let alone provide leadership for world Jewry. But it was becoming organized: in 1906 the American Jewish Committee was established. It was building up numerical, financial, economic and above all political strength, to constitute a huge supportive force once Jews throughout the world reached a majority consensus on their future. All this was the direct consequence of the 1881 tragedy.

But there were other consequences. It was as though history was slowly solving a great jigsaw puzzle, slipping the pieces into their place one after another. The American mass Jewry was one piece. The next piece was the Zionist idea. The events of 1881 pushed that forward too. Before the Russian pogroms, the great majority of Jews saw their future as assimilation in one form or another. After them, some Jews began to look for possible alternatives. The axis of Jewish speculation shifted. It became less optimistic and assured, more agitated – and therefore more imaginative and creative. The Russian horrors made Jews think: was it not possible to bring into existence an ideal community where Jews were not merely safe, not just suffered, or even tolerated, but welcomed, at home: a place where they, and not others, were masters? Of course Zionism was not new. It was as old as the Babylonian exile. Had not the psalmist sung: 'By the rivers of Babylon, there we sat down, yea, we wept, when we remembered Zion'?[128] For more than a millennium and a half, every Jewish generation, in every Jewish community, had contained one or two who dreamed of Zion. Some had fulfilled the dream personally by going there: to Tiberias, to Safed, to Zion itself. Others had thought to found little congregations or colonies. All of these, however, had been religious Zionists. In one way or another they hoped to precipitate the messianic action. That was the idea of the German rabbi Zevi Hirsch Kalischer (1795–1874) who, in 1836, asked the Frankfurt Rothschilds for funds to buy Erez Israel – or at least Jerusalem itself – from Mohammed Ali, in order to start the process of ingathering. In 1840, after Sir Moses Montefiore and Adolphe Crémieux had succeeded in rescuing the Damascus community, Rabbi Judah Alkalai (1798–1878), of Semlin near Belgrade, conceived the notion that this specific operation could serve as a model for a more general coming together of world Jewry as a nation-force, with modernized Hebrew as its language, and Palestine as a future kingdom for the Messiah he almost hourly expected. He propagated this plan in numerous pamphlets and settled in Erez Israel himself, to display his sincerity.

From the 1840s there were secularizers who dreamed of Zion too. Moses Hess (1812–75) went from Hegelianism to socialism, like Marx, but he soon recoiled from the (to him) soulless internationalism of the collective whether in the theoretic version of Marx or the practical efforts of Lassalle in Germany. Like many Jews he began to return to his roots in middle age, but his recovery of Judaism took the form of nationalism rather than religion. The nation-state, he began to see, was the natural unit of historical development. Hence enlightened Jews who went all out for complete assimilation were betraying their own natures. In 1859 he was exhilarated by the way in which Italy, another ancient nation long fragmented, achieved its national identity again. Why could not Jewry stage its own *risorgimento*? In his great book *Rome and Jerusalem* Hess put the case for the Jewish nation-state.[129] It would avoid, on the one hand, the excesses of the *maskils* who wanted to assimilate themselves out of existence and, on the other, the Orthodox who really wished to ignore the world altogether. It would enable the Jews, by the state they created – repudiating both the superstitions of Christianity and the orientalism of Islam – to realize the Jewish idea in practice and so be a political light to the gentiles. At the same time it would allow them to achieve their own redemption not by Marx's negative proposal to destroy their traditional economic functions, but by the positive act of creating an ideal state.[130]

But all these Zionist ideas – and there were many others – envisaged some kind of settlement in or around Jerusalem. Even Mordecai Noah eventually came round to the view that his idealized Jewish community should be nearer the banks of the Jordan than the Niagara. Jews had periodically drifted to Palestine in small numbers. But not even Alkalai had actually set up a colony. Yet without an initial process of colonization, how could a new Zion, religious or secular or both, emerge? Once Jews thought of colonization, they tended to turn to Britain. She was the great colonizing power of the nineteenth century. She was well on her way to acquiring a quarter of the earth's surface. Moreover, Britain was peculiarly receptive to Jewish idealism, especially of the Zionist variety. As we have seen, her great Foreign Secretary, Lord Palmerston, had actively supported a modest resettlement of Palestine. Her great Prime Minister, Benjamin Disraeli, had looked even further. His novel *Alroy* describes its hero's quest to

restore Jerusalem to the Jews. The theme recurs in his more substantial
Jewish novel *Tancred*. Of course Disraeli could be dismissed as a
romantic and highly imaginative Sephardi, who in fact pursued a
pragmatic career in British politics. But Disraeli was quite capable of
realizing his cloud-capped visions. In India he turned a commercial
company into a glittering empire. He usually kept his practical Zionist
schemes to himself, but they were there. In 1851 he took a stroll
through Lord Carrington's park at High Wycombe with his colleague
Lord Stanley. Stanley noted in his journal:

The day was cold; but although usually very sensitive to influence of
weather, he seemed to forget the thermometer in the earnestness with which,
halting to enforce his views the better, and standing by the side of a
plantation, he explained the details of his plan. [Palestine], he said, had ample
natural capabilities: all it wanted was labour, and protection for the labourer:
the ownership of the soil might be bought from Turkey: money would be
forthcoming: the Rothschilds and leading Hebrew capitalists would all help:
the Turkish Empire was falling into ruin: the Turkish govt. would do
anything for money: all that was necessary was to establish colonies, with
rights over the soil, and security from ill-treatment. The question of
nationality might wait until these had taken hold. He added that these ideas
were extensively entertained among the [Jewish] nation. A man who would
carry them out would be the next Messiah, a true Saviour of his people.

Stanley added: 'Though I have many times since seen him under the
influence of irritation or pleasurable excitement, this is the only
instance in which he ever appeared to me to show signs of any higher
emotion.'[131] Disraeli may have reverted to this idea on his death-bed.
There is a tradition that he died muttering to himself in Hebrew.[132]

In his Jewish and Zionist sympathies Disraeli was not merely
reflecting his racial origins; he was also part of the English philosemitic
tradition. English writers in particular, brought up on the King James
Bible, had a profound interest in the Jewish past, often accompanied
by a strong sympathy for their present predicament. Byron's *Hebrew
Melodies* was an instance. There was, of course, the constant
temptation to present Jews in fiction as unpleasant or anti-social
archetypes. Charles Dickens succumbed to this in *Oliver Twist*
(serialized 1837–8), where the evil Fagin is crudely labelled 'Jew',
though his Jewish characteristics are not obvious. There was a lot of
Jewish crime in London, especially among the poor Ashkenazi
community. Jews were among the first of those transported to
Australia; when the system ceased in 1852 at least 1,000 Jews had
taken part in it. Among them was Isaac ('Ikey') Solomons, known as

'the Prince of Fences'.[133] Dickens was supposed to have based Fagin on him. But Dickens hotly resented claims that *Oliver Twist* was anti-Semitic. Almost as if to refute them, in *Our Mutual Friend* (serialized 1864–5), he portrayed one of his most saintly characters, Mr Riah, 'the gentle Jew in whose race gratitude is deep'.

Sometimes it is not clear whether a Jew is intended in a fictional character. Jews were often associated, in Victorian times, with dingy red hair, and some of the more repellent characters possess this attribute: Uriah Heep in *David Copperfield*, for example; or the Rev. Obadiah Slope in Anthony Trollope's *Barchester Towers*. Trollope has sometimes been criticized for portraying bad Jews. He certainly disliked Disraeli (who figures as Mr Daubeney in his political novels). But then so did many other people, including Dickens and Thackeray, not necessarily for racial reasons; and Disraeli returned the compliment, caricaturing both Dickens and Thackeray in his last novel, *Endymion* (1881). Trollope wrote a vast number of novels and portrayed innumerable foreigners (he was the most widely travelled of the nineteenth-century novelists) but a careful reading does not suggest a pattern of prejudice against Jews. Madame Max Goesler, who figures in various of his political novels, is a woman of the highest honour. Anton Trendellsohn, in *Nina Balataka* (1865), is another of Trollope's sympathetic Jews. Even Auguste Melmotte, the larger-than-life financial villain of *The Way We Live Now* (1875), is not actually described as Jewish. Trollope's point was that his origins were obscure. But he was evidently based on Albert Grant, born Abraham Gotheimer in Dublin in 1831, the son of a pedlar. This man became MP for Kidderminster, developed Leicester Square, was general manager of the Credit Foncier and Credit Mobilier of London, and floated fraudulent companies, dying a pauper in 1899.[134]

The Melmotte case was important, however, because it coincided with a watershed in attitudes to Jews. Until the 1870s, educated people in Britain tended to be philosemitic. But during the decade, which was marked by a general economic downturn and many individual financial disasters, there was a subtle change. From the mid-1870s, Jews were associated in many minds with large-scale City manipulation. The same change of mood was observable on the Continent, especially in France, Germany and Austria. But there it was merely an intensification of existing anti-Semitic feelings. In Britain it was new. It distressed the philosemites and inspired some of them to consider ways of tackling what they, too, now recognized as the 'Jewish problem'. One such was the archaeologist Sir Charles Warren, one of the first to excavate the Temple Wall of Jerusalem. In 1875, the same year Melmotte made his appearance, Warren published *The Land of Promise: or, Turkey's Guarantee*. Largely with British help, the number of Jews in the Holy Land had slowly risen, passing the 10,000-mark in the 1840s. Warren now proposed, rather on Disraelian lines, that a British chartered company should be created to colonize Palestine (in return for taking on part of Turkey's national debt), 'with the avowed intention of gradually introducing the Jew, pure and simple, who is eventually to occupy and govern this country'. In Warren's view large-scale finance and systematic and scientific development could eventually enable the country to support fifteen million people.

In the spring of the same year, Warren's voice was joined by a far more influential one in *Blackwood's*, which began serialization of George Eliot's novel *Daniel Deronda*. This book is little read now and was accounted an artistic failure even at the time. But in terms of its practical effects it was probably the most influential novel of the nineteenth century. It was another important piece of the Zionist jigsaw puzzle fitted into place. George Eliot had been passionately interested in the Jews ever since, aged seventeen, she read Josephus. She was immensely learned in Biblical commentary and criticism. She translated Strauss's *Das Leben Jesu* and Spinoza. Anti-Semitic jokes revolted her. She could not decide whether Christian hostility to Jews was 'more impious or more stupid'. In 1866 she met a learned Jew, Emmanuel Deutsch, a book-cataloguer in the British Museum, who had just published a famous article in the *Quarterly Review*, introducing the Talmud to Christian readers and seeking to build a bridge between the two religions. He gave her lessons in Hebrew. In 1869 he visited Palestine and became a fervent Zionist. 'The East!' he wrote from Jerusalem, 'all my wild yearnings fulfilled at last!'[135] Deutsch died of cancer, but George Eliot visited him frequently during his illness and was captured by his enthusiasm. In the early 1870s she began an immense course of reading and visits to synagogues with a view to creating a Jewish novel. She felt, she wrote, 'the urge to treat Jews with such sympathy and understanding as my nature and knowledge could attain to . . . towards the Hebrews we western people who have been reared in Christianity have a peculiar debt and, whether we acknowledge it or not, a peculiar thoroughness of fellowship in religious or moral sentiment'.[136]

The writing and serialization of the novel, completed in 1876, were a tremendous emotional experience for her. She finished it 'with tears in my eyes'. The mentor of the book, the Zionist ideologue, is Mordecai, the dying scholar, based on Deutsch, 'a man steeped in poverty and obscurity, weakened by disease, consciously within the shadow of advancing death, but living an intense life in an invisible past and future'. Through the lips of Deutsch–Mordecai, George Eliot voiced her Zionist hopes: 'The world will gain as Israel gains. For there will be a community in the van of the East which carries the culture and sympathies of every great nation in its bosom; there will be a land set for a halting-place of enmities, a neutral ground for the East as Belgium is for the West.' This famous passage later acquired tragic ironies for the generation of 1914 and still more for our own; but at the time it voiced a sentiment universal among philosemitic intellectuals that rebuilding Zion would pacify and civilize a barbarous area. The sentiment also demanded a Messiah-figure, as in *Tancred*. George Eliot supplied him in the hero of the novel, Daniel Deronda, who is designated by Mordecai. At the end of the story Daniel marries Mirah and prepares to go to the East to restore 'a political existence to my people, making them a nation again, giving them a national centre, such as the English have, though they too are scattered over the face of the globe'.

George Eliot's sales were worldwide and immense. Of all the nineteenth-century novelists, she was the one most respected by intellectuals, on the Continent and in North America as well as in Britain. To all of them, and especially to hundreds of thousands of assimilated Jews, the story presented, for the first time, the possibility of a return to Zion. One of the very few who did not read it was Disraeli. Asked if he had done so, he replied: 'When I want to read a novel, I write one.' But all the rest did. In New York, it exhilarated the young Emma Lazarus. In his article on 'Zionism' in the famous eleventh edition of the *Encyclopaedia Britannica* (1911), Lucien Wolf was to write that the novel 'gave the Jewish national spirit the strongest stimulus it had experienced since the appearance of Shabbetai Zevi'.[137] The book was particularly widely read in political circles. To the generation of Arthur Balfour, who first met George Eliot in 1877, the year after publication, it was their introduction to the Jewish issue.[138] But what everyone wanted to know was: who would be the real Daniel Deronda? When would he emerge? It was, indeed, like waiting for the Messiah.

The real Daniel Deronda emerged on 5 January 1895, in the freezing cold courtyard of the École Militaire in Paris. The occasion was the public degradation of Captain Alfred Dreyfus, the only Jew serving on the French army general staff, who had been accused, tried and convicted – on what subsequently emerged to be fabricated evidence – of handing secrets to the Germans. Watching the ceremony, one of the few journalists allowed to attend, was Theodor Herzl (1860–1904), the Paris correspondent of the Vienna liberal daily, *Neue Freie Presse*. Two weeks before he had attended the courtroom and heard Dreyfus pronounced guilty. Now he stood by as Dreyfus was brought before General Darras, who shouted: 'Alfred Dreyfus, you are unworthy to bear arms. In the name of the French people we degrade you!' Immediately, in a loud voice, Dreyfus shouted: 'Soldiers! An innocent man is being degraded! Soldiers! An innocent is dishonoured! Long live France – long live the Army!' A senior non-commissioned officer cut off Dreyfus' badges and buttons. He took out his sword and broke it across his knee. The prisoner was marched round the courtyard, still shouting that he was innocent. An immense and excited crowd, waiting outside, heard his cries and began to whistle and chant slogans. When Herzl left the building, it was beginning to scream 'Death to Dreyfus! Death to the Jews!'[139] Less than six months later, Herzl had completed the draft of the book which would set in motion modern Zionism, *Der Judenstaat*.

The Dreyfus case and the conversion of Herzl to Zionism both testify to significant developments in Jewish history. They are two more pieces of the jigsaw and both must be examined in detail. In the first place, the Dreyfus affair, and the dark emotions it revealed, brought to a decisive end an epoch of illusion in which assimilated western Jews had optimistically assumed that the process of their acceptance in European society was well under way and would shortly be completed. In 1871 Graetz had concluded the eleventh and final volume of his *History of the Jewish People* almost on a note of triumph: 'Happier than any of my predecessors, I may conclude my history with the joyous feeling that in the civilized world the Jewish tribe has found at last not only justice and freedom but also a certain recognition. It now finally has unlimited freedom to develop its talents not due to mercy, but as a right acquired through thousandfold suffering.'

Nowhere was this feeling of growing security stronger than in France. There, Jews enjoyed the libertarian legacy of the 1789 Revolution. They were few in number. Ironically, France's defeat in 1870, which cost her Alsace-Lorraine, had removed her largest and least popular colony of Alsatian, German-speaking Ashkenazi Jews. At the time of the Dreyfus case Jews in France numbered no more than 86,000 out of a total population of nearly forty million.[140] The community was administered through the government-sponsored Consistoire Central, under the Ministère des Cultes, which laid down rules for the elections of rabbis, fixed and contributed to their salaries.

So French Judaism had some of the characteristics of a state church – and behaved like one. The 'Prayer for France' in its prayer-book read: 'Almighty protector of Israel and humanity, if of all religions ours is the most dear to You, because it is Your own handiwork, France is of all countries the one which You seem to prefer, because it is the most worthy of You.' It ended: 'Let [France] not keep this monopoly of tolerance and of justice for all, a monopoly as humiliating for other states as it is glorious for her. Let her find many imitators, and as she imposes on the world her tastes and her language, the products of her literature and her arts, let her also impose her principles, which it goes without saying are more important and more necessary.'[141]

When J.-H. Dreyfus was installed as Grand Rabbi of Paris in 1891 his theme was the links between 'the French genius' and 'the fundamental spirit of Judaism', especially 'the moral affinities between the two races', the French being 'this elect people of modern times'. Rabbi Kahn of Nîmes called the French Revolution 'our flight from Egypt . . . our modern Passover'. Rabbi Herrmann of Rheims said France was 'designated by Him to direct the destinies of humanity . . . to spread throughout the world the great and beautiful ideas of justice, equality and fraternity which had formerly been the exclusive patrimony of Israel'. Rather like Reform Judaism in America, French Judaism did everything in its power to blend into the local religious landscape. Rabbis dressed almost like Catholic priests. They even considered holding the Sabbath services on Sunday. They had ceremonies for children very similar to baptisms and First Communions. Flowers on coffins, collection-plates, visits to the bedsides of the dying, singing, organs, sermons – all were modelled on Christian practice. It was estimated that there were only 500 true Orthodox Jews in the entire country.

The Jewish laity combined an equally low profile with unctuous patriotism. They competed energetically for the glittering prizes of the French state: admissions to the grandes écoles, the concours, the Académie, the Légion d'Honneur. 'Frenchmen by country and institutions,' wrote Léon Halévy, 'it is necessary that all [French Jews] become so by customs and language . . . that for them the name of Jew become accessory, and the name of Frenchman principal.'[142] 'Let there be neither Jews nor Christians,' wrote Ernest Crémieu-Foa, 'except at the hour of prayer for those who pray!' James Darmesteter, who had risen to be director of the École des Hautes Études, argued in gratitude that Israelite and French cultures were essentially the same. The French Revolution had expressed the ideology of Judaism, and these two chosen peoples with their profound belief in progress would bring about the Messianic Age which would take the form of 'the terrestrial triumph of justice in humanity'. Such men argued that anti-Semitism was an alien German import, which could never gain anything but a superficial hearing in France.

That, alas, was far from correct. The nineteenth century was the great age of pseudo-scientific racial theories and the French played their full part in it. It is true that German philologists, exploring the origins of language, first distinguished between the Aryan or Indo-European peoples, with their roots in Sanskrit, and the Semitic peoples, with their roots in the Hebraic group of languages. But it was the French who popularized these notions, in the process confusing language and race. In 1853 the French diplomat Comte Joseph de Gobineau (1816–82) published his notorious *Essai sur l'inégalité des races humaines*, which distinguished between Aryan virtue and Semitic (and Latin) degeneration. This became the handbook of the German anti-Semites and had an enormous influence on, for example, Richard Wagner. The opinionated polymath Ernst Renan (1823–92) was doing the same for the French, with his *Histoire générale et système comparé des langues sémitiques*, which won the Prix Volnay in 1847, and still more his *Vie de Jésus* (1863), the most successful book published in France during the entire century, read with smug satisfaction by anti-clericals and trembling guilt by Catholics. He believed that 'the Semitic race, compared to the Indo-European race, represents an inferior level of human nature'; and his portrait of Jesus, the humanist hero, was dramatic precisely because it showed him 'immune to almost all the defects of his race . . . whose dominant quality was, indeed, limitless delicacy'. Renan's theory of Jewish racial inferiority was skilfully married to Toussenel's theory of Jewish financial skulduggery by Edouard Drumont to produce his massive two-volume *La France juive* (1886), the most brilliantly written and plausible of all anti-Semitic studies. In a short time it ran into over a hundred editions and enabled him to found the Anti-Semitic League and his vicious daily paper, *La Libre Parole* (1889).

Hence the first layer of French anti-Semitism was pseudo-scientific. The second was envy. If the Jews were racially inferior, why were they so successful? Because they cheated and conspired. Jewish children of the *haute bourgeoisie* tended to carry off all the prizes. Years later, Julien Benda was to write: 'The triumph of the Benda brothers at the *concours général* appeared to me one of the essential sources of the anti-Semitism we had to bear fifteen years later. Whether the Jews realized it or not, such success was felt by other French people as an act of violence.'[143] The immensely clever Reinach brothers, the lawyer–

politician Joseph (1856–1921), the archaeologist Solomon (1858–1932) and the classicist Théodore (1860–1928), were another trio of prize-winning prodigies. They beat the French at their own academic–cultural game every time. Then, in 1892, the Panama scandal broke, an immense labyrinth of financial manipulation and fraud, with their uncle Baron Jacques de Reinach right at the middle of it. His mysterious death, or suicide, merely added to the uproar, and to the angry satisfaction of the Jew-baiters – so they cheated all along! The Union Générale scandal in 1882, the Comptoire d'Escompte scandal in 1889 – both involving Jews – were merely curtain-raisers to this complex crime, which seemed to confirm the financial conspiracy theories outlined in Drumont's book and gave Le Libre Parole's 'investigative journalists' the chance to break a new anti-Jewish story almost daily. After London, Paris was the centre of European finance and its bankers' roll-call was studded with Jewish names: Deutsch, Bamberger, Heine, Lippmann, Pereire, Ephrussi, Stern, Bischoffsheim, Hirsch and Reinach (of course) – that would do to be going on with![144]

There was a third, clerical, layer of French anti-Semitism. The official Roman Catholic hierarchy were in a confused state in the last quarter of the nineteenth century, locked in endless battles with the French state. They had little control over their clergy, still less over the religious orders, especially the Assumptionists, chosen and backed by the papacy to 're-Christianize France' by organizing mass pilgrimages to Rome and new miracle centres such as Lourdes. The Assumptionists were founded in 1847 and were the first order to bring the methods of big business to religious revivalism. They hired special trains to assemble vast crowds of people. They founded an immensely successful publishing house, La Bonne Presse, and a mass-circulation daily, La Croix (1883).[145] Like the Dominican and Franciscan friars before them, whom they resembled in certain ways, they needed an enemy. They produced three, all interconnected: Protestants, freemasons, Jews. As an ultra-Catholic conspiracy theory, the plots of the freemasons long antedated 'scientific' anti-Semitism, going back at least to 1789 in France. Much of masonic lore and ritual could be, and was, linked to Jewish kabbalah, in scores of Catholic pamphlets and books. And, since the Assumptionists believed that many Protestants had been secret Jews and marranos ever since the sixteenth century, it was not hard to tie all together in a satanic trio. When the Catholic banking organization Union Générale collapsed in 1882, the Assumptionists contended that it was the work of this conspiracy. They founded their paper the next year to fight it; and the year after, Leo

XIII, their protector, formally condemned freemasonry as the work of the devil. *La Croix* pledged itself to fight 'the trio of hate ... which includes, one, Protestantism which wants to destroy Catholicism, the *soul of France*; Judaism which wants to rob her national wealth, the *body of France*; freemasonry, the natural compound of the other two, which wants *at the same time* to demolish the *body and the soul of France!*[146]

Against this background of orchestrated hatred and slander, the events of 1881 in Russia, and their consequences, dealt a deadly blow to established French Jewry by giving ordinary Frenchmen, especially in Paris, vivid, ocular evidence of a 'Jewish problem'. Over a generation, France took 120,000 Jewish refugees, more than doubling the size of French Jewry. These were poor, obvious, Ashkenazi Jews, of course, seemingly corresponding to the caricature Drumont and *La Croix* were peddling. Moreover, they were joined by a steady stream of Jews from the Alsace community, who could not abide the German occupation. They included the Dreyfus family who had come to Paris in 1871, but retained business connections with Mulhouse. They were fierce, almost fanatical, French patriots. Getting a commission in the French army had been the boyhood ambition of Alfred Dreyfus. It was a matter of tremendous pride to him that, after the general staff was belatedly reorganized to give it a wider social basis, he had been the first Jew to be selected for staff duties. But of course the patriotism of Alsatian Jews had its ironies. Like anyone else with the faintest German connections they were suspect persons in the France of the 1890s, a paranoid country, still smarting from defeat and territorial robbery, desperate to avenge itself and recover its lost provinces, yet fearful of further German assault. In January 1894 France signed the first secret military convention with her new ally against Germany, Tsarist Russia. This made the Jews still more suspect in French eyes, for they were celebrated for hating the Tsarist regime more than any other. The French Jews did their best. All the Paris synagogues offered up special prayers on the birthday of Alexander III, the most anti-Semitic of the Tsars. It made no difference. Every patriotic gesture the Jews made was received by the anti-Semites with implacable cynicism: 'They would, wouldn't they?'

In July 1894, a spendthrift gambler, Major Count Walsin-Esterhazy, then commanding the 74th Infantry, offered his services to the German embassy. Next month he handed the embassy concierge a letter (the *bordereau*) listing certain papers he intended to hand over in return for cash. On 26 September it reached Major Hubert Henry, of the general staff 'Statistical Section' (a cover for counter-espionage).

Despite its reorganization, the general staff was a morass of incompetence, the Statistical Section being the worst of the lot. It kept virtually no records or registers. It constantly fabricated documents to plant, but did not record them, and often confused false and real. On one occasion it sold an old strongbox; the buyer found top-secret papers in it. That was characteristic. If the Section had possessed a minimum of professional competence, the Dreyfus affair could never have occurred because Esterhazy was a phenomenally incompetent spy. All the internal evidence of the *bordereau* pointed to him. Little or nothing indicated that the culprit was a member of the staff. Some of it positively ruled out Captain Dreyfus. But the head of the section was Colonel Jean-Conrad Sandherr, also an Alastian, but a German-hating, anti-Semitic Catholic convert. When Major Henry, another anti-Semite, produced Dreyfus' name, Colonel Sandherr slapped his forehead and exclaimed: 'I ought to have thought of it!'[147]

Nevertheless, there was no anti-Semitic army plot against Dreyfus. All concerned acted in good faith. The only exception was Henry, who actually forged evidence against Dreyfus. The trouble was started by Drumont and the Assumptionists. It was the *Libre Parole* which first broke the story that a Jewish officer had been secretly arrested for treason. By 9 November 1894, weeks before the trial, it proclaimed that '*toute la Juiverie*' was behind '*le traître*'. *La Croix* joined in the witch-hunt. Appalled, the leaders of the Jewish community, who included five army generals, tried to play things down. When Dreyfus was convicted and sent to Devil's Island, they accepted his guilt; were deeply ashamed of it; wanted the whole thing buried. Dreyfus' own family were convinced of his innocence. But they employed discreet lawyers, working quietly behind the scenes amassing evidence, hoping for a pardon. It was a typical and time-honoured Jewish reaction to injustice.

However, Herzl was not the only Jew who was stirred to anger and action. Another was Bernard Lazare (1865–1903), born Baruch Hagani, a young Symbolist writer from Nîmes. He believed in total assimilation and was, if anything, an anarchist. Now, for the first time, he was stirred on a Jewish issue. He began to make inquiries but was given an icy brush-off by the Dreyfus family. He was revolted by the lack of Jewish outrage. It was, he wrote, 'a deplorable habit from the old persecutions – of receiving blows and not protesting, of bending their backs, of waiting for the storm to pass and of playing dead so as not to attract the lightning'. His own inquiries convinced him Dreyfus was innocent and the victim of a frame-up. At the end of 1896 he published, in Brussels, a pamphlet, *Une erreur judiciaire: la vérité sur l'affaire Dreyfus*. It raised the anti-Semitic issue for the first time on the Jewish side: 'Because he was a Jew he was arrested, because he was a Jew he was convicted, because he was a Jew the voices of justice and of truth could not be heard in his favour.' To Lazare, Dreyfus was the archetype Jewish martyr:

He incarnates, in himself, not only the centuries-old sufferings of the people of martyrs, but their present agonies. Through him, I see Jews languishing in Russian prisons . . . Rumanian Jews refused the rights of man, Galician Jews starved by financial trusts and ravaged by peasants made fanatics by their priests . . . Algerian Jews, beaten and pillaged, unhappy immigrants dying of hunger in the ghettos of New York and London, all of those whom desperation drives to seek some haven in the far·corners of the inhabited world where they will at last find that justice which the best of them have claimed for all humanity.[148]

Lazare did not stop with his pamphlet. He begged prominent Jews to take up the case and work for a revision. He made one early and vital convert: Joseph Reinach, the great Jewish lawyer. This tipped the scales for the Jewish community: the issue became serious. Many young Jews took up the cause, among them Marcel Proust: 'I was the first Dreyfusard', he wrote, 'for it was I who went to ask Anatole France for his signature.'[149] This was for the 'petition of intellectuals', to rope in prominent writers for the cause. It succeeded, in the sense that it got non-Jewish radicals interested. Among them was Émile Zola, then France's most popular writer. He investigated the case, wrote an enormous article in defence of Dreyfus and gave it to the rising politician Georges Clemenceau, who ran the liberal paper *L'Aurore*. It was Clemenceau's idea to print it on his front page (13 January 1898) under the headline 'J'ACCUSE!' That was the real beginning of the Dreyfus affair. Four days later anti-Semitic riots broke out in Nantes and spread to Nancy, Rennes, Bordeaux, Tournon, Montpellier, Marseilles, Toulouse, Angers, Le Havre, Orléans and many other towns. In France it was simply a matter of students and riffraff smashing the windows of Jewish shops, but in Algiers the riots lasted four days and involved the sack of the entire Jewish quarter. None of the ringleaders was arrested.

It was exactly what the Jewish establishment had feared if the Dreyfus case was made into a major issue. But nothing could now stop the polarization. The army, asked to admit it had made a mistake, refused and closed ranks. When one of its number, Major Picquart, produced evidence pointing to Esterhazy, it was Picquart who was arrested and gaoled. Zola was tried and had to flee the country. In February 1898 the Dreyfusards formed a national organization, the

League of the Rights of Man, to get Dreyfus freed. The anti-Dreyfusards, led by the writer Charles Maurras, replied with the League of the French Fatherland, to 'defend the honour of the army and France'. Lazare fought a duel with Drumont (neither was hurt); there were at least thirty-two other duels on the issue, one Jew being killed. In the Chambre des Députés, in January 1898, there was an appalling mass fist-fight while Jean Jaurès was at the tribune and the mob raged outside. The diplomat Paul Cambon, returning to Paris from Constantinople, complained: 'Whatever you may say or do, you are classified as a friend or an enemy of the Jews or the army.'[150]

The Dreyfus affair convulsed France for an entire decade. It became an important event not just in Jewish history but in French, indeed in European, history. It saw the emergence, for the first time, of a distinct class of intellectuals – the word intelligentsia was now coined – as a major power in European society and among whom emancipated Jews were an important, sometimes a dominant, element. A new issue was raised, not just for France: who controls our culture? The French proletariat sat solidly on the sidelines. The mobs were students and petit bourgeois. 'I am bound to admit', Clemenceau confessed, 'that the working class appears to take no interest in the question.'[151] But for the educated classes it became the only thing that mattered in life. A cartoon by Caron d'Ache showed a dining-room with all the furniture smashed and the guests fighting on the floor: 'Someone mentioned It.' Paris society, both aristocratic and bourgeois, divided into two camps. The battle has been repeatedly described, in Proust's *Jean Santeuil*, Zola's *La Vérité*, Anatole France's *L'Île des pinguins* and *Monsieur Bergeret à Paris*, in plays by Lavedan and Donnay, by Charles Maurras, Roger Martin du Gard, Charles Péguy and Jean Barois.[152] The 'Faubourg', the aristocratic quarter, led by the Ducs de Brissac, La Rochefoucauld and Luynes and by the Duchesse d'Uzès, subscribed overwhelmingly to the anti-Dreyfusard cause; they were joined by many writers, such as Paul Valéry and Maurice Barrès; the great painter Edgar Degas found himself at odds with all his Jewish friends. A breakdown of subscribers to the League of the French Fatherland (1899) showed that over 70 per cent were highly educated, composed (in order) of students, lawyers, doctors, university teachers, artists and men of letters; the names included eighty-seven members of the Collège de France and the Institut and twenty-six out of forty members of the Académie Française.[153] The social headquarters of the anti-Dreyfusards was the salon of the Comtesse de Martel, the original of Madame Swann's salon in Proust's *À la Recherche du temps perdu*.[154] They all believed strongly in a (mythical) secret organization of Jews, freemasons and atheists which they called 'the Syndicate'. The Prince de Polignac used to ask Proust: 'What's the good old Syndicate doing now, eh?'

On the Dreyfus side, there was the salon run by Madame Geneviève Strauss, the original of the Duchesse de Guermantes in Proust's novel. Born a Halévy, the greatest of all Jewish–Protestant haute-bourgeois families, with links to the worlds of art, music and letters,[155] she used her salon to organize the great petitions of intellectuals. Its hero was Reinach, now in charge of the Dreyfus campaign. He had, wrote Léon Daudet, 'a voice of wood and leather and used to leap from chair to chair, in pursuit of bare-bosomed lady guests, with the gallantry of a self-satisfied gorilla'. But Daudet was a biased source. Proust put it more mildly: 'He was comic but nice, though we did have to pretend he was a reincarnation of Cicero.' Another Dreyfusard hostess, Madame de Saint-Victor, was known as 'Our Lady of the Revision'. A third, Madame Ménard-Dorien (the original of Proust's Madame Verdurin), ran a violently left-wing salon in the Rue de la Faisanderie known as 'the Fortress of Dreyfusism'; it was there that the philosemitic conspiracy theory, of an (equally mythical) clerical–military plot, originated. But some hostesses, like Madame Audernon, enjoyed having both factions and listening to their rows. Asked by a rival, who had banned her Dreyfusard guests, 'What are you doing about your Jews?', she replied: 'I'm keeping them on.'[156]

But behind the social veneer, real – and for the Jews ultimately tragic – issues were taking shape. The Dreyfus affair was a classic example of a fundamentally simple case of injustice being taken over by extremists on both sides. Drumont and the Assumptionists flourished Dreyfus' conviction and used it to launch a campaign against the Jews. The young Jewish intellectuals, and their growing band of radical allies, began by asking for justice and ended by seeking total victory and revenge. In doing so, they gave their enemies an awesome demonstration of Jewish and philosemitic intellectual power. At the beginning of the Dreyfus case, the anti-Semites, as always in the past, held all the powerful cards, particularly in the world of print. By a significant irony, it was the liberal press law of 1881, lifting the previous ban on criticism of religious groups and designed to expose the Catholic Church to journalistic inquiry, which made Drumont's vicious brand of anti-Semitism legal. Press freedom, at least initially, worked against Jewish interests (as it was later to do under the Weimar Republic). Until the Dreyfus affair, the only Jewish attempt to answer *La Libre Parole*, a journal called *La Vrai Parole* (1893), was an embarrassing failure. At its outset, the press was overwhelmingly anti-Dreyfusard, for in addition to the anti-Semitic papers, which had circulations of between 200,000 and 300,000, the popular papers, *Le Petit Journal* (1,100,000), *Le Petit Parisien* (750,000) and *Le Journal* (500,000), backed the established order.[157]

From 1897, with the founding of papers like *L'Aurore* and the all-woman *La Fronde*, the Jews and their allies began to hit back. They had of course the inestimable benefit of an overwhelming case. But their skill at presenting it grew progressively. It was the first time secular Jews had worked together, as a class, to put their point of view. They invoked the new media of photography and cinema. There were photographic action shots of the Algiers pogrom.[158] As early as 1899 the pioneer *cinéaste* Georges Méliès made eleven short movies re-enacting scenes from the affair; they provoked fights in the audience whenever they were shown.[159] Gradually, the Dreyfusards began to tilt the media balance in their favour, as uncommitted newspapers and magazines swung behind them. Outside France, their capture of public opinion was decisive everywhere. Inside France, as their media power increased, so did their political influence. The affair throughout was propelled forward by weird accidents. The most important, and for the Dreyfusards their real breakthrough, was the sudden death of the violently anti-Dreyfus President, Félix Faure, on 16 February 1899. He had a cerebral haemorrhage while *in flagrante delicto* with his naked concubine, Madame Steinheil, and collapsed clutching her hair in a steely grip – it was her terrified screams which brought the staff rushing to his locked study, whose door they were forced to break down.

After this, the anti-Dreyfusard front began to bend. Dreyfus was brought back from Devil's Island, white-haired, malarial, scarcely able to speak. He was retried, convicted again, offered a free pardon which, under pressure from his family and the old Jewish establish-ment, he accepted. The men who were profiting from the Dreyfus campaign, the radical politicians like Clemenceau, the new intellec-tuals, Jewish and gentile, were furious. 'We were ready to die for Dreyfus,' wrote Charles Péguy angrily, 'but Dreyfus himself is not.'[160] Why should he? He seems to have realized, along with many older Jews, that the pursuit of the case *à l'outrance* was increasing, solidifying and would end by institutionalizing anti-Semitism in France. According to Léon Daudet, he used to say to the fanatics on his side: 'I've never had a moment's peace since leaving Devil's Island,' or 'Shut up, all of you, or I'll confess.'[161] He even remarked, with heavy Jewish irony: 'There's no smoke without fire, you know.' But the new power of the written word in alliance with the radical left was now out of control. It pushed on for revenge and total victory. It got both. The Assumptionists were kicked out of France. The left won an overwhelming electoral success in 1906. Dreyfus was rehabilitated and made a general. Picquart ended up Minister for War. The state, now in Dreyfusard hands, waged a destructive campaign against the church. So the extremists won, both in creating the affair and in winning it.[162]

But there was a price to pay, and in the end it was the Jews who paid it. Anti-Semitism was institutionalized. Charles Maurras's League went on to become, after the 1914–18 war, a pro-fascist, anti-Semitic movement which formed the most vicious element in the Vichy regime, 1941–4, and helped to send hundreds of thousands of French Jews, native and refugee, to their deaths, as we shall see. The victory of the Dreyfusards established in the minds of many Frenchmen the Jewish conspiracy as an incontrovertible fact. One need hardly say that there was no conspiracy, certainly no Jewish one. Joseph Reinach, who not only vindicated his client but wrote the first full history of the affair, showed in his sixth and last volume how much he deplored and feared the excesses of his own supporters.[163] There was no mastermind. The nearest to a master-spirit was Lucien Herr, librarian of the ultra-elitist École Normale Supérieure, and he was the centre of a Protestant, not a Jewish, circle.[164] Yet the demonstration of Jewish intellectual power which the affair provided, the ease with which Jewish writers now strode the French intellectual scene, the fact that nine-tenths of the vast literature which accumulated around the affair was Dreyfusard, all this disturbed Frenchmen who in general sympathized with the Jewish point of view. There is a significant passage in the journals of the Protestant novelist André Gide, 24 January 1914, about his friend Léon Blum, leader of the younger Jewish Dreyfusards and later French Prime Minister:

his apparent resolve always to show a preference for the Jew and to be interested always in him ... comes above all from the fact that Blum considers the Jewish race as superior, as called upon to dominate after having been long dominated, and thinks it his duty to work towards its triumph with all his strength. ... A time will come, he thinks, that will be the age of the Jew; and right now it is important to recognize and establish his superiority in all categories, in all domains, in all the divisions of art, of knowledge and of industry.

Gide then voiced his objections to what he saw as a Jewish takeover of French culture; why could not Jews write in another language – why did they have to write in French?

there is today in France a Jewish literature that is not French literature. ... For what does it matter to me that the literature of my country should be enriched if it is so at the expense of its significance? It would be far better, whenever the Frenchman comes to lack sufficient strength, for him to disappear rather than to let an uncouth person play his part in his stead and in his name.[165]

This was exactly the line of argument which Herzl was beginning to fear. In fact, concern at the resistance the Jews were building up against themselves by their massive and highly successful entrance into European culture was the force edging Herzl towards Zionism even before he watched Dreyfus degraded on that bitter January morning in 1895. For in Vienna, his home city, the Jewish 'invasion' of local culture was even more impressive than in France, and far more bitterly resented. He himself was part of it.

Herzl is one of the most complex characters in Jewish history. Like Disraeli's, his flashy theatrical manner concealed tragic depths. The documentation on him is enormous, as he saved every bit of paper he ever wrote on, down to bills and tickets.[166] He was born in Budapest in 1860: his father, a near-millionaire banker, lost everything in the big 1873 crash; his mother, a German humanist and nationalist, was the hard one, 'the Mother of the Gracchi' as she was called. The family claimed to be Sephardi, in a country where *Ostjuden* was the worst term of abuse; but of course they were Ashkenazi (from Silesia) like nearly everyone else. His Jewish education was scrappy. He never knew Hebrew or Yiddish. His bar-mitzvah was termed 'confirmation'. He grew up aspiring to total assimilation. His aim in life was to be a successful playwright. His marriage to the daughter of an oil millionaire, Julie Naschauer, who brought him a huge dowry, set him up as a man of leisure and letters. He was always superbly dressed. He sported a luxurious, jet-black Assyrian-type beard; his black eyes glittered romantically. Walking past the Vienna Burgtheatre with the young Arthur Schnitzler, he boasted: 'One day I'll get in there.' But he did not look like an Austrian playwright; he looked like a *nasi*, a Prince of Judah. His countenance, wrote Martin Buber, 'was lit by the glance of the Messiah'. It was, said the atheist Max Nordau, 'the work of Providence'. Franz Rosenzweig said it 'proved that Moses was a real person'; Freud claimed he had dreamed of this remarkable man before he ever met him.[167] Others were less flattering. His cousin Raoul Auernheimer said he looked 'like an insulted Arab sheikh'.

Herzl tried to compensate for his looks by cracking anti-Semitic jokes. From Ostend he wrote to his parents: 'Many Viennese and Budapest Jews on the beach. The rest of the holidaymakers very pleasant.' 'Yesterday grande soirée at the Treitels,' he wrote from Berlin. 'Thirty or forty ugly little Jews and Jewesses. No consoling sight.' Viennese Jews specialized in gallows humour and anti-Semitic sneers. When the Austrian Prime Minister, Eduard Taafe, asked the Galician MP Joseph Bloch if the Prince-Archbishop of Olmutz, Dr Theodor Cohen, had converted, he was told: 'Don't worry, Prime Minister, if he were still a Jew he would no longer be called Cohen.' They joked: 'Anti-Semitism didn't begin to succeed until the Jews began to push it.'[168] Some Jews deliberately refrained from having children, so as not to 'hand on the problem'. Others, like Herzl himself, considered having them baptized. 'I myself would never convert,' he wrote,

yet I am in favour of conversion. For me the matter is closed but it bothers me greatly for my son Hans. I ask myself if I have the right to sour and blacken his life as mine has been soured and blackened. . . . Therefore one must baptize Jewish boys before they must account for themselves, before they are able to act against it and before conversion can be construed as weakness on their part. They must disappear into the crowd.[169]

But could a Jew disappear into the crowd? In the Germanic world, anti-Semitism still had a ferocious religious base, particularly in the south; at the popular level it was still symbolized by the *Judensau*. But the further you went up the social scale, the more secular, cultural and racial it became; so baptism did not work. In the nineteenth century, German hatred of the Jews acquired a *völkisch* basis. It started with the nationalist rising against Napoleon. Its first significant event was a mass meeting of the German *Burschenschaften* (fraternity movement) at the Wartburg Castle in 1817 to burn 'foreign' books said to be 'poisoning the *Volk* culture'.[170] This ideology, which slowly became predominant in Germany and Austria during the nineteenth century, drew a crucial distinction between 'culture' (benign, organic, natural) and 'civilization' (corrupt, artificial, sterile). Every culture had a soul; and the soul was determined by the local landscape. German culture, then, was in perpetual enmity with civilization, which was cosmopolitan and alien. Who represented the civilization principle? Why, the one race which had no country, no landscape, no culture of their own: the Jews! The argument was typical of those which caught the Jews whatever they did. If they clung to ghetto Judaism, they were alien for that reason; if they secularized and 'enlightened' themselves, they became part of alien civilization. This *völkisch* rejection of the Jews took many forms. It created a Youth Movement, which wandered through the German landscape, strummed guitars, sang songs by the campfire, and rejected Jews, who had to form a youth movement of their own. It took over the student class, an increasingly important element in German society; they turned the Jews out of their clubs – Herzl was 'cashiered' from his before he could resign – and refused even to fight duels with them, on the grounds that Jews had no 'honour' to lose. It formed a conservationist movement, ancestor of the Greens, which rejected industry and high finance (the Rothschilds) and especially the ever expanding big cities, breeding grounds of the cosmopolitan Jews: Berlin and Vienna were particularly detested among the *Volk*, as 'Jew cities'. Their Bible was *Land und Leute* ('Place and People') by Wilhelm Heinrich Riehl, a Munich university professor and museum curator, who wanted to restore the medieval-type small town and get rid of the 'rootless' (his favourite term of abuse) proletariat, especially migratory workers and, above all, Jews, who had created the big cities, 'the tomb of Germanism'.

Volk-style anti-Semitism was hydra-headed, contradictory, unco-ordinated, ubiquitous. It included many novels dealing with peasant life, such as Wilhelm von Polenz's *Der Büttnerbauer* (1895) and Hermann Lons' *Der Werwolf* (1910), in which Jews were depicted as unscrupulous middlemen and dealers, who cheated the peasants and stole their land; the German Farmer's Union was strongly anti-Semitic. It included a whole school of historians, led by Heinrich von Treitschke, who accused the Jews of an alien and destructive intrusion on Germany's 'natural' historical development, and who first made anti-Semitism respectable in academic circles. It included the scientists and pseudo-scientists who misapplied Charles Darwin's work and created 'social Darwinism', in which races struggled with each other to determine the 'survival of the fittest'; Alfred Krupp sponsored an essay prize on the application of social Darwinism to state policy, winning entries advocating stern policies to preserve the *Volk*, such as sending Jews and other 'degenerate' types to the front as cannon-fodder. It included a new element of German neo-paganism. Thus Paul de Lagarde rejected Christianity, which had been corruptly invented by the Jew, St Paul, and wished it replaced by a specifically German *Volk* religion, which would conduct a crusade to drive the Jews, with their international materialist conspiracy, from the sacred German soil: he predicted a German–Jew armageddon. Then, too, the circle which gathered round Richard Wagner, which dominated much of the German musical scene from the 1870s, absorbed the race teachings of Gobineau and, later, of Houston Stewart Chamberlain, and drew a powerful artistic contrast between the 'purity' of German–pagan folk culture and the Judaic-infected corruption of the cosmopolitan idea.

The violence with which these views were presented was horrifying. De Lagarde, whose original name was Bötticher, demanded a physical campaign against Jewish 'vermin': 'with trichinae and bacilli one does not negotiate, nor are trichinae and bacilli subject to education. They are exterminated as quickly and as thoroughly as possible.' Wagner also advocated the *Untergang* (downfall) of the Jews. 'I regard the Jewish race as the born enemy of pure humanity and everything that is noble in it; it is certain we Germans will go under before them, and perhaps I am the last German who knows how to stand up as an art-loving man against the Judaism that is already getting control of everything.' He wrote this in *Religion and Art* (1881), published the year the great Russian pogroms were driving a new wave of *Ostjuden* refugees into central Europe. Wagner was particularly influential in intensifying anti-Semitism, especially among the middle and upper classes, not only because of his personal standing but because he repeatedly advanced the argument – with innumerable examples – that the Jews were progressively 'taking over' the citadel of German culture, especially its music. Even their so-called 'geniuses', he insisted – men like Giacomo Meyerbeer, Mendelssohn or Heine himself – were not truly creative, and meanwhile a host of Jewish middlemen were taking over the critical press, publishing, theatres and operas, art galleries and agencies. It was Wagner's writings which provoked the furious outpourings of Eugen Dühring, who throughout the 1880s published a succession of widely read racial attacks on the Jews: the 'Jewish question', he declared, should be 'solved' by 'killing and extirpation'.

The attack came from all sides: from the left, from the right; from aristocrats and populists; from industry, from the farms; from the academy and from the gutter; from music and literature and, not least, from science. What were the Jews to do? Was Jewishness, as Heine bitterly remarked, an incurable disease defying all treatment? Jews were attacked whether they were active or passive. 'You had the choice', wrote Arthur Schnitzler, 'of being insensitive, obtuse or cheeky, or of being oversensitive, timid and suffering from feelings of persecution.'[171] In the light of the great Russian pogroms of 1881–2, a Russian Jew, Leon Pinsker, produced a book called *Autoemancipation* (1882), in which assimilation was dismissed as ultimately impossible, since from every viewpoint the Jew could be, and was, attacked: 'for the living, the Jew is a dead man; for the natives, an alien and a vagrant; for property holders, a beggar; for the poor, an exploiter and a millionaire; for the patriot, a man without a country; for all classes, a hated rival'.[172] Viennese Jews knew this better than anyone else. As Jakob Wassermann was to put it so eloquently, the Jews had no real answer to anti-Semitism in its protean form:

Vain to seek obscurity. They say: the coward, he is creeping into hiding, driven by his evil conscience. Vain to go among them and offer them one's hand. They say: why does he take such liberties with his Jewish pushfulness? Vain to keep faith with them as a comrade-in-arms or a fellow citizen. They say: he is a Proteus, he can assume any shape or form. Vain to help them strip off the chains of slavery. They say: no doubt he found it profitable. Vain to counteract the poison.[173]

The growing mood of despair among assimilated Jews was reinforced by the anti-Semitic penetration of politics. In the 1870s anti-Semitism was fuelled by the financial crisis and scandals; in the 1880s by the arrival of masses of *Ostjuden*, fleeing from Russian territories; by the 1890s it was a parliamentary presence, threatening anti-Jewish laws. In 1879 the Hamburg anarchist pamphleteer Wilhelm Marr introduced the term 'anti-Semitism' into the political vocabulary by founding the Anti-Semitic League. The same year the Berlin court preacher Adolf Stoeker persuaded his small Christian Socialist Workers' Party to adopt an anti-Semitic platform. The first International Anti-Jewish Congress met at Dresden in 1882; there were other such gatherings at Kassel (1886) and Bochum (1889). At the same time the Christian socialist and radical Karl Lueger was building up a formidable anti-Semitic movement in and around Vienna. In 1886 Germany elected its first official Anti-Semitic deputy; by 1890 there were four; by 1893 sixteen. By 1895 the anti-Semites were virtually in a majority in the lower diet and in Vienna Lueger had fifty-six seats against seventy-one Liberals. From many German-speaking cities there were reports of physical assaults on Jews and of anti-Semitic students preventing Jewish scholars from lecturing.

It was against this threatening background that Herzl began to abandon his assimilationist position. He had previously considered all kinds of wild ideas to get the Jews accepted. One was a huge programme of social re-education for Jews, to endow them with what he termed 'a delicate, *extremely sensitive* feeling for honour and the like'. Another was a pact with the Pope, whereby he would lead a campaign against anti-Semitism in return for 'a great mass movement for the free and honourable conversion of all Jews to Christianity'.[174] But all these schemes soon seemed hopeless in face of the relentless rise of anti-Semitic hatred. Herzl began to write a play, *The New Ghetto*, showing how the new walls of prejudice surrounding the Jew had replaced the old ones of stone. His stay in France completed the process of disillusionment. Like other educated German Jews, Herzl had always seen France as the citadel of tolerance. In practice he found it riddled with anti-Semitism, and his Paris dispatches reflected his rising anxiety.[175] Then came that fearful scene in the École Militaire. Herzl always saw things, good or bad, in highly dramatic terms: it was the horrific drama of Dreyfus' degradation, and his solitary voice hopelessly intoning his innocence, which finally made up Herzl's mind. Was not Dreyfus the archetypal sufferer in the new ghetto? If even France turned against the Jew, where in Europe could he look for acceptance? As if to reinforce the point, the French Chamber of Deputies only narrowly rejected (268–208) an anti-Semitic motion banning Jews from the public service.

In 1895 Herzl was not to foresee the victory of the Dreyfusards. Looking back from the perspective of a century, we can now identify the 1890s as the culminating point in a wave of European anti-Semitism, provoked by the flood of refugees from the Russian horrors, which was less irresistible than it seemed at the time. But Herzl had not that advantage. The anti-Semites then seemed to be winning. In May 1895 Lueger became Mayor of Vienna. To devise an alternative refuge for the Jews, who might soon be expelled from all over Europe, seemed an urgent necessity. The Jews must have a country of their own!

Herzl completed the text of his book, *Der Judenstaat*, outlining his aims, in the winter of 1895–6. The first extracts were published in the London *Jewish Chronicle*, 17 January 1896. The book was not long, eighty-six pages, and its appeal was simple.

> We are a *people*, *one* people. We have everywhere tried honestly to integrate with the national communities surrounding us and to retain only our faith. We are not permitted to do so. . . . In vain do we exert ourselves to increase the glory of our fatherlands by achievements in art and in science and their wealth by our contributions to commerce. . . . We are denounced as strangers. . . . If only they would leave us in peace. . . . But I do not think they will.

So Herzl proposed that sovereignty be conceded to the Jews over a tract of land large enough to accommodate their people. It did not matter where. It could be in Argentina, where the millionaire Baron Maurice de Hirsch (1831–96) had set up 6,000 Jews in a series of agricultural colonies. Or it could be Palestine, where similar Rothschild-financed colonies were in being. What mattered was the sanction of Jewish public opinion; and they would take what was offered. The work first came out in book form in Vienna, February 1896. It later went into eighty editions in eighteen languages.[176]

With *Der Judenstaat*, Daniel Deronda left the pages of fiction and strode on to the stage of history. Stage is the right word. Herzl could never play the role of cautious, sober Jewish statesman, the

Maimonides type, changing events through quiet words of wisdom. He brought to Jewish world politics the art of show business, the only one he really cared for. He was the actor–manager in a forthcoming production, the return of Israel to a promised land, and though his outline plan was direct and simple, all kinds of glorious details crowded his mind and were jotted down in his notes. There would be a tremendous 'expedition' to 'take possession of the land'. There would be an aristocratic constitution, based on Venice. The first, elected doge would be a Rothschild, with Hirsch perhaps as vice-president. There would be sumptuous squares, like the Piazza San Marco or the Palais Royal. He devised the coronation ceremony, even down to a regiment of life-guards named after himself, the Herzl-Cuirassiers. Entire historic Jewish quarters would be transported and rebuilt. There would be international theatres, circuses, café-concerts, a glittering avenue like the Champs-Élysées, above all a state opera house: 'The gentlemen in full tails, the ladies dressed as lavishly as possible. . . . I shall also cultivate majestic processions on great festive occasions.' Much of his inspiration came from, of all people, Wagner, whose works Herzl constantly attended at this time. 'Only on the nights when no Wagner was performed did I have doubts about the correctness of my idea.' The next exodus to the Promised Land, he boasted, 'compares to that of Moses as a Shrove Tuesday play to a Wagner Opera!'[177] There was a touch of Disraelian fantasy about all this, indeed times when Herzl had something of the huckstering showmanship of a Mordecai Noah.

Some of Herzl's histrionic traits remained with him to the end. He insisted, for instance, that all public Zionist meetings be ceremonious and formal, with delegates wearing full evening dress even if it was only eleven o'clock in the morning. He dressed fastidiously, carefully brushed top hat, white gloves, impeccable frock-coat, when making an official call as Zionist representative. He insisted that all Jews who accompanied him must do the same. It was part of his effort to destroy the old image of the pathetic, shuffling, gaberdine-wearing ghetto Jew. He always organized his meetings and conferences with aplomb and precision. But his theatrical exuberance died as the immensities of the task before him became apparent. The strain of tragedy in his life and features became more apparent.

Herzl began by assuming that a Jewish state would be created in the way things had always been done throughout the Exile: by wealthy Jews at the top deciding what was the best solution for the rest of Jewry, and imposing it. But he found this impossible. Everywhere in civilized Europe the Jewish establishments were against his idea.

Orthodox rabbis denounced or ignored him. To Reform Jews, his abandonment of assimilation as hopeless represented the denial of everything they stood for. The rich were dismissive or actively hostile. Lord Rothschild, the most important man in world Jewry, refused to see him at all and, worse, made his refusal public. In Paris, Edmund de Rothschild, who ran the existing nine small colonies in Palestine, received him (19 July 1896) but made it plain that in his view Herzl's grandiose plans were not only quite unrealizable but would jeopardize what solid progress had already been made. He kept repeating: 'One mustn't have eyes bigger than one's stomach.' Baron Hirsch saw him too but dismissed him as an ignorant theorist. He told Herzl that what Jewish colonization schemes needed were good agricultural workers: 'All our miseries come from Jews who want to climb too high. We have too many intellectuals!' But the intellectuals dismissed Herzl too, especially in the prophet's home town, Vienna. The joke was: 'We Jews have waited 2,000 years for the Jewish state, and it had to happen to me?' Herzl's own paper, the *Neue Freie Presse*, was particularly hostile. Moritz Benedikt (1849–1920), the financial power there, warned angrily: 'No individual has the right to take upon himself the tremendous moral responsibility of setting this avalanche in motion. We shall lose our present country before we get a Jewish state.'[178]

There were exceptions: Nathan Birnbaum, for instance, the leader of the Viennese Jewish students, who had actually coined the word 'Zionism' in 1893. There was the Chief Ashkenazi Rabbi of the British Empire, Hermann Adler, who compared Herzl to Deronda (Herzl had not then read the book), or the Chief Rabbi of Vienna, Moritz Gudemann, who was sceptical of the idea but said to Herzl: 'Perhaps you are the one called of God.' Most important there was Max Nordau (1849–1923), the philosopher, who had achieved a sensational success in 1892 with his book *Entartung* (translated as *Degeneration*, London 1895), diagnosing the malady of the age. He saw anti-Semitism as one of its symptoms and said to Herzl: 'If you are insane, we are insane together – count on me!'[179] It was Nordau who pointed out that, to avoid antagonizing the Turks, the term *Judenstaat* should be replaced by *Heimstätte* (homestead), eventually rendered in English as 'national home' – an important distinction, in terms of winning acceptance. It was Nordau who drew up much of the practical programme of early Zionism.

Nevertheless, what Herzl quickly discovered was that the dynamic of Judaism would come not from the westernized elites but from the poor, huddled masses of the *Ostjuden*, a people of whom he knew nothing when he began his campaign. He discovered this first when he addressed an audience of poor Jews, of refugee stock, in the East End of London. They called him 'the man of the little people', and 'As I sat on the platform . . . I experienced strange sensations. I saw and heard my legend being born.' In eastern Europe, he quickly became a myth-like figure among the poor. David Ben Gurion (1886–1973) recalled that, as a ten-year-old boy in Russian Poland, he heard a rumour: 'The Messiah had arrived, a tall, handsome man, a learned man of Vienna, a doctor no less.' Unlike the sophisticated, middle-class Jews of the West, the eastern Jews could not toy with alternatives, and see themselves as Russians, or even as Poles. They knew they were Jews and nothing but Jews – their Russian masters never let them forget it – and what Herzl now seemed to be offering was their only chance of becoming a real citizen anywhere. To Chaim Weizmann (1874–1952), then a second-year student in Berlin, Herzl's proposals 'came like a bolt from the blue'. In Sofia, the Chief Rabbi actually proclaimed him the Messiah. As the news got around, Herzl found himself visited by shabby, excitable Jews from distant parts, to the dismay of his fashionable wife, who grew to detest the very word Zionism. Yet these were the men who became the foot soldiers, indeed the NCOs and officers, in the Zionist legion; Herzl called them his 'army of schnorrers'.

The 'army' met publicly for the first time on 29 August 1897 in the great hall of the Basel Municipal Casino.[180] It called itself the First Zionist Congress and included delegates from sixteen countries. They were mostly poor men. Herzl had to finance the congress from his own pocket. But he made them dress up: 'Black formal clothes and white ties must be worn at the festival opening session.' Thus attired, they greeted him with the ancient Jewish cry, 'Yechi Hamelech!' ('Long live the King!') Many powerful Jews had attempted to play down the meeting – the Neue Freie Presse refused to report it at all, giving prominence instead to a convention of Jewish tailors in Oxford deliberating on the proper wear for lady-cyclists. But Herzl knew what he was doing: for his first congress he attracted special correspondents from twenty-six papers. By the time the second met in 1898, opening to the rousing strains of Wagner's Tannhäuser overture, it was already an established institution. He was getting able lieutenants too, in addition to his mainstay Nordau, who wrote the policy documents. There was a timber merchant from Cologne, Daniel Wolffsohn, who was to succeed him as head of the organization. From the 1898 congress there was Weizmann too. These men, unlike Herzl, knew eastern Jewry well. Wolffsohn picked blue and white for the Zionist flag, 'the colour of our prayer-shawls'. They understood the religious and political currents within the Jewish masses. Weizmann was already fighting off furious assaults from socialist opponents within the Jewish student movement, remarking: 'Monsieur Plekhanov, you are not the Tsar.'[181] Their idea was to keep Herzl high above the rough waters of internal Jewish faction. 'He does not know the first thing about Jews,' wrote the Russian Zionist Menachem Ussishkin. 'Therefore he believes there are only external obstacles to Zionism, no internal ones. We should not open his eyes to the facts of life, so that his faith remains potent.'[182]

The professional politicians and organizers, who inevitably took over the movement, laughed at Herzl's brand of what they called 'frock-coat Zionism'. But it was a key piece in the jigsaw. Zionism could so easily become, as Herzl realized, yet another grubby international cause, of which there were thousands at the turn of the century. High-level diplomacy at a personal level was essential to make it respectable, to get it taken seriously. Moreover, he was very good at it. Gradually he got admission to everyone in Europe who mattered. He cultivated the great in Turkey, Austria, Germany, Russia. His diaries, which he kept assiduously, record these encounters in fascinating detail.[183] Even anti-Semites could be useful, because they would often help to set up a Zionist project simply to get rid of 'their' Jews. Wenzel von Plehve, the viciously hostile Russian Interior Minister, responsible for organizing pogroms, told him: 'You are preaching to a convert . . . we would very much like to see the creation of an independent Jewish state capable of absorbing several million Jews. Of course we would not like to lose *all* our Jews. We should like to keep the very intelligent ones, those of which you, Dr Herzl, are the best example. But we should like to rid ourselves of the weak-minded and those with little property.'[184] The Kaiser, too, supported another Exodus: 'I am all in favour of the kikes going to Palestine. The sooner they take off the better.' Wilhelm II argued Herzl's case for him in Constantinople with the sultan, and later gave him countenance by meeting him officially in Jerusalem itself. It was an important occasion for Herzl: he insisted his delegation wear full evening dress in the midday heat and carefully inspected their boots, cravats, shirts, gloves, suits and hats – one was made to change his top hat for a better, Wolffsohn to replace dirty shirt-cuffs. But if the Kaiser enhanced Herzl's international standing, the Turks could not be persuaded to grant a national home to Zion, and the Germans, now pursuing an active Turkish alliance, dropped the idea.

That left Britain. Herzl rightly called it 'the Archimedean point' on which to rest the lever of Zionism. There was considerable goodwill among the political elite. A lot had read *Tancred*; even more *Daniel Deronda*. Moreover, there had been a vast influx of Russian Jewish refugees into Britain, raising fears of anti-Semitism and threats of immigrant quotas. A Royal Commission on Alien Immigration was appointed (1902), with Lord Rothschild one of its members. Herzl was asked to give evidence, and Rothschild now at last agreed to see him, privately, a few days before, to ensure Herzl said nothing which would strengthen the cry for Jewish refugees to be refused entry. Rothschild's change from active hostility to friendly neutrality was an important victory for Herzl and he was happy, in exchange, to tell the Commission (7 July 1902) that further Jewish immigration to Britain should be accepted but that the ultimate solution to the refugee problem was 'the recognition of the Jews as a people and the finding by them of a legally recognized home'.[185]

This appearance brought Herzl into contact with senior members of the government, especially Joe Chamberlain, the Colonial Secretary, and the Marquess of Lansdowne, Foreign Secretary. Both were favourable to a Jewish home in principle. But where? Cyprus was discussed, then El Arish on the Egyptian border. Herzl thought it could be 'a rallying-point for the Jewish people in the vicinity of Palestine' and he wrote a paper for the British cabinet bringing up, for the first time, a powerful if dangerous argument: 'At one stroke England will get ten million secret but loyal subjects active in all walks of life all over the world.' But the Egyptians objected and a survey proved unsatisfactory. Then Chamberlain, back from East Africa, had a new idea, Uganda. 'When I saw it', he said, 'I thought, "That is a land for Dr Herzl. But of course he is sentimental and wants to go to Palestine or thereabouts." ' In fact Herzl was so alarmed by the new and far more bloody pogroms now taking place in Russia that he would have settled for Uganda. So Lansdowne produced a letter: 'If a site can be found which the [Jewish Colonial] Trust and His Majesty's Commission consider suitable and which commends itself to HM Government, Lord Lansdowne will be prepared to entertain favourable proposals for the establishment of a Jewish colony of settlement, on conditions which will enable the members to observe their national customs.' This was a breakthrough. It amounted to diplomatic recognition for a proto-Zionist state. In a shrewd move, Herzl aroused the interest of the rising young Liberal politician, David Lloyd George, by getting his firm of solicitors to draft a proposed charter for the colony. He read Lansdowne's letter to the Sixth Zionist Congress, where it aroused 'amazement . . . [at] the magnanimity of the British offer'. But many delegates saw it as a betrayal of Zionism; the Russians walked out.

Herzl concluded: 'Palestine is the only land where our people can come to rest.'[186] At the Seventh Congress (1905), Uganda was formally rejected.

By that time Herzl was dead, aged forty-four. His was a personal tale of exceptional pathos. His heroic efforts over ten crowded years destroyed his body. They killed his marriage too. His family legacy was pitiful. His wife Julia survived him only three years. His daughter Pauline became a heroin addict and died in 1930 of an overdose. His son Hans, under treatment by Freud, committed suicide a little later. His other daughter Trude was starved to death in a Nazi camp, and her son Stephan too killed himself in 1946, wiping out the family. Yet Zionism was his progeny. He told Stefan Zweig in his last months, 'It was my mistake I began too late. . . . If you knew how I suffer at the thought of the lost years.'[187] In fact by the time Herzl died, Zionism was a solidly established movement, with a powerful friend in Britain. By starting it in 1895 he gave Zionism a lead of nearly twenty years over its Arab nationalist equivalent, and that was to prove absolutely decisive in the event. Thus the conviction of Dreyfus, which set it in motion then rather than later, can be seen as the hand of providence too – like the fearful events of 1648 and of 1881.

All the same, at the time of Herzl's death Zionism was still only a minority current in the great religious and secular rivers of Jewish development. Its principal opponent was sheer indifference. But it also had active enemies. Until the First World War, the vast majorities of rabbis everywhere, Reform, Conservative or Orthodox, were strongly opposed to secular Zionism. In the West, they agreed with secular, assimilated Jews who saw it as a threat to their established position, raising doubts about their loyalties as citizens. But in the East, not least in Russia, where most Zionist supporters were to be found, religious opposition was strong and even fanatical. It was to have important consequences for the eventual Israeli state. The founders of Zionism, for the most part, were not merely Westerners, they were (in the eyes of the Orthodox) atheists. When Herzl and Nordau went together to the Sabbath service on the eve of the First Zionist Congress, it was the first time either had done so since childhood – they had to be coached about the benedictions.[188] The Orthodox knew all this. Most of them saw secular Zionism as open to all the objections raised against the enlightenment plus the mighty additional one that it was a blasphemous perversion of one of the central and most sacred Judaic beliefs. The notion that religious and secular Zionism were two heads of the same coin is quite false. To religious Jews the return to Zion was a stage in the divine plan to use the Jews as a pilot-scheme for all humanity. It had nothing to do with Zionism, which was the solution of a human problem (Jewish unacceptability and homelessness) by human means (the creation of a secular state).

By the end of the nineteenth century, there were three distinct traditions among the religious Jews of central and eastern Europe. There was the hasidic strain of Ba'al Shem Tov. There was the strain of *musar* or Moralism, based on the writings of the Orthodox Lithuanian sages, reinvigorated by Israel Salanter (1810–83) and spread by the *yeshivoth*. Then there was the strain of Samson Hirsch, 'Torah with Civilization', which attacked secularization with its own weapons of modern learning and (in Hirsch's words) worked for the kind of reform which 'elevated the age to the level of the Torah, not degraded the Torah to the level of the age'. Hirsch's sons and grandsons demonstrated that secular education could be acquired without loss of faith and helped to organize the Agudath Yisra'el movement. This sought to create a universal Torah organization to co-ordinate Judaic religious forces against secularization and was inspired by the way the relief funds for Russian pogrom victims had fallen into secular hands and were being used to discriminate against pious Jews. But all three of these ways were strongly opposed to Zionism and in particular to its growing claim to speak for all Jewry.[189]

The sages of eastern Europe were passionately opposed to any gesture from which Zionists might profit, even a visit to Erez Israel. One of them, Zadok of Lublin (1823–1900), wrote, characteristically:

> Jerusalem is the loftiest of summits to which the hearts of Israel are directed. . . . But I fear lest my departure and ascent to Jerusalem might seem like a gesture of approval of Zionist activity. I hope unto the Lord, my soul hopes for His word, that the Day of the Redemption will come. I wait and remain watchful for the feet of His anointed. Yet though three hundred scourges of iron afflict me, I will not move from my place. I will not ascend for the sake of the Zionists.[190]

The Orthodox argued that Satan, having despaired of seducing Israel by persecution, had been given permission to try it by even more subtle methods, involving the Holy Land in his wicked and idolatrous scheme, as well as all the evils of the enlightenment. Zionism was thus infinitely worse than a false messiah – it was an entire false, Satanic religion. Others added that the secular state would conjure up the godless spirit of the *demos* and was contrary to God's command to Moses to follow the path of oligarchy: 'Go and collect the elders of Israel' (Genesis 3); 'Heaven forbid', wrote two Kovno sages, 'that the masses and the women should chatter about meetings or opinions concerning the general needs of the public.'[191] In Katowice on 11 May 1912 the Orthodox sages founded the Agudist movement to co-ordinate opposition to Zionist claims. It is true that some Orthodox Jews believed Zionism could be exploited for religious purposes. Rabbi Abraham Isaac Kook (1865–1935) argued that the new 'national spirit of Israel' could be used to appeal to Jews on patriotic grounds to observe and preach the Torah. With Zionist support he was eventually made Chief Rabbi of Jerusalem. But most of the religious Jews already in Erez Israel heard of Zionism with horror. 'There is great dismay in the Holy Land', wrote Rabbi Joseph Hayyim Sonnenfeld (1848–1932), 'that these evil men who deny the Unique One of the world and his Holy Torah have proclaimed with so much publicity that it is in their power to hasten redemption for the people of Israel and gather the dispersed from all the ends of the earth.' When Herzl entered the Holy Land, he added, 'evil entered with him, and we do not yet know what we have to do against the destroyers of the totality of Israel, may the Lord have mercy'.[192] This wide, though by no means universal, opposition of pious Jews to the Zionist pro-gramme inevitably tended to push it more firmly into the hands of the secular radicals.

Yet for the great majority of secular Jews, too, Zionism offered no attraction, and for some of them it was an enemy. In Russia, persecution continued, indeed increased in savagery, the desire of Jews to escape mounted, and whether they were Orthodox or secular, Zionists or not, Palestine was one place to escape to. But among enlightened European Jewry, the panic stirred by the anti-Semitic wave of the 1890s began to subside. The outright victory in France of the Dreyfusards reaffirmed the view that there, at least, the Jews could find not only security but opportunity and a growing measure of political and cultural power. In Germany, too, the anti-Semitic ferment died down, at least in appearance, and it again became the overwhelming consensus of educated Jews that assimilation could be made to work. Indeed it was in this final period before the First World War that German Jews were most insistent in asserting their loyalty to 'the fatherland' and that German and Jewish cultural affinities were most pronounced.

The truth is that, despite Germany's long tradition of vicious anti-Jewish feeling – despite, as it were, the *Judensau* – Jews felt at home in Germany. It was a society which honoured and revered its profes-soriat, and in some respects its values were those of the Jewish cathedocracy. A Jew could slip naturally from a *yeshivah* into one of Germany's universities, now in their golden period of effort and achievement. He relished the opportunities which slowly opened to him in a country where intellectual achievement was justly measured and treated with awesome respect. German Jews worked fanatically hard. They soon began to carry off the new Nobel prizes: two in physiology and medicine, four in chemistry, two in physics, all for work done before the First World War.[193] Ferdinand Julius Cohn founded bacteriology. Paul Ehrlich produced the first practical form of chemotherapy. Franz Boas founded the science of cultural anthropology. German Jews were workaholics, hurrying men. Eduard Devrient wrote of his friend Felix Mendelssohn: 'The habit of constant occupation, instilled by his mother, made rest intolerable to him'; he kept looking at his watch.[194] Gustav Mahler used to run from his apartment to his office at the Opera House in Vienna; on his return, to save time, he would announce his arrival by whistling the opening bars of Beethoven's Eighth Symphony, as a signal for lunch to be served.

But it was not merely intellectual habits Jews shared with the Germans: there was intellectual substance too. Many German Jews felt at one with the politician Gabriel Riesser (1806–63) when he insisted, 'If we are not Germans then we have no homeland.' Jews entering public life, whether socialists like Lassalle or Liberal leaders like Eduard Lasker (1829–84) and Ludwig Bamberger (1823–99), felt there was a strong link between the Jewish rationalizing spirit and the liberalizing aims of modern Germany, attempting patiently to devise and apply rational solutions to all social problems. There were few able German Jews who did not draw nourishment and delight from Kant and Hegel.

This applied, not least, to Jewish religious thinkers. Wilhelmine Germany was on the eve of a great revival in Christian theology, and Jewish writers were affected by the same deep impulses. Hermann Cohen (1842–1918), Professor of Philosophy at Marburg, who might be termed the last follower of Maimonides, argued forcefully that Judaism was the first religion in which the essential insights of what he called 'the religion of reason' were discovered, but that it had no monopoly of the formula. Once a nation reached a certain level of intellectual development, it was ready to receive 'the religion of reason'. Of all the modern nations, he argued, Germany was the one where reason and religious feeling were easiest to reconcile, precisely because Germany, with its philosophical idealism, its reverence for pure religion and its ethical humanism, had been, as it were, anticipated by Jewish history. He rejected the supposed conflict between German culture and Jewish cosmopolitanism as ignorant nonsense. He refuted Professor Treitschke's arguments contrasting

Jew and German point by point, and dismissed his notorious catch-phrase, 'The Jews are our misfortune', as the reverse of the truth. In fact the German spirit was infused with Jewish ideals. They were behind the victory of the Protestant Reformation. The new type of modern religious man, whether Christian Protestant or liberal Jew, ultimately sprang from the religious ideals and energy of the Jewish Bible. Hence, contrary to the views of the anti-clerical rationalists – the detestable French spirit of the secular enlightenment – the German–Jewish ethical interpretation of the Bible made it an instrument of human improvement, not a barrier to it.[195]

Cohen's lectures, indeed, helped to rekindle the Judaism of Franz Rosenzweig (1886–1929), who had earlier come close to conversion, and turn him into one of the greatest of modern Jewish theologians. Rosenzweig conducted a passionate literary debate on the question of conversion with a cousin and contemporary, Eugen Rosenstock-Huessy, who did cross over into Protestantism. Their 'Letters on Judaism and Christianity', written in the years just before the First World War, indicated how closely one strain of Jewish and one strain of Protestant thought could be brought together, and how easily Jews could move within the assumptions of German philosophy.[196] Even German–Jewish thinkers who attacked Christianity, and stressed its differences with Judaism, like Leo Baeck (1873–1956), did so within German terms of reference. In 1905 Baeck published a brilliant reply, *The Essence of Judaism*, to the Protestant theologian Adolf von Harnack's *The Essence of Christianity* (1900), arguing that Judaism was the religion of reason, Christianity of romantic irrationalism. St Paul had been the original villain; but had not Luther, too, written: 'In all who have faith in Christ, reason shall be killed; else faith does not govern them; for reason fights against faith'? Yet this critique of Christianity had distinguished roots and allies in German scepticism, and Nietzsche had already provided guidelines for the attack on St Paul (a favourite target, incidentally, for generations of German anti-Semites). The theological debate, indeed, illustrated how comfortably yet how freely Jews could range within the German mental world, and what a spacious theatre of mind they found it.

In the last generation or two before the First World War – that universal catastrophe of body and spirit which made all human problems more difficult and dangerous – able Jews were emerging into competitive general life in astonishing numbers. Nowhere was their contribution more varied and impressive than in the German-speaking areas. Examining their achievements, one is tempted to conclude that many of these brilliant Jews felt, in their hearts, that Germany was the ideal location for Jewish talents. Was not Germany now aspiring, and on solid grounds, for cultural world leadership? And could not the Jews play a notable, perhaps even a paramount, role in helping the Germans to make good this challenge to all-comers? Was not this the true, modern and secular meaning of the ancient injunction to the Jews to be 'a light to the gentiles'?

There seemed to be all kinds of ways in which the Jews could assist the Germans to world leadership. Germany was now a great industrial as well as the leading intellectual power in the world. Who better to marry these two attributes, in the cause of German-inspired progress, than the Jews, strong in both, always conscious, through their long and painful history, of how economic strength could be created and guided by mental subtlety? One man who was aware of these opportunities was Walther Rathenau (1867–1922), who succeeded his father as head of the great AEG electrical combine, and later was briefly and tragically German Foreign Minister. He was not merely Germany's leading industrialist but one of her most discussed writers on state, society and economics – his essays fill five volumes – and in his own way a visionary. He suffered as much from German anti-Semitism as anyone: 'In the youth of every German Jew', he wrote, 'there comes the painful moment which he will remember for the rest of his life, when for the first time he becomes fully conscious that he has come into the world as a second-class citizen, and that no ability and accomplishment can liberate him from this condition.'[197] Yet Rathenau did not despair. He believed passionately in assimilation. He thought that German anti-Semitism was fundamentally an aristo-cratic creation, and that it would disappear with the end of aristocratic leadership, bound to be eclipsed by the new industrial ruling class.[198] Complete and final assimilation would then follow quickly. This in turn would make it possible for the Jewish element in finance and industry to make a decisive contribution to a new, affluent society, on American lines or better, in which the proletariat disappeared and liberal tolerance reigned.

To men like Rathenau, then, both baptism and Zionism were non-solutions, cowardly escapes from the real task. The Jew should assert his Germanism as well as his humanity, should do the German thing in all spheres. Was physical courage not a Jewish trait? Then let it become one! Jewish students made themselves more hot-tempered duellists than the Junker gentiles. They became feared to the point that gentile clubs had to invent ideological–racial reasons for declining their challenges. They trained. They competed. In the first two decades of the revived Olympics, German Jews won thirteen golds and three silvers in foil and sabre. The German women's fencing champion, Helene Mayer, holder of two golds, was known as *die blonde He*. Jews might, in effect, be banned from the officer corps, but they did their best. Men whose grandfathers had spoken Yiddish, which had no words for war, went on in 1914–18 to amass over 31,500 Iron Crosses.[199]

Yet this Jewish identification with the German was taking place against the background, in the last generation before Armageddon, of a cultural and scientific revolution which was hurtling in quite a different direction, and in which Jews were seen to be at the controls. The military and naval arms race which increasingly divided and electrified Europe was paralleled by an intellectual arms race, which divided society as a whole. The modern movement, affecting every department of artistic and intellectual life, was gathering power and momentum. It was becoming an irresistible force. Tradition and conservatism, though by no means forming an immovable object, offered strong resistance, which became progressively more angry and violent as the full demands of modernism were displayed in the last decade before 1914. The Jews, like everyone else, were on both sides of the battle. Pious Jews, whether Orthodox or hasidic, formed perhaps the most conservative, indeed reactionary, element in Europe, in deploring artistic and scientific change. But in the gentile world nobody took the slightest notice of them, or even knew they existed, except perhaps as a piece of traditional human furniture. They saw the Jews, and Jewishness, as everywhere and always identified with modernism in its most extreme form.

What could not be denied was that the emancipation of the European Jews and their emergence from the ghetto into the intellectual and artistic mainstream greatly accelerated changes which were coming anyway. The Jews were natural iconoclasts. Like the prophets, they set about smiting and overturning all the idols of the conventional modes with skill and ferocious glee. They invaded spheres traditionally alien or banned to Jews and quickly became the chief *foci* of dynamism.

The Jewish musical tradition, for instance, was far older than anyone else's in Europe. Music remained an element in Jewish services, and the cantor was almost as pivotal a figure in local Jewish society as the rabbi. But Jewish musicians, except as converts, had played no part in European musical development. Hence the entry, in considerable numbers, of Jewish composers and performers on the musical scene in the middle decades of the nineteenth century was a phenomenon, and a closely observed one. Judaism was not the issue. Some, like

Mendelssohn, were converts. Others, like Jacques Offenbach (1819–80), were assimilated and indifferent. A few of them, like Jacques Halévy (1799–1862) and Giacomo Meyerbeer (1791–1864), were faithful or observant.* But the musical world was aware of their Jewishness and the influence they wielded, not just as composers but as directors of orchestras, academies, opera houses, musical theatres. Moreover, there was a general belief that many more famous musicians were of Jewish origin. Rossini, present at that famous Rothschild Frankfurt wedding in 1839, was widely believed to be a Jew. Johann Strauss, founder of the famous Viennese musical family, was certainly the son of a baptized Jewish innkeeper in Budapest. Even Wagner had fears he might be Jewish (they were unfounded). There was also a suspicion that radical innovation in music was primarily a Jewish responsibility.

Between 1860 and 1914, public resistance to innovation grew, particularly in centres like Vienna, where they took music very seriously indeed. As one musical historian has put it, the quickening rate of stylistic change and the growth of the musical public combined to make 'the normally difficult relation between artist and public a pathological one'.[200] The musicians became deliberately provocative; the public sometimes responded with force. The iconoclastic Jewish element made both provocation and response more extreme. There was fury in Vienna when Mahler was made head of the court opera in 1897, probably the most important post in German music. He got it on merit: he was one of the leading conductors in Germany and the appointment was abundantly justified by the variety and splendour of the productions which marked his ten-year tenure. But to make himself eligible he had to convert to Catholicism. This, in the eyes of those who hated his innovations, far from removing his Jewish stigma, drew attention to it. 'He was not a man who ever deceived himself,' wrote his wife, 'and he knew that people would not forget he was a Jew. . . . Nor did he wish it forgotten. . . . He never denied his Jewish origin. Rather he emphasized it.'[201]

Mahler's reign in Vienna was stormy, and hostile intrigues eventually drove him to New York. All this took place without even the provocation of his symphonies, which were rarely or never performed in his lifetime. It was a different matter with Arnold

---

* Halévy, with La Juive (1835), created the new French opera form. His daughter Geneviève, later the famous hostess, married his best student, Georges Bizet. His nephew, Ludovic Halévy, wrote the libretto for Bizet's Carmen, most popular of all French operas. His great nephew was the celebrated historian, Élie Halévy. See Myrna Chase, Elie Halévy: An Intellectual Biography (Columbia 1980).

Schönberg (1874–1951), who was born a Jew in Vienna but brought up a Catholic. He caused a scandal at the age of eighteen by converting to Protestantism (he returned to Judaism in 1933). In 1909 his Opus 11, No. 1 for piano dispensed with traditional tonality completely. Two years later, largely on Mahler's recommendation, he was given a minor post in the Viennese Royal Academy of Music, and this produced a stormy protest in the Austrian parliament. Here, it was argued, was Vienna, capital of European music, custodian of one of the crown jewels of world culture – was it to be put into the hands of this Jew, or ex-Jew, or ex-Catholic, or whatever he was, who held it in obvious contempt? The feeling of cultural outrage was much more important than anti-Semitism as such; or rather, it turned into anti-Semites, at any rate for the moment, people who normally never expressed such feelings. It was the Jew-as-Iconoclast which aroused the really deep rage. When Schönberg's enormous traditional cantata *Gurrelieder* was presented in Vienna in February 1913, it was given a fifteen-minute ovation. Next month, in the same city, his Chamber Symphony No. 1 (Opus 9), followed by the *Altenberglieder* of his gentile pupil Alban Berg, generated a vicious riot and police intervention. Mahler had begun it; Schönberg carried it on; both were Jews, and they corrupted young Aryan composers like Berg – so the argument went.

It received a further twist when innovation was accompanied by eroticism. This was precisely the ingredient Leon Bakst (1866–1924) injected into the Ballets Russes, which was primarily a Jewish creation. He was the son of a pedlar who walked all the way from Grodno to St Petersburg with his belongings on his back and then prospered as a Crimean War military tailor. Bakst was red-haired; passionately Jewish in his own way, he believed that most famous artists – Rembrandt and Ruisdael for instance – had Jewish origins and had the Star of David on his monogrammed stationery. He got himself expelled from the Academy of Art in St Petersburg by painting the prize subject, 'The Madonna Weeping over Christ', with a crowd of Lithuanian ghetto Jews to emphasize the Jewishness of Christ and His mother: the outraged judges simply scrawled across his canvas two furious strokes of red crayon.[202]

It was Bakst, the designer of costumes for Pavlova and Nijinsky, who first introduced the latter to Diaghilev. When the company was formed, a Jew, Gabriel Astruc, provided the money, followed in due course by Baron Gunzberg, the Tsarist court Jew. Bakst created the ballets themselves as well as the sets and costumes. He brought to the venture his overwhelming heterosexual eroticism, made more powerful by his skill in covering or constraining, his use of veils. For his ballet *Cléopâtre*, opening the historic programme at the Châtelet Theatre in Paris on 19 May 1909, he announced: 'A huge temple on the banks of the Nile. Columns. A sultry day. The scent of the East and a great many lovely women with beautiful bodies.' He found Ida Rubinstein, a typical Jewish beauty, to play the role, and it was the spectacular appearance of Rubinstein, unveiled on stage, in Bakst's costumes and settings, which launched the movement. As Serge Lifar put it, 'It was painting which first attracted Paris to the Ballets Russes.'[203] Rubinstein, with her long legs, Semitic profile and oriental image was, as Arnold Haskell put it, 'the living picture of Bakst'.[204] The following year he created *Schéhérazade*, the greatest of all the Ballets Russes successes, with a harem of beauties indulging in an orgy of sex with muscular negroes, ending in a bloodbath of vengeance. This was the biggest culture-shock of the entire period.

If Bakst's voluptuousness was Jewish, so was his sense of colour and still more his moral theory of colour, which, as he said, used religious qualities in certain colours ('There is a blue the colour of a Magdalen and the blue of a Messalina') to draw from the spectators the exact emotions he required.[205] He passed this on, in the school he ran for a time in St Petersburg, to his favourite pupil Marc Chagall (1887–1985), the grandson of a Jewish ritual butcher. Again, the arrival of the Jewish artist was a strange phenomenon. It is true that, over the centuries, there had been many animals (though few humans) in Jewish art: lions on Torah curtains, owls on Judaic coins, animals on the Capernaum capitals, birds on the rim of the fountain-basis in the fifth-century Naro synagogue in Tunis; there were carved animals, too, on timber synagogues in eastern Europe – indeed the Jewish wood-carver was the prototype of the modern Jewish plastic artist. A book of Yiddish folk-ornament, printed at Vitebsk in 1920, was similar to Chagall's own bestiary. But the resistance of pious Jews to portraying the living image was still strong at the beginning of the twentieth century. When the young Chaim Soutine (1893–1943), the son of a poor hasidic tailor, painted a portrait from memory of the Smilovichi rabbi, his father flogged him. Chagall's father, who hauled herring-barrels for a living, did not go so far when his son began to study with the portraitist Yehuda Pen, but he flung the five-rouble fee violently on the ground as a gesture of disapproval.[206] So the urge to get away from the religious background was strong. So too was the need to leave Russia. Chagall spent several weeks in gaol for trying to enter St Petersburg without a permit; Bakst was refused entrance (though his father was a 'privileged Jew') as late as 1912, when he was already world-famous.

So Jewish painters went to Paris, and immediately the iconoclastic spirit asserted itself and they passed into the vanguard of artistic adventure. Chagall got there in 1910 and lived in the colony set up in the famous wooden La Ruche, off the Rue de Vaugirard, which once housed Léger, Archipenko and Lenin, among others. There he found the Jewish sculptors Ossip Zadkine (1890–1967) and Jacques Lipchitz (1891–1973). Moise Kisling (1891–1953) was in Paris too. These artists were Polish or Russian Ashkenazis but there were Sephardis too: the Rumanian Jules Pascin (1885–1930) and the Italian from Livorno, Amedeo Modigliani (1884–1920), with whom Soutine, when he too arrived, shared a single cot, taking turns to sleep in it. There had been Jews in the artistic forefront already: Camille Pissarro (1830–1903) and his son Lucien (1863–1944), and Max Liebermann (1847–1935) who took Impressionism to Germany. But these new young Jews were wild men, *fauves*. Except for Chagall, who lived to adorn the new Zion, they had little respect for their religious inheritance. Soutine later denied that he was a Jew or had been born in Vilna and in his will he left 100 francs to the rabbi's children to buy sweets and dance on his grave. But they all had what had now become the characteristic Jewish impulse to push forward ruthlessly into new cultural territory.

It was not that Jews had any general tendency to embrace modernism as such. There was no Jewish world-outlook, let alone a plan to impose modernism on the world. One cultural historian has gone so far as to write that to ascribe modernism to the Jews is 'sheer anti-Semitic tendentiousness or philosemitic parochialism'.[207] Jews who were decisive innovators in their own fields were often highly conservative in every other aspect of life. Thus Max Liebermann, whose paintings once shocked and alarmed Germans – his 'Infant Christ Teaching in the Temple' (1879) showed Jesus as a Jewish boy – boasted that he was 'the complete bourgeois'. He lived in the same house where his parents had lived, and 'I eat, drink, sleep, take walks and work with the regularity of a church clock'.[208] Sigmund Freud (1856–1939), perhaps the greatest of all Jewish innovators, detested 'modernism' in almost all its forms. He had a particular contempt for modern art, accusing those who produced it of having 'congenital defects in their eyesight'.[209] He loved the graven images he collected, from Ancient Egypt, China, Greece and Rome, and he sat at his desk surrounded by them, rather like Abraham with his household gods, but not one was older than the Renaissance. Like Liebermann, Freud had a rigid daily, weekly, monthly, annual routine. Thus: 8–1 p.m., patients. Lunch 1–2, the main meal, which had to be promptly served.

Constitutional walk, 2–3 p.m. (in bad weather and in old age he would take it striding round the vast family apartment). Then, 3–4 p.m. consultation, then patients until a late supper, then another constitutional followed by writing until 1 a.m. The weekly schedule was equally rigid: every Tuesday fortnight, meeting of B'nai B'rith; Wednesday with his professional group; Thursday and Saturday evenings, lectures at the university, followed on Saturday by his one relaxation, a game of four-handed tarok; Sunday morning, visit to his mother.[210] Disciples who wished to see him had either to make an appointment or wait at certain places on his regular walks. Like Marx, who would not allow his daughters to train or work but kept them genteelly at home sewing, painting watercolours and playing the piano, Freud ran his large household in patriarchal fashion. Neither Marx nor Freud applied his theories to his home and family. Freud was the eldest son of a powerful mother and the pair of them bossed around his five younger sisters. In due course his wife took a subordinate role too. She did everything for him, even spreading his toothbrush with paste, like an old-fashioned valet. He never discussed his ideas with his wife, who tended privately to dismiss them: 'Women have always had such troubles, but they needed no psychoanalysis to conquer them. After the menopause, they become quieter and more resigned.' Nor were his ideas applied to his children. He sent his sons to a family doctor to find out the facts of life. His own behaviour was always ultra-respectable.[211]

The case of Freud is worth examining not only because of his enormous intrinsic importance but because of the way his work constantly echoes many of the great themes of the Jewish spirit and history. Indeed, he has some claims to be considered the most representative of all Jews. Not that Freud was a believer, let alone a believer in Torah. He considered all religion to be a form of collective delusion and all his work tended to show that religious (and other) beliefs were wholly man-made. There is some conflict of evidence about how much Hebrew and Yiddish he knew,[212] and his education, rather than Judaic, was European, classical and scientific; he wrote superb German and his style won him the Goethe Prize. But both his parents came from hasidic Galicia, his mother from the ultra-hasidic town of Brody. None of his children converted or married gentiles (his son Ernest became a Zionist). He himself always identified with the Jews and in his last decade he announced that he was neither an Austrian nor a German but a Jew. He knew Herzl and respected him, and he would never take royalties from Hebrew or Yiddish translations of his works. His biographer Ernest Jones wrote that he 'felt himself to be a Jew to the core . . . he made very few friends who were not Jews'.[213] When his discoveries made him unpopular, it was to B'nai B'rith that he turned, as he later explained: 'In my isolation the longing arose in me for a circle of chosen, high-minded men who, regardless of the audacity of what I had done, would receive me with friendliness. . . . That you were Jews only suited me the more, for I myself was a Jew, and it always seemed to me not only shameful but downright senseless to deny it.'[214]

However, Freud turned to his background for more than comfort. He ascribed great powers to the Jewish spirit. 'If you do not let your son grow up a Jew,' he told Max Graf, 'you will deprive him of those sources of energy which cannot be replaced by anything else.' But the Jews not only had immense energy, a quality Freud greatly admired, they placed supreme value on ideas, which he thought even more vital: 'We preserved our unity through ideas', he wrote, 'and because of them we have survived to this day.' He believed in the Jewish cathedocracy, the paramountcy of mind, and said that the founding of the Jabneh academy was 'for me always one of the most significant manifestations in our history'.[215]

Freud's abrupt discovery of psychoanalysis, his move from the posture of a physician to a healer, had something of the nature of a conversion, and of a Jewish kind. Until he was in his mid-thirties, he was a medical scientist. Thereafter he suddenly lost interest in conventional medicine. It was a Jewish tradition that mysteries should be reserved for middle age. Maimonides, rationalist though he was, accepted this view: he did not treat mental cases until well into life. The year thirty-six was considered especially significant. The Ba'al Shem Tov, for instance, revealed himself in his thirty-sixth year. In fact Ernest Jones dates Freud's 'latency period' from the end of 1887, when he was thirty-one, culminating in the publication of 'A Case of Successful Treatment of Hypnosis' in 1892, when he was indeed thirty-six. But Freud himself, while believing in the sudden-miracle theory of scientific discovery, dated it three years later. He said a marble tablet ought to be placed on the house where he had a critical dream. It should read, he said: 'In this house on 24 July 1895, the secret of dreams was revealed to Dr Sigmund Freud.' Jones argued that the actual discovery was preceded by a change in personality. What is clear is that, from this point, Freud was elaborating an entirely new way in which human beings should look at themselves. He was seeking, as Jones put it, the answer to 'the great problem of how man came to be what he is', the ultimate goal of 'the secrets of man's inner nature'.[216]

This is essentially a religious quest and, as with all founders of new religions, Freud distanced himself rapidly from former associates. 'With every step he took in his new venture he became more of a stranger to his colleagues. They could see no link whatever between [his] years of solid and fruitful medical research and his new interests and methods.'[217] The spark of insight broadened out into a whole new faith. 'What was at first a small clue in psychopathology', wrote his colleague Hans Sachs, 'widened out by the untiring concentration of an original mind until eventually it grew into a fundamental concept, of psychology, of human civilization, and lastly of all organic development.'[218]

That Freud had the dynamism of a religious founder or a great heresiarch cannot be doubted. 'Because I was a Jew', he said, 'I found myself free from many prejudices which restricted others in the use of their intellect.' Or again: 'I often felt as though I had inherited all the defiance and all the passions with which our ancestors defended their Temple and could gladly sacrifice my life for one great moment in history.' He was, he confided to his friend Wilhelm Fliess, not so much a scientist, an experimenter or even an observer as a man of action: 'I am nothing but by temperament a conquistador, an adventurer . . . with the curiosity, the boldness and the tenacity that belongs to such a being.'[219] In his view it was Moses, not Abraham, who had founded Judaism, and he was fascinated by the great lawgiver, especially his statue in Rome by Michelangelo: 'For three lonely September weeks in 1913 I stood every day in the church in front of the statue, studied it, measured it, sketched it, until I captured the understanding of it.'[220] He also identified himself with Joseph, the dreamer and seer, and liked to point out that the experts who interpreted dreams were among the most important members of Alexander the Great's staff.

Freud took many elements from Judaism. His technique of interpreting dreams is similar in some ways to the method used in the *Zohar*.[221] From his friend Fliess he derived what he termed (in a letter to Jung) 'the specifically mystic nature of my mysticism', above all a fascination with the significance and predictive quality of numbers.[222] He believed in, to the point of dread, such concepts as the *Doppelgänger* – 'I think I have avoided you', he wrote to a surprised Arthur Schnitzler, 'from a kind of reluctance to meet my double.' He suffered from appalling *Todesangst* (death-anxiety).[223] If Freudianism, like Marxism, is a system of superstition in some ways, if it suffers from the same osmotic quality as Nathan of Gaza's messianic kabbalah – an ability to accommodate inconvenient facts as they emerge – that is not surprising, because it comes from the same background: western science is more a veneer than a substance. But the Jewish element in Freudianism is not primarily hasidic; it is Mosaic. Freud wanted to found a new system of quasi-religious law, with all the power and permanence that implied. As he put it, 'We possess the truth' – no religious leader could have phrased it more dogmatically.[224]

The new creed was Jewish in two more important ways. Its Torah, its essential documents, were Freud's own writings and cases, and they, like the Bible, were the apotheosis of the short story. The skill in illustrating a thesis by a tale had been a characteristic of the sages which had re-emerged in hasidism. Freud gave it scientific and secular status. It was, and to some extent still is, the key to his tremendous power over people. Referring to his 1901 'Fragment of an Analysis of a Case of Hysteria' (the story of Dora), he noted, with authorial satisfaction: 'it is the most subtle thing I have yet written and will produce an even more horrifying effect than usual'.[225] As Steven Marcus has pointed out, Freud is never less convincing than when denying his literary intentions: 'I must now turn', he wrote disingenuously, 'to consider a complication to which I should certainly give no space if I were a man of letters engaged upon the creation of a mental state like this for a short story, instead of being a medical man engaged on its dissection.' Or again: 'It still strikes myself as strange that the case histories I write should read like short stories and that, as one might say, they lack the serious stamp of science.'[226] In fact he took as much trouble with the shape and style of his cases prepared for publication as other contemporary doctor–short-story writers, such as Arthur Conan Doyle and Somerset Maugham – but in addition he brought to them the conviction of truth, the portentousness and the underlying faith of the author of the First Book of Kings. Such cases as those of Dora, the Rat Man, Little Hans, Schreber and the Wolf Man, are the heart and essence of his revelation.

Secondly, Freudianism was a creed spread and practised primarily by Jews. It is not true, as has been often alleged, that it sprang from the treatment of wealthy Jewish women in Vienna. But Josef Breuer, Freud's John the Baptist – in so far as he had one[227] – was a Jew, and so were all the original psychoanalysts. The significance of Jung to Freud was that he was the first important gentile follower he had been able to attract. That was why at the Second Psycho-Analytical Congress at Nuremberg in 1910 he overruled objections and proposed that Jung be made permanent president:

Most of you are Jews, and therefore you are incompetent to win friends for the new teaching. Jews must be content with the modern role of preparing the ground. It is absolutely essential that I should form ties in the world of general science. I am getting on in years and am weary of being perpetually attacked. We are all in danger. . . . The Swiss [Jung] will save us – will save me, and all of you as well.[228]

Freud was Mosaic in his conviction of righteousness too. The alternative Jewish tradition of tolerance, of the polycentric leadership and views, did not appeal to him. Max Graf, father of Little Hans, said the atmosphere in Freud's study was that of 'the foundation of a religion'. The patients were 'the apostles' and Freud himself, 'good-hearted and considerate though he was in private life', was 'hard and relentless in the presentation of his ideas'.[229] Freud had his little court, like a hasidic sage, first formed in 1902, and he never tolerated serious opposition to himself within it. Alfred Adler (1870–1937), one of the first and most brilliant of its members, was treated – once he ventured to disagree – not as a critical colleague but as a heresiarch or, in a term the Marxists would popularize, as a 'defector'. As Graf put it, 'It was a trial and the charge was heresy. . . . Freud, as the head of a church, banished Adler; he rejected him from the official church. Within the space of a few years, I lived through the whole development of a church history.' Thereafter the *herem* was often in use, notably in the case of Jung, the greatest heresiarch of all. The break with Jung was especially bitter because, as Jones put it, he was to have been 'the Joshua to Freud's Moses'. His 'face beamed whenever he spoke of Jung: "This is my beloved son, in whom I am well pleased." ' 'When the empire I have founded is orphaned', he wrote, 'no one but Jung must inherit the whole thing.'[230]

The detection and expulsion of heretics was attended by *odium theologicum*. As Sachs said, Freud was 'hard and sharp as steel, a good hater'. He denounced Albert Moll, author of *The Sexual Life of the Child*, as 'a brute' with 'the intellectual and moral constitution of a pettifogging lawyer', and (throwing him out of his study) 'he has stunk up the room like the devil himself'. Adler was 'trash', 'full of venom and meanness'; 'I have made a pigmy great.' Wilhelm Stekel, another 'apostle', was 'a louse on the head of an astronomer' – a piece of abuse Freud stole from Heine, another good hater. Jung became 'the heretic', 'the mystic', and 'Jungian' the worst term in the Freudian vocabulary. Ex-followers were cut in the street, references to them excised from new editions of Freud's works or changed to 'formerly an analyst'. Jung's letters to Freud were 'lost' for many years.[231] On these searing controversies, Freud quoted Heine again: 'One must forgive one's enemies, but not before they have been hanged.' There is much evidence of hanging, none of forgiveness. When Adler died in 1937 on a trip to Aberdeen, Freud – then over eighty – wrote to Arnold Zweig: 'I don't understand your sympathy for Adler. For a Jew-boy out of a Viennese suburb, a death in Aberdeen is an unheard-of career in itself.'[232]

If Freud had the intolerance of an Ezra and the characteristic faults of the cathedocracy, he also had some of its heroic virtues: dauntless courage in the defence of what he saw as the truth; passionate industry in pursuit of it, right to the end of a life marked by unremitting labour; a saintly death, after a slow cancer for which he refused morphia: 'I prefer to think in torment than not to be able to think clearly.'[233] Arthur Koestler, who saw him at the end, found a 'small and fragile' sage, with 'the indestructible vitality of a Hebrew patriarch'.[234] Freud was in the irrationalist Jewish tradition, more of a Nahmanides or a Besht than a Maimonides. But, perhaps because of this, he became a central pillar of the twentieth-century intellectual structure, itself a largely irrational edifice. To vary the metaphor, he gave humanity a new mirror, and no man has ever changed so radically and irreversibly the way in which people see themselves; or indeed talk about themselves, for he changed the vocabulary of introspection too.

If Freud transformed the way we see ourselves, Albert Einstein (1879–1955) changed the way we see the universe. That made him a central pillar of the twentieth century and perhaps of the twenty-first too, for history shows that great new reformulations of scientific law, such as Galileo's, or Newton's, or Darwin's, continue to impose their consequences on society for huge spans of time. Einstein was a Jew from Ulm, where his father ran a small electro-chemical firm. He worked in the Swiss patent office in Berne, where he formulated the Special Theory of Relativity (1905) and the General Theory (1915). His essential discoveries, like Freud's, were made before the First World War; thereafter, he searched persistently but vainly for a general field theory which would accommodate Quantum Physics, in whose formulation he also played a key role.[235]

Einstein never seems to have been a practising Jew in the ordinary sense. In this he resembled Freud. But unlike Freud he did not dismiss belief in God as an illusion; he sought, rather, to redefine it. Intellectually, he was wholly in the Jewish–rationalist tradition of Maimonides and Spinoza. He was an empirical scientist of the most rigorous kind, formulating his theories specifically to make exact verification possible, and insisting it take place before according his views any validity – almost the exact opposite of Freud's dogmatics. But he was prepared to admit the existence of non-verifiable truth. In this respect too he was more honest than Freud. Freud denied mystic truth while remaining, essentially, a mystic himself; Einstein remained a rationalist, while admitting a mystic sphere. He thought that 'the mysterious', which he saw as emotional rather than factual, 'stands at the cradle of true art and true science'. Beyond 'the profoundest reason and the most radiant beauty' there were impenetrable truths 'which only in their most primitive forms are accessible to our minds'. Awareness of this, he argued, was what constituted true religious feeling and 'in this sense, and this sense alone, I am a deeply religious man'.[236]

The last assertion was a restatement of Maimonides' belief that there are two complementary ways of perceiving truth, reason and Revelation. However, Einstein was much closer to Spinoza, whom he greatly admired, in dismissing Revelation as such. What he did say was that intuitive thinking was essential to the formulation of a great scientific concept, a sort of blind leap into a huge theoretical generalization.[237] Here he had a great deal in common with the French Jewish philosopher Henri Bergson (1859–1941), who shared Einstein's stress on the mystical and intuitive element in science (and the interaction of time and matter).[238] But in Einstein's view and work, once intuition created the elements of an idea, science and reason took over. 'I want to know how God created this world,' he said – almost a mystical aim. But the knowledge had to be acquired by mathematical formulation, verified by astronomy. In a sense, Einstein was doing what the kabbalists had attempted, to describe creation by numbers. But whereas their numbers were intuitive, magic and unverifiable, his were rationally conceived and validated by telescope. There was magic, in the sense that it amazed him to be able to discover that the universe, instead of being chaotic, as one might *a priori* have supposed, was in fact orderly, governed by laws of space–time, which might have to be modified occasionally, as he had modified Newton's, but which were fundamentally accessible to the human intellect. Herein, he said, 'lies the "miracle", which is becoming increasingly deep with the development of our knowledge'.[239]

Einstein believed that the macrocosmic and the microcosmic must be governed by the same laws and that his General Theory of Relativity would ultimately become merely part of a unified theory governing all electromagnetic fields. Every physical relationship of the material world could then be accurately described in a few pages of equations. He felt a deep kinship with Spinoza, who was likewise 'utterly convinced of the causal dependence of all phenomena, at a time when the success accompanying the efforts to achieve a knowledge of the causal relationship with natural phenomena was still quite modest'. He, coming 300 years after Spinoza, might succeed. The quest was peculiarly Jewish, in that it was impelled by an overwhelming need for an enveloping truth-law about the universe, a scientific Torah. The alternative to a general theory was indeterminacy, a concept especially abhorrent to the Jewish mind, since it seems to make impossible all ethics, or certainty in history, politics and law.[240] Hence Einstein's forty-year search, ultimately inconclusive. Like Maimonides, who in his code, his commentary and his *Guide* was trying to reduce his vast Judaic inheritance into a modest-sized, clear and rational body of knowledge – a Judaic *summa* – Einstein was seeking a stark and monumental simplicity, a scientific *summa* which would make plain sense of the universe.[241]

In fact, his achievement stopped with the establishment of relativity theory. The truth of that has been demonstrated many times and it has been for the past sixty years or more a central part of the scientific corpus of knowledge. In the general mind, however, it introduced not a great new simplicity but a great new complexity, for relativity was confused with relativism, and especially with moral relativism. The conjunction of Einstein and Freud, at least in the popular perception, struck a devastating blow at the absolute certainties of Judaeo-Christian ethics, in which Einstein, at any rate, profoundly believed.[242] That was another heavy debt added to the Jewish account in many dark minds. The arrival of relativity theory was the point at which a great many educated and intelligent men gave up trying to keep abreast of scientific discovery. The Jewish literary philosopher Lionel Trilling (1905–75) noted the consequences:

> This exclusion of most of us from the mode of thought which is habitually said to be the characteristic achievement of the modern age is bound to be experienced as a wound given to our intellectual self-esteem. About this humiliation we all agree to be silent; but can we doubt that it . . . introduced into the life of mind a significant element of dubiety and alienation which must be taken into account in any estimate that is made of the present fortunes of mind?[243]

Hence the net result of this furious intellectual activity and cultural innovation at the turn of the century, an activity in which Jews were perceived to be taking a leading part, was to produce not merely an arms race between progressives and conservatives but a widespread feeling of bewilderment and anxiety. The new Jewish secular intellectuals felt this as strongly as anyone, even while they contributed to it with their work. The yearning for remembered certitudes is one of the great engines of Proust's masterpiece, *À la Recherche du temps perdu*.

In the work of Franz Kafka (1883–1924) the entire governing principle appears to be incomprehensible displacement. 'I am here,' one of his stories ends, 'more than that I do not know, further than that I cannot go. My ship has no rudder, and it is driven by the wind that blows in the uttermost regions of death.'[244] Schönberg felt the same, summing up his life in one weird metaphor: 'I had the feeling as if I had fallen into an ocean of boiling water, and not knowing how to swim. . . . I tried with my legs and arms as best I could. . . . I never gave up. But how could I give up in the middle of an ocean?'[245] The expressionist poet Jacob von Hoddis, formerly Hans Davidsohn, epitomized and aggravated the bewilderment by producing in 1910 a short set of verses, 'Weltende' ('The World's End') which briefly became the most famous and notorious poem in Germany. He read it at the poetry-cabaret organized by the expressionist leader, Kurt Hiller, who claimed to be a descendant of the Rabbi Hillel. It began, 'The hat flies off the bourgeois's pointed head', and for reasons now obscure it immediately seemed to sum up modernism both for its proponents and for its enemies, reducing the latter to incoherent rage.[246] In 1914 the young poet went insane, followed immediately after by virtually the whole of Europe, in a vast dance of destruction from which both the prospects and the predicament of the Jews emerged dramatically transformed.

PART SIX

Holocaust

———

On 9 November 1914, in a speech at London's Guildhall, the British Prime Minister, Herbert Asquith, announced dramatically: 'The Turkish empire has committed suicide.' Germany's wooing of Turkey, which had led the Kaiser to abandon his active support of Zionism, had finally succeeded. The sultan had committed himself to a German victory and was about to launch a *jihad* against Britain. Asquith wished to prevent the 100 million Moslem subjects of Britain's own empire from joining it. Hence his speech, committing Britain to breaking up the Ottoman empire at last, and giving freedom to its peoples.[1] But, in making it, he was unconsciously adding another crucial piece to the jigsaw of the Zionist state. For if Turkish rule were removed from Palestine, among other places, there might be nothing to prevent a Jewish national home from moving into the vacuum.

The notion that Jews would benefit from a German defeat in the fearful conflict now beginning would have struck most of them, at the time, as absurd. The mortal enemy of the Jews was Tsarist Russia, which the German army was now trying to tear to pieces. In London's East End, Jews were reluctant to volunteer to fight the Germans for this very reason. Everyone associated Jewish cultural leadership with Germany. Except for the pacifists of the far left, all the leading German-speaking Jewish intellectuals, led by Max Liebermann, signed a petition supporting Germany's war aims – Einstein was almost the only one who refused.

When the German troops, having defeated the Russian army at Tannenberg, pushed into Russian Poland, the Jews hailed them as saviours. One who did so was Ze'ev Dov Begin, father of a future Prime Minister of Israel. In addition to Hebrew and Yiddish he spoke German, in preference to Polish which he called 'the language of anti-Semitism'. He told the young Begin and his sister (later Mrs Halperin): 'You see, the Germans will come, it is a different culture, it is not

Russia.' The Russian army, withdrawing, rounded up entire Jewish communities and drove them, under the lash, to Siberia – a sinister adumbration of Stalin's minorities policy. The Begins watched the Cossacks burn down Jewish villages. When the Germans arrived, Mrs Halperin later recalled, they 'treated the Jews marvellously. . . . They gave each child sweets and biscuits. They were different Germans, a different period.'[2]

Even in the Jewish settlements in Palestine, German tended to be the lingua franca. Many of the settlers wanted German, rather than Hebrew, to be the language of instruction in Jewish schools. It was accepted, without debate, as the official language of Zionist congresses. The Zionist office in Berlin saw itself as the headquarters of the world movement, and its members were calling for a German protectorate over the Jews, as well as over Islam. Many believed it was the big Jewish community of Salonika which had helped to push Turkey into the war on Germany's side.[3]

Nevertheless, the more perceptive realized the immense significance of the British decision to carve up the Ottoman rump. One was Chaim Weizmann, who since Herzl's death had become the most effective proponent of Zionism in the West. 'The time has now come', he wrote with satisfaction after Asquith's speech, 'to speak openly – to point out to the world the attitude of the Jews to Palestine.' Weizmann was one of the noblest and most important figures in Jewish history. As a Zionist leader he was just as skilful as Herzl in handling world statesmen but in addition he could speak for the *Ostjuden* rank and file – he was one. The atmosphere of his home, in the Pripet Marsh town of Motol, was entirely traditional. His father, who cut timber and floated it down to the Baltic, knew Caro's Code by heart and his favourite book was the *Guide of the Perplexed*. It is true that, on the walls of their home, next to Maimonides, was the portrait of Baron Hirsch, but 'the Return' was seen as religious: the local rabbi told Weizmann: 'One has to do much, learn much, know much and suffer much before one is worthy of that.'[4]

Certainly, Weizmann had to suffer much just to acquire a modern education. There were no newspapers in his home. His schoolmaster, a secret *maskil*, had to smuggle in a Hebrew textbook on the natural sciences under cover of teaching the Prophets. Then there was the Tsarist state, whose *numerus clausus* rules allocated a maximum 10 per cent of the grammar-school places to Jews even in towns where they were over 50 per cent of the population. Everything was done to prevent Jews getting to university. Weizmann later wrote: 'as one read, year after year, the complicated *ukases* which poured from St

Petersburg, one obtained the impression that the whole cumbersome machinery of the vast Russian empire was created for the sole purpose of inventing and amplifying rules and regulations for the hedging in of the existence of its Jewish subjects'. So education involved 'ceaseless chicanery, deception and humiliation'.[5] Weizmann acquired monumental patience and persistence, as well as industry, and managed to get to the Berlin Polytechnic, one of the three best science schools in Europe, and later to Switzerland, where he obtained his doctorate in chemistry at Freiburg (1899).

But it was in England, where he came to teach biochemistry at Manchester University, that Weizmann found his life-task: to exploit the existence of the British empire, and the goodwill of its ruling class, to bring the Jewish national home into existence. Weizmann, who became a British subject in 1910, always accepted the British at their own valuation, as tolerant and fair-minded, loving freedom and justice. He banked all his emotional coin in their hearts and on the whole drew a decent dividend. In the years before 1914 he set about cultivating them. He met C. P. Scott, the powerful editor of the Liberal *Manchester Guardian*, and through him such Lancashire MPs as Arthur Balfour, leader of the Conservatives, and Winston Churchill. Scott also introduced him to his closest political friend, Lloyd George. All these men became staunch supporters of Zionism.

Weizmann found an unexpected ally in the Liberal MP Herbert Samuel. He was a member of the Jewish establishment at a time when it was overwhelmingly, sometimes venomously, anti-Zionist. His father had founded the immensely successful banking firm of Samuel Montagu, and his first cousin in the firm, Edwin Montagu, was also in politics and a leading anti-Zionist. Samuel had been to Balliol, that nest of atheism, and was forced to confess to his mother that he lost his faith there. But he conformed outwardly, continued to pay his synagogue dues, and proudly called himself a Jew. So when he got into the cabinet in 1909 he was the first Jew to serve there. He had also done political work in Jewish Whitechapel, and the appalling scenes of poverty and degradation he witnessed there made him a Zionist. This was confirmed by his marginal involvement in the 1911 Marconi case, where he experienced for himself the cruelty of anti-Semitism, even in tolerant Britain.

Samuel was chilly, silent, reserved; he kept his views to himself. Not even Weizmann knew he was a Zionist. But he had privately conceived a plan to exploit the Turkish intervention, and on the day Asquith made his speech Samuel called on Sir Edward Grey, the Foreign Secretary, at the Foreign Office and held a critical conversation there.

What about a national home for the Jews? Grey said 'the idea had always had a strong sentimental attachment to him . . . [and he] would be prepared to work for it if the opportunity arose'. They discussed details. Samuel warned that the area of the national home could not include 'Beirut and Damascus since they contained a large, non-Jewish population which could not be assimilated'. Hence, he added, 'it would be a great advantage if the remainder of Syria were annexed by France, as it would be far better for the state to have a European power as neighbour than the Turk'. The idea took shape for an Anglo-French carve-up, the British getting Palestine, the French Syria–Lebanon, on the lines later drawn in the Sykes–Picot secret agreement, implemented at Versailles. But that did not yet mean the Jews would get their home. Later the same day Samuel strolled across to the Treasury to enlist the help of Lloyd George, now Chancellor of the Exchequer. He 'said to me he was very keen to see a Jewish state established there'.[6]

So Weizmann and Samuel set the campaign in motion. The Fabian *New Statesman*, in a plea for a British protectorate enshrining a Jewish national home, argued: 'The hopes of the Zionists have suddenly passed from an ideal into a matter of practical politics.'[7] In fact there was a long way to go. Asquith, a drawing-room anti-Semite, looked on in disdainful amusement when Samuel put his plan to the cabinet and it was hotly resisted by his anti-Zionist cousin Montagu. The Prime Minister relayed their encounters in his daily letters to his girlfriend Venetia Stanley. '[Samuel] thinks', he wrote (28 January 1915),

we might plant in this not very promising territory about 3 or 4 million Jews, and that this would have a good effect on those (including I suppose himself) who were left behind. . . . It reads almost like a new edition of *Tancred* brought up to date. I confess I am not attracted to this proposed addition to our responsibilities. But it is a curious illustration of Dizzie's favourite dictum that 'race is everything' to find this almost lyrical outburst proceeding from the well-ordered and methodical brain of H.S.[8]

Again, on 13 March 1915 he referred to Samuel's 'almost dithyrambic memorandum' on Palestine, 'into which the scattered Jews could in time swarm back from all quarters of the globe and in due course obtain Home Rule (what an attractive community!). Curiously enough the only other partisan of this proposal is Lloyd George, who I need not say does not care a damn for the Jews' – merely wishing to keep the 'agnostic, atheist French' out of the 'Holy Places'. Four days later, the Prime Minister told Miss Stanley that 'Cousin Montagu', or 'the Assyrian' as he called him, had hit back with a 'racy memorandum' in which he accused 'Cousin Herbert' of being incapable of translating into Hebrew a single phrase of his plan, which was 'a rather presumptuous and almost blasphemous (!) attempt to forestall Divine Agency in the collection of the Jews'. Asquith confessed that the language used by his quarrelling Jewish colleagues 'rather amazes me'.[9] His doubts were confirmed when the War Minister, Lord Kitchener, the only minister who had ever been there, said, 'Palestine would be of no value to us whatsoever.'

However, events moved steadily in the Zionists' favour. Kitchener was forced to relinquish the munitions portfolio to Lloyd George, which brought him into direct professional contact with Weizmann, now working on the war effort. Then Kitchener was drowned on a trip to Russia and Lloyd George took over the War Office completely. This marked the beginning of a transfer of resources to the eastern Mediterranean, making a British conquest of Palestine more likely. Weizmann found it easier to get to see senior members of the government. At the Foreign Office on 18 August 1916 he made a conquest of Lord Robert Cecil, who recorded:

He said with great truth that even in this country a Jew always had to give an explanation of his existence and he was neither quite an Englishman nor quite a Jew, and that the same thing was equally true with much more serious results in other countries. . . . Perhaps a phrase he used may convey something of the impression which he made. He said: 'I am not romantic except that Jews must always be romantic, for to them reality is too terrible.'

Cecil declared himself struck by 'the extraordinary impressiveness of his attitude, which made one forget his rather repellent and even sordid exterior'.[10] Four months later, Asquith was hounded out of office, Lloyd George became Prime Minister and he made Balfour his Foreign Secretary.

This was decisive. Asquith was quite wrong about Lloyd George. He was both a philosemite and a Zionist. Having denounced the Rothschilds in his wilder days, he was impressed by the 1st Lord Rothschild, whom he summoned, along with other financiers, to the Treasury at the outbreak of the war. 'Lord Rothschild,' he began, 'we have had some political unpleasantness.' 'Mr Lloyd George, this is no time to recall those things. What can I do to help?' Afterwards, Lloyd George said, 'Only the old Jew made sense.'[11] Weizmann found that he and Lloyd George 'sympathized on the common ground of the small nationality'. The new premier was a passionate Welsh patriot, and Samuel, when pushing his plan, always made the point that Palestine was 'a country the size of Wales'. Lloyd George was also a Bible-thumper, another point in the Zionists' favour. He noted:

'When Dr Weizmann was talking of Palestine he kept bringing up place-names which were more familiar to me than those on the Western Front.'[12]

Balfour was an equally important ally because behind a diffident manner lurked a steely will, much needed in overcoming the hesitations of Foreign Office officials and colleagues. Once convinced of a case, Balfour was a hard man to deflect, and he was Weizmann's most important convert. The two men first talked at length during the 1906 election, when Balfour upbraided Weizmann for rejecting Uganda. 'Mr Balfour, supposing I were to offer you Paris instead of London, would you take it?' 'But, Dr Weizmann, we have London.' 'That is true, but we had Jerusalem when London was a marsh.'[13] They had a further and decisive talk on 12 December 1914, worth recalling because it illustrates Weizmann's skills as a persuader. After Weizmann had put the Zionist case for action, Balfour told him that, in his view, the Jewish question 'would remain insoluble until either the Jews here became entirely assimilated or there was a normal Jewish community in Palestine'. He added, as a tease, that he had discussed this with the notorious anti-Semite Cosima Wagner in 1912, and she agreed! 'Yes,' replied Weizmann, 'and let me tell you exactly what she said – that the Jews were taking over German culture, science and industry. But', he added,

the essential point which most non-Jews overlook and which forms the very crux of the Jewish tragedy, is that those Jews who are giving their energies and their brains to the Germans are doing it in their capacities as Germans and are enriching Germany and not Jewry, which they are abandoning. . . . They must hide their Judaism in order to be allowed to place their brains and abilities at the disposal of the Germans. They are to no little extent responsible for German greatness. The tragedy of it all is that whereas we do not recognize them as Jews Madame Wagner does not recognize them as Germans, and so we stand there as the most exploited and misunderstood of people.

Balfour was moved to tears, shook Weizmann's hand and said that 'the road followed by a great and suffering nation had been illuminated for him'.[14]

Balfour thus became a staunch Zionist ally and at the Foreign Office moved towards a definite and public British commitment. Events favoured it. In January 1917 British troops began the conquest of Palestine. The same month the Tsar's regime collapsed, thus removing the biggest single obstacle to wholehearted, world-wide Jewish support for the Allied cause. The provisional Prime Minister, Kerensky, ended Russia's anti-Semitic code. And at the end of the month Germany began unrestricted u-boat warfare, making American intervention on the Allied side inevitable. The US government almost automatically became a strong supporter of the Jewish national home in Palestine. There were obstacles. The French hated the idea of the Jews, and still more the Protestant British, instead of Catholic (and atheist) France in Jerusalem. According to Sir Mark Sykes, who was negotiating the secret protectorate treaty, his opposite number, Georges Picot, 'spoke of pogroms in Paris' – the memory of Dreyfus was still vivid – and seemed 'hardly normal on this subject'. There were also stirrings of opposition from Arab interests, or those government departments which represented them. But the Arabs had been slow to get moving, had contributed nothing of substance to the war effort, and their 'Arab Revolt' had been unimpressive; moreover, the man in charge of it, Colonel T. E. Lawrence, favoured the British protectorate and Jewish national home plan. The most formidable opposition came from anti-Zionist Jews, especially Montagu, now in the important and relevant post of India Secretary. This was to have important consequences.

The form the commitment took was to be a letter from Balfour, as Foreign Secretary, to Lord Rothschild, as head of the English Jewish community, with the two sides agreeing on the text beforehand. Walter, 2nd Lord Rothschild, unlike his great father, who had died early in 1915, was a curious choice to take part in one of the most decisive events in Jewish history. It is true that, unlike his father, he had become more or less a Zionist. But he had a speech defect and many other inhibitions, and all his energies had gone, not on public and community affairs, but on the silent amassing of the greatest man-made collection ever assembled. At his Wren house in Tring, once the gift of Charles II to Nell Gwynn, he had accumulated 2,250,000 moths and butterflies, 300,000 bird-skins, 200,000 bird's eggs, and – among many other species – 144 live giant tortoises, including the largest in the world, 150 years old. He had published over 1,200 scientific papers (and books), discovered 5,000 new species, 250 of which had been named after him, including a giraffe, an elephant, a porcupine, a rockwallaby, a bird of paradise, a grackle, a fly with eyes on stalks and an intestinal worm. Unknown to anyone, even his few intimates, he was also being steadily stripped of his fortune by an unscrupulous peeress and her husband, who black-mailed him for over forty years.[15]

However, Rothschild was well advised by Weizmann and others, and his original draft of the British promise, handed to Balfour on 18 July 1917, contained three important elements. The first was the reconstitution of Palestine as a whole as the national home of the Jews. The second was unrestricted right of Jewish immigration. The third was Jewish internal autonomy. These gave the Zionists everything they could reasonably have wished. Weizmann believed to his dying day that, without Montagu's opposition, they would have got all three: 'there cannot be the slightest doubt that, without outside interference – *entirely from Jews!* – the draft would have been accepted [by the war cabinet] early in August, substantially as we submitted it'.[16] As it was, the letter was not approved by the cabinet until 31 October, and it had undergone substantial changes.[17] It no longer equated Palestine with the national home, it had no reference to unrestricted Jewish immigration or internal rule, and it safeguarded the rights of the Arabs. It was dated 2 November 1917 and the essential paragraph read: 'His Majesty's Government view with favour the establishment in Palestine of a national home for the Jewish people, and will use their best endeavours to facilitate the achievement of this object, it being clearly understood that nothing shall be done which may prejudice the civil and religious rights of existing non-Jewish communities in Palestine, or the rights and political status enjoyed by Jews in any other country.' Sykes came out of the decisive cabinet with the text and said: 'Dr Weizmann, it's a boy.' Scrutinizing it, Weizmann commented: 'I did not like the boy at first. It was not the one I expected.'[18]

All the same, the Balfour Declaration was the key piece in the jigsaw, for without it the Jewish state could never have come into existence. Thanks to Herzl and Weizmann, the Jews got in just in time. All over the world, nationalism and irredentism were winning the day. The Allies were besieged by subject peoples demanding that the coming victory and peace should guarantee them territorial rights on the basis of strict numerical head-counting, whether ethnic, linguistic or racial. The Jews had a romantic and historical claim to Palestine, but it was a very old one, and by the criteria applied at the Versailles settlement they had virtually none at all. At the time the Declaration was published, there were between 85,000 and 100,000 Jews living in Palestine, out of a total population of 600,000. Almost all the rest were Arabs. If the Arabs as a whole had been properly organized diplomatically during the war – if the Palestine Arabs had been organized at all – there is not the slightest doubt that the Declaration would never have been issued. Even twelve months later it would not have been possible. As it was, Weizmann pulled the Zionists through a brief window of opportunity, fated never to open again. Thanks to *Tancred* and *Daniel Deronda* he successfully appealed to the romantic instincts of the British ruling class, and thus received perhaps the last *ex gratia* gift of a great power, which went clean against the arithmetical spirit of the age.

In London, Lloyd George and Balfour thought they had taken advantage of the most odious war in human history at least to produce some benefit: to give the Jews a home. When Weizmann lunched with the Prime Minister on Armistice Day he found him reading the Psalms, in tears. Lloyd George often used to say afterwards that, to him, Palestine was 'the one interesting part of the war'.[19] But it was one thing for the enlightened despots in London to make promises; quite another for those on the spot, in Palestine, to deliver them. General Allenby had taken Jerusalem just a month after the Declaration was published and had entered the Holy City, in noble humility, on foot. When Weizmann went to see him in 1918, he found the general friendly but overwhelmed by military and administrative problems. 'But nothing can be done at present. We have to be extremely careful not to hurt the susceptibilities of the population.' Most of the senior British officers knew nothing of the Declaration. One or two were pro-Jewish. Some were anti-Semitic. Some were pro-Arab and expected them to rise up in due course and massacre the Jews. They regarded the local Jewish population as rubbish from Russia, probable Bolsheviks. General Sir Wyndham Deedes handed Weizmann some typewritten sheets: 'You had better read all of it with care. It is going to cause you a great deal of trouble in the future.' It was a copy of *The Protocols of the Elders of Zion*. The document had been brought back by the British Military Mission serving with the Tsarist Grand Duke Nicholas in the Caucasus. All the British officers in Palestine seemed to have it.[20]

Nevertheless, Britain went ahead and secured the Palestine mandate at the peace negotiations.[21] The work of creating the Jewish national home proceeded. The position when the British took over Palestine was as follows. The Jews were of two main types. There were the religious communities of scholars and sages, who had always existed, though their numbers grew steadily in the nineteenth century. In Jerusalem they inhabited the Jewish ghetto quarter. They lived on charitable funds collected from Jews all over the world. Their world did not comprehend the Balfour Declaration. But they were always full of complaints and demands. When Weizmann went to see them, they asked him to persuade Allenby to send a ship to Trieste, where the best myrtles were found, so that they could celebrate the Feast of Tabernacles properly.[22] He was exasperated, but they had their priorities just as he had his, and the Torah – without which a national home was meaningless – was essentially about exact observance; it has been truly observed that 'ritualism' is never a term of abuse in Judaism.

Then there were the agricultural settlers, established with the help of such philanthropists as Montefiore. Some, like those founded and subsidized by Edmund de Rothschild, were almost proprietory colonies. When the 1881 pogroms in Russia provoked the first substantial migration of Jews to Palestine, an event known as the First Aliyah ('ascent'), Rothschild took the new arrivals under his wing. He provided administration, schools and doctors for the new settlements and villages, known as *moshavot*. They included Ekron, Gederah, Rishon le-Zion and Petah Tikva (a revival) in Judaea, Rosh Pinha and Yesud ha-Ma'ala in Galilee, and Zikhron Yacov in Samaria. In 1896 Rothschild added Metullah and the Russian Zionists Be'er Toviyyah. At this stage, of the £1,700,000 so far provided to fund the settlements, all but £100,000 had come from Rothschild's own pocket. He had no time for Herzl, whom he thought of as a political agitator, or Russians like Weizmann, who were, to him, *schlimihls* (simpletons). He told a delegation of Zionists, including Nordau, 'These are my colonies and I shall do what I like with them.'[23] However, he handed the lot over to the new Jewish Colonization Association in 1900, though he continued to provide funds. From the 1890s date such settlement-villages as Rehovot and Hadera, and just after the turn of the century Kefar Tavor, Yavne'el, Menahemya and Kinneret. Not all the colonies were agricultural. Factories were started. New Jewish quarters were added to Jaffa, Haifa and Jerusalem itself.

Then from 1904, in the wake of yet more horrific pogroms in Russia, came the Second, and much larger, Aliyah. This brought over 40,000 immigrants, some of whom set up (1909) the new garden suburb of Jaffa which was to become the great city of Tel Aviv. The same year, the new settlers, who were mostly young, founded the first kibbutz ('collective') at Deganya, to end what they considered the scandal of farms run by Jewish overseers with Arab hired labour doing the actual work. Under the direction of Arthur Ruppin (1876–1943), appointed by Wolffsohn to run the Palestine office of the Zionist movement, the Zionists began systematic settlement work. The kibbutzim, which were voluntary collective farms, were the main type sponsored and funded by the Zionists, and eventually numbered over 200. But there were also *Moshav Ovedim*, agricultural villages whose members possessed individual proprietory holdings but co-operated to buy equipment, and *Moshav Shittifi*, where members owned only their own houses and worked the land as a collective. Ruppin was by origin a Prussian Jew, a sociologist, economist and statistician by training, and he brought this sombre but necessary combination of qualities, plus huge industry, persistence and a grim understanding of Jewish failings, to the business of turning the Zionist idea into a practical reality. More than anyone else, he was responsible for the nuts and bolts, the bread and butter, of the new home.

There was also the problem of protecting the new colonies from marauders. The young men of the Second Aliyah, who had taken part in Jewish self-defence groups to resist pogroms in Russia, set up the society of Shomerin, or Watchmen, in 1909. Photographs taken at the time show them slung with bandoliers and carbines, wearing Russian boots and Arab headdresses, looking like university-educated Cossack sheikhs. Something more was required, and a man emerged to provide it: Vladimir Jabotinsky (1880–1940). Like Herzl, he was a writer and a drama-lover, and he came from that most romantic of Jewish cities, Odessa. This wealthy grain-exporting port on the Black Sea had a special place in Jewish history. It was, to be sure, in Russia, but it had a strongly cosmopolitan, almost Mediterranean flavour, a breath of the warm south. Jabotinsky, characteristically, spoke Russian, German, English, French and Yiddish, as well as Hebrew. Like most Odessan Jews – Trotsky was another example – he was a tremendous orator. By the 1900s there were about 170,000 Jews in Odessa, a third of the city's population, and it was therefore a centre both of anti-Semitism of the most brutal kind and of Jewish culture. But the culture was secular. Odessa's was the first Jewish community to be run by the *maskils*. The Orthodox rabbis hated it and warned pious Jews not to set foot in the place, which they said attracted the sweepings of the Pale and had become another Sodom. It was said: 'The fire of Hell burns around Odessa up to a distance of ten parasangs.' It produced many of the first Zionists, such as Leon Pinsker, author of *Autoemancipation*, and Ahad Ha'Am, the leading philosopher of the early Zionist movement. It had a powerful and strident Jewish press, in which Jabotinsky soon distinguished himself as a militant, aggressive Zionist. He was also an active member of the Odessa self-defence force.

When the First World War broke out, Jabotinsky was appointed a roving correspondent of a Moscow paper and travelled to the Middle East. The Turks were treating the Palestine Jews as potential traitors and their terrorism had reduced a population of over 85,000 to less than 60,000. In Alexandria there were 10,000 Jewish refugees, living in squalor but riven by internal disputes. The Ashkenazis and the Sephardis insisted on separate soup-kitchens. The students from the new Herzl Gymnasium in Tel Aviv would not co-operate at all unless spoken to in Hebrew. Jabotinsky, who is best described as a poetic activist – rather like D'Annunzio – decided that an army was needed both to weld the Jews together and to raise them from their supine acceptance of ill-treatment. He found a fellow spirit in Joseph Trumpeldor (1880–1920), a one-armed conscript-hero of the Russo-Japanese war. Together these two determined men, against much official British resistance, succeeded in creating a specifically Jewish military contribution to the war: first the Zion Mule Corps, then three battalions of the Royal Fusiliers, the 38th (London East End), the 39th (American volunteers) and the 40th, recruited from the *Yishuv* itself.[24] Jabotinsky served in the 38th battalion and led the crossing of the Jordan. But to his dismay and alarm, the Zionist authorities in Palestine showed no particular zeal to keep what had become the Jewish Legion in existence and the British promptly disbanded it. So he formed a covert self-defence organization which was to become the Haganah, embryo of a mighty army.[25]

Jabotinsky's disquiet was prompted by the evident and growing hostility felt by the local Arabs to the Jewish national home project. The Zionists, led by Herzl himself, had tended all along to underestimate the Arabs. On his first visit to London, Herzl had believed Holman Hunt, who knew Palestine well, when he prophesied: 'The Arabs are nothing more than hewers of wood and drawers of water. They don't even have to be dispossessed, for they would render the Jews very useful services.'[26] In fact the Arabs were developing a nationalist spirit just like the Jews. The chief difference was that they started to organize themselves two decades later. Jewish nationalism, or Zionism, was part of the European nationalist movement, which was a nineteenth-century phenomenon. The Arabs, by contrast, were part of the Afro-Asian nationalism of the twentieth century. Their nationalist movement began, effectively, in 1911 when a secret body called Al-Fatah, the Young Arabs, was started in Paris. It was modelled on the Young Turks, and like them was strongly anti-Zionist from the start. After the war the French, who – as we have seen – hated the British mandate from the start and, behind the scenes, fought it inch by inch during the Versailles negotiations, allowed Al-Fatah to set up its base in Damascus, as a centre of anti-British and anti-Zionist activity.[27]

A few Zionists had foreseen that to use Palestine to settle 'the Jewish problem' might, in turn, create 'the Arab problem'. Ahad Ha'Am, who had visited Erez Israel, had written an article 'The Truth from Palestine', in 1891, six years before Herzl launched his movement. He issued a warning. It was a great mistake, he said, for Zionists to dismiss the Arabs as stupid savages who did not realize what was happening. In fact, the Arab, like all semites, possesses a sharp intelligence and great cunning. . . . [The Arabs] see through our activity in the country and its purpose but they keep silent, since for the time being they do not fear any danger for their future. When however the life of our people in Palestine develops to the point when the indigenous people feel threatened, they will not easily give way any longer. How careful must we be in dealing with an alien people in whose midst we want to settle! How essential it is to practise kindness and esteem towards them! . . . If ever the Arab judges the action of his rivals to be oppression or the robbing of his rights, then even if he is silent and waits for his time, the rage will stay alive in his heart.[28]

This warning was largely ignored. The scale of the settlement pushed up the price of land, and Jewish settlers and agencies found the Arabs hard bargainers: 'every dunam of land needed for our colonization work [had] to be bought in the open market', complained Weizmann, 'at fantastic prices which rose ever higher as our work developed. Every improvement we made raised the value of the remaining land in that particular area, and the Arab landowners lost no time in cashing in. We found we had to cover the soil of Palestine with Jewish gold.'[29] Hence the Jews tended to see the Arabs as grasping proprietors – or, indeed, as simple labourers. They eased their consciences by the thought that in this, and many other ways, the Arabs were benefiting from Zionism. But as a rule they ignored them, as merely part of the human scenery. Ahad Ha'Am noted as late as 1920: 'Since the beginning of the Palestinian colonization we have always considered the Arab people as non-existent.'

Arab nationalism at last became dynamic during the war, when Arab troops fought on both sides and were bid for by both sides. The Allies, for their part, issued during the war a lot of post-dated cheques to countless nationalities whose support they needed. When the peace came some of the cheques bounced and the Arabs, in particular, found they had been handed a stumer. Instead of the great Arab state, they got French protectorates in Syria and Lebanon, and British protectorates in Palestine, Transjordan and Iraq. In the dealing and fighting that marked the 'peace', the only Arab clan to emerge triumphant were the Saudis in Arabia. The Emir Feisal, head of the Hashemites, whom Britain had backed, had to be content with Transjordan. He was well disposed towards Jewish settlement, believing it would raise Arab living standards. 'We Arabs,' he wrote to Felix Frankfurter, 3 March 1919, 'especially the educated among us, look with the deepest sympathy on the Zionist movement. . . . We will wish the Jews a most hearty welcome home.'[30]

But Feisal overestimated both the numbers and the courage of Arab moderates prepared to work with the Jews. The British had in fact been warned during the war that if the rumours of the Jewish home proved true, they must expect trouble: 'Politically', wrote one of Sykes' best Arab informants, 'a Jewish state in Palestine will mean a permanent danger to a lasting peace in the Near East.'[31] The British establishment in charge, Allenby, General Bols, the Chief of Staff, and Sir Ronald Storrs, Governor of Jerusalem, knew this very well and tried to play down the national home idea. The Balfour Declaration, ran the order, 'is to be treated as extremely confidential and is on no account for any kind of publication'. At one stage they even proposed that Feisal should be made King of Palestine.[32] But the fact that the British authorities tried hard to calm the Arabs – and so were promptly accused of anti-Semitism by some of the Jews – made no difference. The post-war return of Jewish refugees from Egypt to Palestine, and the arrival of more, fleeing pogroms by the White Russians in the Ukraine, marked the point at which the Arabs, in Ha'Am's words, began to feel threatened. Early in March 1920 there was a series of Arab attacks on Jewish settlements in the Galilee, during one of which Trumpeldor was killed; and they were followed by Arab riots in Jerusalem. Jabotinsky, bringing his self-defence force into action for the first time, was arrested, together with other members of the Haganah, tried by a military court and given fifteen years' hard labour. Arab rioters were convicted and imprisoned too, among them Haji Amin al-Husaini, who fled the country and was sentenced to ten years *in absentia*.

In the uproar that followed the riots, Lloyd George made a fatal error. Seeking to appease the Jews, who claimed that British troops had done little to protect Jewish lives and property, he sent out Samuel as high commissioner. The Jews rejoiced, claimed victory, and the moment Samuel arrived overwhelmed him with complaints and demands. Weizmann was furious. 'Mr Samuel will be utterly disgusted,' he wrote to Dr Edu at the Zionist office in Palestine, 'and will turn his back on the Jewish community, just as the others did, and our best chance will have gone.'[33] In fact that was not the real problem. Samuel did not mind Jewish importuning. What he minded was Arab accusations of unfairness because he was a Jew. Samuel always tried to have things both ways. He wanted to be a Jew without believing in God. He wanted to be a Zionist without joining any Zionist organization. Now he wanted to promote a Jewish national home without offending the Arabs. The thing could not be done. It was inherent in the entire Zionist concept that the Palestine Arabs could not expect full rights within the main area of Jewish settlement. But the

Balfour Declaration specifically safeguarded the civil and religious rights of the 'existing non-Jewish communities' and Samuel took this to mean that the Arabs must have equal rights and opportunities. Indeed, he regarded this phrase as the axiom of his mission. 'The Zionism that is practical', he wrote, 'is the Zionism that fulfils this essential condition.'[34] Samuel believed he could square this particular circle. Not believing in Yahweh, his Bible was Lord Morley's disastrous book, *On Compromise*.

Hence as the Jews quickly discovered, he came not to appease but to lecture. Even before he arrived as high commissioner, he defined 'the Arab problem' as the 'main consideration'. He criticized the Zionists for not having recognized 'the force and value of the Arab nationalist movement', which was 'very real and no bluff'. If anyone had to be appeased, it was the Arabs: 'The only alternative is a policy of coercion which is wrong in principle and likely to prove unsuccessful in practice.' The Jews must make 'considerable sacrifices'. 'Unless there is very careful steering,' he wrote to Weizmann, 10 August 1921, 'it is upon the Arab rock that the Zionist ship may be wrecked.' He told the Palestine Jewish leaders: 'You yourselves are inviting a massacre which will come as long as you disregard the Arabs. You pass over them in silence. . . . You have done nothing to come to an understanding. You know only how to protest against the government. . . . Zionism has not yet done a thing to obtain the consent of the inhabitants, and without this consent immigration will not be possible.'[35]

In a way this was very good advice. The difficulty for the Zionists was that, in the troubled days of the early 1920s, they were finding it very difficult to sustain the effort of settlement at all and had little energy and resources for gestures towards the Arabs. In any case, while giving them such advice Samuel's other actions ruled out the possibility of taking it. He believed in equivalence, in being even-handed. He did not grasp that, just as there was no place for equivalence as between a Jew and an anti-Semite, so you could not be even-handed between Jewish settlers and those Arabs who did not want them there at all. His first act was to amnesty the 1920 rioters. The object was to release Jabotinsky. But equivalence meant a pardon for the Arab extremists who had started the riots in the first place.

Then Samuel, in turn, made a fatal mistake. One difficulty the British experienced in dealing with the Arabs was that they had no official leader, King Feisal's writ running no further than the Jordan. So they invented the title of Grand Mufti of Jerusalem. In March 1921 its existing holder, head of an important local family, died. His younger brother was the notorious rioter Haji Amin al-Husaini, now pardoned and back on the political scene. The procedure for creating a new mufti was for a local electoral college of pious Arab Moslems to choose three candidates and for government to confirm one of them. Haji Amin, then in his mid-twenties, was qualified neither by age nor by learning for the post. He had been passionately anti-British ever since the Balfour Declaration. He had a violent, lifelong hatred for Jews. In addition to his ten-year sentence he was down on the police files as a dangerous agitator. The electoral college was mainly moderate and, not surprisingly, Haji Amin came bottom of the poll, getting only eight votes. A moderate and learned man, Sheikh Hisam al-Din, was chosen and Samuel was glad to confirm him. Then the al-Husaini family and the nationalist extreme wing – those who had led the 1920 riots –began a vicious campaign of denigration. They plastered Jerusalem with posters attacking the electoral college: 'The accursed traitors, whom you all know, have combined with the Jews to have one of their party appointed mufti.'[36]

Unfortunately the British staff contained a former architect and assistant to Sir Ronald Storrs called Ernest T. Richmond, who acted as adviser to the high commissioner on Moslem affairs. He was a passionate anti-Zionist, whom the chief secretary, Sir Gilbert Claydon, termed 'the counterpart of the Zionist organization'. 'He is a declared enemy of the Zionist policy and almost as frankly declared an enemy of the Jewish policy of HM Government,' ran a Colonial Office secret minute; 'government . . . would gain very greatly by excluding from its secretariat so very partisan a figure as Mr Richmond.'[37] It was Richmond who persuaded the moderate sheikh to stand down and then convinced Samuel that, in the light of the agitation, it would be a friendly gesture towards the Arabs to let Haji Amin become Grand Mufti. Samuel saw the young man on 11 April 1921 and accepted 'assurances that the influence of his family and himself would be devoted to tranquillity'. Three weeks later there were riots in Jaffa and elsewhere in which forty-three Jews were murdered.[38]

This appointment to what was regarded as a minor post in an unimportant British protectorate turned into one of the most tragic and decisive errors of the century. It is not clear whether a Jewish–Arab agreement to work together in Palestine would have been feasible even under sensible Arab leadership. But it became absolutely impossible once Haji Amin became Grand Mufti. Samuel compounded his initial misjudgment by promoting the formation of a Supreme Moslem Council, which the mufti and his associates promptly captured and turned into a tyrannical instrument of terror.

Still worse, he encouraged the Palestinian Arabs to make contact with their neighbours and promote pan-Arabism. Hence the mufti was able to infect the pan-Arab movement with his violent anti-Zionism. He was a soft-spoken killer and organizer of killers. The great majority of his victims were fellow Arabs. His prime purpose was to silence moderation in Arab Palestine, and he succeeded completely. He became Britain's outstanding opponent in the Middle East, and in due course he made common cause with the Nazis and strongly supported Hitler's 'Final Solution'. But the principal victims of his unbalanced personality were the ordinary people of Arab Palestine. As the historian Elie Kedourie has well observed, 'It was the Husainis who directed the political strategy of the Palestinians until 1947 and they led them to utter ruin.'[39]

The sombre achievement of the Grand Mufti was to open a chasm between the Jewish and Arab leadership which has never since been bridged. At the San Remo Conference in 1920, a year before he acquired his authority, the British mandate and the Balfour Declaration had been officially confirmed as part of the Versailles settlement, and the Arab and Jewish delegations shared a table together at the Royal Hotel to celebrate the event. By February 1939, when the Tripartite Conference met in London to try to resolve Arab–Jewish differences, the Arabs refused to sit with the Jews under any circumstances.[40] This was the mufti's doing, and in the long run it was the failure to negotiate directly with the Jews, forcing them into unilateral action, which lost the Arabs Palestine.

All the same, there was an inherent conflict of interest between Jews and Arabs which pointed not to a unitary state, in which both races had rights, but to partition in some form. If this fact had been recognized from the start, the chances of a rational solution would have been much greater. Unfortunately, the mandate was born in the Versailles era, a time when it was widely assumed that universal ideals and the ties of human brotherhood could overcome the more ancient and primitive sources of discord. Why could not the Arabs and Jews develop harmoniously together, under the benign eye of Britain and the ultimate supervision of the League of Nations? But Arabs and Jews were not on a level of equivalence. The Arabs already constituted several states; soon there would be many. The Jews had none. It was an axiom of Zionism that a state must come into existence where Jews could feel safe. How could they feel safe if they did not, in some fundamental sense, control it? That meant a unitary, not a binary, system; not power-sharing but Jewish rule.

This was implicit in the Balfour Declaration, as explained to the meeting of the Imperial Cabinet by Winston Churchill, Colonial Secretary, on 22 June 1921. Arthur Meighen, the Canadian Prime Minister, asked him: 'How do you define our responsibilities in relation to Palestine under Mr Balfour's pledge?' Churchill: 'To do our best to make an honest effort to give the Jews a chance to make a national home for themselves.' Meighen: 'And to give them control of the government?' Churchill: 'If in the course of many years they become a majority in the country, they naturally would take it over.' Meighen: 'Pro rata with the Arab?' Churchill: 'Pro rata with the Arab. We made an equal pledge that we would not turn the Arab off his land or invade his political and social rights.'[41]

That being so, the whole future of Palestine turned on the issue of Jewish immigration. It was another axiom of Zionism that all Jews should be free to return to the national home. The British government initially accepted this, or rather took it for granted. In all the early discussions over Palestine as a national home, the assumption was that not enough Jews would wish to go there, rather than too many. As Lloyd George put it, 'The notion that Jewish immigration would have to be artificially restricted in order that the Jews should be a permanent minority never entered the heads of anyone engaged in framing the policy. That would have been regarded as unjust and as a fraud on the people to whom we were appealing.'[42]

Nevertheless, immigration soon became the issue. It was the point on which Arab resistance increasingly concentrated. Nor was this surprising, since the Jews resisted the British desire to develop representative institutions as long as they were in a minority. As Jabotinsky put it, 'We are afraid, and we don't want to have a normal constitution here, since the Palestine situation is not normal. The majority of its "electors" have not yet returned to the country.'[43] As it happened, this vulnerable argument was not put to the test, since the Arabs, for their own reasons, decided (August 1922) not to co-operate with British policy either. But they knew from the start that Jewish immigration was the key to ultimate Jewish political power and their agitation was designed to stop it. Samuel fell for this tactic. One of his gestures towards the Arabs, when he took up his post, had been to allow the reappearance of *Falastin*, an extremist Arab journal closed down by the Turks in 1914 for 'incitement to race hatred'. This, the appointment of the Grand Mufti and similar acts led directly to the pogrom of May 1921, which was incited by the fear of Jews 'taking over'. Samuel's response to the riots was to suspend Jewish immigration completely for a time. Three boatloads of Jews fleeing from massacres in Poland and the Ukraine were sent back to Istanbul.

Samuel insisted that, as he put it, the 'impossibility of mass immigration' must be 'definitely recognized'. He told David Edu that he would not have 'a second Ireland' and that 'Zionist policy could not be driven through'.[44] This led to many bitter Jewish reactions. Edu called Samuel 'Judas'. Ruppin said he had become 'a traitor to the Jewish cause in their eyes'. 'The Jewish national home of the war promises', Weizmann complained to Churchill in July 1921, 'has now been transformed into an Arab national home.'[45]

This was hyperbole. The Jewish national home grew only slowly in the 1920s but British restrictions on immigration were not the main inhibiting factor. After the difficulties of his first year, Samuel emerged as a successful administrator. His successor, Lord Plumer (1925–8), was even better. Modern services were created, law and order imposed and Palestine, for the first time in many centuries, began to enjoy a modest prosperity. Yet the Jews failed to take advantage of this background to create the rapid build-up of the *Yishuv* which the 1917 Declaration had made possible. Why?

One reason was that the Jewish leaders were divided among themselves on both objects and methods. Weizmann was a patient man, who had always believed that the creation of the Zionist state would take a long time, and that the more solidly the infrastructure and foundations were built, the more likely it would be to survive and flourish. He was content to work within Britain's lengthy time-span. What he wanted to see emerge in Palestine, in the first place, were social, cultural, educational and economic institutions which were excellent in themselves and would endure. As he put it, 'Nahalal, Deganiah, the University, the Rutenberg electrical works, the Dead Sea concession, meant much more to me politically than all the promises of great governments and great political parties.'[46]

Other Jewish leaders had different priorities. During the 1920s, the great political force emerging in Israel was David Ben Gurion. For him what mattered most was the political and economic nature of the Zionist society and the state it would create. He came from Plonsk in Russian Poland and, like many thousands of clever young *Ostjuden*, he believed that the 'Jewish question' could never be solved within a capitalist framework. The Jews themselves had to return to their collectivist roots. Most Jewish socialists in Russia went in a Marxist–internationalist direction, arguing that Jewishness was simply an outmoded consequence of a dying religion and a capitalist–bourgeois society, and would disappear along with them. Nachman Syrkin (1868–1924), an early socialist Zionist, insisted that the Jews were a separate people with their own destiny but argued it could only be achieved in a co-operative, collectivist state: therefore the national home must be socialist from the start. Ben Gurion took this side of the argument. His father, Avigdor Gruen, was a strong Zionist who had his son educated at a modernized Hebrew school and with private tutors who taught him secular subjects. Ben Gurion at various times called himself a Marxist but for him, as a result of his upbringing, the Bible, not *Das Kapital*, was the book of life – though he treated it as a secular history and guide. He too was a Jewish prodigy: but one whose tremendous will, passion and energy flowed into activism, not study. At fourteen he was running a Zionist youth group. At seventeen he was an active member of the Zionist workers' organization, the Po'ale Zion. At the age of twenty he was a settler in Erez Israel, a member of the party's central committee and a formulator of its first political platform in October 1906.

As a young man, Ben Gurion moved around the international scene. He lived in the Jewish community in Salonika, in Istanbul and in Egypt. He spent much of the First World War in New York, organizing the He-Halutz bureau which steered potential settlers towards Palestine, though he also served in the Jewish Legion. Yet in all this activity three salient principles remained constant. First, Jews must make it their priority to return to the land; 'the settlement of the land is the only true Zionism, all else being self-deception, empty verbiage and merely a pastime'.[47] Second, the structure of the new community must be designed to assist this process within a socialist framework. Third, the cultural binding of the Zionist society must be the Hebrew language.

Ben Gurion never deviated from these three principles. But the political instruments with which he sought to implement them varied. This was to be a Zionist characteristic. Over the past century, Zionist political parties have undergone constant mutations, and no attempt will be made here to trace them in detail. Ben Gurion in particular was to be a notorious creator and divider of parties. In 1919 he opened the founding conference of Ahdut ha-Avudah. Ten years later (1930) he merged it, with the political wing of Po'ale Zion, into Mapai, the Zionist Labour Party. More solid and permanent was the Histadrut, the Zionist trade union movement, of which he became secretary-general in 1921. He turned it into something much more than a federation of trade unions. In accordance with his principles, he made it into an agent of settlement, an active promoter of agricultural and industrial projects, which it financed and owned, and thus in time a major land- and property-owner, a central pillar of the Zionist–socialist establishment. It was during the 1920s, indeed, that Ben

Gurion created the essential institutional character of what was to become the Zionist state. But this took his time and energy, and though the object of all his efforts was ultimately to accelerate immigration, that was not the immediate consequence. The infrastructure was taking shape, but the people to inhabit it were slow to arrive.

That was the overriding concern of Jabotinsky. His absolute priority was to get the maximum numbers of Jews into Palestine at the earliest possible moment, so that they could be organized politically and militarily to take over the state. Of course it was right, as Weizmann said, to push forward specific educational and economic projects. But numbers must come first. It was right too, as Ben Gurion urged, to settle the land. But numbers must come first. Jabotinsky treated with scorn the notion, held strongly by Weizmann and Ben Gurion, that they should distinguish between types of settlers. Ben Gurion wanted the *chalutzim*, the pioneers, willing to do the back-breaking manual work, to get away from any dependence on Arab labour. Both he and Weizmann were hostile to the religious wing of the Zionists, who founded the Mizrachi ('spiritual centre') Party in 1902, and who moved their operations to Palestine in 1920. The Mizrachi began to build up their own network of schools and institutions, in parallel with the secular Zionists, and to run their own immigration campaigns. In Weizmann's view, Mizrachi was encouraging the wrong type of Jewish immigrant: Jews from the ghettos, especially from Poland, who did not want to work on the land but to settle in Tel Aviv, create capitalist concerns, and – if they were smart – engage in land speculation.

In 1922 Churchill, who was always pro-Zionist, ended the ban on immigration. But his White Paper, published that year, insisted, for the first time, that immigration could be unrestricted but must reflect 'the economic capacity of the country at the time to absorb new arrivals'. In practice, this meant Jews could get settlement visas if they could show $2,500, and it was Weizmann's contention that, in consequence, the capitalist, Mizrachi-type of immigrant was predominating. Jabotinsky thought this of secondary importance. Numbers had to come first. He was not content to see Weizmann and the British government manage matters at their own pace, to ensure that Jewish Palestine was a nation of *chalutzim* even if it took hundreds of years to create it. He wanted rapid growth, and it must be said, in retrospect, that he had a stronger instinct for ugly realities than either of the other two.

Jabotinsky was not prepared to accept British management of

immigration at all. He wanted this to be the exclusive concern of Jewish policy-makers, who in his view should be moving towards setting up state institutions as a matter of urgency. On these grounds he left the Zionist executive in 1923 and two years later he founded the Union of Zionist-Revisionists to use the full resources of Jewish capitalism to bring to Palestine 'the largest number of Jews within the shortest period of time'. He attracted an enormous following in eastern Europe, especially in Poland, where the Revisionist militant youth wing, Betar – of which the young Menachem Begin became the organizer – wore uniforms, drilled and learned to shoot. The object was to achieve the Jewish state in one sudden, irresistible act of will.

In fact, all three Jewish leaders overestimated the actual willingness of Jews to emigrate to Palestine during the 1920s. After the turmoil of the immediate post-war years, especially the pogroms in Poland and the Ukraine, the Jews like everyone else shared in the prosperity of the decade. The urge to take ships to Haifa abated. The riots in 1920 and 1921 were no encouragement. During the 1920s the Jewish population of Palestine did, indeed, double, to 160,000. So did the number of agricultural colonies. By the end of the decade there were 110 of them, employing 37,000 Jewish workers and farming 175,000 acres. But the total number of immigrants was only 100,000 of whom 25 per cent did not stay. So the net rate of immigration was a mere 8,000 a year. Indeed, in 1927, the peak year of twenties prosperity, only 2,713 came and more than 5,000 left. In 1929, the watershed year in the world economy, arrivals and departures just about balanced.

Therein lay a great missed opportunity, and the makings of tragedy. During the calm years, when Palestine was relatively open, the Jews would not come. From 1929 their economic and political position, and still more their security, began to deteriorate all over Europe. But as their anxiety to go to Palestine increased, so did the obstacles to their entering it. There was another Arab pogrom in 1929, in which over 150 Jews were killed. The British response, as before, was to tighten immigration. The Labour Colonial Secretary, Lord Passfield, was unsympathetic: his White Paper of 1930 was the first, unmistakable sign of anti-Zionism in a British state paper. His wife, Beatrice Webb, told Weizmann: 'I can't understand why the Jews make such a fuss over a few dozen of their people killed in Palestine. As many are killed every week in London in traffic accidents and nobody pays any attention.'[48] The British Prime Minister, Ramsay MacDonald, was more sensitive. Thanks to him, immigration was resumed.

Now there were hundreds of thousands of increasingly frightened Jews trying to get in. But with each wave of Jewish immigration, the wave of Arab reaction became more violent. Jabotinsky considered 30,000 a year as satisfactory. The target was passed in 1934, when 40,000 arrived. The following year it rose by more than 50 per cent to 62,000. Then, in April 1936, came a major Arab rising, and for the first time the British began to face the ugly truth that the mandate was breaking down. A commission under Lord Peel, reporting on 7 July 1937, recommended that Jewish immigration be reduced to 12,000 places a year, and restrictions be placed on land purchases too. But it also suggested a three-way partition. The coastal strip, Galilee and the Jezreel valley should be formed into a Jewish state. The Judaean Hills, the Negev and Ephraim should constitute an Arab state. The British would run a mandatory enclave from Jerusalem through Lydda and Ramleh to Jaffa. The Arabs rejected this with fury and staged another revolt in 1937. The next year the pan-Arab conference in Cairo adopted a policy whereby all Arab states and communities pledged themselves to take international action to prevent the further development of the Zionist state. The British dropped partition and, after the failure of the Tripartite Conference in London early in 1939, which the Arabs rendered hopeless from the start, the Balfour Declaration was quietly buried too. A new White Paper, published in May, stipulated that 75,000 more Jews should be admitted over five years, and thereafter none at all, except with Arab agreement. At the same time, Palestine should proceed to gradual independence. By now there were 500,000 Jews in Palestine. But the Arabs were in a large majority still. Hence if the British plan proceeded, the Arabs would control any state that emerged, and the existing Jews would be expelled.

This tragic series of events brought corresponding strains within the Zionist movement as its various factions divided on how to respond to them. In 1931 Weizmann was driven from the presidency of the World Zionist Congress, at the instigation of the Mizrachi. The same year, in Palestine, elections to the Zionist Assembly of Delegates showed a three-way split, with Mapai taking thirty-one out of seventy-one seats, the Revisionists sixteen and Mizrachi five. The division spread to the military arm: the Revisionists and Mizrachi, and other non-socialist Zionists, broke away from the Haganah to form a competitive force, the Irgun.

The fundamental breach, between Mapai on the one hand and the Revisionists on the other, which was to dominate the politics of the Zionist state from its inception, was envenomed by abuse. The Revisionists accused Mapai of collusion with the British and treason to the Jewish cause. The Revisionists were denounced as 'fascists'. Ben Gurion called Jabotinsky 'Vladimir Hitler'. On 16 June 1933 Chaim Arlosoroff, head of the Political Department of the Jewish Agency, which had been formed in 1929 to co-ordinate all Jewish efforts world-wide, was murdered on the sea front of Tel Aviv. He was a passionate Mapai Zionist, and Revisionist extremists were immediately suspected. Two of them, Abraham Stavsky and Zevi Rosenblatt, members of a Revisionist ultra group, Brit Habirionim, were arrested and charged with the murder. Abba Ahimeir, the group's ideologist, was charged with complicity. Stavsky was convicted on the evidence of one witness, sentenced to hang, but acquitted on appeal, under an old Turkish law which said one witness was insufficient in a capital case. The crime was never solved and it continued to fester in the memories of both sides for half a century. To Mapai, the Revisionists would not stop at murder. To the Revisionists, the Mapai had stooped to the age-old device of gentile persecution, the blood libel.

Behind the division was a genuine, agonizing dilemma about Jewish conduct. Some had thought the Balfour Declaration was the beginning of the end of Jewish problems. In the event it merely created an entirely new set of impossible choices. All over the world, Jewish idealists begged their leaders to come to terms with the Arabs. As late as 1938, Albert Einstein, the greatest living Jew, still saw the national home in Utopian terms: 'I would much rather see reasonable agreement with the Arabs on the basis of living together in peace than the creation of a Jewish state . . . my awareness of the essential nature of Judaism resists the idea of a Jewish state with borders, an army and a measure of temporal power, no matter how modest. I am afraid of the inner damage Judaism will suffer – especially from the development of a narrow nationalism within our own ranks.'[49] Others feared this damage too. But they feared still more for Jews caught without a refuge-state to flee to. How could such a state be made with Arab consent? Jabotinsky argued that Jews must assume Arab nationalist emotions to be as strong and obdurate as their own. Hence:

It is impossible to dream of a voluntary agreement between us and the Arabs. . . . Not now, and not in the foreseeable future. . . . Every nation, civilized or primitive, sees its land as its national home, where it wants to stay as the sole landlord forever. Such a nation will never willingly consent to new landlords or even to partnership. Every native-nation will fight the settlers as long as there is a hope of getting rid of them. Thus they behave, and thus will the [Palestine] Arabs behave, so long as there is the glimmer of hope in their hearts that they can prevent the transformation of Palestine into Erez Israel.

Only an 'iron wall of Jewish bayonets', he concluded, could force the Arabs to accept the inevitable.[50]

Jabotinsky made this harsh statement in 1923. The next two decades were to give an ever-growing force to the logic of his argument that the Jews could not afford idealism. It was not just a matter of providing Jewish Palestine with its iron wall of bayonets to ensure its safety. It was a question of whether European Jewry could survive at all, in a world which was turning increasingly and almost universally hostile.

For it was not just in Palestine that the Versailles peace brought bitter disappointment to the Jews. The 1914–18 war was the 'war to end war', which would abolish old-fashioned *realpolitik* and inaugurate an era of justice, sweeping away the old hereditary empires and giving all peoples their due share of self-government. The national home for Jews in Palestine was part of this idealistic pattern. But equally if not more important for most European Jews was the guarantee offered by the peace treaty that they would receive full rights of citizenship throughout the European diaspora. The major powers, under the impulse of Disraeli, had first attempted to ensure minimum rights for Jews at the Berlin Congress in 1878. But the provisions of the treaty had been evaded, notably in Rumania. A second, and much more thorough, attempt was made at Versailles. Jews in Russia had been accorded full rights by Kerensky's provisional government. At Versailles, clauses were written into the treaty giving rights to scheduled minorities, including the Jews, in all the states created, enlarged or delimited by the peace settlement – Poland, Rumania, Hungary, Austria, Czechoslovakia, Yugoslavia, Turkey, Greece, Lithuania, Latvia and Estonia. In theory, then, and certainly in the minds of those, like President Woodrow Wilson and Lloyd George, who shaped the treaty, the Jews were one of its major beneficiaries: they got their national home in Palestine and, if they chose to remain in their adopted homes, they received full and guaranteed citizenship rights.

As things turned out, the Versailles treaty was an important element in the greatest of all Jewish tragedies. For it was a covenant without a sword. It redrew the map of Europe, and imposed new solutions on ancient quarrels, without providing the physical means to enforce either. It thus introduced twenty years of growing instability, dominated by the ferocious hatreds its own provisions had engendered. In this atmosphere of discontent, intermittent violence, and uncertainty, the position of the Jews, far from improving, grew more insecure. It was not just that Jewish communities, as always happened in difficult times, tended to become the focus of any anxiety and antagonism which could be spared from specific and local objects of hatred. The Jews were used to that. But now there was an additional cause of hostility – the Jewish identification with Bolshevism.

For this the Jews bore some responsibility; or rather, the particular type of political Jew which had emerged in radical politics during the second half of the nineteenth century: the Non-Jewish Jew, the Jew who denied there was such a thing as a Jew at all. This group were all socialists, and for a brief period they were of paramount importance in European and Jewish history. The most representative of them was Rosa Luxemburg (1871–1919). She came from Zamosc in Russian Poland and her historical background was impeccably Jewish. She was descended from rabbis going back to at least the twelfth century, and her mother, the daughter and sister of rabbis, quoted the Bible to her endlessly. Like Marx, and with far less excuse, she never showed the slightest interest in Judaism or in Yiddish culture (though she liked Yiddish jokes). As the historian of Jewish socialism, Robert Wistrich, has pointed out, her extraordinary passion for social justice and her fascination with dialectic argument seems to have been bred by generations of rabbinical scholarship.[51] In all other respects, however, she was an ultra-*maskil*. She knew nothing about the Jewish masses. Her father was a rich timber merchant who sent her to an exclusive school in Warsaw, attended mainly by the children of Russian officials. At eighteen she was smuggled across the frontier and travelled to Zurich to complete her education. In 1898 she went through a form of marriage with a German printer in order to obtain German citizenship. Thereafter she devoted her entire life to revolutionary politics.

The parallels with Marx are close in some ways. Like Marx she had a privileged background from which she continued to benefit financially. Like him she knew nothing of the working class, even of the Jewish working class, and like him she never sought to make good her ignorance. Like him, she led a life of middle-class political conspiracy, writing, platform oratory and café argument. But whereas Marx's Jewish self-hatred took the form of crude anti-Semitism, she argued that the Jewish problem did not exist at all. Anti-Semitism, she insisted, was a function of capitalism, exploited in Germany by the Junkers and in Russia by the Tsarists. Marx had settled the matter; he had 'removed the Jewish question from the religious and racial sphere and given it a *social* foundation, proving that what is usually described and persecuted as "Judaism" is nothing but *the spirit of hucksterism and swindle*, which appears in *every* society where *exploitation* reigns'.[52] Actually, that was not what Marx said and her interpretation involved a deliberate distortion of Marx's text. Moreover, her assertion was manifestly untrue. As another Jewish socialist, Eduard Bernstein (1850–1932), pointed out, anti-Semitism had deep popular roots and could not simply be magicked away by Marxism. He much admired Marx's daughter, Eleanor, for proudly telling public meetings in London's East End, 'I am a Jewess.'

By contrast, Rosa Luxemburg never referred to her Jewishness, if she could possibly help it. She tried to ignore anti-Semitic attacks on her, and this was often difficult for the most odious caricatures of her appeared in the German press. Moreover, there was a strong anti-Semitic tinge to the attacks on her by German trade unionists and socialists with working class backgrounds. They disliked her tone of intellectual superiority and her confident assertions of what 'the workers' wanted. She brushed this aside. 'For the followers of Marx,' she wrote, 'as for the working class, the *Jewish question* as such does not exist.' Attacks on the Jews, in her view, were confined to 'small, remote villages in southern Russia and Bessarabia – namely, where the revolutionary movement is weak or non-existent'. She hardened her heart to those who claimed her sympathy for atrocities against Jews. 'Why do you come with your special Jewish sorrows?' she wrote. 'I feel just as sorry for the wretched Indian victims in Putumayo, the negroes in Africa. . . . I cannot find a special corner in my heart for the ghetto.'[53]

Rosa Luxemburg's moral and emotional distortions were characteristic of an intellectual trying to force people into a structure of ideas, rather than allowing ideas to evolve from the way people actually behaved. The Jews of eastern Europe were not an artificial creation of the capitalist system. They were a real people, with their own language, religion and culture. Their sorrows were real enough too, and persecutions were inflicted on them because they were Jews and for no other reason. They even had their own socialist party, the Bund (abbreviation of General Jewish Workers' Union in Lithuania, Poland and Russia), created in 1897. The Bund campaigned vigorously for full civil rights for Jews. But Bundists were divided on whether Jews should be accorded an autonomous state when the 'Workers' Republic' came into existence. They were confused, too, about Zionism, and their ranks were constantly depleted by emigration. Hence they tended to close their ranks around a defence of Yiddish national culture.

This insistence on the uniqueness of Jewish culture made them peculiarly detestable to those Jewish socialists, like Rosa Luxemburg, who denied the Jews any social or cultural particularity at all. They were vehement in repudiating Bundist claims. And their hostility to separate political organizations of Jews shaped the orthodoxy of the revolutionary left. Lenin, in particular, became a fierce opponent of specifically Jewish rights. 'The idea of a Jewish "nationality" is definitely reactionary,' he wrote (1903), 'not only when expounded by its consistent advocates (the Zionists) but likewise on the lips of those who try to combine it with the ideas of social democracy (the Bundists). The idea of a Jewish nationality runs counter to the interests of the Jewish proletariat, for it fosters among them, directly or indirectly, a spirit hostile to assimilation, the spirit of the "ghetto".' Again, in 1913, he wrote: 'Whoever directly or indirectly puts forward the slogan of a Jewish "national culture" is (whatever his good intentions may be) an enemy of the proletariat, a supporter of the *old* and of the *caste* position of the Jews, an accomplice of the rabbis and the bourgeoisie.'[54]

Hence the whole philosophy of the proletarian revolution was based on the assumption that the Jew, as such, did not exist except as a fantasy promoted by a distorted socio-economic system. Destroy that system and the caricature Jew of history would vanish, like an ugly nightmare, and the Jew would become an ex-Jew, an ordinary man. It is hard now for us to get back inside the minds of highly intelligent, well-educated Jews who believed this theory. But many thousands of them did. They hated their Jewishness, and to fight for the revolution was the most morally acceptable means to escape from it. It gave to their revolutionary struggle a peculiar emotional vehemence, because they believed its success would involve a personal liberation from their Jewish burden, as well as a general liberation of humanity from autocracy.

At all events, such non-Jewish Jews were prominent in every revolutionary party, in virtually every European country, just before, during and immediately after the First World War. They took leading roles in the insurrections which followed the defeat of Germany and Austria. Bela Kun (1886–1939) was dictator of the Communist regime which held power in Hungary between March and August 1919. Kurt Eisner (1867–1919) led the revolutionary rising in Bavaria in November 1918 and ran the republic until his murder four months later. Rosa Luxemburg, the brains behind the revolutionary 'Spartacist' group in Berlin, was murdered a few weeks before Eisner.

It was above all in Russia that Jews were most prominently and spectacularly identified with revolutionary violence. There, the architect of the *putsch* which placed the Bolshevik government in dictatorial power in October 1917 was a non-Jew, Lenin. But the executive agent was Leon Trotsky (1879–1940), born Lev Davidovich Bronstein. His father was what he later learned to call a kulak, a Ukrainian farmer, but Trotsky himself was a product of Odessa cosmopolitanism (his school was Lutheran). He claimed that neither Judaism nor anti-Semitism had any effect on his development. It clearly did: there was something unnatural, close to hatred, in his hounding of the Jewish Bundists at the 1903 Congress of the Russian Social Democrats (held in London), which drove them out of the meeting and so prepared the way for the Bolshevik victory. He denounced Herzl as a 'shameless adventurer', a 'repulsive figure'. Like Rosa Luxemburg, he averted his face from specifically Jewish sufferings, however appalling. When in power, he always refused to see Jewish delegations. As with other Non-Jewish Jews, the suppression of feelings which his political posture involved spread to his own family circle: he took no interest in the miseries of his father, who lost all in the revolution and died of typhus.

Trotsky compensated for his indifference as a Jew by his volcanic energy and ruthlessness as a revolutionary. It is most unlikely that the Bolshevik Revolution could have succeeded or endured without him. It was Trotsky who taught Lenin the significance of workers' soviets and how to exploit them. It was Trotsky who personally organized and led the armed uprising which actually overthrew the provisional government and placed the Bolsheviks in power. It was Trotsky who created, and until 1925 controlled, the Red Army, and who ensured the physical survival of the new Communist regime during the Civil War which came close to destroying it.[55] More than anyone else, Trotsky symbolized the violence and daemonic power of Bolshevism and its determination to inflame the world. More than anyone, he was responsible for the popular identification of revolution with the Jews.

The consequences for the Jews, both immediate and long-term, both locally and world-wide, were appalling. The White Russian armies, seeking to destroy the Soviet regime, treated all Jews as enemies. In the Ukraine, the Civil War developed into the most extensive pogrom in Jewish history. There were more than 1,000 separate incidents involving the killing of Jews. Over 700 communities in the Ukraine were involved and several hundred more in Russia. Between 60,000 and 70,000 Jews were murdered.[56] In other parts of eastern Europe, a similar identification of Jews with Bolshevism led directly to murderous attacks on harmless Jewish communities. They were particularly bloody in Poland after the failure of the Bolshevik invasion and in Hungary after the fall of the Bela Kun regime. They occurred intermittently in Rumania throughout the 1920s. In all three countries the local Communist Parties had been largely created and run by Non-Jewish Jews, and in each case it was the unpolitical, traditional, observant Jews of the ghettos and villages who paid the penalty.

To add to the tragic irony of it all, the ordinary Jews of Russia derived no benefit from the revolution. Quite the reverse. They had stood to gain a great deal from the provisional government of Kerensky, which gave them full voting and civil rights, including the right to organize their own political parties and cultural institutions. In the Ukraine, they took part in the provisional government; a Jew ran a separate Ministry for Jewish Affairs; they would have been covered by the minorities provisions of the Versailles treaty. In Lithuania, which the Soviets did not dare annex until 1939, these minority guarantees worked very well, and the large Jewish community there was perhaps the most contented in eastern Europe between the wars.

Hence for Jews, Lenin's *putsch* put the clock back, and ultimately the Communist regime was a disaster for them. It is true that, for a time, the Leninists equated anti-Semitism with counter-revolution. The Council of People's Commissars, in a decree of 27 July 1918, directed 'all soviets of workers, peasants and soldiers' delegates to take such steps as will effectively destroy the anti-Semitic movement at its roots'. The government circulated a gramophone record of a speech by Lenin, denouncing anti-Semitism.[57] But this somewhat feeble effort was wholly cancelled out by Lenin's vicious attacks against the category of 'exploiters and profiteers' he termed 'bagmen', which was intended to refer to Jews, and interpreted as such. A regime based on Marxism, itself rooted (as we have seen) in anti-Semitic conspiracy theory, a regime which set about its business by identifying whole categories of people as 'class enemies' and then persecuting them, was certain to create a climate hostile to Jews. In fact Jewish traders were among the chief victims of Lenin's general policy of terrorism against 'anti-social groups'. Many were 'liquidated'; others, perhaps 300,000 in all, slipped across the borders into Poland, the Baltic States, Turkey and the Balkans.

It is true that Jews were prominent in the Bolshevik Party, in the top echelons as well as among the rank and file: at party congresses, 15–20 per cent of the delegates were Jewish. But these were Non-Jewish Jews; the Bolshevik Party itself was the only post-Tsarist party which was actively hostile to Jewish objectives and interests. Indeed ordinary Jews suffered on account of Jewish involvement with the regime. Jewish Bolsheviks were numerous in the Cheka (secret police), as commissars, tax inspectors and bureaucrats. They took a leading part in the raiding parties organized by Lenin and Trotsky to gouge grain out of hoarding peasants. All these activities made them hated. Thus, as often happened in Jewish history, the Jews were attacked for contradictory reasons. They were 'anti-social bagmen' on the one hand and 'Bolsheviki' on the other. The only Soviet archive ever to reach the West, dealing with Smolensk 1917–38, reveals that, to the peasants, the Soviet regime and the Jewish middlemen were identical. There were threats in 1922 that if the commissars took gold ornaments from the churches, 'not one Jew will survive: we will kill them all during the night'. Mobs roamed the streets: 'Beat the Jews, save Russia.' In 1926 there was even a revival of ritual murder charges. Yet the archive shows that Jews also feared the regime: 'the militia is feared as was the Tsarist gendarme'.[58]

Jewish fear of the soviets was well founded. In August 1919, all Jewish religious communities were dissolved, their property confiscated and the overwhelming majority of synagogues shut for ever. The study of Hebrew and the publication of secular works in Hebrew were banned. Yiddish printing was permitted, but only in phonetic transcription, and Yiddish culture, though tolerated for a time, was placed under careful supervision. The supervising agency consisted of special Jewish sections, Yevsektsiya, set up in Communist Party branches, manned by Non-Jewish Jews, whose specific task was to stamp out any sign of 'Jewish cultural particularism'. They broke up the Bund, then set about destroying Russian Zionism. In 1917 it had become by far the strongest political feature of Russian Jewry, with 300,000 members and 1,200 branches. It was much stronger, numerically, than the Bolsheviks themselves. From 1919 onwards, the Yevsektsiya attacked the Zionists frontally, using Cheka units commanded by Non-Jewish Jews. In Leningrad they took over the Zionist central headquarters, arresting its staff and closing down its paper. They did the same in Moscow. In April 1920, the all-Russian Zionist Congress was broken up by a Cheka squad led by a Jewish girl, who had seventy-five of the delegates arrested. From 1920 onwards, many thousands of Russian Zionists were in the camps, from which few ever emerged. The Zionist Party, said the regime (26 August 1922), 'under the mask of democracy, seeks to corrupt the Jewish youth and to throw them into the arms of the counter-revolutionary bourgeoisie in the interests of Anglo-French capitalism. To restore the Palestine state, these representatives of the Jewish bourgeoisie rely on reactionary forces [including] such rapacious imperialists as Poincaré, Lloyd George and the Pope.'[59]

Once Stalin, who was deeply anti-Semitic, took power, the pressure on the Jews increased, and by the end of the 1920s all forms of specifically Jewish activity had been destroyed or emasculated. He then dissolved the Yevsektsiya, leaving supervision of the Jews to the secret police. By this time, Jews had been eliminated from nearly all senior posts in the regime, and anti-Semitism was once more a powerful force within the party. 'Is it true,' wrote Trotsky in rage and astonishment to Bukharin, 4 March 1926, 'is it possible, that in *our party*, in *Moscow*, in *Workers' Cells*, anti-Semitic agitation should be carried out with impunity?'[60] Not with impunity: with encouragement. Jews, especially within the Communist Party, were to constitute a wholly disproportionate percentage of Stalin's victims.

One of them was Isaac Babel (1894–1940?), perhaps the only great Jewish writer the Russian Revolution produced, whose personal tragedy is a kind of parable of the Jews under the Soviets. Like Trotsky, he was a product of Odessa, where his father kept a shop. In one of his stories he describes how, aged nine, he saw his father, humble and submissive, the archetype ghetto Jew through the centuries, kneel at the feet of a Cossack officer during a pogrom. The officer, said Babel, wore lemon-yellow chamois gloves and 'looked ahead with a distant gaze'. Odessa produced Jewish prodigies, especially performing ones, and Babel was afraid, being clever, that his father would turn him into a 'musical dwarf', one of the 'big-headed, freckled children with necks as thin as flower-stalks and an epileptic flush on their cheeks'. Instead like Trotsky he wanted to become a Non-Jewish Jew, a man of violence, like the notorious Jewish gangsters from the Moldavanka, the Odessa ghetto, or better still like the Cossacks themselves. He fought in the Tsar's army; then, when the revolution came, served in the Cheka and as a Bolshevist thug raiding the farms for food. Finally he got his wish, to fight alongside the Cossacks under General Budënny. From his experiences he produced a masterpiece, *Red Cavalry* (1926), a volume of stories describing in brilliant and often dismaying detail his efforts to acquire, as he put it, 'the simplest of proficiencies, the ability to kill my fellow men'.

The stories succeed, but the effort itself failed. Babel could not become a man for whom violence was natural. He remained the typical Jewish intellectual, 'a man', as he put it in a memorable phrase, 'with spectacles on his nose and autumn in his heart'. The difficulty a Jew finds in escaping from his cultural background, especially in dealing out death, is a recurrent, poignant theme of his stories. A young man dies because he cannot bring himself to shoot a wounded comrade. An old Jewish shopkeeper will not accept that the revolutionary end justifies the means, and calls for an 'International of Good Men'. A young Jewish soldier is killed, leaving in his meagre belongings portraits of Lenin and Maimonides. The two did not consort together, as Babel found from bitter personal experience. The concept of the Non-Jewish Jew did not work. To Stalin, he was a Jew like any other; and in Stalin's Russia, Babel slipped out of favour into limbo. He appeared at the 1934 Writers' Congress, to make a mysterious, ironic speech, claiming that the party, in its infinite benevolence, deprived the writers of only one freedom – the freedom to write badly. He himself, he said, was practising a new literary genre and was becoming 'a master of silence'. 'I have so much respect for the reader', he added, 'that I am dumb.'[61] In due course he was arrested, and disappeared for ever, probably being shot early in 1940. His alleged offence was taking part in a 'literary conspiracy', but the real reason was simply that he had once known the wife of Nicholai Yezhov, the disgraced NKVD boss. In Stalin's Russia, that was enough – especially for a Jew.[62]

In the outside world, however, little was known about the survival of anti-Semitism, in new forms, in Soviet Russia, the destruction of Jewish institutions and the growing physical threat to Jews under Stalinism. It was simply assumed that, since the Jews were among the principal instigators of Bolshevism, they must be among its principal beneficiaries. The all-important distinction between the great mass of Jews, who were observant, assimilationist or Zionist, and the specific group of Non-Jewish Jews who had actually helped to create the revolution, was not understood at all.

But then it had always been an axiom of anti-Semitic conspiracy theory that apparent conflicts of interest among Jews were mere camouflage for an underlying identity of aim. It was the commonest of all anti-Semitic smears that Jews 'worked together' behind the scenes. The notion of a general Jewish conspiracy, involving secret meetings of Jewish sages, was inherent in the medieval blood libel and had reached written form on numerous occasions. Napoleon I's summoning of the Sanhedrin gave it an unfortunate impetus. Thereafter it had become part of the stock-in-trade of the Tsarist secret police, the Okhrana. It was one of the grievances of this body that the Tsars were not sufficiently assiduous in putting down radical conspiracies, especially Jewish ones. At some point in the 1890s, one of their Paris agents was asked to concoct a document which could be used to demonstrate to Nicholas II the reality of the Jewish threat. The forger, whoever he was, used a pamphlet by Maurice Joly, written in 1864, attributing to Napoleon III ambitions to dominate the world. The original had no reference to Jews at all, but for the monarch was now substituted a secret conference of Jewish leaders who stated that, by exploiting modern democracy, they were close to attaining their objectives. This was the origin of the *Protocols of the Elders of Zion*.

The forgery failed in its original object. The Tsar was not deceived, writing on the document: 'A worthy cause is not defended by evil means.' The police then planted it in various quarters and in 1905 it first attained published form as an additional chapter in Serge Nilus' book *The Great in Little*. But it aroused little interest. It was the Bolshevist triumph in 1917 which gave the *Protocols* a second, and far more successful, birth. The association of Jews with Lenin's *putsch* was widely reported at the time, especially in Britain and France, now in the most desperate phase of a long war which had drained their manhood and resources. Kerensky's provisional government had done its best to keep Russia actively in the war against Germany. Lenin reversed its policy and sought an immediate peace on almost any terms. This fearful blow to the Allied cause, which led almost immediately to the transfer of German divisions from Russia to the Western Front, revived in some people's minds the identification of the Jews with Germany. There was in Britain, for example, a small but bellicose group of writers, led by Hilaire Belloc and the brothers Cecil and G. K. Chesterton, who had waged a ferocious campaign, with anti-Semitic undertones, against Lloyd George and his Attorney-General, Sir Rufus Isaacs, over the Marconi case (1911). They now seized on the events in Russia to link the Jews with pacifism in Britain. Early in November 1917, in a speech, G. K. Chesterton issued a threat: 'I would like to add a few words to the Jews. . . . If they continue to indulge in stupid talk about pacifism, inciting people against the soldiers and their wives and widows, they will learn for the first time what the word anti-Semitism really means.'[63]

The rapid circulation of the *Protocols* in the light of the October Revolution had, for a time, a devastating impact even in Britain, where anti-Semitism was a drawing-room, not a street, phenomenon. Both *The Times'* Russian correspondent, Robert Wilton, and the *Morning Post's*, Victor Marsden, were fiercely anti-Bolshevik and inclined to be anti-Semitic too. Both accepted the versions of the *Protocols* they saw as authentic. *The Times* ran a correspondence under the heading 'The Jews and Bolshevism', which included a contribution from 'Verax', 27 November 1919: 'The essence of Judaism . . . is above all a racial pride, a belief in their superiority, faith in their final victory, the conviction that the Jewish brain is superior to the Christian brain, in short, an attitude corresponding to the innate conviction that the Jews are the Chosen People, fated to become one day the rulers and legislators of mankind.' The *Jewish World* commented: 'Verax's letter marks the beginning of a new and evil era. . . . We cannot say any more that there is no anti-Semitism in this country that loved the Bible above everything.'[64] Early the next year, the editor of the *Morning Post*, H. A. Gwynne, wrote an introduction to an unsigned book called *The Causes of World Unrest*, based on the *Protocols*. They might or might not be genuine, he wrote. 'Their chief interest lies in the fact that, while the book which contains them was published in 1905, the Jewish Bolsheviks are today carrying out almost to the letter the programme outlined in the *Protocols*.' He noted that 'over 95 per cent of the present Bolshevik government are Jews'. The publication gave a list of fifty of its members, with their 'pseudonyms' and 'real names', and claimed that of these only six were Russian, one German and all the rest were Jews.[65] *The Times* published an article, 8 May 1920, entitled 'The Jewish Peril', based on the assumption that the *Protocols* were genuine. Had Britain, it asked, 'escaped a *Pax Germanica* to fall into a *Pax Judaica*?'

The agitation was continually refuelled by reports of Bolshevik atrocities. Churchill, a lifelong friend of the Jews, had been badly shaken by the murder of the British naval attaché in the Russian capital. The Jews were the most remarkable race on earth, he wrote, and their religious contribution 'is worth more than all other knowledge and all other doctrines'. But now, he said, 'this amazing race has created another system of morality and philosophy, this one saturated with as much hatred as Christianity was with love'.[66] Victor Marsden, who had been held in a Bolshevik prison, returned with gruesome tales. 'When we besieged Mr Marsden with questions', reported the *Morning Post*, 'and asked him who was responsible for the persecution he had suffered . . . he answered with two words: "The Jews."'[67] Wilton, the *Times* man, published a book claiming that the Bolsheviks had erected a statue to Judas Iscariot in Moscow.[68] Yet in the end it was *The Times*, in a series of articles published in August 1921, which first demonstrated that the *Protocols* was a forgery. After that, the wave of British anti-Semitism subsided as quickly as it had risen. Belloc had taken advantage of the scare to produce a book, *The Jews*, claiming that the Bolshevik outrages had created real anti-Semitism in Britain for the first time. But by the time it appeared, in February 1922, the moment had passed and it was coolly received.

In France, however, it was a different matter, for there anti-Semitism had deep roots, a national culture of its own, and was to yield bitter fruits. The great victory in the Dreyfus case had given

French Jews a false sense of final acceptance, reflected in the extraordinarily small number of legal requests by French Jews to change their names: a mere 377 in the entire period 1803–1942.[69] Leaders of Jewish opinion in France argued strongly that hatred of the Jews was a foreign, German, import: 'Racism and anti-Semitism are a treasonable work,' argued a pamphlet put out by Jewish ex-soldiers. 'They come from abroad. They are imported by those who want civil war and are hoping for a return of foreign war.'[70] In 1906, at the height of the Dreyfus triumph, the Union Israélite pronounced anti-Semitism 'dead'. Yet it was only two years later that Maurras' Action Française and an equally anti-Semitic group, Les Camelots du Roi, came into existence. In 1911, the Camelots organized a violent demonstration against the play *Après Moi* at the Comédie Française; it was written by Henri Bernstein, an army deserter in his youth, and it had to be abandoned as a result of the rioting.[71] In France, unlike Britain, there seems to have been a natural constituency for anti-Semitic agitators. They seized eagerly on the Bolshevik scare and the mythology promoted by the *Protocols*, which went into many French editions. The focus of French anti-Semitism switched from the Jews as 'money power' to Jews as social subversives.

Jewish socialists, like Léon Blum, made no attempt to refute the notion. Blum gloried in the messianic role of Jews as social revolutionaries. The 'collective impulse' of the Jews, he wrote, 'leads them towards revolution; their critical powers (and I use the words in their highest sense) drive them to destroy every idea, every traditional form which does not agree with the facts or cannot be justified by reason.' In the long, sorrowful history of the Jews, he argued, 'the idea of inevitable justice' had sustained them, the belief that the world would be one day 'ordered according to reason, one rule prevail over all men, so that everyone gets their due. Is that not the spirit of socialism? It is the ancient spirit of the race.'[72] Blum wrote these words in 1901. In the post-war context they became more dangerous. Yet Blum, by far the most notable figure in French Jewry between the wars, continued to insist that it was the role of Jews to lead the march of socialism. He seems to have thought that even rich Jews would join it. In fact, while the anti-Semitic right saw Blum as the personification of Jewish radicalism, there were many on the left who abused him as the covert agent of the Jewish bourgeoisie. One-third of the Paris bankers were Jews, and it was a favourite assertion on the left that Jews controlled government finance whoever was in power. 'Their long association with banking and commerce', said Jean Jaurès, 'has made them peculiarly adept in the ways of capitalist criminality.'[73] When, in the post-war years, the socialist left became the French Communist Party, an anti-Semitic element, albeit coded, became part of its bristling armoury of abuse, much of which was directed at Blum personally. The fact that Blum, along with most leading French Jews, consistently underestimated French anti-Semitism, whether from right or left, did not help matters.

It was in the United States, however, that the Bolshevik takeover, and its association with radical Jews, had the most serious consequences. In France, Jews might be assailed from right and left, but the country continued to be generous in receiving Jewish refugees throughout the 1920s and even during the 1930s. In America, however, the Bolshevik scare effectively ended the policy of unrestricted immigration which had been the salvation of east European Jewry in the period 1881–1914, and which had enabled the great American Jewry to come into existence. There had been efforts to impose immigrant quotas even before the war, successfully resisted by the American Jewish Committee, founded in 1906 to combat this and other threats. But the war ended the ultra-liberal phase of American democratic expansion. Indeed it introduced a phase of xenophobia which was to last a decade. In 1915 the Ku-Klux Klan was refounded to control minority groups, including Jews, who (it claimed) challenged American social and moral norms. The same year a book called *The Passing of the Great Race*, by Madison Grant, achieved instant notoriety by its claims that America's superior racial stock was being destroyed by unrestricted immigration, not least of east European Jews. America's intervention in the war was followed by the Espionage Act (1917) and the Sedition Act (1918), which had the effect of associating aliens with treason.

The Bolshevization of Russia put the capstone on this new edifice of fear. The result was the 'Red Scare' of 1919–20, led by the Democratic Attorney-General, Mitchell Palmer, against what he called 'foreign-born subversives and agitators'. He claimed there were '60,000 of these organized agitators of the Trozky doctrine in the US', 'Trozky' himself being 'a disreputable alien . . . this lowest of all types known to New York City'. Much of the material circulated by Mitchell and his allies was anti-Semitic. One list showed that, of thirty-one top Soviet leaders, all but Lenin were Jews; another analysed the members of the Petrograd Soviet, showing that only sixteen out of 388 were Russians, the rest being Jews, of whom 265 came from New York's East Side. A third document showed that the decision to overthrow the Tsar's government was actually taken on 14 February 1916 by a group of New York Jews including the millionaire Jacob Schiff.[74]

The result was the 1921 Quota Act, providing that the number of immigrants admitted in any one year was not to exceed 3 per cent of their existing ethnic stock in the US in 1910. The 1924 Johnson–Reed Act cut the figure to 2 per cent and pushed the base-date back to 1890. The net effect was to cut total immigration to 154,000 yearly, and reduce the Polish, Russian and Rumanian quotas, almost entirely of Jews, to a total of 8,879. It was effectively the end of mass Jewish immigration to the US. Thereafter the Jewish organizations had to fight hard to prevent these quotas from being scrapped completely. They considered it a triumph that in the nine difficult years 1933–41 they managed to get 157,000 German Jews into the US, about the same number as entered in the single year 1906.

Not that the Jewish community in inter-war America should be seen as embattled. Numbering over four and a half million by 1925 it was in the rapid process of becoming the largest, richest and most influential Jewish community in the world. Judaism was America's third religion. The Jews were not merely accepted, they were becoming part of the American core and already making decisive contributions to shaping the American matrix. They never had the financial leverage which, from time to time, they secured in some European countries, because by the 1920s the American economy was so enormous that no one group, however large, could become dominant in it. But in banking, stockbroking, real estate, retail, distribution and entertainment, the Jews occupied positions of strength. More important, perhaps, was the growing Jewish success in the professions, made possible by the enthusiasm with which Jewish families seized on the opportunities open to them in America to secure a higher education for their children. Some colleges, especially in the Ivy League, ran Jewish quota limitations. But in practice there were no numerical restraints on the expansion of Jewish higher education. By the early 1930s, nearly 50 per cent of all college students in New York City were Jewish, and their national total, 105,000, was over 9 per cent of the entire college enrolment.

Hence for the first time since antiquity, Jews were able to deploy, for the benefit of general society, the creative lawmaking talents they had nurtured for so long through the rabbinical tradition. In 1916, after a four-month confirmation battle, Louis Brandeis (1856–1941) became the first Jewish member of the Supreme Court. He was another prodigy, the youngest child of a family of Jewish liberals from Prague. At Harvard Law School he achieved the highest grades so far recorded there, and by the age of forty his practice had brought him a fortune of over $2 million. It was a characteristic of American Jewry that its establishment figures always felt secure enough to embrace Zionism, as soon as they saw it was viable, and Brandeis became the leading US Zionist. But more important was his effort to change the direction of American jurisprudence. Even before he joined the Court, he wrote 'the Brandeis brief' in *Muller* v. *Oregon* (1908), in which he defended a state law limiting the working hours of women. In this he relied not primarily on legal precedents but on general moral and social arguments as to the law's desirability, including over a thousand pages of statistics. This reflected both the creative interpretative philosophy of the liberal cathedocrats, and the industrious energy with which they backed it.

As a Supreme Court Justice, Brandeis was able to push the doctrine of 'sociological jurisprudence' to the centre of America's federal philosophy of law, and thus to turn the Court, under the Constitution, into a creative lawmaking body. As a liberal Jew with a classical education, who saw the American public spirit as a blend of Athens and Jerusalem – a modern Philo, indeed! – he thought that the Court should uphold plurality not just of religions but of economic systems, and still more of opinion. He held it to be true, he ruled in *Whitney* v. *California* (1927), 'that it is hazardous to discourage thought, hope or imagination; that fear breeds repression; that repression breeds hate; that hate menaces stable government; that the path of safety lies in the opportunity to discuss freely supposed grievances and proposed remedies; and that the fitting remedy for evil councils is good ones.'[75]

In 1939 he was joined on the Court by an important follower, Felix Frankfurter (1882–1965), who had immigrated to the Lower East Side at twelve, progressed upwards through the City of New York College to Harvard, and spent most of his professional life debating, in a modern secular context, one of the central problems of Judaic law – how to balance the demands of individual freedom against communal necessities. It was a comforting reflection of the maturity of American Jewry, as a part of the Commonwealth, that Frankfurter sided with the state against a dissenting minority (Jehovah's Witnesses) in the question of saluting the flag: 'One who belongs to the most vilified and persecuted minority in history is not likely to be insensible to the freedom guaranteed by our Constitution. . . . But as Judges we are neither Jew nor gentile, neither Catholic nor agnostic. . . . As a member of this Court I am not justified in writing my private notions of policy into the Constitution, no matter how deeply I may cherish them.'[76]

Jews in America, however, were engaged not merely in fundamentally modifying existing institutions, like jurisprudence, but in introducing and transporting new ones. In Paris and Vienna Jewish musicians, ranging from Halévy through Offenbach to the Strausses, had created new ranges of musical spectacles for the stage, and the theatres, opera-houses and orchestras which made them possible. The same combination of talents soon established itself in New York. Oscar Hammerstein I (1847–1919) arrived there in 1863, working first (like countless other Jews) in a cigar factory. Twenty years later his son Oscar Hammerstein II (1895–1960) went on to play a major part, as librettist, in making the American 'musical play' a new form of integrated drama. From *Rose Marie* (1924) and the *Desert Song* (1926), he joined Jerome Kern (1885–1945), another New Yorker, to create the quintessential American musical, *Show Boat* (1927), and then from the early forties he joined with Richard Rodgers (1902–79) to raise the genre, perhaps the most characteristic of all American art-forms, to a new peak, with *Oklahoma* (1943), *Carousel* (1945), *South Pacific* (1949), *The King and I* (1951) and *The Sound of Music* (1959). These American musical writers came to composition by diverse routes. Rodgers studied at Columbia and the Institute of Musical Art. Irving Berlin (b. 1888), the son of a Russian cantor, came to New York in 1893 and got a job as a singing waiter, had no musical training and never learned to read music. George Gershwin (1898–1937) started as a hack pianist in a musical publishing firm. What they all had in common was ferocious industry and completely new ideas. Kern wrote over 1,000 songs, including 'Ol' Man River' and 'Smoke Gets in Your Eyes', for 104 stage-shows and films. Berlin produced over 1,000 songs too, and scores ranging from *Top Hat* to *Annie Get Your Gun*. His 'Alexander's Ragtime Band' (1911) effectively opened the jazz era. Thirteen years later, Gershwin's *Rhapsody in Blue*, performed by the Paul Whiteman orchestra, made jazz respectable. Frederick Loewe's *My Fair Lady*, Frank Loesser's *Guys and Dolls*, Harold Arlen's *Wizard of Oz* and Leonard Bernstein's *West Side Story* were in the same tradition of perpetual innovation within strict box-office conventions.[77]

American Jews brought the same show-business talents of ideas and organization to the new technologies as they developed. In 1926 David Sarnoff (1891–1971) created the first radio chain, the National Broadcasting System, as the service-arm of the Radio Corporation of America, of which he became president in 1930. At the same time, William Paley (b. 1901) was putting together the rival Colombia Broadcasting System. In due course these two introduced black-and-white television, then colour. Jews also supplied much of the first generation of performing talent for these innovatory media – Sid

Caesar and Eddie Cantor, Milton Berle, Al Jolson and Jack Benny, Walter Winchell and David Susskind.[78] The Broadway musical, radio and TV were all examples of a fundamental principle in Jewish diaspora history: Jews opening up a completely new field in business and culture, a *tabula rasa* on which to set their mark, before other interests had a chance to take possession, erect guild or professional fortifications and deny them entry.

The outstanding example, however, was the movie industry, which was almost entirely put together by Jews. It is a matter of argument, indeed, whether or not it was their greatest contribution to shaping the modern age. For if Einstein created the cosmology of the twentieth century and Freud its characteristic mental assumptions, it was the cinema which provided its universal popular culture. Yet there were ironies in this. Jews did not invent the cinema. Thomas Edison, who developed the first effective cinecamera, the kinetoscope, in 1888, did not design it for entertainment. It was to be, he said, 'the foremost instrument of reason', designed for an enlightened democracy, to show the world as it is and to display the moral force of realism as opposed to 'the occult lore of the east'.[79] Such an exercise in rationalism might well have appealed to Jewish pioneers. In fact they turned it into something quite different. For Edison's vision of the cinema did not work. The educated middle class ignored it. It made little progress in its first decade.

Then, at the end of the 1890s, poor, immigrant Jews married the cinema to another institution they were creating for people like themselves, the amusement arcade. In 1890 there was not a single arcade in New York. By 1900 there were over 1,000, and fifty of them already contained nickelodeons. Eight years later there were 400 nickelodeons in New York alone and they were spreading all over the northern cities. They cost five cents and appealed to the poorest of the urban poor. The hundreds of movie shorts now being made for them were silent. That was an advantage. Most of the patrons knew little or no English. It was entirely an immigrant art-form. So it was the ideal setting for Jewish enterprise.

At first the Jews were not involved on the inventive and creative side. They owned the nickelodeons, the arcades, the theatres. Most of the processes and early shorts were made by American-born Protestants. An exception was Sigmund Lublin, operating from the great Jewish centre of Philadelphia, which he might have turned into the capital of the industry. But when the theatre-owners began to go into production, to make the shorts their immigrant patrons wanted, Lublin joined with the other patent-owners to form the giant Patent

Company, and extract full dues out of the movie-makers. It was then that the Jews led the industry on a new Exodus, from the 'Egypt' of the Wasp-dominated north-east, to the promised land of California. Los Angeles had sun, easy laws, and a quick escape into Mexico from the Patent Company lawyers.[80] Once in California, the Jewish skill at rationalization went into effect. There were more than one hundred small production firms in 1912. They were quickly amalgamated into eight big ones. Of these, Universal, Twentieth-Century-Fox, Paramount, Warner Brothers, Metro-Goldwyn-Mayer and Columbia were essentially Jewish creations, and Jews played a major role in the other two, United Artists and RKO Radio Pictures.[81]

Nearly all these Jewish movie men conformed to a pattern. They were immigrants or of immediate immigrant stock. They were poor, some desperately poor. Many came from families of twelve or more children. Carl Laemmle (1867–1939), the first of them, was an immigrant from Laupheim, the tenth of thirteen children. He worked in clerical jobs, as a bookkeeper and a clothing-store manager, before opening a nickelodeon, turning it into a chain, creating a movie-distribution business, and then founding Universal, the first big studio, in 1912. Marcus Loew (1872–1927) was born in the Lower East Side, the son of an immigrant waiter. He sold papers at six, left school at twelve to work in printing, then furs, was an independent fur-broker at eighteen, had been twice bankrupted by the age of thirty, founded a theatre-chain and put together Metro-Goldwyn-Mayer. William Fox (1879–1952) was born in Hungary, one of twelve children, and came through New York's Castle Garden Immigrant Station as a child. He left school at eleven for the garment industry, set up his own shrinking business, then progressed through Brooklyn penny-arcades to a movie-chain. Louis B. Mayer (1885–1957) was born in Russia, the son of a Hebrew scholar, and also came through Castle Garden as a child, went into the junk trade at the age of eight, had his own junk-business by nineteen, a theatre-chain by twenty-two, and in 1915 made the first big adult movie, *Birth of a Nation*. The Warner Brothers were among the nine children of a poor cobbler from Poland. They worked selling meat and ice-cream, repairing bicycles, as fairground barkers and travelling showmen. In 1904 they bought a film-projector and ran their own show, with their sister Rose playing the piano and twelve-year-old Jack singing treble. In Hollywood they made the breakthrough into sound. Joseph Schenck, co-founder of United Artists, ran an amusement park. Sam Goldwyn worked as a blacksmith's assistant and a glove salesman. Harry Cohn, another Lower East Sider, was a trolley conductor, then in Vaudeville. Jesse Lasky was a cornet player. Sam Katz was a messenger boy but owned three nickelodeons in his teens. Dore Schary worked as a waiter in a Jewish holiday-camp. Adolph Zukor, from a family of rabbis, worked as a fur salesman. So did Darryl Zanuck, who made his first money with a new fur-clasp. Not all the pioneers kept the fortunes and studios they created. Some went bankrupt; Fox and Schenck even went to gaol. But Zukor summed up for them all: 'I arrived from Hungary an orphan boy of sixteen with a few dollars sewn inside my vest. I was thrilled to breathe the fresh strong air of freedom, and America has been good to me.'[82]

These men were underdogs, creating for underdogs. It was a long time before the New York banks would look at them. Their first big backer was a fellow California immigrant, A. P. Giannini, whose Bank of Italy eventually became the Bank of America, the world's biggest. They had centuries of deprivation behind them, and they looked it. They were small in stature. As the film historian Philip French puts it: 'One could have swung a scythe five and a half feet off the ground at a gathering of movie moguls without endangering many lives: several would scarcely have heard the swish.'[83] They were impelled by a strong desire to carry the poor with them in their upward ascent, both materially and culturally. Zukor would boast of turning the proletarian arcades into middle-class palaces: 'Who swept out your dirty nickelodeons? Who put in your plush seats?' he would demand. Goldwyn defined his cultural aim as to make 'pictures built upon the strong foundation of art and refinement'. Their new cinema-culture was not without traditional Jewish characteristics, especially in critical humour. The Marx Brothers provided an underdog view of the conventional world, rather in the way Jews had always seen majority society. Whether examining Wasp society in *Animal Crackers*, culture in *A Night at the Opera*, the campus in *Horse Feathers*, commerce in *The Big Store* or politics in *Duck Soup*, they represented a disconcerting intrusion on established institutions. They disturbed the peace and plunged 'normal' people into confusion.[84]

In general, however, the Hollywood rulers did not wish to disturb. When they gave a haven in the 1930s to the Jewish diaspora from the German movie industry, they tried to impose on it a spirit of conformity. It was their own form of assimilationism. Like the Jews who rationalized the retail trade in the eighteenth century and created the first big stores in the nineteenth, they served the customer. 'If the audience don't like a picture', Goldwyn said, 'they have a good reason. The public is never wrong.'[85] Hence they maximized the market. There was an irony here too. The movie was the first cultural form since the days of classical Greece which presented itself to an entire population. Just as all who lived in the *polis* could fit into the stadium, the theatre, the lyceum or the odeon, so now all Americans could see movies more or less at the same time. A study of Muncie, Indiana, in 1929 found that weekly attendance at its nine cinemas was three times the entire population.[86] The movie, which became the pattern for TV later, was thus a giant step towards the consumer society of the late twentieth century. More urgently than any other institution, it brought to ordinary workers the vision of a better existence. Hence, contrary to what Attorney-General Palmer and Madison Grant had imagined, it was Jews, from Hollywood, who stylized, polished and popularized the concept of the American Way of Life.

Naturally, that American way had its darker sides. Between the wars, American Jews began to approximate to the national profile. They became part of its more repellent features too. As with the Broadway musical and the Hollywood movie, crime and especially new and expanding kinds of crime were areas where enterprising Jews could get in at the beginning without meeting formal gentile barriers. In Europe, Jews had often been associated with certain kinds of poverty-related crimes, such as receiving, pickpocketing and minor fraud. They also developed criminal patterns requiring a high degree of organization and distant networks, such as the white slave-trade. In the late nineteenth century this reached from eastern Europe, with its colossal Jewish birth rate, to Latin America. It was marked by strong Jewish characteristics. A surprising number of Jewish prostitutes observed the Sabbath, Jewish holidays and dietary laws. In Argentina they even had their own synagogue. Moreover, precisely because Jews were prominent in the trade, legitimate Jewish institutions fought to destroy it, all over the world, and created special bodies for this purpose.[87] In New York, Jewish criminals, besides the usual Jewish types of crime, concentrated on protection rackets, arson and horse poisoning. Here again, Jewish society responded with crime-prevention campaigns, including reformatory schools.[88] Such efforts were remarkably effective with small-time Jewish crime. Indeed it is possible that, without prohibition, the Jewish criminal community could have been reduced to a tiny group by the end of the 1920s.

The illegal liquor trade, however, offered irresistible opportunities for clever Jews to rationalize and organize it. Jewish criminals rarely used violence. As Arthur Ruppin, the leading authority on Jewish sociology put it, 'Christians commit crimes with their hands, the Jews use their reason.' A typical Jewish big-time criminal was Jacob 'Greasy Thumb' Guzik (1887–1956), who was Al Capone's bookkeeper and treasurer. Another was Arnold Rothstein (1882–1928), the pioneer of big business crime, who is portrayed as 'The Brain' in Damon Runyon's stories, and by Scott Fitzgerald as Meyer Wolfsheim in *The Great Gatsby*. Then there was Meyer Lansky, who created and lost a gambling empire and had his application for Israeli citizenship turned down in 1971.

But as these upwardly mobile Jewish criminals rose, they found themselves practising violence too. It was Louis Lepke Buchalter (1897–1944), known as 'The Judge' and called by the FBI 'the most dangerous criminal in the United States', who helped to organize the Syndicate, or Murder Incorporated, in 1944, and who was executed for murder in Sing Sing in 1944. On Buchalter's instructions, Syndicate killers murdered Arthur 'Dutch Schultz' Flegenheimer (1900–35), the numbers racketeer who tried, against its orders, to kill Thomas E. Dewey; and the Syndicate was also responsible for the death of Benjamin 'Bugsy' Siegel (1905–47), who organized Las Vegas for it, then broke with it. Finally Jews, led by Samuel 'Sammie Purple' Cohen, organized the notorious Detroit Purple Gang which ran the city's East Side until the Mafia took over. Yet attempts to compare Jewish and Italian crime in the United States fail. A surprising number of notorious Jewish criminals had Orthodox funerals, but organized Jewish crime, unlike the Mafia in Sicily, was not a response to specific social conditions and never enjoyed the slightest communal sanction. Hence it has proved to be a temporary phenomenon.[89]

If the Jewish community reacted to Jewish crime, especially white slavery, with shame and horror, and did all in its power to re-educate the criminal element in its midst, there were many American Jews who disliked the idea of any Jewish propensities, good or bad, and did their best to reject Jewish particularism completely. It was not merely a matter of ceasing to attend synagogue and observing the Law, it was also a conscious effort to stop thinking oneself Jewish. Even Brandeis, as late as 1910, attacked 'habits of living or of thought which tend to keep alive differences of origin' as undesirable and 'inconsistent with the American ideal of brotherhood'. To stress Jewishness was 'disloyal'.[90] But such efforts, as in Brandeis' case, tended to collapse under the sudden impact of an anti-Semitic experience. He ended by going to the opposite extreme: 'To be good Americans', he said, 'we must be better Jews, and to be better Jews we must become Zionists.'[91] Some Jews drifted uneasily between the two poles. A notable example was Bernard Baruch (1870–1965), a figure in the Joseph mould. He advised successive presidents and was reputed, incorrectly as we now know, to have made a fortune in the 1929 crash by selling out just before the market turned down.[92] Father Charles Coughlin, the Jew-baiting Detroit radio priest, used to call him 'Acting President of the United States, the Uncrowned King of Wall Street'. Baruch did his best to escape from the Jewish image. Thanks to his wife's Protestant pull, he got into the *Social Register* at a time when it still banned the Schiffs, Guggenheims, Seligmans and Warburgs. He took vacations in a gentile Adirondack colony. But at any moment there was liable to be a twitch on the thread, telling him: thus far, no further. He was mortified, in 1912, when his daughter Belle was mysteriously refused admission to the Brearley School in Manhattan, though she had passed the entrance exam: 'That really was the bitterest blow of my life,' he wrote, 'because it hurt my child and embittered my whole life for many years afterwards.' He himself had a tremendous struggle to secure election to the fashionable Oakland Golf Club and, though a prominent horse-breeder, to get admittance to the track enclosure at Belmont Park. He never got into the University Club or the Metropolitan.[93] Even in America, a Jew, however rich, influential and well connected he might be, could be pushed back into line; and it was this more than anything else which kept the community together.

Yet some ultra-assimilationists did manage to fight off their Jewishness, at least to their own satisfaction. Walter Lippmann (1889–1974), the newspaper seer, as influential as Baruch in his day, spent his entire life merging with the scenery. His parents, rich clothing manufacturers from Germany, sent him to the upper-class Sachs School for Boys. The family attended the Emanu-El synagogue. They refused to admit they knew Yiddish. Their aim was to avoid being 'oriental', as they put it. The hordes of *Ostjuden* immigrants terrified them. The *American Hebrew*, which voiced their fears, wrote: 'All of us should be sensible of what we owe not only to those ... co-religionists but to ourselves who will be looked upon by our Gentile neighbours as the natural sponsors for these, our brethren.' At Harvard, exclusion from the famous 'Gold Coast' clubs made Lippmann briefly a socialist. But he soon decided that anti-Semitism was to a large extent a punishment the Jews invited, by making themselves 'conspicuous', his favourite term of criticism. 'My personal attitude', he wrote, 'is to be far severer upon the faults of the Jews than of other people.'[94] He attacked the Zionists for their 'dual allegiance' and the 'rich, vulgar and pretentious Jews of our big American cities' as 'perhaps the greatest misfortune which has ever befallen the Jewish people'.[95]

Lippmann was a liberal and civilized man who simply (as he saw it) wanted to avoid Jewish categorization. He could not bring himself to endorse anti-Jewish quotas at Harvard since there should be 'no test of admission based on race, creed, colour, class or section'. On the other hand he agreed that for Jews to exceed 15 per cent of the intake would be 'disastrous'. He thought the solution was for Massachusetts Jews to have a university of their own and for Harvard to draw its students from a wider area, thus diluting the Jewish content. 'I do not regard the Jews as innocent victims,' he wrote. They had 'many distressing personal and social habits, which were selected by a bitter history and intensified by a pharisaical theology'. The 'personal manners and physical habits' of the gentiles were 'distinctly superior to the prevailing manners and habits of the Jews'.[96] This Jewish self-hatred was embittered by the fact that Lippmann could not secure all the social prizes he esteemed. He joined the River in New York and the Metropolitan in Washington, but he could not get into the Links or the Knickerbocker.

Perhaps the most tragic aspect of those Jews who denied their identity, or suppressed the feelings which naturally arose from it, was the almost wilful blindness they thereby inflicted upon themselves. For half a century, Lippmann was perhaps the wisest of all American commentators – on everything except issues affecting Jews. Like Blum in France, he dismissed the anti-Semitic side of Hitler as unimportant and classified him as a German nationalist. After the Nazi burning of Jewish books in May 1933, he said that persecuting the Jews, 'by satisfying the lust of the Nazis who feel they must conquer somebody . . . is a kind of lightning rod which protects Europe'. Germany could not be judged by Nazi anti-Semitism, any more than France by its Terror, Protestantism by the Ku-Klux Klan or, for that matter, 'the Jews by their parvenus'. He called one Hitler speech 'statesmanlike', the 'authentic voice of a genuinely civilized people'.[97] But after these two comments on the Nazis and the Jews, he fell silent on the subject for the next twelve calamitous years and never mentioned the death camps at all. Another form of blindness was the Rosa Luxemburg solution adopted by the brilliant playwright Lillian Hellman (1905–84), whose plays The Children's Hour (1934) and The Little Foxes (1939) were the great Broadway success-scandals of the decade. She tortured her Jewish humanitarianism to fit the prevailing Stalinist mode (as did many thousands of Jewish intellectuals) so that her anti-Nazi play, Watch on the Rhine (1941), gives a weird view of the Jewish predicament in the light of later events. She would not allow her love of justice to find its natural expression in outraged protest at the fate of her race. So it was perverted into a hard-faced ideological orthodoxy defended with rabbinical tenacity. The need to avert the face from the

Jewish facts led her to doctor truth with fiction. As late as 1955 she was associated with a dramatization of the *Diary of Anne Frank* which virtually eliminated the Jewish element in the tragedy.

These confusions, divisions and opacities in the American Jewish community, not least among its intellectuals, help to explain why American Jews, despite the enormous position of power they were beginning to acquire for themselves, were so curiously incapable of affecting events in inter-war Europe, or even of steering opinion in America itself. American anti-Semitism, as revealed by opinion polls, rose steadily throughout the 1930s, peaking in 1944; the polls also showed (in 1938, for instance), that 70–85 per cent of the nation were opposed to raising quotas to help Jewish refugees. The pollster Elmo Roper warned: 'Anti-Semitism has spread all over the nation and is particularly virulent in urban centres.'[98]

It is against this background in Europe and America that we must now examine events in Germany. Germany was the strongest economic, military and cultural power in Europe, and its assault on the Jews, from 1933 to 45, is the central event of modern Jewish history. It is still in many respects a mysterious event: not as regards the facts, which have been documented in stupefying quantity, but as regards the causes. Germany was by far the world's best-educated nation. It was the first to achieve universal adult literacy. Between 1870 and 1933 its universities were the world's finest, in virtually every discipline. Why did this highly civilized nation turn with colossal, organized yet senseless brutality on the Jews? The identity of the victim deepens the mystery. In the nineteenth century the fate of Germany and the Jews was very much interwoven. As Fritz Stern has pointed out, between 1870 and 1914 the Germans suddenly emerged as an actively powerful nation, just as suddenly as the Jews emerged as an actively powerful race.[99] The two helped each other enormously. Among the many things they shared was an almost fanatical devotion to learning. The ablest Jews loved Germany because it was the best place in the world to work in. Modern Jewish culture had an essentially Germanic framework. But in turn, as Weizmann had pointed out in his famous talk with Balfour, the Jews gave all their finest efforts to Germany and helped to make her great. From its inception to 1933, for instance, Germany won more Nobel prizes than any other country, about 30 per cent of the whole; but of Germany's share, the Jews provided nearly a third and in medicine a half.[100] For Germany to turn on the Jews was not just mass murder; it was, in a real sense, mass parricide. How did it happen?

Attempts to provide an explanation are already filling whole libraries, but in the end they always seem inadequate. The greatest crime in history remains, to some extent, baffling. All the same, the chief components can be summarized. The most important, probably, was the First World War. It had the effect of stunning the German nation. They entered it confidently just as their ascent to greatness was reaching its apogee. After fearful sacrifices, they lost it, conclusively. The grief and fury were unhinging; the need for a scapegoat imperative.

The war had a second effect. It transformed the way in which Germany conducted its business. Pre-war Germany was the most law-abiding country in Europe. Civil violence was unheard of, un-German. Anti-Semitism was everywhere, but physical violence to Jews, let alone an anti-Semitic riot, was something which did not, could not, occur in Germany. The war changed all that. It accustomed men to violence everywhere, but in Germany it induced a violence of despair. The 1918 Armistice did not bring peace to central and eastern Europe. It brought a twenty-year interval between two huge, open conflicts, but in those twenty years violence, in varying degrees, was the main arbiter of politics. Both left and right used violence. Lenin and Trotsky set the pattern with their *putsch* in 1917. Their Communist allies and imitators followed suit in Germany, 1918–20. Jews were prominent in all these attempts to overthrow existing order by force. The Communist regime in Bavaria included not only Jewish politicians, like Eisner, but Jewish writers and intellectuals like Gustav Landauer, Ernst Toller and Erich Mühsam. The right responded by organizing private armies of veterans, the Freikorps.

In Russia, the arbitration of violence favoured the left, in Germany the right. Jewish extremists like Rosa Luxemburg and Eisner were simply murdered. It ceased to be unusual for Jewish opponents to be 'dealt with'. In the four years 1919–22 there were 376 political murders in Germany, all but twenty-two of left-wing figures, many of them Jews. One was Walter Rathenau, the Foreign Secretary. The courts dealt lightly with the ex-army thugs. Few were even brought to trial; fewer still sentenced to more than four months.[101] When the old and distinguished Jewish writer Maximilian Harden was nearly beaten to death by two anti-Semites in 1922, the court held that his 'unpatriotic articles' constituted 'mitigating circumstances'.

It was from this background of radical ex-servicemen's violence that Adolf Hitler emerged. He was an Austrian, born on the Austro-Bavarian border in 1889, the son of a petty official. He lived in Linz and then in Karl Lueger's Vienna. He had a distinguished war record and was badly gassed. Hitler later declared in *Mein Kampf* (written in

1924) that he was a young man before he became aware of the 'Jewish problem', but the evidence is clear that his father was an anti-Semite and that he was exposed to anti-Semitic notions all his childhood and youth. The Jews became, and remained, his lifelong obsession. His personal passion, and still more his colossal willpower, were central to Germany's war against the Jews. It could not have taken place without him. On the other hand, he could have done little damage without the destructive elements within Germany which he found to hand. He had unusual skill in creating political dynamism by fusing together two sources of power and making the result greater than the sum of its parts. Thus, he married a small socialist group, the German Workers' Party, to an ex-service strongarm squad, gave it an anti-Semitic platform, and turned it into a mass party, the National Socialist Workers Party (Nazis) with its military wing of stormtroopers, the Sturmabteilung or SA. The SA protected his own meetings and broke up his opponents'. Next, he brought together the two consequences of the war, the need for a scapegoat and the cult of violence, focussing the result on the Jews: 'If at the beginning of the war, and during the war, 12,000 or 15,000 of these Hebrew defilers had been put under poison gas as hundreds of thousands of our very best workers from all walks of life had to endure at the front, then the sacrifice of millions would not have been in vain.'[102]

Hitler's anti-Semitism was composed of all the conventional elements, from the Christian *Judensau* to pseudo-scientific race theory. But it was distinctive in two respects. First, it was to him a complete explanation of the world, a *Weltanschauung*, a world outlook. Other political groups in Germany dabbled in anti-Semitism or even gave it prominence, but the Nazis made it the centre and end of their programme (though they varied the emphasis according to their audience). Second, Hitler was an Austrian by birth but a pan-German by choice, who joined the German, not the Austrian, army in 1914; and his anti-Semitism was a marriage of the German and Austrian models. From Germany, he took the huge and growing fear of 'Jewish–Bolshevist Russia' and the proliferating mythology of the *Protocols of Zion*. Post-war Germany swarmed with Russian refugees of German origin, German Balts, and former members of old Tsarist anti-Semitic groups such as the Black Hundreds, the Yellow Shirts and the Union of the Russian People. All of them stressed the Jewish–Bolshevist connection, which became a central part of Hitler's ideology. Alfred Rosenberg, a German Balt, became the Nazis' chief theorist. The Russian Gertrude von Seidlitz enabled Hitler to acquire (1920) the *Völkischer Beobachter* and turn it into an anti-Semitic daily.[103] In modern times, Germany, and especially Prussia, had been more afraid of the Russian threat than any other. Hitler was now able to place the threat in a plausible anti-Semitic context. But he blended it with the kind of anti-Semitism he had absorbed in Vienna. This concentrated on fear of the Ostjuden, a dark and inferior race corrupting the Germanic blood. Hitler was particularly interested in two topics, both of which he connected with Ostjuden: the white slave-trade, centred in Vienna and run by Jews – or so the moral reformers asserted – and the spread of syphilis, for which as yet there was no antibiotic cure. Hitler believed and taught that there was not only a direct political and military threat to Germany from Jewish Bolshevism but a deeper, biological threat from any contact, but especially sexual congress, with members of the Jewish race.[104]

The sexual–medical aspect of Hitler's anti-Semitism was probably the most important, especially among his own followers. It turned the merely prejudiced into fanatics, capable of any course of action, however irrational and cruel. Rather as the medieval anti-Semite saw the Jew as non-human, a devil or a sort of animal (hence the Judensau), the Nazi extremist absorbed Hitler's sub-scientific phraseology and came to regard Jews as bacilli or a particularly dangerous kind of vermin. Apart from anything else, this approach enabled all Jews to be lumped together, irrespective of their circumstances or views. A Jew who held a professorial chair, who wrote impeccable German, who had served throughout the war and won the Iron Cross, was just as dangerous a racial polluter as a Jewish–Bolshevik commissar. An assimilated Jew carried the bacillus just as certainly as an old rabbi in a kaftan and was more of a threat, since he was more likely to infect, or 'desecrate' as Hitler put it, an Aryan woman. The extent to which he indoctrinated his followers can be seen by a letter written to him, in April 1943, by his Minister of Justice, Thierack:

A full Jewess, after the birth of her child, sold her mother's milk to a woman doctor and concealed the fact that she was a Jewess. With this milk, infants of German blood were fed in a clinic. The accused is charged with fraud. The purchasers of the milk have suffered damage, because the milk of a Jewess cannot be considered food for German children. . . . However, there has been no formal indictment in order to spare the parents, who do not know the facts, unnecessary worry. I will discuss the race-hygienic aspects of the case with the Reich Health Chief.[105]

If it be asked: how could such nonsense be widely believed in a highly educated nation like Germany, the answer is that Hitler never found any difficulty in acquiring intellectual backing, albeit sometimes oblique, for his views. The 'scandal' of Freud and his teachings was an important collateral proof of the Nazi case, since (it was argued) they removed moral guilt from sexual promiscuity and so increased it. Thus Freud enabled Jews to gain greater access to Aryan women. Here, Jung was able to come to Hitler's assistance by drawing a distinction between Freudian–Jewish psychiatry and the rest:

One cannot of course accept that Freud or Adler is a generally valid representative of European mankind. . . . The Jew as a relative nomad has never created, and presumably never will create, a cultural form of his own, for all his instincts and talent are dependent on a more or less civilized host people. . . . In my view it has been a great mistake of medical psychology to apply Jewish categories, which are not even valid for all Jews, to Christian Germans and Slavs. In this way the most precious secret of Teutonic man, the deep-rooted, creative awareness of his soul, has been explained away as a banal, infantile sump, while my warning voice, over the decades, was suspected of anti-Semitism. . . . Has the mighty phenomenon of National Socialism, at which the whole world gazes in astonishment, taught them to know better?[106]

Scientists were similarly found to invalidate Einstein's work as 'Jewish physics'.

Indeed, the German academy, taken as a whole, far from acting as a barrier to Hitlerism, assisted its progress to power. A key element in the Nazi triumph was the generation of schoolteachers who matured in the last decade of the nineteenth century, were infected with *Völkisch* anti-Semitism, and had become senior teachers by the 1920s.[107] The textbooks they used reflected the same influences. The university academics similarly contributed to the rise of Nazi influence by preaching national salvation through panaceas and 'spiritual revivals', instead of sceptical empiricism.[108] Above all, Hitler achieved his greatest success among university students. They were his vanguard. At each stage in the growth of the Nazis, student support preceded general electoral support. The Nazis worked in the first place through the student fraternities, which in 1919 adopted the 'Eisenach Resolution', excluding Jews on racial as well as religious grounds.[109] As they grew more influential, they worked through the students' union, the Hochschulring movement, which dominated student life in the 1920s. Finally, towards the end of the decade they set up their own student party. The success of the Nazis was due to the willingness of enough young fanatics to devote themselves full-time to the effort, to the party's egalitarianism and radical programme.[110] But an important bond between the Nazis and the students was the use of violent demonstrations against Jews. The students were among the first to organize boycotts and mass petitions to force Jews out of government jobs and the professions, especially teaching, and these forms of action soon developed into actual violence. In 1922 the threat of a student riot led to Berlin University cancelling a memorial service for the murdered Walther Rathenau. This would have been inconceivable before the war, and what was most sinister was not just the threat of violence but the pusillanimity of the university authorities in bowing to it. Attacks on Jewish students and on Jewish professors, who were forced to give up their lecture courses, increased to the point in 1927 when the government withdrew recognition from the Deutsche Studentenschaft because of its support for violence. But this made little difference and no resolute action was ever taken by the universities themselves to curb the student thugs. It was not that the professors were pro-Nazi. But they were anti-Weimar and anti-democratic and, above all, they were cowardly in standing up to student acts which they knew to be wrong – an adumbration of the more general cowardice of the nation later. As a result, the Nazis effectively controlled the campuses two or three years before they took over the country.

The climate of actual violence which nourished Nazism was itself sustained by growing verbal and pictorial violence in the media. It is sometimes argued that satire, even of the most savage kind, is a sign of health in a free society and that no restrictions should be placed on it. Jewish history does not lend support to this view. The Jews have been more frequently the target of such attacks than any other group and they know from long and bitter experience that the violence of print is often the prelude to the violence of blood. Weimar was, by German standards, an ultra-liberal society and one of the effects of its liberalism was to destroy most restraints in the press. Just as the Arab extremist newspapers took advantage of Samuel's liberalism in Palestine, so the Nazis revelled in Weimar's licence to insult. There had long been a pornographic side to anti-Semitism, especially in Germany and Austria; the *Judensau* theme itself was often a symptom of it. But Hitler's stress on the sexual, race-defilement issue combined with Weimar permissiveness to produce a peculiarly vicious form of anti-Semitic propaganda epitomized by the weekly *Der Stürmer*, run by the Nazi boss in Middle Franconia, Julius Streicher. It helped to spread and intensify one of the chief, perennial sources of anti-Semitic violence: the notion that Jews are not part of humanity and therefore not entitled to the protection we instinctively accord a human being. It was by no means the only such publication. But it set the increasingly unrestrained tone of visual assault on Jews. Under Weimar's laws it was exceedingly difficult to prosecute, for Streicher enjoyed immunity as a Landtag and later a Reichstag deputy. It seems to have sold only 13,000 copies in 1927 (the only reliable circulation figure), but in the last phases of the Nazi ascent to power it won a national audience.[111]

Unfortunately, the media violence was not one-sided. Just as Communist street gangs, as well as Nazis, took violence systematically into the streets, and so co-operated in preparing national violence, a great deal of verbal savagery was produced from the liberal side, much of it by Jews. Satire came naturally to Jews, and in Germany Heine had forged a powerful and often vicious matrix, the inspiration for many later Jewish writers. Between 1899 and 1936 the Viennese writer Karl Kraus (1874–1936), baptized like Heine, ran a paper called Die Fackel (The Torch), which set new standards in aggressive satire, much of it directed against Jews, such as Herzl and Freud. 'Psychoanalysis', he wrote, 'is the newest Jewish disease' and 'the unconscious is a ghetto for people's thoughts'. His venomous skill in finding the tender spot was widely admired and imitated in Weimar Germany, and used in a highly provocative manner, especially by Kurt Tucholsky (1890–1935) and the journal Weltbühne. It too had only a small sale, 16,000 (1931), but it aroused enormous controversy because of its deliberate attacks on everything right-thinking Germans held dear. Tucholsky's 1929 book, Deutschland, Deutschland über Alles, went for the judiciary, the churches, the police, Hindenburg, Social Democrats and trade union leaders, and contained a brilliant photomontage of German generals entitled: 'Animals are looking at you'.[112]

From the start this media violence from the left played into the hands of anti-Semites. Karl Gerecke made skilful use of Weltbühne in his tract Biblischer Antisemitismus (1920), a Nazi standby. Jewish attacks on the army were particularly dangerous. The Jewish ex-servicemen's association was able to show from official figures that the number of Jews who served in the war, and who were killed, wounded and decorated, was strictly in accordance with the Jewish proportion of the population. But there was a popular belief, shared and propagated by Hitler and the Nazis with relentless persistence, that Jews had evaded service and, indeed, stabbed the army in the back. The most violent satirist of the army–Junker class was, in fact, a non-Jew, George Grosz; but he was closely associated with Jewish artists and writers and so was said to have been 'put up to it'. Tucholsky was Grosz's prose version. Many of his statements were deliberately designed to fill people with rage: 'There is no secret of the German army', he wrote, 'which I would not hand over readily to a foreign power.'[113] But enraged people, especially if they are inarticulate and incapable of replying in kind, may retaliate physically, or vote for those who will; and Tucholsky and his fellow satirists enraged not just professional army officers but the families of countless conscripts killed in the war. The anti-Semitic and the nationalist press ensured that Tucholsky's more wounding attacks were given the widest circulation.

Some Jews tried hard to counter the unpatriotic, Bolshevist image thrust upon them. Jewish children were trained to be artisans and farmers.[114] In the early 1920s, a Berlin lawyer, Dr Max Naumann, a former army captain, formed the League of German Nationalist Jews. There was also the right-wing Jewish youth organization, Kameraden, and the National League of Jewish Frontline Veterans. But Naumann made the mistake of trying to minimize Hitler's hatred of the Jews by praising him as a political genius who could restore German prosperity, and all of them shared the illusion that they could do deals with the Nazis.[115] There is no evidence that anything they did made Jews more popular.

The insuperable difficulty any patriotic German Jew had to contend with was the Weimar Republic itself. It was born of defeat, indissolubly linked with defeat, and, in the minds of most Germans, associated with Jews, the *Judenrepublik*. From beginning to end it was a millstone round the Jewish neck. Yet the Jews played little part in Weimar politics, except at the very beginning. Rathenau and Rudolf Hilferding, Finance Minister in 1923 and 1928, were the first and last Jewish Weimar politicians of any consequence. It is true that Jews were instrumental in creating the German Communist Party. But with the rise of Stalinism they were soon pushed out of its higher ranks, exactly as in Russia. In 1932, when the party ran 500 candidates and got 100 elected, not one was a Jew.[116] The Social Democrat Party was run by gentile working-class trade unionists most of whom actively disliked Jewish left-wingers, whom they saw as undesirable middle-class intellectuals. The actual constitution of Weimar, with its system of proportional representation, strongly favoured extremist parties like the Nazis, who could never have come to power legally under, say, the British first-past-the-post system. And Jewish satirists like Tucholsky went for Weimar as fiercely as the Nazis themselves.

Yet the identification was there, and its roots were cultural. Enemies of the Jews accused them of kidnapping German culture, of transforming it into a new, alien thing, which they termed *Kulturbolschewismus*. The notion of cultural theft was powerful and exceedingly dangerous. Some Jewish writers had warned against it. Jewish use of the German language, as Kafka put it, was 'usurpation of an alien property, which had not been acquired but stolen, (relatively) quickly picked up and which remains someone else's property even if not a single verbal mistake can be pointed out'. Even before the war, Moritz Goldstein had warned in a *Kunstwart* article, 'The German–Jewish Parnassus', that Jews were, in effect, beginning to take charge of the culture of a people which denied them the right to do so.[117] With the creation of Weimar, Jews became more prominent in German cultural life, chiefly for the reason that the advanced ideas with which they had been associated were now beginning to achieve acceptance. Thus in 1920 the Impressionist Max Liebermann was elected the first Jewish president in the history of the Prussian Academy.

Yet the notion that Weimar witnessed a Jewish takeover of German culture is false. The fact is that, during the 1920s, Germany was richer in talent than at any time before or since. It had always been outstanding in music and strong in literature but now it took the lead in the visual arts too. For a time Berlin became the cultural capital of the world. Berlin was much hated by the anti-Semites. Wolfgang Kapp, a proto-Hitler who led a failed *putsch* there in 1920, had as his slogan: 'What has become of Berlin? A playground for the Jews.'[118] Jews were important in Weimar culture. The phenomenon could not have occurred without them. But they were not dominant. In some areas, especially painting and architecture, their contribution was relatively small. There were many Jewish novelists, such as Alfred Doeblin, Franz Werfel, Arnold Zweig, Vicki Baum, Leon Feuchtwanger, Alfred Neuman and Bruno Frank, but the leading figures like Thomas Mann were not Jews. The Jews undoubtedly made a huge contribution to the musical scene, both international and German. There were spectacular prodigy-performers like Jascha Heifetz and Vladimir Horowitz, as well as established masters like Artur Schnabel and Artur Rubinstein. Two of Berlin's leading conductors, Otto Klemperer and Bruno Walter, were Jews. Kurt Weill wrote the music for Brecht's *Threepenny Opera* (1928), which was performed over 4,000 times throughout Europe in its first year. There was Arnold Schönberg and his school, though his two most famous pupils, Berg and Webern, were non-Jews. But German music was so rich at this time that Jewish musicians, despite their numbers and talent, were only one of its elements. The 1929 Berlin Festival featured Richard Strauss, Toscanini, Casals, George Szell, Cortot, Thibaud, Furtwängler, Bruno Walter, Klemperer and Gigli. What did that prove? Only that music was international and Berliners were lucky.

Jews were certainly a principal reason for the enormous success of the German cinemas in the 1920s. During the war, British, French and later American imports were banned. To fill the 2,000 German and

1,000 Austrian cinemas, German production companies jumped from thirty in 1913 to 250 six years later, and after the war German cinema became dominant in Europe. In 1921 it produced 246 feature films, about the same as America; in 1925 its production (228) was twice as many as Britain and France put together.[119] Jews took a leading role in supplying both the quantity and quality of German films. *The Cabinet of Dr Caligari* was scripted by Hans Janowitz and Carl Meyer, and produced by Erich Pommer. *Metropolis* was directed by Fritz Lang. These were only two of the most influential films. Directors like Ernst Lubitsch, Billy Wilder, Max Ophuls and Alexander Korda, and actors like Peter Lorre, Elizabeth Bergner, Pola Negri and Conrad Veidt, were part of a galaxy of Jewish talent which created the golden age of German cinema and then, after the rise of Hitler, led a diaspora to Hollywood, London and Paris. There was undeniably a strong Jewish element in the German cinema, and both Lang and G. W. Pabst were fascinated by the concept of the *golem*.[120] But on the whole the German cinema of the 1920s was brilliant and adventurous rather than politically and culturally committed and its contribution to German cultural paranoia about the Jews is hard to discern now.

The area where Jewish influence was strongest was the theatre, especially in Berlin. Playwrights like Carl Sternheim, Arthur Schnitzler, Ernst Toller, Erwin Piscator, Walter Hasenclever, Ferenc Molnar and Carl Zuckmayer, and influential producers like Max Reinhardt, appeared at times to dominate the stage, which tended to be modishly left-wing, pro-republican, experimental and sexually daring. But it was certainly not revolutionary, and it was cosmopolitan rather than Jewish.

The only Weimar manifestation which to some extent fitted the anti-Semitic stereotype of Jewish *Kulturbolschewismus* was the Frankfurt Institution for Social Research (1923). Its theorists, led by Theodor Adorno, Max Horkheimer, Herbert Marcuse, Erich Fromm and Franz Neuman, preached a humanist version of Marxism in which culture assumed greater importance than practical politics. Jewish attitudes and concepts undoubtedly played a role in their work. They were fascinated by Marx's theory of alienation. They were acutely conscious of the importance of psychoanalysis, and in various ways sought to Freudianize Marxism. They also tried, by using Marxist methods, to demonstrate how socio-economic assumptions determined what most people thought of as cultural absolutes. This was highly subversive, and from the 1950s onwards was to prove influential too. But at the time few Germans had heard of the Frankfurt school. This applied particularly to its most famous alumnus, Walter Benjamin (1892–1940), who found it difficult to formulate his thoughts in publishable shape, and printed comparatively little in his lifetime beyond a few articles and his essays, his doctoral thesis, a book of aphorisms and some annotated letters on the rise of German culture. His lifework was essentially put together and published by Adorno in 1955.

Benjamin was among the most Jewish of modern German thinkers, though he had no religion as such. But, as his great friend Gershom Scholem, the historian, pointed out, his thinking revolved around two basic Jewish concepts: Revelation – truth revealed through sacred texts – and Redemption.[121] Benjamin was always looking for a Messiah-force. Before 1914 it was youth: he was a leader in the largely Jewish radical youth movement created by Gustav Wyneken. But when Wyneken turned patriotic in 1914 Benjamin denounced him, and after the war he turned to literature as the Messiah. Certain outstanding texts, he argued, like the Torah, had to be scrutinized in an exegetical quest for the key to moral redemption. He applied to literature one of the central principles of kabbalah: words are sacred in the same way that the words of the Torah are physically linked to God. As a result of the relationship between divine and human language, man has been charged with the process of completing creation, which he does mainly through words (name-calling) and formulating ideas. He coined the phrase 'the creative omnipotence of language' and he showed that texts had to be explored to detect not merely their surface meaning but their underlying message and structure.[122] Hence Benjamin belonged to the irrational and gnostic Jewish tradition, like Marx himself and Freud, detecting deep, secret and life-explaining meanings beneath the veneer of existence. What he first began to apply to literature, and later to history, was to become in time a more general technique, used for instance by Claude Lévi-Strauss in anthropology and Noam Chomsky in linguistics. Gnosticism is the most insidious form of irrationalism, especially to intellectuals, and the particular variety of gnosticism developed tentatively by Benjamin, expanded into Structuralism, proved a major force among the intelligentsia from the 1950s onwards.

Benjamin was particularly influential in his efforts to show that a ruling class manipulated history to perpetuate its own needs, illusions and deceits. As the scene darkened in the 1930s, he turned to his own version of Marxism as his third Messiah. What he called 'Marxist Time', or the Marxist millennium, was his alternative to the long, unsatisfactory, historical process of reform. It was important, he argued, to 'blast out' (a favourite expression) from the continuum of history 'the past charged with now-time', and for the aims of the enlightenment and social democracy to substitute the revolution: time comes to a stop, the *Stillstand*, when the revolutionary event, alias the messianic happening, occurs. In his *Theses on the Philosophy of History* Benjamin argued that politics was not merely a fierce physical struggle to control the present, and so the future, but an intellectual battle to control the record of the past. In a striking phrase, he insisted that 'even the dead will not be safe from the [fascist] enemy as he wins'.[123] Most forms of knowledge were relativistic, bourgeois creations, and had to be recast to ensure proletarian or classless truth. The irony of these brilliant but destructive insights was that, whereas Benjamin saw them as scientific historical materialism, they were really a product of Judaic irrationality – his was the old tale of how intensely spiritual people, who can no longer believe in God, find ingenious substitutes for religious dogmas.

Moreover, in Benjamin's case, the rejection of religion was by no means complete. His work is full of curious notions of time and fate, even of evil and demons. Without a religious framework, he was lost, and he felt lost. With the rise of Hitler he fled to Paris. There, at the Café des Deux Magots, he drew what he called a diagram of his life, a hopeless labyrinth; and, characteristically, he lost that too.[124] At the end of 1939 he tried to get into Spain, but got stuck on the Franco–Spanish border. One of his best friends had already committed suicide, as had Tucholsky and many other Jewish intellectuals, and in his final phase Benjamin seems to have seen suicide as a form of Redemption-through-death, the Christ–Messiah. At all events, he killed himself and was buried in the cemetery at Port-Bou, overlooking the sea. But no one was present at the actual interment, and when Hannah Arendt came to find his grave, later in 1940, it had disappeared and has never since been identified – a final, unconscious gesture of alienation and confusion, a symbolic reminder that the Jewish intellectuals of the new age (as we have noted already) were as forlorn and adrift in it as anyone else. But though Benjamin was in the long run the most influential of all the Weimar cultural innovators, few people in Germany had then heard of him.

Was the German nationalist accusation that Jews ran Weimar's culture entirely conspiracy theory then? Not quite. Jews ran important newspapers and publishing houses. While it is true that the bulk of German publishing, and the biggest circulation papers in Berlin, Munich, Hamburg and other major towns, were in non-Jewish hands, such Jewish liberal papers as the *Berliner Tageblatt*, the *Vossische Zeitung* and the *Frankfurter Zeitung* had the most brilliant critics and the widest cultural influence. Jewish publishing houses like Kurt Wolff, Carriers and S. Fischer were the most highly regarded. A large percentage of dramatic, music, art and book critics were Jews; and Jews ran important art galleries and other centres of cultural trade. They appeared to be in charge, to set the trends and make the reputations. Their power, such as it was, was confused with the power of the left-intelligentsia as a whole, which aroused envy, frustration and fury. The accusation of Jewish cultural dictatorship was an important weapon in Hitler's campaign to create a real one.

All the same, the Nazis would never have been able to acquire power without the Great Depression, which hit Germany harder than any other country except the United States. In both countries the trough of the crisis came in the summer of 1932, but in both the first glimmer of the upturn was not visible until well into 1933. In both the blame for the phenomenally high level of unemployment was placed by the electors on the political establishment: the Republican Party in America, the Weimar Republic in Germany. The two countries went to the polls within two days of each other in November 1932 and in each the results led, in effect, to a change of regime. There was an element of blind, cruel chance in what happened. On the 6th, the German electorate gave 33.1 per cent of its votes to the Nazis (a drop in their percentage from the previous July). Two days later F. D. Roosevelt won by a landslide in America, an election in which the Jewish vote switched from its traditional Republican (and socialist) allegiance and went 85–90 per cent to the Democrats. The same angry desire for change, which in America gave power to a man whom Hitler quickly identified with the Jews, led in Germany to an electoral deadlock which was resolved, on 30 January 1933, by Hitler becoming chancellor.

There was, then, nothing inevitable about the capture of power in Germany by an anti-Semitic regime. But once Hitler had consolidated his personal and party dictatorship, which took a mere eight weeks in February–March 1933, a systematic attack on the Jews was certain. In particular, Jewish writers, artists and intellectuals knew he would go for them, and most of them left the country quickly. As a result Hitler actually killed fewer Jewish members of the intelligentsia than Stalin did in Russia. Strictly speaking, however, the Nazi policy for the Jews went no further than a reversion to conventional state anti-Semitism. The 1920 party policy provided for Jews to be stripped of German citizenship, including the right to hold office and vote; Jews would become 'guests', and those who had entered since 1914 would be expelled; there was also a vague threat to expropriate Jewish property.[125] But in many of his speeches, as well as in *Mein Kampf*, Hitler had threatened and promised violence against Jews. In a private talk with Major Josef Hell in 1922 he went further. If he won power, he said, 'the annihilation of the Jews will be my first and foremost task. . . . Once the hatred and the battle against the Jews are really stirred up, their resistance will inevitably break down in short order. They cannot protect themselves and no one will stand forth as their defenders.' He explained to Major Hell his belief that all revolutions, like his, needed a focus of hostility, to express 'the feelings of hatred of the broad masses'. He had chosen the Jew not merely out of personal conviction but also out of rational political calculation: 'the battle against the Jews will be as popular as it will be successful'. The conversation with Hell is particularly illuminating because it illustrates the dualism of Hitler's anti-Semitic drive, its mixture of emotional loathing and cool reasoning. He treated Hell not only to his rationale but also to his fury:

I shall have gallows erected, in Munich for example in the Marienplatz, as many as traffic permits. Then the Jews will be hanged, one after another, and they will stay hanging until they stink. . . . As soon as one is untied, the next will take his place, and that will go on until the last Jew in Munich is obliterated. Exactly the same thing will happen in the other cities until Germany is cleansed of its last Jew.[126]

Hitler's dualism expressed itself in two forms of violence to be used against the Jew: the spontaneous, highly emotional, uncontrolled violence of the pogrom, and the cool, systematic, legal and regulated violence of the state, expressed through law and police power. As Hitler moved closer to office, and became more adept at the tactics needed to secure it, he pushed the emotional element into the background, and stressed the legal. One of the chief complaints against Weimar was the political lawlessness on the streets. One of Hitler's chief attractions, to many Germans, was his promise to end it. But Hitler, long before he came to power, had mobilized instruments to express both aspects of his anti-Semitic personality. On the one hand there were the party street-bullies, and in particular the Brownshirts (SA), over 500,000 strong by the end of 1932, who habitually beat up Jews in the steets and even murdered them from time to time. On the other hand there was the elite SS, to run the police power and the camps, to administer the elaborate apparatus of state violence against the Jews.

During Hitler's twelve years in power, the dualism remained throughout. Right to the end, Jews were the victims both of sudden, individual acts of thoughtless violence, and of systematic state cruelty on a mass-industrial basis. During the first six years, in peacetime, there was a regular oscillation between the two. Once war imposed its own darkness and silence, the second gradually became predominant, on an enormous scale. It is true that Hitler was an improviser, a tactician of genius, who often reacted to events. True, also, that the scope of his persecution became so wide and varied as to develop a momentum of its own. Nevertheless, there was always a decisive degree of overall strategy and control, which came from no other mind but his, and expressed his anti-Semitic nature. The Holocaust was planned; and Hitler planned it. That is the only conclusion which makes sense of the whole horrifying process.

When Hitler first took power, his anti-Jewish policy was constrained by two factors. He needed to rebuild the German economy quickly. That meant avoiding the disruption inherent in the immediate dispossession and expulsion of the wealthy Jewish community. He wished to rearm as fast as possible. That meant reassuring international opinion by avoiding scenes of mass cruelty. Hence Hitler adopted the methods used against the Jews in fourteenth- and fifteenth-century Spain. Individual acts of violence were promoted and encouraged, then used as pretexts to introduce formal, legal measures against the Jews. Hitler had agents for his dual purpose. Josef Goebbels, his propaganda chief, was his rabble-rousing Vicente Ferrer. Heinrich Himmler, head of the ss, was his cool, implacable Torquemada. Under the impulse of Goebbels' oratory and media, attacks on Jews by Brownshirts and party members, boycotts and terrorizing of Jewish businesses, began soon after Hitler took power. Hitler let it be known that he disapproved of these 'individual actions', as they were termed. But he left them unpunished, and he allowed them to build up into a climax in the summer of 1935. Then, in a major speech, he used them to justify the introduction of the Nuremberg Decrees on 15 September. These effectively carried out the original 1920 Nazi programme by stripping the Jews of their basic rights and beginning the process of separating them from the rest of the population. It was a reversion to the medieval system at its worst. But because it was a return to the odious but familiar past, it deceived most Jews (and the rest of the world) into believing that the Nuremberg system would give the Jews some kind of legal and permanent, albeit lowly, status in Nazi Germany. What they overlooked was the accompanying warning by Hitler, in the same speech, that if these arrangements for a 'separate, secular solution' broke down, then it might become necessary to pass a law 'handing over the problem to the

National Socialist Party for final solution'.[127] In fact the instrument
for this alternative was already being assembled. Himmler had opened
his first concentration camp, at Dachau, only seven weeks after Hitler
took over, and he had since collected into his hands control over a
repressive police apparatus which had no parallel outside Stalin's
Russia.

On the plinth of the Nuremberg laws, an ever-growing superstructure of regulations restricting Jewish activity was progressively
erected. By the autumn of 1938 the economic power of the Jews had
been destroyed. The German economy was again strong. Germany
was now rearmed. Over 200,000 Jews had fled from Germany. But the
Anschluss with Austria had added as many Austrian Jews to the total.
So the 'Jewish problem' remained unresolved, and Hitler was ready to
move on to the next stage: its internationalization. If Jewish power in
Germany had been destroyed, the power of the Jews abroad, and
especially their power to make war upon him, became a growing
theme of his speeches. The new dimension was dramatically personal-
ized on 9 November 1938 when a Jew, Herschel Grynszpan, murdered
a Nazi diplomat in Paris. This gave Hitler the pretext to move on to the
next stage, using his dualist technique and both his agents. The same
evening Goebbels told a meeting of Nazi leaders in Munich that anti-
Jewish revenge riots had already started. On his suggestion, Hitler had
decided that, if the riots spread, they were not to be discouraged. This
was taken to mean that the party was to organize them. There
followed the Kristallnacht. Party members smashed and looted Jewish
shops. The SA sent out teams to burn down all synagogues. The SS got
the news at 11.05 p.m. Himmler minuted: 'The order was given by the
propaganda directorate, and I suspect that Goebbels in his craving for
power, which I noticed long ago, and also in his empty-headedness,
started this action just at a time when the foreign political situation is
very grave. . . . When I asked the Führer about it, I had the impression
that he did not know anything about these events.'[128] Within two
hours he had ordered out all his police and SS forces to prevent large-
scale looting and to take 20,000 Jews into the concentration camps.

There is little doubt that Hitler, whose orders on important matters
were always oral, gave contradictory ones to Goebbels and Himmler.
That was very characteristic. But there was an element of confusion as
well as planning in this episode. It was used, as Hitler intended, to take
further measures against Jews. They were held responsible for the riot,
and fined a billion marks (about $400 million). But most of the cost of
the damage had to be borne by insurance companies. There were a
great many legal consequences. Jewish claims for damages in the

courts had to be quashed by a special Justice Ministry decree. Cases against twenty-six party members accused of murdering Jews had to be quashed too. Four others who had raped Jewish women had to be expelled, and a distinction made between 'idealistic' and 'selfish' offences.[129] Most disturbing of all, from Hitler's point of view, was that the pogrom was unpopular, not merely abroad but above all in Germany.

Hence he changed his tactics. Goebbels continued his anti-Semitic propaganda, but henceforth he was denied an executive role in anti-Jewish violence. That was now entrusted to Himmler almost entirely. As before, the 'outrage' was used as the pretext for a fresh campaign of legal measures against Jews. But this time the process was made highly bureaucratic. Every move was carefully thought out beforehand by experienced officials, not party theorists, and was made legal and systematic. As Raul Hilberg, the leading historian of the Holocaust, shows, it was this very bureaucratization of the policy which made possible its colossal scale and transformed a pogrom into genocide.

It also ensured that, at one time or another, almost every department of the German government, and large numbers of civilians, were involved in anti-Jewish activities. Hitler's war against the Jews became a national effort. To carry through the policy, the Jews had first to be identified, then dispossessed, then concentrated. Identification involved both the medical profession and the churches. The Nazis found that in practice it was too difficult to define a Jew by race. They had to fall back on religious criteria. Their basic decree of 11 April 1933, needed to throw Jews out of the civil service, defined a 'person of non-Aryan descent' as someone with a parent or grandparent of the Jewish religion. But this led to disagreements. In 1935, a medical conference between Dr Wagner, Chief Medical Officer of the party, Dr Blome, Secretary of the German Medical Association, and Dr Gross, head of the Race Political Office, decided that quarter-Jews were Germans but half-Jews were Jews, since (said Blome) 'among half-Jews the Jewish genes are notoriously dominant'. But the civil service would not accept this definition. They defined Jews as religious half-Jews or those married to Jews. The civil servants got their way because they actually wrote the detailed legislation, including the Reich Citizenship Law of 14 November 1935. Some twenty-seven race-decrees were written at the Interior Ministry by a former customs official, Dr Bernhard Losener, used to making fine distinctions between dutiable goods. Those applying for a wide range of jobs had to produce positive proof of Aryan descent. An ss officer had to produce proof of descent going back to 1750, but even a junior clerk in a government office needed seven authenticated documents. The churches, who had the only records of birth before 1875–6, were thus drawn in. A new profession of *Sippenforscher*, family researcher, was created. A third race of part-Jews, the *Mischling*, came into being, sub-divided into first and second degrees. Demands for reclassification, or 'liberation' as it was termed, multiplied, and as in Tsarist Russia the system led rapidly to every kind of nepotism and corruption. An official in Hitler's Chancellery, whom he liked but who was a second-degree *Mischling*, received a 'liberation' from the Führer, as a personal Christmas present, while he and his family were sitting round the tree on Christmas Eve 1938.[130]

Again, dispossession of Jews, or Aryanization as it was called, brought a large section of the business community into the system. From August 1935, a Boycott Committee, which included Himmler and Streicher, and had all the resources of the state behind it, brought pressure to bear on Jews to sell out and to reduce the sale-price so that Germans could be induced to buy quickly. The banks played a prominent part in this, making a profit at every stage and often ending up with the business themselves. This was part of the process whereby German business was corrupted into taking part in the Final Solution. It was not just a question of benefiting from evil laws. Hitler's dualistic approach was used at every stage. Jews were stripped of their property by thuggery as well as law. IG Farben and the Deutscher Bank swallowed up the Österreichische Kreditanstalt and its industrial subsidiaries, after one of its top men was taken for a ride by the SA and thrown from a moving car, and another kicked to death by the SA during a search of his house. Baron Louis Rothschild was arrested by the police and held as a hostage until the family agreed to be dispossessed of their property at a knock-down price. Afterwards the Dresdner Bank wrote to Himmler's chief of staff thanking the police for help in bringing down the price.[131]

The process of concentrating the Jews, cutting them off from the rest of the population and subjecting them to a completely different regime, also involved the nation as a whole. It was a very complicated and difficult process and demanded a degree of cold-blooded cruelty on the part of scores of thousands of bureaucrats which was almost as pitiless as the eventual killing process itself. Moreover, all Germans were aware of it. Some anti-Jewish regulations were not published in the press. But everyone could see that Jews got different and inferior treatment in every aspect of life. After the Kristallnacht the sex and marriage laws became increasingly severe and were savagely enforced. A Jew caught 'fraternizing' with an Aryan was automatically sent to a concentration camp. The Aryan might be sent there too, for three months' 're-education'. At the same time, November 1938, Jews were expelled from all schools, and trains, waiting-rooms and restaurants were segregated. The shifting of Jews into segregated housing-blocks also began. Some of these actions were in accordance with elaborate decrees. Others had no legal basis at all. From start to finish, Hitler's war against the Jews was a bewildering mixture of law and lawlessness, system and sheer violence. From December 1938, for instance, Himmler reduced Jewish mobility, to assist the concentration process, simply by revoking all Jewish driving licences on his own authority. As the Jews were stripped of their property, they flocked into the big cities. The Jewish relief agencies, similarly impoverished, could not cope. So, under a decree of March 1939, unemployed Jews were pushed into forced labour.

Hence, by the opening of the war in September 1939, many of the eventual horrors had already been foreshadowed, and the system to carry them out was already in embryonic existence. Nevertheless, the war made a difference in two essential ways. First, it changed the emphasis of the moral justification for persecuting Jews which Hitler produced. This moral reasoning, crude though it might be, was an important element in the Holocaust because it was used publicly by Goebbels to secure the acquiescence or indifference of the German people, and by Himmler to promote the enthusiasm of those who manned the repressive machine itself. Until the outbreak of war, the argument ran that, since the Jews had been engaged for generations in defrauding the German people, they had no moral right to their property, and the measures to strip them of it were merely an act of simple restitution, their wealth going back whence it came – to the Reich. With the war, a new argument was added. Hitler had always insisted that, if a war came, it would be the work of the Jews, acting on the international stage; and when it did come, he held the Jews responsible for all the deaths that ensued. The conclusion implicit in this argument was that the Jews had no moral right to their lives either. Indeed, he said on a number of occasions that war would precipitate a 'final solution' of the 'Jewish problem'.

This brings us to the second consequence of war. The experience of government, 1933–9, had led Hitler to modify his views on the popularity of anti-Semitism. It was useful to focus hatred, in the abstract, but he had learned that open, widespread, physical violence against the Jews as a whole was not acceptable to the German people, at any rate in peacetime. War, however, brought its own exigencies, and it also drew a veil over many activities. It was the necessary context in which genocide could be committed. So far from the Jews creating the war, then, it was rather Hitler who willed the war in order to destroy the Jews. Not just German Jews either, but all European Jews, thus providing an international and final solution to what he had always claimed was an international problem. Not only was war necessary, to provide the pretext and concealment the act required; it had to include war against Poland and Russia, to give Hitler access to the principal source of European Jewry.

Hence with the opening of the first phase of the war, pressure on the Jews was rapidly increased. From September 1939 they had to be off the streets by 8 p.m. Then their movements were restricted in all areas at certain times, and in some areas at all times. They were banned from many forms of public transport except at certain inconvenient hours, or at any time. They were deprived of telephones, then forbidden to use them: phone booths were marked 'Use by Jews Forbidden'. Special Jewish identity papers went back to August 1938 and with the coming of war were made the basis for new systems of deprivation. Ration cards were stamped 'J' for deprivation-use in all kinds of ways. From December 1939 Jewish rations were cut, and at the same time Jews were restricted to certain shopping hours. One of Hitler's obsessions was that the First World War had been lost on the Home Front by food shortages often caused by Jewish rackets. He was determined that, this time, no Jew should eat a mouthful of food more than was necessary, and the Ministry of Food played a major part in his anti-Jewish policy. Indeed the bureaucrats there took progressively more severe measures designed, in effect, to starve the Jews to death.

At the same time Jews were being worked to death. They were excluded from the protective provisions of German labour laws. German employers took advantage of this, abolishing holiday pay for Jews. In early 1940 all allowances for Jews were abolished by law. On October 1941 a separate labour code for Jews allowed employers, for instance, to work fourteen-year-old Jewish boys for unlimited hours. Jews were deprived of protective clothing, welders of goggles and gloves. From September 1941 all Jews aged six or over had to wear a Star of David, black with a yellow background, as large as the palm of the hand, with the word *Jude* in the middle. This was an identification system which made it much easier to detect Jews breaking the countless regulations, turned the entire German nation into a police force and participants in the persecution, and demoralized the Jews themselves.

The opening of the war also brought Hitler half Poland and over two million Polish Jews. Moreover, Poland was an occupied country and he could do more or less what he liked there. Again, Hitlerian dualism was applied. First there were 'spontaneous' individual attacks, though on a much larger and more brutal scale than in Germany. Thus over fifty Jews were shot to death in a Polish synagogue. The ss held whipping orgies: at Nasielsky, early in 1940, 1,600 Jews were flogged throughout the night. The German army, which disliked the ss, kept records of these incidents, and some have survived.[132] These violent incidents led to demands for 'orderly' solutions, and these in turn to systematic persecution.

Hence on 19 September 1939, Hitler decided to incorporate much of Poland in Germany proper, move 600,000 Jews from there into a Polish rump called the 'General Government', and ghetto all Jews within it at convenient points along the railways. For good measure he gave orders to shift all Germany's Jews there too. This brought into play the German railway system, the Reichsbahn, with its 500,000 clerical and 900,000 manual workers. Without the railways, the Holocaust would not have been possible. With their deportation trains called Sonderzüge, and their special staff, the Sonderzuggruppe, which co-ordinated the deportation schedules with the rest of the war timetables, the railways made prodigious efforts to get the Jews exactly where the ss wanted them. These trains carrying Jews were given priority over everything else. When a ban on all other uses of railways was imposed in July 1942, during the 266-division offensive in Russia, the ss still ran a daily train carrying 5,000 Jews to Treblinka and a twice-weekly one of 5,000 to Belzec. Even at the height of the Stalingrad panic, Himmler wrote to the Transport Minister: 'If I am to wind up things quickly, I must have more trains for transport. . . . Help me get more trains!' The minister obliged him. Study of the train factor indicates, perhaps better than anything else, the importance of his Jewish policy in Hitler's overall scheme, and the extent to which ordinary Germans helped him to push it to its conclusion.[133]

Once Jews were separated, mobilized and concentrated in the General Government, what Hitler called (2 October 1940) *ein grosses polnisches Arbeitslager*, 'a huge Polish labour-camp', the forced-labour programme could begin in earnest. This was the first part of the Final Solution, of the Holocaust itself, because working to death was the basis on which the system operated. Fritz Saukel, the head of the Allocation of Labour Office, ordered that Jews were to be exploited 'to the highest possible extent at the lowest conceivable degree of expenditure'.[134] The labourers were worked from dawn till dusk seven days a week, dressed in rags and fed on bread, watery soup, potatoes and sometimes meat scraps. The first major slave-labour operation was in February 1940, the construction of a vast anti-tank ditch along the new eastern frontier.[135] Thereafter the system spread to every area of industry. Workers could be 'ordered' by phone and shipped by freight-car just like raw materials. Thus IG Farben got 250 Dutch women Jews freighted from Ravensbrück to Dachau, the same freight-cars taking back 200 Polish women to Dachau.[136] Slave workers were usually forced to move at the double, the 'Auschwitz Trot', even when carrying, for example, bags of concrete weighing 100 lb. At Mauthausen, near Hitler's home town of Linz, where Himmler built a work-camp near the municipal quarry, labourers had only picks and axes, and they had to carry heavy chunks of granite up 186 steep and narrow steps from the quarry to the camp. They had a life expectancy of between six weeks and three months, and this did not include death by accident, suicide or punishment.[137]

There is no doubt at all that forced labour was a form of murder and regarded as such by the Nazi authorities. The words *Vernichtung durch Arbeit*, 'destruction through work', were used repeatedly in discussions which Dr Georg Thierack, the Minister of Justice, had with Goebbels and Himmler on 14 and 18 September 1942.[138] Rudolf Höss, the commandant at Auschwitz May 1940–December 1943, and afterwards office chief at the Main Security Headquarters from which the entire anti-Jewish programme was directed, testified that by the end of 1944 400,000 slaves were working in the German armaments industry. 'In enterprises with particularly severe working conditions', he said, 'every month one-fifth died or were, because of inability to work, sent back by the enterprises to the camps in order to be exterminated.' So German industry was a willing participant in this aspect of the Final Solution. The labourers had no names – just numbers, tattooed on their bodies. If one died, the factory manager did not have to state the cause of death: he merely asked for a replacement. Höss testified that the initiative in securing Jewish slave labour always came from the firm: 'The concentration camps have at no time offered labour to the industry. On the contrary, prisoners were sent to firms only after the firms had made a request for [such] prisoners.'[139] All the companies concerned knew exactly what was happening. Nor was the knowledge confined to very senior managers and those involved in the actual slave-labour operations. There were innumerable visits to the camps. In a few cases written reactions have been preserved. Thus one IG Farben employee, visiting the Auschwitz slave-labour operation, 30 July 1942, wrote to a colleague in Frankfurt, using the tone of joking irony which many Germans adopted: 'That the Jewish race is playing a special part here you can well imagine. The diet and treatment of this sort of people is in accordance with our aim. Evidently an increase of weight is hardly ever recorded for them. That bullets start whizzing at the slightest attempt of a "change of air" is also certain, as well as the fact that many have already disappeared as a result of a "sun-stroke".'[140]

Yet starving and working the Jews to death was not quick enough for Hitler. He determined on mass killing too, in the spirit with which he had discussed it with Major Hell. Signed orders from Hitler of any kind are rare; and rarest of all are those dealing with the Jews. The longest letter Hitler ever wrote about Jewish policy goes back to spring 1933, in reply to a request from Hindenberg to exempt war veterans from anti-Jewish decrees.[141] The absence of written orders led to the claim that the Final Solution was Himmler's work and that Hitler not only did not order it but did not even know it was happening.[142] But this argument will not stand up.[143] The administration of the Third Reich was often chaotic but its central principle was clear enough: all key decisions emanated from Hitler. This applied particularly to Jewish policy, which was the centre of his preoccupations and the dynamic of his entire career. He was by far the most obsessively and fundamentally anti-Semitic of all the Nazi leaders. Even Streicher, in his view, was taken in by the Jews: 'He *idealized* the Jew,' Hitler insisted in December 1941. 'The Jew is baser, fiercer, more diabolical than Streicher depicted him.'[144] Hitler accepted anti-Semitic conspiracy theory in its most extreme form, believing that the Jew was wicked by nature, was indeed the very incarnation and symbol of evil.[145] Throughout his career he saw the 'Jewish problem' in apocalyptic terms and the Holocaust was the logical outcome of his views. His orders to set it in motion were oral but were invariably invoked by Himmler and others as their compelling authority, according to regular formulae: 'the Führer's wish', 'the Führer's will', 'with the Führer's agreement', 'this is my order which is also the Führer's wish'.

The decisive date for the Final Solution was almost certainly 1 September 1939, when hostilities began. Hitler had stated plainly, on 30 January that year, what his reaction to war would be: 'if international-finance Jewry inside and outside Europe should succeed once more in plunging the nations into yet another world war, the consequences will not be the Bolshevization of the earth and thereby the victory of Jewry, but the annihilation [*Vernichtung*] of the Jewish race in Europe.' He regarded the war as his licence for genocide and he set the scientific process in motion the very day war broke out. The first programme, of experimental murder, was conceived in Hitler's

Chancellery and the original order went out on Hitler's personal stationery on 1 September 1939: this authorized the murder of the incurably insane. The programme was code-named T-4 after the Chancellery address, Tiergartenstrasse 4, and from the start it had the characteristics of the genocide programme: ss involvement, euphemism, deception. It is significant that the first man appointed to head the euthanasia programme, ss Obergruppenführer Dr Leonard Contin, was sacked when he asked for written orders from Hitler. He was replaced by another ss doctor, Philip Boyhaler, who accepted oral orders.[146]

The ss experimented with various gases, including carbon monoxide and the cyanide-based pesticide trade-named Zyklon-B. The first gas chamber was set up at a killing centre in Brandenburg in late 1939, Hitler's doctor, Karl Brandt, witnessing a test killing of four insane men. He reported back to Hitler, who ordered only carbon monoxide to be used. Five other killing centres were then equipped. The gas chamber was called a 'shower-room' and the victims, taken in groups of twenty or thirty, were told they were to have a shower. They were sealed in, then the doctor on duty gassed them. This was the same basic procedure later used at the mass-extermination camps. The programme murdered 80,000–100,000 people, but was stopped in August 1941 following protests by the churches – the only occasion when they prevented Hitler from killing people. But by this time it was also being used to kill Jews from concentration camps who were too sick to work. So the euthanasia programme merged into the Final Solution, and there were continuities in methods, equipment and expert personnel.[147]

It should be emphasized that the killing of large numbers of Jews continued in Poland throughout 1940 and the spring of 1941, but the mass-extermination phase did not really begin until Hitler's invasion of Russia, 22 June 1941. This was designed to destroy the centre of the Jewish–Bolshevik conspiracy and to give Hitler access to the five million Jews then under Soviet control. Killing was done by two methods: mobile killing units, and fixed centres or death camps. The mobile killing system dates back to 22 July 1940 when Hitler's idea of total war, involving mass extermination, was first presented to the army. Indeed, the army was heavily involved in the Final Solution since the ss killing units came under its command for tactical purposes. An entry on 3 March 1941 in General Jodl's War Diary records Hitler's decision that, in the coming Russian campaign, ss-Police units would have to be brought right up to front-line army areas in order to 'eliminate' the 'Jewish–Bolshevik intelligentsia'.[148]

This was the origin of the Einsatzgruppen, the mobile killing battalions. They were directed from the Reich Security Main Office (RHSA) under Reinhard Heydrich, the chain of command going Hitler–Himmler–Heydrich. There were four such battalions, A, B, C and D, each 500–900 strong, assigned to each of the four army groups invading Russia. They had a high proportion of high-ranking officers drawn from the SS, Gestapo and police, and included many intellectuals and lawyers. Otto Ohlendorf, who commanded D, had degrees from three universities and a doctorate in jurisprudence. Ernst Biberstein, one of the commanders in C, was a Protestant pastor, theologian and church official.

Of the Jews in Soviet territory, four million lived in areas overrun by the German army 1941–2. Of these two and a half million fled before the Germans arrived. The rest was 90 per cent concentrated in the cities, making it easier for the Einsatzgruppen to kill them. The murder battalions moved directly behind the army units, rounding up Jews before the city populations knew what was in store. In the initial killing sweep, the four groups reported at various dates between mid-October and early December 1941 that they had killed 125,000, 45,000, 75,000 and 55,000 respectively. But many Jews were left behind in the rear areas, so killing teams were sent to catch and murder them. The army co-operated in handing them over, salving its conscience by referring to Jews as 'partisans' or 'superfluous eaters'. Sometimes the army killed Jews themselves. Both they and the SS incited pogroms, to save themselves trouble. There was little resistance from the Jews. Russian civilians were co-operative, though there is one recorded act of a local mayor shot for trying 'to help the Jews'.[149] Quite small groups of killers disposed of enormous numbers. In Riga, one officer and twenty-one men killed 10,600 Jews. In Kiev, two small detachments of C killed over 30,000. A second sweep began at the end of 1941 and lasted throughout 1942. This killed over 900,000. Most Jews were murdered by shooting, outside the towns, at ditches turned into graves. During the second sweep, mass graves were dug first. The killers shot the Jews in the back of the neck, the method used by the Soviet secret police, or by the 'sardine method'. Under this, the first layer stretched themselves at the bottom of the grave and were killed from above. The next layer lay down on top of the first bodies, heads facing the feet. There were five or six layers, then the grave was filled in.

Some Jews hid under floorboards and in cellars. They were blasted out with grenades or burned alive. Some Jewish girls offered themselves to stay alive; they were used during the night but killed all the same the next morning. Some Jews were only wounded and lived hours, even days. There were many sadistic acts. There was reluctance too, even among these picked killers, to slaughter so many people who put up no resistance – not a single member of any of the groups died during an actual killing operation. Himmler paid only one visit to see the work, witnessing 100 Jews shot in mid-August 1941. There is a record of it. Himmler found himself unable to look as each volley rang out. The commander reproached him: 'Reichsführer, those were only a hundred.' Himmler: 'What do you mean by that?' 'Look at the eyes of the men in this *Kommando*. How deeply shaken they are! These men are finished for the rest of their lives. What kind of followers are we training here? Either neurotics or savages.' Himmler then made a speech to the men, calling on them to obey 'the Highest Moral Law of the Party'.[150]

To escape from the degree of personal contact between killers and killed involved in shooting, the groups tried other methods. The use of dynamite proved disastrous. Then they introduced mobile gas vans, and soon two were sent to each battalion. Meanwhile, these mobile killing operations were being supplemented by the use of fixed centres, the death camps. Six of these were built and equipped: at Chelmno and Auschwitz in the Polish territories incorporated in the Reich; and at Treblinka, Sobibor, Majdanek and Belzec in the Polish General Government. In a sense, the term 'death camp' as a special category is misleading. There were 1,634 concentration camps and their satellites and more than 900 labour camps.[151] All were death camps, in that enormous numbers of Jews died there, by starvation and overwork, or by execution for trivial offences or often for no reason at all. But these six camps were deliberately planned or extended for mass slaughter on an industrial scale.

Hitler seems to have given the orders for mass extermination in fixed centres in June 1941, at the same time as the mobile killing units went into action. But as we have seen, large-scale killing by gas was already taking place; and in March 1941 Himmler had already instructed Höss, commandant at Auschwitz, to enlarge it for this purpose. It had been chosen, Himmler told him, because of its easy rail access and isolation from centres of population. Shortly afterwards, Himmler instructed Odilo Globocnik, ss-Police head in Lublin, to build Majdanek, and this official became head of a killing network which included two other death camps, Belzec and Sobibor. The chain of command was as follows. Hitler's orders went through Himmler, and from him to individual camp commanders. But Hermann Göring, as boss of the Four-Year Plan, was involved administratively in arranging the co-operation of various state bureaucracies. This is an important point, showing that, while the executive agent of the Holocaust was the ss, the crime as a whole was a national effort involving all the hierarchies of the German government, its armed forces, its industry and its party. As Hilberg put it, 'The co-operation of these hierarchies was so complete that we may truly speak of their fusion into a machinery of destruction.'[152]

Göring delegated the co-ordinating role to Heydrich, who as head of the RSHA and Chief of Security Police was the junction of state and party, and sent him a written order, 31 July 1941:

As supplement to the task that was entrusted to you in the decree dated 24 January 1939, namely to solve the Jewish question by emigration and evacuation in the most favourable way possible, given present conditions, I herewith commission you to carry out all necessary preparations with regard to the organizational, substantive and financial viewpoints, for a total solution of the Jewish question in the German sphere of influence in Europe. In so far as the competences of other central organizations are hereby affected, these are to be involved.[153]

Heydrich, in turn, gave orders to Adolf Eichmann, his RSHA official in charge of 'Jewish Affairs and Evacuation Affairs'. He had administrative responsibility for the Holocaust as a whole, though Himmler exercised operational responsibility through his camp commanders. It was Eichmann who actually drafted the 31 July 1941 order signed by Göring. But at the same time an additional oral order was given by Hitler to Heydrich and transmitted to Eichmann: 'I have just come from the Reichsführer: the Führer has now ordered the physical annihilation of the Jews.'[154]

Construction of the mass-killing machinery went on throughout the summer and autumn of 1941. Two civilians from Hamburg came to Auschwitz to teach the staff how to handle Zyklon-B, which was the preferred killing method there. In September, the first gassing was carried out, in Auschwitz Block II, on 250 Jewish hospital patients and 600 Russian prisoners. Then work began on Birkenau, the main Auschwitz killing-centre. The first death camp to be completed was Chelmno, near Lodz, which started functioning on 8 December 1941, using exhaust gases from mobile vans. An RSHA conference on the killing had been planned for the next day, at a villa in the Berlin suburb of Wannsee. But it was postponed because of Pearl Harbor, and did not take place until 20 January 1942. By then there was a certain note of anxiety among the top Nazis. The survival of Russia, and the entrance of America into the war, must have convinced many of them that Germany was unlikely to win it. The conference was to reaffirm the object of the Final Solution and to co-ordinate means to carry it through. There was lunch, and while waiters handed round brandy, several present urged the need for speed. It was from this point on that the exigencies of the Holocaust were given priority even over the war effort itself, reflecting Hitler's resolve that, whatever the outcome of the war, the European Jews would not survive it.

Wannsee was followed by rapid action. Belzec became operational the next month. The building of Sobibor began in March. At the same time Majdanek and Treblinka were transformed into death centres. Goebbels, after a briefing by Globocnik, in charge of the General Government camps, noted (27 March 1942): 'A judgment is being visited on the Jews [which is] barbaric. . . . The prophecy which the Führer made about them for having brought on a new world war is beginning to come true in a most terrible manner.'[155]

Goebbels, however, was confiding to his diary. In actual orders, even for very limited circulation, the genocide was invariably described in euphemistic code. Even at the Wannsee conference, Heydrich used code. All Jews, he said, were to be 'evacuated to the East' and formed into labour columns. Most would 'fall away through natural decline' but the hard core, capable of rebuilding Jewry, would be 'treated accordingly'. This last phrase, meaning 'killed', was already familiar from Einsatzgruppen reports. There were many official euphemisms for murder, used by those within the operations and well understood by countless thousands outside them: Security Police measures, worked over in the Security Police manner, actions, special actions, special treatment, moved East, resettlement, appropriate treatment, cleansing, major cleansing actions, conveyed to special measures, elimination, solution, cleaning up, making free, finished, migration, wandering, wandered off, disappeared.

The euphemisms were considered necessary, even among the professional mass-killers, to minimize any brooding on the sheer enormity of what they were doing. There were about 8,861,800 Jews in the countries of Europe directly or indirectly under Nazi control. Of these it is calculated that the Nazis killed 5,933,900, or 67 per cent. In Poland, which had by far the largest number, 3,300,000, over 90 per cent, were killed. The same percentage was reached in the Baltic States, Germany and Austria, and over 70 per cent were killed in the Bohemian Protectorate, Slovakia, Greece and the Netherlands. More than 50 per cent of the Jews were killed in White Russia, the Ukraine, Belgium, Yugoslavia, Rumania and Norway.[156] The six big death camps formed the main killing areas, murdering over two million at Auschwitz, 1,380,000 at Majdanek, 800,000 at Treblinka, 600,000 at

Belzec, 340,000 at Chelmno and 250,000 at Sobibor. The speed with which their gas chambers worked was awesome. Treblinka had ten of them, each accommodating 200 people at a time. It was Höss's boast that at Auschwitz each of his gas chambers could take 2,000. Using Zyklon-B gas crystals, the five Auschwitz chambers could murder 60,000 men, women and children every twenty-four hours. Höss said that he murdered 400,000 Hungarian Jews alone (as well as other groups) during the summer of 1944, and that in total 'at least' 2,500,000 humans (Jews and non-Jews) were gassed and incinerated at Auschwitz, plus another half-million who died of starvation and disease. For many months in 1942, 1943 and 1944, the Nazis were each week killing in cold blood over 100,000 people, mainly Jews.[157]

That atrocities on this scale could have been carried out in civilized Europe, albeit in wartime and behind the protective screen of the German army, raises a number of questions about the behaviour of the German people, their allies, associates and conquests, about the British and Americans, and not least about the Jews themselves. Let us examine each in turn.

The German people knew about and acquiesced in the genocide. There were 900,000 of them in the ss alone, plus another 1,200,000 involved in the railways. The trains were one giveaway. Most Germans knew the significance of the huge, crowded trains rattling through the hours of darkness, as one recorded remark suggests: 'Those damned Jews, they won't even let one sleep at night!'[158] The Germans were beneficiaries of murder. Scores of thousands of men's and women's watches, fountain-pens and propelling pencils, stolen from the victims, were distributed among the armed forces; in one six-week period alone, 222,269 sets of men's suits and underclothes, 192,652 sets of women's clothing, and 99,922 sets of children's clothes, collected from the gassed at Auschwitz, were distributed on Germany's Home Front.[159] The recipients knew roughly where these came from. The Germans did very little to protest about what was being done to the Jews or to help Jews escape. But there were exceptions. In Berlin, at the very heart of Hitler's empire, several thousand of the city's 160,000 Jews managed to escape by going underground, becoming 'u-boats' as they were called. In each case it meant some connivance and assistance by non-Jewish Germans.[160] One such was the scholar Hans Hirschel, who became a u-boat in February 1942. He moved into the flat of his mistress, the Countess Maria von Maltzan, sister-in-law of Field Marshal Walter von Reichenau, an ardent Nazi. She designed for him a box-like bed into which he could climb, with holes drilled for breathing. Each day she put in a fresh glass of water and a cough-suppressant. One day she came back to her flat and heard Hirschel and another u-boat, Willy Buschoff, singing at the top of their voices: 'Hear O Israel the Lord our God, the Lord is one'.[161]

The Austrians were worse than the Germans. They played a role in the Holocaust out of all proportion to their numbers. Not only Hitler, but Eichmann and Ernst Kaltenbrunner, head of the Gestapo, were Austrian. In the Netherlands, two Austrians, Arthur Seyss-Inquart and Hanns Rauter, directed the killing of the Jews. In Yugoslavia, out of 5,090 war criminals, 2,499 were Austrian. Austrians were prominent in the mobile killing battalions. They provided one-third of the personnel of the ss extermination units. Austrians commanded four out of the six main death camps and killed almost half of the six million Jewish victims.[162] The Austrians were much more passionately anti-Semitic than the Germans. Menashe Mautner, a disabled veteran of the First World War with a wooden leg, fell on the icy pavements of Vienna and lay there three hours vainly asking the passers-by for help. They saw his star and refused.[163]

The Rumanians were no better than the Austrians; worse in some ways. There were 757,000 Jews in pre-war Rumania, among the worst-treated in the world. The Rumanian government followed Hitler step by step in his anti-Jewish policy, with far less efficiency but added venom. From August 1940, laws stripped Jews of their possessions and jobs and subjected them to unpaid forced labour. There were pogroms too – in January 1941 170 Jews were murdered in Bucharest. The Rumanians played a major part in the invasion of Russia which for them was also a war against the Jews. They killed 200,000 Jews in Bessarabia. Jews were packed into cattle-trucks without food or water and shunted around with no particular destination. Or they were stripped of their clothes and taken on forced marches, some actually naked, others dressed only in newspapers. The Rumanian troops working with Einsatzgruppe D in southern Russia outraged even the Germans by their cruelty and their failure to bury the corpses of those they murdered. On 23 October 1941 the Rumanians carried out a general massacre of Jews in Odessa, after a land-mine destroyed their army HQ. The next day they herded crowds of Jews into four large warehouses, doused them with petrol and set them alight: between 20,000 and 30,000 were thus burned to death. With German agreement, they carved out the province of Transnistria from the Ukraine, as their own contribution to the Final Solution. In this killing area, 217,757 Jews were put to death (an estimated 130,000 from Russia, 87,757 from Rumania), the Rumanians dispatching 138,957 themselves.[164] After the Germans and Austrians, the Rumanians were the biggest killers of Jews. They were more inclined to inflict beatings and torture, or to rape, the officers being worse than the men since they selected the prettiest Jewish girls for orgies. They were also more mercenary. After they shot Jews they sold the corpses to local peasants who stripped them of their clothes. They were willing to sell live Jews too if they could get enough cash for them. But from 1944 on their attitude became less bellicose as they realized the Allies would win.[165]

In France too there was an important section of opinion willing to take an active part in Hitler's Final Solution. It had never forgiven the Dreyfusard victory in 1906 and its hatred of the Jews was reinforced by the Blum Popular Front government of 1936. As in Germany, the anti-Semites included a great many intellectuals, especially writers. They included a doctor, F. L. Destouches, who wrote under the pen-name Céline. His anti-Semitic diatribe, Bagatelle pour un massacre (1937), written under his real name, was highly influential just before and during the war, arguing that France was already a country occupied (and as a woman raped) by Jews, and that a Hitlerian invasion would be a liberation. This extraordinary book resurrected a deep-seated notion that the English were in unholy alliance with Jews to destroy France. During the Dreyfus case the phrase 'Oh Yes', pronounced in an exaggerated English accent, was an anti-Semitic war-cry, and in Bagatelle Céline lists the slogans of the Anglo-Jewish world conspiracy: 'Taratboum! Di! Yie! By gosh! Vive le Roi! Vivent les Lloyds! Vive Tahure! Vive la Cité! Vive Madame Simpson! Vive la Bible! Bordel de Dieu! Le monde est un lupanar juif!'[166] There were no fewer than ten anti-Semitic political organizations in France, some of them funded by the Nazi government, calling for the destruction of the Jews. Mercifully they could not agree on a common policy. But their moment came when the Vichy government adopted an anti-Semitic policy. Darquier de Pellepoix, who had founded the Rassemblement Anti-Juif de France in 1938, became Vichy Commissaire-Général aux Questions Juifs in May 1942.[167] Most of the French declined to collaborate with the Final Solution policy but those who did were more enthusiastic than the Germans. Thus Hitler contrived to kill 90,000 (26 per cent) of French Jews, and of the 75,000 deported from France, with the help of the French authorities, only 2,500 survived.[168] There was a large element of personal hatred in French wartime anti-Semitism. In 1940, the Vichy and German authorities received between three and five million poison-pen letters denouncing particular individuals (not all of them Jews).[169]

Hitler found his Italian ally much less co-operative. Since the end of the papal states, the Italian Jewish community had become one of the best-integrated in Europe. As King Victor Emmanuel III told Herzl (1904): 'Jews may occupy any position, and they do. . . . Jews for us are full-blown Italians.'[170] It was also one of the oldest in the world. Benito Mussolini liked to joke that Jews 'supplied the clothes after the rape of the Sabine Women'. Jews had produced two Italian prime ministers and one war minister; they provided a disproportionately large number of university teachers, but also of generals and admirals.[171] Mussolini himself oscillated all his life between philo-semitism and anti-Semitism. It was a group of Jews who helped to convert him to intervention in the First World War, the critical moment in his life when he broke with Marxist internationalism and became a national socialist. Five Jews were among the original founders of the *fasci di combattimento* in 1919 and Jews were active in every branch of the Fascist movement. The learned article on anti-Semitism in the *Fascist Encyclopaedia* was written by a Jewish scholar. Both Mussolini's biographer, Margharita Sarfatti, and his Minister of Finance, Guido Jung, were Jews. When Hitler came to power, Mussolini set himself up as the European protector of the Jew and was hailed by Stefan Zweig as '*wunderbar* Mussolini'.[172]

Once the Duce fell under Hitler's spell his anti-Semitic side became uppermost but it had no deep emotional roots. There was a definite anti-Semitic fringe within the Fascist Party and government but it was much less powerful than in the Vichy regime and seems to have had no popular support at all. Italy, in response to German pressure, introduced race laws in 1938 and when war came some Jews were interned in camps. But it was not until the Italian surrender in 1943 delivered half of Italy into German military control that Himmler was able to draw it into the Final Solution. On 24 September he sent instructions to his SS boss in Rome, Herbert Kappler, that all Jews, irrespective of age or sex, were to be rounded up and sent to Germany. But the German ambassador in Rome, whose Italian mistress was hiding a family of Jews in her home with his approval, gave no help and the military commander, Field-Marshal Kesselring, said he needed the Jews to build fortifications. Kappler used his order to blackmail the Jewish community. There was a gruesome, medieval scene in the German embassy, where he saw its two leaders, Dante Almansi and Ugo Foa, and demanded 50 kilos of gold within thirty-six hours; otherwise 200 Jews would be murdered. The two men asked to be allowed to pay in lire but Kappler sneered: 'I can print as much of that as I want.' The gold was delivered to the Gestapo within four days. Pope Pius XII offered to provide as much as was needed but by this time enough had been collected, many non-Jews, especially parish priests, contributing. A more serious loss was the most valuable volumes of *Judaica* in the community library, which went to swell Alfred Rosenberg's private collection.

Himmler, who wanted live Jews to kill, not treasure, was furious with Kappler and sent his round-up expert, Theodor Dannecker, with a team of forty-four SS killers, to conduct a *Judenaktion*; he had carried out similar ones in Paris and Sofia. The German ambassador to the Holy See warned the Pope, who ordered the Rome clergy to open sanctuaries. The Vatican sheltered 477 Jews and a further 4,238 found refuge in convents and monasteries. The raid was a failure. Kappler reported: 'The anti-Semitic section of the people was nowhere to be seen during the action, only a great mass of people who in some cases tried to cut off the police from the Jews.' But it yielded 1,007 Jews, who were sent straight to Auschwitz and all but sixteen were murdered.[173] There were raids in other Italian towns, also largely frustrated by the Italians. One notable survivor was Bernard Berenson, the intensely bookish scion of a Lithuanian rabbinical family who, in a secular age, had become the world's leading authority on Italian Renaissance painting. He was tipped off in code by the local police: 'Dottore, the Germans want to come to your villa but we are not sure exactly where it is. Could you give us instructions for your visit tomorrow morning?' The Italians hid him for the rest of the German occupation.[174]

In other European states, the SS got little or no help. But this did not necessarily mean failure in rounding up Jews. In occupied Greece, without any local help, they murdered all but 2,000 of the ancient 60,000-strong Salonika Jewry. In Belgium, despite local resistance, they killed 40,000 out of 65,000 Jews and almost wiped out the famous diamond-trading quarter of Antwerp. The SS effort in the Netherlands was particularly fierce and unremitting and, although the Dutch went so far as to hold a general strike to protect the Jews, the total loss was 105,000 out of 140,000. The Finns, Germany's ally, refused to yield up their 2,000 Jews. The Danes succeeded in ferrying almost their entire Jewish community of 5,000 into Sweden. On the other hand, the great Hungarian Jewry, the last to be sacrificed, lost heavily: 21,747 were murdered in Hungary, 596,260 were deported, of whom only 116,500 survived.[175]

The mass murder of the Hungarians took place at a time when the Allies had complete air superiority and were advancing rapidly. It raised in acute, practical form the question: could the Allies have done anything effective to save European Jewry? The Russians were closest to the Holocaust but never showed the slightest desire to help the Jews in any way. On the contrary: Raoul Wallenberg, the Swedish diplomat and humanitarian, who tried to save Jewish lives in Budapest, vanished when the Red Army arrived there, the Swedes being told: 'measures have been taken by the Soviet military authorities to protect Mr Raoul Wallenberg and his belongings'. He was never seen again.[176]

The British and American governments were in theory sympathetic to the Jews but in practice were terrified that any aggressively pro-Jewish policy would provoke Hitler into a mass expulsion of Jews whom they would then be morally obliged to absorb. For the Nazis, emigration was always one element in the Final Solution, and although the balance of evidence seems to show that Hitler was determined to murder Jews rather than export them, he was quite capable of modifying his policy to embarrass the Allies if they gave him the opportunity. Goebbels wrote in his diary, 13 December 1942: 'I believe both the British and the Americans are happy that we are exterminating the Jewish riff-raff.' This was not true. But neither power was prepared to save Jewish lives by accepting large numbers of refugees. Of all the major European powers, Britain was the least anti-Semitic in the 1930s. Sir Oswald Mosley's Blackshirt movement, founded in 1932, was a failure, not least because it attacked Jews. The government feared, however, that widespread anti-Semitism would be the inevitable result of a mass immigration of Jews. Nor were they prepared to budge from the immigration restrictions laid down in the 1939 White Paper for Palestine. Winston Churchill, always a Zionist, favoured a larger Jewish intake. But his Foreign Secretary, Anthony Eden, argued that to open up Palestine would alienate all Britain's Arab allies there and destroy her military position in the Middle East. When the New York Jewish leader Rabbi Stephen Wise asked him in Washington (27 March 1943) to support an Anglo-American plea to Germany to let the Jews leave occupied Europe, Eden told him the idea was 'fantastically impossible'. But he privately confessed: 'Hitler might well take us up on any such offer.'[177] The Foreign Office were against taking Jews and resented even Jewish requests to this effect: 'A disproportionate amount of the time of this office', minuted one senior official, 'is wasted in dealing with these wailing Jews.'[178]

The United States could certainly have accommodated large numbers of Jewish refugees. In fact during the war period only 21,000 were admitted, 10 per cent of the number allowed under the quota law. The reason for this was public hostility. All the patriotic groups, from the American Legion to the Veterans of Foreign Wars, called for a total ban on immigration. There was more anti-Semitism during the war than at any time in American history. The polls showed, 1938–45, that 35–40 per cent of the population would have backed anti-Jewish laws. In 1942, according to the polls, the Jews were seen as a bigger threat to America than any other group after Japanese and Germans. In 1942–4, for instance, every synagogue in New York's Washington Heights was desecrated.[179] News of the extermination programme was available from May 1942, when the Polish Jewish Labour Bund got verified reports to the two Jewish members of the Polish National Committee in London. This included descriptions of the gas vans at Chelmno and the figure of 700,000 Jews already murdered. The *Boston Globe* gave it the headline 'Mass Murders of Jews in Poland Pass 700,000 Mark' but buried the story on page 12. The *New York Times* called it 'probably the greatest mass slaughter in history' but gave it only two inches.[180] In general the Holocaust news was under reported and tended to get lost in the general wartime din of horror stories. But there was also great resistance in America to accepting the fact of the Holocaust, even when the US army broke into the camp areas. James Agee, writing in the *Nation*, refused to watch the atrocity films and denounced them as propaganda. The GIs were furious when people back home refused to believe what they had seen or even look at their photos.[181]

A major obstacle to action was F. D. Roosevelt himself. He was both anti-Semitic, in a mild way, and ill informed. When the topic came up at the Casablanca Conference, he spoke of 'the understandable complaints which the Germans bore towards the Jews in Germany, namely that while they represented a small part of the population, over 50 per cent of the lawyers, doctors, schoolteachers, college professors in Germany were Jews' (the actual figures were 16.3, 10.9, 2.6 and 0.5 per cent).[182] Roosevelt seems to have been guided purely by domestic political considerations. He had nearly 90 per cent of the Jewish vote anyway and felt no spur to act. Even after the full facts of systematic extermination became available, the President did nothing for fourteen months. A belated Anglo-American conference on the issue was held in Bermuda in April 1943, but Roosevelt took no interest in it, and it decided that nothing of consequence could be done. Indeed it specifically warned 'that no approach be made to Hitler for the release of potential refugees'.[183] In the end, a War Refugee Board was created. It had little help from the government and 90 per cent of its funds came from Jewish sources. But it did contrive to save 200,000 Jews, plus 20,000 non-Jews.

The question of bombing the gas chambers was raised in the early summer of 1944, when the destruction of the Hungarian Jews got under way. Churchill in particular was horrified and keen to act. The killing, he minutes, 'is probably the greatest and most horrible crime ever committed in the whole history of the world'. He instructed Eden, 7 July 1944: 'Get anything out of the Air Force you can and invoke me if necessary.'[184] An operation was feasible. An oil-refining complex 47 miles from Auschwitz was attacked no less than ten times between 7 July and 20 November 1944 (by which point the Holocaust was complete and Himmler ordered the death machinery to be destroyed). On 20 August 127 Flying Fortresses bombed the Auschwitz factory area less than five miles to the east of the gas chambers.[185] Whether bombing would have saved Jewish lives cannot be proved. The SS were fanatically persistent in killing Jews, whatever the physical and military obstacles. It was certainly worth trying. But Churchill was its only real supporter in either government. Both the air forces hated military operations not directed to destroying enemy forces or war potential. The US War Department rejected the plan without even examining its feasibility.

Here we come to a harsh and important point. The refusal to divert forces for a special Jewish rescue operation was in accordance with general war policy. Both governments had decided, with the agreement of their respective Jewish communities, that the speedy and total defeat of Hitler was the best way to help the Jews. This was one reason why the vast and powerful US Jewish community gave little priority to the bombing issue. But once winning the war was accepted as the overriding objective, the Final Solution had to be seen in this perspective. And, for the Nazi war-effort, it was from first to last a self-inflicted wound. On the German side it was opposed by everyone, whether army or industrial chiefs, who took a rational view of the war. It occupied scores of thousands of military personnel. It often paralysed the railway system, even during critical battles. Most of all, it killed over three million productive workers. Many of these were highly skilled. Moreover, Jewish war-workers, knowing their likely fate, tried fanatically to make themselves indispensable to the war effort. There is a mass of evidence to show that all those Germans involved in production tried hard to keep their Jewish staff. To quote only one of many examples, the organizer of war factories in occupied Russia reported:

Almost insoluble was the problem of finding expert managers. Almost all former owners were Jews. All enterprises had been taken over by the Soviet state. The Bolshevik Commissars have disappeared. The Ukrainian trustee administrators [were] incompetent, unreliable and completely passive. . . . The real experts and real heads are Jews, mostly the former owners or engineers. . . . They try their utmost and extract the very last ounce of production, until now almost without pay, but naturally in the hope of becoming indispensable.[186]

But of course all these Jews were killed. Hence the Holocaust was one of the factors which were losing Hitler the war. The British and American governments knew this. What they did not sufficiently appreciate was that the main military beneficiary of the Holocaust was the Red Army, and the ultimate political beneficiary would be the Soviet empire.[187]

The Allied calculation might have been different if the Jews had produced a resistance movement. None emerged. There were many reasons for this. The Jews had been persecuted for a millennium and a half and had learned from long experience that resistance cost lives rather than saved them. Their history, their theology, their folklore, their social structure, even their vocabulary trained them to negotiate, to pay, to plead, to protest, not to fight. Then too, the Jewish communities, especially in eastern Europe, had been emasculated by many generations of mass migration. The most ambitious had gone to America. The most energetic, adventurous, above all the most militant, had gone to Palestine. This drain of the best and the brightest had continued right up to the war and even during it. Jabotinsky had predicted the Holocaust. But the uniformed, trained, even armed Jewish groups in Poland were designed not to resist Hitler but to get Jews to Palestine. When war broke out, Menachem Begin, for instance, was escorting a group of 1,000 illegal emigrants across the Rumanian frontier on their way to the Middle East. So he got out too.[188] That made sense. The fighting Jews wanted to make their stand in Erez Israel, where they had a chance, not in Europe, where it was hopeless.

The great mass of Jews who remained, overwhelmingly religious, were deceived and self-deceived. Their history told them that all persecutions, however cruel, came to an end; that all oppressors, however exigent, had demands that were ultimately limited and could be met. Their strategy was always geared to saving 'the remnant'. In 4,000 years the Jews had never faced, and had never imagined, an opponent who demanded not some, or most, of their property, but everything; not just a few lives, or even many, but all, down to the last infant. Who could conceive of such a monster? The Jews, unlike the Christians, did not believe the devil took human shape.

The Nazis, precisely to minimize the possibility of resistance, made pitiless use of Jewish sociology and psychology. In Germany they exploited the Jewish Gemeinde in each city, the Landesverbände in each region, and the Reichsvereinigung for the entire country, to get Jewish officials to do the preparatory work for the Final Solution themselves: to prepare nominal rolls, report deaths and births, transmit new regulations, set up special bank accounts open to the Gestapo, concentrate the Jews in particular housing blocks and prepare charts and maps for deportation. This was the model for the Jewish Councils in the occupied countries which unwittingly helped the Nazis push through the Final Solution. About 1,000 of these *Judenrate* were organized, involving 10,000 people. They were formed mainly out of the pre-war religious *kehillot* (congregational bodies). In the Soviet-occupied areas, all the bravest community leaders had already been shot before the Germans arrived. The Germans used the *Judenrate* to spot the actual or potential trouble-makers and kill them instantly. Thus the Jewish leadership tended to be compliant, fearful and sycophantic. The Nazis used them first to despoil the Jews of all their valuables, then to organize bodies of Jews for forced labour and deportation to the killing centres. In return they were given privileges and power over their fellows.[189]

The system was seen at its most odious and formidable in the biggest Polish ghettos, especially Lodz and Warsaw. The Lodz ghetto had 200,000 Jews crowded into it, with a living density of 5.8 a room. It was a killing centre in itself, 45,000 dying there of disease and starvation. The Warsaw ghetto had no less than 445,000 Jews, with a room-density of 7.2; there, 83,000 died of hunger and sickness in less than twenty months. Jews were concentrated in the ghettos, then funnelled out of them into the death trains. Internally, the ghettos were petty tyrannies, run by men like Chaim Mordechai Rumkowski, the strutting dictator of the Lodz ghetto, who even had his head printed on postage stamps. Their power was enforced by unarmed Jewish police (there were 2,000 in the Warsaw ghetto), supervised by Polish police, with the armed German Sip (security police) and the ss watching everyone. The ghettos were not wholly uncivilized. The Jewish social services worked to the best of their meagre resources. Secret *yeshivot* were organized. Warsaw, Lodz, Vilna and Kovno even had orchestras, though they were officially allowed to play only music by Jewish composers. There were clandestine newspapers printed and circu-lated. The Lodz ghetto, as befitted a medieval-type institution, had a chronicle.[190] But there was never any doubt in the minds of the Germans about the function of the ghetto and its Jewish authorities. It was to make what contribution it could to the war effort (Lodz had

117 little war factories, Bialystok twenty) and then, when the deportation orders for the camps came, to ensure that the process was orderly.

To keep resistance to a minimum, the Germans lied at every stage of the process, and employed elaborate deceptions. They always insisted that deportations were to work-sites. They had postcards printed stamped Waldsee, which camp-inmates were made to send home, which read: 'I am well. I work and am in good health.' On the transit to Treblinka, they constructed a dummy station with a ticket office, hand-painted clock and a sign reading: 'In transit to Bialystok'. The death chambers, disguised as shower-rooms, had Red Cross markings on the doors. Sometimes the ss had all-inmate orchestras play music as the Jews were marshalled towards the 'shower-rooms'. The pretence was kept up until the end. A note found in the clothes of one victim reads: 'We arrived at the place after a long journey and at the front of the entrance is a sign "Bathhouse". Outside, people receive soap and a towel. Who knows what they will do with us?'[191] At Belzec, 18 August 1942, an ss disinfectant expert, Kurt Gerstein, heard an ss officer chant, while naked men, women and children were pushed into the death chamber: 'Nothing is going to hurt you. Just breathe deep and it will strengthen your lungs. It is a way to prevent contagious diseases. It is a good disinfectant.'[192]

The deception often worked because the Jews wanted to be deceived. They needed to have hope. The ss skilfully fed rumours into the ghettos that only a portion of Jews were required for deportation, and successfully sold the Jewish leadership the line that a maximum degree of co-operation produced the best chance of survival. The ghetto Jews were reluctant to believe in the existence of the extermination camps. When two young Jews escaped from Chelmno early in 1942 and described what they had seen there, it was argued that they had been unhinged by their experiences and their report was withheld from the underground press. Not until April, when reports from Belzec confirmed the Chelmno story, did the Warsaw Jews believe in the death machinery. In July the Warsaw ghetto boss, Adam Czerniakow, realizing he could not save even the children, took cyanide, leaving a note: 'I am powerless. My heart trembles in sorrow and compassion. I can no longer bear all this. My act will prove to everyone what is the right thing to do.'[193] But even at this stage, many Jews clung to the hope that only some would die. Jacob Gens, the ghetto boss in Vilna, told a public meeting: 'When they ask me for a thousand Jews, I hand them over. For if we Jews do not give of our own, the Germans will come and take them by force. Then they will take not one thousand but many thousands. By handing over hundreds, I save a thousand. By handing over a thousand, I save ten thousand.'[194]

Jewish religious training tended to encourage passivity. The hasidic Jews were the most ready to accept their fate as God's will. They quoted scripture: 'And thy life shall hang in doubt before thee; and thou shalt fear night and day, and shalt have no assurance of thy life.'[195] They got into the death trains wrapped in their prayer-shawls, reciting the psalms. They believed in martyrdom for God's glory. If, by chance or God's mercy, they were spared, then it was a miracle. A whole collection of hasidic tales about the wondrous sparing of individual lives grew up during the Holocaust.[196] One community leader noted: 'The truly pious have become even more pious, for they see God's hand in everything.' A member of the Jewish *Sonderskommando*, who cleared out the Auschwitz death chambers after a gassing, testified that he saw a group of pious Jews from Hungary and Poland, who had managed to get some brandy, dance and sing before entering the gas rooms, because they knew they were about to meet the Messiah. Other, more secular Jews also found joy and acceptance of God's will in the horror. The remarkable diaries which a Dutch–Jewish woman, Ettie Hillesum, kept in Auschwitz show that the tradition of Job lived on in the Holocaust: 'Sometimes when I stand in some corner of the camp, my feet planted on your earth, my eyes raised towards your heaven, tears run down my face, tears . . . of gratitude.'[197]

As the ghettos were gradually emptied, some Jews did determine to fight, though political divisions delayed agreement on a plan. In Warsaw, under pretence of building air-raid shelters, the Jews constructed dug-outs connected to the sewer system. They were led by a twenty-four-year-old, Mordecai Anielewicz, who recruited 750 fighters and contrived to get possession of nine rifles, fifty-nine pistols and a few grenades. The Nazis decided to destroy the ghetto on 19 April 1943, using the Waffen-ss. By that time there were only 60,000 Jews left in it. In the desperate fighting that followed, mainly underground, they killed sixteen Germans and wounded eighty-five. Anielewicz was killed on 8 May, but the rest held out another eight days, by which time several thousand Jews were dead in the debris. Some European countries, with well-equipped armies, had not resisted the Nazis for so long.[198]

There was even a revolt within Auschwitz itself on 7 October 1944. Jews working in a Krupp plant smuggled in explosives; they were turned into grenades and bombs by skilled Soviet POWs. The revolt itself was carried out by the Sonderskommando of Crematoria III and IV. They managed to blow up Crematorium III and kill three SS men. About 250 Jews were massacred by the guards, but twenty-seven escaped. Four Jewish girls who got the explosives in were tortured for weeks, but gave no information. Roza Robota, who died under torture, gave as her last message: 'Be strong and brave.' Two of them survived the torture to be hanged in front of all the women in Auschwitz, one of them with the cry 'Revenge!' as she died.[199]

But as a rule there was no resistance at all, at any stage of the extermination process. The Germans always struck suddenly, with overwhelming force. The Jews were numb with terror and hopelessness. 'The ghetto was encircled by a large SS detachment,' wrote an eye-witness at Dubno (Ukraine),

and about three times as many Ukrainian militia. Then the electric arclights erected in and around the ghetto were switched on. . . . The people were driven out in such haste that small children in bed were left behind. In the street women cried out for their children and children for their parents. That did not prevent the SS from driving the people along the road at running pace, and hitting them until they reached the waiting freight-train. Car after car was filled, and the screaming of women and children, and the cracking of whips and rifle shots, resounded unceasingly.[200]

Many Jews died on the trains, and when the survivors arrived they were hustled straight off to the death chambers. Kurt Gerstein watched, in the early morning, a trainload of 6,700 Jews arrive at Auschwitz in August 1942. There were 1,450 dead on arrival. He saw 200 Ukrainians, armed with leather whips, open up the freight-car doors, order out the living and beat them to the ground. Loudspeakers screamed at them to strip naked. The hair was brutally shorn from the heads of all females. Then the entire shipment, stark naked, were driven towards the gas chambers which they were told were 'disinfectant baths'.[201] At no point did anyone have a chance to resist. The most they could do was to tear up the miserable crumpled dollars they had concealed on their persons, so that the Nazis would not have the use of them – their last and only gesture of protest.[202]

No Jew was spared in Hitler's apocalypse. The Theresienstadt camp in Czechoslovakia, full of old people, was run to preserve the pretence that the Jews were merely being 'resettled'. To it were sent so-called privileged Jews, holders of the Iron Cross First Class or better, and 50-per-cent disabled war veterans. But of the 141,184 sent there, only 16,832 were alive when the camp fell to the Allies on 9 May 1945: more than 88,000, the old and the brave alike, had been gassed.[203] No Jew was too old to be murdered. After the Anschluss, the friends of

Freud, old and dying of cancer, had ransomed him from the Nazis and brought him to England. It did not occur to him, or to anyone, that his four elderly sisters, left behind in Vienna, were at risk. But they too were swept into the Nazi net: Adolfine, aged eighty-one, was murdered in Theresienstadt, Pauline, eighty, and Marie, eighty-two, in Treblinka, Rose, eighty-four, in Auschwitz.

No Jew was too young to die. All women arriving at the death camps were shaved to the skin, the hair being packed up and sent to Germany. If a breast-fed baby was a nuisance during the shaving, a guard simply smashed its head against the wall. A witness at the Nuremberg trials testified: 'Only those who saw these things with their own eyes will believe with what delight the Germans performed these operations; how glad they were when they succeeded in killing a child with only three or four blows; with what satisfaction they pushed the corpse into the mother's arms!'[204] At Treblinka, most babies were taken from their mothers on arrival, killed, and hurled into a ditch, along with invalids and cripples. Sometimes thin wails could be heard from the ditch, whose guards wore Red Cross armbands and which was known as The Infirmary.

The smashing of babies' heads reflects the extent to which the dualism of anti-Semitic violence persisted, with secret, scientific killing proceeding alongside sudden, spontaneous acts of unspeakable cruelty. Jews died in every kind of way known to depraved humanity. At the Mauthausen quarry, an Italian Jew with a good voice was made to stand on top of a rock already wired with dynamite, and then blown to death as he sang 'Ave Maria'. Hundreds of Dutch Jews were forced to jump to their deaths from the cliff overlooking the quarry, known as The Parachutist's Wall.[205] Many thousands of Jews were flogged to death for trivial camp offences: keeping a coin or wedding ring, failing to move Jewish insignia from the clothes of the murdered, having a piece of bread from an outside bakery, drinking water without permission, smoking, poor saluting. There were even cases of beheading. Kurt Franz, deputy commandant at Treblinka, kept a pack of fierce dogs used to tear Jews to death. Sometimes the guards killed with anything that came to hand. A Belzec eye-witness testified about 'a very young boy' who had just arrived at the camp:

He was a fine example of health, strength and youth. We were surprised by his cheerful manner. He looked around and said quite happily: 'Has anyone ever escaped from here?' It was enough. One of the guards overheard him and the boy was tortured to death. He was stripped naked and hung upside down from the gallows; he hung there for three hours. He was strong and still very much alive. They took him down and laid him on the ground and pushed sand down his throat with sticks until he died.[206]

In the end, as the Reich imploded and first Himmler, then his camp commandants, lost control, the scientific side of the Final Solution broke down or was abandoned, and the dualism merged into one insensate force: the desire, right up to the last possible moment, to kill any Jews who remained. The Sonderskommandos, the ghetto bosses, Rumkowski included, the Jewish police and ss spies – all were killed. As the front collapsed, the ss made determined efforts to march columns of Jews away from it, so they could be killed at leisure. The fanaticism with which they clung to their duties as mass murderers, long after the Third Reich was irretrievably doomed, is one of the gruesome curiosities of human history. There was one revolt of the killers. At Ebensee, a Mauthausen satellite camp and the last in German hands, the ss refused to mow down 30,000 Jews who would not march into a tunnel to be blown up. But some killings continued even after camps were liberated. British tanks took Belsen on 15 April 1945 but moved on into action, leaving Hungarian ss guards 'in partial command' for forty-eight hours. During that time they shot seventy-two Jews for such offences as taking potato-peelings from the kitchen.[207]

So nearly six million Jews died. Two millennia of anti-Semitic hatred, of all varieties, pagan, Christian and secular, superstitious and cerebral, folk and academic, had been soldered by Hitler into one overwhelming juggernaut and then driven by his unique energy and will over the helpless body of European Jewry. There were still 250,000 Jews in displaced persons' camps, and scattered survivors everywhere. But the great Ashkenazi Jewry of eastern Europe had, in essence, been destroyed. An act of genocide had indeed been carried out. As the camps were opened and the full extent of the calamity became known, some Jews in their innocence expected an outraged humanity to comprehend the magnitude of the crime and say with one thunderous voice: this is enough. Anti-Semitism must end. We must be done with it once and for all, draw a line under this stupendous outrage, and start history afresh.

But that is not how human societies work. Nor, in particular, is it how the anti-Semitic impulse works. It is protean, assuming new forms as it consumes the old. The effect of the Holocaust was chiefly to transfer the principal focus of anti-Jewish hatred from east-central Europe to the Middle East. What worried some Arab leaders was that Hitler's solution had not, in fact, been final. On 6 May 1942, for instance, the Grand Mufti had protested to the Bulgarian government that Jews were leaving there for Palestine. They should, he said, be sent back to Poland 'under strong and energetic guard'.[208]

Even in Europe, there was often loathing, rather than pity, for the bewildered survivors. Their very nakedness, the habits bred by their atrocious treatment, stirred new waves of anti-Semitism. Among those who yielded to revulsion was General Patton, who had charge of more Jewish DPs than any other commander. He called 'the Jewish type of DP' a 'sub-human species without any of the cultural or social refinements of our time'. No ordinary people, he said, 'could have sunk to the level of degradation these have reached in the short space of four years'.[209] More active hostility to the pitiful survivors was shown in the countries from which they had been drawn, especially Poland. The Jewish DPs knew what awaited them. They resisted repatriation to the best of their strength. A Jewish GI from Chicago, who had to load survivors on to railroad trucks for Poland, related: 'Men threw themselves on their knees in front of me, tore open their shirts and screamed: "Kill me now!" They would say, "You might just as well kill me now, I am dead anyway if I go back to Poland." '[210] In some cases they were proved right. In Poland, anti-Semitic riots broke out in Cracow in August 1945 and spread to Sosnowiec and Lublin. Luba Zindel, who returned to Cracow from a Nazi camp, described an attack on her synagogue on the first Sabbath in August: 'They were shouting that we had committed ritual murders. They began firing at us and beating us up. My husband was sitting beside me. He fell down, his face full of bullets.' She tried to flee to the West but was stopped by Patton's troops. The British ambassador in Warsaw reported that anyone in Poland with a Jewish appearance was in danger. During the first seven months after the end of the war there were 350 anti-Semitic murders in Poland.[211]

Nevertheless, in two important respects the Holocaust, by its sheer enormity, did bring a qualitative change in the way international society reacted to violence inflicted on Jews. It was universally agreed that both punishment and restitution were necessary and to some extent both were carried out. War-crime trials began at Nuremberg on 20 November 1945, with the Final Solution as a principal element in the indictment. The first trial of Nazi leaders ended on 1 October 1946, which coincided with the Day of Atonement, when twelve defendants were sentenced to death, three to life imprisonment, four to prison terms, and three were acquitted. There followed twelve major trials of Nazi criminals, known as Subsequent Nuremberg Proceedings, in four of which the planning and execution of the Final Solution were a chief element. In these twelve trials, 177 Nazis were convicted, twelve sentenced to death, twenty-five to life imprisonment, and the remainder to long prison terms. There were many further trials in each of the three Western occupation zones, nearly all of them involving atrocities against Jews. Between 1945 and 1951 a total of 5,025 Nazis were convicted, 806 being sentenced to death. But in only 486 cases was the death sentence carried out. Moreover, a Clemency Act passed in January 1951 by the US high commissioner in Germany led to the early release of many senior war criminals in US hands. The United Nations War Crimes Commission prepared lists of 36,529 'war criminals' (including Japanese), the majority of them involved in anti-Jewish atrocities. In the first three years after the war, additional trials were held by eight Allied countries of 3,470 on the list, of whom 952 were sentenced to death and 1,905 received prison sentences.

Large numbers of national war-crimes trials were held in nearly all the states involved in the war, involving about 150,000 accused and producing over 100,000 convictions, many of them in punishment of anti-Jewish crimes. Many thousands of Nazis and their allies involved in the Final Solution were swallowed up in the Gulag Archipelago. When German courts began to function again in 1945, they too began to try war criminals, and in the first quarter-century they sentenced twelve to death, ninety-eight to life imprisonment and 6,000 to prison terms.[212] With the creation of Israel in 1948, she also (as we shall see) was able to take part in the retributive process. The pursuit and arraignment of Nazi war criminals continues in the late 1980s, more than forty years after the Holocaust ended, and is likely to last another decade, at the end of which all those involved in perpetrating it will be dead or in extreme old age. No one can say that justice was done. Some of the senior executants of the Final Solution disappeared and lived out their lives in peace or at any rate in hiding. Others received or served sentences which bore no relation to their crimes. Yet equally, no one can doubt the scale of the effort made to punish those who committed history's gravest crime or the persistence with which it has been maintained.

The struggle to secure compensation for the victims produced similar mixed results. Chaim Weizmann, on behalf of the Jewish Agency, submitted a reparations claim to the four occupying powers on 20 September 1945. Nothing came of it, mainly because no general peace treaty was ever negotiated or signed. The three Western powers set aside proceeds from the sale of confiscated Nazi property for Jewish victims. But they had to make individual claims and a well-meant project turned into a bureaucratic muddle. By 1953 only 11,000 claims had been processed, yielding $83 million. In the meantime, in January 1951 the Israeli Prime Minister, David Ben

Gurion, had submitted a collective claim to the federal German government for $1.5 billion, based on Israel's absorption of 500,000 refugees from Germany at a capital cost of $3,000 each. It meant negotiating directly with the Germans, something many camp survivors found unacceptable. But Ben Gurion got majority approval with his slogan: 'Let not the murderers of our people also be their heirs!' Agreement on a figure of $845 million, paid over fourteen years, was reached and, despite attempts by the Arab states to prevent ratification, came into effect in March 1953, and was duly completed in 1965. Moreover, it also provided for the passing of a federal Indemnification Law, indemnifying individual victims or their dependants for loss of life or limb, damage to health, and loss of careers, professions, pensions and insurance. It further made restitution for loss of liberty at a rate of a dollar for each day the victims were imprisoned, forced to live in a ghetto, or wear a star. Those who lost the family breadwinner received a pension, former civil servants got notional promotions and compensation was also given for loss of education. Victims could also claim for loss of property. This comprehensive settlement was administered by a staff of nearly 5,000 judges, civil servants and clerks, who by 1973 had processed over 95 per cent of 4,276,000 claims. For a quarter of a century it absorbed about 5 per cent of the federal budget. At the time of writing, about $25 billion has been paid out, and by the end of the twentieth century the figure will be over $30 billion.[213] These payments cannot exactly be described as generous or even adequate. But they are a great deal more than Weizmann or Ben Gurion ever expected and they represent a genuine desire on the part of the federal government to pay for Germany's crime.

The rest of the reparations story is much less satisfactory. None of the German industrialists involved in the slave-labour programme ever acknowledged the smallest moral responsibility for its atrocious consequences. They argued, in defending themselves against both criminal charges and civil claims, that in the circumstances of total war the forced-labour procedure was not unlawful. They resisted compensation every legal inch of the way and behaved throughout with a striking mixture of meanness and arrogance. Friedrich Flick declared: 'Nobody of the large circle of persons who know my fellow defendants and myself will be willing to believe that we committed crimes against humanity and nothing will convince us that we are war criminals.'[214] Flick never paid out a single deutschmark and was worth over $1,000 million when he died, aged ninety, in 1972. Altogether the German companies paid out a total of only $13 million and fewer than 15,000

Jews got a share of it. The IG Farben slave-workers at Auschwitz got $1,700 each, the AEG–Telefunken slaves $500 or less. The families of those who had been worked to death got nothing.[215] But the behaviour of the German capitalists was no worse than that of the Communist successor states. The East German government never even troubled to reply to requests for compensation. Nor was there any response from Rumania. The whole vast area of oppression controlled by Communist authorities since 1945 yielded the Jews nothing whatever.

Austria's behaviour was the worst of the lot. Though the great majority of Austrians had supported the Anschluss, though nearly 550,000 out of seven million Austrians were actually Nazi Party members, though Austrians had fought alongside Germany through-out and (as we have noted) had killed nearly half the Jewish victims, the Allied declaration of November 1943 in Moscow categorized Austria as 'the first free nation to fall victim to Hitlerite aggression'. Austria was therefore exempted from reparations at the post-war Potsdam Conference. Thus legally absolved, all the Austrian political parties entered into an agreement to evade moral responsibility too, and to claim the status of victim. As the Austrian Socialist Party put it (1946): 'It is not Austria that should make restitution. Rather, it is to Austria that restitution should be made.' Austria was obliged by the Allies to pass a war criminal law, but did not even establish a prosecuting body to enforce it until 1963. Even so, many were amnestied by decree and those trials that did take place usually produced acquittals. Jews claiming compensation were told to apply to Germany, unless they could actually identify their former property in Austria itself; and very few indeed got as much as $1,000.

There was a belated but nevertheless welcome attempt to make moral reparation by the Christian churches. Both Catholic and Lutheran anti-Semitism had contributed, over many centuries, to the Jew-hatred which culminated in Hitlerism. Neither church had behaved well during the war. Pope Pius XII, in particular, had failed to condemn the Final Solution, though he knew of it. One or two isolated voices had been raised on behalf of the Jews. Fr Bernhard Lichtenberg, from St Hedwig's Catholic Cathedral in Berlin, had publicly prayed for the Jews in 1941. His apartment was searched and notes found for an undelivered sermon in which he planned to tell his congregation that they should not believe in a Jewish conspiracy to kill all Germans. For this he served a two-year sentence and on his release was ordered to Dachau. This seems the only case of its kind. Among eye-witnesses of the *Judenrazzia* in Rome on 16 October 1943 was a Jesuit priest,

Augustin Bea, who came from Baden in Germany and acted as Pius XII's confessor. Twenty years later, during the Second Vatican Council, he had the chance, as head of the Secretariat for Christian Unity, to quash, once and for all, the ancient accusation of deicide against the Jews. He took charge of the council *schema*, 'On the Jews', enlarged it into a 'Declaration of the Relations of the Church to Non-Christian Religions', taking in Hinduism, Buddhism and Islam as well as Judaism, and successfully steered it through the council, which adopted it in November 1965. It was a grudging document, less forthright than Bea had hoped, making no apology for the church's persecution of the Jews, and inadequate acknowledgment of the contribution of Judaism to Christianity. The key passage read: 'True the Jewish authorities and those who followed their lead pressed for the death of Christ; still, what happened in his passion cannot be charged against all the Jews, without distinction, then alive, nor against the Jews of today. Although the Church is the new people of God, the Jews should not be represented as rejected of God or accursed, as if this followed from the Holy Scriptures.'[216] This was not much. But it was something. In view of the fierce opposition it aroused, it might even be considered a great deal. Moreover, it was part of a much more general process whereby the civilized world was attempting to strike at the institutional supports of anti-Semitism.

That was welcome. But the Jews had grasped that the civilized world, however defined, could not be trusted. The overwhelming lesson the Jews learned from the Holocaust was the imperative need to secure for themselves a permanent, self-contained and above all sovereign refuge where if necessary the whole of world Jewry could find safety from its enemies. The First World War made the Zionist state possible. The Second World War made it essential. It persuaded the overwhelming majority of Jews that such a state had to be created and made secure whatever the cost, to themselves or to anyone else.

PART SEVEN

Zion

The Holocaust and the new Zion were organically connected. The murder of six million Jews was a prime causative factor in the creation of the state of Israel. This was in accordance with an ancient and powerful dynamic of Jewish history: redemption through suffering. Thousands of pious Jews sang their profession of faith as they were hustled towards the gas chambers because they believed that the punishment being inflicted on the Jews, in which Hitler and the ss were mere agents, was the work of God and itself proof that He had chosen them. According to the Prophet Amos, God had said: 'You only have I known of all the families of the earth, therefore I will punish you for all your iniquities.'[1] The sufferings of Auschwitz were not mere happenings. They were moral enactments. They were part of a plan. They confirmed the glory to come. Moreover, God was not merely angry with the Jews. He was also sorrowful. He wept with them. He went with them into the gas chambers as he had gone with them into Exile.[2]

That is to state cause and effect in religious, metaphysical terms. But it can also be stated in historical terms. The creation of Israel was the consequence of Jewish sufferings. We have used the image of the jigsaw puzzle to show how each necessary piece was slotted into place. As we have seen, the great eastern massacres of 1648 led to the return of a Jewish community to England, and so to America, thus in time producing the most influential Jewry in the world, an indispensable part of the geopolitical context in which Israel could be created. Again, the massacres of 1881 set in motion a whole series of events tending towards the same end. The immigration they produced was the background to the Dreyfus outrage, which led directly to Herzl's creation of modern Zionism. The movement of Jews set in motion by Russian oppression created the pattern of tension from which, in 1917, the Balfour Declaration emerged, and the League of Nations Palestine mandate was set up to implement it. Hitler's persecution of the Jews was the last in the series of catastrophes which helped to make the Zionist state.

Even before the Second World War, Hitler's anti-Jewish policy had the unintended effect of greatly strengthening the Jewish community in Palestine. Hitler eventually came to see the Jewish state as a potential enemy, a 'second Vatican', a 'Jewish Comintern', a 'new power-base for world Jewry'.[3] But for a time in the 1930s the Nazis actively assisted the emigration of German Jews to Palestine. Not only did 60,000 German Jews thus reach the national home, but the assets of these German Jews played an important part in establishing an industrial and commercial infrastructure there. It was the war, bringing with it not only Hitler's outright physical assault on the Jews as his prime enemy, but the chance for Jews to hit back at him with the Allies, which activated the last phase of the Zionist programme. From the outbreak of war in 1939, the creation of the Israeli state, at the earliest possible moment, became the overriding object of the Zionists and spread gradually to the majority of the world Jewish community. The obstacles to a Zionist fulfilment were still considerable. It was not enough to defeat Hitler. It was also necessary to remove any objections from the three victorious Allies, Britain, the United States and Soviet Russia. Let us look at each in turn.

Initially, Britain was the most important, because it was the power in possession. Moreover, the 1939 White Paper policy had, in effect, repudiated the Balfour Declaration and projected a future in which no predominantly Jewish Palestine could emerge. The Jews were Britain's ally in the war. But at the same time they had to overthrow British policy for Palestine. Ben Gurion thought the aims were compatible: 'We must fight Hitler as though there were no White Paper, and fight the White Paper as though there were no Hitler.'[4] He was right, provided the British would allow the Jews to fight the war as a coherent unit, which could later be used to determine events in Palestine. The British authorities, military, diplomatic and colonial, were hostile to the idea for this very reason. Indeed, after the Alamein victory late in 1942 removed the German threat from the Middle East, British HQ there looked with suspicion on any Jewish military activity. But the Jews had one powerful defender: Churchill. He favoured Weizmann's proposal to form a Jewish striking-force from existing small-scale Jewish units. The British army repeatedly blocked the scheme, but Churchill eventually got his way. 'I like the idea', he minuted to the Secretary of State for War, 12 July 1944, 'of the Jews trying to get at the murderers of their fellow countrymen in Central Europe. It is with the Germans that they have their quarrel. . . . I cannot conceive why this martyred race scattered about the world and suffering as no other race has done at this juncture should be denied the satisfaction of having a flag.'[5] Two months later, the Jewish Brigade, 25,000 strong, was formed. Without Churchill the Jews would never have got it, and the experience of working together at this formation level was critical to the Israeli success four years later.

All the same, the British had no intention of reversing their Palestine policy. Overthrowing Hitler impoverished them and made their Middle Eastern oilfields more, not less, important; they had no intention of permitting a level of Jewish immigration which would turn the Arab world implacably hostile. Nor were they ready to move out of Palestine until they could do so in a manner which retained their Arab friendships. So they prevented illegal Jewish immigrants from landing, and if they got through efforts were made to capture and deport them. In November 1940 the *Patria*, about to sail for Mauritius with 1,700 deportees on board, was sabotaged by the Haganah. It sank in Haifa Bay and 250 refugees were drowned. In February 1942 the *Struma*, a refugee ship from Rumania, was refused landing permission by Britain, turned back by the Turks, and sank in the Black Sea, drowning 770.

These tragic episodes did not shake Britain's resolve to maintain her immigration limits throughout the war and even after, when there were 250,000 Jews in DP camps. Nor did the accession to power in 1945 of the British Labour Party, theoretically pro-Zionist, make any difference. The new Foreign Secretary, Ernest Bevin, bowed to the arguments of the diplomats and generals. At that time Britain still ruled a quarter of the earth's surface. She had 100,000 men in Palestine, where the Jews numbered only 600,000. There was no material reason why the Zionists should get their way. Yet eighteen months later Bevin threw in his hand. As Evelyn Waugh, in his book on Jerusalem, bitterly observed of British conduct: 'We surrendered our mandate to rule the Holy Land for low motives: cowardice, sloth and parsimony. The vision of Allenby marching on foot where the Kaiser had arrogantly ridden, is overlaid now by the sorry spectacle of a large, well-found force, barely scratched in battle, decamping before a little gang of gunmen.'[6] How did this happen?

The answer lies in yet another Jewish contribution to the shape of the modern world: the scientific use of terror to break the will of liberal rulers. It was to become a commonplace over the next forty years, but in 1945 it was new. It might be called a by-product of the Holocaust, for no lesser phenomenon could have driven even desperate Jews to use it. Its most accomplished practitioner was Menachem Begin, former chairman of Betar, the Polish youth movement. He was a man in whom the bitterness generated by the Holocaust had become incarnate. Jews formed 70 per cent of his home town, Brest-Litovsk. There had been over 30,000 of them in 1939. By 1944 only ten were left alive. Most of Begin's family were murdered. The Jews were forbidden even to bury their dead. That was how his father died, shot on the spot digging a grave for a friend in the Jewish cemetery.[7] But Begin was a born survivor, and a revenger. Arrested in Lithuania, he was one of the very few men to survive, unbroken, an interrogation by Stalin's NKVD. at the end of it, his interrogator said with fury: 'I never want to see you again.' Begin commented later: 'It was my faith against his faith. I had something to fight for, even in the interrogation room.'[8] Begin was sent to a Soviet slave-camp in the Arctic Circle near the Barents Sea, building the Kotlas–Varkuta railway. He survived that too, benefited from an amnesty for Poles, walked through Central Asia and made his way to Jerusalem as a private in the Polish army. In December 1943 he took over control of the Revisionists' military arm, the Irgun. Two months later he declared war on the British administration.

Among the Jews there were three schools of thought about the British. Weizmann still believed in British good faith. Ben Gurion, though sceptical, wanted to win the war first. Even after it he drew an absolute distinction between resistance and terrorism, and this was reflected in Haganah policy. On the other hand there was an extremist breakaway from the Irgun, known as the Stern Gang after its leader Avraham Stern. He disobeyed Jabotinsky's instructions for a ceasefire with the British on the outbreak of war, and was killed in February 1942. But his colleagues, led by Yizhak Shamir and Nathan Yellin-Mor, carried on an unrestricted campaign against Britain. Begin took a third course. He thought the Haganah too passive, the Stern Gang crude, vicious and unintelligent. He saw the enemy not as Britain but the British administration in Palestine. He wanted to humiliate it; make it unworkable, expensive, ineffective. He had 600 active agents. He rejected assassination but he blew up CID offices, the immigration building, income-tax centres, and similar targets.

Relations between the three groups of Jewish activists were always tense and often venomous. This had grave political consequences later. On 6 November 1944 the Stern Gang murdered Lord Moyne, the British Minister for Middle East Affairs. Haganah, appalled and infuriated, launched what was called the Saison against both Sternists and Irgun. It captured some of them and held them in underground prisons. Worse, it handed over to the British CID the names of 700 persons and institutions. At least 300 and possibly as many as 1,000 were arrested as a result of information supplied by the Zionist establishment. Begin, who got away, accused the Haganah of torture too, and issued a defiant statement: 'We shall repay you, Cain.' But he was too shrewd to get into a war with Haganah. It was during these months, when he was fighting both the British and his fellow Jews, that he created an underground force almost impervious to attack. He believed Haganah would have to join him to get rid of Britain. He was proved right. On 1 October 1945 Ben Gurion, without consulting Weizmann, sent a coded cable to Moshe Sneh, the Haganah commander, ordering him to begin operations against the British forces.[9] A united Jewish Resistance Movement was formed. It began its attacks on the night of 31 October, blowing up railways.

Even so, disagreements on targets remained. The Haganah would not employ terror in any form. It would employ force only in what could plausibly be called a military operation. Begin always rejected murder, such as the cold-blooded killing by the Sternists of six British paratroopers in their beds on 26 April 1946. He repudiated, then and later, the label 'terrorist'. But he was willing to take moral risks, as well as physical ones. How could the Promised Land have been secured in the first place without Joshua? And was not the Book of Joshua a disturbing record of how far the Israelites were prepared to go to conquer the land which was theirs by divine command?

Begin was a leading figure in two episodes which were instrumental in inducing Britain to quit. On 29 June 1946 the British made a dawn swoop on the Jewish Agency. Some 2,718 Jews were arrested. The object was to produce a more moderate Jewish leadership. It failed. Indeed, since Irgun was untouched, it strengthened Begin's hand. He got Haganah to agree to blow up the King David Hotel, where part of the British administration was housed. The agreed object was to humiliate, not to kill. But the risk of mass murder was enormous. Weizmann got to hear of the plot and threatened to resign and tell the world why.[10] Haganah told Begin to call it off but he refused. At lunchtime on 22 July 1946, six minutes ahead of schedule, about 700 lb of high explosive demolished one wing of the hotel, killing twenty-eight British, forty-one Arabs and seventeen Jews, plus five other people. A sixteen-year-old schoolgirl gave a warning phone call as part of the plan. There is a conflict of evidence over what happened next. Begin always insisted that adequate warning was given and blamed the British authorities for the deaths. He mourned the Jewish casualties alone.[11] But, in such acts of terror, those who plant the explosives must be held responsible for any deaths. That was the view taken by the Jewish establishment. The Haganah commander Moshe Sneh was forced to resign. The Resistance Movement broke up into its component parts. Nevertheless the outrage, combined with others, achieved its effect. The British government proposed a tripartite division of the country. Both Jews and Arabs rejected the plan. Accordingly, on 14 February 1947, Bevin announced that he was handing over the whole Palestine problem to the United Nations.

That did not necessarily mean a rapid British withdrawal, however. So the terror campaign continued. A further episode, for which Begin was again responsible, proved decisive. He was opposed to Sternist-type assassinations but he insisted on Irgun's moral right to punish members of the British armed forces in the same way as Britain punished Irgun members. The British hanged and flogged. Irgun would do the same. In April 1947 three Irgun men were put on trial for an attack on the Acre prison-fortress, which freed 251 prisoners. Begin threatened retaliation if the three were convicted and hanged. They were, on 29 July. A few hours later two British sergeants, Clifford Martin and Mervyn Paice, who had been captured for this purpose, were hanged on Begin's instructions by Irgun's operations chief, Gidi Paglin. He also mined their bodies. This gruesome murder of Martin and Paice, who had committed no crime, horrified many Jews. The Jewish Agency called it 'the dastardly murder of two innocent men by a set of criminals'.[12] (It was even worse than it seemed at the time, for it emerged thirty-five years later that Martin had a Jewish mother.) It caused unrestrained fury in Britain. A synagogue was burned down in Derby. There were anti-Jewish riots in London, Liverpool, Glasgow and Manchester – the first in England since the thirteenth century. These in turn produced critical changes in British policy. The British had assumed that any partition would have to be supervised and enforced by them; otherwise the armies of the Arab states would simply move in and exterminate the Jews. Now they decided to get out as quickly as possible and leave Arabs and Jews to it.[13] Thus Begin's policy succeeded, but it involved appalling risks.

The extent of the risks depended to some extent on the two superpowers, America and Russia. In both cases the Zionists benefited from what might be called luck or divine providence, according to taste. The first was the death of Roosevelt on 12 April 1945. In his last weeks he had turned anti-Zionist, following a meeting with King Ibn Saud after the Yalta Conference. The pro-Zionist presidential assistant, David Niles, later asserted: 'There are serious doubts in my mind that Israel would have come into being if Roosevelt had lived.'[14]

F.D.R.'s successor, Harry S. Truman, had a much more straight-forward commitment to Zionism, part emotional, part calculating. He felt sorry for Jewish refugees. He saw the Jews in Palestine as underdogs. He was also much less sure of the Jewish vote than Roosevelt. For the coming 1948 election, he needed the endorsement of Jewish organizations in such swing-states as New York, Pennsylvania and Illinois. Once the British renounced their mandate, Truman pushed for the creation of a Jewish state. In May 1947 the Palestine problem came before the UN. A special committee was asked to submit a plan. It produced two. A minority recommended a federated binational state. The majority produced a new partition plan: there would be Jewish and Arab states, plus an international zone in Jerusalem. On 29 November 1947, thanks to Truman's vigorous backing, it was endorsed by the General Assembly, 33 votes to 13, with 10 abstentions.

The Soviet Union and the Arab states, followed by the international left in general, later came to believe that the creation of Israel was the work of a capitalist–imperialist conspiracy. But the facts show the reverse. Neither the American State Department nor the British Foreign Office wanted a Jewish state. They foresaw disaster for the West in the area if one were created. The British War Office was equally strong in opposition. So was the US Defense Department. Its Secretary, James Forrestal, bitterly denounced the Jewish lobby: 'No group in this country should be permitted to influence our policy to the point where it could endanger our national security.'[15] The British and American oil companies were even more vehement in opposing the new state. Speaking for the oil interests, Max Thornburg, of Cal-Tex, said that Truman had 'extinguished the moral prestige of America' and destroyed 'Arab faith in her ideals'.[16] It is impossible to point to any powerful economic interest, in either Britain or the United States, which pushed for the creation of Israel. In both countries, the overwhelming majority of her friends were on the left.

Indeed, if there was a conspiracy to create Israel, then the Soviet Union was a prominent member of it. During the war, for tactical reasons, Stalin suspended some aspects of his anti-Semitic policies. He even created a Jewish Anti-Fascist Committee.[17] From 1944, for a brief period, he adopted a pro-Zionist posture in foreign policy (though not in Russia itself). His reason seems to have been that the creation of Israel, which he was advised would be a socialist state, would accelerate the decline of British influence in the Middle East.[18] When Palestine first came before the UN in May 1947, Andrei Gromyko, the Soviet Deputy Foreign Minister, caused surprise by announcing that his government supported the creation of a Jewish state, and by voting accordingly. On 13 October Semyon Tsarapkin, head of the Soviet delegation to the UN, offered members of the Jewish Agency the toast, 'To the future Jewish state', before voting for the partition plan. At the decisive General Assembly vote on 29 November the entire Soviet bloc voted in the Israeli interest, and thereafter the Soviet and American delegations worked closely together on the timetable of British withdrawal. Nor was this all. When Israel declared its independence on 14 May 1948 and President Truman immediately accorded it *de facto* recognition, Stalin went one better and, less than three days later, gave it recognition *de jure*. Perhaps most significant of all was the decision of the Czech government, on Stalin's instructions, to sell the new state arms. An entire airfield was assigned to the task of air-lifting weapons to Tel Aviv.[19]

Timing was absolutely crucial to Israel's birth and survival. Stalin had the Russian–Jewish actor Solomon Mikhoels murdered in January 1948, and this seems to have marked the beginning of an intensely anti-Semitic phase in his policy. The switch to anti-Zionism abroad took longer to develop but it came decisively in the autumn of 1948. By this time, however, Israel was securely in existence. American policy was also changing, as the growing pressures of the Cold War dissolved her mood of post-war idealism and forced Truman to listen more attentively to Pentagon and State Department advice. If British evacuation had been postponed another year, the United States would have been far less anxious to see Israel created and Russia would almost certainly have been hostile. Hence the effect of the terror campaign on British policy was perhaps decisive to the entire enterprise. Israel slipped into existence through a fortuitous window in history which briefly opened for a few months in 1947–8. That too was luck; or providence.

However, if Begin's ruthlessness was responsible for the early British withdrawal, it was Ben Gurion who brought the state into being. He had to take a series of decisions each of which could have produced catastrophe for the Jewish people of Palestine. Once the UN partition vote was taken the Arabs were bent on destroying all the Jewish settlements and began to attack them immediately. Azzam Pasha, secretary-general of the Arab League, said on the radio: 'This will be a war of extermination and a momentous massacre.'[20] The Jewish commanders were confident but their resources were small. By the end of 1947 the Haganah had 17,600 rifles, 2,700 sten-guns, about 1,000 machine-guns and between 20,000 and 43,000 men in various stages of training. It had virtually no armour, heavy guns or aircraft.[21]

The Arabs had collected a Liberation Army of considerable size but with a divided leadership. They also had the regular forces of the Arab states: 10,000 Egyptians, 7,000 Syrians, 3,000 Iraqis, 3,000 Lebanese, plus the 4,500-strong Arab Legion of Transjordan, a formidable force with British officers. By March 1948 over 1,200 Jews had been killed, half of them civilians, in Arab attacks. The Czech arms were beginning to arrive and were deployed over the next month. The British mandate was not due to end until 15 May. But early in April Ben Gurion took what was probably the most difficult decision in his life. He ordered the Haganah on to the offensive to link up the various Jewish enclaves and to consolidate as much as possible of the territory allotted to Israel under the UN plan. The gamble came off almost completely. The Jews occupied Haifa. They opened up the route to Tiberias and the eastern Galilee. They took Safed, Jaffa and Acre. They established the core of the state of Israel and in effect won the war before it started.[22]

Ben Gurion read out the Scroll of Independence on Friday 14 May in the Tel Aviv museum. 'By virtue of our national and intrinsic right,' he said, 'and on the strength of the resolution of the United Nations General Assembly, we hereby declare the establishment of a Jewish state in Palestine, which shall be known as the State of Israel.' A provisional government was formed immediately. Egyptian air raids began that night. The next day, simultaneously, the last British left and the Arab armies invaded. They made little difference, except in one respect. King Abdullah's Arab Legion took the Old City of Jerusalem for him, the Jews surrendering it on 28 May. This meant that Jewish settlements east of the Holy City had to be evacuated. Otherwise the Israelis made further gains.

A month's truce was arranged on 11 June. During it the Arab states heavily reinforced their armies. But the Israelis secured great quantities of heavy equipment, not only from the Czechs but from the French too, who provided it chiefly to anger the British. When the fighting resumed on 9 July, it quickly became apparent that the Israelis were in control. They took Lydda, Ramleh and Nazareth and occupied large areas of territory beyond the partition frontiers. The Arabs agreed to a second truce within ten days. But there were occasional outbreaks of violence, and in mid-October the Israelis launched an offensive to open the road to the Negev settlements. It ended in the capture of Beersheba. By the close of the year the Israeli army was 100,000-strong, and properly equipped. It had established a military paramountcy in the area it has never since lost. Armistice talks were opened in Rhodes on 12 January 1949 and were signed with Egypt (14 February), Lebanon (23 March), Transjordan (3 April) and

Syria (20 July). Iraq made no agreement at all, and the five Arab states remained in a formal state of war with Israel.

The events of 1947–8, which established Israel, also created the Arab–Israeli problem, which endures to this day. It has two main aspects, refugees and frontiers, best considered separately. According to UN figures, 656,000 Arab inhabitants of mandatory Palestine fled from Israeli-held territory: 280,000 to the West Bank of the Jordan, 70,000 to Transjordan, 100,000 to Lebanon, 4,000 to Iraq, 75,000 to Syria, 7,000 to Egypt, and 190,000 to the Gaza Strip (the Israelis put the total figure rather lower, 550,000–600,000). They left for four reasons: to avoid being killed in the fighting, because the administration had broken down, because they were ordered to or misled or panicked by Arab radio broadcasts, and because they were stampeded by an Irgun–Stern Gang massacre at the village of Deir Yassin on 9 April 1948.

The last merits scrutiny because it is relevant to the moral credentials of the Israeli state. From 1920 until this point, the Jews had refrained from terrorist attacks on Arab settlements, though the innumerable Arab ones had sometimes provoked heavy-handed reprisals. When the fighting began in the winter of 1947–8, Deir Yassin, an Arab quarrying village of less than 1,000 people, made a non-aggression pact with the nearby Jerusalem suburb of Givat Shaul. But two Jewish settlements nearby were overrun and destroyed, and the Jewish desire for revenge was strong. The Stern Gang proposed to destroy Deir Yassin to teach the Arabs a lesson. A senior Irgun officer, Yehuda Lapidot, testified: 'The clear aim was to break Arab morale and raise the morale of the Jewish community in Jerusalem, which had been hit hard time after time, especially recently by the desecration of Jewish bodies which fell into Arab hands.'[23] Begin agreed to the operation but said a loudspeaker van must be used to give the villagers a chance to surrender without bloodshed. The local Haganah commander also gave his reluctant approval, but laid down further conditions. There were eighty Irgun and forty Sternists in the raid. The loudspeaker van fell into a ditch and was never used. The Arabs chose to fight and were actually stronger and better armed. The Irgun–Sternists had to send for a regular platoon with a heavy machine-gun and 2-inch mortar, and it was these which ended Arab resistance.

It was at this point that the raiding force moved into the village and went out of control. A Haganah spy who was with them described what followed as 'a disorganized massacre'. The raiders took twenty-three men to the quarry and shot them. An Arab eye-witness said ninety-three others were killed in the village, but other accounts put the figure of those killed as high as 250. Begin, before he knew the details of the battle, sent out an order of the day in the spirit of the Book of Joshua: 'Accept my congratulations on this splendid act of conquest. . . . As at Deir Yassin, so everywhere, we will attack and smite the enemy. God, God, thou hast chosen us for conquest.'[24] News of this atrocity, in exaggerated form, spread quickly and undoubtedly persuaded many Arabs to flee over the next two months. There is no evidence that it was designed to have this effect. But in conjunction with the other factors it reduced the Arab population of the new state to a mere 160,000. That was very convenient.

On the other hand, there were the Jews encouraged or forced to flee from Arab states where, in some cases, Jewish communities had existed for 2,500 years. In 1945 there were over 500,000 Jews living in the Arab world. Between the outbreak of the war on 15 May 1948 and the end of 1967, the vast majority had to take refuge in Israel: 252,642 from Morocco, 13,118 from Algeria, 46,255 from Tunisia, 34,265 from Libya, 37,867 from Egypt, 4,000 from Lebanon, 4,500 from Syria, 3,912 from Aden, 124,647 from Iraq and 46,447 from the Yemen. With a total of 567,654, Jewish refugees from Arab countries were thus not substantially smaller in number than Arab refugees from Israel.[25] The difference in their reception and treatment was entirely a matter of policy. The Israeli government systematically resettled all its refugees as part of its national-home policy. The Arab governments, with the assistance of the UN, kept the Arab refugees in camps, pending a reconquest of Palestine which never came. Hence, as a result of natural increase, there were more Arab refugees in the late 1980s than there had been forty years before.

This contrasting attitude towards refugees itself sprang from a fundamentally different approach towards negotiations. The Jews had been for two millennia an oppressed minority who had never possessed the option of force. They had therefore been habitually obliged to negotiate, often for bare existence, and nearly always from a position of great weakness. Over the centuries they had developed not merely negotiating skills but a philosophy of negotiation. They would negotiate against impossible odds, and they had learned to accept a negotiated status, however lowly and underprivileged, knowing that it could later be improved by further negotiations and their own efforts. The paramountcy of settlement, as opposed to force, was built into their very bones. That was one reason they found it so difficult, even when the evidence became overwhelming, to take in the magnitude of Hitler's evil: it was hard for them to comprehend a man who wanted no settlement at all with them, just their lives.

The Arabs, by contrast, were a conquering race whose sacred writings both inspired and reflected a maximalist position towards other peoples, the despised *dhimmi*. The very concept of negotiation towards a final settlement was to them a betrayal of principle. A truce, an armistice might be necessary and was acceptable because it preserved the option of force for use later. A treaty, on the other hand, appeared to them a kind of surrender. That was why they did not want the refugees resettled because it meant the final disposal of a moral asset. As Cairo Radio put it: 'The refugees are the cornerstone in the Arab struggle against Israel. The refugees are the armaments of the Arabs and Arab nationalism.'[26] Hence they rejected the 1950 UN plan for resettlement without discussion. Over the subsequent quarter century they refused even to receive repeated Israeli proposals for compensation. The result was disastrous for the refugees themselves and their progeny. It was a source of instability for the Arab states also. It came near to destroying Jordan in the 1960s. It did destroy the finely balanced structure of Lebanon in the 1970s and 1980s.

The different approach to negotiating played a still more important part in determining Israel's frontiers. For Jews there were three possible ways of looking at their recreated country: as a national home, as the Promised Land and as the Zionist state. The first can be quickly disposed of. If all the Jews wanted was a place where they could be safe, it might be anywhere: Argentina, Uganda, Madagascar, for instance, were all proposed at one time or another. But it quickly became clear that few Jews were interested in such schemes. The only one with the slightest practical appeal was the El Arish proposal, precisely because it was near Palestine.

So we move on to the second notion: the Promised Land. In one way or another, this had a theoretical appeal to all Jews, secular and religious, except to pious Jews who insisted that any return to Zion must be part of a messianic event, and assimilated Jews who had no intention of returning anywhere. But what exactly was this land? As we have already noted, when God gave it to Abraham he did not define it with any precision.[27] Was it then to consist of the territories the Israelites had actually occupied? If so, at what period? There had in fact been two commonwealths as well as two temples, the Davidic and the Hasmonean. Some Zionists saw (and see) the state as the Third Commonwealth. But to which was it the successor-state? David's kingdom (but not Solomon's) had included Syria. The Hasmoneans had also ruled at one time over a vast territory. Both ancient commonwealths had been mini-empires at their greatest extent, and had included subject people who had been only semi-Jewish or not

Jewish at all. They could scarcely serve as models for a Zionist state whose primary purpose was to provide a national home for Jews. On the other hand there was a strong emotional belief in the Jews' right to claim those parts of Palestine where they had been predominant in antiquity. This found expression in the plan put forward by the Zionists to the Paris Peace Conference in 1919. It gave the Jews the whole coast from Rafah to Sayda and both banks of the Jordan, the eastern frontier running just west of the Damascus–Amman–Hijaz railway.[28] The plan, as expected, was turned down, but its claims lingered on in the programme of Jabotinsky's Revisionists.

We turn then to the Zionist state as such, the territory which in practice Jews could acquire, settle, develop and defend. This empirical approach was the one the main Zionist bodies adopted and which became in practice the policy of the state itself. It was a sensible approach because it offered the widest possible scope to Jewish negotiating skills. It allowed the Jewish leaders to say that they would settle for any frontiers which included the areas occupied by Jews and which were themselves coherent and defensible. Hence at every stage, during the mandate and after, the Jews were flexible and willing to accept any reasonable partition proposal put to them. In July 1937 the Peel Commission Partition Plan offered them only Galilee from Metulla to Afula, and the coastal strip from a point 20 miles north of Gaza up to Acre, the latter being broken by a corridor to a British-held enclave round Jerusalem.[29] The Jews were reluctant but they accepted it. The Arabs, who would have been given three-quarters of Palestine, turned it down without discussion.

At the time of the next partition proposal, by the UN in 1947, settlement had moved on and the plan reflected it. It did not give the Jews Acre and western Galilee, which were then mainly Arab, but it added to the Jewish portion almost the whole of the Negev and part of the Dead Sea area. Whereas Peel had given the Jews only 20 per cent of Palestine, the UN now gave them 50 per cent. It was not the Promised Land by any definition because it excluded Judaea and Samaria, the whole of the West Bank and, above all, Jerusalem itself. But the Jews, however reluctantly, accepted it. Their empirical philosophy was lucidly explained by the former Oxford academic, Abba Eban, who was for many years to be the Foreign Minister and chief negotiator of the new state. The Jews agreed to lose areas of religious and historical significance to them, he said, because there was 'a partitionist implication inherent in the development of Jewish statehood' from the very moment when it became 'a concrete political prospect' – that is, the League mandate. Zionist settlement policy was 'based on the idea of avoiding any conflict with existing demographic realities. The idea was to settle Jews where Arabs were *not* in firm possession.' Since Arab settlements followed ancient Israelite ones, the modern Jews went to the old coastal plain of the Philistines and the valley of Jezreel, which the Arabs had avoided because of malaria. 'The principle of Jewish settlement', said Eban, 'was always empirical and contemporary, never religious and historical.' Hence in the UN negotiations,

we relied on the general premise of a historical connection, but made no claims whatever for the inclusion of particular areas on our side of the Partition boundary on the grounds of ancient connections. Since Hebron was full of Arabs, we did not ask for it. Since Beersheba was virtually empty, we put in a successful claim. The central Zionist thesis was that there existed sufficient room within Eretz Israel for a densely populated Jewish society to be established without displacing Arab populations, and even without intruding upon their deep-rooted social cohesion.[30]

This philosophy led the Jews to accept the UN partition plan even though the state thereby delimited would have been extremely awkward to run and defend. But the Arabs again rejected the plan, which would have given them a Palestinian state, without any discussion at all and immediately sought the arbitration of force. As a result of the war that followed, and the Israeli conquests between June and November 1948, the Israeli state ended with 80 per cent of Palestine and frontiers which, though still awkward, made a state which was workable and could be defended. The Palestinian Arabs ended with no state at all: just the Gaza Strip, and the West Bank run by Jordan.

Despite their earlier experience of Arab unwillingness to negotiate, the Israelis attempted, on the basis of the 1949 armistice lines, to get agreement on permanent frontiers. This would have meant surrendering some territory. That would have been acceptable if, in return, Israel could have secured a final settlement. But such a bargain was never on offer. The Arabs refused direct talks with the Israelis. Various talks conducted through the UN Palestine Conciliation Commission made it clear that the Arabs insisted that Israel retire behind the 1947 UN partition lines (which they had never accepted or recognized) without even, in return, granting the new state recognition. Whereas Israel saw the armistice as a prelude to peace, the Arabs saw it as no more than a truce, and a prelude to war when it should become convenient to them. Moreover, the Arab states were unwilling to keep to the terms of the various armistice agreements. They were used as a protective screen behind which *fedayeen* raids and terrorism could be launched against Israel's citizens, and boycotts and blockades organized against her economy. For the Arabs, armistice was the continuation of war by other means. Hence in a real sense Israel has been at war with most of her Arab neighbours from November 1947 until this day.

This brought about a fundamental reappraisal of the nature of the Zionist state. The secular pioneers had seen it as a pacifist, collectivist Utopia. The religious pioneers had seen it as a holy theocracy. Now both were alike obliged to invest their energies in a maximum-security state. In a sense the development was natural. The modern settlers had always been obliged to put up perimeter fences guarded against Arab marauders. In the inter-war period these had gradually become more elaborate and professional. But what had to be accepted from 1949 onwards, albeit slowly and reluctantly, was that security must become the overriding and permanent priority of the entire state. Not only had the Israelis to devise increasingly elaborate internal security measures to meet the growing sophistication of Arab terrorism, but they also had to adopt a multi-power standard of external defence: their armed forces had to be capable of meeting an assault from all the Arab states at once. These considerations determined the new state's budget; they dominated its external relations.

Indeed, for the first thirty years of its existence, 1948–78, Israel had a constant and sometimes vertiginous struggle for her existence. The armistice proved worthless. In its first seven years, over 1,300 Israelis were murdered during Arab raids and Israel's retaliatory attacks against terrorist bases became increasingly severe. On 20 July 1951 the last of the Arab moderates, King Abdullah of Jordan, was assassinated. On 23 July 1952 a military junta ousted the Egyptian monarchy, leading in turn (25 February 1954) to the populist dictatorship of Gamal Abdul Nasser, dedicated to Israel's destruction. Stalin had broken off relations with Israel in February 1953, a month before he died. From September 1955 onwards, with the signature of the Egyptian–Czech arms agreement, the Soviet bloc began to supply a growing quantity of modern weapons to the Arab forces. With the security this new ally gave him, President Nasser put into motion a plan for the strangulation and extinction of Israel. Though the practice was condemned by the UN Security Council in September 1951, Egypt had always refused Israeli ships the right to use the Suez Canal. From 1956 Nasser denied them access to the Gulf of Aqaba too. In April he signed a military pact with Saudi Arabia and Yemen, in July he seized the Suez Canal and on 25 October he formed a unified military command with Jordan and Syria. Feeling the noose tightening round its neck, Israel launched a pre-emptive strike on 29 October, dropping paratroops to seize the Mitla Pass in Sinai. During the brief war that followed, and in conjunction with Anglo-French forces landed in the Canal Zone, Israel conquered the whole of Sinai, took Gaza, ended the *fedayeen* activities and opened up the sea route to Aqaba.[31]

The Sinai War demonstrated the ability of Israel to preserve its security even against the new Soviet weapons, though its military significance was obscured by Anglo-French involvement. The agreement which followed the end of the fighting was again inconclusive. Israel undertook to withdraw from Sinai provided Egypt did not remilitarize it and UN forces formed a protective *cordon sanitaire*. This arrangement, however unsatisfactory, lasted a decade. But raids and terrorism continued. Syria too was armed by the Soviet bloc. In 1967 Nasser, his forces reorganized and re-equipped, decided to make another attempt. On 15 May he remilitarized Sinai, moving in 100,000 men and armour and ordering out the UN force (which complied). On 22 May he again blockaded Aqaba by closing the Tiran Straits to Israeli shipping. Eight days later, the noose was tightened when King Hussain of Jordan signed a military agreement in Cairo. The same day Iraqi forces took up positions in Jordan. Hence on 5 June the Israelis again felt compelled to launch a pre-emptive strike. That morning they destroyed virtually the entire Egyptian air force on the ground. Jordan and Syria were misled about Israel's success and duly entered the war on Egypt's side. In reply, Israel felt at liberty to remove the (to her) worst anomalies left by the War of Independence. On 7 June she took the Old City, thus securing the whole of Jerusalem as her capital. By the end of the next day she had occupied the entire Left Bank. During the next two days she stormed the Golan Heights in Syria and established positions only 30 miles from Damascus. At the same time she reoccupied all Sinai. As a result of the Six Day War, Israel had obtained defensible frontiers for the first time, as well as the capital and a famous portion of her historic heritage.[32]

Yet this celebrated victory did not bring security. Quite the contrary. It induced a mood of illusory confidence and a false dependence on fixed-line defences such as the so-called Bar Lev Line east of the Suez Canal. Nasser, who had won every public-relations battle and lost every military one, died and was succeeded by a more formidable colleague, Anwar Sadat. To increase his freedom of action Sadat threw out Egypt's Soviet military advisers in July 1972, though this in no way cut Egypt off from Soviet equipment. He dispensed with Nasser's spectacular politico-military alliances with other Arab powers, contenting himself with secret co-ordinations of plans.

Hitherto, Israeli forces had been theoretically inferior. Israel had therefore felt herself obliged, in April 1948, in October 1956 and in June 1967, to attack pre-emptively, with all the tactical advantage of surprise. Now she believed herself superior, and it was Sadat, in concert with the Syrians, who struck without warning on the Day of Atonement or Yom Kippur (6 October) 1973, achieving complete surprise in turn.

Both the Egyptians and the Syrians broke through the Israeli lines. An element of technological surprise in the effectiveness of Arab anti-tank and anti-aircraft missiles enabled them to inflict disturbing losses on Israeli planes and armour. For the first time in the quarter-century of the state's existence, Israel faced the possibility of a major defeat and even of a second holocaust. But the Syrian advance had been stemmed on 9 October; the next day, in response to desperate Israeli pleas, the American President, Richard Nixon, began an emergency airlift of advanced weapons. Two days afterwards the Israeli forces began an audacious counter-attack on Egypt, crossing on to the West Bank of the Canal, and threatening to cut off all the advancing Egyptian forces in Sinai. This was the turning-point and Israel moved swiftly towards a victory as decisive as that of 1967, when a cease-fire came into force on 24 October.[33]

Israel's willingness to accept a cease-fire was dictated more by political and psychological than by military factors. In each of the four wars there was a complete lack of symmetry. The Arab countries could afford to lose many wars. Israel could not afford to lose one. An Israeli victory could not win peace. But an Israeli defeat meant catastrophe. Israel had always regarded Egypt as her most dangerous enemy, the one most likely to deliver the knock-out blow. But Egypt was also the most synthetic of Israel's opponents. Her people were not true Arabs. She was in the struggle to make good her claims to Middle Eastern leadership and to secure prestige rather than from any deep emotional commitment. The Egyptian territory Israel held, however useful (a substantial oilfield was developed there 1967–73), was not part of the historic heritage of the Jews. For all these reasons a peace with Egypt was possible. What prevented it was Egypt's bruised sense of military honour. But this was healed by her initial success in 1973, which time and propaganda could make seem more substantial than it was.

There was another obstacle. Israel had been ruled since its inception by a Labour-dominated coalition whose flexibility on frontiers was expressed by the pragmatic philosophy already summarized in Abba Eban's words. But the Opposition maintained the Jabotinsky maximalist tradition on frontiers. Peace with Egypt would involve heavy Israeli territorial sacrifices, actual and potential. That in turn would require a national consensus. The Opposition would deny it. Hence, when Labour's coalition lost the May 1977 elections and handed over power for the first time to the Revisionists in the shape of Begin's Likud, the change, by a paradox familiar to democratic societies, made peace more likely. Begin, precisely because of his maximalist commitment, was in a position to trade land for security in a manner which no Labour leader since Ben Gurion would have dared.

Sadat, the first Arab realist since Abdullah, recognized this key point. Less than six months after Likud's victory, on 9 November 1977, he offered to negotiate peace terms. The peace process was long, complex and hard. It was stage-managed by President Jimmy Carter and underwritten financially by the generosity of the American taxpayer, an indispensable element. It culminated in a marathon thirteen-day session, beginning on 5 September 1978, at the presidential summer home, Camp David – what Begin characteristically called 'a concentration camp de luxe'. It required a further six months to embody the agreement reached there in a detailed treaty.

The compromise reached was a genuine one; hence it endured. Egypt recognized Israel's right to exist, provided cast-iron guarantees for Israel's southern border, in effect withdrew from the military equation and thus for the first time gave Israel some measure of genuine security. In return Israel handed over Sinai, including its oilfields, air-bases and settlements, all of profound emotional significance to her. She also undertook to negotiate away much of the West Bank and even to make concessions over Jerusalem, in return for a complementary treaty with the Palestinians and the other Arab states. But these last sacrifices were not, in the event, exacted. Camp David offered the Palestinian Arabs their best chance since the UN partition plan of 1947. Once more they threw it away without even attempting to negotiate. That left Israel with Judaea and Samaria, albeit as 'occupied territories' still, rather than internationally recognized freeholds. The treaty, as such historic compromises will, demanded heavy sacrifices from its signatories too. It cost Begin some of his oldest political friends. It cost Sadat, most dangerous-treacherous and courageous-generous of Israel's enemies, his life.[34]

In a historical context, the Israeli–Egyptian peace treaty was of incalculable importance not only in itself but in its timing. From the 1920s, the source of Arab power, both economic and diplomatic, had always been the oilfields of the Persian Gulf and upper Iraq. In the second half of the 1970s this oil power increased dramatically. Demand for oil had been rising faster than supply in the 1960s. In

1973 this trend was radically reinforced by political actions of the Middle Eastern oil states in response to the Yom Kippur War. Oil prices tripled, from $3 a barrel to $10. By the end of 1977 the price had risen to $12.68; in 1979–80 it tripled again, reaching a price of $38.63 a barrel at the end of 1980. By raising Arab oil revenues more than tenfold, the oil-price revolution made available huge sums for Arab arms-purchases and for financing anti-Israeli terrorism. It also increased Arab diplomatic leverage with both Western and Third World nations. France, for instance, built Iraq an advanced nuclear reactor, whose rapidly developing war-potential obliged Israel to destroy it by a bombing raid on 7 June 1981. Some Third World states, in response to Arab pressure, broke off diplomatic relations with Israel. At the UN there was an extraordinary growth in Arab influence. As a result, in 1975 the General Assembly passed a resolution equating Zionism with racialism. The mufti's successor, Yasser Arafat, leader of the main Arab terror group, the Palestine Liberation Organization, was accorded head-of-government status by the UN and by numerous states hitherto friendly to Israel. There was a real danger of Israel being driven into an international ghetto occupied solely by South Africa.

Against this background, the Egyptian peace-treaty and the fact that it was fully implemented on both sides was the great sustaining force of Israel's position on the world scene. Had the Palestinians negotiated seriously at this time, there can be little doubt that Israel would have been obliged to yield most of the West Bank. But the chance was missed in favour of fruitless terrorism and the window of opportunity closed. From 1981 to 1985 the oil price drifted slowly downwards as supply came into balance with demand. By January 1986 it was $25 a barrel and in April that year it went below the $10 mark, less – allowing for inflation – than it had been before the Yom Kippur War. The balance of economic and diplomatic power once more began to shift back in Israel's favour. By this stage, in the late 1980s, Israel had been in possession of the West Bank for twenty years and her frontiers, though 'temporary' in places, had begun to acquire an air of permanence.

Indeed, the underlying assumption beneath the Arab refusal to negotiate, that time was on their side, not Israel's, and the misleading analogy with the medieval Crusader states which they were fond of adducing, were both falsified by the first forty years of Israel's existence. Israel had become a successful maximum-security state without sacrificing her basic aim or freedoms, and while retaining the negotiating flexibility and empiricism of her founding fathers. Time had proved to be on the side not of the Arabs but of the Israelis. Moreover, the very fact that the Arabs continued to prefer the option of war encouraged the habit of thinking, to be found even among Israeli empiricists, in terms of Israel's historic frontiers. The official *Government Year Book 1951–2* had noted: 'The state has been established in only a portion of the Land of Israel.' There were many Jews who saw Israel's repeated victories as a moral mandate for wider boundaries. For pious Jews it was the hand of providence, for secular Jews a form of manifest destiny. In 1968 the Sephardi Chief Rabbi argued that it was a religious obligation not to return the newly conquered territories. The same year the Kibbutz Dati, representing the religious collectives, intoned a prayer for Independence Day: 'Extend the boundaries of our land, just as Thou hast promised our forefathers, from the river Euphrates to the river of Egypt. Build your holy city, Jerusalem, capital of Israel; and there may your temple be established as in the days of Solomon.' Dr Harold Fisch, rector of Bar-Ilan University, insisted: 'there is only one nation to whom the land belongs in trust and by covenant promise, and that is the Jewish people. No temporary demographic changes can alter this basic fact which is the bedrock of the Jewish faith; just as one wife does not have two husbands so one land does not have two sovereign nations in possession of it.'[35] The 1967 victory also produced a multi-party movement known as the Land of Israel, which argued that it was not within the moral authority of the Israeli state, representing only Israeli citizens, to give up any conquered portion of the Promised Land, since this was the property of the entire Jewish people, and must be preserved for their eventual ingathering or Aliyah. This form of neo-Zionism, which could quote in its support from Herzl and Ben Gurion as well as Jabotinsky, argued that only one-fifth of world Jewry was yet settled in Israel. The ultimate aim of Zionism must be the return of the entire nation; and to accommodate them the entire land was required.[36]

This of course was hyperbole and ideological politics of the kind which, in practice, Israel always rejected. On the other hand, in some respects the Israeli state was constitutionally idealistic. It accepted the inescapable duty to receive as an immigrant any Jew who wished to come as an *oleh*, defined as 'a Jew immigrating to Israel for settlement'. This was the primary purpose of its creation. It was so laid down in the original Basel Programme of 1897, in Article 6 of the 1922 mandate, in the Declaration of Independence, 14 May 1948, and formally enacted in the Law of Return of 1950.[37] Section 4B of the Law defined a Jew as 'a person who was born of a Jewish mother or has become converted to Judaism and who is not a member of another religion'. But settling in practice who was a Jew was not easy. It was one of the most vexed problems of Jewish history, from the time of the Samaritans onward. With the growth of secularism it became even more difficult. In modern Europe Jews were often defined not by themselves but by the anti-Semites. Karl Lueger used to say: 'A Jew is anyone I say is a Jew.' Most modern Jews agreed that a Jew was someone who felt himself Jewish. But that was not good enough for the courts. Halakhic law insisted on the religious element. This meant that in Israel the offspring of a mixed marriage where the mother was non-Jewish, though an Israeli citizen, speaking Hebrew, educated in the spirit of Jewish history, and serving in the Israeli army, could not legally be called a Jew without going through a specific process of conversion. On the other hand, halakhic law laid down that even a converted Jew remained a Jew. The inability to achieve a purely secular definition of a Jew led to cabinet crises and litigation. When a born Jew, Oswald Rufeisen, who had converted and become a Carmelite as 'Brother Daniel', sought entry under the Law of Return, the case went to the Supreme Court (*Rufeisen* v. *Minister of the Interior*, 1962). Judge Silberg (for the majority) held that the Law of Return was a secular enactment. For its purposes, a Jew was defined not according to halakhah but as Jews in general understood the term: 'The answer to this question is in my opinion sharp and clear – a Jew who has become a Christian is *not* deemed a Jew.'[38]

But in the overwhelming majority of cases there was no problem of definition. Israel was thrown open to the *oleh* from her inception. She had to receive not only the refugees from Arab countries but all the Jewish DPs of Europe who wished to come. In Israel's first three and a half years a rush of 685,000 immigrants, 304,000 from Europe, doubled the population. There was a second great wave of immigrants (160,000) in 1955–7, a third (215,000) in 1961–4. The Six Day War stimulated the immigration figures yet again. Jews from Arab lands were balanced by Jews from Europe, nearly 600,000 European Jews reaching Israel in the twenty-two years 1948–70. The largest group came from Rumania (229,779), the next from Poland (156,011), but there were big contingents from Hungary (24,255), Czechoslovakia (20,572), Bulgaria (48,642), France (26,295), Britain (14,006) and Germany (11,522). There were also 58,288 Jews from Turkey, over 60,000 from Persia and about 20,000 from India. Russia continued to be the great reservoir of would-be immigrants, but the numbers who actually came from there depended on fluctuations in Soviet policy. In the period 1948–70, only 21,391 Jews reached Israel from Russia, but in the four years 1971–4 more than 100,000 were released.[39]

In its first quarter-century, largely through immigration, Israel's population rose from the initial 650,000 to well over three million. Receiving, housing, educating and employing the new arrivals became a priority second only to basic security and, after defence, the biggest item in Israel's budget. Getting Jews out of what were termed 'lands of stress' sometimes involved special efforts, such as the sea- and air-lift which brought 43,000 Jews out of the Yemen in a single year, June 1949–June 1950, or the secret air-lift of 20,000 Falasha Jews from Ethiopia in the mid-1980s.

In the business of blending this new national community together the two most important instruments were the army and Hebrew. The Israel Defence Force, thanks to Arab intransigence, succeeded the kibbutz as the most characteristic product of the Zionist state, and was most influential in transforming the world's vision of the Jew. It also became the means whereby the children of immigrants achieved emotional equality within society. The acceptance of Hebrew was an even more remarkable achievement. Until late in the nineteenth century no one at all spoke Hebrew as his or her first language. Indeed as a spoken language it had been succeeded by Aramaic (except for liturgical purposes) in late Biblical times. It remained of course the primary written language of Judaism. Jewish scholars meeting in Jerusalem found they could speak it to each other, though the varying Ashkenazi and Sephardi pronunciations made understanding difficult. The Zionist state might easily have spoken German or Yiddish, both of which would have proved disastrous. Eliezer ben Yehuda (1858–1922), who went to Palestine in 1881, made the adoption of Hebrew possible by his vigorous campaigning. When he and his wife, born Deborah Jonas, arrived in Jaffa, he insisted that henceforth they spoke only Hebrew to each other. Theirs was the first Hebrew-speaking household in the country (indeed in the world) and Ben Yehuda's first son, Ben Zion, was the first Hebrew-speaking child since antiquity. Hebrew succeeded as a modern tongue, where many other linguistic revivals, such as Irish, failed, partly because Judaism, working in Hebrew, had always dealt in infinite detail with practical matters: work, housing, cooking, lighting and heating, travelling and living. Of course its main power was as a language of prayer, but it was also a language of conduct. Once people forced themselves to speak it they found it met the needs of everyday life remarkably quickly and soon displayed an organic capacity to grow. Its development as an official language of government was dramatically assisted by the British decision (1919) to give it equal status with English and Arabic under the mandate. The rival claims of German were destroyed by Hitler, and of Yiddish, spoken by over ten million Jews in the late 1930s, by the mass immigration of Sephardi Jews from Arab countries after 1945. Hebrew worked because the new army spoke it. The army worked because it spoke Hebrew. Thus Israel went against all the laws of modern linguistic sociology and made the revival into a self-sustaining process.

There was some bullying, especially over names. Of course since Abraham's time Jews had been inured to name changing, in order to make religious, patriotic or cultural points. Ben Yehuda began the new Hebrew practice, changing his own name from Perelman. Many of the settlers in the first three Aliyahs followed suit at the same time as they began to learn Hebrew. Thus David Gruen, or Green, became David Ben Gurion. Later an element of compulsion was added. There were poignant ironies in this. In the nineteenth century German- and Austrian-ruled Jews had been forced to Teutonize their names. Hitler reversed the process. In 1938 German Jews were forbidden to change their family names and forced to resume Jewish ones. For given names, Jews were limited to 'official Jewish names', 185 for men, 91 for women. These excluded certain Biblical names fancied by German non-Jews, such as Ruth, Miriam, Joseph and David. Jews with forbidden names had to assume in addition the name Israel if male, Sarah if female. The Vichy regime in France and the Quisling regime in Norway passed similar laws. But none of this deterred Ben Gurion, whose vigorous, indeed belligerent, support for Hebrew was one of the factors that ensured its success. Hearing that a visit to South Africa had been paid by an Israeli ship commanded by a Captain Vishnievsky, he laid it down that from then on 'no officer will be sent abroad in a representative capacity unless he bears a Hebrew family name'.[40]

The Israeli ruling establishment followed Ben Gurion's lead. Moshe Sharett changed his name from Shertok, Eliahu Elath from Epstein, Levi Eshkol from Shkolnic. A Commission for Hebrew Nomenclature was set up and produced lists of Hebrew names, together with rules for changing, for instance, Portnoy into Porat, Teitelbaum into Agosi, Jung into Elem, Novick into Hadash and Wolfson into Ben Zev. The iniquities of malevolent Austrian bureaucrats were expunged by changing Inkdiger (lame) into Adir (strong) and Lügner (liar) into Amiti (truth-teller). Given names were Hebraized also. Pearl became Margalit, for instance. Jews proved less willing to change their given than their surnames. Goldie Myerson, in accordance with Israeli Foreign Office practice, changed her surname to Meir when she became Foreign Minister in 1959, but she refused to switch to Zehavah, simply turning Goldie into Golda. The need for Hebrew given names led to a scouring of the Bible for novelties. Thus Yigal, Yariv, Yael, Avner, Avital and Hagit came into fashion, and even Omri and Zerubavel. There were also invented names: Balfura after Balfour, Herzlia after Herzl. According to Rabbi Benziob Kaganoff, the leading expert on Jewish names, the Biblical revival led to deliberate defiance of many Judaic taboos, especially the ban on Biblical names before Abraham. Israelis broke this by calling their children Yuval, Ada, Peleg and, above all, Nimrod, referred to in the Talmud as one of the five wickedest men in the entire history of mankind. Other 'wicked' names which became fashionable were Reuma, Deliah, Ataliah and Tzipor. Begin himself was called after Menachem, of whom the Bible said: 'And he did that which was evil in the sight of the Lord.'

Hebrew was not just a binding force. It prevented Israel from developing a language problem, the curse of so many nations, especially new ones. This was fortunate, for Israel had many other fundamental fissures. The fact that, in the Warsaw ghetto in late 1942, the Jewish political parties could argue bitterly on how they were to resist the Nazis gave some indication of the depth of the ideological divisions, all of which (and more) were endemic in Israel too. The basic division between the Labour Party (sometimes called Mapai), with its Histadrut trade union wing and its Haganah military arm, and the Revisionists, who in other incarnations were called Herut, Gahal and finally Likud, had been envenomed (as we have noted on page 446) by the Arlosoroff murder in 1933 and its aftermath. They worsened still further as a result of a shocking episode during the War of Independence. Ben Gurion had feared all along that Begin, who rejected the UN partition frontiers, would fight to enlarge them if the Irgun was allowed to operate as a separate force. Begin agreed to merge Irgun with the national army on 1 June 1948 but he maintained his own arms supply. When, during the first truce, the Irgun arms-ship *Altalena* arrived off Tel Aviv, the government denied him its contents. Ben Gurion told the cabinet: 'There are not going to be two states and there are not going to be two armies. . . . We must decide whether to hand over power to Begin or tell him to cease his separatist activities. If he does not give in we shall open fire.'[41] The cabinet instructed the Defence Minister to enforce the law of the land. Fighting broke out on the beach and Begin scrambled aboard to protect his arms. Yigal Allon, commander in chief of the Haganah's full-time force, the Palmach, and his deputy Yitzhak Rabin, directing operations from the Ritz Hotel, decided to shell the ship and sink it. Begin was forced to swim ashore, fourteen Irgun men were killed, and it was the effective

end of the organization. Begin called the Labour coalition 'a government of criminals, tyrants, traitors and fratricides'.[42] Ben Gurion
called Begin simply 'Hitler'.

Thereafter the Labour Party and its allies ruled Israel until 1977.
With the kibbutzim, the Histadrut, the Haganah and their dominance
within the Jewish Agency, they had formed the establishment under
the mandate. After Independence they continued to form the
establishment, controlling the armed forces, the civil service and,
through the trade union holdings, Israeli industry. Israel inherited
from the mandate many British political, constitutional and legal
institutions. But in one respect it was quite unlike Britain. It drew from
the socialist parties of eastern Europe the notion of the party becoming
the state. In this respect it was more like the Soviet Union. The
distinction between professional politicians and professional civil
servants, so salient to the British style of parliamentary democracy,
scarcely existed in Israel. Allon went from the Palmach command to
become a minister and Deputy Prime Minister. Rabin was Chief of
Staff of the IDF and later Prime Minister. Two other IDF chiefs,
Haim Bar-Lev and David Elazar, also came up through the Labour
movement. Moshe Dayan, the most celebrated of all the IDF
commanders, rose through the Mapai youth movement, or Zeirim, as
did Shimon Peres, who ran the Defence Ministry bureaucracy under
Ben Gurion and in time became Prime Minister himself. A man might
be in turn a member of the Knesset, a general, a cabinet minister, an
ambassador and head of the state radio. Israel was a party state though
never a one-party state. The most important decisions were not
necessarily taken inside the cabinet. Civil service appointments were
based, as a rule, on a party spoils system which distributed them
according to electoral strength. Each party tended to decide who
served and who did what and who was promoted in the ministries it
controlled. The Labour movement as a whole formed an agricultural–industrial settlement complex embracing much of the arms
industry, housing, health insurance and distribution. It dominated,
through its own machinery, huge areas of what would normally be
government functions: labour relations, education, public health and
immigration. Much of this arose through the way the land was
settled under the mandate.[43] In its post-Independence structure Israel
had some of the weaknesses of a typical Third World ex-colony which
came into being through resistance, a dominant nationalist movement, even terrorism, and then transformed itself into a regime.

The multi-party structure preserved democracy. But parties were in
constant osmosis, splitting, regrouping, renaming themselves, form-

ing *ad hoc* coalitions. Between 1947 and 1977 Mapai–Labour never fell below 32.5 per cent of the vote but never rose over 40 per cent. The result was a high degree of instability within the general structure of Labour movement dominance, with difficult coalition bargaining after each election and often between elections. Ben Gurion was Prime Minister 1948–63, except for a brief period 1953–5 when he made way for Moshe Sharett. Many of his most arbitrary dismissals or appointments – of generals, for instance – were in reaction to internal political manoeuvres. His long vendetta against Pinhas Lavon, a Defence Minister whom Ben Gurion held responsible for a costly intelligence fiasco in Egypt, was prompted as much by internal party as by public factors. Parties were interests as well as ideological entities. They recruited accordingly, especially among the immigrants. This went back to the inter-war period when land settlement was largely a party function. In the early 1930s there was an inter-party agreement for the division of scarce land. After Independence there was really enough land for all with agricultural leanings, so the party officials toured the transit camps to get people. There were unofficial carve-ups on an ethnic–religious basis. The Rumanians, Bulgarians and Yugoslavs, for instance, went to the secular parties (chiefly Mapai), the North Africans to the religious group, Mizrachi, which formed part of the coalition. Thanks to the skill of Mapai's Yemeni agents, the party established a virtual monopoly over Yemeni immigrants, though after a Mizrachi protest its share was reduced to 60–65 per cent. Mapai and Mizrachi also did a deal over 100,000 Moroccan immigrants, Mapai organizing the emigration from the South Atlas area, Mizrachi from the North Atlas. A revolt of some of the Moroccans, who resented being owned and indoctrinated, brought this arrangement into the open in 1955.[44]

Weizmann hated all this aspect of Zionist politics. When the state was formed he became its first president but lost the battle to secure presidential powers on American lines. Hence he was not in a position to uphold the state–public interest against the party. The job was left to Ben Gurion and, to do him justice, he tried to fight the party system. He had been a professional party activist all his life and he remained, to the last, an aggressive political bruiser. But as Prime Minister he did his best to effect a separation between party and state, to rescue the state from the party grip, to fight the Labour movement machine (most of which he had created himself) over policy, appointments, and not least the investigation of abuses. He wrenched the Prime Minister's office, the Defence Ministry, the army and the schools out of the party's possession. But he failed with the health system, which the

Histadrut in effect retained. In the end he grew disgusted with his political colleagues, created a new party of his own (1965) and, when it failed, retired to an angry internal exile at his kibbutz of Sedeh Boker.[45]

Unlike Herzl, Weizmann and even Jabotinsky, Ben Gurion did not see himself as a European but as a Jewish Middle Easterner. He placed his trust in the *sabras*, the Israeli-born natives of pioneer stock, who would transform Israel from a European colony into a genuine Asian state, albeit one which was unique. He was a Moses with a grim message, offering his people blood and tears, toil and sweat. 'This is not a nation, not yet,' he said in 1969 at the end of his life.

It is an exiled people still in the desert longing for the flesh-pots of Egypt. It cannot be considered a nation until the Negev and Galilee are settled, until millions of Jews emigrate to Israel and until moral standards necessary to the ethical practice of politics and the high values of Zionism are sustained. This is neither a mob nor a nation. It is a people still chained to their Exilic past – redeemed but not fulfilled.[46]

Yet the animating spirit of the Labour movement remained European socialism. It was a party of city intellectuals whose kibbutzim were their weekend cottages. It was university-educated, culturally middle class. To the workers, especially to the Afro-Asian Sephardi immigrants, it turned a face of well-meaning condescension, patiently explaining what was good for them, rather as Rosa Luxemburg had once tried to lecture the German proletariat. They were the natural aristocrats of the new state, or perhaps one should call them a secular cathedocracy. Gradually an illuminating sartorial distinction appeared between the government and the opposition. Labour statesmen affected a rustic informality of open-necked shirts. Begin's Likud sported smart suits and ties. It was the difference between a socialist intelligentsia and instinctive populists.

After Ben Gurion's retirement the Labour movement's dependence on European-stock support, a diminishing asset, became more pronounced. By contrast the new arrivals from the Arab territories drifted towards the opposition. This dated back to the inter-war period. Jabotinsky had always drawn a following from the Sephardis of the Levant. He learned to speak Ladino. He stuck up for the Sephardi pronunciation of Hebrew. Begin fell effortlessly into this tradition. As a Polish Jew, one of a tiny remnant, he had a natural affinity of circumstances with Jews who had been brutally expelled from Arab lands. Like them, he felt no need to apologize for being in Israel. He shared their hatred of the Arabs. He too put Jewish interests before any other consideration, by the moral right of suffering. Like the oriental Jews, he regarded the notion that the Arabs had the choice of granting or withholding Israel's right to exist as an insult to the dead. 'We were granted the right to exist by the God of our fathers,' he insisted, 'at the glimmer of the dawn of human civilization nearly 4,000 years ago. For that right, which has been sanctified in Jewish blood from generation to generation, we have paid a price un-exampled in the annals of the nations.'[47] In strict contrast to the Labour establishment, he and the oriental Jews had a common and precious characteristic: a complete absence of any feelings of guilt.

Labour's grip on the regime was immensely strong and only slowly loosened. Begin must have been the only party leader in history to lose eight elections in a row and retain his post. But under successive Prime Ministers, Levi Eshkol (1963–9), Golda Meir (1969–74), Yitzhak Rabin (1974–7), Labour's electoral support gradually declined. Towards the end of its long rule, and not surprisingly, granted its refusal to heed Ben Gurion's warning and separate party from state, there were several major scandals. Hence at the May 1977 elections Labour at last lost its paramountcy. It dropped 15 per cent of its vote and emerged with only thirty-two seats. Begin's Likud had forty-three and he had no real difficulty in forming a coalition government. He won the following election too in June 1981. After his retirement Likud fought the Labour movement to a draw in 1984, leading to an arrangement in which a Labour–Likud coalition, with alternating premiers, governed the country. Thus Israel eventually acquired a two-party system of a kind and the dangers of a permanent one-party regime were avoided.

At bottom, however, the differences between Israel's political parties, however deep and poisoned by violent historical events, concerned secular matters and thus in the end always yielded to pragmatic compromises. More serious was the chasm between the secularity of the Zionist state and the religiosity of Judaism itself. The problem was not new. The demands of the Law and the demands of the world produced tensions in any Jewish society. They broke to the surface in open conflict immediately Jews were given charge of their own affairs. That was why many pious Jews believed it was preferable for Jews to live under gentile sovereignty. But this left them at the mercy of gentile goodwill. The experience of modern times showed that it could not be relied upon. The new Zion had been conceived in response to nineteenth-century anti-Semitism and born in the immediate aftermath of the Holocaust. It was not a blueprint for a Jewish theocracy but a political and military instrument for Jewish survival. In short the situation was fundamentally the same as in the prophet Samuel's day. Then the Israelites were in danger of extermination by the Philistines and had turned to monarchy to stay alive. Samuel had accepted the change with sorrow and misgivings because he saw clearly that the monarchy, or as we would say the state, was in irreconcilable conflict with rule by the Law. In the end he was proved right. The Law was defied, God angered, and the Babylonian Exile followed. The Second Commonwealth ran into exactly the same difficulties and likewise perished. Thus the Jews went into the diaspora. It was the essence of Judaism that the exile would be ended by a metaphysical event, in God's good time, not by a political solution devised by man. The Zionist state was simply a new Saul. To suggest it was a modern form of the Messiah was not only wrong but blasphemous. As the great Jewish scholar Gershom Scholem warned, it could only produce another false Messiah: 'The Zionist ideal is one thing and the messianic ideal another, and the two do not touch except in pompous phraseology at mass rallies, which often infuse into our youth a spirit of new Shabbateanism which must fail.'[48] It is true that the Zionists, who were mostly non-religious or even anti-religious, invoked the aid of Judaism. They had no alternative. Without Judaism, without the idea of the Jews as a people united by faith, Zionism was nothing, just a cranky sect. They invoked the Bible too. They drew from it all kinds of political morals, campaign rhetoric and idealistic appeals to youth. Ben Gurion used it as a guide to military strategy. But that was merely an eastern European form of the Jewish enlightenment. Zionism had no place for God as such. For Zionists, Judaism was just a convenient source of national energy and culture, the Bible no more than a State Book. That was why from the start most religious Jews regarded Zionism with suspicion or outright hostility and some (as we have noted) believed it was the work of Satan.

But just as Samuel agreed to anoint Saul, so religious Jews had to recognize the existence of Zionism and take up attitudes towards it. There were several streams of thought, each modified over time. All were Orthodox. Reform Judaism played no part in the settlement of Palestine and the creation of Israel. The first Reform synagogue was not built in Jerusalem until 1958. But Orthodoxy varied in the degree to which it acknowledged Zionism. Just as Zionists used Judaism to create their state, so some pious Jews believed the Zionist national spirit could be exploited to bring Jews back to Judaism. Abraham Isaac Kook (1865–1935), appointed European Chief Rabbi with Zionist support, took the view that Torah observance could be fuelled by the new patriotic spirit among Jews provided observant Jews organized themselves. So after the 10th Zionist congress (1911) decided in favour of secular as opposed to Torah schools, the first religious political party, the Mizrachi, came into being to fight for the Torah within Zionism. Hence it worked with the Zionists throughout the mandate and was a partner in government from the inception of the state. It was instrumental in avoiding a complete breach between secular and religious Jews in Israel but it tended to be more of an intermediary between the two camps than a religious force in itself.

In response to the 'treason' of Mizrachi, the Orthodox sages founded the Agudist movement in 1912. It did not become organized and active until the British took over Palestine. Under Turkish rule the old system of delegating power to minorities through their religious leaders had been maintained, and this naturally favoured the Orthodox. But under Article 4 of the 1922 mandate, the British handed the political representation of all Jews to the Zionists. Their National Council was firmly in secular hands, and it simply syphoned off the religious aspects of its work to the Mizrachi. In response the Agudists formed in 1923 a mass movement, run by a 'Council of Great Men of the Torah', whose branches trained observant Jews to exercise their votes in favour of its nominees. So a second religious party developed. In eastern Europe it was extremely powerful, with its own press and lobbies, and remained strongly anti-Zionist. But in Palestine it was forced to compromise after the rise of Hitler set up a panic demand for immigrant visas. These all went through the Zionist Jewish Agency, which also controlled the central funds to finance new settlement. The truth is, like the Israelites faced with the Philistines, Agudah did not know how to maintain its principles in the face of Hitlerism. Might not the Balfour Declaration be a divinely ordained mode of escape? In 1937 one of its leaders, Issac Breuer, a grandson of the famous Rabbi Hirsch, asked the Council of Great Men a formal question: did the Balfour Declaration impose a divinely ordained task on the Jews to build a state, or was it a 'satanic contrivance'? They could not agree on an answer so he worked one out for himself, against the background of the Holocaust, which produced still more compelling reasons for coming to terms with Zionism. Breuer's eventual argument, that the state was Heaven's gift to martyred Israel and could be 'the beginning of the Redemption' provided it was developed under guidance from the Torah, became the basis of Agudah's ideology.[49]

Hence when the state was about to be founded, Agudah demanded that it should have a Torah legal basis. This was rejected. The Jewish Agency wrote to Agudah, 29 April 1947: 'The establishment of the state requires the confirmation of the UN and this will be impossible without a guarantee of freedom of conscience in the state for all its citizens and without it being made clear that it is not the intention to establish a theocratic state.' The state had to be secular. On the other hand the Agency agreed to bow to the religious viewpoint on the Sabbath, food laws and marriage, and to allow full religious freedom in the schools. This compromise made it possible for Agudah to belong to the Provisional Council of Government at the inception of the state and, as a member of the United Religious Front, to form parts of governing coalitions 1949–52. The Agudah viewpoint was set out as follows (10 October 1952):

> The world was created for the sake of Israel. It is the duty and merit of Israel to maintain and fulfil the Torah. The place where Israel is destined to live and, therefore, to maintain the Torah is Israel. This means that the *raison d'être* of the world is the establishment of the regime of the Torah in the land of Israel. The foundation of this ideal has been laid. There are now Jews living in their homeland and fulfilling the Torah. But completion has not yet been attained, for all Israel does not yet live in its land and [not even] all Israel is yet fulfilling the Torah.[50]

In short, Agudah pledged itself to use Zionism to complete the ingathering and transform the result into a theocracy.

Just as Mizrachi's compromises produced Agudah's, so Agudah's in turn produced a rigorist group which called itself the Guardians of the City ('Neturei Karta'). This broke away from Agudah in 1935, opposed the foundation of the state root-and-branch, boycotted elections and all other state activities, and declared that it would rather Jerusalem were internationalized than run by Jewish apostates. The group was comparatively small and to the secular mind extreme. But the whole history of the Jews suggests that rigorous minorities tend to become triumphant majorities. Like Judaism itself, moreover, its members exhibited (granted their initial premise) strong logical consistency. The Jews were 'a people whose life is regulated by a supernatural divine order ... not dependent on normal political, economic and material successes or failures'. The Jews were not 'a nation like any other nation', subject to the factors 'which cause all other nations to rise and fall'.[51] Hence the creation of the Zionist state was not a Jewish re-entry into history, a Third Commonwealth, but the start of a new and far more dangerous Exile, since 'full licence has now been given to tempt through the success of the wicked'. They frequently quoted the statement of a group of Hungarian rabbis who, on their arrival at Auschwitz, acknowledged the justice of their punishment from God for their too feeble opposition to Zionism. The

Zionist masqueraders, pretending to represent the people of Israel, were incinerating Jewish souls, whereas Hitler's ovens only burned their bodies and released their souls for eternal life. They deplored alike the Sinai and the Six Day Wars as calculated, by their glamorous success, to lure Jews to Zionism and so to eternal destruction. Moreover, such victories, being the work of Satan, would merely culminate in colossal defeat. The Guardians rejected the 'deliverance and protection' of Zionism, together with its wars and conquests:

We do not approve of any hatred or hostility and above all any fighting or war in any form against any people, nation or tongue, since our Holy Torah has not commanded this of us in our Exile, but the reverse. If, through our many sins, we are apparently joined in the destiny of these rebels [against God], Heaven forbid! All we can do is to pray to the Holy One, blessed be He, that He may release us from their destiny and deliver us.

The Guardians saw themselves as a 'remnant' who 'refused to bow the knee to Baal' as in 'the time of Elijah', or to 'dine at Jezebel's table'. Zionism was 'a rebellion against the King of Kings' and it was implicit in their theology that the Jewish state would end in a catastrophe worse than the Holocaust.

Hence from its inception the secular Zionist state faced a tripartite religious opposition: from within the government coalition, from outside the coalition but within the Zionist consensus, and from outside the consensus but within the country. The opposition took an infinite variety of forms, from the childish to the violent: sticking stamps on letters upside down and omitting 'Israel' from the address; tearing up identity cards; boycotting elections; demonstrations; full-scale riots. The Israeli state, like its Hellenistic and Roman predecessors, faced a section of the population, especially in Jerusalem, easily and often unpredictably outraged by minor and unconsidered government decisions. As a rule, however, religious power expressed itself by fierce bargaining within the Knesset and especially within the cabinet. In Israel's first four governments no less than five cabinet crises were provoked by religious issues: in 1949 over importing forbidden food, in February 1950 over the religious education of Yemeni children in transit camps, in October 1951 and again in September 1952 on the conscription of girls from Orthodox homes, and in May 1953 over schools. This pattern continued for the first forty years of Israel's existence, religion proving a far greater source of coalition disharmony than differences over ideology, defence or foreign affairs.

The Jewish religion being rich in strict moral theology, the area of conflict was very wide. Thus, on the Sabbath, which was given legal and constitutional status, there are thirty-nine principal and many subsidiary categories of forbidden work, including riding or travelling in a vehicle, writing, playing an instrument, telephoning, turning on a light or touching money. Moreover, the commonest of Judaic codes states that 'everyone who openly desecrates the Sabbath is like a non-Jew in all respects, his touch causes wine to be forbidden, the bread that he bakes is like the bread of a non-Jew, and his cooking is like that of a non-Jew'.[52] Hence the Sabbath law, with its knock-on effect, raised serious problems in the armed forces, the civil service and the huge public and collective sector of industry and agriculture. There were bitter battles over Sabbath milking of cows in kibbutzim and TV broadcasting, massive legislative enactments and conflicts of bye-laws. Thus buses ran in Haifa but not Tel Aviv; cafés were open in Tel Aviv but not in Haifa; Jerusalem banned both. There was another cabinet crisis over El-Al, the state airline, flying on the Sabbath. There was an even more protracted struggle within the government over the serving of non-kosher food on the state shipping-line, the food laws being a fertile field for political rows. Hotels and restaurants needed a 'certificate of correctness' from the rabbinate. Under a law of 1962 pig-farming was banned except in Christian Arab areas near Nazareth or for scientific purposes; and in 1985 a legislative campaign began to ban the sale and distribution of pork products also. Government and rabbis alike examined the credentials of the East Indonesia Babirusa hog, declared by its breeders to be a mammal, have hooves and chew the cud. There were cabinet rows over autopsies and over burials in consecrated ground.

Education raised immense complexities. Under the mandate there were four kinds of Jewish school: General Zionist (secular), Histadrut (secular–collective), Mizrachi (Torah–secular) and Agudah (Torah only). The 1953 Unified Education Act conflated these into two types: government–secular and government–religious schools. Agudah withdrew its schools from the system, but found it lost its government grants if it failed to devote sufficient time to secular subjects. Secularists complained that Agudah schools devoted eighteen periods out of thirty-two a week to Bible, Talmud and Hebrew (girls getting more Bible, less Talmud, than boys), at the expense of science, geography and history. Religious Jews complained that state schools gave only eight out of thirty-two to religion, three of which were Hebrew, and that the Bible was taught in a secular spirit, as myth, except for certain bits presented as early Zionist history.[53] In the late 1950s, a muddled cabinet compromise plan, to promote 'Jewish consciousness' in secular schools and 'national–Israel consciousness' in religious schools, led to more trouble.[54] In 1959 there were riots in three places against secular propaganda among the children of Orthodox orientals, one of whose rabbis complained bitterly:

[They] raised the youth that was lacking in wisdom to the heights, and clothed them with pride, while casting in the dust the elders who had acquired wisdom. They taught the child at school that here – in the land of Israel! – there was no need to observe the commandments of the Torah. When the boy came home from school and his parents told him to pray, he answered that the teacher said it was unnecessary or that the instructor had called it nonsense. When the rabbi came and told the boys to observe the Sabbath, they would not listen to him because the club was organizing a football match or the car was waiting to take them to the beach . . . if the Rabbi pleaded and wept, they laughed in his face, because that was what the instructor had ordered. . . . Sages of the Torah were thrust into a corner while boys rose to greatness because they held party cards.[55]

The Orthodox were also outraged over the way in which many institutions broke the ancient rules over segregation of the sexes. Near centres of Orthodoxy there were angry scenes over dance-halls and mixed bathing. Over the conscription of girls into the army the Council of the Great Men stigmatized the law as one to be defied even at the risk of death. That was one of many battles the religious element won.

They also won on the central issue of marriage. The secular state of Israel was obliged to forego the institution of civil marriage. It imposed Orthodox law even on secular unions, under the provisions of Sections 1 and 2 of the Rabbinical Courts Jurisdiction (Marriage and Divorce) Law of 1953. Secularist members of the Knesset voted for the law because otherwise Israel would gradually have split into two communities which could not intermarry. But the law led to hard cases and protracted litigation, involving not only non-Jews and secularized Jews but Reform rabbis and their converts, since the Orthodox rabbinates enjoyed the sole right to recognize conversions and would not accept Reform ones. The Orthodox marriage and divorce experts, quite legitimately from their point of view, subjected entire categories of Jewish immigrants to the strictest tests. Thus in 1952 the divorce practices of 6,000 Bene Israels (Jews from Bombay) were scrutinized as irregular (though eventually validated) and the marriages of the Falasha Jews from Ethiopia were queried in 1984.

There were many bitter disputes over remarriage and divorce. Deuteronomy 25:5 imposes levirate marriage on a childless widow and the brother of the deceased husband. The obligation is ended by the *halizah* or refusal of the brother-in-law. But if he is a minor the widow must wait. If he is deaf and dumb and cannot say, 'I do not wish to take her', she may not remarry. This case actually occurred in 1967 in Ashdod; moreover, the deaf and dumb man was already married. So the rabbinate arranged a bigamous marriage and supervised the divorce the next day.[56] Hard cases also arose when one party to a marriage refused a divorce. If the refusal came from the woman, a divorce became difficult but if it came from the man it was impossible. In a 1969 case, for instance, a husband was sentenced to fourteen years in prison for six indecent assaults and three rapes. The wife sued for a divorce, the man refused and the couple remained married under rabbinic law, the wife having no civil remedy in Israel. On such cases, Rabbi Zerhah Warhaftig, a former Minister of Religion, took a relaxed view: 'We have a legal system which has always sustained the people. It may contain within it some thorn that occasionally pricks the individual. We are not concerned with this or that individual but with the totality of the people.'[57]

The point might have been better put but it contained the truth, to which the difficulties of the new state drew attention, that Judaism is a perfectionist religion. It contains the strength of its weaknesses. It assumes that those who practise it are an elite since it seeks to create a model society. That made it in many ways an ideal religion for a new state like Israel, despite the fact that its law was in process of being formed about 3,200 years before the state was founded. Because of Judaism's unique continuities, many of its most ancient provisions were still valid and observed by the pious. They often reflected the form rather than the content of religious truth but it must be stressed again that 'ritualistic' is not a term of reproach for Jews. As Dr Harold Fisch, the rector of Bar-Ilan University, put it:

The very word 'ritual' in English carries a pejorative quality derived from the Protestant tradition. The word in Hebrew is *Mizvot* (religious command) and these have the same moral force whether involving relations between man and man or between man and God. It is the latter part of the code that embodies the so-called ritual commandments and these are on any proper appraisal as indispensable as the ethical commandments.[58]

The essence of the ritual spirit is punctilious observance, and that again is a Judaic strength particularly well adapted to a new state. All states need to hallow themselves with the dignity of the past. Many of the hundred or more countries which became independent after 1945 had to borrow institutions and traditions from their former colonial rulers or invent them from a past which was largely unrecorded. Israel was fortunate because her past was the longest and richest of all, was copiously chronicled and kept fresh by absolute continuities. We have noted that the Jewish genius for writing history lapsed between the time of Josephus and the nineteenth century. Once the Zionist state was founded it expressed itself not merely in history but above all in archaeology. Statesmen and generals, like Ben Gurion, Moshe Dayan and Yigael Yadin, and thousands of ordinary people, became passionate archaeologists, both amateur and professional. The study of deep antiquity rose to the height of an Israeli obsession.

That was an important element in creating an organic nation. But it was insignificant compared to the living force of a religion which had formed the Jewish race itself and whose present custodians could trace their rabbinical succession back to Moses. The Jews had survived precisely because they were punctilious about their rituals and had been prepared to die for them. It was right and healthy that the respect for strict observance should be a central feature of the Zionist community.

The outstanding example was the attitude of the Jews towards the Temple Mount, when courage and providence at last restored it to them, along with the rest of the Old City, during the Six Day War of 1967. It was a simple decision to restore the ancient ghetto, from which the Jerusalem Jews had been driven in 1948. But the Temple posed difficulties. It had been completely destroyed in antiquity. But no less an authority than Maimonides had ruled that, despite the destruction, the site of the Temple retained its sanctity for all time. The *Shekinah* never departed, and that was why Jews always came to pray near the site, especially at the Western Wall, traditionally believed to be close to the west end of the Holy of Holies. Since the Temple site retained its sanctity, however, it also required Jews to be ritually pure before actually entering it. The purity rules surrounding the Temple were the strictest of all. The Holy of Holies was banned to all except the high-priest, and even he entered it only once a year on the Day of Atonement. Since the Temple area was equated with the Mosaic 'camp of Israel' which surrounded the sanctuary in the wilderness, the purity provisions of the Book of Numbers applied to it.[59] In this book, God defined to Moses both the causes of impurity and its cure. A person became defiled by touching a corpse, a grave or a human bone, or by being under the same roof as any of these. Then it adds: 'And for an unclean person they shall take of the ashes of the burnt heifer of purification for sin, and running water shall be put thereto in a vessel: And a clean person shall take hyssop, and dip it in the water, and sprinkle it upon the tent, and upon all the vessels, and upon the persons that were there, and upon him that touched a bone, or one slain, or one dead, or a grave.'[60]

The heifer had to be red and 'without spot, wherein is no blemish, and upon which never came yoke'. Most important of all, the critical part of the operation had to be carried out, to avoid defilement, by Eleazar, the heir-apparent of Aaron. When he had produced the mixture, it was stored 'in a clean place' and kept for when needed. The authorities insisted that the heifers were rare and costly: if only two hairs of the animal were not red, its ashes were invalid. They disagreed on how many heifers had been burned. Some said seven. Others said nine. After the destruction of the Temple it was impossible to prepare new ashes. A supply remained, and it was apparently used to purify those who had been in contact with the dead as late as the Amoraic period. Then it ran out, and purification was no longer possible until the Messiah came to burn the tenth heifer and prepare a new mixture. Because the purity rules, especially over the dead, were and are so strict, rabbinical opinion agrees that all Jews are now ritually impure. And, since no ashes exist for their purification, no Jew can enter the Temple Mount.[61]

The Law of the Red Heifer has been cited as an outstanding example of *hukkah*, a Judaic statute for which there is no rational explanation but which must be strictly observed because divinely commanded in the clearest possible manner. It is just the kind of rule for which gentiles always derided the Jews. It is also the kind of rule which Jews insisted on observing whatever the disadvantages, and so retained their Jewish identity. So, from 1520 at least, Jews prayed at the Western Wall but not beyond it. After the Jewish quarter of Jerusalem fell in 1948, Jews were prevented by the Arabs from using the Western Wall or even from looking at it from afar. This denial lasted nineteen years. With the recapture of the Old City in 1967, the Wall was available again and on the first day of Shavuot that year a quarter of a million Orthodox Jews tried to pray there at once. The entire area in front of it was then cleared and a fine, paved open space created. But nothing could be done about Jews entering the Temple Mount itself. All kinds of ingenious rabbinical arguments were put forward to allow Jews to enter at least part of the area. But in the end the consensus of rabbinical opinion was that the entire site had to remain out of bounds to Jews who really believed in their faith.[62] So the Chief Rabbinate and the Ministry of Religions put up notices forbidding Jews to go on the Mount under pain of *Karet* ('extirpation' or loss of eternal life). The fact that thousands of Jews ignored the warning was cited as evidence of the impotence of the rabbis. Its observance by large numbers of pious Jews, despite their intense anxiety to enter the area, was equally if not more significant.

The Jerusalem rabbis had a collateral reason for taking a strict line on this issue. They wanted to discourage, in the minds of ordinary Jews, any equation of Zionist military triumphs, such as the recapture of the Old City, with messianic fulfilment. The same argument also applied to proposals to rebuild the Temple itself. Any such scheme would of course have run into violent opposition from the entire Moslem world, since the Temple platform was occupied by two Islamic structures of immense historic and artistic importance. Nevertheless the idea was argued through with characteristic rabbinical thoroughness. Did not the Jews, by divine command, rebuild the Temple on the return from their first, Babylonian Exile, and was not this a precedent to follow now the great Exile was over? No: the precedent applied only when the majority of Jews 'live upon the land', and that had not yet happened. Yet at the time of Ezra was not the Temple rebuilt even though the number of Jews returning from Babylon was smaller than today? True, but no divine command has been received; the Third Temple will be erected in a supernatural manner by God's direct intervention. But this argument was once used against Zionism itself, was it not, and falsified by events? And the first Temple, undoubtedly built by Solomon, was also ascribed to God. It was; on the other hand, the Temple could not be built in David's time because he was a man of war; it had to wait until Solomon's time of peace. So today: not until a final peace comes could a Third Temple be built. Even then a true prophet would be required to inspire the event, if for no other reasons than that the details, given by God to David in His own hand, were lost.[63] Yes, they were: but details of the Third Temple are given in the Book of Ezekiel. Perhaps; but leaving aside the technical arguments, the present generation was neither prepared nor willing to restore the Temple and its mode of worship: to become so would require a religious awakening. Exactly: and what better way of creating one than starting to build the Temple again?[64] So the arguments went on, leading to the majority conclusion that nothing could yet be done. Even a proposal to offer a ritual sacrifice of the paschal lamb was dropped because the exact site of the altar could not be discovered, there was doubt about the priestly lineage credentials of present-day Cohens or *Kohanim*, and (not least) too little was known of the priestly garments to recreate them exactly.[65]

The Temple, and the arguments surrounding it, symbolized the religious past which was a living, binding force in the new Israeli community. But there was a secular past too, to escape from which the

Zionist state had been created. There the symbol was the Holocaust: more than a symbol indeed, an awesome reality which had over-shadowed the state's creation and which, rightly, continued to be the salient fact in the nation's collective memory. Judaism had always been concerned not only with the Law but with (in human terms) the ends of law, justice. An endlessly recurrent and pitiful feature of Jewish history in the Exile had been the injuries inflicted on Jews as Jews and the failure of gentile society to bring their perpetrators to justice. The Jewish state was, in part at least, a response to the greatest injustice of all. One of its functions was to be an instrument of retribution and display to the world that Jews at long last could strike back and execute their Law against those who wronged them. The Holocaustal crime was so gigantic that the Nuremberg trials and other machines of justice operated by individual European countries, which we have already described, were plainly not enough. As early as 1944 the research department of the Jewish Agency's Political Office, then run by the future Prime Minister Moshe Sharett, had begun to collect material on Nazi war criminals. After the foundation of the state, tracing the guilty and bringing them to justice was part of the duties of several Israeli agencies, some secret. The effort was not confined to Israel. Many Jewish organizations, national and international, including the World Jewish Congress, joined in. So did the survivors themselves. In 1946 Simon Wiesenthal, a thirty-eight-year-old Czech Jew who had survived five years in various camps, including Buchen-wald and Mauthausen, set up with thirty other camp inmates the Jewish Historical Documentation Centre, which eventually found a permanent home in Vienna. It concentrated on the identification of Nazi criminals not yet tried and sentenced. The Holocaust was intensively studied for academic and educational as well as retributive purposes. By the 1980s there were ninety-three courses in Holocaust studies in United States and Canadian universities alone and six research centres entirely devoted to the subject. At the Wiesenthal Center for Holocaust Studies in Los Angeles, for example, the latest technology was invoked to create what was called a 'multi-screen, multi-channel-sound, audio-visual experience of the Holocaust', using a 40-foot-high and 23-foot-long screen in the configuration of an arch, three film projectors and a special Cinemascope lens, eighteen slide projectors and pentaphonic sound, all linked to a central computer for simultaneous control. This dramatic recreation of the event might not seem excessive at a time when anti-Semites were beginning to make determined attempts to prove that it had never taken place at all or had been grotesquely exaggerated.[66]

But the primary object of Holocaust documentation remained justice. Wiesenthal himself was responsible for bringing over 1,100 Nazis to prosecution. He supplied much of the material which allowed the Israeli government to identify, arrest, try and sentence the man who, after Himmler himself, was the chief administrator–executant of the Holocaust, Adolf Eichmann. He was arrested by Israeli agents in Argentina in May 1960, brought to Israel secretly, and charged on fifteen counts under the Nazis and Nazi Collaborators (Punishment) Law, 1950.[67] For a number of reasons the Eichmann trial was an important event, actual and symbolic, for the Israelis and for the entire Jewish people. It demonstrated in the most striking manner that the age of impunity for those who murdered Jews was over and that there was no hiding-place for them anywhere in the world. It was covered by 976 foreign and 166 Israeli correspondents and, because of the nature of the indictment, embracing the Holocaust as a whole as well as events leading up to it, it was a process of education for millions in the facts of mass murder. But it was also a meticulous demonstration of Israeli justice in this most emotional of fields.

Eichmann's first reaction to capture was to admit his identity and guilt and to concede the Jewish right to punish him. He said on 3 June 1960: 'If it would give greater significance to the act of atonement, I am ready to hang myself in public.'[68] Later he became less co-operative and fell back on the defence familiar from Nuremberg that he was a mere cog in the machine executing the orders of someone else. In the event, then, the prosecution faced an active, cunning and obstinate, if ignoble, defence. The Knesset passed a law allowing a foreigner (the German counsel Dr Robert Servatius) to defend Eichmann and the Israeli government provided the fee ($30,000). The trial was a long and thorough affair and the judgment, delivered on 11 December 1961, went to great trouble to assert and argue the competence of the court and its right to try the accused despite the circumstances of his arrest, as well as the substance of its findings. The overwhelming evidence made the verdict inevitable. Eichmann was sentenced to death on 15 December and his appeal dismissed on 29 May 1962. President Yitzhak ben Zvi received a petition for clemency and spent a day in solitude considering it. Israel had never executed anyone before (or since) and many Jews, there and abroad, wanted to avoid the rope. But the great majority believed the sentence was right and the President could find no mitigating circumstances whatever in the case. A room in the Ramla Prison was specially converted into an execution chamber, with a trap-door cut in the floor and a gallows above, and Eichmann was executed near midnight on 31 May 1962, his body being burned and the ashes scattered at sea.[69]

The Eichmann affair demonstrated Israeli efficiency, justice and firmness, and went some way to exorcising the ghosts of the Final Solution. It was a necessary episode in Israel's history. But the Holocaust continued to be a determining fact in Israel's national consciousness. In May 1983 the Israeli polling firm Smith Research Center conducted an exhaustive survey of Israeli attitudes to the Holocaust. This revealed that the overwhelming majority of Israelis (83 per cent) saw it as a major factor in how they saw the world. The Center's director, Hanoch Smith, reported: 'The trauma of the Holocaust is very much on the minds of Israelis, even in the second and third generations.' The view of the Holocaust, indeed, went right to the heart of Israel's purpose. An overwhelming majority (91 per cent) believed that the Western leaders knew of the mass killings and did little to save the Jews; only slightly fewer (87 per cent) agreed with the proposition: 'From the Holocaust we learn that Jews cannot rely on non-Jews.' Some 61 per cent considered the Holocaust the main factor in the establishment of Israel and 62 per cent believed its existence made a repetition impossible.[70]

Hence, just as the collective memory of pharaonic bondage dominated the early Israelite society, so the Holocaust shaped the new state. It was, inevitably, pervaded by a sense of loss. Hitler had wiped out a third of all Jews, especially the pious and the poor, from whom Judaism had drawn its peculiar strength. The loss could be seen in secular terms. In the nineteenth and early twentieth centuries the world had been immeasurably enriched by the liberated talent streaming out of the old ghettos, which had proved a principal creative force in modern European and North American civilization. The supply continued until Hitler destroyed the source for ever. No one will ever know what the world thereby sacrificed. For Israel the deprivation was devastating. It was felt at a personal level, for so many of its citizens had lost virtually all their families and childhood friends, and it was felt collectively: one in three of those who might have built the state was not there. It was felt spiritually perhaps most of all. The supreme value Judaism attached to human life, to the point where the Israeli nation debated long and anxiously before it deprived even Eichmann of his, made the murder of so many, especially of the poor and the pious, whom God specially loved, an event hard to comprehend. It required another Book of Job even to state the problem. It was touched on by the great Judaic theologian Abraham Joshua Herschel (1907–73), who had been fortunate to get out of Poland just six weeks before the disaster. 'I am', he wrote, 'a brand plucked from the fire of an altar of Satan on which millions of human lives were exterminated to evil's greater glory, and on which so much else was consumed: the divine images of so many human beings, many people's faith in the God of justice and compassion, and much of the secret and power of attachment to the Bible bred and cherished in the hearts of men for nearly 2,000 years.'[71] Why had it happened? The new Zion began with an unanswered, perhaps unanswerable, question.

Yet there were some ways in which the world position of the Jews had been fundamentally improved since the days before the Holocaust. The Jewish national state had been established. That did not end the Exile of course. How could it? The Exile, as Arthur Cohen observed, was not an accident of history corrected by creation of a secular, national state; it was, rather, a metaphysical concept, 'the historical coefficient of being unredeemed'.[72] Most of Jewry remained outside the state. That had been so ever since the Babylonian Exile. The Third Commonwealth, like the Second, contained only about a quarter of all Jews. There was no sign, as Israel completed its fourth decade, of a fundamental change in this proportion. All the same, realization of a secular Zion gave to world Jewry a living, beating heart it had not possessed for two millennia. It provided a focus for the global community which the old pious settlements and the idea of Return, however cherished, had not supplied. The building of Israel was the twentieth-century equivalent of rebuilding the Temple. Like the Temple under Herod the Great, it had unsatisfactory aspects. But it was there. The very fact that it existed, and could be visited and shared, gave a completely new dimension to the diaspora. It was a constant source of concern, sometimes of anxiety, often of pride. Once Israel had been established and proved it could defend and justify itself, no member of the diaspora ever had to feel ashamed of being a Jew again.

This was important because even near the close of the twentieth century the diaspora continued to maintain its characteristics of extremes of wealth and poverty and baffling variety. Total Jewish population had been nearly 18 million at the end of the 1930s. By the mid-1980s it had by no means recovered the Holocaust losses. Of a total of 13.5 million Jews, about 3.5 million lived in Israel. By far the largest Jewish community was in the United States (5,750,000) and this, combined with important Jewish communities in Canada (310,000), Argentina (250,000), Brazil (130,000) and Mexico (40,000), and a dozen smaller groups, meant that nearly half world Jewry (6.6 million) was now in the Americas. The next largest Jewish community, after the US and Israel, was Soviet Russia's, with about 1,750,000. There were still sizeable communities in Hungary (75,000) and Rumania (30,000), and a total of 130,000 in Marxist eastern Europe. In western Europe there were a little over 1,250,000 Jews, the principal communities being in France (670,000), Britain (360,000), West Germany (42,000), Belgium (41,000), Italy (35,000), the Netherlands (28,000) and Switzerland (21,000). In Africa, outside the South African Republic (105,000), there were now few Jews except in the diminished communities of Morocco (17,000) and Ethiopia (perhaps 5,000). In Asia there were still about 35,000 Jews in Persia and 21,000 in Turkey. The Australian and New Zealand communities together added a further 75,000.[73]

The history, composition and origin of some of these communities were of great complexity. In India, for instance, there were about 26,000 Jews in the late 1940s, composed of three principal types. About 13,000 formed the so-called Bene (Children of) Israel, living in and around Bombay on the west coast. These Jews had lost their records and books but retained a tenacious oral history of their migration, put into written form as recently as 1937.[74] Their story was that they had fled from Galilee during the persecution of Antiochus Epiphanes (175–163 BC). Their ship was wrecked on the coast about 30 miles south of Bombay, and only seven families survived. Though they had no religious texts and soon forgot Hebrew, they continued to honour the Sabbath and some Jewish holidays, practised circumcision and Jewish diet and remembered the *Shema*. They spoke Marathi and adopted Indian caste practices, dividing themselves into Goa (whites) and Kala (blacks), which suggests there may have been two waves of settlement. Then there were the Cochin Jews, about 2,500 at one time, living 650 miles further south down the west coast. They had a foundation document of a kind, two copper plates engraved in old Tamil, recording privileges and now dated between 974 and 1020 AD. There were certainly several layers of settlement in this case, the Black Cochin Jews being the earliest, joined by whiter-skinned Jews from Spain, Portugal and possibly other parts of Europe (as well as the Middle East) in the early sixteenth century. Both black and white Cochin Jews had sub-divisions and there was a third main group, the Meshuararim, who were low-caste descendants of unions between Jews and slave-concubines. None of the three main Cochin groups worshipped together. In addition, there were about 2,000 Sephardi Jews from Baghdad, who arrived in India during the decade 1820–30, and a final wave of European refugee Jews who came in the 1930s. These two last categories associated with each other for religious (not social) purposes, but neither would attend the same synagogues as the Bene Israel or Cochin Jews. All the white-skinned Jews and many of the blacks spoke English, and they flourished under British rule, serving with distinction in the army, becoming civil servants, tradesmen, shopkeepers and craftsmen, attending Bombay University, studying Hebrew, translating the Jewish classics into Marathi and graduating as engineers, lawyers, teachers and scientists. One of them became Mayor of Bombay, the centre of all Jewish groups of India, in 1937. But independent India was less congenial to them and with the creation of Israel most chose to migrate, so that by the 1980s there were not much over 15,000 Bene Israel and only 250 Jews on the Cochin coast.[75]

That such groups should survive at all testified not to the proselytizing power of Judaism but to its tenacious adaptability even in the most adverse circumstances. But it cannot be denied that the cataclysmic events of the twentieth century virtually destroyed dozens of Jewish communities, many of them ancient. The post-war Communist regime in China, for instance, imposed its own final solution on China's Jewish population, much of it a refugee exodus from Soviet Russia and Hitler's Europe, but including descendants of Jews who had been in China from the eighth century onwards. All fled or were driven out, Hong Kong alone, with about 1,000 Jews, and Singapore with 400, constituting lonely outposts in the Far East.

Throughout the Arab world, during the late 1940s and 1950s, the historic Sephardi communities were reduced to a fraction of their pre-war size or eliminated altogether. In large parts of Europe, the Jews who survived or returned after the ravages of the Holocaust were winnowed further by emigration, especially to Israel. Salonika's Ladino-speaking population, 60,000 strong in 1939, was a mere 1,500 in the 1980s. Vienna's vast and fertile Jewry, perhaps the most gifted of all, shrank from 200,000 to less than 8,000, and even the mortal remains of Herzl himself, buried in the city's Doebling cemetery, left for reinterment in Jerusalem in 1949. Amsterdam Jewry, nearly 70,000 in the 1930s, was scarcely 12,000 forty years later. The Jews of Antwerp, who had made it the diamond centre of the West, continued to work in the trade but the city's Jewry had fallen from 55,000 to about 13,500 in the 1980s. The ancient Frankfurt Jewry, once so famous in finance, fell from 26,158 in 1933 to 4,350 in the 1970s. In Berlin where, in the 1920s, nearly 175,000 Jews had made it the cultural capital of the world, there were in the 1970s only about 5,500 (plus another 850 in East Berlin). The most desolate vacuum of all was in Poland, where by the 1980s a pre-war Jewish population of 3,300,000 had dropped to about 5,000. Scores of towns there, once rich in synagogues and libraries, knew the Jew no more.

Yet there was continuity too and even growth. Italian Jewry survived the Nazi era with remarkable tenacity. The 29,000 left at the end of the German occupation rose slowly in the post-war period to 32,000; but this was due to emigrants reaching Italy from the north and east. A study by the Hebrew University of Jerusalem in 1965 showed that the Italian community, like many others in the advanced countries, had a vulnerable demographic profile. The birth rate for Italian Jews was only 11.4 per 1,000 compared to 18.3 for the population as a whole. Fertility and marriage rates were also much lower; only the mortality rate and the average age (forty-one against thirty-three) were higher.[76] In Rome, the core of the Jewish community still lived in what, until 1880, had been the old ghetto area in Trastevere where Jews had eked out a precarious existence, as rag-pickers and pedlars, since the time of the old kings of Rome. Here, rich Jews lived virtually next door to the very poorest, as they always had done. The thirty chief families, the *Scuola Tempio*, could trace their ancestry back to the time of the Emperor Titus 1,900 years ago, when they had been brought to Rome in chains after the destruction of the Temple. The Roman Jews had lived in the shadow of the majestic church that had in turn exploited, persecuted and protected them. They had sought both to defy and to blend with it, so that their principal synagogue, in the Lungotevere Cenci, just outside the old ghetto gates, was a spectacular exercise in Italian church baroque. There, in April 1986, Pope John Paul II became the first pontiff to attend a synagogue service, taking turns with the Chief Rabbi of Rome to read the psalms. He told the Jewish congregation: 'You are our dearly beloved brothers, and in a way you are our elder brothers.' The intention was good, the stress on 'elder' a little too apposite.

In France, the post-war period saw undeniable growth, in both numbers and intensity. The Nazis and their Vichy allies had killed 90,000 of France's pre-war Jewish population of 340,000, and the tragedy had been envenomed by the knowledge that France's established and highly assimilated native community had in some ways collaborated in deporting the refugee element. But this loss was more than made good by a huge influx of Sephardi immigrants from the Moslem world in the three decades after the war: 25,000 from Egypt, 65,000 from Morocco, 80,000 from Tunisia and 120,000 from Algeria, as well as smaller but substantial numbers from Syria, the Lebanon and Turkey. As a result, French Jewry more than doubled to over 670,000, and became the fourth largest in the world.

This huge demographic expansion was accompanied by a profound cultural change. French Jewry had always been the most assimilationist of all, especially since the French Revolution had allowed it to identify almost completely with republican institutions. The vicious behaviour of many Frenchmen under Vichy had produced some loss of confidence, and one index of it was that six times as many French Jews changed their names in the twelve years 1945–57 as in the entire period 1803–1942.[77] Even so, the number was small, and ultra-assimilation remained the distinguishing characteristic of French Jewry even in the post-war period. Writers like Raymond Aron stood at the very centre of contemporary French culture and the quiet, unostentatious, highly sophisticated Jewish upper-middle class provided notable prime ministers, such as René Mayer and Pierre Mendès-France under the Fourth Republic, and Michel Debré and Laurent Fabius under the Fifth. Nevertheless, the influx of Sephardis from Africa greatly intensified the Jewishness of French Jewry. Francophone most of them might be, but a high proportion of them read Hebrew. French Jews of the nineteenth century had a 'theory of three generations': 'The grandfather believes, the father doubts, the son denies. The grandfather prays in Hebrew, the father reads the prayers in French, the son does not pray at all. The grandfather observes all the holidays, the father Yom Kippur, the son no holidays at all. The grandfather has remained Jewish, the father has been assimilated, and the son has become a mere deist . . . if he has not become an atheist, a Fourierist or a Saint-Simonian.'[78] In post-war France this theory no longer worked. The son was now just as likely to return to the religion of his grandfather, leaving the father isolated in his agnosticism. In the south, the influx of Algerian Jews resurrected the dead or dying communities of the Middle Ages. In 1970, for instance, the celebrated composer Darius Milhaud laid the foundation-stone of a new synagogue in Aix-en-Provence – the old one having been sold in the war and turned into a Protestant church.[79] Nor were new synagogues the only sign of a revived Jewishness which was both religious and secular. In the 1960s and 1970s the leaders of the old Alliance Israélite Universelle tended to be practising Jews with militant attitudes to Jewish causes at home and abroad. A much higher percentage of Jews observed the Law and learned Hebrew. The continuing existence of a residual anti-Semitic movement in France, though weaker than in the 1930s, tended to reinforce Jewish militancy. When it found parliamentary form, as with the Poujadists in the 1950s or the National Front in the 1980s, Jewish organizations reacted vigorously and asserted their Jewish convictions. The bomb attack on the Liberal synagogue on the Rue Copernic on 3 October 1980, one of several at that time, served to stimulate *Le Renouveau*

Juif as it was called. French Jewry, even as enlarged by immigration from Africa, remained strikingly resistant to Zionism as such: French Jews would not actually go to Israel to live in any numbers. But they identified themselves with the survival of Israel in 1956, 1967, 1973 and again in the early 1980s. They reacted strongly against French government policies which were inimical to Jewish and Israeli interests as they saw them. They constituted, for the first time, a Jewish lobby in France, and in the 1981 elections the Jewish vote was an important element in replacing the Gaullist–right-wing regime which had governed France for twenty-three years. A new and far more vigorous and visible Jewish establishment was emerging in France, conscious of its numerical strength and youth, and likely to play in the 1990s a more significant role in forming opinion throughout the diaspora.

A strong French voice in the diaspora could be welcome, par-ticularly since the German voice was virtually silenced as a result of the Hitler age. Necessarily in recent decades, and particularly with the decline of Yiddish, the voice of the diaspora has been English. Indeed, it is some measure of the importance of the return of the Jews to England in 1646 that more than half of the world's Jews now speak English, 850,000 in the countries of the British Commonwealth (plus South Africa) and nearly six million in the United States. The real British moment in the history of the Jews came and went with the birth of modern Zionism, the Balfour Declaration and the mandate. British Jewry became and remained the most stable and contented and the least threatened of the major Jewries. It took in 90,000 refugees in the 1930s, to its great enrichment, and expanded from about 300,000 just before the First World War to well over 400,000 at the end of the Second. But, like Italian Jewry, it developed demographic weaknesses which became progressively more marked in the 1960s and 1970s. In the years 1961–5, for instance, the English synagogue marriage rate was an average of 4.0 per thousand compared to a national average of 7.5. The total number of Jews slipped from 410,000 in 1967 to below 400,000 in the 1970s and probably to below 350,000 in the second half of the 1980s. There was no lack of energy in modern British Jewry. Jewish enterprise was active in finance, as always, and it was of critical importance in entertainment, property, clothing, footware and the retail trade. It created national institutions like Granada TV. The Sieff dynasty turned the successful firm of Marks & Spencer into the most enduring (and popular) triumph of post-war British business, and Lord Weinstock transformed General Electric into the largest of all British companies. The Jews were vigorous in the publishing of books and newspapers. They produced the best of all diaspora journals, the *Jewish Chronicle*. In growing numbers they adorned (if only occasionally) the benches of the House of Lords. There was a time, in the mid-1980s, when no fewer than five Jews sat in the British cabinet. But this impressive energy did not take philoprogenitive forms. Nor was it collectively exerted to constitute a leading influence within the diaspora or on the Zionist state. In this respect British Jewry behaved, and perhaps was obliged to behave, like Britain herself: it handed over the torch to America.

The expansion and consolidation of United States Jewry in the late nineteenth and twentieth centuries was as important in Jewish history as the creation of Israel itself; in some ways more important. For, if the fulfilment of Zionism gave the harassed diaspora an ever-open refuge with sovereign rights to determine and defend its destiny, the growth of US Jewry was an accession of power of an altogether different order, which gave Jews an important, legitimate and permanent part in shaping the policies of the greatest state on earth. This was not fragile *Hofjuden* influence but the consequences of democratic persuasion and demographic facts. At the end of the 1970s the Jewish population of the United States was 5,780,960. This was only 2.7 per cent of total US population but it was disproportionately concentrated in urban areas, particularly big cities, which notoriously exert more cultural, social, economic and indeed political influence than small towns, villages and rural districts. Towards the end of the twentieth century the Jews were still big-city dwellers. There were 394,000 in Tel Aviv–Jaffa, over 300,000 in Paris, 285,000 in Moscow, 280,000 in Greater London, 272,000 in Jerusalem, 210,000 in Kiev, 165,000 in Leningrad, 115,000 in Montreal and 115,000 in Toronto. But the most impressive urban concentration was in the United States. Metropolitan New York, with 1,998,000 Jews, was by far the largest Jewish city on earth. The second largest was Los Angeles with 455,000. Then followed Philadelphia (295,000), Chicago (253,000) Miami (225,000), Boston (170,000) and Washington DC (160,000). Altogether there were sixty-nine American cities with a Jewish population of over 10,000. There was also a demographic concentration in key states. In New York State 2,143,485 Jews constituted 12 per cent of the population. They formed 6 per cent in New Jersey, 4.6 per cent in Florida, 4.5 per cent in Maryland, 4.4 per cent in Massachusetts, 3.6 per cent in Pennsylvania, 3.1 per cent in California and 2.4 per cent in Illinois. Of all the great American ethnic votes, the Jewish vote was the best organized, the most responsive to guidance by its leaders and the most likely to exert itself effectively.

However, it was possible to exaggerate the direct political impact of

Jewish voters, however well schooled. Since 1932 the Jews had voted overwhelmingly Democratic, sometimes by as high a proportion as 85–90 per cent. There was no clear evidence that Jewish influence on Democratic presidents or policy was proportionately decisive. In fact during the 1960s and 1970s the continuing fidelity of the Jewish voter to the Democratic Party appeared to be based increasingly on emotional–historic grounds rather than on a community of interests. In the 1980s most Jews, somewhat to the surprise of psephologists, still voted Democrat, though the majority fell to around 60 per cent. In the 1984 election they were the only religious group (apart from atheists) to give the Democratic candidate majority support, and the only ethnic group (apart from blacks). The Jews voted as they did not for communal economic or foreign policy reasons but from a residual sympathy for the poor and the underdog.[80] By the last quarter of the twentieth century, the notion of the 'Jewish lobby' in American politics had become to some extent a myth.

What had happened, in the relationship of Jewish citizens to America as a whole, was something quite different and much more important: the transformation of the Jewish minority into a core element of American society. Throughout the twentieth century American Jews continued to take the fullest advantage of the opportunities America opened to them, to attend universities, to become doctors, lawyers, teachers, professional men and women of all kinds, politicians and public servants, as well as to thrive in finance and business, as they always had. They were particularly strong in the private enterprise sector, in press, publishing, broadcasting and entertainment, and in intellectual life generally. There were certain fields, such as the writing of fiction, where they were dominant. But they were numerous and successful everywhere. Slowly, then, during the second half of the century, this aristocracy of success became as ubiquitous and pervasive in its cultural influence as the earlier elite, the White Anglo-Saxon Protestant. Jews ceased to be a lobby in American society. They became part of the natural organism itself, a limb, and a powerful one. They began to operate not from without the American body inwards, but from within it outwards. With their historic traditions of democracy, tolerance and liberalism, they assumed to some extent the same role in America as the Whigs had once played in England: an elite seeking moral justification for its privileges by rendering enlightened service to those less fortunate. In short, they were no longer a minority seeking rights but part of the majority conferring them; their political activity switched imperceptibly from influencing leadership to exercising it.

Hence it became hard to distinguish specifically Jewish elements in American culture. They had become an integral and harmonious part of it. It was still harder to identify American policies which were in response to supposed Jewish interests. Such interests tended to become increasingly coterminous with America's as a whole. This principle operated forcibly in the case of Israel. It was no longer needful to argue America's leaders into guaranteeing Israel's right to survive. That was taken for granted. Israel was a lonely outpost of liberal democracy, upholding the rule of law and civilized standards of behaviour in an area where such values were generally disregarded. It was natural and inevitable that Israel should receive America's support and the only argument was about how that support could be most judiciously provided. By the 1980s the realities of the world were such that Israel would have remained America's most reliable ally in the Middle East, and America her most trustworthy friend, even if the American–Jewish community had not existed.

Yet that community did exist and it had achieved a unique status in the diaspora not merely by its size but by its character. It was a totally assimilated community which still retained its Jewish consciousness. Its members thought of themselves as wholly American but as Jews too. Such a phenomenon had never existed before in Jewish history. It was made possible by the peculiar circumstances of America's growth and composition. The Jews, the eternal 'strangers and sojourners', at last found permanent rest in a country where all came as strangers. Because all were strangers all had comparable right of residence until the point was reached when all, with equal justice, could call it home. Then too, America was the first place in which the Jews had settled where they found their religion, and their religious observance, an advantage, because all religions which inculcated civic virtue were honoured. Not only that: America also, and above all, honoured the umbrella religion of its own, what might be called the Law of Democracy, a secular Torah which Jews were outstandingly well equipped to observe. For all these reasons it became perhaps misleading to see the American Jewish community as part of the diaspora at all. Jews in America felt themselves more American than Jews in Israel felt themselves Israeli. It was necessary to coin a new word to define their condition, for American Jews came to form, along with the Jews of Israel and the Jews of the diaspora proper, the third leg of a new Jewish tripod, on which the safety and future of the whole people equally depended. There was the diaspora Jew, there was the ingathered Jew and, in America, there was the possessing Jew.

American Jewry formed the mirror-image of Russian Jewry. In

America a Jew helped to own his country; in Russia he was owned by it. The Soviet Jew was possessed, a property of the state, as he had been in the Middle Ages. One of the lessons we learn from studying Jewish history is that anti-Semitism corrupts the people and the societies possessed by it. It corrupted a Dominican friar as effectively as it corrupted a greedy king. It turned the Nazi state into a heaving mass of corruption. But nowhere were its corrosive effects more apparent than in Russia. The ubiquitous petty corruption engendered by the Tsarist laws against the Jews has already been noted. More important in the long run was its moral corruption of state authority. For in harassing the Jews, the Tsarist Russian state became habituated to a close, repressive and highly bureaucratic system of control. It controlled the internal movements and residence of the Jews, their right to go to school or university and what they studied there, to enter professions or institutes, to sell their labour, to start businesses or form companies, to worship, to belong to organizations and to engage in an endless list of other activities. This system exercised monstrous, all-pervading control of the lives of an unpopular and underprivileged minority and a ruthless invasion of their homes and families. As such, it became a bureaucratic model, and when the Tsars were replaced first by Lenin, then by Stalin, the control of the Jews was extended to the control of the entire population, and the model became the whole. In this system, in which all were harried and all underprivileged, the Jews were further depressed to form a sump or sub-class in which the degree of state control was deliberately intense.

Stalin's use of anti-Semitism in the leadership struggles of the 1920s and the purges of the 1930s was characteristic of him. His wartime creation of the Jewish Anti-Fascist Committee and publication of the Yiddish magazine *Aynikayt* ('Unity') were merely tactical moves. Stalin's daughter Svetlana has described his personal connections with Jews. He had some Jews in his household, including the foreign ministry official Solomon Lozowsky. When Svetlana, then seventeen, fell in love with a Jewish scriptwriter, Stalin had him deported. Later she succeeded in marrying a Jew, Gregory Morozov. Her father accused him of evading military service: 'People are getting shot and look at him – he's sitting it out at home.' Stalin's oldest son Yakov also married a Jewish wife and, when he was taken prisoner, Stalin claimed she had betrayed him. 'He never liked Jews,' Svetlana wrote, 'though in those days he wasn't yet as blatant about expressing his hatred for them as he was after the war.'[81]

There was really no pause in Soviet anti-Semitism, even during the war. It was very marked in the Red Army. 'Anti-Semitism in the Soviet

Union', a former army captain stated, 'is rampant to an extent that it is impossible for anyone never having lived in that accursed country to imagine.'[82] Towards the end of the war, some government departments, notably the Foreign Ministry, were largely cleared of Jews and no more Jews were accepted as trainees. The post-war attack, of which the murder of Mikhoels in January 1948 was a foretaste, began the same year in September. It was signalled by an Ilya Ehrenburg article in *Pravda* – Stalin often made Non-Jewish Jews the agents of his anti-Semitism, rather as the ss used the Sonderskommandos – denouncing Israel as a bourgeois tool of American capitalism. The Jewish Anti-Fascist Committee was disbanded, *Aynikayt* closed and the Yiddish schools shut down. Then began a systematic attack on Jews, especially writers, painters, musicians and intellectuals of all kinds, using terms of abuse ('rootless cosmopolitanism') identical with Nazi demonology. Thousands of Jewish intellectuals, including the Yiddish writers Perez Markish, Itzik Fefer and David Bergelson, were murdered, as was any Jew who happened to catch Stalin's eye, such as Lozowsky. The campaign was extended to Czechoslovakia, where on 20 November 1952 Rudolf Slánsky, the Czech party general secretary, and thirteen other leading Communist bosses, eleven of them Jews, were accused of a Troskyite–Titoist–Zionist conspiracy, convicted and executed. Supplying arms to Israel in 1948 (actually on Stalin's own orders) formed an important element in the 'proof'.[83] The climax came early in 1953 when nine doctors, six of them Jews, were accused of seeking to poison Stalin in conjunction with British, US and Zionist agents. This show-trial was to have been a prelude to the mass deportation of Jews to Siberia, as part of a Stalinist 'Final Solution'.[84]

Stalin died before the doctors came to trial and the proceedings were quashed by his successors. The plan for a mass deportation came to nothing. But it was significant that anti-Semitism was not one of the aspects of Stalin's behaviour Nikita Khrushchev denounced in his famous Secret Session speech. As first secretary in the Ukraine he shared the endemic anti-Semitism there and, immediately after the war, had stopped returning Jewish refugees from claiming their old homes. 'It is not in our interests', he stated, 'that the Ukrainians should associate the return of Soviet power with the return of the Jews.'[85] Indeed there were several post-war Ukrainian pogroms under Khrushchev's rule. Once in power, he switched the thrust of anti-Jewish propaganda from spying to 'economic criminality', large numbers of Jews, their names prominently displayed, being convicted and sentenced to death in nine show-trials. He closed down many synagogues, their total falling during his rule from 450 to sixty. He permitted the publication, by the Academy of Sciences of the Ukrainian Soviet Republic, of the notorious anti-Semitic tract, *Judaism Without Embellishment*, by the Communist Rosenberg, Trofim Kychko. The Khrushchev era witnessed an outbreak of blood libels, anti-Semitic riots and synagogue burning.

There was a brief respite for Soviet Jewry after Khrushchev's fall in 1964. But, following the Six Day War in 1967, the campaign was openly resumed and intensified. In some respects Soviet anti-Semitism was very traditional. The Soviet rulers, like early medieval societies, like the Spaniards until the late fourteenth century, employed Jews in the economy until sufficient non-Jews had acquired the skills to replace them. The top Jewish Bolsheviks were nearly all murdered in the 1920s and 1930s. Thereafter Jews remained over-represented in the bureaucratic elites but never at the top political level: like the court Jews, they were allowed to help but never to rule. Even in the 1970s a Jew occasionally got as far as the Party Congress – there were four in 1971 and five in 1976 – and it was not unknown for a Jew to be on the Central Committee. But such men had to earn their jobs by violent anti-Zionism. In 1966 Jews accounted for 7.8 per cent of academics, 14.7 per cent of doctors, 8.5 per cent of writers and journalists, 10.4 per cent of judges and lawyers and 7.7 per cent of actors, musicians and artists. But in every case the percentage was being pushed down by party and bureaucratic action. Thus Jews provided 18 per cent of Soviet scientific workers in 1947, only 7 per cent by 1970. As under the Tsars, the squeeze was applied particularly at the university level. The number of Jewish students declined in absolute terms, from 111,900 in 1968–9 to 66,900 in 1975–6, and still more heavily relative to the population as a whole. In 1977–8 not a single Jew was admitted to Moscow University.[86]

Soviet anti-Jewish policy, like Tsarist – and even Nazi policy in the 1930s – showed some confusions and contradictions. There were conflicting desires to use and exploit the Jews, to keep them prisoners, and also to expel them, the common factor in both cases being an anxiety to humiliate. Thus in 1971 Brezhnev decided to open the gates, and during the next decade 250,000 Jews were allowed to escape. But with every increase in emigration there was a sharp rise in trials of Jews, and the actual exit visa procedure itself was made as complex, difficult and shameful as possible. The need for a character-reference from the applicant's place of work often led to a sort of show-trial there, in which the Jew was publicly discussed, condemned and then dismissed. So he was often jobless, penniless and liable to be gaoled for 'parasitism' long before the visa was granted.[87]

The exit procedures became more onerous in the 1980s, recalling the labyrinthine complexities of Tsarist legislation. Fewer visas were granted and it became common for a family to wait five or even ten years for permission to leave. The procedure could be summarized as follows. The applicant had first to get a *visov*, a legally attested invitation from a near-relative living in Israel, with an Israeli government guarantee to issue an entry visa. The *visov* entitled him to go to the Emigration Office and be issued with two questionnaires for each adult member of the family. The applicant filled these in, then added the following: an autobiography, six photographs, copies of university or other diplomas, a birth certificate for each member of the family, a marriage certificate if married, and, where parents, wife or husband were dead, the appropriate death certificates; a certificate showing possession of a legal residence; an officially certificated letter from any member of the family being left behind; a certificate from their place of work or, if not working, from the House Management Office of their place of residence; and a fee of 40 roubles (about $60). When all these had been handed in, the decision whether or not to grant a visa took several months. If a visa were granted (but not yet issued), the applicant had then to resign from work (if not already dismissed); get an official estimate of the cost of repairing his flat; pay the estimate; pay 500 roubles a head ($750) as a penalty for giving up Soviet citizenship; surrender his passport, Army Registration Card, employment record book and his flat-clearance certificate; and pay a further 200 roubles ($300) for the visa itself. Applicants refused a visa had the right to apply again at six-month intervals.[88]

The Soviet campaign against the Jews, after 1967 a permanent feature of the system, was itself conducted under the code-name of anti-Zionism, which became a cover for every variety of anti-Semitism. Soviet anti-Zionism, a product of internal divisions within the east European Jewish left, was in turn grafted on to Leninist anti-imperialism. At this point we need to retrace our steps a little, in order to show that the Leninist theory of imperialism, like Marx's theory of capitalism, had its roots in anti-Semitic conspiracy theory.

The theory arose from the development of South Africa from the 1860s onwards, the outstanding example of the application of large-scale capital to transform a primitive into a modern economy. South Africa had been a rural backwater until the discovery of the diamond fields of Kimberley in the 1860s, followed by the goldfields of the Rand twenty years later, opened up its interior and mineral wealth. What made South Africa different was the use of a new institution, the mining finance house, to concentrate claims and to raise and deploy enormous capital sums in high-technology deep mining. The institution itself was invented by an Englishman, Cecil Rhodes. But Jews had always been involved in precious stones (especially diamonds) and bullion, and they played a notable part both in the South African deep-level mines and in the financial system which raised the capital to sink them.[89] Such men as Alfred Beit, Barney Barnato, Louis Cohen, Lionel Phillips, Julius Wehrner, Solly Joel, Adolf Goertz, George Albu and Abe Bailey turned South Africa into the world's largest and richest mining economy. A second generation of mining financiers, led by Ernest Oppenheimer, consolidated and expanded the achievement.[90]

The rapid fortunes made (and sometimes lost) on the Rand by Jews aroused great jealousy and resentment. Among their critics was the left-wing polemicist J. A. Hobson, who went out to South Africa to cover the outbreak of the Boer War in 1899 for the *Manchester Guardian*. Hobson regarded the Jew as 'almost devoid of social morality', possessing a 'superior calculating intellect, which is a national heritage' allowing him 'to take advantage of every weakness, folly and vice of the society in which he lives'.[91] In South Africa he was shocked and angered by what he saw as the ubiquitous activity of Jews. The official figures, he wrote, stated there were only 7,000 Jews in Johannesburg but 'The shop fronts and business houses, the market place, the saloons, the "stoops" of the smart suburban houses are sufficient to convince one of the large presence of the chosen people.' He was particularly disgusted to find that the stock exchange was closed on the Day of Atonement. In 1900 he published a book, *The War in South Africa: Its Causes and Effects*, which blamed the war on 'a small group of international financiers, chiefly German in origin and Jewish by race'. British troops were fighting and dying 'in order to place a small international oligarchy of mine-owners and speculators in power in Pretoria'. 'Not Hamburg,' he wrote in disgust, 'not Vienna, not Frankfurt but Johannesburg is the new Jerusalem.'[92]

Hobson's explanation of the origin of the war was false. The fighting, as was foreseeable, was disastrous for the mine-owners. As for the Jews, the whole of modern history proved them strongly pacific by inclination and interest, especially in their capacity as financiers. But Hobson, like other conspiracy theorists, was not interested in facts but in the beauty of his concept. Two years later he expanded his theory into a famous book, *Imperialism: A Study*, which revealed international finance capital as the chief force behind colonies and wars. His chapter, 'Economic Parasites of Imperialism', the heart of his theory, contained this key passage:

Those great businesses – banking, brokering, bill discounting, loan floating, company promoting – form the central ganglion of international capitalism. United by the strongest bonds of organization, always in closest and quickest touch with one another, situated in the very heart of the business capital of every state, controlled, so far as Europe is concerned, chiefly by men of a single and peculiar race, who have behind them many centuries of financial experience, they are in a unique position to control the policy of nations. No great quick direction of capital is possible save by their consent and through their agency. Does anyone seriously suppose that a great war could be undertaken by any European state, or a great state loan subscribed, if the house of Rothschild and its connections set their face against it?[93]

When Lenin came to write his own thesis on the subject, at Zurich in the spring of 1916, he complained of a shortage of books. 'However,' he wrote, 'I made use of the principal English work on imperialism, J. A. Hobson's book, with all the care that, in my opinion, this work deserves.'[94] Hobson's theory, in fact, became the essence of Lenin's own. The result, *Imperialism: The Highest Stage of Capitalism* (1916), laid down the standard doctrine on the subject for all states under Communism, from 1917 to the present day. Leninist theory, in one form or another, likewise formed the attitudes of many Third World states towards imperialism and colonialism, as they acquired independence in the 1950s and 1960s.

Granted the theory's anti-Semitic roots, it was not difficult to fit into it the concept of Zionism as a form of colonialism and the Zionist state as an outpost of imperialism. There were, it was true, the awkward historical facts of Israel's birth, with Stalin acting as one of the principal midwives. These in themselves demolished the Soviet theory of Zionism completely. But like many other facts in Soviet history, they were buried and forgotten by the official propagandists. In any case the entire history of anti-Semitism demonstrates how impervious it is to awkward facts. That 'Zionism' in practice stood for 'the Jews' became quickly apparent. The 1952 Slánsky trial was the first occasion in the history of Communism that the traditional anti-Semitic accusation of a world-wide Jewish conspiracy, with the American Jewish Joint Distribution Committee and the Israeli government constituting the modern Elders of Zion, was put forward officially by a Communist government – an ominous milestone. The reality behind the scenes was even worse. The Jewish Deputy Foreign Minister Artur London, sentenced to life imprisonment but released in the 'Prague Spring' of 1968, was then able to reveal the anti-Semitic fury of the chief prosecutor, Major Smole: '[He] took me by the throat and in a voice shaking with hatred shouted: "You and your dirty race, we shall exterminate it. Not everything Hitler did was right. But he exterminated Jews and that was a good thing. Far too many of them managed to avoid the gas chamber but we shall finish where he left off." '[95]

From the early 1950s, Soviet anti-Zionist propaganda, growing steadily in intensity and comprehensiveness, stressed the links between Zionism, the Jews in general, and Judaism. 'Judaic sermons are the sermons of bourgeois Zionists,' announced a Ukrainian-language broadcast from Korovograd, 9 December 1959. 'The character of the Jewish religion', the Kuibyshev newspaper *Volszhskaya Kommuna* wrote on 30 September 1961, 'serves the political aims of the Zionists.' 'Zionism', wrote *Kommunist Moldavia* in 1963, 'is inseparably linked to Judaism . . . rooted in the idea of the exclusiveness of the Jewish people.'[96] Hundreds of articles, in magazines and newspapers all over the Soviet Union, portrayed Zionists (i.e. Jews) and Israeli leaders as engaged in a world-wide conspiracy, along the lines of the old *Protocols of Zion*. It was, *Sovietskaya Latvia* wrote, 5 August 1967, an 'international Cosa Nostra' with 'a common centre, a common programme and common funds'. The 'Israeli ruling circles' were only junior partners in its global plots.[97]

In the twenty years after the 1967 Six Day War, the Soviet propaganda machine became the main source for anti-Semitic material in the world. In doing so it assembled materials from virtually every archaeological layer of anti-Semitic history, from classical antiquity to Hitlerism. The sheer volume of the material, ranging from endlessly repetitive articles and broadcasts to full-scale books, began to rival the Nazi output. Trofim Kychko's book, *Judaism and Zionism* (1968), spoke of the 'chauvinistic idea of the God-chosenness of the Jewish people, the propaganda of messianism and the idea of ruling over the peoples of the world'. Vladimir Begun's *Creeping Counter-Revolution* (1974) called the Bible 'an unsurpassed textbook of bloodthirstiness, hypocrisy, treason, perfidy and moral degeneracy'; no wonder the Zionists were gangsters since their ideas came from 'the scrolls of the "holy" Torah and the precepts of the Talmud'.[98] In 1972 the Soviet embassy journal in Paris actually reproduced parts of a Tsarist anti-Semitic pamphlet put out in 1906 by the Black Hundred, who organized the pre-1914 pogroms. In this instance it was possible to take action in the French courts, which duly found the publisher (a prominent member of the French Communist Party) guilty of incitement to racial violence.[99] Some of the Soviet anti-Semitic material, circulated at a very high level, almost defied belief. In a Central Committee memorandum of 10 January 1977, one Soviet anti-Semitic expert, Valery Emelianov, claimed that America was controlled by a Zionist–masonic conspiracy ostensibly led by President Carter but actually under the control of what he called the 'B'nai Brith Gestapo'. The Zionists, according to Emelianov, penetrated goy society through the masons, each one of whom was an active Zionist informer; Zionism itself was based on 'the Judaic–masonic pyramid'.[100]

The keystone of the new Soviet fantasy-edifice of anti-Semitism was provided in the 1970s, when the charge that the Zionists were the racist successors of the Nazis was 'proved' by 'evidence' that Hitler's Holocaust itself was a Jewish–Nazi conspiracy to get rid of poor Jews who could not be used in Zionist plans. Indeed, it was alleged, Hitler himself got his ideas from Herzl. The Jewish–Zionist leaders, acting on orders from the millionaire Jews who controlled international finance capital, helped the ss and the Gestapo to herd unwanted Jews either into the gas ovens or into the kibbutzim of the Land of Canaan. This Jewish–Nazi conspiracy was used as background by the Soviet propaganda machine to charges of atrocities against the Israeli government, especially during and after the Lebanon operations of 1982. Since the Zionists were happy to join with Hitler in exterminating their own discarded people, wrote *Pravda* on 17 January 1984, it was not surprising that they were now massacring Lebanese Arabs, whom they regarded as sub-human anyway.[101]

These sinister developments in the anti-Semitic policy of the Soviet government were more than a reversion to traditional Tsarist practice, though they included most of the familiar Tsarist mythology about Jews. For one thing, Tsarist governments always allowed the Jews escape through mass emigration. For another, the Soviet regime had a record second only to Hitler's in exterminating entire categories of people for ideological purposes. The equation of Jews with Zionism, a capital offence in Soviet doctrine, would make it the easiest thing in the world for the Soviet leadership to justify in ideological terms extreme measures against Russia's 1,750,000 Jews, such as reviving Stalin's 1952–3 plan to deport them *en masse* to Siberia, or even worse.

Another disturbing factor was the close resemblance between Soviet anti-Jewish propaganda and similar material put out by Russia's allies in the Arab world. The difference was more of form than of substance. The Arabs were less thorough in their use of ideological jargon and they sometimes openly used the word 'Jews' where the Russians were usually careful to employ the code-term 'Zionists'. Where the Russians drew from the *Protocols of Zion* without acknowledgment, the Arabs published it openly. This tract had circulated widely in the

Arab world, published in innumerable different editions, ever since the early 1920s. It was read by such diverse Arab leaders as King Feisal of Saudi Arabia and President Nasser of Egypt. The latter evidently believed it, telling an Indian journalist in 1957: 'It is very important that you should read it. I will give you a copy. It proves beyond a shadow of a doubt that three hundred Zionists, each of whom knows all the others, govern the fate of the European continent and that they elect their successors from their entourage.'[102] Nasser was so impressed by the book that yet another Arab edition was published by his brother in about 1967. Extracts and summaries were used in Arab school textbooks and in training material for the Arab armed forces.[103] In 1972 yet another edition of it appeared at the top of the Beirut best-seller list.

All these editions, it should be added, were specially edited for Arab readers and the Elders were presented in the context of the Palestine problem. The *Protocols* were not the only anti-Semitic classic to live on in the post-war Arab world. Blood-libel material, published in Cairo in 1890 under the title *The Cry of the Innocent in the Horn of Freedom*, resurfaced in 1962 as an official publication of the UAR government called *Talmudic Human Sacrifices*.[104] Indeed the blood libel periodically reappeared in Arab newspapers.[105] But the *Protocols* remained the favourite, and not only in Arab Islamic countries. It was published in Pakistan in 1967 and extensive use was made of it by the Iranian government and its embassies after the Ayatollah Khomeini, a fervent believer in anti-Jewish conspiracy theory, came to power there in 1979. In May 1984, his publication *Imam*, which had already printed extracts from the *Protocols*, accused the British task force in the Falklands of conducting atrocities on the advice of the Elders of Zion.[106] Khomeini's propaganda usually portrayed Zionism (alias the Jews), which had been at work 'for centuries everywhere, perpetrating crimes of unbelievable magnitude against human societies and values', as an emanation of Satan. Khomeini followed the medieval line that Jews were sub-human or inhuman, indeed anti-human, and therefore constituted an exterminable category of creature. But his anti-Semitism hovered confusingly between simple anti-Judaism, Islamic sectarianism (Sunni Moslems ruling his enemy Iraq were Zionist puppets as well as devils in their own right) and hatred of America, 'the great Satan'. He found it difficult to decide whether Satan was manipulating Washington via the Jews or vice versa.

Arab anti-Semitism too was an uneasy blend of religious and secular motifs. It was also ambivalent about the role of Hitler and the Nazis.

The Grand Mufti of Jerusalem had known of the Final Solution and welcomed it. Hitler told him that when his troops reached the Middle East they would wipe out the Jewish settlements in Palestine.[107] After the war, many Arabs continued to regard Hitler as a hero-figure. When Eichmann was brought to trial in 1961–2, the English-language Jordanian newspaper, *Jerusalem Times*, published a letter congratulating him for having 'conferred a real blessing on humanity'. The trial would 'one day culminate in the liquidation of the remaining six million to avenge your blood'.[108] On the other hand, Arab anti-Semitic propagandists often followed the Soviet line that Jews and Nazis had worked hand-in-glove, and that the Zionists were the Nazis' natural successors. Particularly in their propaganda directed at the West, Arab governments compared the Israeli air force to the Luftwaffe and the IDF to the SS and Gestapo. At one time or another (sometimes simultaneously) Arab audiences were informed that the Holocaust had been a fortunate event, a diabolical plot between Jews and Nazis, and had never occurred at all, being a simple invention of the Zionists. But when had anti-Semitic theorists ever been disturbed by internal contradictions in their assertions?

The quantity of anti-Zionist material flooding into the world, from both the Soviet bloc and the Arab states, was augmented first by the 1967 Six Day War, which acted as a powerful stimulant to Soviet propaganda against Israel, then by the oil-price revolution following the 1973 Yom Kippur War, which greatly increased Arab funds made available for anti-Zionist propaganda. Inevitably the scale and persistence of anti-Israeli abuse had some effect, notably in the United Nations. The old League of Nations had shown itself singularly ineffective in protecting Jews during the inter-war period. But at least it had not actively encouraged their persecution. The 1975 session of the United Nations General Assembly came close to legitimizing anti-Semitism. On 1 October it received in state President Idi Amin of Uganda, in his capacity as Chairman of the Organization of African Unity. Amin was already notorious for his large-scale massacres of the Ugandan population, some of which he had carried out personally. He was also well known for the violence of his anti-Semitic statements. He had sent a cable to the UN secretary-general on 12 September 1972 applauding the Holocaust, and he announced that, since no statue to Hitler had been erected in Germany, he proposed to set one up in Uganda. Despite this, or perhaps because of it, he was well received by the General Assembly. Many UN delegates, including the whole of the Soviet and Arab blocs, gave him a standing ovation before he began his speech, in which he denounced the 'Zionist–American conspiracy' against the world and called for the expulsion of Israel from the UN and its 'extinction'. There was frequent applause during his grotesque philippic and another standing ovation when he sat down. The following day the UN secretary-general and the president of the General Assembly gave a public dinner in his honour. A fortnight later, on 17 October, the professional anti-Semites of the Soviet and Arab publicity machines achieved their greatest triumphs when the Third Committee of the General Assembly, by a vote of 70 to 29, with 27 abstentions and 16 absent, passed a motion condemning Zionism as a form of racism. On 10 November the General Assembly as a whole endorsed the resolution by 67 to 55 with 15 abstentions. The Israeli delegate, Chaim Herzog, pointed out that the vote took place on the thirty-seventh anniversary of the Nazi *Kristallnacht* against the Jews. The US delegate, Daniel P. Moynihan, announced with icy contempt: 'The United States rises to declare before the General Assembly of the United Nations, and before the world, that it does not acknowledge, it will not abide by, and it will never acquiesce in this infamous act.'[109]

One of the principal lessons of Jewish history has been that repeated verbal slanders are sooner or later followed by violent physical deeds. Time and again over the centuries, anti-Semitic writings created their own fearful momentum which climaxed in an effusion of Jewish blood. The Hitlerian Final Solution was unique in its atrocity but it was none the less prefigured in nineteenth-century anti-Semitic theory. The anti-Semitic torrent poured out by the Soviet bloc and the Arab states in the post-war period produced its own characteristic form of violence: state-sponsored terrorism. There was irony in this weapon being used against Zionism, for it was militant Zionists, such as Avraham Stern and Menachem Begin, who had (it could be argued) invented terrorism in its modern, highly organized and scientific form. That it should be directed, on a vastly increased scale, against the state they had lived, and died, to create could be seen as an act of providential retribution or at any rate as yet another demonstration that idealists who justified their means by their ends did so at their peril. The age of international terrorism, created by post-war Soviet–Arab anti-Semitism, effectively opened in 1968 when the Palestine Liberation Organization formally adopted terror and mass murder as its primary policy. The PLO, and its various competitors and imitators, directed their attacks primarily against Israeli targets but they made no attempt to distinguish between Israeli citizens, or Zionists, and Jews, any more than traditional anti-Semitic killers distinguished between religious Jews and Jews by birth. When members of the Baader–

Meinhof gang, a German fascist left organization inspired by Soviet anti-Semitic propaganda, hijacked an Air France aircraft flying from Paris to Tel Aviv on 27 June 1976, and forced it to land in Idi Amin's Uganda, the terrorists carefully separated the non-Jews from the Jews, who were taken aside to be murdered. One of those they planned to kill still had the ss concentration camp number tattooed on his arm.[110]

Terrorism on the scale and of the sophistication employed by the PLO was a menacing novelty. But to the Jews there was nothing new in the principle of terrorism. For terror had been used against Jews for 1,500 years or more. The pogrom was a typical instrument of anti-Jewish terrorism, designed not primarily to kill Jews but to inculcate submissive fear and resignation to ill-treatment, to instil the habitual docility which led the Jews to submit to the Final Solution almost without a struggle. But those days were over. Terrorism was still employed by Jews but no longer with impunity. The planned murder of Jews aboard the Air France aircraft was an instance. The Israeli Entebbe raid which rescued them (all save one old lady, killed by Amin) demonstrated the ability of the Zionist state to aid Jews in peril more than a thousand miles beyond its borders. Israel could and did act directly against terrorist bases also. The greatest of them was the southern Lebanon, effectively occupied by the PLO in the years 1970–82. From 6 June 1982 the Israel Defence Forces demolished the bases and cleared the entire area of the PLO, which was forced to retreat to a reluctant Tunisia; and even there, in 1985, it was shown that the PLO headquarters was not beyond the reach of Israeli retribution. Such Israeli exercises of the right of self-defence were sometimes misjudged or ill executed. They provoked criticism, on occasion from Israel's friends. The occupation of the southern Lebanon in 1982, which involved heavy Israeli bombing and many Arab casualties and homeless, was a bitter source of discord between Israel and her allies and even within Israel. It was also the background to a slaughter of Moslem refugees, by Christian Falangist Arabs, in the Sabra and Shatilla camps on 16 September. This episode was skilfully exploited by Arab and Soviet propagandists and presented in the Western media as an Israeli responsibility. Begin, then still Israel's prime minister, commented bitterly to a cabinet meeting three days later: 'Goyim kill goyim, and they blame the Jew.'[111] The Israelis wisely ordered an independent judicial inquiry which established the facts and placed some blame on the Israeli Minister of Defence, Ariel Sharon, for not having foreseen and prevented the killings.[112]

The spectacle of Jews killing, especially killing unjustly, was deeply disturbing to them. The possibility had been foreseen in Judah

Halevi's *Kuzari*, written in about 1140, in dialogue form between a rabbi and the wise King of the Khazars. Thus: '*Rabbi*: Our relation to God is a closer one than if we had already reached greatness on earth. *King*: That might be so if your humility were voluntary. But it is involuntary, and if you had power you would slay. *Rabbi*: Thou hast touched our weak spot, O King of the Khazars.' Yet the right to kill in self-defence was inherent in the human condition. Every man possessed it. The state merely exercised it vicariously, on the community's behalf, and on a greater scale. Jews, perennially pre-occupied, almost obsessed, with the sanctity of life, found the killing role of the state hard to accept. To them it was the curse of Saul. It had cast a shadow on the life of their greatest king, so that David, being a man of blood, could not build the Temple. But between the curse of Saul and the reality of Auschwitz there could be no real choice. The Jews had to have their state, with all its moral consequences, to survive.

The need for a secular Zion did not diminish during the first forty years of its history. It increased. It had been created to receive the victims of European anti-Semitism and, in the aftermath of the Holocaust, to house its shattered survivors. It had served to accommodate those expelled from Arab Jewries. These fulfilled purposes alone justified its existence. But new tasks emerged. It became clear, during the post-war decades, that the Soviet regime was no more likely to reach a peaceful accommodation with its Jewish citizens than its Tsarist predecessor. The evidence suggested that they might be in greater collective peril than ever before. So one prime aim of the Israelis was to get their 1,750,000 Russian brethren out of the power of the Soviet system. They had to be prepared, at short notice, to accept a mass migration of the kind that Tsarist cruelties had provoked. They had equally to be ready to move heaven and earth if the hatred of the Soviet regime for the Jews took other forms.

The state of Israel acquired an even more sombre purpose. It was the sovereign refuge of the imperilled Jew anywhere in the world. It was the guardian of gathered Jews already within its borders. It was the only physical guarantee that another Holocaust would not occur. The unremitting campaign of violent anti-Semitism by its Soviet and Arab enemies suggests that separately or conjointly they might seek to impose another Final Solution if they got the opportunity. Israel had to assume such a possibility, and arm against it. It had reliable promises of United States protection but in the last resort a sovereign state must look to its own defences. Hence Israel had to possess the means to inflict unacceptable damage on a would-be aggressor, however powerful. If David had to meet Goliath, he must possess a sling. During the Second World War Jewish scientists had played a critical part in making the first nuclear weapons. They had done so because they feared Hitler would develop an atomic bomb first. In the 1950s and 1960s, as Soviet and Arab hostility to Israel grew, Israeli scientists worked to equip the state with a means of deterrence. In the late 1970s and 1980s they created a nuclear capability, whose existence was secret but understood in the quarters where it would have most effect. Thus Israel was in a position to fulfil the second of the two new tasks which circumstances had placed upon her.

But it would be wrong to conclude a history of the Jews on this grim note. Jewish history can be presented as a succession of climaxes and catastrophes. It can also be seen as an endless continuum of patient study, fruitful industry and communal routine, much of it unrecorded. Sorrow finds a voice while happiness is mute. The historian must bear this in mind. Over 4,000 years the Jews proved themselves not only great survivors but extraordinarily skilful in adapting to the societies among which fate thrust them, and in gathering whatever human comforts they had to offer. No people has been more fertile in enriching poverty or humanizing wealth, or in turning misfortune to creative account. This capacity springs from a moral philosophy both solid and subtle, which has changed remarkably little over the millennia precisely because it has been seen to serve the purposes of those who share it. Countless Jews, in all ages, have groaned under the burden of Judaism. But they have continued to carry it because they have known, in their hearts, that it carried them. The Jews were survivors because they possessed the law of survival.

Hence the historian must also bear in mind that Judaism has always been greater than the sum of its adherents. Judaism created the Jews, not the other way round. As the philosopher Leon Roth put it: 'Judaism comes first. It is not a product but a programme and the Jews are the instruments of its fulfilment.'[113] Jewish history is a record not only of physical facts but of metaphysical notions. The Jews believed themselves created and commanded to be a light to the gentiles and they have obeyed to the best of their considerable powers. The results, whether considered in religious or in secular terms, have been remarkable. The Jews gave the world ethical monotheism, which might be described as the application of reason to divinity. In a more secular age, they applied the principles of rationality to the whole range of human activities, often in advance of the rest of mankind. The light they thus shed disturbed as well as illuminated, for it revealed painful truths about the human spirit as well as the means to uplift it.

The Jews have been great truth-tellers and that is one reason they have been so much hated. A prophet will be feared and sometimes honoured, but when has he been loved? Yet a prophet must prophesy and the Jews will persist in pursuing truth, as they see it, wherever it leads. Jewish history teaches, if anything can, that there is indeed a purpose to human existence and that we are not just born to live and die like beasts. In continuing to give meaning to creation, the Jews will take comfort from the injunction, thrice repeated, in the noble first chapter of the Book of Joshua: 'Be strong and of good courage; be not afraid, neither be thou dismayed: for the Lord thy God is with thee whithersoever thou goest.'[114]

Epilogue

In his *Antiquities of the Jews*, Josephus describes Abraham as 'a man of great sagacity' who had 'higher notions of virtue than others of his time'. He therefore 'determined to change completely the views which all then had about God'. One way of summing up 4,000 years of Jewish history is to ask ourselves what would have happened to the human race if Abraham had not been a man of great sagacity, or if he had stayed in Ur and kept his higher notions to himself, and no specific Jewish people had come into being. Certainly the world without the Jews would have been a radically different place. Humanity might eventually have stumbled upon all the Jewish insights. But we cannot be sure. All the great conceptual discoveries of the intellect seem obvious and inescapable once they have been revealed, but it requires a special genius to formulate them for the first time. The Jews had this gift. To them we owe the idea of equality before the law, both divine and human; of the sanctity of life and the dignity of the human person; of the individual conscience and so of personal redemption; of the collective conscience and so of social responsibility; of peace as an abstract ideal and love as the foundation of justice, and many other items which constitute the basic moral furniture of the human mind. Without the Jews it might have been a much emptier place.

Above all, the Jews taught us how to rationalize the unknown. The result was monotheism and the three great religions which profess it. It is almost beyond our capacity to imagine how the world would have fared if they had never emerged. Nor did the intellectual penetration of the unknown stop at the idea of one God. Indeed monotheism itself can be seen as a milestone on the road which leads people to dispense with God altogether. The Jews first rationalized the pantheon of idols into one Supreme Being; then began the process of rationalizing Him out of existence. In the ultimate perspective of history, Abraham and Moses may come to seem less important than Spinoza. For the Jewish impact on humanity has been protean. In antiquity they were the great innovators in religion and morals. In the Dark Ages and early medieval Europe they were still an advanced people transmitting scarce knowledge and technology. Gradually they were pushed from the van and fell behind until, by the end of the eighteenth century, they were seen as a bedraggled and obscurantist rearguard in the march of civilized humanity. But then came an astonishing second burst of creativity. Breaking out of their ghettos, they once more transformed human thinking, this time in the secular sphere. Much of the mental furniture of the modern world too is of Jewish fabrication.

The Jews were not just innovators. They were also exemplars and epitomizers of the human condition. They seemed to present all the inescapable dilemmas of man in a heightened and clarified form. They were the quintessential 'strangers and sojourners'. But are we not all such on this planet, of which we each possess a mere leasehold of threescore and ten? The Jews were the emblem of homeless and vulnerable humanity. But is not the whole earth no more than a temporary transit-camp? The Jews were fierce idealists striving for perfection, and at the same time fragile men and women yearning for flesh-pots and safety. They wanted to obey God's impossible law, and they wanted to stay alive too. Therein lay the dilemma of the Jewish commonwealths in antiquity, trying to combine the moral excellence of a theocracy with the practical demands of a state capable of defending itself. The dilemma has been recreated in our own time in the shape of Israel, founded to realize a humanitarian ideal, discovering in practice that it must be ruthless simply to survive in a hostile world. But is not this a recurrent problem which affects all human societies? We all want to build Jerusalem. We all drift back towards the Cities of the Plain. It seems to be the role of the Jews to focus and dramatize these common experiences of mankind, and to turn their particular fate into a universal moral. But if the Jews have this role, who wrote it for them?

Historians should beware of seeking providential patterns in events. They are all too easily found, for we are credulous creatures, born to believe, and equipped with powerful imaginations which readily produce and rearrange data to suit any transcendental scheme. Yet excessive scepticism can produce as serious a distortion as credulity. The historian should take into account all forms of evidence, including those which are or appear to be metaphysical. If the earliest Jews were able to survey, with us, the history of their progeny, they would find nothing surprising in it. They always knew that Jewish society was appointed to be a pilot-project for the entire human race. That Jewish dilemmas, dramas and catastrophes should be exemplary, larger than life, would seem only natural to them. That Jews should over the millennia attract such unparalleled, indeed inexplicable, hatred would be regrettable but only to be expected. Above all, that the Jews should still survive, when all those other ancient people were transmuted or vanished into the oubliettes of history, was wholly predictable. How could it be otherwise? Providence decreed it and the Jews obeyed. The historian may say: there is no such thing as providence. Possibly not. But human confidence in such an historical dynamic, if it is strong and tenacious enough, is a force in itself, which pushes on the hinge of events and moves them. The Jews believed they were a special people with such unanimity and passion, and over so long a span, that they became one. They did indeed have a role because they wrote it for themselves. Therein, perhaps, lies the key to their story.

Glossary

Aggadah: The non-legal part of the Talmud and midrash, tales, folklore, legends etc., as opposed to the Law itself (halakhah).

Aliyah: 'Ascending'; emigrating to Israel; being called to read the Law in synagogue.

Am Ha-arez: Lit. 'people of the land'; can mean 'natives', and sometimes used pejoratively, as denoting ignorance; the common people; the population as a whole.

Amoraim: Jewish scholars, third to sixth centuries AD, who produced the *Gemara*.

Ashkenazi: German Jews; west, central and east European Jews, in contrast to Sephardi Jews.

Ba'al shem: 'Master of the Holy Name'; a learned kabbalist who knew how to use the power of the Holy Name; a learned man, usually hasidic.

Bar: 'Son of' (Aramaic) in personal names. 'Ben' (Hebrew) means the same.

Bar-mitzvah: Initiation of thirteen-year-old Jewish boy into the community.

Bet din: Rabbinical law court.

Cohen: Jew of priestly or Aaronic descent.

Conservative Judaism: Term used in the United States for Jewish worship which modifies the Law to meet modern needs while avoiding the wholesale changes of Reform Judaism.

Conversos: Spanish medieval and Renaissance term for Jews who converted to Christianity, and their descendants.

Dayyan: Judge in rabbinic court.

Diaspora: Collective term for the dispersal and Jews living in it, outside Erez Israel.

Erez Israel: Land of Israel; the Promised Land; Palestine.

Exilarch: Lay head of the Jews in Babylonia.

Galut: The Exile; the exiled community.

Gaon: Head of Babylonian academy.

Gemara: Rulings, etc., of the amoraim, supplementing the Mishnah and forming part of the Talmud.

Genizah: Depository of sacred writings; usually refers to the one in Fustat (Old Cairo).

Get: A Jewish bill of divorce.

Golem: An artificial man brought to life by magic.

Haganah: Jewish defence force under the British mandate, which became the basis of the Israeli army.

Halakhah: A generally accepted ruling in rabbinical law, and the part of the Talmud dealing with legal matters, as opposed to the aggadah.

Hanukkah: Feast commemorating the victory of the Maccabees over the pagan Greeks.

Hasidim: Followers of devout form of Judaism with strong mystical element, usually in eastern Europe.

Haskalah: Jewish form of the eighteenth-century European enlightenment. One who believed in it was a *maskil*.

Hazzan: Liturgical prayer-leader.

Heder (or *cheder*): Judaic primary school.

Herem: Excommunication.

Histadrut: Israeli labour federation.

Irgun: Underground military wing of the Revisionist movement in Israel, 1931–49.

Kabbalah: Jewish mysticism. 'Practical kabbalah' is a form of magic.

Karaite: Member of eighth-century Jewish sect which rejected the Oral Law or post-Biblical rabbinic teaching, and stuck to the Bible alone.

Ketubbah: Jewish marriage contract.

Kibbutz: Jewish settlement, usually agricultural, owning property in common.

Kiddush: Blessing over wine, preceding Sabbath or festival meal.

Knesset: Israel's parliament.

Kosher: Food conforming to Jewish dietary laws or *kashrut*.

Levirate marriage: Obligatory marriage of childless widow with deceased's brother (Deuteronomy 25:5).

Maggid: Popular hasidic preacher.

Marranos: Secret Jews, descended from Spanish and Portuguese forced converts.

Maskil: Member of the Jewish enlightenment or haskalah.

Masoretic: Word used of the accepted tradition for spelling and pronouncing the Bible.

Menorah: The seven-branched lamp used in Temple; the eight-branched candelabrum used on Hanukkah.

Mezuzah: Torah verses fixed to doors of Jewish houses.

Midrash: An exposition of Scripture or collection of such.

Minyan: Quorum (ten adult Jews) for community prayers.

Mishnah: Codified version of Jewish Oral Law.

Mohel: Circumciser.

Moshav: Smallholders' co-operative in Israel.

Nagid: Medieval head of Jewish community.

Nasi: President of the Sanhedrin; a Jewish prince; a descendant of Hillel recognized as Jewish patriarch.

Oral Law: As opposed to the written Torah or Bible; first found written form in the Mishnah.

Orthodox Judaism: Traditional Judaism based on strict observance of the Law.

Pale: The twenty-five Tsarist provinces where Russian Jews were granted permanent residence.

Palmah: The full-time section of the Haganah.

Parnas: The chief synagogue official or elected head of the laity.

Pilpul: A talmudic discussion or dispute, often hair-splitting.

Piyyut: Liturgical poetry in Hebrew.

Purim: Festival commemorating deliverance of the Persian Jews by Esther.

Rabbi: Literally 'master'; religious teacher.

Reform Judaism: Jewish worship modifying the Law to meet modern conditions.

Responsum: Written opinion in reply to query about the Law.

Revisionist: Follower of breakaway Zionist movement led by Jabotinsky.

Rosh Ha-Shanah: Jewish New Year holiday.

Sanhedrin: Supreme Court of religious scholars in Second Commonwealth.

Schnorrer: A professional beggar.

Shabbat: Dusk Friday till darkness Saturday.

Shabbetean: Follower of the false Messiah, Shabbetai Zevi.

Shadchan: A match-maker. A match is a *shidduch*.

Shammos: Synagogue sexton-beadle.

Sheitl: Wig worn by Orthodox woman in public.

Shekhinah: lit. 'dwelling'; the numinous presence of God in the world.

Shema: Judaic confession of faith (Deuteronomy 6:4).

Shiksa: Young gentile woman.

Shofar: Liturgical ram's horn.

Shohet: Ritual slaughterer.

Shtetl: Small Jewish town in eastern Europe.

Shulhan Arukh: Joseph Caro's famous code of Jewish law.

Siddur: Prayer-book.

Sukkot: Festival of Tabernacles.

Tallit: Prayer-shawl.

Tannaim: Rabbinical scholars of Mishnah period.

Targum: Aramaic translation of Hebrew Bible.

Tefillin: Phylacteries or small leather boxes fixed to the arm or forehead during prayers.

Torah: The Pentateuch, or scroll thereof; the entire body of Jewish law and teaching.

Tosefta: Collection of tannaic teaching related to Mishnah.

Yeshivah: A rabbinical academy. The *rosh yeshivah* is head of it.

Yishuv: A settlement; the Jewish community in Erez Israel before the state was created.

Yom Kippur: Day of Atonement.

Zaddik: A hasidic leader or holy man.

Zohar: The principal work of kabbalah, being a mystical commentary on the Pentateuch.

Source Notes

PART ONE: ISRAELITES

1. For a description and plan of the tombs, see L. H. Vincent *et al.*, *Hebron: Le Haram El-Khalil. Sépulture des Patriarches* (Paris 1923); *Encyclopaedia Judaica*, xi 671.
2. G. L. Strange, *Palestine Under the Moslems* (London 1890), 309ff.
3. E. Sarna, *Understanding Genesis* (London 1967), 168ff.
4. Herbert Han, updated by H. D. Hummel, *The Old Testament in Modern Research* (London 1970); R. Grant, *A Short History of the Interpretation of the Bible* (New York 1963).
5. English translation published Edinburgh 1885; New York 1957.
6. M. Noth, *The History of Israel* (2nd edn, London 1960); A. Alt, *Essays on Old Testament History and Religion* (New York 1968).
7. G. Mendenhall and M. Greenberg, 'Method in the Study of Early Hebrew History', in J. Ph. Hyatt (ed.), *The Bible in Modern Scholarship* (Nashville, New York 1964), 15–43.
8. See W. F. Albright, *Archaeology and the Religion of Israel* (3rd edn, Baltimore 1953) and *Yahweh and the Gods of Canaan* (London 1968); Kathleen Kenyon, *Archaeology in the Holy Land* (4th edn, London 1979) and *The Bible and Recent Archaeology* (London 1978).
9. Deuteronomy 4:19.
10. R. D. Barnett, *Illustrations of Old Testament History* (London 1966), ch. 1, 'The Babylonian Legend of the Flood'.
11. Genesis 11:31.
12. L. Woolley *et al.*, *Ur Excavations* (British Museum, London, 1954–); L. Woolley, *The Sumerians* (London 1954).
13. M. E. L. Mallowan, 'Noah's Flood Reconsidered', *Iraq* 26 (1964).
14. W. G. Lambert and A. R. Millard, *Atrahasis: The Babylonian Story of the Flood* (London 1970); E. Sollberger, *The Babylonian Legend of the Flood* (3rd edn, London 1971).
15. *Cambridge Ancient History*, I i (3rd edn 1970), 353ff.
16. Genesis 9:18.
17. *Encyclopaedia Judaica*, v 330; Michael Grant, *A History of Ancient Israel* (London 1984), 32.
18. For a summary of the calculations, see R. K. Harrison, *Introduction to the New Testament* (London 1970).

19. See Kenyon, *Archaeology of the Holy Land* (London 1960), for the concordance between the Middle Bronze Age tombs outside Jericho and the Cave of Machpelah; Nelson Glueck, 'The Age of Abraham in the Negev', *Biblical Archaeologist* 18 (1955).

20. A. Parrot, *Mari, une ville perdue* (Paris 1935).

21. D. H. Gordon, 'Biblical Customs and the Nuzi Tablets', *Biblical Archaeologist* 3 (1940).

22. P. Matthiae, 'Ebla à l'Époque d'Akkad', *Académie des inscriptions et belles-lettres, compte-rendu* (Paris 1976).

23. A. Malamat, 'King Lists of the Old Babylonian Period and Biblical Genealogies', *Journal of the American Oriental Society* 88 (1968); 'Northern Canaan and the Mari Texts', in J. A. Sanders (ed.), *Near Eastern Archaeology in the Twentieth Century* (Garden City, NY 1970), 167–77; and 'Mari', *Biblical Archaeologist*, 34 (1971).

24. Genesis 23:29–34.

25. Quoted in R. K. Harrison, *Introduction to the Old Testament* (London 1970).

26. C. H. Gordon, 'Abraham of Ur', in D. Winton Thomas (ed.), *Hebrew and Semitic Studies Presented to G. R. Driver* (Oxford 1962), 77–84; E. A. Speiser, *Genesis, Anchor Bible* (Garden City, NY 1964). See also M. Grunberg, 'Another Look at Rachel's Theft of the Terraphin', *Journal of Biblical Literature* 81 (1962).

27. Kenyon, *The Bible and Recent Archaeology*, 7–24.

28. J.-R. Kupper, *Les Nomades de Mésopotamie au temps des rois de Mari* (Paris 1957); I. J. Gelb, 'The Early History of the West Semitic Peoples', *Journal of Cuneiform Studies*, 15 (1961).

29. E. A. Speiser, 'The Biblical Idea of History in its Common Near Eastern Setting', in Judah Goldin (ed.), *The Jewish Experience* (Yale 1976).

30. Genesis 26:16.

31. Genesis 16:12.

32. J. L. Myers, *The Linguistic and Literary Form of the Book of Ruth* (London 1955); Albright, *Yahweh and the Gods of Canaan*, 1–25; S. Daiches, *The Song of Deborah* (London 1926).

33. S. W. Baron, *Social and Religious History of the Jews* (2nd edn, New York 1952), i 1 44. Grant, *A History of Ancient Israel*, 32ff.

34. Joshua 24:2.

35. Isaiah 29:22.

36. Speiser, *op. cit.*

37. G. E. Wright, 'How Did Early Israel Differ from Her Neighbours?', *Biblical Archaeology* 6 (1943); Baron, *op. cit.*, i 1 48.

38. Genesis 22:2 says 'thine only son Isaac', meaning of course by Sarah.

39. *Encyclopaedia Judaica*, ii 480–6; Philo, *De Abrahamo*, 177–99, 200–7; Maimonides, *Guide of the Perplexed*, 3:24; Nahmanides, *Works*, ed. C. B. Chavel (London 1959), i 125–6.

40. *Fear and Trembling* (trans.), Penguin Classics (Harmondsworth 1985).

41. Ernst Simon in *Conservative Judaism* 12 (Spring 1958).

42. Genesis 22:14.

43. *Ibid.*, 22:18.

44. This theme is ingeniously discussed in Dan Jacobson, *The Story of the Stories: The Chosen People and its God* (London 1982).

45. Abot 6:10 (baraita, Kinyan Torah); quoted in Samuel Belkin, *In His Image: The Jewish Philosophy of Man as Expressed in the Rabbinical Tradition* (London 1961).

46. Midrash Tehillim 24:3.

47. Leviticus 25:23; I Chronicles 29:15; Psalms 39:12.

48. Genesis 15:1–6.

49. Genesis 17:8.

50. W. D. Davies, *The Territorial Dimensions of Judaism* (Berkeley 1982), 9–17.

51. Gerhard von Rad, *The Problem of the Hexateuch and Other Essays* (trans., Edinburgh 1966); J. A. Sanders, *Torah and Canon* (Philadelphia 1972).

52. In Genesis 32:28 and 35:10.

53. In Genesis 37:1.

54. Genesis 29:30; 35:16–18; 48:5–6.

55. Genesis 25:13–16; 22:20–4; 10:16–30; 36:10–13.

56. W. F. Albright, 'The Song of Deborah in the Light of Archaeology', *Bulletin of the American School of Oriental Research*, 62 (1936); H. M. Orlinsky, 'The Tribal System of Israel and Related Groups in the Period of Judges', *Oriens Antiquus*, 1 (1962).

57. O. Eissfeld in *Cambridge Ancient History*, II ii ch. xxxiv, 'The Hebrew Kingdom', 537ff.

58. Genesis 14:18–20; 17:1; 21:33.

59. For Shechem, see W. Harrelson, B. W. Anderson and G. E. Wright, 'Shechem, "Navel of the Land" ', in *Biblical Archaeologist*, 20 (1957).

60. Genesis 48:22.

61. Joshua 8:30–5.

62. *Cambridge Ancient History*, II ii 314–17.

63. Baron, *op. cit.*, i I 22.

64. Genesis 41:39.

65. *Encyclopaedia Judaica*, x 205.

66. Exodus 1:11.

67. *Cambridge Ancient History*, II ii 321–2.

68. H. H. Ben Sasson (ed.), *A History of the Jewish People* (trans., Harvard 1976), 42ff.

69. I Kings 1:6 refers to 'the 480th year after the children of Israel were come out of the land of Egypt, in the fourth year of Solomon's reign over Israel. . . .' Solomon's reign is the first in Israel's history for which we have absolute dating.

70. B. Couroyer, 'La résidence Ramesside du Delta et la Rames Biblique', *Revue biblique* 53 (1946).

71. Ben Sasson, *op. cit.*, 44; *Cambridge Ancient History*, II ii 322–3.

72. Deuteronomy 4:23–4; Exodus 19:4–6.

73. Exodus 4:10ff.

74. Exodus 18:14–24.

75. Sifra 45d; *Encyclopaedia Judaica*, xii 568.

76. Eusebius (died *c.* 359 AD) summarized much of this tradition in his *Praeparatio Evangelica*, 9:26–7 etc.

77. Josephus, *Contra Apion*, 2:154.

78. Philo, *Questiones et Solutiones in Gesesin*, 4:152; *De Providentia*, 111.

79. Numenius, *Fragments* (ed. E. A. Leemans, 1937), 19, 32.

80. Reproduced in Josephus, *Contra Apion*, 1:228ff; Theodore Reinach, *Textes d'auteurs grecs et romains rélatifs au Judaisme* (Paris 1895).

81. Marx to Engels, 10 May 1861; 30 July 1862: *Marx–Engels Works*, vol. xxx, 165, 259.
82. *Moses and Monotheism* (London 1939).
83. Exodus 1:9–10.
84. C. J. Gadd, *Ideas of Divine Rule in the Ancient Near East* (London 1948).
85. Speiser, *op. cit.*
86. Enid B. Mellor (ed.), *The Making of the Old Testament* (Cambridge 1972).
87. For examples of codes see James B. Pritchard (ed.), *Ancient Near Eastern Texts Relating to the Old Testament* (3rd edn, Princeton 1969).
88. Moshe Greenberg, 'Some Postulates of Biblical Criminal Law', in Goldin, *op. cit.*
89. Deuteronomy 22:22–3; Leviticus 20:10.
90. Exodus 21:22ff.
91. Exodus 21:29; see A. van Selms, 'The Goring Ox in Babylonian and Biblical Law', *Archiv Orientali* 18 (1950).
92. Deuteronomy 24:16; 5:9; Exodus 20:5. There are, however, examples of the law of talion applying in the Biblical narratives, for example Saul's sons. Joshua 7; ii Samuel 21.
93. Deuteronomy 25:3; E. A. Hoebel: *The Law of Primitive Man* (Harvard 1954); G. R. Driver and J. C. Miles, *The Babylonian Laws*, 2 vols (Oxford 1952); W. Kornfeld, 'L'Adultère dans l'orient antique', *Revue biblique* 57 (1950).
94. J. J. Stamm and M. E. Andrew, *The Ten Commandments in Recent Research* (New York 1967).
95. Pritchard, *Ancient Near Eastern Texts*, 35.
96. G. Mendenhall, *Biblical Archaeology* 17 (1954).
97. Set out conveniently, with Biblical text references, in *Encyclopaedia Judaica*, v 763–82.
98. Exodus 21:1 to 22:16; O. Eissfeldt in *Cambridge Ancient History*, ii ii ch. xxxiv, 563: see J. P. M. Smith, *The Origin and History of Hebrew Law* (Chicago 1960).
99. A. van Selms, *Marriage and Family Life in Ugaritic Literature* (New York 1954).
100. D. R. Mace, *Hebrew Marriage* (New York 1953).
101. Roland de Vaux, *Ancient Israel: Its Life and Institutions* (trans., New York 1961), 46–7.
102. J. M. Sasson, 'Circumcision in the Ancient Near East', *Journal of Biblical Literature*, 85 (1966).
103. Exodus 4:25; Joshua 5:2–3.
104. Baron, *op. cit.*, i i 6–7.
105. Ezekiel 20:12.
106. Leviticus 17:14; Genesis 9:4; Genesis 38:24. See I. M. Price, 'Swine in Old Testament Taboos', *Journal of Biblical Literature* 44 (1925).
107. i Kings 22:11.
108. ii Kings 2:23.
109. A. H. Godbey, 'Incense and Poison Ordeals in the Ancient Orient', *American Journal of Semitic Languages*, 46 (1929–30).
110. See examples with references in George Fohrer, *History of Israelite Religion* (trans., London 1973), 233.
111. Von Rad, *op. cit.*, 'Some Aspects of the Old Testament World View'.
112. Exodus 34:13–16.

113. This was the view of the Mishraic sage Simeon ben Assai; Sifra on Leviticus 19:18.
114. *Contra Apionem* (Loeb Classic 1951), ii 165.
115. Berakot 2, 2.
116. *De Specialibus legibus* (Loeb Classics 1950), iv 237.
117. Belkin, *op. cit.*, 15–18.
118. I Corinthians 1:19–20.
119. For a discussion of the site of Mt Sinai, see *Cambridge Ancient History*, II ii 324ff.
120. Baron, *op. cit.*, i I 48–9.
121. *Ibid.*, i I 23.
122. Cf. W. F. Albright, 'Exploring in Sinai with the University of California Expedition', *Bulletin of the American School of Oriental Research*, 109 (1948).
123. *Cambridge Ancient History*, II ii 327.
124. Exodus 17:8–13.
125. Numbers 27:15–21; Deuteronomy 34:9.
126. Joshua 6:16–20.
127. Joshua 6:21, 26; Kathleen Kenyon, *Digging Up Jericho* (London 1957).
128. Joshua 9:27.
129. James B. Pritchard, *Gibeon, Where the Sun Stood Still: The Discovery of a Biblical City* (Princeton 1962).
130. Joshua 10:9–13.
131. Joshua 11:4–11.
132. Yigael Yadin, *Hazor: The Rediscovery of a Great City of the Bible* (London 1975).
133. Joshua 24:13.
134. W. F. Albright, *From the Stone Age to Christianity* (Baltimore 1946), 194, 212, and *Archaeology and the Religion of Israel* (3rd edn, Baltimore 1953), 3, 102.
135. Baron, *op. cit.*, II 55.
136. Judges 4:8.
137. Judges 3:15–30.
138. Judges 4:17–21.
139. Judges 11:1–3.
140. Judges 11:37.
141. Judges 16:28.
142. See A. van Selms in *Journal of Near Eastern Studies*, 9 (1950).
143. Judges 12:5–6.
144. I Samuel 21:13–14.
145. II Samuel 23:20–1.
146. Judges 9.
147. Joshua 24:8, 13; Judges 11:17ff.; II Samuel 7:23; Numbers 33:50ff.
148. Deuteronomy 9:4ff.; see also 18:9–14, 29:22ff. and Psalms 44:3.
149. T. Dothan, 'Archaeological Reflections on the Philistine Problem', *Antiquity and Survival* 2, 2/3 (1957).
150. J. A. Montgomery, 'Archival Data in the Book of Kings', *Journal of Biblical Literature*, 53 (1934).
151. I Samuel 10:5.
152. II Kings 3:15.
153. Isaiah 28:7.
154. I Samuel 2:19.

155. I Samuel 15:22.
156. Grant, *History of Ancient Israel*, 118.
157. I Samuel 7:16–17.
158. I Samuel 10:17; 12:1–25.
159. I Samuel 10:25.
160. S. Mowinckel, 'General Oriental and Specific Israelite Elements in the Israelite Conception of the Sacral Kingdom', *Numen*, iv (1959).
161. I Samuel 8:22.
162. I Samuel 15:3.
163. I Samuel 14:52.
164. I Samuel 17:39.
165. I Samuel 16:18.
166. *Cambridge Ancient History*, II ii 579–80.
167. II Samuel 20:1.
168. Albright, *Archaeology and the Religion of Israel*, 158ff.
169. II Samuel 5:8.
170. Kathleen Kenyon, *Royal Cities of the Old Testament* (London 1971) and *Digging Up Jerusalem* (London 1974); *Encyclopaedia Judaica*, ix 1379–82.
171. Belkin, *op. cit.*, 117.
172. I Kings 5:3.
173. De Vaux, *op. cit.*, 253–65.
174. I Kings 2:3–4.
175. II Samuel 18:7.
176. I Kings 5:13–16.
177. I Kings 9:15.
178. Kenyon, *The Bible and Recent Archaeology*, ch. 4, 'Palestine in the Time of David and Solomon', 44–66.
179. *Cambridge Ancient History*, II ii 589.
180. Kenyon, *Royal Cities*.
181. I Kings 4:7–19.
182. I Kings 11:1.
183. See Nelson Glueck's findings in the *Bulletin of the American School of Oriental Research* (1938–40); I Kings 9:26.
184. I Kings 7:1–12.
185. Kenyon, *Royal Cities*.
186. Joan Comay, *The Temple of Jerusalem, with the History of the Temple Mount* (London 1975).
187. Haran, *Temples and Temple Service*, 28f.
188. Numbers 10:35–6.
189. De Vaux, *op. cit.*, 305ff.
190. I Kings 12:4.
191. I Kings 12:14.
192. I Kings 22:34–7.
193. Deuteronomy 27:17.
194. I Kings 17: 3–4.
195. I Kings 21:25–6.
196. II Kings 2:23–4.
197. Grant, *History of Ancient Israel*, ch. 11, 'Northern Prophets and History', 122–34.
198. II Kings 10.

199. I Kings 21:19–20.
200. Amos 5:21–4.
201. Amos 7:10–13.
202. Baba Batra 9a; Shalom Spiegel, 'Amos v. Amaziah', in Goldin, *op. cit.*
203. II Kings 7:23–4.
204. For textual analysis of Hosea, see *Encyclopaedia Judaica*, viii 1010–25.
205. Hosea 8:7; 10:13.
206. Hosea 4:11.
207. Hosea 5:9; 4:5; 9:7. See Grant, *History of Ancient Israel*, 129ff.
208. Hosea 6:1–2.
209. II Kings 11:15–17.
210. II Chronicles 32:3–5.
211. Kenyon, *Royal Cities*.
212. II Kings 19:35; Herodotus, *Histories*, book II:141.
213. II Kings 18:21.
214. II Kings 23:21–3.
215. *Encyclopaedia Judaica*, ix 44–71; O. Eissfeldt, *The Old Testament, an Introduction* (London 1965), 301–30.
216. Grant, *History of Ancient Israel*, 148–9.
217. Isaiah 21:11; 22:13; 38:1; 5:8; 3:15.
218. Isaiah 1:18; 6:3; 2:4; 35:1.
219. Isaiah 7:14; 11:6; 9:6.
220. H. H. Rowley, *The Faith of Israel* (London 1953), 122; Isaiah 42:1–4; 49:1–6, etc.
221. II Kings 3:27; Psalms 89:6–9; Genesis 20:1ff.; 12:10ff.; Exodus 7:8ff.
222. Isaiah 44:6.
223. Fohrer, *op. cit.*, 172ff., 324–5, 290; see also N. W. Snaith, 'The Advent of Monotheism in Israel', *Annual of Leeds Univ. Oriental Society*, v (1963–5).
224. J. P. Hyatt, *Jeremiah, Prophet of Courage and Hope* (New York 1958).
225. Jeremiah 5:23; 5:31.
226. Jeremiah 20:14; 15:18; 11:19.
227. II Kings 24:14ff.
228. II Kings 25:18ff.
229. Jeremiah 44:28.

PART TWO: JUDAISM

1. For Ezekiel, see G. von Rad, *Old Testament Theology* II (1965), 220–37; *Encyclopaedia Judaica*, vi 1078–98.
2. Ezekiel 1:3.
3. Ezekiel 37:1–10.
4. Ezekiel 18:1ff.
5. Deuteronomy 6:6–8.
6. Isaiah 40:4; see also 10:33; 14:12; 26:5–6; 29:18; 47:8–9.
7. I Samuel 2:1–10.
8. S. W. Baron, *Social and Religious History of the Jews* (2nd edn, New York 1952), i I 22.
9. B. Porten, *Archives from Elephantine: The Life of an Ancient Jewish Military Colony* (New York 1968).

10. W. D. Davies, *The Territorial Dimensions of Judaism* (Berkeley 1982), 70.
11. For Cyrus' religious beliefs and consequences see W. D. Davies and Louis Finkelstein (eds), *Cambridge History of Judaism* (Cambridge 1984), i 281ff.
12. Quoted in *ibid.*, 287.
13. Isaiah 45:1.
14. Ezra 1:1–4.
15. Ezra 4:1ff.
16. *Cambridge History of Judaism*, 70–4, 135–6.
17. Nehemiah 4:18.
18. *Cambridge History of Judaism*, 344.
19. *Ibid.*, 398–400.
20. Nehemiah 10:28.
21. Judges 8:14.
22. Baron, *op. cit.*, i i, footnote 8, 323.
23. *Contra Apionem*, 1:37.
24. R. K. Harrison, *Introduction to the Old Testament* (London 1970).
25. Deuteronomy 4:2; also 12:32.
26. i Chronicles 2:5.
27. Sanhedrin 12:10.
28. C. D. Ginsburg, *Introduction to the Maseretico-Critical Edition of the Hebrew Bible* (1966 edn by H. M. Orlinsky); H. B. Swete, *An Introduction to the Old Testament in Greek* (London 1968); F. G. Kenyon, *Our Bible and the Ancient Manuscripts* (London 1965); M. Gaster, *The Samaritans: Their History, Doctrine and Literature* (London 1925); Harrison, *op. cit.*; *Encyclopaedia Judaica*, iv 814–36; v 1396ff.
29. Joshua 8:29; 4:20.
30. Psalms 3, 5, 6, 7, 9–10, 13, 17, 22, 25–8, 31, 35, 36, 38, 39, 41, 42, 43, 51, 52, 54–7, 59, 61, 63, 64, 69, 71, 77, 86, 88, 102, 120, 123, 130, 140–3.
31. Proverbs 22:17 to 23:11.
32. For Job see especially H. H. Rowley, 'The Book of Job and its Meaning', in *From Moses to Qumran: Studies in the Old Testament* (London 1963) and his *Submission in Suffering and Other Essays* (London 1951); Harrison, *op. cit.*; E. F. Sutcliffe, *Providence and Suffering in the Old and New Testaments* (London 1955); for the literature on the Book of Job, see C. Kuhl in *Theological Review*, 21 (1953).
33. Ecclesiasticus 24:3–10.
34. i Corinthians 1:19–27; see Gerhard von Rad, *Problems of the Hexateuch and Other Essays* (trans., Edinburgh 1966).
35. i Maccabees 9:27.
36. Zechariah 13:3ff.
37. Ecclesiasticus 24:33; Enid B. Mellor (ed.), *The Making of the Old Testament* (Cambridge 1972).
38. Roland de Vaux, *Ancient Israel: Its Life and Institutions* (trans., New York 1961), 343–4; for earliest references, see *Encyclopaedia Judaica*, xv 579–81.
39. Ezra 2:64–5; pop. of Jerusalem in Pseudo-Hecateus, quoted by Josephus: *Contra Apionem*, 1:197; *Encyclopaedia Judaica*, xiii 870.
40. Daniel 7:7.
41. Ecclesiastes 5:8ff.; 6; see Martin Hengel, *Judaism and Hellenism* (trans., 2 vols, London 1974), i 14–31.
42. Davies, *op. cit.*, 61; Harrison, *op. cit.*

43. Jonah 4:11. See Michael Grant, *A History of Ancient Israel* (London, 1984), 194–5.
44. Hengel, *op. cit.*, i 65–9; ii 46, notes 59–61.
45. *Ibid.*, i 55–7.
46. E. Bickermann, *From Ezra to the Last of the Maccabees: The Foundations of Post-Biblical Judaism* (New York 1962); Hengel, *op. cit.*, i 270.
47. Jad. 4:6 (first century AD).
48. Isocrates, *Panegyr*, 4:50; H. C. Baldry, *The Unity of Mankind in Greek Thought* (Cambridge 1966), 69ff.
49. Sota 49b; quoted Hengel, *op. cit.*, i 76; see also *ibid.*, 300ff.
50. II Maccabees 4:12–14.
51. H. H. Ben Sasson (ed.), *A History of the Jewish People* (trans., Harvard 1976), 202ff.
52. Sukk. 56b.
53. Ezra 7:26.
54. II Maccabees 13:3ff.; Josephus, *Antiquities*, 12:384.
55. I Maccabees 13:42.
56. I Maccabees 13:51. For details of the crisis, see Ben Sasson, *op. cit.*, 202–16.
57. Hengel, *op. cit.*, 291ff.
58. E. Ebner, *Elementary Education in Ancient Israel during the Tannaitic Period* (New York 1956).
59. Deuteronomy 31:19.
60. Josephus, *Antiquities*, 13:280.
61. *Ibid.*, 13:300.
62. Sanhedrin 19a; Sot. 47a; Kid. 66a.
63. Josephus, *Antiquities*, 14:380.
64. For Herod see Stewart Perowne, *The Life and Times of Herod the Great* (London 1956); F. O. Busch, *The Five Herods* (New York 1958).
65. *Encyclopaedia Judaica*, xiii 871.
66. Deuteronomy 16:16; Exodus 23:17.
67. For Herod's Temple, see Joan Comay, *The Temple of Jerusalem, with the History of the Temple Mount* (London 1975); Kathleen Kenyon, *Digging Up Jerusalem* (London 1974); *Encyclopaedia Judaica*, viii 383–5; xv 961ff.
68. *Antiquities*, 15:380–425; *Wars*, 5:184–247.
69. Josephus, *Wars*, 4:262; 5:17; *Antiquities*, 16:14.
70. Josephus, *Wars*, 6:282.
71. For Greeks and Jews, see Hengel, *op. cit.*, esp. 310ff.; W. W. Tarn and G. T. Griffith, *Hellenist Civilization* (3rd edn, London 1952).
72. Thanksgiving Psalm from Qumran Cave One; cf. *Encyclopaedia Judaica*, iii 179ff.
73. Daniel 12:1–2.
74. Enoch 1–5; 37–71. See H. H. Rowley, *The Relevance of Apocalyptic* (London 1947).
75. Numbers 25:7–15.
76. Josephus, *War*, 2:118.
77. See, for instance, S. G. F. Brandon, *Jesus and the Zealots* (London 1967) and *The Trial of Jesus of Nazareth* (London 1968); W. R. Farmer, *Maccabees, Zealots and Josephus* (London 1956).
78. A. Dupont-Sommer, *The Jewish Sect of Qumran and the Essenes* (New York 1954); H. A. Butler, *Man and Society in the Qumran Community* (London 1959).

79. Ben Sasson, *op. cit.*, 253–4; C. F. Kraeling, *John the Baptist* (London 1951).
80. Isaiah 40:3.
81. II Samuel 7; 23:1–5; 22:44–51.
82. For instance, Psalm 18; Amos 9:11–12; Hosea 11:10; Ezekiel 37:15ff.
83. Acts of the Apostles 5:34–40.
84. M. Hooker, *Jesus and the Servant* (London 1959).
85. John Bowker, *Jesus and the Pharisees* (Cambridge 1983), esp. 1–20.
86. G. F. Moore, *Judaism in the First Centuries of the Christian Era* (London 1927) i 72–82; Bowker, *op. cit.*, 32–3.
87. Pes. 66a; Suk. 20a; see *Encyclopaedia Judaica*, viii 282–5.
88. Shab. 31a.
89. Mark 7:14–15; Bowker, *op. cit.*, 44ff.
90. E. Bamel (ed.), *The Trial of Jesus* (London 1970), esp. 'The Problem of the Historicity of the Sanhedrin Trial'.
91. J. Blinzner, 'The Jewish Punishment of Stoning in the New Testament Period', and E. Bammel, 'Crucifixion as a punishment in Palestine', in E. Bammel, *op. cit.*, 147–61 and 162–5.
92. *Encyclopaedia Judaica*, x 12–13 and bibliography; H. Cohn, *The Death of Jesus* (New York 1971); S. G. F. Brandon, *The Trial of Jesus of Nazareth* (London 1968).
93. By, for example, E. R. Goodenough, 'Paul and the Hellenization of Christianity', in J. Neusner (ed.), *Religions in Antiquity* (Leiden 1968), 22–68.
94. Samuel Sandmel, *Judaism and Christian Beginnings* (Oxford 1978), 308–36.
95. E. P. Sanders, *Paul and Palestinian Judaism* (London 1977), 555–6.
96. Mark 14:24–8.
97. Galatians 3:29; Romans 4:12–25.
98. Paul to the Colossians, 3:9–11.
99. Acts of the Apostles, 7:48–60.
100. Acts 15:5ff.; Galatians 2:6–9.
101. J. N. Sevenster, *The Roots of Pagan Anti-Semitism in the Ancient World* (Leiden 1975), 89ff.
102. Quoted in *ibid.*, 90.
103. *Contra Apionem*, 1:71.
104. Diodorus, *Bibliotheca*, 34:1,1ff.; quoted in *Encyclopaedia Judaica*, iii 87ff.
105. Wisdom of Solomon 12:3–11.
106. Sevenster, *op. cit.*, 8–11.
107. Josephus, *Antiquities*, 14:187, 190ff.
108. *Ibid.*, 19:286ff.
109. Quoted in *Encyclopaedia Judaica*, iii 90.
110. Tacitus, *Histories*, 5:13.
111. Ben Sasson, *op. cit.*, 296ff.
112. Shaye J. D. Cohen, *Josephus in Galilee and Rome: His Vita and Development as a Historian* (Leiden 1979), appendix 1, 243ff.; 253ff.
113. Listed in *ibid.*, 3–23.
114. *Ibid.*, 238–41.
115. *Ibid.*, 181.
116. For analysis of Josephus' account, see *ibid.*, 230ff.
117. Josephus, *Wars*, 2:408, 433.
118. Yigael Yadin, *Masada: Herod's Fortress and the Zealots' Last Stand* (London 1966).

119. For Tacitus' anti-Semitism, see *Histories*, 5:1–13; *Annals*, 15:44; see also Juvenal's poem, *Saturae*, 14:96ff.
120. Cassius Dio, *Roman History*, book 69.
121. Eusebius, *Ecclesiastical History*, 4:6, 2; Numbers 24:17.
122. Jerusalem Talmud, Ta'an 4:7, 68d; quoted *Encyclopaedia Judaica*, ii 488–92.
123. For Akiva see L. Finkelstein, *Akiva, Scholar, Saint and Martyr* (New York, 1962 edn). On the question of his joining the revolt see Chaim Raphael, *A Coat of Many Colours* (London, 1979), 190–8.
124. Ta'an 4:68d; *Encyclopaedia Judaica*, vi 603.
125. Yigael Yadin, *Finds from the Bar Kokhba Period in the Cave of Letters* (New York 1963).
126. Cassius Dio, *Roman History*, book 69.
127. Quoted in Comay, *op. cit.*; Kenyon, *Digging Up Jerusalem*.
128. S. G. Wilson, *Luke and the Law* (Cambridge 1983), 103–6.
129. S. G. F. Brandon, *The Fall of Jerusalem and the Christian Church* (2nd edn, London 1957).
130. Barnabas Lindars, *Jesus Son of Man: A Fresh Examination of the Son of Man Sayings in the Gospels in the Light of Recent Research* (London 1983).
131. See, for instance, Geza Vermes, *Jesus and the World of Judaism* (London 1984).
132. Franz Mussner, *Tractate on the Jews: The Significance of Judaism for Christian Faith* (trans., Philadelphia 1984), 180ff.
133. 4 Q Fl 1:8, quoted in Mussner, *ibid.*, 185; John 8:37–44.
134. Matthew 27:24ff.
135. E. Hennecke and W. Schneemelcher, *New Testament Apocrypha* (Philadelphia 1965), 1:179ff.
136. Ecclesiasticus 36:7.
137. Wayne A. Meeks, *The First Urban Christians* (Yale 1984).
138. Philo's *Complete Works*, ed. and trans. F. H. Colson and G. H. Whitaker, are in 12 vols (Cambridge 1953–63); E. R. Goodenough, *Introduction to Philo Judaeus* (London 2nd edn 1962).
139. Aboth Derabbi Nathan B, 31.
140. G. Bader, *Jewish Spiritual Heroes* (New York 1940), i 411–36.
141. Rachel Wischnitzer, *The Messianic Theme in the Paintings of the Dura Synagogue* (Chicago 1948).
142. C. Hollis and Ronald Brownrigg, *Holy Places* (London 1969); Moshe Perelman and Yaacov Yanni, *Historical Sites in Israel* (London 1964).
143. For the full list of subjects covered, see *Encyclopaedia Judaica*, xv 751.
144. *Ibid.*, 1283–5.
145. Leviticus Rabbah 34,3; Philo, Leg. All. 3:69; De Pot. 19–20; Taanit 11a; Yer. Nedarim 9,1 (41b); quoted in Samuel Belkin, *In His Image: The Jewish Philosophy of Man as Expressed in the Rabbinical Tradition* (London 1961).
146. Sanhedrin 4, 5.
147. Hilkot Rozeah 1, 4.
148. Sifra on Leviticus 22:6; Mekilta on Exodus 22:6; quoted in Belkin, *op. cit.*
149. Deuteronomy 17:15; Philo, *Spec. Leg.*, 4:157, quoted in Belkin, *op. cit.*
150. Abot 4, 8.
151. Berakot 55a.
152. Yer. Shabbat 3d.
153. Horayot 3, 7–8, quoted in Belkin, *op. cit.*
154. Baba Kamma 8, 1.

155. Baba Bathra 2b; Baba Metziah 108b; Baba Bathra 6b, 21a. Quoted in Belkin, *op. cit.*
156. Belkin, *op. cit.*, 134ff.
157. Philo, *De Sacr. Ab.*, 121–5.
158. Proverbs 3:17.
159. Psalms 29:11; Tractatus Uksin 3:12; quoted in Meyer Waxman, *Judaism, Religion and Ethics* (New York 1958).
160. Isaiah 52:7.
161. Quoted in Waxman, *op. cit.*, 187–90.
162. *Contra Apionem*, ii 177–8.
163. Kiddushin 71a.
164. Ben Sasson, *op. cit.*, 373–82.
165. F. Holmes Duddon, *The Life and Times of St Ambrose*, 2 vols (Oxford 1935).
166. Charles C. Torrey, *The Jewish Foundation of Islam* (Yale, new edn 1967).

PART THREE: CATHEDOCRACY

1. A. Adler (ed.), *The Itinerary of Benjamin of Tudela* (London 1840–1, reprinted New York 1927).
2. Andrew Sharf, *Byzantine Jewry from Justinian to the Fourth Crusade* (London 1971), 21.
3. *Ibid.*, 25–6.
4. Quoted in *ibid.*, 136.
5. Cecil Roth, *Personalities and Events in Jewish History* (Philadelphia 1961), 'The Jew as European'.
6. *Ibid.*, 40–4.
7. Irving A. Agus, *Urban Civilization in Pre-Crusade Europe*, 2 vols (Leiden 1965), i 9.
8. Fritz M. Heichelheim, *An Ancient Economic History*, 2 vols (trans., Leiden 1965), i 104–56.
9. For example, I Samuel 22:2; II Kings 4:1; Isaiah 50:1; Ezekiel 22:12; Nehemiah 5:7; 12:13.
10. BM 5:11, 75b; Yad, Malveh 4:2; BM 5:2; BM 64b; BM 5:10, 75b; Tosef, BM 6:17.
11. BM 65a, 68b, 104b, 61b; Tosef, BM 5:22, 5:23; Sanh.:3; BM 61b, 71a etc. *Encyclopaedia Judaica*, xii 244–56; xvi 27–33.
12. Philo, *De Virtutibus*, 82.
13. Mekhilta of R. Ishmael on Exodus 22:25; Mak, 24a; BM 70b.
14. Tos. to BM 70b.
15. Responsa Maharik 118, 132.
16. Bat Ye'or, *The Dhimmi: Jews and Christians Under Islam* (London 1985) 45–55.
17. S. Katz, *The Jews in the Visigothic Kingdoms of Spain and Gaul* (Cambridge 1937).
18. Proverbs 8:22ff.; Ecclesiastes 1:1–5, 26; 15:1; 24:1ff.; 34:8.
19. Avot 3:14; Lev. R. 19:1; ARN 31:91; II Moses 2; 14, 51.
20. Proverbs 8:14.
21. Sifre, Deuteronomy 41; Ex. Rabbah 30, 10; Tanhumah, Mishpatim 2; Philo, *Spec. Leg.*, iii 1–7. Quoted in Samuel Belkin, *In His Image: The Jewish*

Philosophy of Man as Expressed in the Rabbinical Tradition (London 1961).
E. R. Goodenough: *The Politics of Philo Judaeus* (Yale 1938), 16ff.

22. S. D. Goitein, *A Mediterranean Society* (California 1971), ii The Community, 205–6.

23. *Ibid.*, 198–9.

24. Quoted in Mark R. Cohen, *Jewish Self-Government in Medieval Egypt* (Princeton 1980), 7–9.

25. *Ibid.*, 94ff.

26. Goitein, *op. cit.*, iii The Family, 3–5.

27. *Ibid.*, i 1–28, and S. D. Goitein, *Studies in Islamic History* (Leiden 1966), 279–95; *Encyclopaedia Judaica*, vii 404–7; xiv 948–9.

28. S. D. Goitein, *Letters of Medieval Jewish Traders* (Princeton 1973), 227–9.

29. Genesis 37:35; letter quoted in Goitein, *Letters of Medieval Jewish Traders*, 207.

30. 'Moses Maimonides', in Alexander Marx, *Studies in Jewish History and Booklore* (New York 1969), 42.

31. Quoted Marx, *ibid.* 38.

32. *Ibid.*, 31.

33. *Ibid.*, 32–3.

34. Goodenough, *op. cit.*, 8–19.

35. Marx, *op. cit.*, 29–30.

36. 'Maimonides and the Scholars of Southern France', in *ibid.*, 48–62.

37. Arthur Hyman, 'Maimonides' Thirteen Principles', in Alexander Altmann (ed.), *Jewish Medieval and Renaissance Studies* (Harvard 1967), 119–44.

38. Erwin I. J. Rosenthal, 'Maimonides' Conception of State and Society', in *Studia Semitica*, 2 vols (Cambridge 1971), i 275ff.

39. *Guide of the Perplexed*, 3:27; Hyman, *op. cit.*

40. Cecil Roth, 'The People and the Book', in *Personalities and Events in Jewish History*, 172ff.

41. Isadore Twersky, 'Some Non-Halakhic Aspects of the Mishneh Torah', in Altmann, *op. cit.*, 95–118.

42. Marx, *op. cit.*, 38–41.

43. *Guide of the Perplexed*, 2:45; Alexander Altmann, 'Maimonides and Thomas Aquinas: Natural of Divine Prophecy', in *Essays in Jewish Intellectual History* (Brandeis 1981).

44. Ecclesiastes 7:24.

45. 'Free Will and Predestination in Saadia, Bahya and Maimonides', in Altmann, *op. cit.*

46. Quoted in H. H. Ben Sasson (ed.), *A History of the Jewish People* (trans., Harvard 1976), 545.

47. Shir Hashérim Rabbah 2:14; quoted in *ibid.*

48. Quoted in Beryl Smalley, *The Study of the Bible in the Middle Ages* (Oxford 1952), 78.

49. Norman Golb, 'Aspects of the Historical Background of Jewish Life in Medieval Egypt', in Altmann, *op. cit.*, 1–18.

50. Samuel Rosenblatt (ed.), *The Highways to Perfection of Abraham Maimonides* (New York 1927), i Introduction.

51. S. D. Goitein, 'Abraham Maimonides and his Pietist Circle', in Altmann, *op. cit.*, 145–64.

52. Some scholars think Philo himself was a mystic and dealer in symbols. Cf. E. R. Goodenough, *Jewish Symbols in the Graeco-Roman Period*, 12 vols (New York, 1953–68).
53. For kabbalah, see G. Scholem's article in the *Encyclopaedia Judaica*, x 489–653, and his *Major Trends in Jewish Mysticism* (New York 1965).
54. 'Moses Narboni's "Epistle on Shi'ur Qoma"', in Altmann, *op. cit.*, 228–31; G. Scholem, *Jewish Gnosticism, Merkabah Mysticism and Talmudic Tradition* (2nd edn, New York 1965), 36–42.
55. R. Kaiser, *Life and Times of Jehudah Halevi* (New York 1949).
56. Goitein, *A Mediterranean Society*, ii The Community, 241–5; 255–64.
57. *Ibid.*, iii The Family, 17–35.
58. *Ibid.*, 46.
59. Meyer Waxman, *Judaism: Religion and Ethics* (New York 1958), 'Marriage', 113ff.
60. Goitein, *A Mediterranean Society*, iii 209–11.
61. Waxman, *op. cit.*, 118 footnote.
62. Goitein, *A Mediterranean Society*, iii 50.
63. Malachi 2:16.
64. Goitein, *A Mediterranean Society*, iii 260ff.
65. Yevamot, 14, 1.
66. Goitein, *A Mediterranean Society*, iii 352.
67. *Ibid.*, ii 211.
68. *Ibid.*, 148–60.
69. Waxman, *op. cit.*, 32–6.
70. *Ibid.*, 108ff.; Goitein, *A Mediterranean Society*, ii 225.
71. Waxman, *op. cit.*, 112.
72. Mattenot Aniyim 9:3; quoted in Israel S. Chipkin, 'Judaism and Social Welfare', in Louis Finkelstein (ed.), *The Jews*, 2 vols (London 1961), i 1043–76.
73. Baba Batra 8a.
74. Quoted in Goitein, *A Mediterranean Society*, ii 142.
75. Baba Batra 110a; Pesahim 113a; quoted in Chipkin, *op. cit.*, 1067.
76. Goitein, *A Mediterranean Society*, ii 138–42, and appendices A, B, C.
77. *Ibid.*, ii 287.
78. *Ibid.*, ii 279.
79. B. Blumenkranz, *Juifs et Chrétiens dans le monde occidental 430–1096* (Paris 1960).
80. Quoted in Cecil Roth, 'The Medieval Conception of "The Unbelieving Jew"', in *Personalities and Events*.
81. A. M. Haberman (ed.), *Massacres of Germany and France* (Jerusalem 1946).
82. *Ibid.*, 94; quoted in Ben-Sasson, *op. cit.*
83. Cecil Roth, *The Jews of Medieval Oxford* (Oxford 1951), 83.
84. Nikolaus Pevsner and John Harris, *The Buildings of England: Lincolnshire* (Harmondsworth 1964), 158–9.
85. V. D. Lipman, *The Jews of Medieval Norwich* (London 1967).
86. Cecil Roth, *Intellectual Activities of Medieval English Jewry* (British Academy, London 1949), 65, gives list of doctors.
87. Lipman, *op. cit.*, ch. 6, 95–112.
88. Augustus Jessop and M. R. James (eds), *The Life and Miracles of St William of Norwich by Thomas of Monmouth* (Cambridge 1896).
89. Lipman, *op. cit.*, 54.

90. Roth, *Personalities and Events*, 62–6, and his *The Ritual Murder Libel and the Jews* (London 1935); see also G. I. Langmuir, *Speculum* (1972), 459–82.

91. Ralph de Diceto, *Imagines Historiarum*, ii 78, quoted in Lipman, *op. cit.*

92. Roth, *Personalities and Events*, 61–2.

93. Lipman, *op. cit.*, 59–64.

94. Roth's book on ritual murder prints the refutation by Pope Clement XIV in 1759.

95. Richard W. Emery, *The Jews of Perpignan* (New York 1959), ch. 4.

96. M. D. Davis, *Shetaroth: Hebrew Deeds of English Jews Before 1290* (London 1888), 298ff, quoted in Lipman, *op. cit.*, 88; Lipman prints a number of debt-bonds and quit-deeds, 187ff.

97. Quoted in Lipman, *op. cit.*

98. *Ibid.*, 68.

99. H. G. Richardson, *English Jewry under the Angevin Kings* (London 1960), 247–53; 127–73.

100. J. W. F. Hill, *Medieval Lincoln* (London 1948), 217–22.

101. Richardson, *op. cit.*, 184–6: M. Adler, *Jews of Medieval England* (London 1939).

102. *Ibid.*, 313–33.

103. Solomon Grayzel, *The Church and the Jews in the Thirteenth Century* (New York, new edn 1966), 108.

104. 'The People and the Book', in Cecil Roth, *Personalities and Events*, 174–5.

105. 'The Medieval University and the Jew', in *ibid.*, 91ff.

106. Translated, 1933, *My Life as German and Jew*.

107. Jeremy Cohen, *The Friars and the Jews: The Evolution of Medieval Anti-Semitism* (Cornell 1982), 14.

108. *Ibid.*, 242.

109. Pierre Mandonnet, *St Dominic and His Work* (trans., St Louis 1944), 61.

110. Cohen, *op. cit.*, 13.

111. A. G. Little, 'Friar Henry of Wadstone and the Jews', *Collecteana franciscana* 11 (Manchester 1922), 150–7; quoted in Cohen, *op. cit.*

112. Quoted in Ben Sasson, *op. cit.*

113. *Encyclopaedia Judaica*, iv 1063–8; P. Ziegler, *The Black Death* (London 1969).

114. See map in *Encyclopaedia Judaica*, iv 1066, for towns where atrocities occurred.

115. Hyam Maccoby (ed. and trans.), *Judaism on Trial: Jewish–Christian Disputations in the Middle Ages* (New Jersey 1982).

116. Quoted in Grayzel, *op. cit.*, 241, note 96.

117. Quoted in Maccoby, *op. cit.*, 32.

118. *Ibid.*, 25ff.

119. Quoted in Ben Sasson, *op. cit.*, 557–8.

120. Maccoby, *op. cit.*, 54.

121. Cecil Roth, 'The Disputation at Barcelona', *Harvard Theological Review*, xliii (1950).

122. Martin A. Cohen, 'Reflections on the Text and Context of the Disputation at Barcelona', *Hebrew Union College Annual* (1964); Y. Baer, *A History of the Jews in Christian Spain*, 2 vols (trans., Philadelphia 1961–6), i 150–62.

123. Maccoby, *op. cit.*, 50.

124. Quoted in Gershom Scholem, *Sabbatai Sevi: The Mystical Messiah 1626–76* (trans., London 1973), 12.

125. Peter Lineham, *Spanish Church and Society* (London 1983).

126. M. M. Gorce, *St Vincent Ferrer* (Paris 1935).

127. For Tortosa, see Maccoby, *op. cit.*; A. Pacios Lopez, *La Disputa de Tortosa*, 2 vols (Madrid 1957).
128. Quoted in Maccoby, *op. cit.*, 84.
129. *Ibid.*, 86.
130. A. Farinelli, *Marrano: storia di un vituperio* (Milan 1925), 36.
131. Quoted in Haim Beinart, *Conversos on Trial: The Inquisition in Ciudad Real* (Jerusalem 1981), 3.
132. Quoted in *ibid.*, 3, footnote 4.
133. Quoted in *ibid.*, 6.
134. Baer, *op. cit.*, ii 292.
135. Quoted in Beinart, *op. cit.*, 66.
136. *Ibid.*, 10–19.
137. *Ibid.*, 34, footnote 40; H. C. Lea, *A History of the Inquisition in Spain*, 4 vols (New York 1906–7), vol. i for origins.
138. For detailed figures see Elkan Nathan Adler, *Auto da Fé and Jew* (Oxford 1908), esp. ch. viii, 39ff.
139. Beinart, *op. cit.*, 36–42.
140. Lea, *op. cit.*, i 178.
141. G. A. Bergenroth (ed.), *Calendar of Letters . . . from Simancas* (London 1861), i Henry VII, xxxivff.; quoted in Beinart, *op. cit.*, 28.
142. Quoted in Baer, *op. cit.*, ii 382.
143. Beinart, *op. cit.*, 130–5; 204–31. See also his *Records of the Trials of the Spanish Inquisition in Ciudad Real*, 3 vols (Jerusalem 1974–80).
144. Lea, *op. cit.*, iii 83ff.
145. Beinart, *op. cit.*, 194.
146. For distinctions see H. J. Zimmels, *Askenazim and Sephardim* (New York 1958).
147. M. Kaiserling, *Christopher Columbus and the Participation of the Jews in the Portuguese and Spanish Discoveries* (London 1907); Cecil Roth, 'Who Was Columbus?', in *Personalities and Events*, 192ff.
148. Cecil Roth, 'The Jewish Ancestry of Michel de Montaigne', in *Personalities and Events*, 212ff., prints his family tree on p. 324. See also Chaim Raphael, 'The Sephardi Diaspora' in *The Road from Babylon: The Story of Sephardi and Oriental Jews* (London 1985), 127–58.
149. Leon Poliakov, *Les Banquiers juifs et le Saint Siège du xiii au xvii siècles* (Paris 1965), 80–4, 147–56.
150. Isaiah Shachar, *The Judensau: A Medieval Anti-Jewish Motif and its History* (London 1974).
151. H. C. J. Duijker and N. H. Frijda, *National Character and National Stereotypes* (Amsterdam 1960); see also H. Fiscg, *The Dual Image* (New York 1971).

PART FOUR: GHETTO

1. G. K. Anderson, *The Legend of the Wandering Jew* (London 1965); S. W. Baron, *Social and Religious History of the Jews* (2nd edn, New York, 1952), 11 177–82; *Encyclopaedia Judaica*, xvi 259–63.
2. Quoted in Lionel Kochan, *The Jew and his History* (London 1977), 39; see also Arthur A. Cohen, *The Natural and Supernatural Jew* (London 1967), 12ff.
3. *Encyclopaedia Judaica*, viii 1203–5.

4. Cecil Roth, *Jewish Communities: Venice* (Philadelphia 1930), 49ff.
5. Cecil Roth, 'The Origin of the Ghetto', in *Personalities and Events in Jewish History* (Philadelphia 1961), 226ff.
6. Roth, *Venice*, 106–7.
7. *Ibid.*, 46.
8. Simhah Luzzatto, *Essay on the Jews of Venice* (trans., Jerusalem 1950), 122–3.
9. Esther 2:3.
10. Quoted in H. H. Ben Sasson (ed.), *A History of the Jewish People* (trans., Harvard 1976), 691.
11. J. Bloch, *Venetian Printers of Hebrew Books* (London 1932), 5–16; *Encyclopaedia Judaica*, v 197; xvi 101; iv 1195–7.
12. Quoted in Cecil Roth, 'The Background of Shylock', in *Personalities and Events*, 237ff.
13. Quoted in *ibid.*, 250.
14. *Ibid.*, 288–9.
15. Israel Adler, 'The Rise of Art Music in the Italian Ghetto', in Alexander Altmann (ed.), *Jewish Medieval and Renaissance Studies* (Harvard 1967), 321–64.
16. Roth, *Personalities and Events*, 1–3.
17. Alexander Marx, 'A Jewish Cause Célèbre in Sixteenth Century Italy', *Studies in Jewish History and Booklore* (New York 1969), 107–54.
18. Cecil Roth, 'The Amazing Abraham Colorni', in *Personalities and Events*, 296ff.
19. Cecil Roth, 'A Community of Slaves', in *Personalities and Events*, 112ff.
20. Quoted in *ibid.*, 114–15.
21. W. L. Gundersheimer, 'Erasmus, Humanism and the Christian Kabbalah', *Journal of the Warburg and Courtauld Institute*, 26 (1963), 38–52.
22. Quoted in Jonathan I. Israel, *European Jewry in the Age of Mercantilism* (Oxford 1985), 15.
23. Cf. W. Linden (ed.), *Luther's Kampfschriften gegen das Judentum* (Berlin 1936).
24. Baron, *op. cit.*, xiii 281–90.
25. Israel, *op. cit.*, 13.
26. *Ibid.*, 16.
27. K. R. Stow, *Catholic Thought and Papal Jewry Policy 1555–1593* (New York 1977).
28. Brian Pulhan, *The Jews of Europe and the Inquisition of Venice 1550–1670* (Oxford 1983), ch. 2.
29. *Ibid.*, 21.
30. See, for instance, H. R. Trevor-Roper, *Religion, the Reformation and Social Change* (London 1967).
31. Manasseh ben Israel, 'The Hope of Israel' (London 1652), printed in Lucien Wolf (ed.), *Manasseh ben Israel's Mission to Oliver Cromwell* (London 1901), 50–1.
32. Quoted in Ben Sasson, *op. cit.*, 391.
33. Quoted in *Encyclopaedia Judaica*, xii 244–56.
34. Deuteronomy 7:13.
35. Deuteronomy 15:6.
36. Psalms 34:10.
37. Quoted in Werner Sombart, *The Jews and Modern Capitalism* (trans., London 1913), 36.

38. Ben Sasson, *op. cit.*, 670–9.
39. Israel, *op. cit.*, 27–30.
40. Erhard Oestreich, *Neostoicism and the Early Modern State* (Cambridge 1982), 45–56; Israel, *op. cit.*, 38.
41. Roth, *Venice*, 305–6; Benjamin Ravid, *Economics and Toleration in Seventeenth Century Venice* (Jerusalem 1978), 30–3; Israel, *op. cit.*, 47–8.
42. H. I. Bloom, *The Economic Activities of the Jews of Amsterdam in the Seventeenth and Eighteenth Centuries* (London 1937).
43. O. Muneles, *The Prague Ghetto in the Renaissance Period* (London 1965).
44. Israel, *op. cit.*, 96; 88–90; 102ff.; 117.
45. S. Stern, *Court Jew* (London 1950).
46. For Oppenheimer see Israel, *op. cit.*, 123ff.; Stern, *op. cit.*; M. Grunwald, *Samuel Oppenheimer und sein Kreis* (Frankfurt 1913); *Encyclopaedia Judaica*, xii 1431–3.
47. Quoted in *Encyclopaedia Judaica*, iii 402–5.
48. Israel, *op. cit.*, 121.
49. B. D. Weinryb, *The Jews of Poland: A Social and Economic History of the Jewish Community in Poland from 1100 to 1880* (Philadelphia 1972), 192–9; *Encyclopaedia Judaica*, v 480–4.
50. See Gerhard Scholem, 'Zohar: Manuscripts and Editions', *Encyclopaedia Judaica*, xvi 211–12.
51. For Luria see Gerhard Scholem, *Major Trends in Jewish Mysticism* (New York 1965), 244–86, 405–15; and *Sabbatai Sevi: The Mystical Messiah 1626–76* (trans., London 1973), 28–44.
52. Quoted in Scholem, *Sabbatai Sevi*, 18.
53. For Reubeni and Molcho, see Roth, *Venice*, 72ff.
54. R. J. Z. Werblowsky, *Joseph Caro, Lawyer and Mystic* (Oxford 1962).
55. Quoted in H. H. Ben Sasson, 'Messianic Movements', *Encyclopaedia Judaica*, xi 1426.
56. Isaiah 28:15–18; 34:14; Habakkuk 3:5; Chronicles 21:1; Leviticus 16:8. J. Trachtenberg, *The Devil and the Jews* (Philadelphia 1943).
57. J. Trachtenberg, *Jewish Magic and Superstition* (New York 1939).
58. Psalms 139:14–16.
59. Roth, *Personalities and Events*, 78ff.
60. Quoted by Ben Sasson, *Encyclopaedia Judaica*, xi 1425–6.
61. Scholem, *Sabbatai Sevi*, 3ff.
62. Quoted in *ibid.*
63. Quoted in Scholem, *Encyclopaedia Judaica*, xiv 1235.
64. Cecil Roth, *Essays and Portraits in Anglo-Jewish History* (London 1962), 139–64; *Encyclopaedia Judaica* vi 1159–60.
65. For his life see Cecil Roth, *Life of Manasseh ben Israel* (London 1934).
66. 'Jewish Physicians in Medieval England', in Roth, *Essays and Portraits*, 46–51; Lucien Wolf, *The Middle Ages of Anglo-Jewish History 1290–1656* (London 1888).
67. P. M. Handover, *The Second Cecil* (London 1959), ch. xiii, 'The Vile Jew'.
68. Cecil Roth, 'Philosemitism in England', in *Essays and Portraits*, 10–21.
69. For this episode see Cecil Roth, 'The Mystery of the Resettlement', in *Essays and Portraits*, 86–107.
70. Joseph J. Blau and S. W. Baron, *The Jews in the United States 1790–1840: A Documentary History*, 3 vols (New York 1963), i, Introduction, xviiiff.

71. Quoted in *ibid.*, xxi.
72. *Ibid.*, xxixff.
73. Quoted in Israel, *op. cit.*, 134.
74. *Ibid.*, 129.
75. Quoted in *ibid.*
76. *Ibid.*, 130; O. K. Rabinowicz, *Sir Solomon de Medina* (London 1974).
77. For the Salvadors, J. Picciotto, *Sketches of Anglo-Jewish History* (London 1956), 109–15, 153–6; for Gideon, A. M. Hyamson, *Sephardim of England* (London 1951), 128–33.
78. The book is translated as *The Jews and Modern Capitalism* (London 1913).
79. Alexander Marx, *Studies in Jewish History and Booklore* (New York 1969), 'Some Jewish Book Collectors', 198–237.
80. Commentary to Mishnah Sanhedrin, x 1, quoted in Kochan, *op. cit.*, 20.
81. *Ibid.*, 55–7; M. A. Meyer (ed.), *Ideas of Jewish History* (New York 1974), 117ff.; S. W. Baron, 'Azariah dei Rossi's Historical Method', *History and Jewish Historians* (Philadelphia 1964), 205–39.
82. Byron L. Sherwin, *Mystical Theology and Social Dissent: The Life and Works of Judah Loew of Prague* (New York 1983).
83. For the biography, see R. Kayser, *Spinoza: Portrait of a Spiritual Hero* (New York 1968); R. Willies (ed.), *Benedict de Spinoza: Life, Correspondence and Ethics* (London 1870).
84. Text from Willies, *op. cit.*, 34–5, and *Encyclopaedia Judaica*, xv 275–84.
85. Willies, *op. cit.*, 35.
86. Quoted in *ibid.*, 72.
87. L. Strauss, *Spinoza's Critique of Religion* (trans., New York 1965).
88. For documents, see *Chronicon Spinozanum*, 3 vols (Leiden 1921–3), i 278–82.
89. Jonathan Bennett, *A Study of Spinoza's Ethics* (Cambridge 1984), 32ff.
90. Quoted in *ibid.*, 34.
91. For an appreciation of Spinoza's thought see Bertrand Russell, *History of Western Philosophy* (London 1946), book iii, part 1, ch. 10.
92. Deuteronomy 21:18–20; Sanhedrin 8, 5; 71a; Yebamoth 12, 1–2; quoted by Samuel Belkin, *In His Image: The Jewish Philosophy of Man as Expressed in the Rabbinical Tradition* (London 1961).
93. J. R. Mintz, *In Praise of Ba'al Shem Tov* (New York 1970); *Encyclopaedia Judaica*, ix 1049ff.; Martin Buber, *Origins and Meaning of Hasidism* (London 1960).
94. R. Schatz, 'Contemplative Prayers in Hasidism', in *Studies in Mysticism and Religion Presented to Gershom G. Scholem* (Jerusalem 1967), 209ff.
95. Quoted in *ibid.*, 213.
96. *Ibid.*, 216.
97. L. Ginzburg, *The Gaon, Rabbi Elijah* (London 1920).
98. Quoted in *Encyclopaedia Judaica*, vi 653.
99. Arthur A. Cohen, *The Natural and Supernatural Jew* (London 1967), 20ff.
100. Quoted in *ibid.*, 24.
101. Isaac Eisenstein Barzilay, 'The Background of the Berlin Haskalah', in Joseph L. Blaud *et al.* (eds): *Essays on Jewish Life and Thought* (New York 1959).
102. Quoted in Cohen, *op. cit.*
103. Alexander Altmann, *Essays in Jewish Intellectual History* (Brandeis 1981), and *Moses Mendelssohn: A Biographical Study* (University of Alabama 1973).
104. Quoted in Altmann, *Essays*.

105. Cohen, *op. cit.*, 27–9.
106. Quoted in *Encylopaedia Judaica*, vi 153.
107. Blau and Baron, *op. cit.*, xxii–xxiii.
108. Roth, *Personalities and Events*, 256–70.
109. See B. C. Kaganoff, *A Dictionary of Jewish Names and their History* (London 1977).
110. A. Herzberg, *The French Enlightenment and the Jews* (New York 1968).
111. Z. Sjakowlski, *Jews and the French Revolutions of 1789, 1830 and 1848* (New York 1970).
112. Quoted in Cecil Roth, 'Lord George Gordon's Conversion to Judaism', in *Essays and Portraits*, 193–4.
113. Quoted in *ibid.*, 205.
114. Cecil Roth, *A History of the Great Synagogue* (London 1950), 214ff.
115. Quoted in *Encyclopaedia Judaica*, viii 1390–1432.
116. Quoted in Ben Sasson, *History of the Jewish People*, 745; see Herzberg, *op. cit.*
117. Quoted in Ben Sasson, *History of the Jewish People.*
118. See R. Anchel, *Napoléon et les Juifs* (Paris 1928).
119. F. Pietri, *Napoléon et les Israélites* (Paris 1965), 84–115.

PART FIVE: EMANCIPATION

1. Quoted in M. C. N. Salbstein, *The Emancipation of the Jews in Britain* (New Jersey 1982), 98.
2. Quoted in W. F. Moneypenny, *Life of Benjamin Disraeli*, 6 vols (London 1910), i 22.
3. Fritz J. Raddatz, *Karl Marx: A Political Biography* (London 1979), ch. 1; for Marx's family background, see Heinz Monz, *Karl Marx: Grundlagen der Entwicklung zu Leben und Werk* (Trier 1973).
4. Emile Marmorstein, *Heaven at Bay: The Jewish Kulturkampf in the Holy Land* (Oxford 1969), 32.
5. Quoted in H. H. Ben Sasson (ed.), *A History of the Jewish People* (trans., Harvard 1976), 826.
6. *Erstlingswerk* (Leipzig 1894), 233; quoted in Marmorstein, *op. cit.*
7. The best is Bertrand Gille, *Histoire de la Maison Rothschild*, 2 vols (Geneva 1965–7).
8. Quoted in Miriam Rothschild, *Dear Lord Rothschild: Birds, Butterflies and History* (London and Philadelphia 1983), 295–6.
9. *Ibid.*, 301.
10. David Landes, *Bankers and Pashas* (London 1958), ch. 1.
11. Harold Pollins, *Economic History of the Jews in England* (East Brunswick 1982), 95–6.
12. S. D. Chapman, *The Foundation of the English Rothschilds, 1793–1811* (London 1977), 20ff.
13. See Edward Herries, *Memoirs of the Public Life of John S. Herries* (London 1880); Gille, *op. cit.*, i 45ff.; F. Crouzet, *L'Économie Britannique et le blocus continental 1806–13* (Paris 1958), 842.
14. Gille, *op. cit.*, i 458.
15. Pollins, *op. cit.*; K. Helleiner, *The Imperial Loans* (Oxford 1965).
16. Gille, *op. cit.*, ii 571; see Pollins, *op. cit.*, 245, table 5.

17. G. Storey, *Reuters* (London 1951); F. Giles, *Prince of Journalists* (London 1962); Ronald Palin, *Rothschild Relish* (London 1970), quoted in Pollins, *op. cit.*

18. Miriam Rothschild, *op. cit.*, 9.

19. Cecil Roth, *The Magnificent Rothschilds* (London 1939), 21.

20. L. H. Jenks, *The Migration of British Capital to 1875* (London 1963).

21. Salbstein, *op. cit.*

22. Quoted in *ibid.*, 165.

23. Gille, *op. cit.*, ii 591–616.

24. Richard Davis, *The English Rothschilds* (London 1983).

25. For details, see Roth, *op. cit.*

26. Miriam Rothschild, *op. cit.*, 298.

27. *Ibid.*, 33.

28. For an account of 1st Lord Rothschild, see *ibid.*, 30–50.

29. *Ibid.*, 40.

30. Quoted in Roth, *op. cit.*

31. Quoted in Salbstein, *op. cit.*, 44.

32. Cecil Roth, *Essays and Portraits in Anglo-Jewish History* (London 1962), 18–20.

33. Geoffrey Finlayson, *The Seventh Earl of Shaftesbury* (London 1981), 112–16, 154–9 etc.

34. Quoted in Ronald Sanders, *op. cit.*, 5.

35. L. Loewe, *The Damascus Affair* (New York 1940).

36. For Montefiore, see Lucien Wolf, *Sir Moses Montefiore* (London 1885).

37. Roth, *Essays and Portraits*, 19–20.

38. Robert Blake, *Disraeli's Grand Tour: Benjamin Disraeli and the Holy Land, 1830–1* (London 1982), 107ff.

39. Daien Schwarz, *Disraeli's Fiction* (London 1979), 99–100.

40. 'Benjamin Disraeli, Marrano Englishman', in Salbstein, *op. cit.*, 97–114.

41. This was the view of Judah Halevi; see H. J. Zimmels, *Ashkenazim and Sephardim* (New York 1959).

42. Quoted in Blake, *op. cit.*, 126.

43. Quoted in Salbstein, *op. cit.*

44. M. A. Meyer, *The Origins of the Modern Jew* (New York 1968); Wolf's article 'On the Concept of a Science of Judaism' (1822) is in *Leo Baeck Institute Yearbook II* (London 1957).

45. Quoted in Lionel Kocham, *The Jew and his History* (London 1977), 66.

46. Arthur A. Cohen, *The Natural and Supernatural Jew* (London 1967), 46.

47. Quoted in Kocham, *op. cit.*, 66.

48. Babylon Talmud, Berakhoth 3a, quoted in *ibid.*

49. For Hirsch's writings see I. Grunfeld (ed.), *Judaism Eternal*, 2 vols (London 1956).

50. *Ibid.*, i 133–5, quoted in Kocham, *op. cit.*

51. Kochan, *op. cit.*, 79–80; Cohen, *op. cit.*, 34; N. Rotenstreich, *Jewish Philosophy in Modern Times* (New York 1968), 136–48.

52. The English translation, by P. Bloch, is in 6 vols (London 1892–8) and 5 vols (London 1919).

53. Quoted in Kochan, *op. cit.*

54. H. Graetz, *Historic Parallels in Jewish History* (London 1887).

55. Alexander Altmann, 'The New Style of Preaching in Nineteenth Century German Jewry', in *Essays in Jewish Intellectual History* (Brandeis 1981).

56. W. D. Plaut, *Rise of Reform Judaism* (London 1963); D. Philipson, *Reform Movement in Judaism* (New York 1967).

57. M. Weiner (ed.), *Abraham Geiger and Liberal Judaism* (New York 1962).

58. Quoted by Marmorstein, *op. cit.*, 36.

59. English translation by M. M. Kaplan (2nd edn, London 1964).

60. S. Ginzburg, *The Life and Works of M. H. Luzzatto* (London 1931).

61. Quoted in Marmorstein, *op. cit.*, who gives a summary of Luzzatto's teaching, 5–11.

62. See Leo Rosen, *The Joys of Yiddish* (Harmondsworth 1971), xviff.

63. *The Renaissance of Hebrew Literature, 1743–1885* (New York 1909), quoted in Marmorstein, *op. cit.*

64. Laura Hofrichter, *Heinrich Heine* (trans., Oxford 1963), 1–2.

65. Jeffrey L. Sammons, *Heinrich Heine: A Modern Biography* (Princeton 1979), 40.

66. *Ibid.*, 171.

67. The most important is S. S. Prawer, *Heine's Jewish Comedy: A Study of his Portraits of Jews and Judaism* (Oxford 1983).

68. Heine to Moses Moser, 23 August 1823; quoted in Sammons, *op. cit.*

69. Heine to Immanuel Wohlwill, 1 April 1823; quoted in *ibid.*

70. Heine to Ferdinand Lassalle, 11 February 1846, quoted in *ibid.*

71. Heine to Moser, 14 December 1825, quoted in Hofrichter, *op. cit.*, 44.

72. Ernst Elster (ed.), *Heines samtliche Werke*, 7 vols (Leipzig and Vienna 1887–90), vii 407.

73. Sammons, *op. cit.*, 249–50.

74. *Ibid.*, 288.

75. *Ibid.*, 25–6.

76. *Ibid.*, 166.

77. *Ibid.*, 308.

78. For their relations see Raddatz, *op. cit.*, 42–3; Sammons, *op. cit.*, 260ff.

79. Paul Nerrlich (ed.), *Arnold Ruges Briefwechsel und Tagebuchblatter aus der Jahren 1825–1880* (Berlin 1886), ii 346.

80. Robert S. Wistrich, *Revolutionary Jews from Marx to Trotsky* (London 1976), 40, shows that an article by Marx on Jerusalem, printed in the *New York Daily Tribune* in April 1854, sometimes quoted to disprove this assertion, in fact confirms it.

81. To Engels, 11 April 1868, *Karl Marx–Friedrich Engels Werke* (East Berlin 1956–68), xxxii 58.

82. Karl Jaspers, 'Marx und Freud', *Der Monat*, xxvi (1950), quoted in Raddatz, *op. cit.*

83. See Raddatz, *op. cit.*, 143 for references.

84. François Marie Charles Fourier, *Théorie des quatres mouvements* (Paris 1808); for Fourier see L. Poliakov, *History of Anti-semitism* (trans., London 1970–   ).

85. *Carnets* (Paris 1961), ii 23, 337.

86. Wistrich, *op. cit.*, 6ff.

87. For Börne see Orlando Figes, 'Ludwig Börne and the Formation of a Radical Critique of Judaism', *Leo Baeck Institute Year Book* (London 1984).

88. See Prawer, *op. cit.*; Nigel Reeves, 'Heine and the Young Marx', *Oxford German Studies* viii (1972–3).

89. *Herr Vogt* (London 1860), 143–4; quoted in Wistrich, *op. cit.*
90. Karl Marx, *Neue Rheinische Zeitung*, 29 April 1849.
91. *Marx–Engels Works*, ii iii (Berlin 1930), 122.
92. *Marx–Engels Werke*, xxx 165.
93. *Ibid.*, 259.
94. See Figes, *op. cit.*
95. Bruno Bauer, *Die Judenfrage* (Brunswick 1843).
96. I have used T. B. Bottomore (ed. and trans.), *Karl Marx: Early Writings* (London 1963). Also in *Karl Marx–Engels Collected Works* (London 1975ff.), iii 146–74.
97. Bottomore, *op. cit.*, 34.
98. *Ibid.*, 37.
99. *Ibid.*, 35–6.
100. *Ibid.*, 34–5.
101. *Capital*, i ii, ch. 4.
102. *Capital*, ii vii, ch. 22.
103. Karl Marx, 'The Russian Loan', *New York Daily Tribune*, 4 January 1856.
104. Quoted by S. W. Baron, 'Population', *Encyclopaedia Judaica*, xiii 866–903.
105. Quoted in Ben Sasson, *op. cit.*
106. Paul Lindau (ed.), *Ferdinand Lassalles Tagebuch* (Breslau 1891), 160–1; quoted in Wistrich, *op. cit.*
107. A. F. Day, *The Mortara Mystery* (London 1930).
108. For Jews under the Tsars see J. Frumkin *et al.* (eds), *Russian Jewry 1860–1917* (London 1966); S. W. Baron, *The Russian Jew under Tsars and Soviets* (New York 1964).
109. See Alexis Goldenweiser, 'Legal Status of Jews in Russia', in Frumkin, *op. cit.*
110. Lucien Wolf (ed.), *Legal Sufferings of the Jews in Russia* (London 1912).
111. *Ibid.*, 41.
112. *Ibid.* 44–6, 71–6.
113. *Ibid.*, 2–6.
114. *Ibid.*, 9.
115. I. M. Dijur, 'Jews in the Russian Economy', in Frumkin, *op. cit.*, 120–43.
116. Quoted in Amos Elon, *Herzl* (London 1976).
117. Quoted in Ben Sasson, *op. cit.*
118. Joseph L. Blau and S. W. Baron, *The Jews in the United States 1790–1840: A Documentary History*, 3 vols (New York 1963), ii 576.
119. *Ibid.*, iii 809.
120. *Ibid.*, ii 327.
121. A. B. Makover, *Mordecai M. Noah* (New York 1917); I. Goldberg, *Major Noah: American Jewish Pioneer* (New York 1937); text of his proclamation in Blau and Baron, *op. cit.*, iii 898–9.
122. *Ibid.*, 176–81.
123. For Leeser, see Murray Friedman, *Jewish Life in Philadelphia 1830–1940* (Philadelphia 1984).
124. Text in full in *Encyclopaedia Judaica*, xiii 570–1.
125. H. E. Jacobs, *The World of Emma Lazarus* (New York 1949); E. Merriam, *Emma Lazarus: Woman with a Torch* (New York 1956).
126. *Encyclopaedia Judaica*, xii 1092.
127. Richard Siegel and Carl Rheins (eds), *The Jewish Almanack* (New York 1980), 509.

128. Psalms 137:1.
129. Moses Hess, *Rome and Jerusalem* (trans., New York 1918).
130. Cohen, *op. cit.*, 57–9; for Hess, see also Isaiah Berlin, *The Life and Opinions of Moses Hess* (Cambridge 1959).
131. J. R. Vincent (ed.), *Disraeli, Derby and the Conservative Party: The Political Journals of Lord Stanley* (London 1978), 32–3.
132. J. A. Gere and John Sparrow (eds), *Geoffrey Madan's Notebooks* (Oxford 1984).
133. J. J. Tobias, *The Prince of Fences: The Life and Crimes of Ikey Solomons* (London 1974).
134. L. Hyman, *The Jews of Ireland, London and Jerusalem* (London 1972), 103–4.
135. Emily Strangford, *Literary Remains of the Late Emanuel Deutsch* (New York 1974).
136. Gordon S. Haight, *George Eliot* (Oxford 1968), 487.
137. *Encyclopaedia Britannica* (London 1911), xxviii 987.
138. For the influence of George Eliot, see Ronald Sanders, *The High Walls of Jerusalem: A History of the Balfour Declaration and the Birth of the British Mandate for Palestine* (New York 1984), 14ff.
139. Guy Chapman, *The Dreyfus Case* (London 1955), 99.
140. For French Jewry during the Dreyfus case see Michael R. Marrus, *The Politics of Assimilation: The French Jewish Community at the Time of the Dreyfus Affair* (Oxford 1971).
141. Quoted in *ibid.*, 118.
142. Léon Halévy, *Résumé de l'histoire des juifs modernes* (Paris 1828), 325–6; quoted in Marrus, *op. cit.*, 90.
143. Julien Benda, *La Jeunesse d'un clerc* (Paris 1936), 43; quoted in Marrus, *op. cit.*
144. Herbert Feis, *Europe the World's Banker 1870–1914* (New York 1965), 33ff.
145. For the church see R. P. Lecanuet, *L'Église de la France sur la troisième république* (Paris 1930), 231–3; Robert L. Hoffman, *More Than a Trial: The Struggle over Captain Dreyfus* (New York 1980), 82ff.
146. *La Croix*, 13 November 1896, quoted in Pierre Sorin, *La Croix et les Juifs 1880–1899* (Paris 1967), 117.
147. Chapman, *op. cit.*, 59.
148. *L'Aurore*, 7 June 1899; quoted in Marrus, *op. cit.*, who has a chapter on Lazare, 164–95; B. Hagani, *Bernard Lazare* (Paris 1919).
149. George D. Painter, *Marcel Proust*, 2 vols (London 1977), i 210.
150. Paul Cambon, *Correspondance*, 2 vols (Paris 1945), i 436.
151. Quoted in Chapman, *op. cit.*, 199.
152. Christophe Charles, 'Champ littéraire et champ du pouvoir: les écrivains et l'affaire Dreyfus', *Annales*, 32 (1977).
153. Jean-Pierre Rioux, *Nationalisme et conservatisme: la Ligue de la Patrie française 1899–1904* (Paris 1977), 20–30; quoted in Marrus, *op. cit.*, 148–9.
154. Painter, *op. cit.*, i 220.
155. Alain Silvera, *Daniel Halévy and his Times* (Cornell 1966).
156. Painter, *op. cit.*, i 214ff.
157. Janine Ponty, 'La Presse quotidienne et l'Affaire Dreyfus en 1898–99', *Revue d'histoire moderne et contemporaine*, 21 (1974).
158. Found in a scrapbook compiled for Drumont and now (along with a mass of other Dreyfus case material) in the Houghton Library at Harvard.
159. Frederick Busi, 'The Dreyfus Affair and the French Cinema', *Weiner Library Bulletin*, 39–40 (1976).

160. Painter, *op. cit.*, i 226.
161. *Ibid.*, 233.
162. R. D. Mandell, 'The Affair and the Fair: Some Observations on the Closing Stages of the Dreyfus Case', *Journal of Modern History* (September 1967); Douglas Johnson, *France and the Dreyfus Affair* (London 1966).
163. Joseph Reinach, *Histoire de l'Affaire Dreyfus*, 6 vols plus index (Paris 1901–8).
164. Chapman, *op. cit.*, 359; Charles Andler, *La Vie de Lucien Herr* (Paris 1932).
165. André Gide, *Journals 1889–1949* (trans., Harmondsworth 1978), 194ff.
166. Of the many books on Herzl, I have chiefly followed Elon, *op. cit.*
167. *Ibid.*, 9.
168. Quoted in *ibid.*, 66.
169. *Ibid.*, 115.
170. For the rise of *völkisch* anti-Semitism, see George L. Mosse, *The Crisis in German Ideology* (London 1966).
171. Quoted in Elon, *op. cit.*, 64.
172. First English translation, *Autoemancipation: An Admonition to his Brethren by a Russian Jew* (New York 1906).
173. Quoted in Walter Laqueur, *Weimar: A Cultural History 1918–1933* (London 1974).
174. Elon, *op. cit.*, 114.
175. Pierre van Passen, 'Paris 1891–5: A Study of the Transition in Theodor Herzl's Life', in Meyer W. Weisgal (ed.), *Theodor Herzl, Memorial* (New York 1929).
176. *Der Judenstaat: Versuch einer modernen Loesung der juedischen Frage* (Vienna 1896); H. Abrahami and A. Bein, *The Editions of the Jewish State by Theodor Herzl* (New York 1970).
177. Elon, *op. cit.*, 142–7.
178. *Ibid.*, 175ff.
179. For Nordau see A. and M. Nordau, *Max Nordau* (trans., London 1943).
180. I had the privilege of addressing an international congress of Zionists and Christians from this same platform in August 1985.
181. Chaim Weizmann, *Trial and Error* (London 1949), 71.
182. Elon, *op. cit.*, 186.
183. His *Tagebücher*, trans. Harry Zohn, ed. R. Patai, were published New York 1960.
184. Elon, *op. cit.*, 379–80.
185. Sanders, *op. cit.*, 29–30.
186. *Ibid.*, 37–8.
187. Elon, *op. cit.*, 405–6, 397.
188. *Ibid.*, 237.
189. Marmorstein, *op. cit.* 60–70.
190. Quoted in I. Domb, *Transformations* (London 1958), 192–5.
191. Quoted in Marmorstein, *op. cit.*, 71–2.
192. Quoted in *ibid.*, 79–80.
193. T. Levitan, *The Laureates: Jewish Winners of the Nobel Prize* (New York 1906); see list of Jewish Nobel prizewinners in *Encyclopaedia Judaica*, xii 1201–2.
194. Frederick V. Grunfeld, *Prophets Without Honour* (London 1979), 10.
195. For Cohen see Cohen, *op. cit.*, 70ff.; Alexander Altmann, 'Theology in Twentieth-century Jewry', in *Essays in Jewish Intellectual History*.

196. For Rosenzweig and Rosenstock-Huessy see Altmann, *op. cit.*, and N. N. Glatzer (ed.), *Franz Rosenzweig: His Life and Thought* (2nd edn, New York 1961).

197. Quoted in Grunfeld, *op. cit.*, 17.

198. Hartmut Pogge von Strandmann (ed.), *Walter Rathenau: Notes and Diaries 1907–22* (Oxford 1985), 98–9.

199. Quoted in Grunfeld, *op. cit.*

200. Charles Rosen, *Schoenberg* (London 1976), 16–17.

201. Alma Mahler, *Gustav Mahler: Memories and Letters* (trans., New York 1946), 90.

202. Charles Spencer, *Léon Bakst* (London 1973).

203. Serge Lifar, *A History of the Russian Ballet* (London 1954).

204. Quoted in Spencer, *op. cit.*, 127.

205. For Bakst's moral theory of colour see Mary Franton Roberts, *The New Russian Stage* (New York 1915).

206. Sidney Alexander, *Marc Chagall* (London 1978).

207. Peter Gay, *Freud, Jews and Other Germans* (Oxford 1978), 21.

208. *Ibid.*, 101ff.

209. Letter to Karl Abraham, quoted in Jack J. Spector, *The Aesthetics of Freud* (London 1977), 22.

210. Paul Roazen, *Freud and his Followers* (London 1976), 192–3.

211. *Ibid.*, 75ff.; for Freud and his wife see letter from his daughter Matilda Freud Hollitscher to Ernest Jones, 30 March 1952, in the Jones archives, and Theodor Reik, 'Years of Maturity', *Psychoanalysis*, iv i (1955).

212. David Bakan, *Sigmund Freud and the Jewish Mystical Tradition* (Princeton 1958), 51–2; Sigmund Freud, Preface to *Totem and Taboo* (1913).

213. Ernest Jones, *Life and Work of Sigmund Freud*, 3 vols (New York 1953–7), i 22, 184.

214. 'On Being of the B'nai B'rith', *Commentary* (March 1946).

215. Max Graf, 'Reminiscences of Sigmund Freud', *Psychoanalytic Quarterly*, xi (1942); Jacob Meotliz, 'The Last Days of Sigmund Freud', *Jewish Frontier* (September 1951); quoted in Bakan, *op. cit.*

216. Jones, *op. cit.*, i 25, 35. For Freud's own account, see M. Bonaparte, A. Freud and E. Kris (eds and trans.), *Freud, Origins of Psychoanalysis: Letters to Wilhelm Fliess, Drafts and Notes 1887–1902* (New York 1954), 322; Bakan, *op. cit.*

217. E. Stengel, 'A Revaluation of Freud's Book "On Aphasia" ', *International Journal of Psychoanalysis* (1954).

218. H. Sachs, *Freud, Master and Friend* (Harvard 1944), 99–100; quoted in Bakan, *op. cit.*

219. Jones, *op. cit.*, i 348.

220. *Ibid.*, ii 367; Sigmund Freud, 'The Moses of Michelangelo', *Collected Papers*, iv 251–87.

221. Bakan, *op. cit.*, 246–70.

222. Robert S. Steele, *Freud and Jung: Conflicts of Interpretation* (London 1982); W. McGuire (ed.), *Freud–Jung Letters* (Princeton 1974), 220.

223. Max Schur, *Freud Living and Dying* (London 1972), 337.

224. Jones, *op. cit.*, ii 148.

225. Steven Marcus, *Freud and the Culture of Psychoanalysis* (London 1984), 50–3.

226. Quoted in *ibid.*, 83.

227. For Breuer, see Sigmund Freud, 'Origins and Development of Psychoanalysis', *American Journal of Psychology*, xxi (1910), 181; Roazen, *op. cit.*, 93–9.

228. Fritz Wittels, *Sigmund Freud* (New York 1924), 140; quoted in Bakan, *op. cit.*
229. Quoted in Roazen, *op. cit.*, 197.
230. Jones, *op. cit.*, ii 33.
231. For Freud's rows, see Roazen, *op. cit.*, 194ff., 204ff., 220ff., 234ff. etc.
232. Jones, *op. cit.*, iii 208.
233. *Ibid.*, iii 245.
234. Arthur Koestler, *The Invisible Writing* (London 1955).
235. For Einstein's contribution to quantum theory see Max Jammer, 'Einstein and Quantum Physics', in Gerald Holton and Yehuda Elkana (eds), *Albert Einstein: Historical and Cultural Perspectives* (Princeton 1982), 59–76.
236. 'What I Believe', *Forum and Century* 84 (1930); quoted in Uriel Tal, 'Ethics in Einstein's Life and Thought', in Holton and Elkana, *op. cit.*, 297–318.
237. Einstein, *Physics and Reality* (New York 1936).
238. Henri Bergson, *Two Sources of Morality and Religion* (trans., London 1935).
239. Einstein to Solovine, 30 March 1952, quoted in Yehuda Elkana, 'The Myth of Simplicity', in Holton and Elkana, *op. cit.*, 242.
240. Milic Capek, *The Philosophical Impact of Contemporary Physics* (Princeton 1961), 335ff.; see also William James, 'The Dilemma of Determinism', in *The Will to Believe* (London 1917).
241. Yehuda Elkana, *op. cit.*
242. For this, see my *Modern Times: The World from the Twenties to the Eighties* (New York 1983), ch. 1, 'A Relativistic World'.
243. Lionel Trilling, *Mind in the Modern World* (New York 1973), 13–14.
244. 'The Hunter Graccus'. *Graccus* or *graculus* is Latin for jackdaw, Czech *kavka*, and Kafka's father, whom he hated, had a jackdaw sign over his shop. See Lionel Trilling, *Prefaces to the Experience of Literature* (Oxford 1981), 118–22.
245. Quoted in Rosen, *op. cit.*, 10.
246. Grunfeld, *op. cit.*, 23–4.

PART SIX: HOLOCAUST

1. Asquith speech in *The Times*, 10 November 1914.
2. Interview with Mrs Halperin in Eric Silver, *Begin* (London 1984), 5, 9.
3. Ronald Sanders, *The High Walls of Jerusalem: A History of the Balfour Declaration and the Birth of the British Mandate for Palestine* (New York 1984), 315ff.
4. Chaim Weizmann, *Trial and Error* (London 1949), 15–25.
5. *Ibid.*, 29, 44.
6. Sanders, *op. cit.*, 64–9.
7. *New Statesman*, 21 November 1914, article signed A.M.H. (Albert Montefiore Hyamson).
8. Michael and Eleanor Brock (eds), *H. H. Asquith: Letters to Venetia Stanley* (Oxford 1952), 406–7.
9. *Ibid.*, 477–8; 485.
10. Quoted in Sanders, *op. cit.*, 313–14.
11. Miriam Rothschild, *Dear Lord Rothschild: Birds, Butterflies and History* (London and Philadelphia 1983), 45.
12. Sanders, *op. cit.*, 69, 133.
13. Weizmann, *op. cit.*, 144; doubts have been cast on this story; see Sanders, *op. cit.*, 94–6.

14. Quoted in Sanders, *op. cit.*

15. For the collections see Miriam Rothschild, *op. cit.*

16. Weizmann, *op. cit.*, 257.

17. Montagu was not present at the war cabinet of 31 October 1917; see Sanders, *op. cit.*, 594–6, which also gives text of the final letter.

18. Weizmann, *op. cit.*, 262.

19. *Ibid.*, 298; Sanders, *op. cit.*, 481.

20. Weizmann, *op. cit.*, 273–4.

21. Text of the mandate in David Lloyd George, *The Truth About the Peace Treaties*, 2 vols (London 1938), ii 1194–1201.

22. Weizmann, *op. cit.*, 288.

23. *Ibid.*, 67.

24. Vladimir Jabotinsky, *The Story of the Jewish Legion* (trans., Jerusalem 1945); P. Lipovetski, *Joseph Trumpeldor* (trans., London 1953).

25. Yigal Allon, *The Making of Israel's Army* (New York 1970); J. B. Schechtman, *The Vladimir Jabotinsky Story*, 2 vols (New York 1956–61).

26. Amos Elon, *Herzl* (London 1976), 179.

27. Neil Caplan, *Palestine Jewry and the Arab Question 1917–25* (London 1978), 74, 169ff.

28. Quoted in S. Clement Leslie, *The Rift in Israel: Religious Authority and Secular Democracy* (London 1971), 32.

29. Weizmann, *op. cit.*, 316.

30. *Ibid.*, 307–8.

31. Sanders, *op. cit.*, 569–70, for full text of message.

32. Elie Kedourie, 'Sir Herbert Samuel and the Government of Palestine', in *The Chatham House Version and Other Middle East Studies* (London 1970), 57.

33. 8 June 1920; *Letters and Papers of Chaim Weizmann* (New Brunswick 1977), xi 355.

34. Quoted in Kedourie, *op. cit.*, 55–6.

35. Quoted in Neil Caplan, 'The Yishuv, Sir Herbert Samuel and the Arab Question in Palestine 1921–5', in Elie Kedourie and Sylvia G. Haim (eds), *Zionism and Arabism in Palestine and Israel* (London 1982), 19–20.

36. Kedourie, *op. cit.*, 60–2.

37. Quoted in *ibid.*, 65.

38. Bernard Wasserstein, 'Herbert Samuel and the Palestine Problem', *English Historical Review*, 91 (1976).

39. Kedourie, *op. cit.*, 69.

40. Weizmann, *op. cit.*, 325, 494.

41. Lloyd George, *Peace Treaties*, 1123ff.

42. *Ibid.*, 1139.

43. Caplan, 'The Yishuv', 31.

44. Quoted in Wasserstein, *op. cit.*, 767.

45. Quoted in R. H. S. Crossman, *A Nation Reborn* (London 1960), 127.

46. Weizmann, *op. cit.*, 418.

47. Quoted in *Encyclopaedia Judaica*, iv 506.

48. Weizmann, *op. cit.*, 411.

49. Quoted in Leslie, *op. cit.* (1938 interview).

50. 'On the Iron Wall', 1923; quoted in Silver, *op. cit.*, 12.

51. Robert S. Wistrich, *Revolutionary Jews from Marx to Trotsky* (London 1976), 77ff.; see also J. P. Nettl, *Rosa Luxemburg*, 2 vols (London 1966).

52. Quoted in Wistrich, *op. cit.*, 83.
53. Letter to Mathilee Wurm, 16 February 1917, quoted in *ibid*.
54. *Collected Works* (London 1961), vii 100ff.; 'Critical Remarks on the National Question', 1913; quoted in Wistrich, *op. cit.*
55. Isaac Deutscher, *The Prophet Armed: Trotsky, 1879–1921* (Oxford 1965).
56. See K. Pindson (ed.), *Essays in Anti-Semitism* (2nd edn, New York 1946), 121–44. The *Encyclopaedia Judaica*, xiv 459, gives the figure as 60,000; H. H. Ben Sasson (ed.), *A History of the Jewish People* (trans., Harvard 1976), gives 75,000; the Soviet figure is 180,000–200,000.
57. Bernard D. Weinryb, 'Anti-Semitism in Soviet Russia', in Lionel Kochan (ed.), *The Jews in Soviet Russia* (Oxford 1972).
58. J. B. Schechtman, 'The USSR, Zionism and Israel', in Kochan, *op. cit.*, 101.
59. *Ibid.*, 107; Guido D. Goldman, *Zionism under Soviet Rule 1917–28* (New York 1960).
60. Isaac Deutscher, *The Prophet Unarmed: Trotsky 1921–29* (Oxford 1965), 258.
61. Quoted in Lionel Trilling, 'Isaac Babel', in *Beyond Culture* (Oxford 1980), 103–25; see also Trilling's edition of Babel's *Collected Stories* (New York 1955), and R. Rosenthal in *Commentary*, 3 (1947).
62. Robert Conquest, *Inside Stalin's Secret Police: NKVD Politics 1936–39* (London 1985), 99.
63. *Jewish Chronicle*, 2 November 1917.
64. Quoted in Leon Poliakov, *History of Anti-Semitism*, vol. iv, Suicidal Europe, 1870–1933 (Oxford 1985), 209.
65. *The Cause of World Unrest*, 10, 13, 131–2.
66. *Illustrated Sunday Herald*, 8 February 1920, quoted in Poliakov, *op. cit.*
67. *Morning Post*, 6 October 1921, quoted in Poliakov, *op. cit.*
68. Robert Wilson, *The Last Days of the Romanovs* (London 1920), 148.
69. P. Lévy, *Les Noms des Israélites en France* (Paris 1960), 75–6.
70. Quoted in Paul J. Kingston, *Anti-Semitism in France during the 1930s: Organization, Personalities and Propaganda* (Hull 1983), 4.
71. Paul Hyman, *From Dreyfus to Vichy: The Remaking of French Jewry* (Columbia 1979), 35.
72. Léon Blum, *Nouvelles Conversations de Goethe avec Eckermann* (Paris 1901), quoted in Wistrich, *op. cit.*
73. Harvey Goldberg, 'Jean Jaurès on the Jewish Question', *Jewish Social Studies* (April 1958).
74. A. Mitchell Palmer, 'The Case Against the Reds', *Forum*, February 1920; Poliakov, *op. cit.*, 231–2.
75. For Brandeis' legal philosophy, see Philippa Strum, *Louis D. Brandeis: Justice for the People* (Harvard 1985).
76. *West Virginia State Board of Education* v. *Barnette* (1943).
77. G. Saleski, *Famous Musicians of Jewish Origin* (New York 1949).
78. T. Levitan, *Jews in American Life* (New York 1969), 96–9, 199–203, 245–6.
79. Quoted in Lary May, *Screening Out the Past: The Birth of Mass Culture and the Motion-Picture Industry* (Oxford 1980).
80. See Philip French, *The Movie Moguls* (London 1967).
81. *Ibid.*, 21.
82. For biographical details see French, *op. cit.*; May, *op. cit.*, 253, table iiia, 'Founders of the Big Eight', and table iiib for biographies.
83. French, *op. cit.*, 28.

84. Raymond Durgnat, *The Crazy Mirror: Hollywood Comedy and the American Image* (London 1969), 150–61; 78–83.

85. May, *op. cit.*, 171.

86. Helen and Robert Lynd, *Middletown* (New York 1929).

87. Edward J. Bristow, *Prostitution and Prejudice: The Jewish Fight Against White Slavery 1870–1939* (New York 1984).

88. Jenna Weissman Joselit, *Our Gang: Jewish Crime and the New York Jewish Community 1900–1940* (New York 1983).

89. For Jewish gangsters see Albert Fried, *The Rise and Fall of the Jewish Gangster in America* (New York 1980).

90. Melvin Urofsky, *American Zionism: From Herzl to the Holocaust* (New York 1975), 127.

91. Quoted in Ronald Steel, *Walter Lippmann and the American Century* (London 1980), 187.

92. James Grant, *Bernard Baruch: The Adventures of a Wall Street Legend* (New York 1983), 223ff., shows that he merely salvaged most of his fortune after the market broke; he was never worth more than between $10 million and $15 million.

93. *Ibid.*, 107–9.

94. Steel, *op. cit.*, 189.

95. 'Public Opinion and the American Jew', *American Hebrew*, 14 April 1922.

96. Quoted in Steel, *op. cit.*, 194.

97. Quoted in *ibid.*, 330–1.

98. *New York Times*, 11 April 1945; for polls see Davis S. Wyman, *The Abandonment of the Jews: America and the Holocaust 1941–45* (New York 1984), 8–9.

99. Fritz Stern, 'Einstein's Germany', in Holton and Elkana, *op. cit.*, 322ff.

100. *Ibid.*, 324–5.

101. E. J. Gumpel produced a statistical survey of these murders and sentences, *Vier Jahre politisches Mord* (Berlin 1922), quoted in Grunfeld, *op. cit.*

102. *Mein Kampf* (1962 edn), 772.

103. Walter Laqueur, *Russia and Germany: A Century of Conflict* (London 1962), 109ff.; Poliakov, *op. cit.*, iv 174.

104. Robert Wistrich, *Hitler's Apocalypse: Jews and the Nazi Legacy* (London 1986), 14–19.

105. Quoted in Raul Hilberg, *The Destruction of the European Jews* (rev. edn, New York 1985), i 20–1.

106. *Zentralblatt für Psychotherapie*, vii (1934); quoted in Grunfeld, *op. cit.*

107. Fritz Stern, *The Politics of Cultural Despair* (Berkeley 1961), 291.

108. Fritz K. Ringer, *The Decline of the German Mandarins: The German Academic Community 1890–1933* (Harvard 1969), 446.

109. George L. Mosse, *The Crisis in German Ideology* (London 1966), 196.

110. Michael S. Steinberg, *Sabres and Brownshirts: The German Students' Path to National Socialism, 1918–35* (Chicago 1977), 6–7; P. G. J. Pulzer, *The Rise of Political Anti-Semitism in Germany and Austria* (New York 1964), 285ff.

111. Dennis E. Showalter, *Little Man, What Now? Der Stürmer in the Weimar Republic* (Hamden, Connecticut 1983).

112. Istvan Deak, *Weimar Germany's Left-wing Intellectuals: A Political History of the Weltbühne and its Circle* (Berkeley 1968); Harold L. Poor, *Kurt Tucholsky and the Ordeal of Germany 1914–35* (New York 1968).

113. Quoted in Walter Laqueur, *Weimar: A Cultural History 1918–1933* (London 1974), 45.

114. Mosse, *op. cit.*, 144.

115. Donald L. Niewyk, *The Jews in Weimar Germany* (Manchester 1981), has a chapter on this subject, 'The Jew as German Chauvinist', 165–77.

116. Laqueur, *Weimar*, 72.

117. *Ibid.*, 75ff.

118. Mosse, *op. cit.*, 242.

119. Roger Manvell and Heinrich Fraenkel, *The German Cinema* (London 1971), 7ff.

120. Laqueur, *op. cit.*, 234ff.

121. Gershom Scholem, *Walter Benjamin: The Story of a Friendship* (London 1982); *Jews and Judaism in Crisis* (New York 1976), 193.

122. Richard Wolin, *Walter Benjamin: An Aesthetic of Redemption* (New York 1982), 40–3.

123. Walter Benjamin, *Illuminations* (trans., New York 1969), 255: Wolin, *op. cit.*, 50ff.

124. Terry Eagleton, *Walter Benjamin, or Towards a Revolutionary Criticism* (London 1981).

125. Hilberg, *op. cit.*, i 30ff.

126. *Institut für Zeitgeschichte*, Munich; quoted in Wistrich, *Hitler's Apocalypse*, 31–2.

127. Max Domarus (ed.), *Hitler: Reden und Proklamationen 1932–45* (Würzburg 1962), i 537.

128. Hilberg, *op. cit.*, i 39.

129. *Ibid.*, 46, footnote 1.

130. *Ibid.*, 69–75.

131. *Ibid.*, 96–107.

132. *Ibid.*, 190–1.

133. *Ibid.*, ii 416; Lucy S. Davidowicz, *The War Against the Jews, 1933–45* (London 1975), 141; Martin Gilbert, *The Holocaust* (New York 1986), 526.

134. Benjamin Ferencz, *Less than Slaves: Jewish Forced Labour and the Quest for Compensation* (Harvard 1979), 25.

135. Hilberg, *op. cit.*, i 254.

136. Ferencz, *op. cit.*, 28.

137. Robert H. Abzug, *Inside the Vicious Heart: Americans and the Liberation of Nazi Concentration Camps* (Oxford 1985), 106.

138. Ferencz, *op. cit.*, 22.

139. *Ibid.*, appendix 3, 202ff.; Höss affidavit, 12 March 1947.

140. Ferencz, *op. cit.*, 19.

141. Hilberg, *op. cit.*, i 87.

142. David Irving, *Hitler's War* (London 1977).

143. Gerald Fleming, *Hitler and the Final Solution* (Berkeley 1984), refutes it.

144. H. R. Trevor-Roper (ed.), *Hitler's Table Talk 1941–44* (London 1973), 154.

145. Wistrich, *Hitler's Apocalypse*, 37; and see his ch. 6, 'Hitler and the Final Solution', 108ff.

146. Davidowicz, *op. cit.*, 132.

147. *Ibid.*, 134; Alexander Mitscherlich and Fred Mielke, *Doctors of Infamy: The Story of the Nazi Medical Crimes* (New York 1949), 114.

148. Hilberg, *op. cit.*, i 281.

149. *Ibid.*, 308.
150. *Ibid.*, 332–3.
151. The camps were listed by the German government, *Bundesgesetzblatt*, 24 September 1977, pp. 1787–1852; the figure of 900 labour camps was given by Höss.
152. Hilberg, *op. cit.*, i 56.
153. Davidowicz, *op. cit.*, 130.
154. Jochen von Lang, *Eichmann Interrogated* (New York 1973), 74–5.
155. Louis P. Lochner (ed.), *The Goebbels Diaries 1942–43* (New York 1948).
156. Figures taken from Davidowicz, *op. cit.*, appendix B, 402f.
157. The basic evidence for Nazi killings comes from *Trials of Major War Criminals before the International Military Tribunal*, 44 vols (Nuremberg 1947), *Nazi Conspiracy and Aggression*, 8 vols plus supplement (Washington DC 1946), and *Trials of War Criminals before the Nuremberg Military Tribunals under Control Council Law No. 10*, 15 vols (Washington DC).
158. Luba Krugman Gurdus, *The Death Train* (New York 1979); Martin Gilbert, *Final Journey* (London 1979), 70.
159. Hilberg, *op. cit.*, i 581; Gilbert, *Final Journey*, 78.
160. For case histories see Leonard Gross, *The Last Jews in Berlin* (London 1983).
161. *Ibid.*
162. Austria's anti-Jewish war-record is summarized in Howard M. Sacher, *Diaspora* (New York 1985), 30ff.
163. Hilberg, *op. cit.*, ii 457–8.
164. Figures from Julius S. Fischer, *Transnistria, the Forgotten Cemetery* (South Brunswick 1969), 134–7.
165. Davidowicz, *op. cit.*, 383–6.
166. *Bagatelle pour un massacre* (Paris 1937), 126; for Céline see Paul J. Kingston, *Anti-Semitism in France during the 1930s* (Hull 1983), 131–2.
167. Jean Laloum, *La France Antisémite de Darquier de Pellepoix* (Paris 1979).
168. M. R. Marrus and R. O. Paxton, *Vichy France and the Jews* (New York 1981), 343.
169. André Halimi, *La Délation sous l'occupation* (Paris 1983).
170. Herzl's diary, 23 January 1904; Cecil Roth, *The History of the Jews of Italy* (Philadelphia 1946), 474–5.
171. Meir Michaelis, *Mussolini and the Jews* (Oxford 1978), 52.
172. *Ibid.*, 11ff., 408; Gaetano Salvemini, *Prelude to World War II* (London 1953), 478.
173. Michaelis, *op. cit.*, 353–68.
174. Oral History Collection, *The Reminiscences of Walter Lippmann*, 248–50; Meryl Secrest, *Being Bernard Berenson* (New York 1979).
175. Holocaust statistics vary. I have taken the Hungarian figures from Monty Noam Penkower, *The Jews Were Expendable: Free World Diplomacy and the Holocaust* (Chicago 1983), 214. See the set of figures, and sources, in *Encyclopaedia Judaica*, viii 889–90.
176. F. E. Werbell and Thurston Clarke, *Lost Hero: The Mystery of Raoul Wallenberg* (New York 1982); Alvar Alsterdal, 'The Wallenberg Mystery', *Soviet Jewish Affairs*, February 1983.
177. David S. Wyman, *The Abandonment of the Jews: America and the Holocaust, 1941–5* (New York 1984), 97.
178. Penkower, *op. cit.*, 193.

179. Charles Stember (ed.), *Jews in the Mind of America* (New York 1966), 53–62; Wyman, *op. cit.*, 10–11.

180. *Boston Globe*, 26 June 1942; *New York Times*, 27 June 1942. The *Times* had an extensive summary of the report on 2 July, however.

181. *Nation*, 19 May 1945; Abzug, *op. cit.*, 136–7.

182. Wyman, *op. cit.*, 313 and footnote.

183. *Ibid.*, 112ff.

184. Penkower, *op. cit.*, 193.

185. Wyman, *op. cit.*, 299.

186. Hilberg, *op. cit.*, i 358.

187. Wyman, *op. cit.*, 4–5.

188. For Betar see Marcus, *Social and Political History of the Jews in Poland 1919–38*, 271–3; Silver, *op. cit.*, 19ff.

189. Hilberg, *op. cit.*, i 186–7.

190. About one-third of it has been published: Lucjan Dobroszynski (ed.), *The Chronicle of the Lodz Ghetto, 1941–44* (Yale 1984).

191. Penkower, *op. cit.*, 292, 337–8, note 10.

192. Gilbert, *The Holocaust*, 426–7.

193. Davidowicz, *op. cit.*, 301.

194. *Ibid.*, 289.

195. Deuteronomy 28:66–7.

196. Yaffa Eliach (ed.), *Hasidic Tales of the Holocaust* (Oxford 1983).

197. Arnold J. Pomerans (trans.), *Etty: A Diary, 1941–3* (London 1983).

198. For Warsaw, see Yisrael Gutman, *The Jews of Warsaw, 1939–43: Ghetto, Underground, Revolt* (trans., Brighton 1982); Hilberg, *op. cit.*, ii 511–12.

199. See 'Rose Robota, Heroine of the Auschwitz Underground', in Yuri Suhl (ed.), *They Fought Back* (New York 1975); Philip Muller, *Auschwitz Inferno: The Testimony of a Sonderskommando* (London 1979), 143–60.

200. Ferencz, *op. cit.*, 21.

201. *Ibid.*, 20.

202. Gilbert, *The Holocaust*, 461.

203. Hilberg, *op. cit.*, ii 438.

204. Gilbert, *The Holocaust*, 457.

205. Abzug, *op. cit.*, 106.

206. Gilbert, *The Holocaust*, 419.

207. *Ibid.*, 808, 793.

208. International Military Tribunal Nuremberg, Document NG-2757, quoted in Gilbert, *The Holocaust*, 578.

209. Abzug, *op. cit.*, 152ff.

210. *Ibid.*, 160.

211. Gilbert, *The Holocaust*, 816ff.

212. For statistics of war trials, see *Encyclopaedia Judaica*, xvi 288–302.

213. For a useful summary, see Howard Sachar, *op. cit.*, 7–13.

214. Quoted in Ferencz, *op. cit.*, Introduction, xi.

215. *Ibid.*, 189.

216. The Council debates are summarized in Bea's own book, *The Church and the Jewish People* (London 1966), which gives the text of the Declaration in appendix I, 147–53.

PART SEVEN: ZION

1. Amos 3:2.
2. Arthur A. Cohen, *The Natural and Supernatural Jew* (London 1967), 180–2.
3. Robert Wistrich, *Hitler's Apocalypse: Jews and the Nazi Legacy* (London 1986), 162ff.
4. Quoted in H. H. Ben Sasson (ed.), *A History of the Jewish People* (trans., Harvard 1976), 1040.
5. Churchill to Sir Edward Grigg, 12 July 1944; Monty Noam Penkower, *The Jews Were Expendable: Free World Diplomacy and the Holocaust* (Chicago 1983), ch. 1, 'The Struggle for an Allied Jewish Fighting Force', 3ff.
6. Evelyn Waugh, *The Holy Places* (London 1952), 2.
7. Eric Silver, *Begin* (London 1984), 8.
8. Menachem Begin, *White Nights* (New York 1977).
9. Michael Bar-Zohar, *Ben Gurion: A Biography* (London 1978), 129.
10. Thurston Clarke, *By Blood and Fire* (London 1981), 116.
11. Silver, *op. cit.*, 67–72.
12. Nicholas Bethell, *The Palestine Triangle: The Struggle Between the British, the Jews and the Arabs* (London 1979), 261ff.
13. Michael J. Cohen, *Palestine and the Great Powers* (Princeton 1982), 270–6, for the British decision to withdraw.
14. Alfred Steinberg,*The Man from Missouri: The Life and Times of Harry S. Truman* (New York 1952), 301.
15. *The Forrestal Diaries* (New York 1951), 324, 344, 348.
16. *Petroleum Times*, June 1948.
17. Leonard Schapiro, 'The Jewish Anti-Fascist Committee . . .', in B. Vago and G. L. Mosse (eds), *Jews and Non-Jews in Eastern Europe* (New York 1974), 291ff.
18. Howard Sachar, 'The Arab–Israel Issue in the Light of the Cold War', *Sino-Soviet Institute Studies* (Washington DC), 1966, 2.
19. Howard Sachar, *Europe Leaves the Middle East 1936–54* (London 1974), 546–7; Netanel Lorch, *The Edge of the Sword: Israel's War of Independence 1947–9* (New York 1961), 90; David Horowitz, *The State in the Making* (New York 1953), 27.
20. Rony E. Gabbay, *A Political Study of the Arab–Jewish Conflict* (Geneva 1959), 92–3.
21. Edward Luttwak and Dan Horowitz, *The Israeli Army* (New York 1975), 23ff.
22. For the course of the fighting see Edgar O'Ballance, *The Arab–Israeli War 1948* (London 1956).
23. Jabotinsky Archives; quoted in Silver, *op. cit.*, 90.
24. For an account of the Deir Yassin affair, see *ibid.*, 88–95.
25. See maps and figures on the provenance and distribution of Arab and Jewish refugees in Martin Gilbert, *The Arab–Israel Conflict: Its History in Maps* (London 1974), 49, 50.
26. Cairo Radio, 19 July 1957.
27. Genesis 15:1–6; 12:1–3.
28. Gilbert, *op. cit.*, 11, for map of 1919 proposal. See also maps in *Encyclopaedia Judaica*, ix 315–16.
29. Gilbert, *op. cit.*, 24, for map of Peel proposal.
30. Quoted in W. D. Davies, *The Territorial Dimension in Judaism* (Berkeley 1982), 114–15; see also Ben Halpern, *The Idea of the Jewish State* (2nd edn, Harvard 1969), 41ff.

31. For the Sinai War see Chaim Herzog, *The Arab–Israeli Wars* (London 1982).
32. For the Six Day War see Terence Prittie, *Israel: Miracle in the Desert* (2nd edn, London 1968).
33. For the Yom Kippur War see Herzog, *op. cit.*
34. For the Israel–Egypt peace negotiations see two eye-witness accounts, Moshe Dayan, *Breakthrough* (London 1981); Ezer Weizman, *The Battle for Peace* (New York 1981).
35. Quoted in S. Clement Leslie, *The Rift in Israel: Religious Authority and Secular Democracy* (London 1971), 63ff.
36. Amos Perlmutter, *Israel: the Partitioned State: A Political History since 1900* (New York 1985), ch. 7; R. J. Isaacs, *Israel Divided: Ideological Politics in the Jewish State* (Baltimore 1976), 66ff.
37. Text of the Law of Return (as amended 1954, 1970) is given in Philip S. Alexander, *Textual Sources for the Study of Judaism* (Manchester 1984), 166–7.
38. For this ruling see *ibid.*, 168–71.
39. For immigrants from Europe see map in Gilbert, *op. cit.*, 51; detailed immigration figures up to 1970 are in *Encyclopaedia Judaica*, ix, 534–46.
40. B. C. Kaganoff, *A Dictionary of Jewish Names and their History* (London 1977).
41. Bar-Zohar, *op. cit.*, 171–2.
42. Silver, *op. cit.*, 99–108.
43. Dan Horowitz and Moshe Lissak, *Origins of the Israeli Polity: Palestine Under the Mandate* (Chicago 1978).
44. Emile Marmorstein, *Heaven at Bay: The Jewish Kulturkampf in the Holy Land* (Oxford 1969), 142–3.
45. For Ben Gurion's struggles see Perlmutter, *op. cit.*, 15–17, 131–5.
46. Quoted in *ibid.*, 145.
47. Speech in the Knesset, 20 June 1977.
48. 'With Gershom Scholem: An Interview', in W. J. Dannhauser (ed.), *Gershom Scholem: Jews and Judaism in Crisis* (New York 1976).
49. Marmorstein, *op. cit.*, 80–9.
50. *Ibid.*, 108ff.
51. I. Domb, *Transformations* (London 1958).
52. Solomon Granzfried, *Kissor Shulan 'Arukh*, ch. 72, paras 1–2.
53. Leslie, *op. cit.*, 52ff.
54. Z. E. Kurzweil, *Modern Trends in Jewish Education* (London 1964), 257ff.
55. Quoted in Marmorstein, *op. cit.*, 144.
56. Case quoted in Chaim Bermant, *On the Other Hand* (London 1982), 55.
57. Quoted in *ibid.*, 56.
58. Quoted in Leslie, *op. cit.*, 62.
59. Numbers 5:2–3.
60. Numbers 19:17–18.
61. N. H. Snaith, *Leviticus and Numbers* (London 1967), 270–4.
62. Immanuel Jacobovits, *The Timely and the Timeless* (London 1977), 291.
63. I Chronicles 28:19.
64. For the arguments, see Jacobovits, *op. cit.*, 292–4.
65. *Encyclopaedia Judaica*, xv 994.
66. Such as Richard Harwood, *Did Six Million Really Die?* (New York 1974) and Arthur Butz, *The Hoax of the Twentieth Century* (New York 1977).

For the charges see Moshe Pearlman, *The Capture and Trial of Adolf Eichmann* (London 1963), appendix 633–43.

68. *Ibid.*, 85.
69. *Ibid.*, 627.
70. Hanoch Smith, 'Israeli Reflections on the Holocaust', *Public Opinion* (December–January 1984).
71. Quoted in John C. Merkle, *The Genesis of Faith: The Depth Theology of Abraham Joshua Herschel* (New York 1985), 11.
72. Cohen, *op. cit.*, 6–7.
73. See the useful map, 'World Jewish Population 1984', in Howard Sachar, *Diaspora* (New York 1985), 485–6.
74. H. S. Kehimkan, *History of the Bene Israel of India* (Tel Aviv 1937).
75. For Indian Jews see Schifra Strizower, *The Children of Israel: The Bene Israel of Bombay* (Oxford 1971) and *Exotic Jewish Communities* (London 1962).
76. Quoted in *Encyclopaedia Judaica*, ix 1138–9.
77. P. Lévy, *Les Noms des Israélites en France* (Paris 1960), 75–6.
78. Quoted in P. Girard, *Les Juifs de France de 1789 à 1860* (Paris 1976), 172.
79. Domenique Schnapper, *Jewish Institutions in France* (trans., Chicago 1982), 167, note 22.
80. Irving Kristol, 'The Political Dilemma of American Jews', *Commentary* (July 1984); Milton Himmelfarb, 'Another Look at the Jewish Vote', *Commentary* (December 1985).
81. Quoted in Bernard D. Weinryb, 'Anti-Semitism in Soviet Russia', in Lionel Kochan (ed.), *The Jews in Soviet Russia* (Oxford 1972), 308; for Stalin's anti-Semitism, see Svetlana Alliluyeva, *Twenty Letters to a Friend* (trans., London 1967), 76, 82, 171, 193, 206, 217.
82. Quoted in Weinryb, *op. cit.*, 307.
83. See Peter Brod, 'Soviet–Israeli Relations 1948–56', and Arnold Krammer, 'Prisoners in Prague: Israelis in the Slansky Trial', in Robert Wistrich (ed.), *The Left Against Zion: Communism, Israel and the Middle East* (London 1979), 57ff., 72ff.
84. See Benjamin Pinkus, 'Soviet Campaigns against Jewish Nationalism and Cosmopolitanism', *Soviet Jewish Affairs* iv 2 (1974); Leonard Schapiro, 'The Jewish Anti-Fascist Committee and Phases of Soviet Anti-Semitic Policy during and after World War II', in B. Gao and G. L. Mosse (eds), *Jews and Non-Jews in Eastern Europe* (New York 1974), 291ff.; Wistrich, *Hitler's Apocalypse*, ch. 10, 'The Soviet Protocols', 194ff.
85. Joseph B. Schechtman, *Star in Eclipse: Russian Jewry Revisited* (New York 1961), 80.
86. W. D. Rubinstein, *The Left, the Right and the Jews* (London 1982), 'The Soviet Union', 180–99, gives numerous statistics.
87. Philippa Lewis, 'The Jewish Question in the Open, 1968–71', in Kochan, *op. cit.*, 337–53; Ilya Zilberberg, 'From Russia to Israel: A Personal Case-History', *Soviet Jewish Affairs* (May 1972).
88. 'A Short Guide to the Exit Visa', issued by the National Council for Soviet Jewry, London, 1986.
89. D. M. Schreuder, *The Scramble for Southern Africa, 1877–1895* (Oxford 1980), 181ff.; Freda Troup, *South Africa: An Historical Introduction* (London 1972), 153ff.

90. For the Jewish pioneers see Geoffrey Wheatcroft, *The Randlords: The Men Who Made South Africa* (London 1985), 51ff., 202ff. For the second generation see Theodore Gregory, *Ernest Oppenheimer and the Economic Development of Southern Africa* (New York 1977).

91. Quoted in Wheatcroft, *op. cit.*, 205 footnote.

92. J. A. Hobson, *The War in South Africa: Its Cause and Effects* (London 1900), esp. part II, ch. 1, 'For Whom Are We Fighting?'

93. J. A. Hobson, *Imperialism: A Study* (London 1902), 64.

94. V. I. Lenin, preface to *Imperialism: The Highest Stage of Capitalism* (rev. trans., London 1934), 7. See also R. Koebner and H. D. Schmidt, *Imperialism: The Story and Significance of a Political Word, 1840–1960* (Cambridge 1965), 262.

95. Artur London, *L'Aveu* (Paris 1968), quoted in W. Oschlies, 'Neo-Stalinist Anti-Semitism in Czechoslovakia', in Wistrich, *The Left Against Zion*, 156–7.

96. Quoted in J. B. Schechtman, 'The USSR, Zionism and Israel', in Weinryb, *op. cit.*, 119.

97. *Ibid.*, 124.

98. Quoted in Wistrich, *Hitler's Apocalypse*, 207.

99. *Ibid.*, 207–8; Emmanuel Litvinov, *Soviet Anti-Semitism: The Paris Trial* (London 1984).

100. Howard Spier, 'Zionists and Freemasons in Soviet Propaganda', *Patterns of Prejudice* (January–February 1979).

101. Quoted in Wistrich, *Hitler's Apocalypse*, 219. See his entire chapter, 'Inversions of History', 216–35.

102. R. K. Karanjia, *Arab Dawn* (Bombay 1958); quoted in Wistrich, *Hitler's Apocalypse*, 177. See Y. Harkabi's important compilation, *Arab Attitudes to Israel* (Jerusalem 1976).

103. For instance *The Palestine Problem* (1964) published by the Jordanian Ministry of Education, and a handbook under a similar title put out by the Indoctrination Directorate of the United Arab Republic Armed Forces.

104. *Encyclopaedia Judaica*, iii 138, 147.

105. D. F. Green (ed.), *Arab Theologians on Jews and Israel* (3rd edn, Geneva 1976), 92–3.

106. Wistrich, *Hitler's Apocalypse*, 181.

107. For Hitler's relations with the Grand Mufti, see Joseph Schechtman, *The Mufti and the Führer: The Rise and Fall of Haj Amin el Huseini* (New York 1965).

108. Quoted in Harkabi, *op. cit.*, 279.

109. For the events leading up to the resolution, see Daniel Patrick Moynihan, *A Dangerous Place* (Boston 1978), ch. 9, 169–99.

110. Jillian Becker, *Hitler's Children: The Story of the Baader–Meinhof Gang* (London 1977), 17–18.

111. Silver, *op. cit.*, 236.

112. *Final Report of the Commission of Inquiry into the Events at the Refugee Camps in Beirut* (Jerusalem 8 February 1983, English/Hebrew).

113. Leon Roth, *Judaism: A Portrait* (London 1960).

114. Joshua 1:9.

Index